Johannes Bähr, Paul Erker

BOSCH

History of a
Global Enterprise

Johannes Bähr, Paul Erker

BOSCH

History of a
Global Enterprise

Translated by J. A. Underwood

C. H. Beck

With 88 illustrations, 18 figures, and 21 tables

German edition C. H.Beck oHG, München 2013
© Verlag C. H. Beck oHG, Munich 2015
Typeset: Janß GmbH, Pfungstadt
Produced by: CPI – Ebner & Spiegel, Ulm
Printed on acid-free, age-resistant paper
(manufactured from non chlorine-bleached cellulose)
Printed in Germany
ISBN 978 3 406 68359 6

www.beck.de

Contents

Appendix:

Introduction

On July 10, 1996, Hans L. Merkle sent a memorandum to Hermann Scholl, the chairman of the Bosch board of management, and to Marcus Bierich, the chairman of the industrial trust Robert Bosch Industrietreuhand KG. Merkle was alarmed by an article about Bosch that had appeared in a recent issue of the German business weekly *Wirtschaftswoche*. In the memorandum, Merkle drew attention to obvious factual errors, for example the suggestion that the foundation Robert Bosch Stiftung GmbH somehow "oversaw" the company's affairs. More importantly, however, he warned of possible consequences that "might arise from claims by heirs of Robert Bosch" and that "threaten our [corporate] constitution. I would see a comparable risk in the proposed scholarly appraisal of our company's history."[1] At the time, of course, Merkle had long since retired from all his executive positions at Bosch, but as honorary chairman he still wielded considerable influence. His memorandum alludes to two cardinal areas of corporate history – problem areas which had remained largely taboo, though they had no bearing on what had long been seen as the dubious role played by the company in National Socialist Germany. The first of these concerned the distribution of voting rights between management and the Bosch family, culminating in the establishment of a new, foundation-based Bosch constitution and the 1964 reformulation of the "Bosch basic law." The second was the importance of Robert Bosch Industrietreuhand KG. This was the real center of power, direction, and control at Bosch, one which had emerged from the group of executors installed by Robert Bosch to manage his estate. The doubts and misgivings expressed by Merkle in his memorandum were the main reason why, during Merkle's lifetime, despite numerous false starts and notwithstanding all potentially fitting occasions arising from company-internal anniversary celebrations, no source-based corporate history of Bosch had ever been published. Even after his death, all efforts in this direction had failed – for a wide variety of reasons. No fault attaches to the successors of Robert Bosch. The members of the family had been pressing for such a publication for years.[2]

So it is by no means a matter of course that a Bosch corporate history has now been published – and here the 125th anniversary celebrated in 2011 was in fact more occasion than actual cause. The cause lies in a recent opening up of the company under the leadership of Hermann Scholl and Franz Fehrenbach, as well as in the express readiness of the most senior Bosch executives to subject themselves to the complex and – for them – often difficult task of having a source-based analysis and evaluation conducted by business historians from outside the company. As it happened, the anniversary gave rise not only to an official general history of the company compiled by staff at Bosch Historical Communications to mark 125 years of the company's existence,[3] but also to the present analysis compiled by independent business historians, now published quite some time after the company's milestone anniversary. For the first time, this analysis goes beyond the period from 1886 to 1945, which for all intents and purposes has already been examined, to look at developments up to and including the present. That said, it also brings to light new findings about the National Socialist era and places points of emphasis slightly differently than previous research has done. Naturally, the project has been accompanied by many consultations, debates, and informal discussions between the authors and members of Bosch management. The slant that such individuals have on the history of the company, the way they remember things – particularly when it comes to phases that they themselves crucially helped to shape – inevitably diverges in many respects from insights gained through external examination of documents. At all times, however, the principle of scholarly independence that governed the study was respected. The authors enjoyed unrestricted access to all relevant papers and files – not only in the Bosch Archives (unique in the quality and availability as well as in the sheer extent of its content) but also, in certain instances, in the management's own files. Here, the authors drew mainly on the minutes of meetings of the Bosch board of management and of the group of executors, as well as on those of subsequent meetings of the shareholders of Robert Bosch Industrietreuhand KG. In doing so, they gained insight into an area of Bosch history that for a long time, both outside and inside the company, was veiled in secrecy. In addition, they carried out supplementary research work in national and municipal archives and evaluated assorted accounts given by the people involved.

The study itself falls into four parts. The first two parts describe and analyze the beginnings and rise of Bosch up to 1914 as well as the company's progress in the Weimar Republic and the Third Reich. During these years, the company stood under the dominant leadership of its larger-than-life founder Robert Bosch, the entrepreneur who left such an indelible mark on the company. The second part, entitled "Bosch in the Third Reich," is a rather special case. Bosch was hugely important to the armaments industry during these years, and during the war the company became involved in using forced labor. At the same time, Bosch management tried to keep its distance from the National Socialists – to the point of backing the resistance movement against Hitler. However, in contrast to the study by Joachim Scholtyseck,[4] the present work highlights the ambivalence that was characteristic of Bosch, and which is manifested in a balancing act between compliance and opposition. In other words, it looks at the entire range of ways in which Bosch workers and managers reacted to the National Socialists. The subsequent period, following Robert Bosch's death in 1942, and particularly from the immediate postwar years to the early 1980s, is marked by processes of adaptation and transformation in an economic environment that swung repeatedly from boom to bust and back again. It constitutes a pivotal phase in Bosch history, one of decisive importance. This phase is the subject of the third part. During this period, management of the company passed into the hands of non-family members, and a new, foundation-based constitution was introduced. Both these things were carried out in a complex process of negotiation, against the background of the legacy handed down by the company founder. Finally, the fourth part examines the corporate policies and strategies formulated in response to the many challenges posed by globalization and the fundamental upheaval in customer-supplier relations that began in the early 1980s – challenges that still call for responses today. It is largely accidental that the four phases defined here broadly coincide with the terms of office served by the company's first four chairmen of the board of management. In any event, it has nothing to do with any methodological approach.

What this first truly complete history of the Bosch Group enables us to do is to compare the individual phases of the company's development over time. For many of the challenges of postwar history, one can find comparable phenomena in the 1920s and earlier – crises and diversification conflicts, attempts to achieve internationalization, arguments about legal forms and experiments in business organization, and efforts to use engineering expertise and high levels of research and development outlay to work on innovations and technological improvements in the fields of processes, products, and manufacturing. At all points across these decades, something akin to a strategic path providing Bosch management with crucial guidance can be seen. One of the aims of this study, therefore, is to reveal the long-term learning effects and experiential processes running through the history of the company – processes which, because they exist beyond the personal sphere and, indeed, are handed down from one generation to the next, might well be described as collective.

The common thread running through our study is woven from three main themes:

– *Corporate constitution, corporate leadership, and corporate principles.* What makes the history of Bosch special is the fact that it has for the most part been a privately owned family company. Even so, it is a company that, over the years, has modified its corporate constitution several times. Starting as a sole proprietorship, in 1917 it became the stock corporation Robert Bosch AG, which in 1937 was transformed into the close corporation or private limited company Robert Bosch GmbH, eventually adopting a distinctive foundation-based solution in 1964. It is also in this context that the values and principles of the owners and managers of Bosch have to be discussed. In addition, the study focuses on the fundamental matter of corporate governance (the defining lines along which the company is organized and managed), the role of internal stakeholders (shareholders, associates), and issues relating to corporate financing and social benefits for the workforce.

–   *Technical orientation and competitive structure.* From the outset, Bosch has been an innovation-driven engineering enterprise. In all phases of its history, the company has come up with groundbreaking developments and important technical changes; changes which have extended to manufacturing technology and production systems. As a result, the company has held a special competitive position – and this from the beginning of the twentieth century – as one of a bare handful of suppliers of choice for automotive technology and the original-equipment business.

–   *Internationalization and globalization.* Bosch was represented outside Germany from an early stage, with 88 percent of its sales being generated outside Germany as early as 1913. This makes it all the more important to ask how the company managed to conquer markets outside Germany, to return to world markets after two world wars, and to cope with changing patterns of globalization over recent decades.

In addition to these main strands, the study deals with other themes:

–   *Corporate strategies.* What plans were drawn up and what decisions were made that led not only to changes in production and competition structure but also to some companies being taken over and others sold? In the course of its history, Bosch has managed to navigate several key junctures of this sort – the decision, for example, to enter the household-appliances sector, or the sortie into communications technology, later abandoned.

–   *Crises and crisis management.* The present study analyzes how Bosch has conducted itself in a number of economic crises, looking at the Great Depression of the 1930s and the slumps of the 1970s, 1990s, and the first decade of the new millennium. Particular attention is paid to the crises of 1926 and 1993, which the Bosch management boards of those years found especially traumatic.

In all this, our focus is not only on how decisions were made but also on processes of perception and negotiation. The latter may relate to internal struggles for power between workforce and management or to wrangles about how to interpret the "constitutional principles" contained in Robert Bosch's will and set out in guidelines – wrangles first played out between family shareholders and the executors named by Robert Bosch himself, and later between the family and the select circle of independent businessmen appointed as shareholders of Robert Bosch Industrietreuhand KG. These processes were also evidenced in the way Bosch defined its future market and competitive positions, and in efforts within management to find the optimum growth and crisis strategies for the company. Viewed from outside in the mirror of documentation, the "Bosch world" often appears more sharply defined in this connection, but at the same time many facets remain concealed and can only be inferred – and then only in part – by speaking to those who were involved. However, what we want to show is not only how Robert Bosch practiced his own brand of business management and, later on, what made company headquarters at the Schillerhöhe tick. We also want to demonstrate how Bosch engineers and plant managers sought, in each of these different periods, to deal with the production problems facing them. It is extremely important in this regard that the wealth of options and the complexity of developments that were faced by all concerned should also be brought out in full. Many negotiations about investments or new orders ultimately came to nothing, collapsed, or dragged on interminably. If these developments are not reflected, corporate policy and corporate action will ultimately, in hindsight, assume a pleasing linearity, cohesion, and developmental logic that in historical terms they never in fact possessed. Seen in their proper historical perspective, processes of change within companies are far more complex, drawn out, and disjointed than they appear in the eyes of management today or were regarded by those in charge at the time.

Our concern, therefore, is to take a historico-critical approach to the "Bosch phenomenon," with the central question being: what has made this company so special and so unmistakable, even where the paths it took were by no means unusual? The answer must be sought in the specific manner in which decisions have been made and business operations have been run. In other words, it must be sought in corporate culture. This leads back to the founder, Robert Bosch, and his ubiquitous presence which continues even today, decades after his death. The power of his legacy has made itself felt not only in the annual remembrance of the anniversary of his birth and death, the celebrations to mark the day the company was founded, and the articles in the *Bosch-Zünder* containing his sayings and anecdotes about him. The way in which business operations are invariably governed by testamentary principles and directives – for instance, in connection with whether borrowed capital or projected partnerships are acceptable or not – likewise testifies to the enduring influence of the founder. Strict though the rules are that have been imposed by the "Bosch basic law" and the quasi-permanent "jurisdiction" of the executors of Robert Bosch and (later) the shareholders of Robert Bosch Industrietreuhand KG, at the same time the ruling doctrine has been one of a corporate culture that has foregone rigid rules and regulations and remained open to constant reform. Ultimately, therefore, the question around which our whole study revolves is this: how has Bosch mastered this ongoing, dual task of guarding its own identity and corporate culture while at the same time – indeed, with the very aid of this cultural grounding – remaining as far as possible ahead of the processes of economic and technological change?

Thanks are due in large measure to the skilled and tireless assistance of the Historical Communications team of Robert Bosch GmbH under the direction of Dr. Kathrin Fastnacht, with special mention going to Dieter Schmitt for helping us find our way through the vast store of the Bosch Archives. Thanks are also due to present and former members of the company's supervisory and management committees, as well as to the works council and to the members of the Bosch family, for their full and frank responses to our queries. The authors are grateful to J. A. Underwood for his translation of the revised edition, and to Philip Mann and Stephen Smith (Bosch Corporate Communications) for their editing of the manuscript. Our hope is that this study, rather than representing the last word on Bosch, marks the beginning of further detailed studies of the many aspects of Bosch history that could often only be touched on here.

I Early years and rise of the company (1886–1932)

1 Robert Bosch – portrait of a founder

Robert Bosch was born in Albeck, a village near Ulm in the Swabian Jura, on September 23, 1861. He was the eleventh of twelve children born to a couple who worked as innkeepers and farmers. Their inn, the "Gasthaus zur Krone" in Albeck, with its approximately 75 hectares of arable land and forest, had been in the Bosch family for several generations. Robert's father, Servatius Bosch, an educated, well-read man, was also a freemason and someone who held firm principles.[1] His mother, Maria Margaretha Bosch, née Dölle, came from an innkeeper family in nearby Jungingen, and despite her huge brood helped out tirelessly in the inn. The couple, while not being particularly rich, were very comfortably off.[2] Today we would say the parents belonged to the prosperous middle class.[3]

"We children were fond of our parents; they showed us understanding," Robert Bosch wrote in his 1921 "Memoirs."[4] In fact, the parental home exerted a stronger influence on him than might be assumed at first glance. His parents may not have been responsible for his fascination with electrical engineering and precision mechanics, but they did instill in him a head for business, a disciplined approach to work, and a love of farming. For Robert Bosch, his father was in many respects an exemplar. He grew up sharing his father's political stance, understanding of social affairs, and highly developed sense of justice. As a social-liberal democrat with a commitment to the "ideas of 1848," Servatius Bosch felt a deep aversion to Prussian militarism. In Albeck, he had a certain reputation as a stubborn opponent of the mayor. He is said to have taken matters into his own hands when a broom-maker was imprisoned on what he considered unjust grounds, freeing the man from his cell – which cost Servatius a two-month spell in the state penitentiary at Hohenasperg.[5] "Never forget your humanity, and respect human dignity in your dealings with others," was a motto that Robert Bosch ascribed not only to himself but also to his father.[6] Servatius Bosch was a member of the local railroad committee, from which we can infer that he took a forward-looking attitude toward the technological and industrial developments of the age. In 1867, the landlord of Albeck's "Zur Krone" is said to have visited the World Exhibition in Paris.[7] Robert Bosch was also shaped by the region into which he was born. To his dying day he saw himself as a *Schwabe*. "The Swabian," Theodor Bäuerle writes in his biography of Robert Bosch, "was for him the epitome of the good German, the industrious worker, a pillar of German civilization."[8] Robert Bosch not only spoke the local dialect in the family and among friends and associates, he was also the living embodiment of several qualities often attributed to the Swabian: thoroughness, conscientiousness, dependability, and a certain mulish obstinacy.

In 1869, when Robert Bosch was just under eight years old, the family moved to Ulm. His father sold the house and land in Albeck, since none of the older sons wished to take over the inn. In addition, it was becoming apparent that the place was not going to lie on the new Ulm-Heidenheim railroad. In Ulm, Robert Bosch attended the *Realschule*, the secondary-technical school, while his parents now lived from private means.[9] Robert's brothers had in the meantime gone their own ways. The eldest, Jakob, became an innkeeper, taking over the "Adler" in Jungingen from his maternal grandfather.[10] His brother Karl, with whom Robert Bosch was subsequently on closer terms than with any of his other siblings, went into partnership with their sister Caroline's husband, Gustav Haag. Together they founded an installation business for gas and water appliances in Cologne. Karl's elder son Carl later became president of the board of IG Farben and in 1931 received the Nobel Prize for Chemistry. Carl's career filled Robert Bosch with pride that "the rustic farmland of the Ulm Jura has produced two men who are a glorious credit to the German nation."[11] Another brother, Albert, studied architecture, settled in Ulm in that profession, and worked as a stonemason at the minster there.[12]

Following his father's advice, having completed *Realschule*, Robert Bosch began an apprenticeship in precision mechanics – although at the time his interest lay more with the natural sciences.[13] During his three-year training under the Ulm mechanic and optician Wilhelm Maier, he made his first acquaintance with electrical apparatus. Later, he was to describe this apprenticeship as deeply disappointing. His master, he complained, had "not even encouraged learning."[14] The experience made a profound impression on him and was later to play a major role in shaping apprenticeship training at his own company.

His apprenticeship completed, the "years of travel" then customary for young journeymen began for Robert Bosch. Initially, he worked at his brother Karl's company in Cologne, where he also learned basic bookkeeping. He then moved to Stuttgart and joined C. & E. Fein, one of the earliest electrical engineering businesses to operate in the city. He did not stay for long there, either, switching to a jewelry workshop in Hanau that manufactured foxtail necklaces.[15] In the autumn of 1880, he entered military service with an engineering battalion in Ulm. One of his friends from this time, Eugen Kayser, subsequently became his brother-in-law, and later still a close colleague. At the end of his term of military service, Robert Bosch was given the chance of pursuing

Robert Bosch (1881)

an officer's career. However, he decided against it and instead resumed his "travel years," first taking a job at the Schuckert works in Nuremberg, then working for the mechanic Gottlob Schäffer in Göppingen. Clearly, Robert Bosch found it hard to make up his mind between precision mechanics and electrical engineering.[16] So he decided to enroll as an auditor at what would later become the Stuttgart Polytechnic in order to tackle the theoretical principles of electrical engineering.[17] After only one semester, he felt the urge to move on. In the spring of 1884, together with a friend from Ulm, his former fellow-apprentice Leonhard Köpf, he took ship for the United States. In retrospect, Robert Bosch wrote that he had embarked for America "partly to see the world but partly also because that country, the land of freedom, held a particular attraction for me. After all, by upbringing and after the example of my father and my elder brothers, I saw myself as a young democrat."[18]

   On the basis of references he brought with him from Germany, Robert Bosch found employment in New York City as a technician at the company run by the German-American entrepreneur Sigmund Bergmann. Bergmann, an immigrant from Thuringia, had jointly developed the first light bulb with Thomas Edison in 1879. His business was a forerunner of the General Electric

Company, which Edison set up subsequently. In New York City, the young technician not only became acquainted with the world but also suffered the hardships of having a job with no security. As soon as the next slump arrived he was laid off, and although he quickly found a new position at the Edison Machine Works it was an experience that left its mark on him. Robert Bosch promptly joined a worker organization named the Knights of Labor and in a letter to his future wife, Anna Kayser, declared himself a socialist.[19] He was disillusioned with the "land of freedom" because, as he later wrote, "the cornerstone of justice was missing: equality before the law."[20]

Following such disappointments, it was likely his engagement to Anna Kayser (which had ensued by correspondence) that persuaded him to leave the U.S. after only a year and return to Europe. Robert Bosch spent the first six months working for Siemens Brothers outside London, but at Christmas 1885 he went back to Germany and became officially engaged to marry Anna Kayser. She lived in Obertürkheim, just outside Stuttgart, so it made sense for him to move to the Stuttgart region. Before he finally settled there, Bosch worked for a few months for Buss, Sombart & Co., a gas-powered engine manufacturer in Magdeburg.[21] He was drawn to Stuttgart for personal reasons in the main, and not because the city was a particularly important industrial center (in fact, at the time it was by no means a big place). But after many "travel years," it is likely that Robert Bosch also felt the need to return to his Swabian homeland, and calculated that there were good career prospects for him in the Württemberg capital, with its roughly 130,000 inhabitants.

At the time when Robert Bosch settled in Stuttgart he was 25 years old. Seven years had passed since the completion of his apprenticeship – a lengthy total of "travel years," measured by the standards of the time. There is a strong sense that he did not find it easy to commit to a specific occupation. His letters, however, show that he had decided some time back to opt for self-employment, and now had personal reasons for taking the plunge. In Robert Bosch's view, setting up his own company would give him the kind of assured income that at the time was deemed essential for a man contemplating marriage. Sure enough, the business was launched in November 1886, and one year later the wedding took place. The young Mrs. Bosch, the daughter of a timber merchant in Obertürkheim, had almost as many brothers and sisters as her husband. And over the next seven years the couple had four children of their own: their daughters Margarete (born 1888) and Paula (b. 1889), a son Robert (b. 1891), and a further daughter, Elisabeth (b. 1893), who died prematurely. For a time the family lived in rented accommodation in the west end of Stuttgart, not far from the new company's workshop – on Schwabstraße, initially, then on Rotebühlstraße, then on Moltkestraße. For several years, the Bosch family were

Anna Kayser (1886)

neighbors of the Kautskys, with whom they became friends. Through Karl Kautsky, the leading contemporary theoretician of social democracy, they also came to know the emigrant Clara Zetkin, who worked under Kautsky as a journalist on the magazine *Die Neue Zeit*. The Social Democratic Party's celebrated "Erfurt Program" of 1890 is said to have been drawn up in the flat above the Bosch apartment at 145 Rotebühlstraße.[22]

As the business grew, Robert Bosch prospered, and in 1902 the family moved into a small detached town house. Eight years later, the entrepreneur built the rather more splendid villa on Heidehofstraße in eastern Stuttgart – a building that is today the head office of Robert Bosch Stiftung. Soon afterwards it emerged that the son, Robert, who was designated to succeed his father at the helm of the company, was incurably ill with multiple sclerosis. In 1913, he had to break off his studies at the Stuttgart Polytechnic, and from that time on he was an invalid in need of constant nursing.[23] Family life was overshadowed by the son's serious illness. In addition, there were clashes between Robert Bosch and his daughters, who had joined a left-wing socialist group. Paula Bosch, the younger daughter, began a relationship with the painter Georg Friedrich Zundel, who was married to Kautsky's former associate, Clara Zetkin. Zetkin hesitated for a long time before agreeing to a divorce, and the couple were not able to marry until 1926. The elder daughter, Margarete, studied political science at Tübingen University, receiving a doctorate in 1920.[24] Aged just 30, the son, Robert, died on April 6, 1921, while his father was away on a business trip to South America. In 1917, the then "crown prince" in the management team, Gustav Klein, had been killed in a plane crash, and the following year Robert Bosch's brother-in-law, Eugen Kayser, committed suicide. For Robert Bosch, this was probably the worst period in

Paula, Margarete, and Robert Bosch (who died in 1921). Photo taken around 1903.

his life. He was suffering from cardiac dilation, his company was going through a difficult time, and his own marriage was on the rocks. According to Robert Bosch's own account, following the death of their son, his wife had sunk into a series of depressions. The couple were divorced in 1927. But things soon looked up again. He remarried immediately after the divorce, having met his second wife, the singer and forester's daughter Margarete Wörz, when she applied to him for a scholarship.[25] As a result, at an advanced age Robert Bosch became a father again. In 1928, a son was born, he too receiving the name Robert, and three years later a daughter, Eva.

Robert Bosch was an entrepreneur in Joseph Schumpeter's sense – a creative, dynamic founder who implemented new ideas and never once rested on his laurels.[26] However, unlike Werner von Siemens, for instance, Robert Bosch was no inventor. His saying "I think I can say it was never my ambition to actually make something myself" is among the classics in the long list of Robert Bosch quotes.[27] Robert Bosch's strengths were the skills of the precision mechanic: exactness and quality. In this respect he was a perfectionist who would not tolerate the slightest negligence and could never accept compromise. His business principles included a determination to manufacture "the best of the best."[28] A demanding entrepreneur needs above all able colleagues.

Robert Bosch with his second wife Margarete and their son Robert Bosch Jr. (1931)

One of the reasons Robert Bosch was so successful was that he knew how to pick gifted technicians, engineers, and sales personnel and, having picked them, to motivate them and win their loyalty to his organization. The rapid rise of Bosch from workshop to global brand rested on the new magneto ignition systems for internal-combustion engines developed by Bosch's associates Arnold Zähringer and Gottlob Honold. But of course these inventions alone would not have been enough to achieve such great things; they also had to be marketed, and here Robert Bosch showed his good head for business. The economic historian Toni Pierenkemper points out that the kind of business success enjoyed by Robert Bosch involved "a certain amount of luck": "He entered the right market with the right product at the right time."[29]

The distinctive characteristics of Robert Bosch included a special ability to instill and communicate his ideas within and through the workshop (and later factory) environment. He did not spoon-feed staff, and he gave those in charge extensive freedom. In return, however, he expected them to live up to his standards. Robert Bosch had very precise ideas about what principles should govern work in his organization and how business should be conducted. Those principles were not enshrined in any in-house regulations, but everyone in the company knew what they were and complied with them as unwritten rules. Indeed, many employees referred to the founder as "Father Bosch," the label remaining in use even after his death. The fact was that Robert Bosch exuded a natural authority within the company. He was generous in his praise, but his criticism could also be unsparing.

Robert Bosch expected entrepreneurs to "recognize staff as contractual partners enjoying equal rights."[30] His company, too, had its fixed hierarchies, but the kind of "master in the house" mentality championed by many industrialists in the Ruhr district of Germany and elsewhere was not something the Swabian democrat Robert Bosch ever entertained. He invariably accepted works councils as part of corporate structure. In his view, they served to promote understanding between management and workforce. But trade-union representatives who tried to be something more found him to be an unsympathetic opponent. A further component of Robert Bosch's conception of the entrepreneur's task was that it included a duty of care towards employees.[31] This view matched his own conviction that well paid and well looked-after workers will also work well. Robert Bosch therefore paid good wages and was one of the first employers in Germany to introduce (in 1906) the eight-hour working day. Not only did he consider both to be his social duty; he also saw both as contributing to a perfectly sober business-management calculation.[32] Altogether, he remained firmly convinced that good behavior, besides carrying its own reward, paid for itself commercially, and that reprehensible practices would be punished by the market.

Robert Bosch's social openness was in stark contrast to the thinking of most members of his class. Consequently, among broad sections of the public he enjoyed a popularity accorded to few captains of industry. In his "character sketches" of German entrepreneurs published in 1924, the journalist Felix Pinner wrote this about Robert Bosch: "But what marks him out, almost uniquely, as a glorious exception, not merely from the typical German entrepreneur of his day, is his attitude towards social-policy matters."[33] This did not make him popular among his fellow entrepreneurs. Early on he acquired the nickname "Bosch the Red."[34] Nor was the sobriquet wholly unjustified. During his time in the U.S., he had believed in socialism, his friend Kautsky had taught him a lot about social democracy, and up until the years following the First World War, he consistently voted for the Social Democratic SPD.[35] However, he rejected out of hand any encroachment on the autonomy of the entrepreneur, to say nothing of full-scale nationalization of industry. In matters of economic policy, he was a staunch liberal: for free trade and against any kind of national regulation. How these potentially disparate stances fitted together was indicated by Bosch in his 1921 memoirs, where he admits to having "sympathized with the Socialist Party out of despair at the bourgeoisie."[36] But later, under the influence of the circle that gathered around Ernst Jäckh and Friedrich Naumann, Robert Bosch shifted closer to a social-liberal position, and in the Weimar Republic his sympathies lay with the German Democratic Party (DDP), also founded by Naumann. In the 1925 presidential election, he publicly issued an appeal for the electorate to vote for the centrist politician Wilhelm Marx, who was standing against Hindenburg. Seven years later, he backed Hindenburg as being, compared to Hitler, the lesser of two evils.[37] In any case, Robert Bosch remained a committed democrat, as his father had been before him, and he stayed true to his principles throughout the Third Reich.

Robert Bosch can be seen as a Swabian *Eigenbrötler* – in other words, as something of a loner, as we might say nowadays. But he was undoubtedly also a citizen of the world and a pioneer of globalization. As a result of the development of his company, but also – even earlier – as a result of the time that he himself had spent abroad, he was a cosmopolitan. He had no difficulty in doing business in Paris, New York City, or Buenos Aires, and his partners never had the feeling they were dealing with a narrow-minded German businessman. By this time, his deep commitment to international understanding was by no means confined to commercial interests alone. Robert Bosch was also firmly convinced that political chest-beating and militant nationalism operate to people's detriment by inhibiting justice and social equilibrium. He reached this attitude under the impression of the First World War. From this point on, he particularly strove for détente between Germany and France, and from the late 1920s he committed himself equally to the Paneuropean Union founded by Coudenhove-Kalergi, fired by his vision of "a united Europe, living in peace."[38]

Robert Bosch was thrifty, but he was not miserly. He despised any squandering of money, but he often gave generously to causes that seemed to him worth supporting. As early as 1910, the Stuttgart Polytechnic received a donation from him of one million marks for promoting research and training in physics, mechanical engineering, electrical engineering, and construction.[39] At the end of 1916, he donated 13 million marks of his war profits to "building the Neckar Canal" – a project that was thwarted by the high inflation of the postwar years.[40] Robert Bosch also gave money to, among other things, the Markel Foundation for Furthering Gifted Students, the Society for the Advancement of Popular Education founded by Theodor Bäuerle, the Berlin College of Politics where his subsequent biographer Theodor Heuss taught, the *Deutscher Werkbund* association for the applied arts, the foundation that ran Stuttgart's Homeopathic Hospital, and the House of German-Turkish Friendship in Istanbul. Hans-Erhard Lessing's biography of Robert Bosch lists over 30 endowments and major donations made by the entrepreneur, primarily to colleges, educational societies, and medical and charitable organizations.[41] To mark his 75th birthday, Robert Bosch set up something of a monument to himself by endowing a homeopathic hospital in Stuttgart, now known as the Robert Bosch Hospital [*Robert-Bosch-Krankenhaus*].[42]

Of great importance in the life of Robert Bosch was his interest in agriculture, which he also inherited from his parents. He acquired an estate of his own when, in 1912, he bought shares in an undertaking that produced peat briquettes from a large moor in the vicinity of Mooseurach in Upper Bavaria. Ammonia and nitrogen were also extracted from the peat for the manufacture of artificial fertilizers, although such operations had to be halted following the introduction of the Haber-Bosch process for synthesizing ammonia, developed by Robert Bosch's nephew Carl Bosch in conjunction with Fritz Haber. In December 1913, Robert Bosch bought the Mooseurach estate, and during the First World War he had it drained and the peat extracted. After the war, he acquired several adjoining farms in order to combine them into a major agricultural holding. At the beginning of the 1930s, more than 300 people worked there. Under its manager Walther Mauk, the estate experienced a boom following the Great Depression, but in commercial terms it remained very much a loss-making business. Here, too, Robert Bosch developed a certain technical ambition, but for him the farm (known as the *Boschhof*) was more an important place of retreat where he could busy himself encouraging swallows to nest and planting fruit trees. For the family, it became a second home. After Robert Bosch's death, the family continued to run the *Boschhof*, and today it is farmed by Christof Bosch, a grandson of the founder.[43]

Hunting lodges were further places of retreat for Robert Bosch. Hunting was indeed his greatest leisure-time passion, and he did not feel this conflicted in any way with his commitment to the lifestyle reform [*Lebensreform*] movement. He owned several shoots simultaneously: the so-called "Bosch-Jagd" near Pfronten in the Allgäu, the Wespental preserve near Dottingen in the Swabian Jura, and a third one at Kastelalmen, Scharnitz, in Austria's Tyrol region. His interest in hunting was not so much fuelled by social needs. It was a private passion. That said, he did on many occasions invite work associates and business partners to Pfronten or Wespental. "Hunting reveals a completely different side to people," Robert Bosch would say frequently, or so we are told.[44] Hunting gave rise to friendships such as those with the Stuttgart city official Otto Metzger and the professional hunter Georg Escherich – a Bavarian monarchist who in the early 1920s had founded a right-wing, paramilitary self-protection league and certainly will not have shared Robert Bosch's political opinions. As a hunter,

Robert Bosch hunting (1941)

too, Robert Bosch set himself the highest standards. Escherich, one of the most prominent forestry people of his time, wrote of the Wespental shoot, "Robert Bosch's hunting preserve in the Rauhe Alb is the best shoot I know of in present-day Germany. It was not money alone that created this jewel of a hunting preserve but primarily the sympathy and skill of the proprietor."[45]

Robert Bosch was not an easy man to get on with. He could fly into a dreadful temper when something did not suit him or failed to come up to his high standards. It is said that those around him often had to suffer a seemingly "total lack of manners and respect."[46] People who knew him only as a caring employer and generous patron never suspected this side of his character and therefore often found such behavior puzzling. Theodor Bäuerle, who knew Robert Bosch well, had the feeling that, however successful and popular this entrepreneur was, "in the deepest part of his being, he was a lonely and unhappy man."[47] Robert Bosch had very few close friends. From the early years, there was only really Eugen Kayser, who subsequently became the first head of the metal-working business that Robert Bosch set up in Feuerbach. His longest friendship was probably that with Paul Reusch, managing director of the Gutehoffnungs-hütte mining and industrial engineering group. Robert Bosch had met him in 1888–89, through the *Akademischer Verein Hütte Stuttgart*, a student organization. Both men remained friends until Robert Bosch's death, although politically the national conservative Reusch took a different view from Robert Bosch in many respects. Another close friendship began in the 1920s with Hermann Bücher, whom Robert Bosch got to know through the *Reichsverband der Deutschen Industrie* ("National Association of Industrialists"), even before Bücher became president of AEG. Skeptical by nature, Robert Bosch was no fan of formal social occasions, clubs, or high society. He would rather go walking with the family in the Alps, and even there he was not drawn to the five-star hotels favored by the industrialist class.

Robert Bosch became involved in the lifestyle reform movement early on. His parents had already been great believers in natural healing. He was also influenced by Gustav Jäger, whom he met during his brief period of study as an academic teacher. Jäger was keen for people to wear only clothing made from natural fabrics, and from that time on Robert Bosch wore what was called "natural clothing" or "Jäger underwear" made from wool.[48] Around the turn of the century, Robert Bosch began campaigning for homeopathy. He joined the "Stuttgart Homeopathic Hospital" association, and in 1915 donated nearly three million marks to build such a hospital in the city. Since this project could not be brought to fruition, he later supported the construction of an "interim" homeopathic hospital.[49] Robert Bosch also financed homeopathic training courses and in 1925 founded the homeopathic publishing house Hippokrates, which today still specializes in literature on the subject of natural healing processes.[50]

Despite his sparse leisure time, Robert Bosch was widely read. He was interested in publications to do with the natural sciences but also in history. On the other hand, he had no feeling for music, and also viewed the fine arts more through the eyes of a craftsman, concerned mainly with technical aspects.[51] Unlike many of his bourgeois contemporaries, Robert Bosch never dreamed of building an art collection. He felt a deep aversion for the metaphysical, the transcendent – in any shape or form. He was an engineer, and that was the way he saw the world; he could not be doing with anything intangible. Bäuerle writes in his memoir about Robert Bosch, "He took no interest in theoretical questions. He avoided philosophical, ideological, or religious literature."[52] The same stance determined what Robert Bosch thought of the church. He was unable to believe in God because God was invisible. He is reported as often saying, "If there is a personal God, he should have created me in such a way that I too can believe in him."[53] It was no more than consistent

Robert Bosch with an apprentice (1938)

with such an attitude that Robert Bosch resigned his church membership. However, the entrepreneur felt no reservations toward associates who were devout Christians, for in his eyes religion and ideology were private matters; they did not concern other people.

A major interest of Robert Bosch's was adult education, as championed by the reformist educational movements of the day. He supported the association for the promotion of adult learning founded by Bäuerle and backed educational provision for his own employees in the form of lectures and a works library. By contrast, he was very distrustful of the educated classes with their grounding in the classics. Heuss tells us that Robert Bosch detested intellectual snobbery and above all rejected the humanist education provided at high-school level by the Gymnasium.[54] One of the rules that he introduced into his company was a renunciation of personal titles. He himself was awarded an honorary doctorate in 1910 for his generous donation to the Stuttgart Polytechnic but made virtually no use of it, having people address him as "Mr. Bosch" ["Herr Bosch"].

A fascinating side of Robert Bosch's personality was and is that he was invariably true to his own character and to his own style. Although as an entrepreneur he enjoyed an extraordinarily rapid rise, he continued (as Hans Walz put it in a speech to mark the man's 80th birthday) to evince "an inconspicuous simplicity."[55] Granted, Robert Bosch lived in a splendid town house and owned a country estate and several hunting preserves, but not even in his appearance did he conform to what people at the time expected of a wealthy industrialist. He kept his full beard, stayed true to his woolen clothing, and was happier in the mountains than on the Côte d'Azur. All these things lent him a certain authenticity, and the message he conveyed was universally understood. A Robert Bosch does not need to adapt. Robert Bosch succeeded in communicating deeply held principles in such a way that they became part of the corporate culture – like the unwritten rule that politics and ideology were private matters and had nothing to do with an employer, for instance, or that it was not a person's title that counted but what that person achieved. In particular, though, it was his commercial principles – a striving for quality, total reliability, and a customer-friendly atmosphere – that came to characterize his company.[56] These things were so influential not only because they carry messages of timeless actuality but also because Robert Bosch saw himself and his company as being integrally linked; his personal ethic of behavior in no way diverged from the principles that governed his business activities. Nothing illustrates this better than his best known dictum, taken from an article that he wrote in September 1918 for the manuscript collection of the Prussian National Library in Berlin. For more than 90 years, it has formed part of the Bosch Group's corporate identity: "I have always acted according to the principle that I would rather lose money than trust. The integrity of my promises, the belief in the value of my products and in my word of honor have always had a higher priority for me than a transitory profit."[57] With such utterances Robert Bosch was able to win associates over, since he gave them values and inspiration. Of course, the ability (shared by many owner-entrepreneurs) to feel integrated in one's corporation has its down side. Robert Bosch expected all his employees to work in accordance with his own principles. He was incapable of accommodating other ideas. Until the end, Robert Bosch could not bear to think that his life's work might develop differently than intended. His testamentary arrangements are imbued with this concern. To supplement those arrangements he left an extensive framework of guidelines designed to guarantee continuance of his corporation in line with his conception. It was not his aim to bequeath the greatest possible fortune but to ensure that, within the company and beyond, his ideas should remain exemplary.

2 The difficult early years

"I started out with a technician and an errand boy." That was how Robert Bosch described in his memoirs the beginnings of the operation that he set up in Stuttgart on November 15, 1886, under the name "Werkstätte für Fein-mechanik und Elektrotechnik" [Workshop for precision mechanics and electrical engineering].[1] The company began modestly in the courtyard-entrance building at 75B Rotebühlstrasse, opposite the Feuersee lake in the western part of the city.[2] There, not far from the furnished room in which he lived, the founder had rented a ground-floor apartment that he used as business premises. According to a later account by Robert Bosch, at the time he had an office, one larger and one smaller workshop, and a windowless room containing a portable forge.[3] As a kind of company sign, he installed an electric clock on the front building. Apart from Robert Bosch's workshop, the courtyard-entrance building at 75B Rotebühlstraße was also home to a bottled-beer store and a coachbuilder. The building that fronted onto the street housed a cigar business owned by Otto and Max Rosenfeld.[4]

The 25-year-old founder contributed a handsome 10,000 marks as capital stock for the new company. However, he had no fixed business plan beyond simply the "intention of building appliances, if possible of an electrical nature."[5] It would have to be seen what kind of orders would come his way. As was to be expected, in the early days the workshop was mainly asked to do installation and repair jobs. Robert Bosch and his technician laid telephone cables, fitted bells, and mended typewriters. For the Rosenfeld cigar business at the front of 75B Rotebühlstraße, the workshop manufactured cigar holders. The range of the workshop's activity is illustrated by an advertisement that appeared in the Stuttgart daily newspaper *Der Beobachter* on February 2, 1887: "Telephones, house telegraphs, expert testing and installation of lightning rods, installation and repair of electrical appliances, and all types of precision-engineering work."[6] "House telegraph" was the term used at the time for an electrical bell pull for summoning domestic servants.[7] The market for such systems can hardly have been very large, and in those days telephones were still seen as "toys for the rich." They were rented out at a high price, mainly to companies and wealthy households.[8] And initially, Robert Bosch could not afford a telephone connection for his workshop either. More generally,

Bosch's first workshop at 75B Rotebühlstraße (1886)

electrification made slow progress in Stuttgart, since the city still did not have its own electricity works, but just one power station to supply a block of buildings.[9]

The ledger kept by Robert Bosch tells us that on January 4, 1887, he issued his first invoice (for the installation of an electric bell) and that in the company's first financial year it had a total of 66 customers. Its largest order – to install a telephone system – had come from a publishing house, the Süddeutsches Verlagsinstitut. The company's earnings clearly did not cover its costs. According to a later reconstruction, the workshop generated sales in the region of 5,000 marks in its first financial year, but made an overall loss of 1,540 marks. The technician's annual salary alone amounted to 1,200 marks (the average annual salary of a worker in mechanical engineering at that time was about 820 marks), while Robert Bosch also had personal expenses of 1,600 marks. Nonetheless, the founder placed great importance on having good equipment, so in that first year he invested some 1,100 marks in buying a lathe, a workbench, and various tools.[10] In his memoirs, Robert Bosch wrote that his earnings enabled him to "get married approximately one year after launching my business."[11] And in fact, he married his fiancée Anna Kayser in October 1887, even if the company was not yet turning a profit. Clearly, also within the minds of the families of the young couple, starting the business was closely bound up with the expectation of an early marriage. The 10,000 marks capital stock that Robert Bosch invested in his company came from the inheritance of his father, who had died in 1880. Each of his brothers had already received such a sum when they married.[12]

But Robert Bosch's beginnings as an entrepreneur cannot fairly be described simply by conjuring up the modest image of his first workshop. He himself encouraged this version of the story in later writings, but the fact was that he started out with far more than "a technician and an errand boy." He was also an exceptionally well-informed man, he had a wide range and variety of contacts, and he came from a well-to-do family. Given his extensive access to information, he could be in no doubt that electricity was the future. After all, he had worked for Thomas Edison in New York City, where the world's first electricity works had gone into operation in 1882, and it was common knowledge that Emil Rathenau's German Edison Society (soon to become AEG) had already built a central power station in Berlin. He could expect a strong demand for electrical appliances to come into play locally as soon as Stuttgart had its own electricity works.

A number of companies had already tried to persuade the city of Stuttgart to grant them a license to build an electricity works. In 1884, the Elektrotechnische Fabrik Cannstatt submitted such an application to the municipal authorities. Two years later, Wihelm Reißer, a company which had acquired the German Edison Society's sole agency for Württemberg, applied for a license. However, the city of Stuttgart was not prepared to cede. The powers-that-be were reluctant to upset the gas company with which they had concluded a street-lighting contract, and many Swabians still saw electricity as a needless luxury.[13] It is possible, however, that the authorities were simply being cautious, aware as they were that the Berlin electricity works was in financial difficulties – difficulties which had temporarily brought Rathenau's company to the verge of bankruptcy.[14]

Robert Bosch likely knew that the electrification boom in Stuttgart was not going to start immediately after the launch of his workshop. Accordingly, he created a second pillar for his business – the distribution of medical appliances powered by electricity. In medical practices and hospitals, electricity was in wider use than in private households, and there was brisk demand for laryngoscopes, induction appliances, and microscope lamps. In 1883, an old friend of Robert Bosch, a precision mechanic by the name of Karl Friedrich Schall, had opened a workshop in Stuttgart for various illuminated endoscopes. At the beginning of 1886, Schall and his partner Max Gebbert joined forces with a technician named Ernst Moritz Reiniger, who manufactured electromedical appliances in Erlangen. The new company, known as Reiniger, Gebbert & Schall, a forerunner of Siemens-Reiniger AG, had its registered office in Erlangen. Although it abandoned its Stuttgart workshop soon after it was set up, the company was reluctant to give up its clientele in the city. Schall therefore asked Robert Bosch to represent Reiniger, Gebbert & Schall in Stuttgart on a commission basis.[15] The Schall connection gave Robert Bosch a certain customer base. Of the 66 customers that his company supplied in its first financial year, 21 were physicians and medical institutes. Two of them were among Bosch's most important customers, including the eye clinic run by a certain Dr. Königsdorfer.[16]

Automotive technology was not something Robert Bosch had in mind when he set up his company. At the time, motorization of road traffic was still an exotic idea. Granted, Robert Bosch knew Gottlieb Daimler, who together with Wilhelm Maybach had set up an experimental workshop in Cannstatt, just outside Stuttgart. When Bosch as a company came into being, Daimler and Maybach had recently succeeded in building the world's first four-wheeled automobile, a motor carriage, and shortly before that Carl Benz had manufactured his three-wheeled patent motor vehicle in Mannheim. However, it was to be some time before a market grew out of these beginnings. By contrast, stationary engines had long been commonplace, even in the Swabian hinterland. So it was that in August 1887 an engineering works in Möckmühl gave Robert Bosch his first order to construct an ignition device. In his memoirs he wrote: "In the summer of [1887], a small mechanical engineering company approached me and asked me whether I could make it a device like the one Gasmotorenfabrik Deutz in Cologne was using in its gasoline engines. I was told I could have a look at one of the devices in Schorndorf. I went over to Schorndorf, and there I found the low-voltage magneto ignition device fitted with break-spark rodding."[17] Robert Bosch first asked Gasmotorenfabrik Deutz whether this ignition device was protected by patent. Although he received no reply, luck was on his side. Nicolaus Otto, one of the founders of Gasmotorenfabrik Deutz, had invented the device just three years earlier, but had not taken out a patent on it.[18] Robert Bosch copied the device in less than six weeks, improving it in the process, and sold it for 216.50 marks to his customer, the Schmehl & Hespelt engineering works – a company that no one would remember today had they not, back then, bought the first Bosch magneto. So the low-voltage magneto was not a Bosch invention, but reproducing and reworking it certainly was a remarkable achievement. The order likely presented an opportunity of another kind for the young entrepreneur. Here was a chance to make something. His primary intention, after all, was to build appliances, and not to carry out installation and repair work or to supply goods on a commission basis.

Having come to Bosch as a result of the Schmehl & Hespelt order, the business of building magnetos for internal-combustion engines quickly grew into a further pillar of business for the new workshop. When Robert Bosch read in a newspaper advertisement that the reputable Swiss engineering works and soon-to-be automobile manufacturer F. Martini & Co. in the Thurgau canton was on the lookout for magnetos, he supplied the company with a low-voltage magneto based on the one he had adapted from the model made by Gasmotorenfabrik Deutz. He traveled to the headquarters of F. Martini & Co. in Frauenfeld himself and, during the course of 1888, managed to sell a further four ignition devices in Switzerland.[19] These were his company's first orders outside Germany. The following years saw a marked increase in orders for the construction of ignition devices, and thus for the manufacturing side of his business. By 1891, 58 percent of sales were already accounted for by ignition devices, and Bosch magnetos were being supplied as far afield as Dresden, Kiel, and Vienna – even to a customer in the U.K.[20] Nonetheless, Robert Bosch wrote in his memoirs that unit sales of the magnetos he built for stationary engines in those years were "unimpressive."[21] To some extent this was quite true, since customer numbers were extremely modest. In 1891, Bosch had only 11 customers ordering ignition devices as compared with 157 for installation work. The likely reason for this was that the only companies ordering Bosch ignition devices were those already equipped with the new gasoline engines. These were an innovation which displaced gas-powered engines only gradually, and even where companies already possessed a gasoline engine, most of these likely operated with the original ignition devices supplied by Gasmotorenfabrik Deutz. But while the installation business was largely local, the market for ignition devices was supra-regional, with the major customers in that market each ordering a number of devices each year. To take two examples, of the 130 ignition devices sold in 1891, 72 went to Gasmotorenfabrik Moritz Hille in Dresden alone, and a further 25 to the F. Martini & Co. engineering works in Frauenfeld.[22] At that time, Bosch did no business at all with such important engineering companies as Maschinenfabrik Esslingen, Motorenfabrik Benz & Co. in Mannheim, or Daimler-Motoren-Gesellschaft in nearby Cannstatt.

Profits still eluded Robert Bosch as many as five years after opening his workshop. The losses of 1887–91 had swallowed up most of the capital stock. Evidence for this comes from the reconstruction of the company's balance sheets and profit-and-loss accounts for the early financial years drawn up by Otto Fischer in 1942 on the basis of the surviving ledgers. In this regard, Fischer wrote: "Sales had gone up fivefold in the first half-decade, with the ignition-device business even increasing almost tenfold in four years, yet the bottom line was depressing. Capital was virtually exhausted, and the business survived essentially on family and bank loans. As a company, Bosch was in a bad way!"[23] The data reconstructed by Fischer do not give any clues as to what caused those losses. Profitability can hardly have been the reason, since the ratio of profit to sales increased from 25.3 percent in 1888 to 36.5 percent in 1892.[24] Yet in none of those years did gross profit suffice to cover "administrative costs." Also included in that item were the requirements of Robert Bosch and his family, which (Fischer suggests) had increased markedly as a result of his marriage and the arrival of the children. Following the births of Margarete, Paula, and Robert, the family moved into a larger apartment at 145 Rotebühlstraße, and this doubtless had an impact on expenses. But the reconstruction also shows that, in the period 1886–91, wage costs went up steeply from 1,440 to 9,750 marks, the reason for this being that the workshop had long since ceased to employ only "a technician and an errand boy." The workforce is now more likely to have numbered ten.[25] The business also needed more and more space. In the spring of 1890, the workshop moved to 9 Gutenbergstraße, and a year and a half later to 109 Rotebühlstraße.[26]

All in all, there is plenty to suggest that the rising sales from the ignition-device business were simply not adequate to fund the entrepreneur's growing family and the ever-expanding workforce. Gottlob Honold, who had begun his apprenticeship with Bosch in 1891, later recalled that at that time the workshop employed six assistants, two apprentices, and two errand boys.[27] According to the memoirs of Richard Schyle, one of Bosch's earliest associates, the workshop employed as many as 24 people in 1892, though this is likely an overestimate.[28] Nonetheless, it could be inferred from Schyle's assertion that Robert Bosch tended to employ more staff than the business could reasonably support. Schyle also recalls a serious crisis in 1892, when Robert Bosch was obliged to lay off the entire workforce except for two associates.[29] This first crisis in the history of the company may have been due to payment difficulties suffered by a major customer, the Stuttgart photographer Hackh.[30] The crisis cannot have lasted long, though, since Fischer was unable to find any indication of such a drastic drop in headcount in the company ledgers.[31] The wage bill did in fact sink in May 1892 from 1,509 to 774 marks, and that October it went down to 439 marks.[32] Yet in 1892, the company was able to record a substantial profit for the first time, which made up for the losses of the previous years.[33] It is possible that the surplus had to do with an electrical engineering exhibition that took place in Stuttgart in February 1892, attracting 20,000 visitors.[34]

Bosch now increasingly took on orders of all kinds. Among other things, the company produced fountain pens, speedometers, gas lighters, gelding forceps, and typewriters – including one for blind typists. Its most successful product was an electric water-level meter, used in connection with the work then being carried out to supply homes in the Swabian Jura with water.[35] This "shambles," as Robert Bosch later called it,[36] was likely the fault of Stuttgart's municipal authorities and their reluctance to build an electricity works. Bosch had presumably not reckoned with such a lengthy dry spell before the start of Stuttgart's electrification boom, and the ignition-device business did not at first provide an adequate substitute, gasoline engines being still relatively uncommon. Looked at in this light, the economic troubles of the company's first decade of operation stemmed ultimately from Robert Bosch's reliance on new technologies for which there was as yet no market of any size.

In this critical phase from the autumn of 1891 to the spring of 1892, the only thing that kept the company from insolvency was the loans that Robert Bosch had secured from his relatives – especially from his mother. Maria Margaretha Bosch initially lent her son 10,000 marks, but by late 1893 this amount had risen to approximately 14,000 marks. In addition, she acted as guarantor for a credit facility granted to Robert Bosch by the Stuttgarter Gewerbekasse on March 16, 1891. In May 1893, Robert Bosch had drawn on this to the tune of 10,000 marks.[37] In connection with this, in March 1891 Robert Bosch asked the Stuttgarter Gewerbekasse to give him his first bank account. His brothers-in-law Carl Kayser and August Grünzweig contributed further loans of around 5,100 marks and 2,500 marks respectively. By the end of 1893, Robert Bosch had received family loans totaling 21,641 marks. On top of this came the Gewerbekasse credit facility for which his mother had acted as guarantor, and which was still drawn to the tune of 6,211 marks. He also had outstanding debts of 2,634 marks.[38]

At this point, however, there was a turn for the better. In November 1893, the Stuttgart municipal authorities decided in favor of a power station, which was then built by a subsidiary of Elektrizitäts AG (formerly Schuckert). Crucial to the decision were the interests of the streetcar company. Its horse-drawn carriages could not deal with the many steep climbs in the city. Moreover, it had already conducted successful trials of electrically powered units on a test track.[39] In September 1895, Stuttgart's first electricity works, a steam power station in Marienstraße, went into operation. In the same month, the first electrified section of the streetcar network was opened between Charlottenplatz and Berg.[40] For Bosch, the inauguration of the electricity works was a crucial turning point. The company now received sizeable installation contracts, securing its livelihood. In the 1896 financial year, it was able to make a profit larger than total losses incurred since the day of its founding.[41]

The atmosphere at Bosch at that time was still that of an artisanal workshop. The entrepreneur taught the apprentices himself – and did so with great commitment, partly because of the negative experience of his own apprenticeship. He did not take on more than two apprentices at one time. Some of his earliest associates proved disappointing, as was the case with the errand boy employed at the time the company was founded, a young man named Michel Dentz.[42] The identity of Bosch's first technician can no longer be established, but several of his successors stayed with the company for lengthy periods. One stroke of luck turned out to be the hiring of a technician named Arnold Zähringer, who came to Bosch – temporarily at first – in 1889, departed for a year, then returned, and was soon put in charge of the workshop. Zähringer, a trained watchmaker from Furtwangen in the Black Forest, brought with him the precision-mechanical skills of his trade. He witnessed the transformation of Bosch from workshop to major company, until in late 1914 he was obliged to retire for health reasons.[43] Another good choice was Richard Schyle, who joined the company as an assistant technician in 1891. He later became its longest-serving associate and the subject of numerous anecdotes.[44] After a number of disappointments, Bosch became more cautious in his choice of apprentices, but here too he had clearly acquired a surer touch. Two of his apprentices from this period, Gottlob Honold and Max Rall, later rose to senior-management and even board level. Honold, who was introduced to the company by his father, a teacher from Langenau near Ulm who was also a former friend of Bosch's father, began his apprenticeship in 1891. Honold subsequently invented the high-voltage magneto, which made a crucial contribution to the rise of the company. In 1917, he became a member of the board.[45] Max Rall came from a business family and joined Bosch as an apprentice in 1894. He subsequently built up the business in France, was elected to the board in 1926, and remained a member of senior management until 1942.[46]

Honold later reported that associates in the workshop would often sing together as they worked, and Schyle gives a detailed account of this in his memoirs. Apparently, Robert Bosch asked the singers to keep their voices down, since he did not want people thinking the place was a conservatory.[47] But despite such reminiscences, Theodor Heuss rightly stresses that the company of that time was no "olde-worlde idyll."[48] Robert Bosch knew how to make use of the media, placing advertisements in the press and issuing catalogues. To keep himself informed, he subscribed to the *Centralblatt für Elektrotechnik*, unusually for a workshop the size of his. From 1889, he had his own telephone connection, for which the high annual rental of 150 marks had to be paid, and in 1890 he purchased a bicycle to enable him to keep a closer eye on his associates as they performed jobs in different parts of the city.[49] There were not many bicycles in Stuttgart at the time – they were classed as a luxury at first, rather like riding horses – but mounted on his latest model he attracted the attention of many passers-by, which was doubtless good for publicity too.[50]

Reports from the initial phase of the company's history show that Robert Bosch already displayed the typical characteristics of his entrepreneurial approach, namely high standards of quality and openness to social welfare considerations. Work was done with a high degree of precision under the strict eye of the founder. "Botchers and bunglers were not tolerated in the Bosch workshop," recalled Adolf Krauß, who was taken on in 1894 as a technician.[51] Yet Robert Bosch was extremely keen on having a good atmosphere in the workshop and good relations with workers. He paid what were already high wages for the time, and he *did* tolerate singing in the workshop, provided that it was not detrimental to work. Decades later, Honold wrote of his apprenticeship years: "Mr. Bosch knew how to secure the good will of his employees by treating them fairly, paying them well, and making their working conditions as comfortable as possible."[52] When in 1894 four associates approached Robert Bosch with the request that the working day be shortened from ten hours to nine, he did not refuse – although the company was still losing money. He introduced the nine-hour working day and held out the promise of a further reduction to eight hours if other companies dropped the ten-hour day.[53]

3   The period of rapid growth

The irresistible rise of the Bosch magneto

The electrification of Stuttgart and the installation work that resulted from it secured the bare existence of Robert Bosch's new company. But its rapid growth in the years after 1895 was attributable to the magneto ignition business, and thus to a product manufactured in-house. Electrification had been a foreseeable development when Robert Bosch ventured into the world of business, but when he became involved in magneto production, it was still unclear what course automotive technology would take. When Robert Bosch produced his first ignition device in 1887, this was simply one field of business among many, since gasoline engines were still quite rare. However, when the gasoline engine did gain wide acceptance – in factories at first, then on the road – the company was able to draw on its accumulated expertise in producing ignition devices. But this does not explain how Bosch could become an international brand in this field in less than a decade. It happened because the company made a number of groundbreaking inventions. These in turn prompted it to start up export operations, which then expanded rapidly.

The low-voltage magneto ignition device developed by Nicolaus Otto at Gasmotorenfabrik Deutz in the 1880s was a huge advance, crucial to the replacement of gas engines by gasoline-powered ones. Current generated by an armature revolving between the poles of a magnet was fed to a piece of apparatus comprising a fixed trigger electrode and an ignition lever. Sudden opening of the ignition lever, which had the effect of breaking the power circuit, produced a spark in the combustion chamber. In other words, ignition took place as a result of the revolutions of the engine alone. No external source of power was required. The pioneering Otto had of course designed his magneto for stationary engines. There were no automobiles as yet. The first automakers were forced to concede that the magnetos built by Gasmotorenfabrik Deutz were unsuitable for vehicle engines, which ran at higher speeds. The heavy armature was too cumbersome. Most of the early automobiles therefore had battery-powered ignition systems, but the major disadvantage of these was that power used for ignition could not be replenished while the vehicle was on the move. Drivers had to stop after only a short stretch to recharge the vehicle's batteries. For his part, Gottlieb Daimler fitted the gasoline engines built by his company with glow-tube ignition. However, the high fire risk involved made this a very dangerous construction. So as automobile numbers increased, a new solution to the ignition problem became more and more urgent. In his memoirs, Carl Benz referred to the question of how to provide ignition as "the trickiest problem" in engine design.[1] The first drivers had to put up with many trials and tribulations in this regard, particularly since there were no automobile repair workshops at this time. They sometimes spent whole days tinkering with their ignition systems, cooling them down, installing new ones, and replacing damaged parts.[2]

There were plenty of attempts to find an ignition system suitable for automobiles. Up to a certain engine speed, the low-voltage magneto ignition device built by Bosch seems to have proved comparatively acceptable. The first company to fit automobiles with such magnetos was a small engine builder in Thuringia. The two devices that Bosch sold to Thüringische Motorenwerke in Neustadt an der Orla in 1894 were demonstrably the first Bosch magnetos to be installed in automobile engines. Indeed, they were satisfactory enough for the customer to order three more ignition devices from Bosch. However, financial difficulties forced Thüringische Motorenwerke out of business shortly afterwards, in 1895.[3] In the same year, another Bosch magneto was successfully incorporated into a Benz automobile running at a lower engine speed.[4] And while Bosch produced 157 magnetos in 1895, the number rose to 528 the following year. But nearly all these were destined for installation in stationary engines. Fewer than 1 percent of the low-voltage magnetos manufactured by Bosch in 1896 were in fact installed in automobiles.[5] Production of the 1,000th magneto was marked on September 6, 1896, by Robert Bosch inviting his entire staff on a works outing to Geradstetten in the Rems Valley.[6] Clearly, the expanding company was to retain something of the convivial atmosphere of the earlier workshop.

In 1896, Bosch was approached by the Augsburg motorcycle manufacturer Rüb & Wegelin. It had been disappointed by battery-powered ignition systems, and the engine designer Ludwig Rüb considered Daimler's glow-tube system too much of a hazard. Rüb needed an ignition system for engine speeds in excess of 1,000 rpm – faster than existing magneto ignition devices could cope with.[7] Bosch's works manager Arnold Zähringer took up the challenge. Experiments showed him that the double-T armature situated between the poles of the magnet need not move at all. The same effect could be achieved if the armature remained still and a sleeve rotated around it. The spark was still triggered by breaking the circuit with an ignition lever, but with the sleeve being so much lighter than the armature, higher engine

Works outing (1896)

speeds could be attained. Bosch received a patent for this break-spark ignition device in June 1897, and the device went into production immediately,
Zähringer's reward being a share in future license revenue.[8] His invention
was the first ignition device designed specifically for automobile engines.
Such vehicles could now cover longer distances without interruption than
had been possible before. The first customer for the new break-spark ignition
device, the Rüb & Wegelin company, was convinced of its advantages.[9] There,
the ignition system was successfully incorporated into motorcycles and subsequently into motorized three-wheelers.[10] However, in the case of another
motorcycle manufacturer (based near Hamburg) trials of the Bosch magneto
were unsuccessful.[11]

Robert Bosch brought Zähringer's invention to the attention of the Ger-
man-British entrepreneur Frederick R. Simms. At the time, Simms was looking for suitable ignition devices for automobiles, since battery ignition had
left him unconvinced. Having failed to find what he was looking for in the
U.K., he had widened the search to include Germany, where he was told that
Gasmotorenfabrik Deutz and Bosch were two leading producers.[12] A pioneer

of the European automobile industry, Simms was as influential as he was self-opinionated. He had acquired an exclusive agency agreement with Daimler-Motoren-Gesellschaft for the United Kingdom and the Commonwealth, and by setting up Daimler Motor Company in Coventry in 1896 had brought the automobile industry to the U.K.[13] Simms had already purchased several magneto ignition devices from Bosch. Hearing of Zähringer's design, he placed an order for it to be fitted into the gasoline engine of a three-wheeler. The vehicle that Simms dispatched to Bosch in November 1897 was a British version (manufactured under license) of the then very popular three-wheeler produced by the French company De Dion-Bouton. Test drives at Bosch, which were entrusted to an apprentice named Max Rall, established that the engine worked at a minimum speed of 500–600 rpm. Robert Bosch later put this figure even higher – at 1,800 rpm.[14] Be that as it may, the new break-spark ignition device survived even this trial unscathed. On December 21, 1897, Bosch successfully demonstrated the three-wheeler in the presence of Daimler and Maybach, and at the beginning of January 1898 – eight weeks after placing the order – Simms took delivery of his converted De Dion-Bouton three-wheeler.[15] It was the first automobile to be fitted with the new Bosch magneto designed by Zähringer.

Soon afterwards, Robert Bosch received his first order from Daimler-Motoren-Gesellschaft for the new low-voltage magneto ignition device. Simms had convinced the Daimler supervisory board of the advantages of this design, though not Gottlieb Daimler himself, who wanted to stick with the glow-tube system. Personal animosities may well have played a role here, since Daimler and Bosch did not get on.[16] In retrospect, Robert Bosch wrote: "Daimler detested me and created as many problems for me as he could."[17] Daimler, who was far older (he died in March 1900), apparently regarded Robert Bosch as a young whippersnapper; and Bosch, for his part, doubtless thought Daimler an incorrigible mule head. At Simms's urging, the supervisory board of Daimler-Motoren-Gesellschaft opened negotiations with Bosch. The Daimler directors Maybach and Vischer even considered acquiring the magneto producer and sent Bosch a corresponding enquiry. But Robert Bosch was not prepared to sell his company, so Daimler-Motoren-Gesellschaft attempted to secure the exclusive rights to sell the Bosch magneto ignition device. In exchange, Bosch expected an assurance that Daimler would use Bosch magnetos exclusively. In the end, negotiations were broken off, since Daimler-Motoren-Gesellschaft would only agree to purchase 100 magnetos a year, which was approximately what Bosch was selling at the time for use in automobile engines. He was still selling a great many more for stationary engines. In fact, his company was already producing in excess of 1,000 of these annually. So he asked Daimler to guarantee that it would purchase 3,000 magnetos per annum – and this for 14 years. In addition, Daimler was to take over distribution of magnetos for stationary engines, since the customers for these were often the same as for "cycle ignition systems."[18] But, as already mentioned, no agreement was reached, so Bosch as a company did not fall under Daimler's control. Instead, it remained an independent supplier.[19]

Nonetheless, Daimler-Motoren-Gesellschaft was unable to avoid buying the new break-spark ignition device from Bosch. The man who made sure of this was Emil Jellinek, one of the most enigmatic figures among the automobile pioneers of the day. Jellinek, who came from a family of scholars, had made a substantial fortune in the tobacco trade and through insurance and stock-exchange transactions. As the Austro-Hungarian consul general in the Principality of Monaco, he lived in a splendid villa in Nice much frequented by the local upper crust. The moneyed aristocracy in France were very keen at the time on this new means of individual mobility, and the rich and beautiful of the Côte d'Azur were no exception. Automobiles were *le dernier cri*, and those who could afford them were all "car-crazy." Being very expensive, motor vehicles were symbols of luxury and exclusivity. And there was the added attraction of the automobile races staged in France from 1894 onwards. These were social events, rather like horse racing, except that there was an extra thrill involved: accidents were frequent.[20] Having grasped early on what business possibilities this opened up, Emil Jellinek got in touch with Daimler. He distributed Daimler automobiles in France from 1898 and began putting his name down for races. Before long, he was urging Daimler to design a new, lighter model more suited to racing than the existing motorized carriages and fitted not with glow-tube ignition systems but with the break-spark magneto ignition devices by Bosch. Jellinek being one of its biggest customers, Daimler-Motoren-Gesellschaft consented.[21]

The new vehicle, a four-seater, six-liter car designed by Wilhelm Maybach, met Jellinek's requirements in full. It was named for Jellinek's daughter Mercedes. The vehicle's presentation at the Nice Motor Show in late March 1901 was a huge success. The new 35-horsepower Mercedes won the Nice-Salon-Nice race by a large margin, and the secretary-general of the French automobile club talked of the "Mercedes era" as having dawned. Jellinek's order books were now so full that he was able to secure from Daimler a purchase option for the entire vehicle production of 1901 and 1902.[22] Winning races boosted not only the automobile's reputation but also its price, and there were times when Jellinek was able to charge double what the manufacturer had stipulated. His customers included not only Kaiser Wilhelm II but also the king of Württemberg and a number of American billionaires.[23] Since the Mercedes operated with a Bosch magneto ignition device, some of its fame rubbed off on Robert Bosch's company in Stuttgart. By this time, if not before, the name Bosch was familiar throughout the automobile world – relatively small though that world still was in the early years of the twentieth century.[24]

The company achieved a further spectacular triumph in July 1900 when the first of Graf Zeppelin's airships (LZ 1), equipped with a Bosch break-spark magneto ignition device, completed a successful test flight. Zeppelin had had Daimler engines fitted but had understandably asked that they be equipped not with glow-tube ignition systems but with magnetos.[25] Of course, it was still too early to consider a business producing aviation-engine ignition systems. Zeppelin, incidentally, soon had to abandon his test flights for lack of money and was unable to build another airship until 1904.

As part of the negotiations with Daimler in the spring of 1898, Robert Bosch had intended to transfer the entire distribution of his products to Daimler-Motoren-Gesellschaft. For him, the main argument in favor of this solution was the prospect of business outside Germany. Internationally, Daimler was already well set up. With Simms and Jellinek, Daimler-Motoren-Gesellschaft had influential representatives in the U.K. and France. Robert Bosch was eager to gain entry to the markets in these countries. He was looking for an agent especially for the U.K., since in that country virtually no one was yet producing magneto ignition devices. At first glance, it may perhaps appear over-ambitious for a relatively small company – one, moreover, that had been flourishing for only a few years – to be looking to open agencies in other countries. The fact is that Bosch was *obliged* to make the venture. The success of his ignition-system business depended crucially on his being able to establish a foothold outside Germany. In France and in the U.K., automobiles were much more common than in Germany. If a company operating in this sector wished to grow, it had to be represented in those two countries. By this time, Daimler and Benz were already sending the bulk of their output to France.

Robert Bosch initially believed it was best to secure an agreement with Daimler that would allow him to use the excellent export operations of Daimler-Motoren-Gesellschaft for his products, thus avoiding the high costs involved in building up sales offices outside Germany on his own. Bosch may have been pursuing the same strategy when in April 1898 he granted Simms, the Daimler-Motoren-Gesellschaft agent in London, the exclusive right to represent his products throughout the United Kingdom.[26] Talks with Daimler were still in progress at the time. At the end of April, Robert Bosch received a draft agreement from Daimler-Motoren-Gesellschaft. Several weeks went by before he finally decided not to transfer sale of Bosch magnetos to

Daimler after all.[27] By then, Simms had already begun selling Bosch magnetos in the United Kingdom. Simms was sure he was on to a winner, and was not willing to let this business opportunity slip through his fingers, even after the collapse of talks between Bosch and Daimler. So alongside his work for Daimler-Motoren-Gesellschaft, Simms continued to serve as Bosch agent for the U.K., and he and Robert Bosch continued to forge plans together. On the advice of Daimler-Motoren-Gesellschaft, Bosch had already filed for patents in Russia, Italy, and Belgium. As early as July 1898, he and Simms agreed that a joint company should be set up in Paris.[28] For Bosch, the strategy of using his connection with Simms to enter the export business was in many respects more advantageous than the arrangement with Daimler would have been. By working with Simms, his company was represented outside Germany at no great expense. In addition, Bosch was able to secure a greater measure of independence for his company. Simms had good connections with London's financial world. He contributed the funds for their business partnership, and Robert Bosch supplied the patents. At the same time, Simms had excellent contacts within the automobile sector, having founded one of Britain's leading automobile clubs in 1897. Two years after the agency agreement, Simms and Bosch set up a joint company in London. Even at this early stage, the Simms-Bosch magneto ignition device had a large and virtually dominant share of the U.K. market.

As early as February 27, 1899, Bosch and Simms set up a joint company in Paris, but one that operated under British law. Named Automatic Magneto Electric Ignition Co., it was later renamed Cie. des Magnétos Simms-Bosch.[29] Part of the plan was to manufacture magneto ignition devices in Paris. However, as this initial, still very modest production of Bosch magnetos outside Germany got under way there, technical problems arose. Finding himself obliged to send an experienced technician to Paris, Robert Bosch chose Max Rall. This was the man who had test-driven Simms's three-wheeler several years earlier, while still an apprentice. When it first set up business operations outside Germany, the company did not yet have an associate with international experience. Robert Bosch could only hope that the young Rall, even without such experience, would do the Paris job well. Rall did not let him down.

In the space of only five years, the company's rise had been positively sensational. From being a loss-making workshop in Stuttgart, it was now an internationally reputed manufacturer with sales offices in London and Paris. Such an accomplishment would of course have been impossible on the basis of the electrical installation business. Even in the magneto business, it was possible only because the company had developed a technical innovation and brought it to the market at the right time – and also because there was little competition in the field. Neither automakers nor engine builders had made any serious attempt to get into ignition-device manufacturing themselves, and if they had at all (like Daimler with its glow-tube system), they had persisted with inauspicious technologies. Robert Bosch wrote to Simms in November 1898: "German companies are either so busy or have to devote so much time to other problems with their engines that they haven't looked seriously into ignition." In the same letter, Bosch gave an insight into his marketing strategy: "I am now working on the major automakers to get them to ask engine builders for my ignition system. Benz will be the first. *C'est seulement le premier pas, qui coûte.*"[30] For a supplier to win over manufacturers (i. e., engine builders) as customers by convincing their own customers (i. e., automakers) of the value of its products seemed a thoroughly modern concept at the time. Robert Bosch may have been thinking of Jellinek here, who had made Daimler undertake not to incorporate glow-tube ignition systems into its Mercedes engines but magnetos instead. It is also clear that, in these early years, there was still a dividing line between engine builders and automakers, and that Bosch's position vis-à-vis engine builders was not an easy one.

This strong growth in the ignition business led the company to move as early as 1897 to 22 Kanzleistraße, to a building that offered larger premises. Soon not even this building was big enough, and additional premises had to be rented on Kasernenstraße. By the turn of the century, Robert Bosch was so prosperous that he was able to buy and build on industrial land. There cannot have been many companies in Germany at that time that had sales offices in other countries before having industrial premises of their own in the city in which they were based. On April 12, 1900, Bosch purchased a house on Militärstraße (today's Breitscheidstraße), together with the adjacent plot at 11 Hoppenlaustraße, on which the company was able to erect its own office and factory premises for the first time. Here, too, Robert Bosch knew exactly what he wanted. This was the first building in Stuttgart to use reinforced-concrete construction, although outwardly it had the look of an upper-class town house with a "Renaissance-style sandstone façade." A "plain shed" would not do.[31] The company was no longer called "Werkstätte für Feinmechanik und Elektrotechnik." Now it had a new name: Elektrotechnische Fabrik Robert Bosch. And at the time of the move to Hoppenlaustraße, it had a workforce of roughly 40. The new facility was designed for future expansion and could accommodate up to 200 workers. Between 1898 and 1901, sales had more than doubled from 163,000 marks to 369,000 marks, with 15 percent already accounted for by export business.[32]

The factory building at 11 Hoppenlaustraße (1910)

As a result of the success of the break-spark low-voltage magneto ignition device developed by Zähringer in 1897, production at Bosch had focused increasingly on the magneto business. At the same time, production of ignition devices for automobiles increased faster than that of ignition devices for stationary engines. From 1901 onwards, the chief focus of production lay quite clearly on low-voltage magnetos for automobiles and motorcycles.[33] However, the rapid growth in this area notwithstanding, Robert Bosch had his doubts whether magneto production would in the long run constitute an adequate foundation for his company. During his first decade in business, he had not let the problems confronting his company knock him off course. And now, he did not let success go to his head either. He was well aware of the risk of being heavily dependent on a single product. As he wrote in his memoirs some twenty years later: "I was constantly plagued by the possibility that our specialty, magnetos, might be a flash in the pan, and one day be superseded or become completely obsolete. I never ceased to consider what other products I might manufacture as well."[34]

In addition to magneto production, Robert Bosch kept up the electrical installation work. There was now a separate electrical-engineering department headed by Heinrich Stütz. Around the turn of the century, Bosch even expanded this business by agreeing with Sigmund Bergmann, his former employer in New York, to act as an agent for insulated conduit tubing. The fact was that in 1900, installations in the field of electrical engineering still accounted for 21 per cent of Bosch company sales.[35] In the meantime, Robert Bosch had even considered including typewriter production in his manufacturing program. However, he had dropped the idea in order to avoid competing with an important customer, the Frankfurt company Adlerwerke, formerly known as H. Kleyer AG, a bicycle and automobile manufacturer that had just begun making typewriters.[36]

Robert Bosch was also loath to sit back on the laurels of his ignition-device triumph, despite the fact that here was a guaranteed source of handsome profits for the foreseeable future. Together, he and Zähringer kept looking for an even better design. Zähringer's break-spark low-voltage magneto had the disadvantage that its unwieldy break-spark rodding was prone to break down and made even higher engine speeds impossible. The battery-operated ignition systems widely used outside Germany, but also by Carl Benz, were regarded as more reliable. In these systems, an electric arc was generated between the electrodes of a spark plug. On the other hand, the big disadvantage of battery-operated ignition was that after only a short distance the batteries went flat and needed recharging. The man at Bosch who tackled this problem was Gottlob Honold, who was taken on in 1901. The company urgently needed an electrical engineer, since the growing number of challenges in this area could no longer be dealt with by technicians alone. Having served his apprenticeship in the Bosch workshop, Honold had left to join Hartmann & Braun in Frankfurt, where he worked on electrical measuring equipment. He had also attended Stuttgart Polytechnic, where he studied electrical engineering. He had been offered a position as a research assistant there, but opted instead to become chief engineer at Bosch.[37]

In December 1901, after months of experimentation, Honold came up with a brilliant solution – one that combined the advantages of the magneto with those of battery ignition. In contrast to the traditional low-voltage magneto, he designed one with two windings around the armature. This produced a high voltage that was then conducted to a spark plug via a wire. The high voltage caused an arc (i. e., the ignition spark) to be generated between the two fixed electrodes of the spark plug. In other words, Honold's invention made it possible to replace the vulnerable break-spark mechanism with a spark plug while at the same time retaining the fundamental advantage of magneto ignition. After all, the new design was also driven by the revolutions of the engine and therefore needed no outside power source. With his high-voltage magneto ignition system, which at the time was also called "arc ignition," Honold had thus found a reliable, high-performance ignition system for high-speed internal-combustion engines. When he showed the new design to Robert Bosch, Bosch is said to have exclaimed, "You have hit the bull's eye!"[38] Admittedly, the founder did concede later that he had not immediately grasped the full significance of the invention, since the spark plugs in common use at the time were not suited to high-voltage magnetos.[39] In retrospect, Robert Bosch also described Honold's achievement as the product of a common development effort.[40] Heuss, on the other hand, presents the high voltage magneto as more of a solo effort on Honold's part.[41] Certainly, Honold had the groundbreaking idea, but it is also true that designing the high-voltage magneto ignition system was a drawn-out process involving lengthy trials.

It was to be some time before the high-voltage magneto went into production. First, new insulating materials had to be found and new spark plugs developed. It was also necessary to run test drives to find out whether the new design would work in automobiles.[42] When the high-voltage magneto was first presented to the public at the Paris Motor Show in November 1902, it received some skeptical looks. Most racing drivers preferred to rely on the low-voltage magneto, regarding it as too risky to drive with an ignition system that was relatively untried.[43] The breakthrough did not come until 1906, when a Renault fitted with a high-voltage magneto won the Grand Prix.[44] The entire automotive world switched to Bosch technology. The trickiest contemporary problem facing automotive technology had been solved. By 1909, 92 percent of all ignition systems manufactured were high-voltage magnetos, and in the following year magneto production at Bosch passed the 200,000 mark – only 14 years after the workforce had been treated to a works outing to celebrate the manufacture of the thousandth ignition device.[45]

Gottlob Honold filed for a patent for the high-voltage magneto. In June 1904, following prolonged examination, it was granted to the company with retrospective effect from January 7, 1902.[46] Three years later, a rival challenged this with a plea of nullity since an earlier patent for a similar device (developed by Paul Winand but never used by Gasmotorenfabrik Deutz) had come to light. Robert Bosch reacted by ceasing payment of maintenance fees, which meant that the patent for the high-voltage magneto lapsed. Clearly he was quite confident that, even without patent protection, he need have no fear of the competition. And he was right. The Karlsruhe company Underberg & Henle did copy the Bosch high-voltage magneto, and Ernst Eisemann & Co., a

Gottlob Honold (1910)

Stuttgart company whose plant was immediately adjacent to the Bosch complex, also started manufacturing high-voltage magnetos. However, the Bosch ignition system was so highly developed technically that it could not be imitated to the same standard. In 1921, Honold wrote in the company newspaper, which took its name ("Bosch-Zünder") from the device, "The Bosch ignition system was imitated by all, but bettered by none."[47]

The company's dispatch books show Simms to have been Bosch's biggest customer for automotive magnetos from 1899 onwards, which likely had to do with supplies to the companies set up jointly by Simms and Bosch in London and Paris. According to the records, 21 percent of Bosch's automotive magneto production went to Paris and London in 1899. Only a year later, the figure was 31 percent.[48] In second place was Daimler-Motoren-Gesellschaft, with a share of just under 11 percent in 1900. The automakers Opel and Adler had been customers of Bosch since 1899, while the following year saw the first deliveries to Fiat and Peugeot.[49] The success of the Bosch ignition device put the company in a very strong position vis-à-vis customers, particularly since there were many automakers but no magneto producers that could seriously compete with Bosch. But Robert Bosch also knew how to keep customers loyal through incentives, offering preferential prices if they would undertake to use Bosch magnetos exclusively. In fact, such an agreement existed with Daimler-Moto-ren-Gesellschaft.[50]

Simms and Jellinek each contributed to the rapid rise of Bosch in their different ways. They brought to the table what Bosch did not yet have, namely international connections and a wide variety of contacts inside the automobile industry. Jellinek persuaded Daimler to collaborate with Bosch, thus establishing the highly successful business relationship between what would later be Stuttgart's two largest companies. Simms facilitated an early and low-cost entry into the export market. For as long as he still feared the magneto might turn out to be a flash in the pan, as he called it, Robert Bosch might well have been put off making larger investments of his own outside Germany. He was also keen to avoid taking out bank loans, always keeping his distance from banks. He stayed true to his commercial principles, relying on self-financing wherever possible in order to protect his company's independence.[51] And indeed, the success of the Bosch magneto meant that the entrepreneur had meanwhile amassed such a fortune as to be able to afford such a point of view. When asked about Bosch in February 1908, the Stuttgart credit inquiry agency Wilhelm Schimmelpfeng reported: "Its profitability is deemed high and according to informed sources the current wealth of its proprietor comes to 11 million marks."[52] Not that Robert Bosch had been miserly about investing. His company grew so successfully that, in the decades preceding the First World War, its expansion could be financed entirely from profits.

The first regional subsidiaries and the conquest of the U.S. market

Much has been written about why automobiles spread earlier in France than in Germany, where Carl Benz and Gottlieb Daimler had invented them. Authors now see this as due to several factors. Roads in France were better developed, and French automakers more innovative, but the motor races that burgeoned in that country also played a major role, exerting an attraction that can scarcely be exaggerated.[53] The German automobile industry turned out high-quality vehicles, but its urge for technical perfection tended to stand in the way of higher-volume production. There were also too many manufacturers in Germany, each producing a number of different models.[54] In 1907, one automobile was produced per 6,953 inhabitants in Germany; in France, the ratio was already one per 1,255.[55]

For a while, France was the world's leading market for automobiles, and for a long time it remained the largest one in Europe. Passenger cars lost their exclusive stamp earlier there than in Germany. They were increasingly used less for pleasure, and more for the professional needs of doctors, engineers, and traveling salesmen.[56] Not until the years immediately preceding the First World War did Germany begin to catch up. Europe as a whole lay well behind the U.S., where cheaper cars were already being manufactured in large numbers. When Ford introduced the world's first conveyor-belt production line in 1913, that company on its own exceeded Germany's entire automobile production several times over. The U.S. then accounted for 80 percent of global automobile production (in 1903 the figure had been 38.9 percent), France for 7.4 percent (1903: 48.5 percent), and Germany for 3.4 percent (1903: 5.0 percent).[57] In Europe, France remained the largest automobile market, but the most coveted automobile engines came from Germany – from Daimler-Motoren-Gesellschaft and Benz & Cie. Both companies were manufacturing under license in France and sold most of what they produced to that country.

The above clearly illustrates how important to Robert Bosch the subsidiary company was that he and Simms had set up jointly in Paris. The German market of those years was not large enough for a German automotive supplier to attain and hold a strong market position. In forming the alliance with Simms, Bosch was following in the footsteps of the German engine builders and automakers Daimler and Benz. However, Robert Bosch was also after something more: he aimed to do business directly with French automakers. In the U.K., where there was virtually no engine and automobile industry, the situation was different, and Simms-Bosch had barely any competitors.

From Bosch's point of view, the agreements with Simms were at first ideal. Little by little, however, it emerged that Simms practiced a different business style than Robert Bosch, to put it mildly. Subsequently, the two men leveled severe accusations at each other – with what justification can no longer be ascertained in detail. But there is plenty of evidence that Bosch paid dearly for his entry into the export market, placing too much trust in a wily businessman. According to the contract with Bosch, Simms was entitled only to sell products in the U.K. under the Simms-Bosch label, not to manufacture them. For that he would have had to take out a license, paying a fee of 120,000 marks. But according to Robert Bosch's account, Simms had failed to abide by this agreement. Bosch claimed that Simms had secretly, and without a license, produced spark plugs patented by Bosch. He also claimed that Simms had sold Bosch magneto ignition devices under his name alone. As for the Paris company, Simms secured a 51 percent majority holding for himself, despite the fact that Robert Bosch had agreed parity with him.[58] Simms for his part claimed later that Bosch had copied his own (i. e., Simms's) design models. He further alleged that the agreements entitled him to produce anything else that Bosch later invented in the field of ignition technology – including the high-voltage magneto.[59]

Robert Bosch felt betrayed by Simms and regretted having left overall control of the regional subsidiaries in the hands of a business partner with greater international experience than himself. He now insisted on concluding firm supply agreements for the future, but Simms was not prepared to comply. Instead, he asked to become a partner in Bosch's company. Finally, in 1905, he offered to buy Robert Bosch out for 5 million marks.[60] Bosch was not averse. For a company with annual sales of 1.7 million marks that he had founded 19 years earlier with a starting capital of 10,000 marks, a purchase price of 5 million marks was not a bad offer. Agreement was swiftly reached over the main issues of management participation. Robert Bosch was to withdraw from the company and Honold and Zähringer were to take charge, together with a friend of Honold's from college days, Gustav Klein. However, events took a different turn. The purchase agreement collapsed because Simms was unable to raise the 5 million marks in cash and instead offered Robert Bosch a shareholding, which Bosch understandably declined.[61]

Determined to part from Simms, Robert Bosch now went on the offensive. He threatened to discontinue supplies to their joint venture in Paris and to sell Bosch magneto ignition systems in France without any middleman. Then he recalled Max Rall from Paris and deliberately delayed deliveries to the Paris company, with the result that Simms was unable to fill a major order from Renault. Simms now had no alternative but to sell out. For the substantial sum of 1.2 million French francs (equivalent to 600,000 marks), he ceded his shares in the Paris company to Bosch in 1906. Six months later, Simms was also obliged to sell his share in the joint venture in the U.K., Robert Bosch having threatened to discontinue supplies to that company, too, as well as to set up a branch of his Paris regional subsidiary in London.[62] The dispute between Bosch and Simms rumbled on in the British courts, where Robert Bosch was able to secure two rulings in his favor.

The lesson that Robert Bosch learned in his attempts to enter the international market with Simms was one he never forgot. Ever afterwards he held a deep distrust of businessmen with a reputation for shady dealings, no matter how sophisticated an impression they gave. A further lesson learned from this period was the principle that a supplier must never compete with its customers, as Simms had tried in vain to do with an engine and automobile production of his own. Indeed, the commercial principles of Robert Bosch, principles that he later professed repeatedly, read like a counter-blast to the practices of Frederick R. Simms. The same conclusion is suggested by the memoirs that Bosch wrote at a later date. In his "Lebenserinnerungen," drawn up in 1921, he wrote of the dispute with Simms: "Had Simms been a right-thinking man of business, I might never have broken free of him, nor might I ever have been in a position to develop as I did. In the long term, an honest and fair approach to doing business will always be the most profitable. And the business world holds such an approach in much higher esteem than is generally imagined."[63]

After the break with Simms, Robert Bosch ran the companies in London and Paris himself. The Paris company, now called Bosch Magneto Ltd. and still incorporated under British law, had started up manufacturing operations as early as 1905. It was the first Bosch plant outside Germany. Managed by Max Rall, the French business grew fast, and U.K. sales also rose steeply. In the meantime, other sales agencies had opened in Vienna, Budapest, Amsterdam, Milan, Geneva, and Moscow. In the Swedish engineer Fritz Egnell, Bosch had also found an agent for Scandinavia in 1904. And while his collaboration with Simms had enabled Robert Bosch to extend his business successfully to Britain and France, it had not helped him gain a foothold in the United States, now rapidly becoming the world's largest market for automobiles. Bosch and Simms had in fact filed jointly for U.S. patents, but to Bosch's dismay his partner had not wished to take advantage of these rights.[64] Since Robert Bosch wanted to benefit from the flourishing automotive industry in the U.S. at all costs, he sent his authorized representative Hugo Borst to New York to sound out the American market.[65] Borst made numerous contacts and, on his return to Stuttgart, launched a professional advertising campaign directed at the U.S. market. The advertisements he placed in trade journals such as *The Horseless Age* had a ring of promise to them: "At Last You Can Get Them – The Long Missed and Long Wanted Bosch-Magnetos."[66] Some 100 interested parties in the U.S. received letters offering to send them sample devices.

Meanwhile, Robert Bosch had found the right man to develop his U.S. business: Gustav Klein, Honold's friend from his college days. Honold had wanted to recruit Klein for his senior management team in the event Robert Bosch decided to sell his company to Simms. Bosch had taken to Klein immediately. When the Simms deal fell through, he put him in charge of sales – quite possibly with a future assignment overseas in mind. Klein, who had worked for Maschinenfabrik Esslingen in Argentina for three years, was a fascinating character. Heuss saw him as a "guy who got things done," and as one "who could win people over to a cause," while Lessing simply calls him "one hell of a guy."[67] Robert Bosch himself wrote of the globe-trotting engineer who had grown up in modest circumstances in Sulzbach an der Murr: "Klein worked hard and was up to any job. He was supremely talented, flexible, and industrious. He was everywhere at once and this in the best sense of the

Newspaper ad (1906)

term."[68] For building up a business in the "land of unlimited opportunity," he was, in a word, the ideal choice.

In July 1906, Klein set out across the Atlantic, accompanied by his friend Otto Heins. His visit had been announced in the letters sent out to prospective customers by Hugo Borst. Klein's success in the United States exceeded all expectations. Within no time at all, he had collected orders worth more than a million dollars – more than the company's annual sales up to that time.[69] Automotive fever had broken out later in the U.S. than in France, but subsequent demand had grown more quickly. Because of the greater distances in the United States, motor vehicles there had always been not so much status symbols as a means of transportation.[70] For Bosch, the U.S. market was a challenge because there was strong competition. Battery-powered ignition was prevalent there, and American engineers were already working on a new electrical ignition system. But the U.S. at this time represented an automotive market on a completely different scale than in France or indeed Germany, with the result that Bosch was able to generate a high level of sales there.

However, before a sales company could be set up in New York City, one hurdle had to be overcome. Robert Bosch instructed an attorney by the name of Carl Schurz to file a complaint against the high import duty of 45 percent, and the complaint was successful. On September 6, 1906, Robert Bosch New York Inc. was then set up. The offices and salesrooms initially occupied a building on the corner of Broadway and 66th Street in Manhattan. Because the imported ignition devices soon became known in the U.S. as "Bosch magnetos," the operation was renamed Bosch Magneto Company in 1908. The company was headed up by Klein's friend Otto Heins. Heins decided to start up manufacturing operations as well, so Bosch Magneto Company moved into a four-story building on 46th Street, where a workforce of nearly 350 was soon working shifts to assemble magneto ignition devices. In 1908, the company opened up sales branches in Chicago and San Francisco, and two years later a further sales office opened in Detroit.[71]

Because of the dynamic growth of the American automotive market, the sales figures of Bosch Magneto Company broke ever-new records. The need for more workers and larger premises increased accordingly, so Heins began looking for a greenfield site for a new factory. His choice fell on the city of Springfield, Massachusetts, which offered ideal conditions – sufficient workers with industrial training, and inexpensive transport links. At this time, when Detroit was still in the early stages of its development as the car-making center of the U.S., Springfield was already a key location for the American automotive industry. The brothers Charles and Frank Duryea had set up the first automobile plant in the U.S. there, designing America's first motorized vehicle with a gasoline engine.[72] The gun maker Smith & Wesson had also long been based there.

In 1910, the foundation stone of a four-story factory building for Bosch Magneto Company was laid on the edge of Springfield, and the new plant was able to begin manufacturing in January 1912. It was regarded as exemplary, not only because of its architecture but also in terms of manufacturing technology and work organization. The technical manager was Karl Martell Wild, a future board member of Robert Bosch AG. The new plant enabled Bosch to serve the U.S. market much better. But there were problems: it turned out to be difficult to recruit workers capable of manufacturing goods to the high quality standards that Bosch required, and for many materials it was nearly impossible to find suitable suppliers. Moreover, capacities at the Springfield plant were inadequate to meet the demand for Bosch magnetos in the United States. Some of what the company supplied to American customers still had to be imported from Stuttgart.[73] As early as 1911, Bosch Magneto Company generated sales of 11 million marks, which was around half the sales volume of all Bosch operations taken together. Three years later, it had a greater manufacturing capacity than even the parent company.[74] In 1913,

The Bosch plant in Springfield (1911)

Bosch Magneto Company produced 226,000 magneto ignition devices, some of them for airplanes and motorboats. In addition, there were now generators. In the summer of 1914, just before the war began, Bosch further expanded its U.S. business by buying Rushmore Dynamo Works in Plainfield, New Jersey, which specialized in electric starters.[75] Bosch's trade activities in the U.S. were carried out not only by sales offices, but also by independent franchises. Each of these "Official Bosch Distributors" covered a certain area, often in conjunction with workshops, known as "Official Bosch Supply Stations," which did servicing and repair work. By 1913, Bosch already had over 700,000 customers in the United States.[76]

In the pre-war era, there were not many German companies operating a manufacturing facility of their own in the U.S. coupled with such an extensive sales and service network. For Bosch it was the natural thing to do, given the importance of the U.S. market. This was undoubtedly where the automotive industry of the future would arise. Yet it is unlikely that even Robert Bosch himself had reckoned with such success in the United States. Looking back on the trip to America that he had taken with his wife and son in April 1911 to watch the new Springfield plant being built, he wrote that the trip had been a "triumph."[77] With his successful U.S. venture, Robert Bosch also freed himself from the culture of the German engine-building and automaking industries. Daimler-Motoren-Gesellschaft scored no great successes in the U.S. market in those years because its vehicles were substantially more expensive that those of American automakers. Against this background, Bosch's decision to enter the U.S. market was a very bold one. But the gamble paid off. Bosch magnetos became established in America long before European automobiles attained any appreciable share of the U.S. market. Up until the outbreak of the First World War, Bosch experienced a boom sustained by the rapid growth of the automotive market in the United States.

By 1906, Bosch was already generating 79 percent of its sales outside Germany. A year later, the figure was nearly 87 percent, and more than one in four Bosch magnetos was being delivered to the United States.[78] The fact that sales more than quadrupled between 1904 and 1908 was due exclusively to export demand. Even allowing for the strong growth in German exports in those years, there were likely only few companies for which export sales were so important. These most likely included the chemicals companies Bayer, BASF, and Agfa, which in 1913 generated nearly 82 percent of their dye sales outside Germany. At Benz & Cie. and Daimler-Motoren-Gesellschaft, exports in the years preceding the First World War accounted for more than 50 percent of sales; at Siemens and Halske, the figure was 35 percent.[79] It should be stressed once again, though, that Bosch's extraordinarily high level of exports reflected not only its own international competitiveness but also the limitations of the German automotive market. Had there been the same level of demand for motor vehicles in Germany in those years as for electrical products or stationary engines, Bosch export figures would have been very much lower.

The transition to a large-scale enterprise and the introduction of the eight-hour working day

A serious banking crisis in the U.S. in the autumn of 1907 resulted in a slump on both sides of the Atlantic. The slump hit the young automotive industry hard, and also led to a temporary crisis at Bosch. "The disaster came out of the blue, so to speak," Robert Bosch wrote in retrospect.[80] In the months leading up to the slump, the company's sales had picked up considerably. In the wake of the crisis, however, several hundred workers were laid off and construction of a new factory building had to be called off.[81] Since the U.S. and the U.K. were more seriously affected by this economic crisis than Germany, Bosch felt the drawbacks of its heavy export bias. That said, the crisis of 1907 soon passed. As early as February 1908, Robert Bosch was able to write to his brother-in-law, Eugen Kayser, that he had "got off very lightly up to now so far as losses are concerned."[82] In the ensuing months, the order books filled up again, and many of the dismissed workers could be reinstated. By the autumn of 1908, the company's manufacturing capacity was under such a strain that Robert Bosch impatiently demanded greater haste in the work on the new factory buildings on Stuttgart's Forststraße.[83]

In the years that followed, the marked increase in sales led to a further rapid rise in headcount. In 1908 alone, the blue- and white-collar workforce increased by 91 percent. For the first time, headcount passed the 1,000 mark. Ten years earlier there had been only nine associates.[84] The transition from an artisanal workshop to a large-scale industrial enterprise called for new methods of manufacturing and involved radical changes not only in the composition of the workforce and their status in the workplace but also in the structure of the company and in industrial relations. No other company in Stuttgart was growing at such a pace. In 1904, Daimler-Motoren-Gesellschaft still employed more than ten times as many people as Bosch, but by 1913, Bosch employed more than Daimler.[85] However, this position as the largest company in the city was only short-lived, since during the First World War Daimler-Motoren-Gesellschaft grew much faster. In Stuttgart, which had not yet developed to the same extent industrially as the Ruhr area or Berlin, people were proud of the rapid rise of Bosch as a company. The press spoke of Bosch as a model for other companies, and the daily newspaper *Der Beobachter* went so far as to refer to it as "setting an example for the entire country."[86]

The company's strong growth notwithstanding, Robert Bosch had for a long time declined to build a new plant outside Stuttgart. His view was that he could take on skilled workers more easily in Stuttgart than elsewhere and that his industrial premises in the west end of Stuttgart could easily be rented out if demand for magneto ignition devices ever collapsed.[87] But with sales having once again increased sharply in 1908, the founder had no choice but to look for a location that offered greater potential for long-term expansion than his present facility in the west part of town. He decided to buy a large tract of land in Feuerbach, just outside Stuttgart, as a site for a new factory. The town still offered sufficient vacant plots at relatively low prices, and enjoyed a favorable transport link in the shape of the *Nordbahn* train from Stuttgart to Bietigheim. His purchase of the land in 1909 marked the beginning of the history of the largest industrial location of today's Robert Bosch GmbH.

The new plant in Feuerbach was referred to as the press works [*Presswerk*]. Later it became the metal works [*Metallwerk*].[88] The man appointed head of the Feuerbach plant was Robert Bosch's brother-in-law and old friend, Eugen Kayser. For a while Bosch was worried that putting Kayser in charge of the press works might lead to accusations of nepotism being leveled against him. Arnold Zähringer, the works manager, also had reservations, regarding Kayser as "Prussianized."[89] Since Kayser was unwilling to become head of the press works so long as such doubts existed, and since Robert Bosch was keen to have an objective opinion, Gustav Klein was asked to assess Kayser's suitability. The upshot was described by Bosch in his memoirs, written a decade later: "Klein came back and said in so many words, 'We can use Kayser, I've put him to the test.' What he meant was, he had spent a night drinking with him and found him to be authentic in character."[90]

The company was growing so rapidly at this time that a large part of the workforce always comprised recently hired employees. In 1911, no more than 20 percent of blue- and white-collar workers – but likely far fewer – had been with Bosch longer than five years. Between the beginning of 1904 and the beginning of 1911, total headcount rose twelve-fold. Up until 1910, there was a strong influx of skilled workers – in the main, presumably, from the artisanal and small businesses in the mid-Neckar region. At the beginning of April 1910, skilled workers made up 40.8 percent of the workforce; three years later it was only 30.2 percent. So most of those taken on after 1910 were semi-skilled or unskilled workers.[91] Women were scarcely represented on the payroll; in mid-1912, they accounted for only 3.7 percent of the Bosch workforce.[92] In fact, for a long time this technically oriented company remained a purely male domain. The first female member of staff was taken on when a secretary was employed on March 1, 1905 – nearly 19 years after the company was set up. This woman – and women like her – were "typists," so it stood to reason that female employment at Bosch began with the introduction of the typewriter.[93] Not until later were they also employed on the shop floor.

For Robert Bosch, who had always placed great value on a good working atmosphere in his company, the sudden rapid rise in headcount meant that his relations with his workforce were changed fundamentally. The founder was nonetheless determined to stay true to his principles. One of those was that he paid good wages. In the period 1910–12, the wages of Bosch workers were between 60 and 63 percent higher than those of their colleagues in other companies in the electrical-engineering and precision-mechanical sectors of industry in and around Stuttgart.[94] This kind of concern for staff was of course not entirely altruistic, any more than it had been in the first years of the century. As a rapidly growing company, Bosch had a seemingly inexhaustible need for suitable workers, and the only way it could meet that need was by paying higher wages than its competitors in the labor market. It had long been common knowledge in the Stuttgart region that workers at Bosch earned more than elsewhere, and a good number of the workers taken on at that time may well have switched to Bosch because of its better wage levels in comparison with other companies. Robert Bosch is often quoted as having said, "You might think I pay good wages because I am wealthy. Far from it. I am wealthy because I pay good wages." In light of the above, his observation seems more than just an offhand remark.[95]

However, the transition to large-scale industrial structures also called for organizational changes, which caused a certain amount of difficulty. Bosch was still a sole proprietorship, not legally separate from the person of its founder. Development of a management team was not keeping pace with the company's rapid growth. True, since the turn of the century, Bosch had taken on people with a business, rather than technical, background, but it was only gradually that these people gained influence. As a rule, shift supervisors and senior shift supervisors performed administrative tasks in addition to their technical work.[96] The first commercial associate taken on by Robert Bosch (in 1900) was Hugo Borst, a nephew of his wife's who had just completed a commercial apprenticeship.[97] Six months later, the company took on an experienced commercial associate: Ernst Ulmer, then 28 years of age. Ulmer took over the accounts, where there had previously been some embezzlement, and was then also made responsible for purchasing and human resources.[98] In 1902, Honold and Ulmer were made authorized representatives. In practical terms, therefore, the company now had a technical and a commercial manager. Initially, however, a separate sales department was not set up. In 1904, Robert Bosch entrusted responsibility for sales in Germany, Switzerland, and Russia to an agent in Frankfurt, August Euler, a retired racing cyclist who later rose to be permanent secretary at the Imperial Air Ministry. After only a few years, there were clashes between Bosch and Euler. While they were not as serious as those with Simms, they nonetheless led to a parting of ways in 1908.[99] Robert Bosch was now convinced of the advantages of a separate internal sales organization, and in the ensuing years one was developed by Hugo Borst. In Paris (1909), Berlin (1909), and Geneva (1910), sales offices were set up, which in addition to salesrooms were also equipped with installation workshops.[100]

In 1906, Robert Bosch was reminded by associates of his promise, given a dozen years earlier, to introduce the eight-hour working day.[101] The condition that the founder had tied it to – namely that other companies should have moved from the ten-hour to the nine-hour working day – had been met. Daimler-Motoren-Gesellschaft was now also working a nine-hour day.[102] That said, circumstances were now fundamentally different. Introducing the eight-hour working day in a company with a workforce of 600 was quite a different matter from doing so in a workshop with only a handful of associates. But Bosch kept his word. On August 1, 1906, to mark the production of the 100,000th magneto ignition device, a new working regulation came into effect, stipulating that the working day would be eight hours in duration. From now on, in summer work at Bosch began at 7:30 a.m. and finished at 5:30 p.m., with a two-hour lunch break. In winter, work began and ended half an hour later.[103]

The introduction of the eight-hour working day caused a sensation. As a result, Bosch became a household name well beyond the (still very confined) bounds of the automotive world. Only two companies of any size in Germany – namely the venetian blind manufacturer Heinz Freese in Berlin and the foundation-owned Carl Zeiss in Jena – had already taken this step.[104] Cutting the length of the working day was also a political issue, the eight-hour working day being one of the key demands of the fast-growing labor movement – a demand which employer associations rejected firmly. Robert Bosch's fellow entrepreneurs were unenthusiastic (to say the least) about his decision. In the eyes of many of them he was suspect anyway, particularly since he refused to join the regional employers' federation, the *Verband Württembergischer Metallindustrieller*. In Stuttgart business circles there was once again talk of "Bosch the Red." In Robert Bosch's view, however, bringing in the eight-hour working day was by no means simply the action of a pioneer of social justice keeping an old promise. He also saw it as "advantageous from a business standpoint if maximum performance can be attained within fewer working hours."[105] The company was now able to structure its working processes more efficiently and to introduce two-shift operation. Like the higher wage levels, the shorter working day was a further incentive that may well have persuaded many workers to apply for jobs at Bosch. The company's manpower requirements increased enormously as a result of its rapidly expanding export business. In 1906 alone, headcount went up by more than half. Taking our cue from Robert Bosch, we might say that the eight-hour working day was introduced so early not because the company was making such a profit but in the expectation that a shorter working day would lead to increased workforce productivity.

However, considerations of this kind were not the only motive behind Robert Bosch's achievements as a social pioneer. For him, doing more for his own associates than other employers did for theirs was something close to his heart. He introduced paid vacation as early as 1910, and where other companies' workers faced dismissal if they did not show up for work on May Day (i. e., Labor Day in Germany), Bosch workers had the day off. Robert Bosch also paid a voluntary contribution towards sickness and disability insurance for his workforce – directly at first, then (from December 1913) through a be-

1906 works regulations setting out
an eight-hour working day

nevolent fund that he himself set up. Offering benefits such as these put Robert
Bosch well ahead of his time. The legally binding eight-hour working day was
not introduced in Germany until 1919, and it was 1933 before May Day became
a statutory holiday.

There were limits, admittedly, to Robert Bosch's willingness to grant social benefits. This became clear when, a year after the introduction of the eight-
hour working day, a workforce meeting demanded that the founder declare
Saturday afternoons work-free.[106] Bosch refused. His introduction of the eight-
hour working day had aroused hopes of further reductions – hopes which
workers were reluctant to abandon. When the demand for work-free Saturday
afternoons was raised once more in April 1909, Robert Bosch again refused,
insisting that "precisely the short eight-hour working day should be managed
in a way that maximum performance can be achieved within that time."[107] But
free Saturday afternoons were in fact introduced a year later.

For the workforce, "maximum performance" was the flip side of the
eight-hour working day. For Bosch, it was no doubt an established fact from
the outset that a shorter working day had to go hand in hand with the intro-

duction of new production methods. The deluge of incoming orders could not be dealt with by new appointments alone – certainly not if the standard of quality on which the reputation of the Bosch magneto rested was to be maintained. Dealing with these orders also called for significant increases in productivity. At Bosch, they were now using the latest machine tools from the United States and developing plans for rationalizing work processes. Piecework wages were introduced and processing times measured by stop-watch. There had been a certain level of automation since 1904. Bosch was among the pioneers of rationalization in Germany, management seeing it as a sure-fire method of boosting production beyond the limits to growth imposed by location factors. Moreover, manufacturing processes at Bosch were particularly suited to such an approach, since the company specialized in the mass-production of magneto ignition systems, and since magneto production itself involved working with small components that did not require long processing times.[108]

Management soon realized that Bosch could learn a lot from the U.S. in this respect. There, an engineer by the name of Frederick Taylor had developed a theory of what he called "scientific management," which was concerned with how the output of workers in a factory could be increased by optimizing their work processes.[109] Bosch's sales director Hugo Borst went to see Taylor in the spring of 1913. Impressed by what he saw, he reported back to Stuttgart about the findings of scientific management. After the First World War, Taylor's theory once again exercised great influence at Bosch. It seemed to be just what the company needed.[110] Workers, on the other hand, soon started talking about "being rushed off their feet." They were required to work faster now, and the work was becoming more monotonous. Much of the discontent concerned the practice of using time-and-motion studies to tie piecework wages to shorter and shorter processing times. This method, also developed by Taylor, led to workers not being rewarded for working fast but having to work fast in order not to be paid less.[111] This "piecework spiral" changed the roles of shift and workshop supervisors on the factory floor. Workers saw their supervisors as slave drivers, since now part of their job was to monitor work rates. A further effect of rationalization was that, from 1910, numbers of semi-skilled and un-skilled workers at Bosch increased.[112] Given the mechanized tasks, they were forced into their first experience of performing an interchangeable operation on an industrial scale at what was called "the Bosch pace." For their part, the skilled workers at Bosch increasingly had the feeling that the decline in their number was going hand in hand with a decline in their status.

The strike of 1913

For an entrepreneur of his day, Robert Bosch was unusually sympathetic toward the labor movement. During his time in the U.S. as a young man, he had belonged to a labor organization himself and taken an enthusiastic interest in socialism. So Bosch had no objection when his company's workers began to organize themselves in a socialist trade union, the "Association of German Metal Workers" [*Deutscher Metallarbeiter-Verband* or DMV]. Before long the company was a DMV stronghold, with 94 percent of Bosch workers belonging to that union in 1912.[113]

The union did not have to fight for recognition in this case. Robert Bosch respected them as representatives of the workforce, negotiated with union functionaries, and concluded agreements with the DMV regarding wages and working-time regulations within the company. Since there was no official company-internal representation of Bosch workers, internally the DMV took on the character of a works council. If shorter working weeks had to be introduced in certain departments or there had to be layoffs, management cleared these decisions with the DMV. When rationalization was brought in, the union did not object in principle, preferring to settle such matters by negotiation and agreement as well.[114] Robert Bosch for his part preferred to deal directly with the DMV as representing his workforce. He was not a member of the employers' federation, and had no wish to have anyone else dictate his wage and working-time regulations.

At the beginning of 1913, this cooperation suddenly, almost overnight, turned into bitter conflict. On January 17, following a two-month decline in order intake, eight workers from the Feuerbach plant were given notice of dismissal, including a union representative. The colleagues of the dismissed men promptly stopped all the machines in the department. Management reacted to this wildcat strike by threatening more dismissals. Further escalation resulted. The DMV called for a sit-down strike – initially for the Feuerbach plant, then for the main Stuttgart factory as well. No more workers were to accept employment at Bosch, and no one there was to do overtime. In return, Robert Bosch cancelled all agreements with the DMV, cut the wages of female temps, raised the prospect of setting up a works committee, and declared that only once the strike had been lifted was he prepared to reopen negotiations with the union.[115] In the end, Bosch and the DMV reached an agreement before the court of arbitration, and the strike was lifted on February 5, 1913. One of the things agreed in the judicial settlement was the election of a works committee.[116]

However, the clashes surrounding the strike were merely the prelude to the conflict that broke out a few months later. During the negotiations regarding the constitution of the new works committee, Robert Bosch and Karl Vorhölzer, the DMV district head, fell out.[117] There was already tension in the air when several union representatives were sacked in May 1913. Then, on May 31, two toolmakers received notice of dismissal. The chairman of the works committee demanded that they be reinstated, but the senior shift supervisor and plant management refused. At this point, workers in the toolmaking shop downed tools, followed by those in the grinding shop. Once again, these were wildcat strikes. No ballot had been taken, nor had the union issued a strike call, although it did subsequently support the strikers. Some 240 workers or about 6 percent of the Bosch workforce were involved at most.[118]

On June 2, Robert Bosch responded with a lockout, ordering the two factories in Stuttgart and Feuerbach to be shut down. All that remained in the company were the approximately 560 office staff, the apprentices, and just over 100 workers.[119] In justification of his actions, Robert Bosch pointed out that the departments hit by the strike were essential to production.[120] His biggest concern, though, was not to let control of events be taken out of his hands. Aware that the company could survive a labor dispute lasting several weeks, he was determined to bring the union to its knees. He paid maintenance to the non-unionized workers, in the same way the DMV gave its workers strike pay. There was sufficient inventory to keep customers supplied even if production was halted for quite some time. As Gustav Klein wrote in a letter dated June 10, 1913, to his friend Otto Heins at Bosch Magneto Company in New York, where concern had obviously been expressed that there might be no deliveries from Stuttgart for a considerable period, "The situation at present is quite favorable so far as the company is concerned. There being large amounts of stock everywhere, the factory can be down for several months before we need fear any serious harm."[121]

In Stuttgart, the labor dispute at Bosch dominated the headlines. Mayor Lautenschlager offered his services as mediator, and the strike was debated in the regional parliament, the *Landtag*. An article in the June 10, 1913 edition of the liberal daily, *Der Beobachter*, included the observation: "Everywhere I go: in restaurants, on the tram, in the cigar shop – nothing but Bosch, Bosch, and more Bosch!"[122] Throughout Germany, newspapers carried the "Bosch strike" story. Politicians and journalists of every persuasion were preoccupied with the question of why, particularly in what was reckoned to be a model operation socially, such a bitter labor dispute was being waged – each of them blaming the opposite side. Robert Bosch had the bulk of public opinion behind him, while the union was having trouble explaining its support for a strike at a company that paid its workers well and had introduced the eight-hour working day years earlier. Even among workers in other companies, solidarity with the Bosch lockout victims was stretched to the limit.[123]

On July 16, 1913, after a six-week shutdown, Bosch reopened the factory gates. The terms of employment were the same as before. The company had no wish, after all, to risk throttling customer supplies – particularly not in the United States. The DMV had presumably realized by now that this was one labor dispute they were not going to win, but neither did the union want to lose face, so the call was issued for the strike to continue. Meanwhile, the workshops were filling up with workers who were not prepared to heed the union's call. At first there were around 750, but six days later the number was up to 1,600 – another source putting the number at 1,800.[124] Prior to the lockout, some 3,700 workers of both genders had been employed by the company. That meant the workforce was split into two almost equal camps.[125] On July 19, Robert Bosch announced he was joining the employers' federation. The DMV now had to negotiate with this association, not with Bosch alone. Not that there was much room for negotiation. On July 26, 1913, once the two sides had reached an agreement, the workforce elected (with two votes against) to resume work.[126]

Robert Bosch had got his way – but at a high price. A nearly two-month loss of production was difficult to deal with, inventories notwithstanding, and the industrial climate had been poisoned. Bosch and the union both reckoned the strike had cost the company in the region of 700,000 marks.[127] For the DMV, the outcome of the Bosch strike was a disaster. Membership numbers crashed, the strike fund was empty, nothing tangible had been achieved, and in the Bosch plants the union had no further say. From now on the DMV had to negotiate with the employers' federation. It was not permitted to operate in the company in any way. Robert Bosch asked his workers to sign a written undertaking to resign from the DMV, and in 1914 he had a "savings and benevolent association" [*Spar- und Unterstützungsverein*] set up to represent the workforce. The DMV lost some 2,700 of its members at Bosch – either because they had been excluded as strikebreakers or because they voluntarily left the union in the aftermath of the strike.[128]

Regarding the causes of what is probably the best-known labor dispute in the history of the company, historians disagree. Heidrun Homburg traces the 1913 strike back to the Taylorist system that had been introduced there. She claims the workers were resisting the disempowerment that came with the pressures of rationalization and "the Bosch pace."[129] Similarly, Uta Stolle argues that Bosch took advantage of an economic downturn to lay off workers and to increase the speed of rationalization, provoking a labor dispute in order to sideline the union and cut wages.[130] In the most thorough investigation yet devoted to the 1913 Bosch strike, Marlis Prinzing reaches a different conclusion. According to her account, worker protest against the drive toward rationalization did not cause the strike, nor can wage cuts be shown to have resulted from the strike. It was more that the DMV and the left wing of the SPD had stirred up the conflict for reasons of political expediency.[131] There is much to indicate that the Bosch strike of 1913 had more than one cause, with other factors playing a role. The first of those is the sharp rise in headcount, which affected the workforce quite as much as mechanization and division of labor. A large portion of the company's workforce at any given time was new. Most of these had never worked in a large-scale industrial operation before. For such workers, being faced with piecework and division of labor represented an immense burden of adjustment. Unlike previously, most Bosch workers now had no sense of loyalty toward their employer, not yet having worked for the company for long. But neither was the management team attuned to the different conditions in a large-scale industrial enterprise. Robert Bosch believed that he could create the same kind of consensus with a trade union as he had enjoyed with his associates when the company was still a workshop operation. He did not expect associates to feel resentment at the pace of work when they were getting good money for a relatively short working day.

Such a mixture was already quite explosive. But there were also political interests involved. The DMV belonged to the left wing of the Social Democratic movement of the day, and was especially active in Stuttgart, having its headquarters there. It had very close ties with the Stuttgart branch of the SPD, which was seen within the party as being particularly radical – partly because of the influence of Robert Bosch's former neighbor Karl Kautsky and of the Marxist Clara Zetkin, whose husband was now having an affair with one of Bosch's daughters. Both the DMV and SPD had firm roots in the Bosch workforce, not least because of the working men's clubs founded by the Socialist workers' movement, together with such leisure facilities as the *Waldheim* in Sillenbuch, but also because of the Social Democratic daily newspaper, *Schwäbische Tagwacht*, and educational programs that appealed above all to skilled workers.[132] The chairman of the local SPD branch, Friedrich Westmeyer, was obeying political motives in fanning the flames of such discontent as had built up among workers, and he roped the DMV in as well.[133] Opponents within the party, such as the moderate Social Democrat Wilhelm Keil, later accused him of sole responsibility for the unsuccessful labor dispute.[134] In reality, though, not even the rhetorically gifted local party chairman could ever have achieved anything, had the Bosch workers been content with their employer. Westmeyer merely touched off what had already been seething under the surface.

When the DMV announced the sit-down strike in January 1913, it was looking for a fight. The recent sackings were not a compelling reason; there had already been such sackings before. The strike was something new, representing an interference in industrial decision-making. Robert Bosch rose to the bait. While respecting the union as a negotiating party, he did not want it telling him how to run his company. Looked at in this light, the cooperation that had existed up to that point had not been a "stable social partnership,"[135] but instead an arrangement that Robert Bosch was willing to tolerate – within bounds set by himself. In January, the DMV had deliberately overstepped those bounds, and from Bosch's viewpoint it was simply a logical consequence that he should promptly cancel all agreements with the union. A workers' union that resorted to industrial action was not something he was prepared to accept, as became apparent later with the establishment of the savings and benevolent association in the aftermath of the strike – an association conducive to good relations between management and workforce. The fact that he had employed harsh methods during the strike, methods that neither the trade-union camp nor the employers' federation would have expected of "Bosch the Red," was no doubt partly connected with his regarding the strikers and the union as "ungrateful." The fact that his two daughters sided with Westmeyer and now felt more comfortable in the *Waldheim* in Sillenbuch than in the parental home on the Heidehofstraße cannot have made things any easier.[136]

The labor dispute that took place at Bosch in 1913 can also be seen as a learning experience in the evolution of industrial relations. Robert Bosch learned that a trade union is not the same thing as a works council and that it is an advantage for an employer to belong to an employers' federation. The DMV, on the other hand, learned that it was ill-advised to let itself be roped into a labor dispute by organizations with a political agenda, and that a strike cannot succeed without the broad consent of the union's base. It was learning experiences of this kind behind which the outlines of collectively bargained pay agreements took shape – outlines that in 1913, even in the case of Bosch, did not yet exist. However, the route to a proper social partnership did not remain blocked by industrial action for long. Despite the dispute, Robert Bosch kept his fundamental sympathy for the labor movement. Associates continued to think of him and refer to him in fatherly terms, but they wanted their interests represented by a trade union, not by a company-engendered savings and benevolent association. In the worker committee elections of 1917, the DMV prevailed against this association.[137]

The company on the eve of the First World War

In 1913, the workforce of "Elektrotechnische Fabrik Robert Bosch" first passed the 5,000 mark. That made it the largest industrial enterprise in the Kingdom of Württemberg. At the time, it was generating 88.7 percent of its sales in export markets – a figure it has never attained since. Looking back six years later, Robert Bosch wrote that in 1913 his company had enjoyed a "quasi-monopolistic world position."[138] In the U.K., Bosch's market share in magneto ignition systems was a full 90 percent, while in France and Italy it stood at around 85 percent. In the U.S., the company had 65 percent of the market, its name being almost as well known there as in Germany. And in the German market, no companies from outside Germany could rival Bosch at all.[139]

With the establishment of the manufacturing facilities of Bosch Magneto Ltd. in Paris and Bosch Magneto Company in Springfield, MA, Bosch had become a multinational company. Following the example of multinational companies in the U.S., Bosch had first built up an international presence through exports and sales offices outside Germany and then started up manufacturing operations there.[141] At the same time, the network of sales offices was constantly extended. The company now had sales offices in 30 countries, including Australia, Russia, China, Brazil, and South Africa. There were few European countries where Bosch was not represented.

Sales offices outside Germany were often managed by trading companies that specialized in the countries concerned and were familiar with local conditions there. For instance, trade in China was covered by an agency agreement concluded in 1909 with the Bremen-based trading company Walter Schärff & Co., which had a branch office in Shanghai.[142] Two years later, the Canadian company Andrews George & Co. was entrusted with the Bosch sales office for Japan.[143] In Argentina, Bosch was represented from 1908 by Carlos A. Pugni, and in Brazil from 1910 onward by the Rio de Janeiro operation Schlosser & Co.[144] How business was actually handled with sales offices outside Germany is no longer documented. Orders were no doubt cabled through, but it would be several weeks before ships arrived with the deliveries. This meant that the sales agents had to be far-sighted in their scheduling and keep consignment stocks.

The Bosch trademark that became known all over the world in the years prior to 1914 was the Mephistophelean figure known as the "red devil." This advertising motif was quite modern for the time, and allowed the company to exploit the popularity of automobile racing to enhance its brand image.

Table 1 Bosch sales offices outside Germany (1898–1914)[140]

Year set up	Country	Head office
1898	U. K.	London
1899	France	Paris
	Austria*	Vienna
	Hungary*	Budapest
1903	Netherlands	Amsterdam
1904	Italy	Milan
	Sweden, Denmark, Finland***, Norway	Stockholm
	Switzerland	Geneva
	Russia	Moscow
1906	USA	New York City
	South Africa	Johannesburg
	Romania	Bucharest
1907	Australia	Melbourne
	Belgium	Brussels
1908	Argentina	Buenos Aires
	Spain	Barcelona
	Ireland**	Dublin
1909	China	Shanghai
1910	Brazil	Rio de Janeiro
	Turkey****	Constantinople
1911	Canada	Toronto
	Portugal	Porto
	Japan	Yokohama
	Finland***	Helsinki
1913	Chile	Santiago
	Greece	Athens
	Egypt	Cairo

* up to 1918, Austria-Hungary   ** up to 1921, U. K.   *** up to 1917, Russia   **** up to 1922, Ottoman Empire

The "red devil" is said to have borne some resemblance to the Belgian Ca-
mille Jenatzy, the most famous racing driver of the years before the First
World War. His "red devil" nickname came not only from his red beard but
also from his driving style. He was the first person to drive a road vehicle at
more than 100 kilometers per hour. In 1903, Jenatzy won the famous Gordon
Bennett Cup race in Ireland at the wheel of a Mercedes fitted with a Bosch
low-voltage magneto ignition system.[145] Hugo Borst, Bosch's sales director at
the time, wrote in later life that the first sketch for the famous "red devil"
poster had been presented to him by the Stuttgart advertising agency
Münch & Grieshaber.[146] The design is sometimes credited to the renowned
graphic designer Julius Klinger, but there is no proof of this. Beginning in
1911, the "red devil" featured in advertisements for Bosch magnetos the world
over, becoming particularly well known in the United States. It was the company's first advertising poster. Up to that point, Robert Bosch had kept faith
with the old engineering principle that products constituted their own best
publicity and good products did not need to advertise themselves. It was
Hugo Borst who instigated the poster campaign, commissioned agencies,
and worked with noted artists.[147] Borst later wrote to Theodor Heuss that he
had never been keen on the "red devil" idea, also disputing that Jenatzy had
provided the model.[148] A different motif, the exploding spark of a spark plug,
was designed by Lucian Bernhard, whom Borst commissioned to design advertising posters. It first appeared on spark plug packaging before also being
printed in poster format from around 1914. For a long time it was the best-
known motif in all Bosch advertising.[149]

In 1913, the company launched new products: generators and headlights.
These were followed a year later by electric starters. The generators enabled
electricity to be produced while the vehicle was in motion. The importance of
this principle as regards the development of automotive equipment can hardly
be exaggerated. Passenger cars now had their own power source, and current
generated during driving could be stored in a battery and called up from there.
This electrical circuit made it possible to include electric headlights and electric starters. Under the general term "Bosch automotive lighting system," an
entire package could now be placed on the market.[150] Electric headlights not
only improved road safety. They also enabled automobiles to be used in bad
weather or at night. They offered substantially better performance and also
required less maintenance than the carbide lamps used previously. Work on
developing headlights had begun at Bosch as early as 1911. Special reflectors
had first to be designed for the purpose, and light-bulb manufacturers had to
develop a special filament bulb that cast an even light over the road surface
ahead.[151]

1^{00}
BOSCH
PLUGS
AS GOOD AS
BOSCH MAGNETOS

Bosch ad featuring the
"Red Mephisto" (1913)

Bosch was not the first company capable of producing generators and electric headlights. As early as 1912, General Motors in the U.S. brought out the Cadillac Model 30 fitted with headlights and electric starters by Delco (Dayton Engineering Laboratories Company). In fact, Delco had been mass-producing electric starters since 1910. Bosch lagged behind developments in this area and faced the realization that the starters made by American manufacturers were protected by a whole range of patents. When in 1914 the chance came up to buy the Rushmore Dynamo Works in Plainfield, New Jersey, thus acquiring a starter patent that opened up fresh possibilities, Robert Bosch did not hesitate: "[…] Rushmore […] had a patent that looked better, and this we bought, together with his company, after talks lasting only a few days."[152] Another reason why the new products were so important to the company was that up to that time, Bosch had made hardly anything but magneto ignition systems, and had thus become dependent on the demand for a single product. For its part, the electrical installation business by now accounted for less than 3 percent of sales. Following the introduction of generators, Robert Bosch wanted to give up this business entirely, but then retained it because of a short-term contract

Bosch ad by Lucian Bernhard (*c.* 1914)

with the Upper Swabian electricity works, hiving it off only in 1917.[153] Magneto ignition systems had made the company highly successful, but Robert Bosch was aware that times could change and that he had to be prepared for the downside. Generators held the key to an entirely new sphere of automotive technology. Not only could they power electric starters, they also offered a way to overcome the old disadvantages of battery-powered ignition systems. Now that automobiles had their own power source, drivers no longer needed to stop to recharge. The electricity needed for ignition could be regenerated while the vehicle was in motion. This kind of improved battery ignition system had been developed in the United States by Charles Kettering. General Motors had been mass-producing it since 1910. Granted, magneto ignition was still thought to be more reliable, but battery ignition was a lot cheaper, and at Bosch they may well have suspected that the new technology, once it had been further improved, would render the magneto redundant. That made it even more important that the company should acquire a high level of competence in this area as well.

For the manufacture of generators and headlights, Robert Bosch built a new factory, the light works [*Lichtwerk*], in Feuerbach, where the press works had been erected in 1910. In May 1914, the first section of the *Lichtwerk* was taken into operation. Three months later, the First World War broke out, whereupon Bosch had to interrupt its promising venture into automotive lighting technology. Because of the war, the company fell even further behind the American manufacturers in this area.

All in all, the outbreak of the First World War marked the end of a golden era for Bosch. Never again would the company dominate the world market with a single product, as had been the case with the high-voltage magneto ignition system in the years before 1914. In fact, it would be a long time before the company could pick up on its former successes at all.

4 The First World War and its aftermath

The war – a turning point

Although international tensions had been on the increase for some time, people at Bosch had not expected war to break out among the great European powers. The company was quite unprepared for this turn of events. No attempt had been made to pave the way for arms contracts, and in the sales offices outside Germany no precautions had been taken for the eventuality of a war. For business reasons, if for no other, Robert Bosch cannot have been interested in war, since nearly 90 percent of his company's sales were generated in markets outside Germany. But also given his political stance and his aversion to Prussian militarism, he had no sympathy with the saber-rattling and world-power ambitions of the hawkish elements in society. In his memoirs, written after the war, Bosch stated that as early as 1912, against the background of the Balkan conflict (then just beginning), he had told a hunting friend, "I will happily pay 10 million marks if my doing so helps avoid war."[1] On July 31, 1914, the day before war was declared, he wrote to his wife, Anna, "I refuse, actually, to abandon hope that it will not come to war."[2]

However, his letters after the declaration of war change their tune. In one written to his agent in neutral Sweden, Fritz Egnell, on September 28, 1914, we read, "If I now say to you: I am of the opinion that we shall overcome most of our enemies, I am voicing the general opinion. We shall attack Britain and the British on their own soil."[3] These words hardly express the kind of depression that Robert Bosch felt at the start of the Second World War. Yet he had a presentiment that the war would bring untold suffering, and he was determined to help. On August 4, 1914, only days after war was declared, he handed Stuttgart's mayor, Karl Lautenschlager, the sum of 100,000 marks for welfare purposes.[4] An even larger amount was donated shortly afterwards to another organization, "War Aid for Commerce and Industry" [*Kriegshilfe für Handel und Industrie*], that Bosch had helped to set up. Robert Bosch also supported around 1,200 families of associates who had been drafted, and in the new Lichtwerk in Feuerbach that had been inaugurated only shortly before the war, a 400-bed hospital for war-wounded was established.[5]

The outbreak of war hit Elektrotechnische Fabrik Robert Bosch extremely hard. Some 52 percent of the male blue-collar workforce had been drafted into the military – approximately 45 percent of the entire workforce.[6] Even greater than the drop in the number of active employees was the drop in sales. According to Heuss, some 82 percent of sales – practically the company's entire export business – was either with countries with which Germany was at war or with neutral countries that were also, from now on, no longer supplied by German companies or were no longer allowed to take deliveries from Germany in case they aided the enemy war effort.[7] The company's sales offices in Paris and in London (where new business premises at Tottenham Court Road had just been acquired and occupied) were confiscated as enemy assets. In the U.S., the new plant in Springfield was now left to fend for itself, there being no further possibility of supplying it from Stuttgart. Hermann Waker, who had worked there during the war, reported later, "The outbreak of war in Europe in the late summer of 1914 struck us like a bolt from the blue. The fact was, Stuttgart was still the main source for our requirements."[8] Conversely, bottlenecks were now experienced by manufacturers of engines and automobiles in France and the U.K., since Bosch had enjoyed an 85 to 90 percent share of the magneto ignition market in those countries before the war. The Bosch sales offices and regional companies outside Germany that had been confiscated were no more able to fill these gaps than their former competitors domiciled in the countries concerned. German producers of ignition systems, soon catching on to the fact that British and Russian companies were going to great lengths to get hold of such systems for aviation and truck engines through neutral countries, undertook not to supply such technology either directly or indirectly to enemy countries.[9] However, there was a breach in this front that could not be controlled from Germany: Bosch Magneto Company in the United States.

In August 1914, many of the associates still left in the Stuttgart and Feuerbach factories received letters like the one addressed to Gotthilf Wezel: "War has made it impossible for me to export my goods, and as yet there is no end to the war in sight. But since, as you know, only a tiny part of my output stays in this country, I cannot say how long I shall be able to keep the factory running. For this reason I am obliged to give notice of termination, with effect from September 30, 1914, of the contract of employment entered into with you. I can offer to continue to employ you on the same terms as before, but with one month's notice of termination only."[10] Orders from within Germany and those from countries allied to Germany were insufficient to fully utilize Bosch's magneto-producing capacity. Fuel shortages forced the prohibition of private automobile journeys in Germany for the duration of hostilities, and the German army's magneto requirements were not exactly large, given that the armed forces were only lightly motorized in Germany at that time. To maintain the company's production facilities after being deprived of more than four-fifths of its sales, and to make further use of its technical and human capital, there was only one possibility, and that was switching to ordnance, whatever changes that might entail. Having made up his mind to negotiate for military contracts, Robert Bosch traveled to Berlin in September 1914. He came back full of optimism. In the above-mentioned letter to Fritz Egnell, he wrote, "I believe we can gradually find employment for the core of associates remaining to us by turning out ignition systems for aircraft and airships, ignition systems for export to neutral countries, and ordnance."[11]

Table 2 Sales and workforce of Bosch and Robert Bosch AG (1913–18)[12]

Year	Total sales in marks	Export sales as percentage	Sales of ordnance as percentage	Headcount
1913	26,861,569	88.7		4,542
1914	23,560,221	77.1	0.3*	3,611
1915	33,126,325	12.7	62.3	3,895
1916	47,512,944	9.8	69.5	5,639
1917	77,462,421	8.5	69.6	8,253
1918	73,462,273	8.5	37.0**	9,249

* second half year **first half year

The trouble was, at the beginning of the war, aircraft numbers were still very low, and even if exports to neutral countries were included (possible only with special permits), this was still not enough to keep the already reduced workforce at the Stuttgart and Feuerbach factories employed. However, they could be kept on if ordnance were produced. Within a short space of time, the company switched from producing magneto ignition systems to producing technically simple weapons. A world-renowned automotive supplier was now producing *flechettes* (airplane darts), detonators for hand-grenades to be thrown from aircraft, detonators for shells, and gun parts. By 1915, the company was already achieving more than 60 percent of its sales through ordnance.[13] Robert Bosch may initially have seen this as a stopgap solution, since in early 1915 he still believed that the war would not last long.[14] Nonetheless, turning out ordnance accounted for most of the company's production for the next four years. It was what ensured its survival.

In 1917, ordnance made up some 70 percent of Bosch sales, while export sales sank to an all-time low of 8.5 percent. The vast majority of ordnance produced consisted of detonators for grenades to be thrown from aircraft. This form of ammunition alone accounted for around 37 percent of the company's sales in 1916. A year later, that share had risen to almost half.[15] On the other hand, production of high-voltage magneto ignition systems fell with the outbreak of war. In 1916, Bosch manufactured only about 59,000 of these systems, compared with some 198,000 in 1913. In the last two years of the war, production of these systems rose again, very likely since the armed forces were increasingly being equipped with military vehicles and heavy trucks. Altogether, the war reduced the company's status from that of a high-export supplier of state-of-the-art automotive technology to that of a manufacturer of mass-produced goods. The focus of production was no longer on electrical engineering (manufacturing ignition systems for internal-combustion engines) but on pyrotechnics – notably, turning out vast numbers of detonators for grenades.

Table 3 Composition of the Bosch workforce (1914–18)[16]

Date	Blue-collar workers (m)	Blue-collar workers (f)	White-collar workers (m/f)	Apprentices	Total headcount
Aug 1,1914	3,375	580	930	70	4,955
Sept 1,1914	1,598	541	555	79	2,773
Jul 1,1915	1,693	887	570	88	3,238
Jul 1,1916	2,160	3,255	519/213	102	6,249
Jul 2,1917	2,583	4,469	684/336	102	8,174
Mar 11,1918	2,669	4,977	789/425	90	8,950

Conscriptions and arms production led to radical changes in the make-up of the workforce during the First World War. Female employment rose sharply, as it did in nearly all large-scale enterprises at the time. Women constituted virtually the only labor resource available, once a large part of the core male workforce had been drafted. By October 1915, the number of women blue-collar workers had passed the 1,000 mark, and by mid-1916 more women were employed than men – in a company that had begun to employ women only 11 years earlier. Leaving aside the apprentice department, which still trained no females, it was only among white-collar staff that men still outnumbered women. Toward the end of the war, there were roughly 4,300 more women blue-collar workers than at the beginning. The documentation that survives does not allow any conclusions to be drawn as to how many of the new blue-

Women leaving the Stuttgart plant (1916)

collar workers had had industrial jobs previously, how many came from the agricultural sector, and how many had never been in paid employment before.[17]

In September 1914, Robert Bosch was alerted to a very special arms project by Gustav Klein, his sales director. Count Ferdinand von Zeppelin, whose airship-building activities had enjoyed a brief revival with the outbreak of war, wished to construct a giant airplane more suited to bombing enemy cities and ports than his cumbersome airships. He summoned a number of experts to the Grand Hotel in Metz on September 5, 1914, Gustav Klein among them.[18] Hellmuth Hirth, the son of the Stuttgart industrialist Albert Hirth, had got Klein interested in aviation and given him some flying lessons. Klein and Hirth, together with Karl Maybach, had been planning to fly the giant airplane (which was by no means a new idea) to San Francisco for the 1915 world exhibition.[19] Now that the military was interested in building giant airplanes and the venture was taking concrete form, there was no holding Klein in Stuttgart. Bosch had to second him, along with several other associates, lending them to this still-secret project. The work of actually constructing the giant airplane – the first in the world – began in a shed belonging to Waggonfabrik Gotha, and initially went by the name of Gothaer Versuchs-Abteilung [Gotha

Research Department].[20] On October 1, 1915, a separate company was set up to build giant airplanes, Versuchsbau GmbH Gotha-Ost (VGO), with Gustav Klein as managing director.[21] While not owning this research company, Bosch did in fact fund it – a fact that the company kept quiet about after the war, allegedly out of concern for its British customers.[22] Following completion of the research phase, construction of the giant airplane was removed to Luftschiffwerft Staaken near Berlin at the beginning of 1916. There production was to be started, using one of the hangars that Zeppelin's company had had built for airship construction. VGO now became Flugzeug-Werft GmbH. Employing around 700 persons, at the end of 1916 the renamed company began building giant airplanes, several dozen of which were subsequently deployed as "long-range bombers," dropping bombs on French and British cities but never achieving any great military significance.[23]

On March 10, 1917, Gustav Klein, accompanied by the pilot Hans Robert Vollmoeller and three mechanics, took off for a further test flight in a giant aircraft. Coming back, the airplane struck the hangar and crashed. Vollmoeller was killed instantly, Klein died only hours later, and none of the mechanics survived.[24] The news of Klein's death came as a shock to the entire Bosch management, but most of all to Robert Bosch himself. Klein had given impressive evidence of his commercial skills in building up the Bosch business in the U.S., and had long been Robert Bosch's personal favorite among the company's top managers. Ever since it had become clear that his son, Robert, was incurably ill, the founder had had his eye on Klein to succeed him. Inside the company, Klein was generally regarded as the "crown prince." In his memoirs, Robert Bosch wrote, "Klein's death deprived me of someone so valuable that no single individual could ever replace him."[25]

During the First World War, Robert Bosch gradually assumed a public role. He forged political alliances, adopted a public stance, and became a prominent figure in Berlin as well as in Stuttgart. The way for this new role was paved by Ernst Jäckh, the former editor-in-chief of the Heilbronn-based newspaper, *Neckar-Zeitung*, and the brother-in-law of Hugo Borst, a member of the Bosch management. He had moved to Berlin in 1912 as chief executive of the *Deutscher Werkbund*, and made a wide variety of contacts in a short time. Together with Paul Rohrbach, Jäckh had been editing the periodical *Das größere Deutschland* ["Greater Germany"] since the spring of 1914, with Robert Bosch supporting the venture to the tune of between 100,000 and 150,000 marks.[26] Through Jäckh, Bosch also became a co-founder and patron of the "1914 German Society" [*Deutsche Gesellschaft 1914*], an association of distinguished people from public life that came into existence in November 1915 in order to bolster the feeling of national solidarity invoked at the start of the

Gustav Klein (1900)

war, the so-called "spirit of 1914." The "1914 German Society" was where the elite of the German empire or Reich assembled. Members included major industrialists such as Carl Duisberg, Gustav Krupp von Bohlen und Halbach, Walther Rathenau, and August Thyssen, but also the banker Max Warburg, the publisher Louis Ullstein, the writer Gerhart Hauptmann, and the composer Richard Strauss. The founding president was the statesman Wilhelm Solf, but politics and the armed forces were nothing like as well represented as the business world. Jäckh was the society's chief executive. Robert Bosch was a member of the executive committee, and for a small rent placed at the club's disposal rooms in a fine building that he had acquired, the Pringsheim Palace on Berlin's Wilhelmstraße.[27]

At the beginning of 1916, Robert Bosch joined a "Working Committee for Central Europe" [*Arbeitsausschuß für Mitteleuropa*] that had been launched by the liberal politician Friedrich Naumann. Here again, the chief executive was Ernst Jäckh. Its members were prominent citizens with largely liberal views from the worlds of business, science, and politics. Their concern in this committee was with the future shape of central Europe, as well as to influence Germany's war aims.[28] Bosch had shared such concerns for some time. He had been a co-signatory of the "Delbrück-Dernburg Petition" of July 9, 1915, in which several public figures from the moderate liberal camp, including Max Weber and Albert Einstein, had called for territorial annexations. The petition was in fact intended as an alternative to the highly immoderate demands of the national conservative "Pan-German League," but its terms hardly suggested a desire for a peaceful settlement.[29] As had become evident at the start of the war, Robert Bosch was by no means averse to the "ideas of 1914." In all likelihood, he was particularly impressed by the idea of political and social tensions being transcended by what was called *Kriegsgemeinschaft* – the sense of community and solidarity brought about by the war. However, over the course of 1916, he very likely came to realize that his stance was placing him in the company of extreme nationalists and advocates of an authoritarian state. For whatever reason, the periodical edited by Jäckh and funded by Bosch changed its name at that time from *Das größere Deutschland* to the less aggressive *Deutsche Politik* [German Politics].[30]

At the end of that year, Robert Bosch decided to make a major donation. As he remarked in his memoirs: "I made up my mind to use my war profits to set up a foundation to build the Neckar Canal."[31] The profits that his company had made from the war up to that time were not exactly small. After all, the amount that Bosch donated to set up the *Neckarkanal-Stiftung* was 13 million marks. If we add two further large donations that Robert Bosch made around that time – one to the Society for the Promotion of the Gifted and another (presumably made in 1915) to the Homeopathic Hospital Society – the total comes to 20 million marks.[32] Bosch later disclosed that the sum was the entire fortune he had amassed since December 31, 1913.[33] A grateful Stuttgart awarded him honorary citizenship. Whether these major donations also expressed a change of attitude toward or even a protest against the war has to be doubted. Robert Bosch had made major donations before – as soon as the war began – moved by a need to relieve suffering. The new donations were also entirely consistent with the "spirit of 1914," but there was also a truly mundane reason for them: the introduction of a war-profits tax. Previously, war profits had been tax-free – which had repeatedly led to vigorous protest that tax-free war profits were not befitting of the "spirit of 1914."[34] In mid-1916, a new tax was imposed on excess profits since the outbreak of war. Evidence that this was what prompted Robert Bosch's donations is given by a chronicle produced by the company's sales organization: "When the excess profits tax was levied for the first time, the tax authorities asked Robert Bosch to declare by how much his assets had grown since 1913. He responded by saying that he not only had no intention of paying this tax but also that he renounced all the assets he had amassed during this period. 'I have no wish to become even a penny richer as a result of this war.'"[35]

If Robert Bosch underwent a change, it was only during 1917, because of the way the war was going and because of the growing political influence of the military under Hindenburg and Ludendorff. Contributing factors may also have been his own very low mood at the time as well as his poor state of health. His later outright opposition to war may well have taken root in the experiences of this period. In business terms, too, the war was becoming disastrous for Bosch. Only a few weeks after the death of Gustav Klein had robbed him of a ray of hope for the future, the United States declared war on Germany. Robert Bosch likely suspected that this declaration meant his company could say goodbye to its largest export market for the indefinite future. Nor was it going to recover its former international status in any hurry. In conjunction with the Friedrich Naumann circle, to which Theodor Heuss also belonged, he now placed his hopes in a negotiated peace. He also moved closer to the labor movement again. Jointly with the trade union presidents Carl Legien and Adam Stegerwald, Bosch, Naumann, and the economist Alfred Weber sent a memorandum to the German High Command in February 1918. In it, they called for the abandonment of a planned major offensive, and demanded a peace initiative as well as a declaration of intent with regard to "restoring the sovereignty and integrity of Belgium."[36] At the end of October, Bosch wrote to Naumann that the Reichstag should address "that great obstacle to peace, the Kaiser," and force him to resign. Yet at this point Bosch was still able to imagine that the Kaiser's grandson might succeed him and thus secure the survival of the monarchy.[37]

The repercussions and consequences of the First World War were painful for Bosch as a company. In all, 453 associates had been killed, others returned severely disabled.[38] For four years, the company had for the most part produced goods that did not belong to its product portfolio. As a result, it had lost touch with technological developments in its traditional areas of expertise. All its assets outside Germany had been confiscated, and its principal export markets were gone. In the U.S., Bosch Magneto Company had in fact managed to keep producing independently of supplies from Germany, but it had forfeited its former market position long before the U.S. entered the war. Hermann Waker's memoir describes this vividly: "Before the war, the Bosch spark plug was the undisputed market leader. Then supplies dried up owing to the Allied blockade. Automakers had to look for alternative sources of supply. General Motors had its own brand, while A. C. Ford and the rest turned to Champion. The Bosch spark plug was forgotten."[39]

Conversion to a stock corporation and establishment of VVB

When it came to the question of who would succeed him, Robert Bosch had originally regarded his son, Robert (born 1891), as the prime candidate. When it emerged, however, that his sons's illness was incurable, Gustav Klein became the "crown prince." Klein's death in March 1917 left the then 55-year-old founder obliged to look for another solution. At this point, Bosch decided to legally separate his company from his own person and to cede part of his share in it. He did so on the basis of agreements that also contained provisions for the period following his own death.

There had been a time when Robert Bosch had been able to envisage selling his company – on the condition that the price was right. In 1905, he had accepted a purchase offer from Frederick Simms. The only reason the sale fell through was that Simms did not have enough liquid funds to pay in cash. Three years later, Bosch was still thinking in similar terms. In a letter to Eugen Kayser he wrote, "Starting up a stock corporation merely in order to have a family business is not something I consider necessary just now, and if I want to sell the risk, then I really do need to sell it properly – that is to say, come away with a respectable pile of cash."[40] By now, the sum he had in mind was 15 million marks.[41] He would have accepted 5 million marks from Simms.

Four years later still, Robert Bosch was thinking very differently. On February 27, 1912, he told his nephew Hermann Bosch that "in the end, I may well have to change the constitution of my company in order to secure its continuation after my death. Whether this will result in a general partnership [*Offene Handelsgesellschaft*] or a stock corporation or something else, I do not know."[42] Bosch now regarded his company as his life's work, as something that needed to be "secured." And by this time, he was likely also aware that he was not going to be able to hand it down to his son. Robert Bosch's legal adviser, the attorney Paul Scheuing, who had been with him since the legal disputes with Simms, doubtless urged him to convert his company into a stock corporation.[43] As long as the company remained in sole proprietorship [*Personengesellschaft*], the whole company would pass to his heirs when he died, including all liabilities within and outside Germany. As a general partnership or stock corporation, on the other hand, the company would constitute its own legal person. In that case, only Robert Bosch's shares would fall to his estate when he died.

There were no changes to the make-up of the company before the First World War. But according to Heuss, work on the change was already far advanced in 1913.[44] In Bosch's memoirs we read that Gustav Klein advised against turning Bosch into a stock corporation or public limited company.[45] Whether that was so can no longer be established. Nonetheless, things got moving after Klein's death, with the sole proprietorship becoming a stock corporation [*Aktiengesellschaft*] only months later. It is also conceivable that the one event had only indirectly to do with the other, in the sense that this experience persuaded the founder that the future of his company should not lie in the hands of a single person. Robert Bosch's core idea in placing the company on a joint-stock basis was to have his most important associates on board as shareholders. He wanted them to be committed partners, so that the company would remain in tried and tested hands following his own death. There was no plan to have the shares traded on the stock exchange. His intention instead was to form a kind of extended family business. Naturally, the same objective could have been achieved by forming a close corporation or private limited company [*Gesellschaft mit beschränkter Haftung* or GmbH]. But Scheuing seems to have held out for the legal form of a stock corporation. He later explained that this legal form had been chosen in 1917 to make it easier to accept additional capital – in the form of new shareholdings, for instance – should this become necessary.[46] Since this notion is not entirely in line with Bosch's ideas, it makes sense to assume that it was put forward either by Scheuing or by another adviser. In any case, it was sound advice considering the situation in 1917. By then, it looked likely that Germany would suffer defeat in the First World War and that Bosch, faced with the prospect of losing its holdings outside Germany, was going to need a correspondingly large injection of capital to rebuild its export business in the aftermath of war.

The idea of involving associates is the likeliest explanation for the way in which the stock corporation was set up. Under this scheme, the directors were not to purchase their shareholdings from Robert Bosch directly. Instead, it was agreed that they would set up a new organization together with him. Accordingly, Aktiengesellschaft für Kleinmaschinen- und Apparatebau came into existence on July 6, 1917, with a capital stock of 12 million marks. Just over a month later, on August 9, 1917, the company was renamed Robert Bosch AG.[47] Robert Bosch himself acquired shares in Aktiengesellschaft für Kleinmaschinen- und Apparatebau worth a face value of 6.12 million marks, which gave him 51 percent of the entire capital stock. The remaining 49 percent (with a total face value of 5.88 million marks) was subscribed by six directors: Gottlob Honold, Hugo Borst, Eugen Kayser, Heinrich Kempter, Ernst Ulmer, and Max Rall. Members of this group were permitted to sell their share packages by majority agreement only. It was also planned that Otto Heins would be a shareholder. As he had been in the U.S. since the outbreak of war, the other directors were expected to hold his shares for the time being. Eugen Kayser transferred his share package to the remaining directors even before the company changed its name to Robert Bosch AG.

On July 16, 1917, Robert Bosch and the other shareholders concluded an agreement. This stated that, on Robert Bosch's demise or in the event of his becoming legally incompetent, Honold, Borst, Kempter, Ulmer, and Rall should be entitled to acquire 240 shares from his possession, worth a nominal

240,000 marks. This would bring their combined shareholding up to 51 percent. Until that time, those 240 shares were to be held in trust. Alternatively, they could subsequently be sold to a new member of the company's management board if a majority was in favor.[48] In the newly formed Robert Bosch AG, Bosch himself chaired the supervisory board. Gottlob Honold and Hugo Borst were appointed to the board of management as full members, while Heinrich Kempter, Max Rall, and Ernst Ulmer became deputy members. In setting up the AG, Robert Bosch wanted individual manufacturing operations to become separate companies. It is unclear why he wanted this, and 11 years later the separation was reversed. But this is how the press works in Feuerbach became a separate organization in 1917, trading as Robert Bosch Metallwerk AG with a nominal 1.2 million marks of capital stock. The electrical installation business was also hived off as Elektra-Installations GmbH, with authorized capital of 300,000 marks.[49]

Now that Robert Bosch's personal assets had been separated from his company assets, and the stock corporation had been set up, Scheuing pushed for arrangements for Robert Bosch's personal assets to be made. He presented his first proposals in September 1917. Working in conjunction with Hans Walz, the founder's private secretary, Bosch and Scheuing drafted proposals for a non-profit organization structured as a trust administration company [Treuhand-GmbH für Vermögensverwaltung]. Under these proposals, Robert Bosch would contribute his shareholding in Robert Bosch AG to this new organization, which was conceived of as a "focus for the many civic initiatives" pursued by the founder.[50] After the war, these considerations resulted in a new company devoted to the administration of Robert Bosch's assets and called "Vermögensverwaltung Bosch GmbH" or VVB. The company was set up on March 9, 1921, with a capital stock of 280,000 marks. Of this amount, Robert Bosch himself held 230,000 marks (82.14 percent). The remainder was shared among Hugo Borst, Gottlob Honold, Arthur Leinss, Paul Scheuing, and Richard Stribeck, each of whom had a shareholding of 10,000 marks (3.57 percent).[51] Two days after this new company had been set up, Robert Bosch concluded an agreement with it, under which VVB would purchase 9,500 Robert Bosch AG shares for 12.35 million marks.[52] That was no less than his entire shareholding in Robert Bosch AG. The purchase agreement was not authorized by the shareholders' meeting of VVB, so did not come into effect – a curious turn of events, considering that the shareholders concerned were all close colleagues of Bosch and had his confidence.[53]

One possible explanation for this turn of events is that Robert Bosch postponed the sale because of mounting inflation. However, it is more likely that the agreement was intended from the outset to be held in abeyance as a documented sale offer that could be returned to later. On April 30, 1924, Bosch made VVB a further sale offer, and once again the offer was put on the shelf.[54] There is written confirmation that Robert Bosch did at the time intend to sell his shareholding in Robert Bosch AG to VVB. A letter that Hans Walz wrote many years later to Willy Schloßstein, his successor as head of the private secretariat, contains the following passage: "In earlier circumstances (that is, in the period following the First World War), the intention was that Mr. Bosch should not bequeath his shares in what was then Robert Bosch AG, but instead transfer them to Vermögensverwaltung Bosch GmbH (VVB), in return for which the latter would have been required to pay him or his successors the purchase price in installments. It was further intended that the transfer should take place in Mr. Bosch's lifetime and that Mr. Bosch should be appointed the first managing director."[55]

Why should an industrialist of the stature of Robert Bosch have been planning to have himself appointed managing director of a company that he himself had set up? If we are to believe Walz, then while he was still alive, Bosch intended, "through the way in which he and the other directors meant to run the affairs of VVB, to establish a precedent for the proper administration of the shares of Robert Bosch AG and the proper interpretation of the VVB guidelines after his death."[56] In other words, Robert Bosch had no intention of retiring, for instance, or of simply selling his company. Instead, as was already evident in part when the AG was set up in 1917, he wanted to give his own ideas the force of guidelines for his associates and for posterity. At a time when he was having to come to terms with his no longer having a son and heir, he wanted a way of making sure that the company would continue to be run as he intended.

Changing times: Robert Bosch AG and the aftermath of war

On December 7, 1918, an employee of the U.S. Office of Alien Property Custodian, A. J. M. Palmer, sold by auction Bosch Magneto Company, which had been confiscated at the end of the war. At a price of 4.15 million U.S. dollars (less than half its actual value) the company and all its patent rights were awarded to a man by the name of Martin E. Kern, one of two bidders. A number of issues later emerged. First, Kern should not have been allowed to bid at all, since he held German nationality at the time. Second, he was simply acting as a front for a group of investors. Third, he and the auctioneer had long been friends; and, finally, the two were acting in cahoots. As a result, Bosch was not alone in suing the buyers. The American government did so, too.[57] These developments, however, speak volumes about the situation in which Bosch found itself at the end of the First World War. How could what had once been the company's most valuable asset possibly be sold off so cheaply? Clearly, Bosch was going to find it difficult to regain a foothold in the international marketplace. Over the next decade and a half, the key question underlying the company's development was whether it would manage to return to its most important export market and pick up from where it had left off.

Circumstances were anything but favorable. The liberal world economic order of the prewar years and the international monetary system of the gold standard were both shattered. Many countries had put up high tariff barriers, and the economies of Europe – Germany's especially – were badly hit by the aftermath of war. As a company that prior to 1914 had generated nearly 90 percent of its sales from exports and from manufacturing outside Germany, Bosch was particularly hard hit by this "de-globalization,"[58] as it has been called. The competitive situation had changed completely as a result of the war. In the U.K., many companies had begun producing their own magnetos during the war years, the French market was shielded by massive protective duties, and in the U.S., Bosch's former customers now had to turn to the company set up in 1919 by Martin E. Kern's backers under the name American Bosch Magneto Corporation (ABMC). The new word across the Atlantic was "Bosch, I am an American!" – a slogan that had a nightmarish ring for Stuttgart ears.[59] Even the well-known Bosch "red devil" was used by ABMC for its publicity, since Robert Bosch AG had lost all trademark rights in the U.S. The "red devil" was now worthless so far as the Stuttgart company was concerned.[60] Consequently, the search was on for a fresh, unmistakable symbol, and the design eventually chosen was one that Gottlob Honold had hit on in November 1918. It showed a stylized double-T armature inside a circle. Honold's design became the symbol of the company, and has remained so – with slight amendments – to the present day.

Following the end of the war, the Bosch head office on Stuttgart's Militärstraße was initially unable to contemplate a return to export markets, since it faced problems resulting from supply bottlenecks, revolutionary protests, and demobilization. On November 12, 1918, several representatives of the business world met in Stuttgart at the office of the Lord Mayor Karl Lautenschlager. Their spokesman was Robert Bosch. Bosch undertook to reinstate all blue- and white-collar workers returning from the field, and not to dismiss any associates until they had found new jobs.[61] However, Robert Bosch AG already had a big manpower surplus. The many orders for war materials received in the last two years of the war had more than doubled the company's headcount. With the war ending, those orders had abruptly dried up.

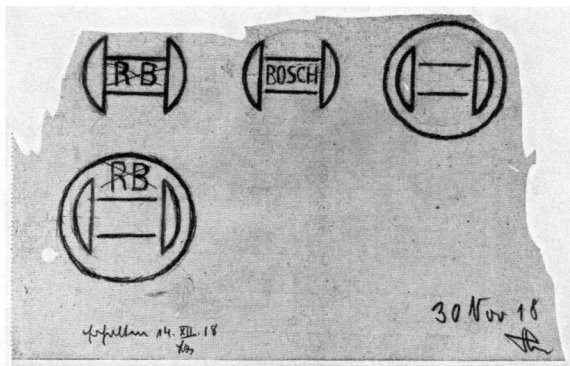

Gottlob Honold's sketch of the new logo (1918)

Many of the women workers taken on in the meantime now had to leave their jobs, their contracts being valid only for the duration of the war. But at nearly 1,500, the number of returnees was far greater.[62] In an appeal to the workforce dated November 15, 1918, Bosch management asked all associates who could do so to return to their former employers.[63] However, there was no great inclination to comply with this appeal, since Bosch paid better than anyone else. Out of some 1,400 office staff, only 73 gave notice.[64] The next few months saw a drastic fall in headcount that can only have resulted from mass dismissals. At the end of September 1918, Robert Bosch AG and Robert Bosch Metallwerk AG employed a total workforce of 9,870. The appeal of November 15, mentioned above, speaks of a workforce of 10,400.[65] By the end of January 1919, despite 624 re-employed returnees from military service and from the confiscated companies abroad, the number was down to 6,788.[66] Even when measured against the situation at the end of September 1918, that was a fall of more than 30 percent. The majority of those dismissed were women. The number of female blue-collar workers then employed at Bosch, as compared with the beginning of 1918, was down by at least 2,700 or 60 percent – but was still markedly higher than before the war.[67] Dismissals at Daimler-Motoren-Gesellschaft were on an even greater scale than at Bosch. In 1920, therefore, Bosch was once again the largest company in Stuttgart in terms of headcount – and so it remained until the Daimler-Benz merger of 1926.[68]

In January 1919, Stuttgart had its share of the violent clashes following the "Spartacist Uprising." The German Communist Party (KPD), founded shortly before by Karl Liebknecht and Rosa Luxemburg, called for an armed revolt aimed at preventing the National Assembly elections. In Stuttgart, the revolt was put down by temporarily mobilized security forces under the command of Paul Hahn, a man who later acted as an adviser to Robert Bosch.[69] Street fight-

Spark-plug production at the Feuerbach plant (1920)

ing broke out again in early April 1919. When the unions called a general strike, the Württemberg government under its Social Democratic prime minister, Wilhelm Blos, responded by declaring a state of siege in Stuttgart. Several hundred Spartacists threw up barricades but were eventually defeated by the military. Robert Bosch had no sympathy with the soviet republic the Communists were calling for, but condemned the brutal treatment meted out to the rebels in Berlin, where Liebknecht and Luxemburg had been murdered.[70] The fact was, the founder sympathized with a commission which had tasked itself with examining the feasibility of nationalizing important sectors of German industry, and described himself in 1919 (to a trade unionist) as a socialist. Yet at the same time he spoke against what he termed "nationalization frenzy" [*Sozialisierungswut*] and government intervention in commercial affairs.[71]

Following the spring of 1919, political relations in the Württemberg capital quickly stabilized. Yet at the end of August 1920, there were further vehement protests at a number of Stuttgart companies, including the Bosch factories. As part of his program of financial reforms, Matthias Erzberger, Vice-Chancellor of Germany and Minister of Finance, had introduced a national income tax. Prior to this, such taxation had been levied by individual states only, at varying but on the whole very low rates. Many Bosch and Daimler workers refused to accept this new deduction from their wages imposed by Berlin, and the more radical Socialist and Communist works councils declared a "tax war" [*Steuerkampf*]. There were walkouts and sit-ins at the Bosch factories. When it began to be rumored in Stuttgart that Communist elements were planning acts of sabotage, the authorities arranged for plants that had been hit by wildcat action to be closed down and surrounded by armed police units. At this, the works councils concerned went against the union leadership and called a general strike. For ten days, the main Bosch factory resembled a fortress before the strike had to be called off without result.[72]

Among the greatest attainments of the revolution of 1918–19 was a new framework governing working conditions and welfare arrangements. It was a framework which Robert Bosch AG had no difficulty in adopting. Some of its regulations had been brought in at the company long ago, the eight-hour working day being one example. And there had been a workers' committee [*Arbeiterausschuss*] at Bosch since before the war. The introduction of official works councils [*Betriebsräte*], laid down by law in 1920, was something Robert Bosch had explicitly endorsed in a letter to the presiding council of the *Reichsverband der Deutschen Industrie* written the year before. He believed it would help to overcome the "fundamental confrontational stance" [*grundsätzliche Kampfstellungnahme*] between employers and employees. Robert Bosch was prepared to give works councils a right of co-determination regarding "internal factory affairs" and personnel issues, but not where commercial and technical matters were concerned.[73] When the first *Betriebsrat* elections were held, it emerged that the radical left still wielded great influence among the Bosch workforce. For some time to come, Communists chaired the *Betriebsräte* of Robert Bosch AG and Robert Bosch Metallwerk AG as well as the combined works council.[74] It is striking that at Bosch the KPD could rely on the support of skilled workers, whereas elsewhere its membership tended to consist of less-qualified workers.[75] To an even greater extent than during the labor struggles of 1913, this had to do with the political orientation of the unions. Skilled workers had always been more heavily represented in trade-union organizations than unskilled, and since the DMV belonged to the left wing of the socialist-oriented unions, many skilled workers at Bosch backed the KPD.

Business developments in the years following the war were influenced by Germany's increasing inflation, and so cannot be measured by sales figures. Headcount numbers give a different picture than in prewar years. The fact was, Bosch was no longer growing at the same exceptional pace. Numbers of blue-collar and white-collar workers at the end of 1921 were scarcely greater than they had been in 1919. But within two years they shot up by something like half.[76] The growth was due in part to the de facto re-integration of the Feuerbach metal

works, but that is not the whole story. In export markets, Bosch actually benefited at that time from the collapse of the German currency. The downward slide
of the mark meant that goods produced in Germany could be sold abroad at
cheaper and cheaper prices. At the same time, German companies were to all
extents and purposes shielded from international competition, since exchange
rates put U.S., French, and even Swiss products virtually beyond the reach of
German purchasers. This has to be borne in mind when looking at the company's exports, which in 1920 once again accounted for over 50 percent of Bosch
sales. But while the collapse of the German currency eased German companies'
return to the world market, this collapse led to a price advantage that was merely
artificial, and that only temporarily enabled them to surmount the obstacles
they faced there. The important French market was now protected by a 45 percent tariff barrier, and in the U.K. 14 companies had begun producing their own
ignition devices during the war years – mostly copies of the Bosch magneto.[77]
Even so, in 1920 Bosch was able to open a new sales office in London, using a
company called J. A. Stevens Ltd. In the same year, an engineer by the name of
Ferdinand Péan became the Bosch agent in Paris. One by one, nearly all the
company's prewar sales offices outside Germany were restored. The Geneva
"sales house" (as the sales offices were called in the company) reopened for business as early as 1919.[78]

   With tariff barriers blocking access to the major European export markets,
Bosch proceeded to develop its presence farther afield, particularly since motorization of road traffic was clearly making great headway in Asia and Latin
America. In the space of only a few years, fresh sales offices sprang up on all five
continents – in New Zealand, India, Kenya, and Mexico, as well as in some of
the new European countries. In the Far East, the Shanghai branch of Jebsen &
Co. took over the China sales office in 1921, and in the same year the Hamburg
commercial giant C. Illies & Co. was granted the Bosch agency in Japan. Robert
Bosch personally traveled to Buenos Aires and Rio de Janeiro in 1921 to assess
the potential for business in South America. And he was impressed by what he
found. Three years later, on April 14, 1924, a separate subsidiary was set up in
Argentina: Robert Bosch S. A., Buenos Aires.[79] By the mid-1920s, Bosch already
had a denser network of sales offices outside Germany than before the First
World War. Particularly in Asia and Latin America, the company was now more
strongly represented. Seen in this light, there can be no question of any "de-
globalization" during this period. On the contrary, Bosch reacted to its market-
share losses in Europe by deliberately targeting what were still, for the most
part, peripheral markets in Latin America and Asia. Bosch may no longer have
enjoyed its earlier prominence in world markets, but by the mid-1920s its presence was more global than before the outbreak of hostilities in 1914.

The heaviest blow that Bosch had suffered as a result of the war was undoubtedly its expulsion from the U.S. market, the largest automobile market in the world. The rapid growth of the U.S. automobile industry during the war had passed Bosch by, and the Bosch name had now been supplanted in the U.S. by ABMC – the heir to Bosch Magneto Company, the company that had been sold off cheaply at the war's end and was now producing in the modern environment of the former Bosch factory in Springfield. Bosch had filed an appeal against the confiscation in the hope of regaining possession of Bosch Magneto Company, but this had only wasted more time. Not until it had become clear that the loss of the old U.S. subsidiary was going to have to be accepted did the company begin to build up a new distribution organization in America. Otto Heins, the former head of Bosch Magneto Company, traveled back to New York City in 1921, where he set up a new company, Robert Bosch Magneto Company (RBMC), to handle the U.S. market. The distribution network that Heins and his business manager Hermann Waker then built up was based more strongly than in the prewar years on the notion of "preferred dealerships." These were capable of delivering customer services and were equipped with workshops for installation and repair. Before the war, too, what were called "Official Bosch Distributors" had formed an important pillar of commercial business in the U.S. in addition to showrooms. These were supplemented by "Official Bosch Supply Stations" – independent workshops that acted as Bosch dealers and provided customer services. Only a few years later there were 1,500 such stations in existence.[80]

The U.S. supply stations could well have been the model for the "Bosch Service" workshops introduced in Germany during the 1920s.[81] The first Bosch Service Station was opened in Hamburg in 1921 by Max Eisenmann & Co. (today's Kruse Car Service).[82] Not until several years later did Bosch Service workshops spread throughout Germany. In 1926, there were 20 such workshops; by 1930 there were 113.[83] Like the U.S. supply stations, these service stations were independent workshops that, as well as selling and installing Bosch products on a franchise basis, offered maintenance services and carried out repairs. At a time when there were only very few car dealerships and filling stations, Bosch Service workshops filled a gap in the market. This pioneering after-sales service concept was of course also excellent publicity for Bosch – publicity that was soon global in its effect. Bosch Service workshops and "Bosch Departments" also sprang up in countries such as Egypt and Japan.[84]

These years also saw the spread of sales offices [Verkaufsbüros] in Germany, which came to be referred to as sales houses [Verkaufshäuser], even though the official renaming took place only in 1937.[85] The first such sales office for Germany had been set up in Berlin in 1909. During the First World War, a

Bosch Car Service repair shop in Manila (1939)

five-story office block to house the premises was built in the Charlottenburg district to designs by the renowned architects Richard Bielenberg and Josef Moser. The building (which also contained a small apartment for Robert Bosch) was taken into service in 1917. In February 1919, the Berlin sales office already had a staff of 78, and by May 1922 that number had risen to 160.[86] This building in Charlottenburg at 71 Bismarckstraße was also used as the company's liaison office in the national capital, and serves this purpose there to this day. There had been a sales office in Stuttgart since 1911. At first it was on the factory site, then in 1926 it moved into the former Kuhn'sche Maschinenfabrik in the Berg district. A further sales house opened in Frankfurt am Main in April 1919. By the autumn of 1924, Bosch sales operations already had over 14 sales houses with seven branch offices.[87]

Given the altered conditions of the postwar world, Bosch was unable to regain its earlier stature in international markets with its magneto ignition business alone. So the company further extended its product range. In the shape of the "oiler," a lubricating pump that could be used in stationary engines as well, Bosch had for some time been turning out a product that appealed not only to automakers. The company's reaction to rising demand had been to build a separate oiler factory, completed in 1923.[88] Above all, however, the company now gave itself a broader base in automotive technology. In a process that had begun before 1914, the manufacturer of ignition devices became a supplier of automotive components and systems. Bosch now mass-produced headlights, too, which it improved with a new low-beam function. Headlight production passed the 100,000 mark in 1922, and the manufacture of generators kept pace.[89] Little by little, Bosch succeeded in recovering the ground lost to the U.S. in the field of automotive lighting.

The innovation of these years with the greatest public appeal, however, was the Bosch horn designed by Gottlob Honold – an electric device with a steady, sonorous tone. Before its introduction, drivers were obliged to alert other road users by means of bells, bulb horns, sirens, and pea whistles. The Bosch horn was a big improvement. It could be operated from the steering wheel, and its sound was unmistakable. And as an unintentional by-product, the new accessory generated excellent publicity for its manufacturer. The Bosch horn was the talk of the October 1921 Motor Show. It soon found acceptance on the streets and roads of the world and was also, apparently, used at meetings of the Frankfurt city council.[90] Sales of the Bosch horn topped 100,000 in the space of only two years, with more being sold than there were automobiles in Germany.[91] Outside Germany, too, the horn proved hugely popular. The head of Tokyo's Bosch Department, Friedrich Reiser, reported that "the Bosch horn sounds its own hymn of praise through the streets of Kobe, Osaka, Tokyo, and the other cities, and its spread is vigorously backed by generous advertising."[92]

With the introduction of the windshield wiper in 1926, Bosch further extended its range of automotive electric equipment. Once again, this was an innovation made possible by the fact that automobiles now generated their own electricity. Two years later, the Bosch direction indicator followed, making it easier for drivers to show when they were turning or changing lanes. Many innovations now indelibly associated with automotive technology were introduced into Germany by Bosch in those years. As motorization spread and vehicle requirements multiplied, the Bosch brand acquired a modern image even among the general public. Technologically speaking, however, things like headlights, horns, and windshield wipers were not exactly – well, futuristic. The war had left a technology gap that was beginning to become noticeable. At Bosch, people realized that a truly groundbreaking innovation was needed if the company was to make its presence felt in the international markets as one of the world's leading automotive suppliers.[93]

Robert Bosch was not one of those businessmen who took advantage of Germany's inflation to buy up competitors with cheap money, and much less to establish entire industrial groups. During the years of inflation, Robert Bosch AG did not take over a single company. Only outside Germany did it have subsidiaries at that time, and those were all sales operations. However, in 1924 an agreement was reached with Eisemann-Werke AG, a company that Bosch regarded as its "most significant competitor in Germany."[94] Founded by Ernst Eisemann in the 1890s, Eisemann-Werke AG not only had a similar profile to Bosch; it was also located in the immediate vicinity of its larger rival – on Stuttgart's Rosenbergstraße. Eisemann-Werke had also been extremely successful in the United States before the First World War, which is likely one reason why Robert Bosch had always felt respect for it. In fact, to prevent the Eisemann factory from becoming reliant on banks Bosch had even (secretly) taken a capital holding in it.[95] Altered market conditions now led to Eisemann-Werke AG coming entirely under the umbrella of its mighty neighbor. Purchasing and production for both companies were first merged at Bosch. A full takeover followed in 1926, and from that point on Eisemann-Werke was run as the first subsidiary of Robert Bosch AG in Germany. For Robert Bosch AG this not only brought the advantage of removing a competitor from the market. It also gave the company the use of Eisemann's well-established sales organization with its sales houses, and enabled Bosch to extend its own factory facilities in Stuttgart onto the adjacent site belonging to its old rival.[96]

Relations between Robert Bosch AG and its neighboring company in Feuerbach, AEG-Mea, were very different. The history of the latter company is referred to in Bosch documents as "a permanent cross we must bear" [*ein dauernder Leidensweg*].[97] The history of the "Mea Factory for Magneto-Electrical Appliances" started with a company that a Stuttgart electrician named Max Wild had set up in 1903 in the wake of Bosch's success. Wild, who specialized in bell magnetos, received financial backing first from the tobacco wholesaler Max Rosenfeld – Robert Bosch's neighbor when he had lived at 75B Rotebühlstraße – and then from a Stuttgart businessman and industrialist named Eduard Scharrer, a son-in-law of the American beer magnate Adolphus Busch. In 1910, Wild and Scharrer merged their two companies to form Unionwerk Mea GmbH, based in Feuerbach. But it was only after AEG took over Union Mea in 1922 that the rivalry became troublesome so far as Bosch was concerned. The two companies were now competing in Feuerbach for skilled workers, and AEG-Mea began offering its bell magneto at cut-throat prices to automakers such as Opel and Adler. A possible solution emerged when Hermann Bücher joined the board at AEG. He was someone Robert Bosch knew through the *Reichsverband der Deutschen Industrie*, and the two subsequently became close friends. AEG-Mea was losing money anyway, and in 1928 Bücher let it go. Bosch took over the land and the company's technical facilities.[98]

For some time now, Robert Bosch had been personally involved in equity interests and acquisitions in the media world. He had acquired the folk-culture newspaper *Die Lese* in 1912, although after eight years it had to be closed down. During the First World War he had set up a publishing company called Rhein-Verlag in Basel, but that was similarly unsuccessful. And in the spring of 1917 he failed once again when he tried to take over the renowned *Vossische Zeitung* in Berlin. Between 1917 and 1920 Robert Bosch became involved in another publishing company, Deutsche Verlags-Anstalt (DVA) in Stuttgart, where he took on a majority holding of 54.56 percent. DVA for its part held 50 percent of the capital of Stuttgarter Zeitungsverlag, which published the time-honored *Stuttgarter Neues Tagblatt,* the newspaper with the largest circulation in the state capital, and the *Württemberger Zeitung.*[99] Regarding Bosch's motives, Heuss reports that the founder was trying to protect DVA from possible attack by the German-nationalist press baron Alfred Hugenberg.[100] This explanation may well be correct – although it cannot be proved on the basis of the company's surviving documentation. One argument in its favor is that Robert Bosch never developed media-political ambitions of his own, though as owner of the *Stuttgarter Neues Tagblatt* and the *Württemberger Zeitung* he was probably the most powerful figure on Württemberg's media scene. Unlike his friend Paul Reusch, who was involved with another newspaper published in Stuttgart, the *Schwäbischer Merkur,* Bosch never tried to use his publishing company's newspapers as his own personal forum or to influence the way they reported events.[101]

A shadow was cast over the development of Robert Bosch AG in these postwar years by a depressing number of deaths within the inner circle of the company's management. Gustav Klein's passing had already left a very large gap. The men now talked of as the founder's potential heirs were Gottlob Honold, known as the company's "inventor-in-chief," and Hugo Borst, its head of sales.[102] In December 1918, Robert Bosch's brother-in-law and long-time friend Eugen Kayser, who headed the Metallwerk division, took his own life.[103] Gottlob Honold took over at Metallwerk temporarily until Karl Martell Wild came back from internment in America and was able to relieve him. In the autumn of 1919, another board member, Heinrich Kempter, succumbed to a lung infection at the age of 48. The gaps that the deaths of Kayser and Kempter left in senior management were hard to fill. Robert Bosch brought in two family members for the purpose: Hermann Bosch, one of the sons of his favorite brother Karl, was appointed to help Wild run the Metallwerk, while Hermann Borst, a brother of Hugo Borst and a nephew of the founder's wife, was asked to assist Ernst Ulmer, the overworked head of personnel, and to build up a unit for white-collar workers within the personnel department.[104] Two further members of senior management died only a few years later. Gottlob Honold, designer of the high-voltage magneto ignition system, was only 46 when he succumbed to appendicitis in 1923. And in 1925, Ernst Ulmer suffered a fatal heart attack. He, too, was only 51 and in the prime of his life. Of the six members of the initial board of management of Robert Bosch AG (founded in 1917), only two were still alive: Hugo Borst and Max Rall.

Organizational development and the evolution of a sense of identity

The in-house newspaper Bosch-Zünder   Just as in the technical field, many plans and initiatives for internal development from the pre-1914 period had to be postponed because of the outbreak of hostilities. The 1913 strike had made two things clear. First, top management at Bosch was ill-prepared for the tensions that can arise in a large-scale industrial enterprise. Second, the rapid growth of the workforce meant that the founder's business principles had lost some of their immediate influence among associates. Due to the high rates of turnover during the war, management could only react to these changes after the fighting was over. And Robert Bosch himself was determined to firmly cement his principles in the company, even if that company was now a large industrial enterprise in an unsettled political environment. He wanted to strengthen the bond between the company and its associates.

Following the strike of 1913, thought had already been given to establishing an in-house publication. Such "works journals" were unusual at the time, and even where they existed their chief purpose was to provide the workforce with edification and other forms of instruction.[105] Robert Bosch seems to have been skeptical about the project, and was reluctant to go ahead until a suitable editor was found. This proved difficult, although Hugo Borst and indeed Bosch himself had excellent contacts at the *Neckar-Zeitung*, published in Heilbronn, where Borst's brother-in-law Ernst Jäckh had for a long time been editor-in-chief. According to Heuss, after the start of the war Borst did chance upon a good candidate. In Ulm while on military service, he met Otto Debatin, then editor of *Kosmos,* a monthly popular-science journal. Wounded in 1916, Debatin returned to Stuttgart, where, at Borst's suggestion, he drew up a plan for an in-house newspaper. This found favor with Robert Bosch, and within weeks of submitting a second memorandum in April 1918, Debatin was hired.[106] Robert Bosch AG was the tenth company in Germany to publish its own newspaper.[107]

The first issue of the *Bosch-Zünder* appeared on March 15, 1919, as a "Journal for all associates of Robert Bosch AG and Bosch-Metallwerk AG in Stuttgart and Feuerbach." The preface set out the principles that would guide editorial policy – an appeal to the togetherness and "Bosch spirit" of the workforce: "All of us, from the chief to the latest unskilled recruit, are bound together by working for a greater whole, by committing ourselves to a manufacturing company that is proud to bear the name of its founder, and of the man who is still at the helm." Debatin made it plain that the *Bosch-Zünder* would set out to strengthen the bond between workforce and company and instill a sense of shared identity in all employed there. The preface referred explicitly to the division of labor typical of a large-scale industrial enterprise, as a result of which "the individual learns and witnesses but little of events and processes outside his own, closely restricted field of operation." The *Bosch-Zünder*, on the other hand, would strive to give associates the feeling that they were "part of the whole."[108] The preface also specified what this would mean for the articles printed there. Debatin announced that the *Bosch-Zünder* would "report facts" (i. e., would not content itself with anecdotes), that it would introduce new products, and that alongside communications from management it would offer contributions from the shop floor.

Even in the proposals sent to Hugo Borst in April 1918, Debatin had stressed how an in-house newspaper could promote a "sense of belonging" and foster what he called "factory pride" [*Fabrikstolz*] among associates. Possible topics ranged from "Development of the Bosch manufacturing sites" through "What is a patent?" all the way to "The significance of the Neckar Canal project for the business life of Württemberg." Debatin also considered a separate supplement entitled "House and Garden." He was particularly interested in linking the *Bosch-Zünder* to lecture and entertainment evenings on company premises. Such plans were reflective of the educational policies of the *Reform* movement of the day, something which likely appealed to Robert Bosch. Debatin may well have emphasized this link between publication and events since he knew the founder was supportive of this kind of "practical adult education." In fact, it was soon after this that Robert Bosch became chairman of the newly founded "Society for the Promotion of Adult Education".[109]

Debatin had already suggested several names for the newspaper in his April 1918 proposal: "The Bosch Associate," "Our Factory," "The Spark Plug," or "The Magneto." He wanted it to be a name that related to the company.[110] This, too, was in line with what was then a new concept of the in-house newspaper as an "internal consultation tool" [*innerbetrieblicher Sprechsaal*].[111] The self-imposed goal of dealing with the industrial realities of the workplace was one that the *Bosch-Zünder* subsequently lived up to, devoting much space to describing products and discussing production technology, rationalization, and industrial organization and training.[112] In contrast to other internal publications, it did not set out to censure. Politics and religion were both excluded from its pages. At Bosch, these were deemed private matters to be left outside the factory gates. Of course, such reticence did not prevent the *Bosch-Zünder* from propagating democracy as a political ideal.[113]

Launched in 1919 as a monthly publication of 16–20 pages, the *Bosch-Zünder* was no crude management mouthpiece, let alone a "weapon of class warfare" – as the German Communist Party termed in-house newspapers.[114] It made a point of being open-minded, even when discussing union matters. It also combined technological information with training objectives and avoided indoctrination. This approach made the *Bosch-Zünder* a major success. By 1923, 13,000 copies were being printed, which was well in excess of the Bosch headcount of around 10,000 at the time.[115] Moreover, unlike some other in-house newspapers, the *Bosch-Zünder* was no flash in the pan. It is still published today – in ten languages.

Debatin doubtless realized that an in-house newspaper was not going to enhance associates' feeling of belonging unless it was popular. This was an objective which, in line with the principles of Robert Bosch, the *Bosch-Zünder* pursued by insisting on high quality, tolerance, and freedom from prejudice. Even a Communist works-council member could browse this publication without having to fear that it would contain spiteful articles about the KPD.

Accordingly, Debatin did not position the *Bosch-Zünder* unilaterally in the service of the board of management. That would not have chimed with company ethos. But neither was this newspaper just another tabloid. It saw itself as being committed to the spirit of the founder, and its job as being to instill the principles of Robert Bosch in the now expanded workforce. That became crystal clear as early as the second issue – which was published in unusual circumstances, delivery having been held up by the general strike of early April 1919 and by the state of siege declared in Stuttgart.[116] Under the headline "I would rather lose money than trust," the journal reprinted on its first page a document setting out the business principles of Robert Bosch in their clearest form: his letter of September 1918 to the Autograph Collection of the Prussian National Library. Those words still form an integral part of Bosch's corporate culture today. Back then, just after the general strike, they must have had a profound impact on everyone employed at the company's Stuttgart and Feuerbach plants.[117]

The workforce at Robert Bosch AG could now read the *Bosch-Zünder* each month. But that was not all. The company had begun offering training and cultural programs. Not on the scale, admittedly, that Debatin had outlined in his 1918 proposal. Nonetheless, since the end of the war the company had had a large library – an object of such pride that the numbers of books it contained were occasionally cited in the annual report. In the spring of 1922, it already contained 4,500 books. Fifteen years later, the number stood at eight thousand.[118] Echoing the attitude of Robert Bosch himself, this was an area in which the company was particularly keen to avoid talking down to either blue-collar or white-collar staff. So the library included works by Marx, Bebel, Lenin, and Trotsky.[119] Many of the cultural events provided by the company comprised concerts put on by associate ensembles. Before the Second World War, Robert Bosch AG had two brass bands, a string orchestra, and both male- and female-voice choirs. For these orchestras and choirs, the company had appointed its own music director.[120]

Bosch-Hilfe (a retirement and surviving dependents' providence fund) Securing a comfortable livelihood for the workforce had always been one of the entrepreneurial principles of Robert Bosch. He took the view that corporate welfare should not be allowed to take the form of making associates' minds up for them – spoon-feeding them, in other words. He declined as a matter of principle to build special housing developments, regarding this as an invasion of associates' freedom of movement. For the same reason, there were no company pensions at Robert Bosch AG even in the mid-1920s. Until then, what the company did for its workforce extended solely to the contract of employment itself and to working conditions. This was where Robert Bosch felt that the social responsibility of the entrepreneur lay, and it was here that he had performed the pioneering work on which his reputation as a socially open-minded industrialist rested. Rather than build company-owned housing, he preferred to pay his workers good wages that would motivate them to do good work. What workers spent their wages on was not, as he saw it, of any concern to the employer. It was something they could decide for themselves as responsible citizens. For Robert Bosch, the best kind of welfare a company could provide for its workers was a good environment in which to work – not extra benefits in other areas of their lives. It was to this end that he had introduced the eight-hour working day, as one of the first entrepreneurs to do so. Also, Bosch employees received paid vacation well before workers in most other companies.

After the First World War, Robert Bosch felt forced to rethink his position with regard to social welfare in the workplace. As a result of the war, the need for welfare had grown beyond recognition. Many company employees had become invalids, while the death toll had left women without husbands and children without fathers. In the face of such distress, the social responsibilities of Robert Bosch AG could no longer be confined to the industrial sphere alone or to the actual workforce. Moreover, galloping inflation was producing fresh hardships. The national pension-insurance scheme, then largely financed on a fully funded basis, was losing its capital stock. With no company pension to look forward to, members of the Bosch workforce faced poverty in their old age. Their high wages were of little use to them now. With the currency rapidly collapsing, they were hardly worth saving. Furthermore, social-security provision was expanding under the Weimar Republic and spreading its net wider than it had under the German Empire. No entrepreneur with a highly developed sense of social responsibility, certainly not Robert Bosch, could or would stand idly by.

Robert Bosch AG gave employment to greater numbers of war wounded, including those who had lost their sight, than it was legally obliged to do.[121] In 1922, the company set up its *Robert-Hilfe*, named after the founder's first son. This scheme provided educational support grants for the children of associates who had fallen in battle. It started off helping 302 children. Later, in 1927, the number was down to 222, many of those children having meanwhile become adults.[122] A benevolent scheme for white-collar staff at Bosch came into existence on October 1, 1921. It took the form of a life-assurance scheme (*Angestellten-Hilfe*) that staff qualified for after more than ten years' service. According to Heuss, the main aim of this "white-collar benevolent scheme" was to compensate for inflation.[123] Savings dramatically lost value in the early 1920s, and this hit white-collar staff especially hard. They were in a position to save up for old age, and thus tended to have more money put by than their colleagues on the shop floor. When hyperinflation hit in 1923, the assets of the benevolent scheme for white-collar staff lost all their value, although subsequently, by switching them to the new gold standard, the company revalued them. By the end of 1927, the white-collar benevolent scheme had 417 members.[124]

Blue-collar workers at Bosch can hardly have been happy about this special provision for white-collar staff. Privileged treatment was by no means the company's usual practice. However, inflation had also shrunk the financial reserves of Robert Bosch AG badly, and it was not until some time after the stabilization of the currency that the human resources department could start making plans to introduce a more comprehensive benefits scheme. Those plans, already well advanced by 1926, had to be shelved because of the severe crisis affecting the company at that time.[125] It was Christmas 1927 before Otto Debatin, now the director of industrial relations, was able to tell shop-floor associates that the company had a special present for them: a company pension scheme was being introduced.[126] This retirement and surviving dependents' providence fund, which went back to a proposal by Robert Bosch (hence the name, *Bosch-Hilfe*) was financed purely from the company's current income.

In other words, employees were not required to pay contributions, though nei-ther could they claim such benefit as a right. The pension rights of blue- and white-collar employees who had worked for Bosch for a minimum of ten years became vested on their 40th birthday. Benefits began at 20 percent of earnings and rose with years of service at Bosch to 45 percent at age 65 and 35 years' service. The scheme also included widows' allowances and educational sup-port grants. If someone left the company, their pension remained vested, but they could not take the reserves they had accrued with them. The assets of this pension scheme were administered by a trustee separately from the business assets of Robert Bosch AG. If the company became insolvent, the assets were to pass to the city of Stuttgart.[127]

The introduction of the company pension scheme was a generous move because it was charged to the dividends and hence the income of Robert Bosch. Although the scheme was not officially set up until 1929, it had already re-ceived 1 million reichsmarks from the profit disclosed for the 1927 business year. In the following year, 2 million reichsmarks were transferred to it. De-spite the effects of the Great Depression, in 1937 it had assets of some 18 million reichsmarks. Two years later, it was converted into a membership corporation [*eingetragener Verein*].[128] According to the 1928 annual report, the board of management saw the pension scheme "not [as] an act of charity but [...] as an economic measure in the company's interest, with the aim of preserving and increasing the good will of our workforce at the same time as giving concrete expression to the solidarity of all involved in the House of Bosch."[129] The expression "House of Bosch" [*das Haus Bosch*] was becoming increasingly common. In fact it was popular even in the 1930s, but in the long term it failed to catch on.[130]

The *Bosch-Hilfe* was not only designed to give security to employees and strengthen their loyalty to the company. It could also make loans to Robert Bosch AG and as such was by no means entirely altruistic. It made the com-pany even more independent of the capital market, which may also have been a lesson from the acute shortage of capital experienced during the years of hyperinflation, as well as from the 1926 crisis. It certainly proved its worth in the Great Depression of 1929 and after. As Heuss wrote, "The *Bosch-Hilfe* in fact became very important as a sort of savings bank for the company, placing operating capital at its disposal. In that respect it served both sides."[131] This is a classic example of Bosch reasoning, given that Robert Bosch firmly believed that looking after the workforce did not simply cost the company. It also paid the company.

Not even in the 1920s could Robert Bosch make up his mind to build company-owned housing on any large scale. The primary task of the housing company Bosch Haus-Gesellschaft mbH, set up in 1923, was to replace any homes that had to make way for industrial expansion.[132] However, from 1926 employees of Robert Bosch AG were able to obtain from their company building loans at favorable rates of interest.[133] This was the time when the building society idea was taking hold in Germany, inflation having destroyed much private capital. The country's first building society was set up in Wüstenrot near Heilbronn in 1924. Cooperative building societies, too, now put forward savings models that were hugely popular with the notoriously house-proud Swabians.[134] Robert Bosch will hardly have wanted his employees to miss out on such an offer when many of them had seen the money set aside for "building a little place of their own" wiped out during the inflationary years.

Principles and reform of apprentice training   The first dedicated workshop for apprentices had been set up at Bosch in 1913. Its purpose was to systematize the training of apprentices, to which Robert Bosch always attached great importance, and adapt it to an industrial environment. Moreover, the rapid growth of the company had increased the need for skilled workers – a need that the labor market could no longer satisfy. Until 1922, the training workshop was headed by the Swiss-born August Utzinger, an exceptionally thorough man who had an especially formative influence on apprentice training at Bosch. Utzinger had previously worked in a lighting-technology laboratory at the Siemens-Schuckert factory. Robert Bosch had been a friend of his since his own time at Schuckert and had complete faith in Utzinger's skills as an instructor.[135] In addition to Utzinger, Ernst Durst served in the apprentice workshop for some considerable time. Durst had had to instruct many newly appointed women workers during the First World War, and later he published a textbook on the subject of teaching technicians their trade.[136]

Robert Bosch had clear ideas about training apprentices. He attached great importance to their receiving comprehensive instruction in their trade and not simply in the special requirements of his own company.[137] That was partly why apprenticeships at Bosch were so sought-after, but one result of this form of training was that most Bosch apprentices later moved elsewhere. Only about a quarter of them stayed with the company.[138] Robert Bosch was aware of this, of course, and likely regarded his company's apprentice workshop as also helping to promote technical training throughout the state of Württemberg. August Utzinger, too, had his own ideas. He insisted that apprentices should receive instruction solely in their own workshop, quite separately from the plant itself. Only a small number of companies had such an arrangement.[139] This principle was not uncontroversial, since it meant that apprentice training became increasingly incompatible with the speed and specialization of work processes on the shop floor. Just like Robert Bosch, Utzinger laid great stress on the training of apprentices not being confined to imparting technical ability alone. Trainees should also feel they were being addressed personally and be helped to develop a sense of responsibility and interpersonal skills as well. The teaching of such "soft skills" was almost a trademark of a Bosch apprenticeship. The same was true later of the "Bosch Service" workshops, which arose in the 1920s and adopted their own system of apprentice training. The guidelines laid down for Bosch Service stated: "Apprentice training is a responsible job that demands a great deal from the instructor. It does not stop at imparting expert knowledge but extends to teaching the apprentice to be an independent person whose behavior demonstrates character. In other words, the instructor must also possess educational skills, and be an example to the apprentice not only in the field of expertise but also in behavior and attitude."[140]

Under Utzinger's successors Adolf Ottmann (1921–27) and Wilhelm Bernhardt (1927–44), the apprentice department was enlarged and training courses changed. While only technicians were originally trained at Bosch, a course for toolmakers followed in 1924, and from 1928 it was also possible to serve a commercial apprenticeship at Bosch. The strict separation of apprentice workshops and shop floor was no longer adhered to, with apprentices now spending part of their training time on the latter. Also, theoretical instruction was moved from the city's trade school (where there had been separate Bosch classes) to the apprentice training department.[141]

In the period after the First World War, Robert Bosch AG took on between 30 and 35 apprentices annually. Invariably, there were far more applicants than available places. An initial selection process was based on school grades. There followed an entrance examination in which applicants had to demonstrate their knowledge of mathematics, physics, and German.[142] Apprenticeships took three and a half years (before the turn of the century that had even been four years), and they began with a three-month, unpaid probationary period. For the first two apprenticeship years (this was true even under Utzinger's successors), all training took place in the apprentice department, where apprentices were instructed by company engineers, their instruction also covering operational matters. After that, for a year they were allocated to an operational department, and for the last six months they were recalled to the training workshop. Journeyman examinations were initially taken at the chamber of crafts, later at the chamber of commerce. These comprised a theory section, manufacture of a sample of work, and a journeyman's piece.[143] It was the company's ambition that all Bosch apprentices should pass the journeyman exam,

Aptitude test for apprentices (1925)

and this was indeed the case – almost always with good marks. In the period 1927–35, only three of 473 Bosch apprentices taking the examination failed to receive the grades "good" or "very good."[144] Among applicants for apprenticeships, preference was given to sons of Bosch associates. Successful completion of the eighth *Volksschule* class was a prerequisite. At the start of the 1920s, 50 percent of apprentices had completed *Volksschule*, 25 percent had been through *Realschule*, and 25 percent had attended *Bürgerschule*, a kind of *Gymnasium* without the upper level.[145] Following the introduction of the commercial training system there were also apprentices who were high school graduates.[146]

Extension of plants The manufacturing facilities of Robert Bosch AG in Stuttgart and Feuerbach were greatly extended during the 1920s. The company's very rapid growth before the First World War had led to cramped conditions in many areas of production. Despite the construction of new buildings in Feuerbach, that growth had failed to keep pace with rising headcount. The overcrowding had less to do with total floor space and more with covered area. Expansion led mainly to roomier and more functional manufacturing facilities, not necessarily to larger offices. In 1931, the covered area at the Stutt-

Feuerbach plant (1925)

gart and Feuerbach sites was more than four times greater than it had been in 1914. Much of the expansion was centered on Feuerbach, since here a very much larger area of land was available than in the west end of Stuttgart, where the main plant still stood. Yet during the 1920s, the site in Stuttgart was considerably extended as well.

Table 4 Surface areas and headcount at the Bosch plants in Stuttgart and Feuerbach (1906–31)[147]

Year	Plot size in m^2		Covered area in m^2		Total floor space in m^2		Headcount
	Stuttgart	Feuerbach	Stuttgart	Feuerbach	Stuttgart	Feuerbach	
1906	3,230		2,130		9,480		611
1914	12,500	71,300	8,250	11,600	45,100	19,300	3,611
1918	13,200	91,700	8,500	29,800	46,100	63,600	9,249
1931	35,200	206,000	20,000	63,800	63,500	114,100	8,658

The main plant site in Stuttgart had grown historically. Being in the city center, it could expand only to a limited extent. As the oldest industrial site in this location, the building that Robert Bosch had put up on Hoppenlaustraße (later no. 11) looked architecturally like a prestigious town house. The plot adjoined the office building at 4 Militärstraße (now 4 Breitscheidstraße) that comprised the company's headquarters and included Robert Bosch's own

Office building at
4 Militärstraße (*c.* 1935),
now 4 Breitscheidstraße

office. Within ten years, repeated extensions meant that the magneto works and the spark-plug works had grown to cover nearly the entire area lying between Hoppenlaustraße, Militärstraße, Seidenstraße, and Forststraße. From the mid-1920s the main plant, which now consisted principally of the magneto works, was joined by the former Eisemann site between Forststraße and Rosenbergstraße, on which a new building for the sales bureau and parts of the administration was constructed in the years 1933–35.[148]

Table 5 Bosch plants in Stuttgart and Feuerbach (early 1930)[149]

Section/works	Location	Headcount
Administration	Stuttgart	1,370
Administration	Feuerbach	813
Magneto works	Stuttgart	2,893
Light works	Feuerbach	2,651
Metal works	Feuerbach	725
Oiler works	Feuerbach	508
Isolit works	Feuerbach	614

In Feuerbach, which until 1933 was a separate municipality to the north of Stuttgart, Bosch was able to acquire a very much larger site and build more spacious production facilities consisting of large single-story buildings with sawtooth roofs. Unlike in Stuttgart, here separate factories could be devoted to individual areas of production. The first factory in Feuerbach was the press works, later called the metal works, which made semi-finished products for the main plant in Stuttgart. It went into operation in 1911, two years after the foundation stone had been laid. From 1917 to 1928 the metal works traded as a separate stock corporation under the name of Robert Bosch Metallwerk AG. It was in 1912 that Bosch began building the light works in Feuerbach, moving into a first finished part in May 1914, only months before the First World War broke out. The light works brought the company's latest technology to Feuerbach – namely generators and headlights (integrated within the Bosch automotive lighting system). During the First World War, the spark-plug works moved out to Feuerbach, and after the war the company was able to build another factory there to produce oilers and to start work on the isolit works, which went into operation in 1923. The oiler works turned out the then very popular lubrication pumps known as "oilers," while the isolit works produced spark-plug insulators. Virtually all that remained in the principal factory in Stuttgart was magneto production.

5 The 1926 crisis, and diversification in the Great Depression

Causes, course, and repercussions of the great crisis of 1926

In November 1923, with hyperinflation overcome and a new, stable currency introduced, Germans could finally breathe again. It seemed they had escaped by the skin of their teeth once more. For the weeks and months preceding the introduction of the new currency, organized existence had no longer been possible. A tram ticket had cost up to 150 billion marks, and wages had become worthless almost as soon as they were paid. The country itself had threatened to come apart. In Hamburg, the Communist Party had staged an uprising, while in Munich Hitler had attempted a putsch. In light of these events, the years following the stabilization of the currency were also a time of political stabilization. However, the German economy was by no means out of the woods. Symptoms of grave weakness appeared even before 1929 and the advent of the Great Depression. This was particularly true of the German automotive industry, which had fallen even further behind its international competitors during the years of inflation. Initially, there was very little demand for passenger cars in Germany after the war. Inflation then created a bubble for the country's automakers. The depreciation of the mark gave the German automotive industry such a price advantage outside the country that vehicles could be sold there which would normally have been uncompetitive.[1] In terms of vehicle density, Germany lagged far behind in 1923. The U.S. at that time had one passenger car per 8.3 inhabitants, and in France the ratio was 1 to 136. In Germany, by contrast, it was one automobile to 625 inhabitants – which approximated the figures for the U.S. as far back as 1907.[2]

After currency stabilization, it was no longer possible to shield the German market against imports for long. German automakers knew what they would be facing when they had to compete with Ford and General Motors. So they persuaded their national government to slap a hefty import duty on automobiles coming into the country. But not even that could prevent U.S. automakers from conquering the German market in the ensuing years. Ford and General Motors were offering inexpensive middle- and compact-class cars which were mass-produced on the assembly line. During the period in which they had had no outside competition to fear, German automakers had failed to recognize the trend toward small cars. At most companies, manufacturing was also still based on prewar methods. Moreover, the number of German automakers had increased during the era of hyperinflation. Measured against the relatively modest size of the German market, there were just too many of them, and most of them were making too many different models to boot. Being produced in low volumes, German automobiles cost a lot more than U.S. imports. This was particularly true of the models made by companies such as Daimler and Horch, in which high quality and features mattered more than price. But expensive automobiles that only few people could afford were no longer in demand in the German market. Instead, people wanted entry-level models such as the Model T Ford. The so-called "Tin Lizzy" was the world's most widely sold car at the time. Gone were the days when the passenger car was a luxury item. Now it was price that determined market success. On this point, U.S. automakers had a dual advantage. As well as inexpensive cars, they could also offer financing on the installment plan – a retail instrument completely new to Germany at the time. Moreover, the German automotive market's markedly lower vehicle density made it particularly attractive to U.S. and French automakers, since high growth rates could be expected. As late as in 1923, imported products accounted for only 5 percent of new automobile registrations in Germany. By 1929, this figure had risen to 38.5 percent.[3] By then, the U.S. automotive industry already had eight assembly plants in Germany, while French automakers had three subsidiaries there.[4]

When it came to production methods, most German manufacturers were in no position to catch up. They had lost too much capital owing to inflation. The result was a number of insolvencies and a process of concentration. Of the 65 automakers that Germany boasted in 1924, only 17 were still in existence in 1929. Companies forced out of production or taken over by rivals included not only the "flowers of inflation," as the ones who had entered the market in the years 1922–23 were called, but also some well-known and distinguished names. The two oldest manufacturers in the German automotive industry, Daimler-Motoren-Gesellschaft and Benz & Cie., formed a strategic alliance in 1924. Daimler-Motoren-Gesellschaft had deliberately chosen to stay with high-quality, expensive models – and nearly driven itself into bankruptcy as a result. In June 1926, its largest creditor, Deutsche Bank, forced it to merge with the similarly struggling Benz & Cie. to form Daimler-Benz AG.[5] Other mergers planned at the time – between Opel and BMW, for instance – failed to materialize.[6] A notable exception among German automakers was Adam Opel AG. It switched to assembly-line production as early as 1924, and with the Opel 4 PS (nicknamed the "tree frog" [*Laubfrosch*]), a copy of the Citroën 5CV, it launched a model that followed the trend. The Laubfrosch made Opel the largest automaker of the day in Germany, with a market share of some 27 percent and a more than 40 percent share of production (1928).[7] In March 1929, the owners sold 80 percent of their shares to General Motors, and two years later Adam Opel AG passed wholly into GM ownership. Ford expanded its presence in Germany in the early 1930s by building a new plant in Cologne.

Bosch, too, had escaped competitive pressure during the years of inflation. In the domestic market, the company was protected against competition from other countries. Outside Germany, it was able to sell its products at favorable prices. This advantage facilitated its return to the international marketplace. Like the German automotive industry, there was no need for Bosch to offer new designs. Nor was the company exposed to any cost pressure so long as production in Germany could be financed with cheaper and cheaper money and every magneto sold for export brought in hard currency. However, people at Bosch also realized that a boom based on a devaluing currency could not last. As early as 1922, preparations began for an innovation in the field of diesel technology that the company hoped would open up opportunities in the longer term.[8] Once inflation had been overcome, cost pressure from the market could be expected to hit the company. To meet it, the prototype of a new series of magneto (the "F Series") had been designed as early as 1921. The FB 1 single-cylinder magneto ignition device assembled a number of components inside an aluminium housing, simplifying the design and making it less expensive than previous ignition devices. In 1923, Bosch brought out an entire range of F-Series magnetos. These included the FF 4A-type for four-cylinder engines, which was then installed in the Opel Laubfrosch.[9] Another "first" in the same year was the introduction, in one department, of U.S.-style assembly-line production. Instead of teamwork, the manufacture of Bosch horns now used this new method, cutting turnaround time from 14–16 days to 4 days.[10]

Following stabilization of the currency, U.S. companies crowded onto the German market with inexpensive products and new technology. Automotive equipment was no exception. The triumph that Bosch had enjoyed in the U.S. before the First World War was now enjoyed in Germany by the U.S. manufacturers Bendix and Delco. The Bendix electric starter gained worldwide acceptance at this time. Ford, General Motors, and Citroën all used it in their vehicles. Delco, which had meanwhile passed into the ownership of General Motors, was the leading producer of battery-powered ignition systems. The GM subsidiary had built its first ignition systems with high-performance batteries in 1910, combining the technology with a generator which could produce current while the vehicle was in motion.[11] But pressure on Bosch came not only from competitors in other countries. It also came from German automakers who, finding that the new competition with Ford and General Motors exposed them to cost pressure, sought to shift this onto suppliers, demanding that Bosch either reduce its prices or manufacture more cheaply. Robert Bosch would complain bitterly about such behavior on the part of his major German customers. He pointed out in the *Bosch-Zünder* that Ford could build 1.5 million ignition systems a year, whereas in Germany only 60,000 were required – and this for some 50 automakers. "Most of those companies want custom-made equipment. And then German manufacturers have nothing better to do than demand that I charge the same low prices as the Americans."[12]

The year 1925 began auspiciously for Robert Bosch AG. Despite a difficult market situation, the order books were bulging. Demand was rising so fast that headcount reached a new high.[13] However, there was a clear drop in order intake in September 1925, and many orders already placed were cancelled. Two months on, the decline in orders became a full-blown crisis – the most serious the company had faced yet. By January 1926, headcount was down to 10,986. Recalling the 1907 crisis, Robert Bosch drew hope that orders would begin to recover as they had then.[14] However, this time the crisis took a different course. It was to last for almost a year, even casting a shadow over celebrations to mark the company's 40th anniversary in September 1926. As the founder wrote in the in-house newspaper at the time, "Bosch is celebrating its 40th birthday in the severest crisis it has ever faced."[15] A month after the anniversary the headcount figure reached a low of 6,149 – some 56 percent of where it had been at the start of the year.[16] Despite schemes for reduced working hours, more than 40 percent of jobs were shed, most of these cuts no doubt resulting from dismissals. Socially, this was a disaster that inevitably shook the way the company saw itself, as well as its protestations of solidarity within the "House of Bosch," to the core. Sacked associates who failed to find a job elsewhere received out-of-work pay only for the regulation 28 weeks. Not until two years later was unemployment insurance introduced in Germany.[17]

Many accounts of the history of the company have glossed over the serious crisis of 1926. Only in the chronicle published to accompany the 125th corporate anniversary celebrations was the veil of silence covering this chapter of Bosch history lifted.[18] The "interim crisis" [*Zwischenkrise*] of 1925–26, as economic historians now call it,[19] was triggered by a slump that was confined to Germany, where for the first time the jobless figure topped two million. Part of the cause lay in the aftermath of war and the years of inflation. But the crisis also stemmed from structural problems in the entire German economy. The automotive industry, already suffering, was hit particularly hard. Year on year, automobile production in Germany in 1926 was down by something like a quarter. More than half the country's 65 automakers still producing in 1924 and 1925 failed to survive the "interim crisis."[20] But for Bosch to dismiss over half of its associates, orders must have dipped by more than a quarter. In other words, the crisis that befell Bosch in 1926 was due to more than just a decline in German automobile production. Instead, it seems likely that German automakers were also beginning to turn away from Bosch, since its products were now just too expensive for them. They could cut costs by switching to less expensive suppliers.

Even before the war a start had been made on broadening the Bosch product range to include generators and headlights, making the company less dependent on the ignition business. But this was of little use to Bosch now, since these additions were also products that rivals, too, could offer more cheaply. No one at Bosch had expected the magneto ignition system to last forever as the rock on which Bosch was built. However, the company was simply not prepared for a sudden collapse of the entire automotive market – even if some lessons might have been learned from the 1907 crisis. Outside automotive technology, Bosch had nothing in its product range but lubrication pumps for stationary engines. The "interim crisis" also challenged Bosch's reputation as a high-quality supplier, the linchpin on which the self-image of the company and its workforce rested. It was one of the business principles of Robert Bosch to make "the best [product] from the best [materials]" [*Vom Besten das Beste*].[21] His company's success was based on the high quality of its products – and quality, of course, does not come cheap. The company had hoped that its decision to shift to assembly-line production, combined with the new, simplified magneto design, would reduce costs to such an extent that Bosch would remain competitive, even when working to the highest standards.

Now the company had to say goodbye to that idea. It faced a choice: abandon the former standard of quality, or vanish from the market. Although the very survival of the company was at stake, those in charge found the decision hard to take. Many *Boschler* (as associates were called) doubtless hated the idea of abandoning perfectionism and of copying – under license – cheap American designs they had once looked down upon. Many likely found the prospect humiliating. No other explanation is possible for the lengthy delay in accepting the inevitable, a delay which is mentioned in an article that Robert Bosch wrote for the company's 40th anniversary in

Table 6 Headcount at Robert Bosch AG (1926)[22]

Month	White-collar workers	Blue-collar workers	of which skilled workers	of which women workers	Total headcount
January	2,295	8,691	2,366	3,315	10,986
March	2,010	6,600	1,948	2,385	8,610
May	1,876	6,034	1,793	2,163	7,910
July	1,739	4,903	1,398	1,696	6,642
September	1,595	4,596	1,415	1,569	6,191
October	1,566	4,583	1,409	1,555	6,149
December	1,493	4,902	1,419	1,789	6,395

the autumn of 1926. But in the end, the company did force itself to sell cheaper designs – designs that were no longer produced according to the principle of "selling only the very best, in terms of both design and manufacture."[23]

At the same time, Bosch now started producing batteries and battery-powered ignition systems for passenger cars, although in doing so the company was itself competing with its own biggest product, the magneto.[24] Yet here, too, the crisis left Bosch with no alternative. The fact was, battery-powered ignition systems cost less than magneto ignition systems. The know-how for this new line had long been in existence at Bosch, since it had also been selling motorcycle batteries since 1922.[25] Technically, Bosch batteries and battery-powered ignition systems were good, and were also quite soon a market success. But they were not an original design. Instead, they were manufactured under license, even if with technical improvements. It was also during this time that Bosch obtained a license from Bendix in the U.S. to manufacture electric starters. In a report written later by the first head of the Bosch archives, Friedrich Schildberger, we read, "As regards starters, [...] Bendix has virtually conquered the entire world market. In 1926, we ourselves were forced by price pressure to begin producing its starters, although we subsequently improved them greatly."[26] In the summer of 1926, it looked as if Bosch would be confined to just such license production in the future, if the age of the magneto really was nearly at an end. Bosch was still struggling to come up with a key innovation in the field of diesel technology, but so far had little to show for its efforts.[27]

The collapse of orders in winter 1925–26 also put Robert Bosch AG under pressure financially. Decades later, Hans Walz wrote that the company had been "on the verge of ruin" at that time, having fallen into an "awkward liquidity and payments squeeze."[28] Bosch appears to have been at risk of illiquidity, since most of its assets (the real estate in Stuttgart, for example, and the holdings outside Germany) were not available as short-term liquid assets, and inflation had robbed the company of much of its capital. However, in his remarks in retrospect quoted above, Walz blamed the liquidity crisis on the leadership of the company itself: "The rules of consistently directed management and proper financial conduct had been grossly flouted."[29] To clarify the financial position of the company, the Berlin branch of Price, Waterhouse & Co. was asked to audit the accounts.[30]

Here, too, financial necessity forced Robert Bosch AG to depart from its traditional principles by resorting to the capital market. The company had already received a private loan of 10 million reichsmarks from its founder, which was to be converted into shares if necessary.[31] Now it placed a bond issue. At the end of March 1926, Robert Bosch traveled to Berlin, where he met with Jakob Goldschmidt, head of Danatbank (Darmstädter- und National-bank), then one of the largest commercial banks in Germany.[32] Goldschmidt was the star of the Berlin banking world, and his bank was among the first ports of call where industrial finance was concerned. On April 2, 1926, Danat-bank in the Netherlands issued a Robert Bosch AG bond worth three million U.S. dollars, as a debenture paying 7 percent interest.[33] Plots of land in Stuttgart and Feuerbach were put up as collateral. Bosch had in fact issued debentures during the years of inflation, but the fall in the value of the currency meant that those bonds did not have any major significance. Heuss was the first to remark that the 1926 bond marked a new departure in financing at Bosch. However, contrary to his account, the bond was not used primarily to finance further rationalization measures and research on the diesel injection pump. It was used to keep Robert Bosch AG solvent.[34]

The capital market in Germany had dried up as a result of the repercussions of inflation and the restrictive monetary policy of the *Reichsbank*, which was determined to avoid a further devaluation of the currency. Accordingly, many German companies borrowed money abroad during this period. Banks outside Germany readily granted German companies loans, since interest rates in Germany were higher than in the countries in which the creditors were domiciled, which made even short-term loans a lucrative business. The Bosch bond had a 20-year term, and viewed in that light it was a rock-solid deal. The only trouble was, it was not matched by a correspondingly high level of equity. In all likelihood, Robert Bosch would have done all he could to prevent an equity investment by a bank, a financially strong industrial group, or an international investor. Yet AEG, by then Bosch's neighbor in Feuerbach as a result of having acquired Mea, had already made tentative inquiries about his company, as we know from a later account: "When Bosch itself presented a most illiquid balance sheet in 1925, AEG had high hopes of possibly securing a major deal, i. e. merging with Bosch."[35] Merger plans enjoyed a boom in the "interim crisis" of 1925–26. That was when Daimler and Benz tied the knot. Robert Bosch, however, wished to remain independent. As the founder wrote to his daughter Margarete in the following year, he wanted his company "to stay on its own two feet while maintaining good relations with AEG and S&H [Siemens and Halske]."[36]

During the 1925–26 crisis, Robert Bosch also found himself in a difficult situation personally. His marriage had failed, his son had died only a few years previously, and now his life's work was threatening to come unraveled. Robert Bosch AG was unable to pay a dividend for the 1925 financial year, and in the years immediately thereafter, shareholders likewise received no dividend. As a result, the crisis affecting the company was also reflected in its founder's income. In a continuation of his memoirs composed several years later, he wrote: "Accordingly, having no further revenue from the company, I was obliged to live off the interest I earned."[37] Robert Bosch could undoubtedly live very well off this interest. He was a wealthy man. Still, no longer receiving income from the company that he had created must have been a humiliating experience for him.

It is in this context that a change in his behavior has to be seen. In the course of the year 1926, Robert Bosch began to behave in ways that were new to his associates. The crisis facing the company brought personal dramas at management level in its wake. Seeking scapegoats, Bosch accused three members of the Bosch board of management – Hugo Borst, Hermann Bosch, and Otto Heins – of having failed in their duty. All three were dismissed and forced to leave the company formally on October 25, 1926. For outsiders, the accusations that Robert Bosch leveled at the three men were puzzling. Paul Scheuing, Bosch's legal adviser, tried to temper his client's behavior, explaining that he was particularly wrong to point the finger at Hugo Borst, the company's commercial head. But all such efforts were in vain.[38]

In later years, too, Robert Bosch said bitter and insulting things about the members of the board of management he had dismissed. Hermann Bosch, he alleged, was "incapable of doing a proper day's work," while Otto Heins had "failed completely" in connection with the purchase of the Acro engine [editor's note: see the chapter "Trial and tribulation on the way to the diesel injection pump"]. Hermann Bosch was admittedly something of a problem. After working in Japan for 13 years, he had been forced to return to Germany because of the war and never really succeeded in re-settling there. Otto Heins, by contrast, as head of Bosch Magneto Company, had been part of Bosch's U.S. success story in the years before the First World War and had built up the U.S. business again after it. As for the Acro engine, Otto Heins had not been the only one to make a mistake. Robert Bosch himself had made an even bigger one.[39] Hugo Borst, however, was the subject of revilement. Robert Bosch saw him as the chief wrongdoer, yet there is not a shred of real evidence for this. In the contracts to acquire Acro licenses, Borst had clearly made concessions that went too far for the founder's liking, but it was Borst who had built up the commercial side of the company since 1900 and had headed it for years. Since Gustav Klein's death he had seen himself in the role of "heir apparent." Now he was in disgrace. Robert Bosch wrote in the continuation to his memoirs that Borst had become "extremely idle" and a "useless prattler." [40] When Theodor Bäuerle wrote his biography of Robert Bosch, the founder informed him that he wished to see no mention of Borst in it. Borst, he said, had been "nothing more to the company than an administrative assistant, a civil servant if you will, and a disloyal one at that."[41] After the founder's death, Theodor Heuss corresponded with Hugo Borst in connection with his own Bosch biography. He discovered that Borst, still searching for an explanation of the events of 1926, hoped that Heuss would manage to "solve the riddle that has been plaguing me for 18 years."[42] But not even Heuss could find a plausible explanation. The issue was clearly awkward and possibly even embarrassing for him. In any case his treatment of it in the book goes no further than vague hints.[43]

Apart from the difficult personal situation facing the founder and the crisis threatening his company, the key to the solution of the whole 1926 dispute undoubtedly lies in the relationship between Bosch and Borst. The son of an Esslingen businessman, the then 19-year-old Borst had joined the company founded by his "Uncle Robert" – his mother was one of Anna Bosch's sisters. In the early years a good, almost friendly relationship existed between the two. When the company was transformed into a stock corporation in 1917, Bosch gave Borst a seat on the board of management and a stake in the company. The breakdown of Robert Bosch's marriage must surely have had some effect on the relationship with his nephew. But this cannot have been the main reason for the clash.

When no dividend was paid for 1925 in view of the critical financial situation, Robert Bosch had no claim to revenue from his company. Hugo Borst, on the other hand, did. As a member of its board of management he drew a fixed salary. That the directors of a company he had set up should earn more from it

Hugo Borst (1917)

than he himself did was an idea Bosch found intolerable. That alone would have infuriated him. And he blamed Borst. In the continuation of his memoirs, begun in 1930, he wrote that Borst "tried to cheat me to benefit the stock corporation" and contrived that the chairman of the supervisory board – namely, Robert Bosch – should receive no fixed remuneration.[44] Paul Scheuing, who had been Bosch's legal adviser when the stock corporation was set up, told him he was mistaken, but Bosch clung to the idea.[45]

Neither had Hugo Borst, unlike other members of the board of management, ever made a secret of his wealth. His lifestyle was one that Bosch might have considered fit for the proprietor of a company but not for an employee. Borst accumulated a large art collection, and in the early 1920s he moved into a house occupying a fine situation on Gähkopf, a hill in the north part of Stuttgart.[46] Robert Bosch, no friend of the fine arts, will have had little sympathy with his head of sales spending so much time in the company of artists and tending to his collection. That could account for the finger-pointing, but there is no other evidence to suggest that Borst neglected his duties to the company. We are inclined to assume that it was not the art collecting per se that upset Robert Bosch so much as the fact that Borst had a life outside work and the company's sphere of influence, and one that suited him nicely. In a nutshell: in the years before his dismissal Borst had not behaved as Robert Bosch expected a senior executive to behave. Hugo Borst saw himself more as an associate than as a member of the founder's retinue – despite being the man's nephew.

This might have found expression in business matters as well. Robert Bosch claimed that Borst felt the U.S. rights belonged not to Robert Bosch personally, but to the company. It is only in such a light that the founder's protestations of disloyalty can possibly make any sense.[47]

Bosch might have been able to accept Borst's lifestyle had the man not been a close relative and a candidate for the corporate succession. Moreover, Borst, like Heins, owned part of the company's share capital. Other blocks of shares belonged to the heirs of Eugen Kayser – the family to which Anna Bosch and Hugo Borst's mother Emilie Borst both belonged. These links may have led Robert Bosch to fear that his life's work was slipping through his fingers. If we further take into account that Robert Bosch was in any case irritable by nature, that he was undergoing a personal upheaval at the time, and that his company faced the gravest crisis since its foundation, we may have found the answer to the riddle that for so long would give Borst no peace. Following his dismissal, Hugo Borst's art-buying activities intensified, and he also assembled a highly esteemed library. On his death in 1967 he handed down the largest private art collection in Stuttgart.[48]

The restructuring of 1926–27 and the resolution of the crisis

The dismissals of Hugo Borst, Otto Heins, and Hermann Bosch went hand in hand with an extensive restructuring of the board of management, which was drastically reduced from eleven members to six and given additional powers through the formation of an executive committee.[49] The number of full members went down from six to three, and it was those three – Hans Walz, Karl Martell Wild, and Hermann Fellmeth – who made up the executive committee, which was now the supreme managerial body of the company. The Walz-Wild-Fellmeth trio continued to head the organization until 1945, and among the deputy members there were only minor changes over the next 19 years.

Within the executive committee Hans Walz was deemed "primus inter pares," even though he did not formally chair the board of management. A qualified bank clerk, Walz had joined the company in 1912. He became head of Robert Bosch's private office, and in 1919 he was appointed to the supervisory board of Robert Bosch AG. Five years later, he switched to the board of management. No doubt the founder himself already had him in mind for the succession. Enjoying Robert Bosch's trust and equipped with his own business skills, Walz was a particularly suitable candidate. At the time when he joined the board of management, it was plain that Robert

Bosch would be retiring from day-to-day business sooner or later (to assume chairmanship of the supervisory board). Walz did not fall short of Bosch's expectations. Although he was not an engineer, was quite different in temperament from the founder, and, quite unlike Bosch, was a committed church member, the two men always saw eye to eye. Like Robert Bosch, Walz was a dyed-in-the-wool democrat. He belonged to the social-liberal German Democratic Party [*Deutsche Demokratische Partei* or DDP] founded by Friedrich Naumann – a party for which Bosch had a lot of sympathy. And like Robert Bosch, he saw his position as one of social responsibility. Finally, since he had headed up Bosch's private office for many years, he was familiar with all the founder's ideas.

Only months after this restructuring of the board of management, the company itself was reorganized. Previously, alongside the board of management, there had been a central administration encompassing two main groups: technical general management and commercial general management. The former covered matters to do with engineering on a company-wide basis – product design, research, materials inspection, but also occupational training. In addition, each plant had its own commercial administration, dealing with orders, accounts, wages, human resources, and so on.[50]

In January 1927, a new organizational structure was introduced – one based on functional criteria. At the top was the board of management. At the next level down, corporate departments for engineering, sales, and administration came into being, each responsible for that particular area on a company-wide basis and each headed by one of the three full members of the board of management. Manufacturing, as well as the development, testing, and incoming inspection departments, now reported to the corporate engineering department headed by Karl Martell Wild, which in turn oversaw two offices for factory issues, one commercial and one technical. The corporate administrative department under Hans Walz oversaw human resources management and tax matters, while the responsibilities of the corporate sales department under Hermann Fellmeth included advertising and the sales houses. Special status attached to purchasing, which also reported directly to the board of management but was not regarded as a corporate unit.[51] The restructuring of early 1927 also saw the introduction of abbreviations (so popular at Bosch even today) to denote individual departments and plants, which the in-house newspaper justified as "simplifying spoken and written communication."[52] The new structure involved above all a centralization of commercial and administrative spheres, now combined in the corporate administrative department. It gave commercial managers new powers that had previously lain with individual plants.

A distinguishing feature of this reform was that, within the board of management, the commercial sphere now gained in importance at the expense of engineering. This was also reflected in the make-up of the board of management.[53] Businessmen had already outnumbered engineers on the old board. The big difference now was that a businessman headed the company, in the shape of Hans Walz. At the lower levels, too, the balance between commercial and technical personnel now began to be redressed. In 1928, the occupational training department also started offering training for commercial positions.[54] Among senior management, there was a conviction that the new situation called for a strengthening of the company's business expertise. In a memorandum drawn up in November 1929 we read: "For success in today's global competition, outstanding engineering alone is not enough. Commercial and business competence are least as crucial."

This stronger emphasis on business management was a lesson Bosch drew from the crisis of 1926. Indeed, it was what chiefly enabled the company to survive that crisis. The diesel injection pump, on which the company pinned high hopes, could not be taken into production until the autumn of 1927, by which time a brief but powerful upswing had already set in. Bosch came through the crisis mainly because it changed gear cost-wise and because its new products, which it had included in its portfolio as a response to the pressure engendered by the crisis, sold well. Production statistics show that the years 1926–28 saw a sharp rise in the quantities of batteries, ignition coils, and distributors manufactured. And spark plugs also showed a more than twofold increase in quantity over the same period.[55] The magneto remained in great demand and continued to constitute the company's business foundation. It was nowhere near obsolescence. The trouble was, Bosch had been producing its core product too expensively for too long. Now Bosch battery ignition systems were cheaper. With simpler models being manufactured, production costs could be cut by rationalization. The fact was, it was not rationalization that made the 1926 crisis so severe and the ensuing mass lay-offs so damaging, as Stolle writes. These things sprang from its delayed implementation.[56]

Surprisingly, Bosch had been one of the pacemakers of industrial rationalization in Germany in the years preceding the First World War. And even in the mid-1920s, when the company built its first assembly lines, Bosch was perceived as being at the forefront of rationalization in Germany. In May 1925, Robert Bosch and Ernst Durst gave a talk on the new efficiency measures to the annual meeting of the Association of German Engineers [*Verband Deutscher Ingenieure*].[58] However, because of inflation, even at Bosch this drive for greater efficiency was late getting started and was launched on too narrow

Fig. 1 Management structure of Robert Bosch AG (January 1927)[57]

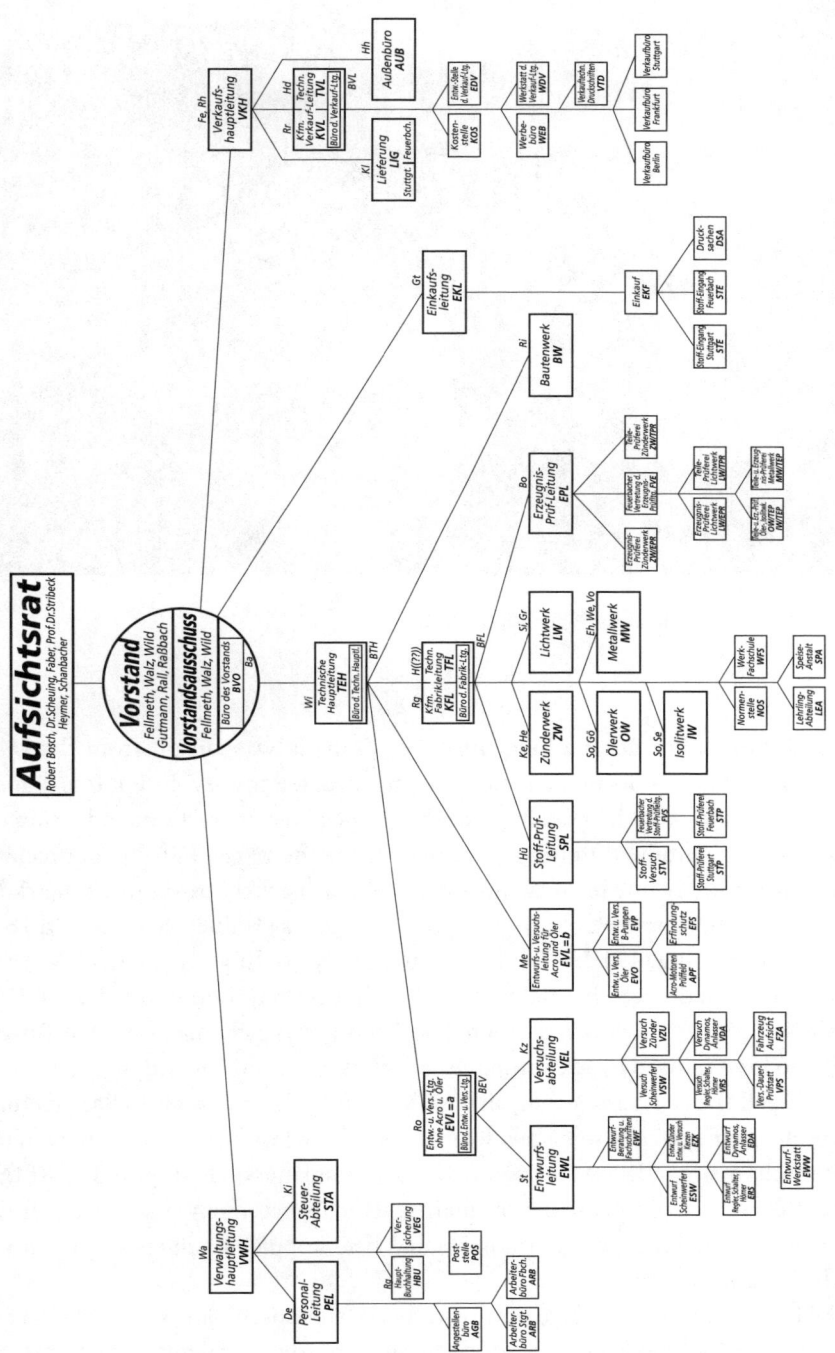

Assembly-line production of headlights (1926)

a capital base. For quite a long time the company was cut off from the U.S. market. As a result, its management underestimated the revolution in production technology that had taken place there since Henry Ford's introduction of assembly-line production in 1913. In much the same way, it failed to appreciate how the assembly line had transformed a sellers' market into a buyers' market. Before that, Bosch now noted, selling the company's products had been "no big deal" since, "shielded by a virtual monopoly, selling to a clientele that everywhere had eager hands outstretched hardly required enormous skill – really it didn't."[59] Meanwhile, there had been a game change, one that Bosch had too long refused to acknowledge. Why? Because the new rules of the game challenged the company's commitment to quality. The 1926 crisis changed that attitude. Management was now determined to take its cue from the new market mechanisms. "The American principle of business has imposed itself the world over. The old principle of quality, which once reigned so successfully because it suited the old requirements, has been toppled by the laws governing today's business world."[60]

New assembly lines were now installed in the Bosch plants. Assembly-line production had been brought into the ignition-device plant as early as the spring of 1926 and soon afterwards into the light works as well. Coordinated by a rationalization team under Ernst Durst, the number of types manufactured was cut, and standardization was introduced for more and more components. Additional cost reductions were successfully achieved by using cheaper raw materials and semi-finished goods.[61] Stolle calculates that the wage bill for ignition was cut by between 17 percent and 21 percent, while the saving in spark-plug production reached as much as 28 percent.[62] Even so, Bosch still did not have U.S.-style assembly-line production. Production quantities were still too low for that.[63]

Table 7 Composition of Bosch workforce in percentages (1926–29)[64]

	skilled associates	semi-skilled associates	unskilled associates	women associates
June 1926	28.3	18.5	17.1	36.1
December 1926	28.9	20.1	14.5	36.5
June 1927	24.3	18.9	13.3	43.4
December 1927	25.3	20.8	11.8	42.0
June 1929	24.5	19.9	10.3	45.3

As the factory office's monthly employment statistics show, the more widespread assembly-line working became, the more substantially did it alter the composition of the workforce. Relative numbers of skilled associates remained fairly constant at some 25 percent (having risen sharply during the 1926 crisis). However, the share of unskilled workers declined steeply in the 1926–29 period, while the share of women workers showed a steady increase, reaching 45 percent by mid-1929. Clearly, rationalization eliminated many jobs previously performed by unskilled workers, whereas for the new assembly-line work it was primarily women who were taken on. The relative number of women workers at Bosch had briefly peaked at 43.7 percent in July 1923, although that was in the extreme situation of the hyperinflation then prevailing. This figure is therefore of little use as a benchmark. Instead, it can be assumed that the upward trend in the number of women workers at Bosch was a result of rationalization.[65]

Trial and tribulation on the way to the diesel injection pump

Although rationalization had proved successful and the company had adopted "American" commercial principles, Robert Bosch was in no doubt that more would be needed if the company was to reassert its former position in the world market. Recognizing that good engineering was no longer a sure-fire recipe for success in the marketplace, he had come to terms with manufacturing goods under license. But he remained firmly convinced that only another innovation of the order of the high-voltage magneto ignition system could give his company the same sort of unassailable market position that the magneto had delivered for many years.

In their search for a promising technology, researchers had focused on diesel injection systems as early as 1922.[66] The assumption was that diesel engines, which consumed less fuel than gasoline engines, would play a major role in the automobility of the future. It was felt that the diesel engine would be especially suitable for trucks, which were being built in ever-increasing numbers in the 1920s. Indeed, production of trucks had risen sharply during the First World War, achieving practically a breakthrough. But while diesel engines had existed for some time, no one had yet managed to develop a diesel engine for road vehicles. For these, an entirely different design was required. To power any kind of road vehicle, a diesel engine had to run at higher speeds. It also needed to be much lighter and much more compact than conventional diesels, which were so weighty and cumbersome as to be practical only as stationary engines (mostly in factories) or to power ships. Daimler, Benz, and MAN (Maschinenfabrik Augsburg-Nürnberg) were already engaged in intensive development work aimed at producing a diesel engine for road vehicles.[67] The first models were expected to come onto the market in only a few years' time. Robert Bosch reckoned that if his company could produce the first properly developed diesel injection system, the automotive industry would turn to the Bosch product en masse, just as it had with the magneto ignition system. The diesel engine needed no ignition system. Injected at high pressures, diesel fuel ignited spontaneously because of the very high compression in the combustion chamber and the resultant high temperatures there. For such a technology, the expertise already available in a company that produced high-pressure lubrication pumps could be harnessed without difficulty.[68]

This time, in contrast to the way Bosch engineers had devised the high-voltage magneto, the innovation process was approached with careful planning and with the benefit of scientific advancements. The company now had its own physics laboratory, which was given the knotty task of working out a recommendation as to how the research should proceed. When work was being done to develop the Bosch magneto, an engine had been available for test purposes. In this case there was none. So the laboratory began by addressing two questions: what parts would an injection system for an automotive diesel engine comprise, and what designs should the developers focus on? In other words, the correct course had to be set from the beginning, yet there could be no ultimate certainty about the design of an engine that did not yet exist. There was a constant risk that the work on an automotive diesel engine being done at Daimler, Benz, and MAN might take a direction that called for a completely different injection-system design. If that happened, Bosch would have bet on the wrong horse. However, if the company wished to become the market leader in diesel injection technology it had to launch its product as soon as possible. There was no time to be lost. On February 20, 1923, the physics laboratory recommended development of a "diesel injection system using a sleeve-valve pump and a liquid-controlled, enclosed nozzle."[69]

The testing department now began trying out pumps. A wide variety of types were tested, but again there was the problem that no automotive diesel engine yet existed. The Bosch engineers tried converting engines to run on diesel. They even designed their own experimental engine, but they made little progress.[70] Meanwhile, the chief designer at Benz & Cie., Prosper L'Orange, had succeeded in actually building the first automotive diesel engine. And Daimler-Motoren-Gesellschaft soon followed suit. Both companies had fitted their engines with their own injection systems, and in October 1923 Benz and Daimler presented their new diesel-powered trucks at the Berlin Motor Show.[71]

Only in the early autumn of 1924 was Bosch able to buy a truck with a prechamber diesel engine from Benz & Cie.[72] And now that engineers and mechanics at Bosch no longer needed to work in the dark but had a real engine available on which whole series of tests could be run, development of the injection pump proceeded apace. In a matter of months a pump had been designed that met the requirements of the earliest automotive diesel engines. It is referred to expressly in the publication accompanying Bosch's 50th corporate anniversary: "So by early 1925 we had a pump design that, in terms of its performance, its durability, and its surprisingly small size, was fully equal to the demands of the only two truck diesel engines in existence at the time (both of which could be seen at the Berlin Motor Show of December 1924) – namely, the prechamber engine from the Benz plant at Gaggenau and the jet-injection engine from the Nuremberg plant of Maschinenfabrik Augsburg-Nürnberg."[73] The quote is reproduced here in full because it was tantamount to an admission. Only after a suitable lapse of time, here on the occasion of the company's

1936 anniversary, was this made with such clarity. The fact was, Bosch had never exploited the pump that had been available in the winter of 1924–25. Instead, it had made a costly detour.

Over the course of 1924, Robert Bosch had become restless over the diesel injection pump. His company's flagship project had yet to yield tangible results. He was beginning to feel that "my own people's efforts were leading nowhere," and he took matters in hand personally.[74] He spoke to various experts in the engine-building industry and learned that the Munich engineer Franz Lang had successfully designed a diesel engine that used a new kind of injection technology, known as the "air-chamber method."[75] Lang had made a cavity in the diesel engine's cylinder head, into which thin jets of fuel known as "horsehair fuel streams" were injected through a nozzle. The fuel ignited spontaneously inside this cavity, while any leftover fuel vaporized.[76] For this design Lang had developed an injection pump and an injection nozzle. He had sold the design rights to Süddeutsche Motorengesellschaft, who then hired him to work for them. The company belonged to three brothers and had a subsidiary in the U.S., American Crude Oil Corporation (Acro) by name, which is why Lang's invention became known generally as the "Acro engine."

Bosch now turned to the head of Acro, the German-American Albert Wielich, who was also one of the proprietors of Süddeutsche Motorengesellschaft. Wielich was not particularly cooperative at first. He was prepared only to grant Bosch supply contracts. But then he invited Bosch to the United States, and the two men got on better when in August 1924 they went hunting together in Canada for bear and elk. Wielich offered Bosch a share in all Acro's patents.[77] That was not quite what Bosch had in mind. He was interested only in injection technology, not the engine itself. Still, here was a chance of obtaining Lang's patents, and after all, so far as the engine was concerned, licenses could be granted to third parties. Bosch saw Wielich's offer as a major opportunity, although his fellow senior executives – the experienced engineer Karl Martell Wild in particular – strongly advised against acceptance. Yet Süddeutsche Motorengesellschaft could present positive testimonials from some noted experts.[78] Robert Bosch made another trip to the U.S. to inspect the only Acro engine already in operation. The matter was of huge importance, so he took several members of the board of management with him – Hugo Borst, Otto Heins, and the very man who had expressed grave doubts, Karl Martell Wild. Together they visited Sterling Engine Corporation in Buffalo, New York, where they had the Acro engine presented to them several times. Lang had altered his design in the meantime, incorporating a diffusor in the pistons. The trials proved thoroughly "satisfactory," as Wild had to admit in a confidential letter to Max Rall.[79] With Wild now persuaded, Robert Bosch left further negotiations to him and Hugo Borst. Both reached agreement with Wielich, although the price was high. Through a 15 percent commission, Wielich contrived to obtain a share of profits. Süddeutsche Motorengesellschaft now passed into the ownership of a holding company, Acro AG, founded in Küssnacht (Switzerland) by Bosch and Wielich. The inventor, Franz Lang, switched to Robert Bosch AG, together with several colleagues, to head a test shop there for the Acro engine.[80]

At Robert Bosch AG, there had been much skepticism concerning the Acro engine from the outset. When it came to Wielich and Lang, both of whom constantly shrouded themselves in mystery, this skepticism was even more pronounced. The patent engineer Alfred Meyer vehemently opposed signing the Acro contracts. Lang's inventions, he said, were worth only a fraction of the price.[81] By February 1925, experts at Bosch had established that the Acro engine functioned differently than had first been assumed. A note dated February 4, 1925, reads: "No one talks any more about the pump and nozzle being the secret of the success of Acro engines. What accounts for their success is the special design of the piston – in other words, a product that has not been part of our portfolio up to now."[82] Yet it was precisely because of the pump and nozzle that Bosch had acquired the license for the Acro engine. Nonetheless, the work being done under Lang went on unabated. Unwilling simply to write off the hefty price paid for the licenses, those responsible at Bosch remained convinced that studying this injection technology would help them to build a fully engineered diesel injection pump. The fact that Bosch engineers had meanwhile developed a pump of their own – albeit by no means a high-performance one – seems to have made no difference.

It was in the autumn of 1926 that Bosch began making Acro pumps. However, the emphasis now shifted to a preoccupation with the Acro engine itself. Samples were urgently needed if licenses were to be issued and some of the steep purchase price recouped. Numerous test drives were undertaken with diesel trucks converted to the Acro system. Bosch engineers even fitted an automobile with an Acro engine that covered more than 36,000 kilometers and proved its worth in test drives that took it to Berlin and Paris.[83] Franz Lang had meanwhile fallen out with the Bosch engineers, resigning from the company in October 1926. As we know from the anniversary publication that appeared ten years later, the Bosch engineers made better progress without the inventor. They went back to concentrating on pump development, with the result that "there now emerged in a relatively short time today's renowned Bosch diesel injection pump."[84]

How much the Acro patents contributed to the development of this diesel injection pump was disputed among experts at the time. In fact, it may never be explained in full. The anniversary publication quoted above tells us that Bosch's preoccupation with the Acro engine had "enabled [it] to supply some useful diesel engine equipment."[85] The patent engineer Alfred Meyer wrote later that "the Acro engine helped us to develop Bosch injection equipment. The question is, couldn't we have gained this knowledge much more cheaply?"[86] There was something of an epilogue in the courts. Robert Bosch challenged the Acro contracts, maintaining that Wielich had cheated him. When the engine was demonstrated in Buffalo it had (he alleged) been tampered with.[87] Eventually an agreement – the "Lanova Treaty," it was called – finally released Robert Bosch AG from its Acro commitments in 1931. Robert Bosch himself blamed the fiasco on two members of the board of management, Hugo Borst and Otto Heins. As mentioned above, they were both dismissed in October 1926.[88] Yet he himself had insisted on buying the Acro patents in the face of misgivings voiced by associates. As a matter of fact, Franz Lang's design subsequently came into its own in connection with a new development – that of the Lanova engine. From 1932, the German producer Henschel fitted heavy trucks and locomotives with the Henschel-Lanova engine designed by Lang.[89]

As early as April 1927 Bosch manufactured an initial sample of the diesel injection pump, and in late November this was ready to go into series production. The invention enabled automotive diesel engines to run with a constant fuel flow over the entire engine speed range. The injection nozzle, which was now also made by Bosch, was still based on Lang's design. It was incorporated into the engine as an enclosed nozzle. A needle with a pintle attached made it possible to keep the nozzle-hole clean. Apart from Bosch, only the Munich-based Deckel GmbH offered diesel-injection technology of this kind. Truck manufacturers now opted for these new products from the equipment suppliers and decided to stop producing their own injection pumps.[90] This also charted the way ahead for the subsequent development of diesel-powered passenger cars. Hans Walz was able to tell the supervisory board in September 1932 that Bosch now enjoyed "the same status [in the field of diesel injection pumps] as it had in the field of magnetos before the war."[91] Following the launch of the diesel injection pump, Robert Bosch was told by his older daughter from his first marriage Margarete: "Going into diesel pump production is as though you were setting up your company for a second time."[92] This would seem to explain why the years 1924–28 came to be described as the "second creative period" in the history of the company.[93] Even though diesel vehicles only gradually gained acceptance, Bosch was once again at the cutting edge in a segment with great promise. This was not like the magneto. This was a business field that was in no danger of becoming obsolete in a few decades' time. Bosch still leads the world market in diesel-injection technology – 85 years after introducing its first diesel injection pump.

Building up a presence outside Germany and battling for the U.S. market

Ten years after the First World War had ended, Bosch management decided to go on the offensive internationally. Their aim was to sweep aside all adverse consequences of the war, including the auction of the U.S. regional subsidiary. The 1926 crisis had been overcome, and introducing the diesel injection pump looked as if it had secured the company's future. Now international expansion was the chief objective. Bosch was determined not to let its U.S. rivals force it onto the defensive any longer. As a memorandum of November 1929 warned, Bosch feared that continued inferiority to U.S. companies might easily lead to a loss of independence.[94] Considerations like these are understandable, given that only a few months earlier, Germany's largest automaker, Adam Opel AG, had passed into the ownership of General Motors (GM). The sale of Opel can hardly have aroused enthusiasm at Bosch, which had a sole-supply agreement with the Rüsselsheim-based company.[95] As a result of this agreement, Opel may well have been Bosch's largest customer at the time. Now there was a danger of Opel giving preferred-supplier status to the GM-controlled Bendix – under license from which Bosch, too, produced starters. Connections such as those between GM and Bendix or Delco were viewed with growing concern from the Bosch boardroom on Militärstraße. Bosch, which valued its independence highly, now had to compete with conglomerates of automakers and automotive suppliers that were worryingly large and had considerable financial clout.

In the face of such rivals, winning through in international markets meant above all being able to produce in far larger volumes than before. This was the only way Bosch could achieve the low prices that U.S. competitors were offering. Sales inside Germany were never going to be enough. The German market was just too small. So Bosch adopted the strategy of boosting its market share in the U.K. and France and producing series of a size that would in turn enable it to challenge its rivals in the United States. "Our task is clearly mapped out before us," says the above-mentioned memorandum of November 28, 1929: "It is imperative that as soon as possible we should lower our prices to the point where the Americans cease to be cheaper than us in Europe and instead become more expensive. To succeed in this we must put ourselves in a position to satisfy most of the non-American – notably the European – demand for our goods."[96]

In the markets of the smaller European countries, Bosch had already regained a respectable position. Here, there was little or no competition in the ignition business. Bosch also enjoyed a large share of the market in Spain, where it had set up a subsidiary by the name of Equipo Bosch S. A. in 1926.[97] This was not the case in France, and certainly not in Britain. Here, numerous companies had begun producing magnetos during the First World War, since Bosch, the previous market leader, could no longer supply customers. In England, a new automotive equipment company, Joseph Lucas Ltd. of Birmingham, was by now almost as large as Bosch. In Stuttgart, Lucas was viewed as "a particularly dangerous rival, very strong in terms of both engineering and finance."[98] Bosch was also keeping a very close eye on the Swiss company Scintilla AG, which had been producing magneto ignition systems since 1917. Granted, Scintilla was only a small operation, but in Stuttgart they were afraid it could easily fall into American hands and be used by U.S. companies as a bridgehead from which to enter the German and French markets.[99]

Clearly, the Bosch board of management realized full well that they would not be able to deprive the competition of any substantial market share very soon. So they sought to form a "European community of interest" in the hope this would allow them to mount a challenge to the companies in the United States. Bosch had already made substantial progress in France, where it had successfully embarked on a joint-venture project – one that was also to serve as a model for later projects. Since the First World War, the French magneto market had been protected by a 45 percent tariff barrier. This was primarily aimed at warding off the former market leader from Stuttgart. Bosch had in fact been represented again in France since 1920, but the protective duty proved a near-insurmountable barrier. The company's French business also suffered from Franco-German disputes over reparation payments, which brought further instances of reciprocal trade discrimination in their wake.

In 1928, a prominent French industrialist, Count Henri de la Valette, contacted Robert Bosch. The two had been acquainted for some time. The count was, so to speak, the founder of the French magneto industry. He had formerly produced under license from Eisemann-Werke AG, which now belonged to Bosch. He suggested to Bosch that they set up a plant together. This was an offer the Bosch board of management could hardly refuse: having a manufacturing facility of its own in France would allow Bosch to sidestep the tariff-barrier problem. Meanwhile, Franco-German relations in general had also improved under the policy of rapprochement advocated and practiced by Stresemann and Briand, so the timing couldn't have been better. Moreover, Count de la

Valette was a renowned and well-connected businessman. Together with André Michelin, Jules Verne, and others, he had founded the famous Aéro-Club de France. Bosch lost no time in reaching agreement with him, handing over the company's French agency rights, and taking a 50 percent holding in his Société des Ateliers de Construction Lavalette. In 1929, work began on a new plant in the Paris suburb of St. Ouen, which then manufactured and traded under the name Lavalette-Bosch.[100] It was only a joint venture, but even so, Lavalette-Bosch was the first manufacturing facility outside Germany that Bosch had had since the war.

In the U.K., the company had more difficulty in finding joint-venture partners. Bosch supplied only 4 percent of the U.K. market in 1928, compared to the 90 percent market share it had possessed in 1913.[101] But by the spring of 1929, talks were under way simultaneously with three potential alliance partners: Joseph Lucas Ltd. (the market leader), a Scottish finance group, and a consortium headed by a banker called Myers. Lucas was prepared to cede a 49 percent holding in its heavy-trucks business, the Scots offered parity, and Myers even offered a 51 percent share. So far as Bosch was concerned, Lucas was its first choice, but the Stuttgart company was unwilling to accept the proposed limitation to the truck business, which accounted for only one-fifth of the automotive market. Negotiations dragged on for some time, even though at Bosch the executive committee of the board of management pressed for a quick decision as early as June 1929. They took the view that "the British problem is extremely urgent and needs to be solved as soon as possible."[102] The main reason the talks with Lucas were prolonged was likely the onset of the Great Depression. Not until the spring of 1931 did the two sides reach agreement – after Bosch had launched preparations to build its own plant in England. The Lucas subsidiary C.A.V. in Acton, a western suburb of London, was converted into a joint venture under the name of C.A.V. Bosch. Lucas retained 51 percent of the capital of C.A.V. Bosch, while Bosch acquired the remaining 49 percent.[103]

In the meantime it had become apparent that Bosch's idea of a "European community of interest" was not working out. Despite successes in France, volumes were still inadequate. The Great Depression had thwarted the company plans. In the supervisory board meeting of June 6, 1930, Karl Martell Wild pointed out that "the prices of our competitor products are still so low that we shall need to concern ourselves intensively with rationalization for several years yet."[104]

However, by this time Bosch had scored a success in the U.S. that would have been unimaginable even as recently as 1928. Ever since Otto Heins had set up Robert Bosch Magneto Company (RBMC) in New York in 1921, this com-

pany had been in fierce competition with American Bosch Magneto Corporation (ABMC), which had emerged from the Bosch Magneto Company that had
been expropriated and auctioned off after the war. RBMC advertised Bosch
ignition systems as "original Bosch" while ABMC countered with its "Buy
American" slogan. The American clientele followed this Bosch v. Bosch contest with a certain sporting interest, while benefiting from its downward effect
on prices. The Bosch subsidiary RBMC offered products of substantially
higher quality. However, it had had to start out business from an unfavorable
position, and held a smaller share of the market. Furthermore, it was only a
distribution company, having no manufacturing facility of its own in the
United States. ABMC, by contrast, owned the huge Springfield plant, received
orders from Ford, and was also looking to position itself in the European market. In 1926, it generated sales of 12.5 million U.S. dollars, as compared to a
figure of 1.7 million U.S. dollars for RBMC.[105] However, RBMC held its own
against a superior competitor very well. In 1927, it moved into larger premises
on Queens Boulevard in Long Island City, and with the diesel injection pump
it was able to offer a widely acclaimed innovation. By 1929, RBMC sales were
up to 3.6 million U.S. dollars, while at 11.7 million U.S. dollars those of ABMC
were slightly down.[106]

The U.S. public was even treated to the Bosch v. Bosch match in the court-
room. One Harvey T. Andrews, RBMC's tireless attorney, discovered that
Martin E. Kern had, in December 1918, come into possession of Bosch Magneto Company, ABMC's predecessor, by fraudulent means. Andrews exposed
the scandal and filed legal proceedings. A. J. M. Palmer, Kern's accomplice,
was arraigned in Massachusetts by the U.S. government.[107] At the same time,
however, ABMC's complaint against RBMC for infringement of trademark
rights got as far as the New York Supreme Court. Its argument was that a
regional subsidiary of a non-American company – namely, Robert Bosch AG –
ought not to be allowed to use the Robert Bosch name or the Bosch trademark.
The Bosch legal team in New York soon gained the impression that their opponent was going to win its case in the appeal stage. They urgently advised the
founder to settle out of court.[108] In June 1929, the chief judge in New York ruled
in favor of ABMC. It was a disastrous judgment, not only for RBMC but for
the Bosch Group as a whole. Bosch's legal advisers were afraid that the legal
principle of Anglo-Saxon "case law" would mean that Robert Bosch AG now
faced lengthy legal proceedings throughout the English-speaking world regarding use of its name. Bosch was therefore prepared to settle with ABMC,
which ABMC agreed to do against payment of 400,000 U.S. dollars.[109] ABMC
too was under pressure, since the Kern and Palmer case was becoming the
subject of more and more U.S. media attention. Other cases of fraud in what

was known as the "Office of Alien Property Custodian" (the department for administering confiscated foreign assets) had come to light in the meantime, and Congress was now looking into these in Washington.[110]

On October 26, 1929, ABMC and Robert Bosch AG signed what both sides termed a "peace treaty" in Paris. Robert Bosch AG paid 400,000 U.S. dollars (the profits of RBMC for the period 1926–29) and gave a further 200,000 U.S. dollars in escrow. In return, Robert Bosch AG and its subsidiary companies in the rest of the world (including RBMC) could continue using the name Bosch internationally – though not in conjunction with the word "American." ABMC for its part could use the term "American Bosch" world-wide but not in conjunction with the name "Robert." In addition, Robert Bosch AG ceded its rights to the "red devil" advertising motif – which it was in any case no longer using.[111]

Two days before the signing of the "peace treaty" between the two Bosch companies, Wall Street experienced a stock-market crash that went down in history as "Black Friday." In the space of only a few hours, a record number of shares – nearly 13 million – were dumped in panic. Share prices continued to fall over the ensuing weeks. The Dow Jones index plummeted to something like half its September 1 level.[112] In contrast to Robert Bosch AG, ABMC was a publicly traded company, and the stock-market crash led to the collapse of its own share price. Robert Bosch quickly saw the opportunity offered by these developments and gave his New York bank (Kuhn, Loeb & Co.) instructions to buy. What had eluded the lawyers in court, the investment bankers were now able to achieve in the marketplace. Apart from Kuhn, Loeb & Co., the Amsterdam branch of the Mendelssohn & Co. Bank and Jakob Goldschmidt's Danatbank were also involved in the buying that went on during the course of 1930. The fear in Stuttgart was that ABMC would take refuge under the umbrella of General Motors, but once Bosch had quickly acquired a 25 percent blocking minority, it was clearly too late for that.[113] Kuhn, Loeb & Co. purchased ABMC shares for a total of 3.4 million U.S. dollars – chiefly with the help of a 2.5-million-dollar loan that the bank, acting jointly with Danatbank, granted Bosch for the purpose. Other ABMC shares were amassed by Mendelssohn Bank in Amsterdam for 1.28 million U.S. dollars. The total was further boosted by the large blocks of shares that Industria Kontor AG, a Swiss asset management company belonging to the Bosch Group, purchased from two private individuals for around 1.3 million U.S. dollars. The buying was halted in the autumn of 1930, since Bosch by then owned 77.2 percent of the share capital of ABMC.[114]

On November 3, 1930, just over a year after the stock-market crash, the two companies, enemies for so long, merged. In what was termed a "reorganization agreement" it was decided that RBMC should be consolidated with ABMC. The resultant company was called United American Bosch Corporation (UABC). It was headed by the former president of ABMC, A. T. Murray.[115] In 1938, UABC changed its name to American Bosch Corporation (ABC). As a result of the merger, Bosch recovered its dominant position in the U.S. market for magnetos and, despite the setbacks of the Great Depression, was able to grow successfully there. The merger agreement of 1930 meant that, 12 years after the end of the First World War, Robert Bosch AG was able to draw a line under the immediate repercussions of the war so far as its U.S. business was concerned, notably the trauma of the auction proceedings of December 7, 1918.

Between sackings and shorter working weeks: Bosch in the Great Depression

The stock-exchange crash on Wall Street in the autumn of 1929 ushered in the Great Depression, an economic crisis such as the world had never seen before. The German economy was particularly badly affected. Together with the U.S., Germany experienced the sharpest drop in production and the highest unemployment. Its automotive industry was once again among the sectors that saw an exceptionally steep decline in manufacturing. In 1930, passenger-car production stood at only 71 percent of its 1928 level. Two years later, at the peak of the crisis, it was down to 40 percent. Even so, in 1932 (with the crisis still raging), more passenger cars were produced in Germany than during the "interim crisis" of 1926. The degree of motorization had risen in the meantime, and more automakers had rationalized their production to enable them to offer lower-cost vehicles.[116]

From mid-1930 onward Bosch felt the full force of the Great Depression. Sales within Germany dropped by 25 percent, export sales by 15 percent.[117] But the company now stood on a much broader footing, and the board of management reacted with a different strategy from the one it had adopted in 1926. Bosch now sought to avoid mass lay-offs, relying on shorter working weeks and further price reductions instead. In the annual report for 1930 we read: "Considering our [difficult] business situation and the [unsatisfactory] capacity utilization in our manufacturing facilities, more people ought to have been laid off [than actually were]. We avoided this by reducing our associates' working hours as far as possible, despite the substantial problems and extra cost this involved."[118]

Bosch appears not to have been alone in adopting such a strategy at this time. A study carried out by Württemberg's Ministry of Economic Affairs in 1927 established that companies in the state placed greater reliance on shorter working weeks and were less inclined to shut down manufacturing facilities than in other parts of the country. This was attributed to the manpower shortages which were quick to appear when business was good. "When business turns bad," the study went on, these companies sought to "keep their workers on board as long as possible, since they cannot count on being able to re-recruit them when the economic climate improves once again."[119] This reasoning, together with other factors (notably, the particular structure of Württemberg's industry and the prevalence of part-time farming in rural areas), contributed to Württemberg's having by far the lowest unemployment in Germany during the Great Depression.[120] "The figures are better in Württemberg," the *Bosch-Zünder* wrote at the time.[121]

In June 1930, shorter working hours accounted for 16.2 percent of all hours worked at Bosch, as compared to the previous month's figure of 7.2 percent. In September, it peaked at 31.2 percent. Even so, headcount declined over the course of 1930 by some 15 percent, from around 9,500 to around 8,100. In June 1930 alone, the workforce was reduced by some 9 percent. At the same time, the number of associates calling in sick fell sharply – a clear indication that more and more people were afraid of losing their jobs.[122] However, a year later these reductions in headcount came to a halt. In stark contrast to the trend, headcount at Bosch started to rise again. From July 1931 (the month of the severe banking crisis in Germany), the figure was up year on year, and by the end of 1931 Bosch was employing 389 more associates than at the end of 1930 – an increase of some 6 percent.[123] Over the same period, the total of registered unemployed in Germany went up by around 3.7 million to nearly 5.1 million.[124] During the first few months of 1932, too, headcount at Bosch remained surprisingly stable. But from May onward it fell below the previous year's level. Nor did the situation change until the end of 1932, although from October of that year the number of workers bucked the seasonal trend by increasing again.

Table 8 Number of workers (both men and women) and share of shorter working hours at Robert Bosch AG (1931–32)[125]

	Jan	Feb	Mar	Apr	May	Jun	Jul	Aug	Sep	Oct	Nov	Dec
1931	6,077	6,195	6,237	6,225	6,260	6,425	6,514	6,501	6,470	6,450	6,428	6,404
	11.3%	7.1%	5.7%	7.4%	5.1%	4.0%	2.8%	4.7%	10.7%	21.3%	31.3%	31.7%
1932	6,389	6,366	6,340	6,348	6,242	6,208	6,179	6,159	6,195	6,254	6,259	6,372
	35.6%	30.6%	17.9%	19.2%	19.5%	22.7%	22.3%	21.0%	20.9%	19.1%	14.6%	9.6%

To put it another way, the employment statistics show that Bosch experienced a temporary respite between the summer of 1931 and the spring of 1932, when the Great Depression was becoming more severe in Germany. For a company to have more employees at the end of 1931 than at the end of 1930 was a rare occurrence, and one that Bosch duly highlighted in its annual report.[126] The business result for 1931 tells a different story. Sales for the year were down 16 percent year on year, and the income statement disclosed a loss of more than 1.6 million reichsmarks.[127]

Over the course of 1932, the situation worsened, also for Bosch. Even over the summer, the only way of avoiding further lay-offs was by increasing the percentage of people working shorter hours. Like many German companies, Bosch fell back on exports. For the first time since the years of inflation, sales outside the country accounted for more than 50 percent of sales revenue. However, this was more a sign of a decline in domestic sales. Exports themselves were stagnating.[128] It was Bosch's magneto production that was particularly hard hit by the Great Depression. Between 1929 and 1931, production of magnetos declined by 37 percent. On the other hand, volumes of some of the products introduced since the mid-1920s showed a marked increase. Production of ignition coils rose by 33 percent between 1929 and 1931, and in the case of injection pumps the figure even exceeded 40 percent.[129]

Table 9 Headcount at Bosch, Daimler-Benz, BMW, MAN, and Siemens (1928–32)[130]

year	Bosch (ave)*	%	Daimler-Benz (Dec. 31)	%	BMW (N/A)	%	MAN (Jul.1)	%	Siemens (ave)**	%
1928	10,925	*100.0*	16,733	*100.0*	4,676	*100.0*	15,300	*100.0*	88,327	*100.0*
1929	10,566	*96.7*	14,870	*88.9*	3,309	*70.8*	15,030	*98.2*	106,713	*120.8*
1930	8,635	*79.0*	10,142	*62.2*	3,150	*67.4*	14,050	*91.8*	86,135	*97.5*
1931	8,052	*73.7*	9,686	*57.9*	2,370	*50.7*	11,400	*74.5*	73,385	*83.1*
1932	7,961	*72.9*	9,148	*54.7*	3,148	*67.3*	7,400	*48.4*	57,529	*65.1*

ave = average for the year   N/A = basis of calculation unknown
* = excluding sales houses   ** = Siemens & Halske, Siemens-Schuckert plants, and Siemens-Reiniger

Comparison with other major companies shows how untypical headcount fluctuation was at Bosch during these years. The Bosch workforce declined in number by around 27 percent between 1928 and 1932, while at Daimler-Benz the figure was 45 percent, in the key Siemens companies 35 percent, and at MAN as high as 52 percent.[131] So while lay-offs at Bosch during the Great Depression were substantial, they were not as extreme as at other large companies. This is due to a combination of three factors:

- At Bosch, sales did not collapse to the same extent, no doubt partly because of the new products the company had introduced in the preceding years. Between 1929 and 1932, sales fell by 42 percent at Bosch, by 56 percent at Siemens, by almost 62 percent at MAN, by 50 percent at Daimler-Benz, and by 49 percent at BMW.[132]
- The share of people working shorter hours increased massively at Bosch. In the winter of 1931–32, shorter working hours made up a constant 30–35 percent of all hours worked, but even in the summer of 1932 the figure was still more than 20 percent. In 1932, the average Bosch worker was down to just over a 38-hour working week.[133] This was less than at Daimler-Benz.[134]
- At Bosch, headcount had fallen particularly sharply as early as 1926, and rationalization measures in the ensuing years meant it did not return to its 1925 peak. To put it another way, as a result of the company having undergone a serious crisis only three years earlier, Bosch started out from a lower level when the Great Depression hit.

It was likely a result of lessons learned from the 1926 crisis that the Bosch board of management placed so much importance on extending schemes for shorter working hours as a way of avoiding more extensive lay-offs. The policy of mass dismissals adopted during that crisis had meant that the company had lost many key associates for good – men and women whom it was unable to re-employ in the ensuing upturn, and who were sorely missed. As the above-mentioned 1927 report by the Württemberg Ministry of Economic Affairs pointed out, the state of the labor market in Stuttgart meant that other employers had already mopped them up. An important role was also played by Bosch's launch, in the autumn of 1927, of an innovation on which it pinned high hopes. The board of management was convinced that the Bosch injection pump would support the rapid spread of diesel-powered automobiles, which would then form the basis of its future business. So it was important to retain as many associates as possible. Once the crisis had passed, Bosch would be able to swiftly ramp up production, and would not be left behind in the anticipated diesel boom. The associates who kept their jobs in these years of mass unemployment and dire poverty were no doubt grateful to the company. Bosch was able to regain its reputation as a caring employer, so badly damaged in the 1926 crisis. Granted, collectively bargained wage scales had been lowered several times by emergency presidential decree. However, directors' salaries, being linked at Bosch to sales, had also dropped – by 40 percent between 1929 and 1931.[135]

Male white-collar and semiskilled blue-collar workers were least affected by dismissals at Bosch during the Great Depression. Women blue-collar workers bore the brunt of these measures. The fact that numbers of women workers declined to a disproportionate extent does not primarily reflect a squeezing out of less qualified employees. Actually, the number of unskilled women workers increased – albeit from a very low starting point. Most likely, it was due to a cutback in female employment generally. The total number of semiskilled women workers shrank by 1,574 over this period, while that of their male equivalents shrank by only 196.[136] The dismissals are likely to have included a particularly large number of the women taken on at the time of the rationalization measures of 1927–28. On the other hand, the number of apprentices rose during the Great Depression. Where this kind of investment in the future was concerned, Bosch was not prepared to make cuts.

Table 10 Headcount at Bosch, grouped by wage/salary levels and by gender (1929–32)[137]

Year	White-collar workers		Blue-collar workers (men)			Blue-collar workers (women)	Appren-tices	Total headcount
	male	female	skilled	semi-skilled	un-skilled	semi-skilled		
1930	97.8	89.7	85.5	87.7	71.9	71.0	110.0	81.7
1931	90.5	81.6	80.3	87.2	54.1	63.2	116.7	76.2
1932	89.3	79.6	80.8	88.7	52.0	59.2	118.6	75.3

Percentage figures; 1929 = 100 % (averaged out over the year)

In 1932, Robert Bosch published an essay entitled "How to prevent future crises in the world economy," in which he developed his business principles into a full-scale economic-policy program. Drafting policy statements of this kind was not exactly something which reflected his strongest talents, as he presumably realized himself, since he never again referred to the publication or to the proposals it contained. Nonetheless, his exposé is worth noting as a document of its time. Bosch saw it not as a recipe for overcoming crises so much as a plan for avoiding them in future. Mass unemployment was in his view a result of technological progress, as well as of the reluctance to abandon over-long working hours. He called for the time spent working by able-bodied people to be reduced from some 2,400 hours a year to 1,800 hours, which in practice meant bringing in the six-hour working day. Bosch conceded that this was not financially viable. So he suggested further measures: boosting purchasing power by lowering prices, and abolishing customs barriers. Apart from thoughts that today we may find it difficult to relate to, the essay – like many of his writings – contains statements of timeless relevance. Advertising is described, for example, as something that "misleads the consumer." And: "The purpose of the world economy is to secure the greatest possible well-being for the planet's inhabitants."[138]

Power tools, refrigerators, radios, and gas-fired water heaters: the first phase of diversification and the rise of a conglomerate

Even before the 1926 crisis was fully overcome, the Bosch board of management began efforts to widen the company's product range. The aim was to reduce the company's dependence on the automotive market. The lessons of the crisis undoubtedly played an important role in this decision. Not only had Bosch been seriously affected by the sales slump in the German automotive industry, it had also felt the effect of automakers turning to less expensive equipment suppliers. So it made sense to diversify, as well as to manufacture articles from other areas of electrical engineering, since this would allow the company to better spread its risks. However, for the first broadening of the production program, which Bosch embarked on in 1927–28 with the manufacture of power tools and hair-trimming machines, the crucial motive may well have been different. Judging the earnings potential of the automotive business to be slim, management was keen to branch out into what it deemed more profitable fields. This rationale is evident from a letter that Robert Bosch wrote to Max Fischer (for many years commercial director of Carl-Zeiss-Werk in Jena) on April 5, 1928: "We ourselves are looking to move away from automotive work if we can, or, to be more precise, to add more strings to our bow. If our German automotive industry fails to prosper, this could have disastrous consequences for a company such as mine. Granted, we can go on selling things abroad to some extent, but no longer always at prices that would allow us to keep operating at a decent, secure level. For this reason, we have begun manufacturing an electric hair trimmer as well as an electrically heated curling iron."[139]

Outside automotive technology, Bosch had previously offered only a limited number of products and services: lubrication pumps (*Öler*, as they were called), which were also in demand for stationary engines, the plumbing and fittings business handled by Elektra GmbH, and some of the semi-finished goods turned out by the Metallwerk plant. If it wanted to diversify into new areas of manufacturing, therefore, it either had to accept longish lead times or take over companies with alternative production programs. Bosch initially decided to develop and manufacture the new products itself. Buying up existing companies seems to have been out of the question, no doubt because of the tight financial situation. Taking over Eisemann-Werke AG in 1926 and re-incorporating Metallwerk two years later did not involve enormous outlay, but nor did either transaction result in any change in product portfolio. Moving into a different industrial sector was not considered at first. Again, it would have meant buying up other companies. Bosch was looking for new products that it could develop with its own know-how and bring to market quickly. Electrical consumer goods seemed particularly suitable.

How a company goes about deciding which new items to produce is an interesting matter. At its meeting of October 12, 1926, the executive committee of the Bosch board of management examined several proposals (which had doubtless already gone through a pre-selection process). New products up for discussion included fire extinguishers for automobiles, vacuum cleaners, and components for typewriters. Anticipated sales and market saturation were major considerations. Something called a "type adder" (an adding machine and typewriter combined) failed to win acceptance, since prospective sales were not considered promising. With vacuum cleaners, the company would have been up against strong competition.[140] Thought had already been given to producing radios. However, this was still a small market in Germany, where the first radio broadcast had been transmitted only in the autumn of 1923. Anyway, producing radio receivers required a license from Telefunken, where AEG carried a lot of weight. Relations between AEG and Bosch were strained at the time.[141]

It was decided that Bosch would start by making hair trimmers and power tools. The company already had a certain level of expertise in connection with electric motors, and Bosch apparently believed that this could be exploited further. In 1928, the company began producing power tools, and in the same year it launched the Forfex hair trimmer.[142] It was the model for the design principle of power tools with their "electric motor in the handle," as engineers liked to call the Forfex. Distribution was via the Bosch-owned Eisemann-Werke AG. In the first year, Bosch produced 5,711 hair trimmers. The figure rose to 11,481 in the following year, after which sales declined because of the Great Depression.[143] Rather less successful were the carpet clippers and pet clippers that followed on from the Forfex. As further "electric motor in the handle" lines, grinders, screwdrivers, polishers, thread-cutters, and drills were manufactured, which soon outstripped hair trimmers in sales. In 1931, Bosch acquired a Swedish patent for an electric hammer with torsion gearing. Moreover, the partial acquisition of the Berlin-based Ernst Heubach & Co. helped further expand this area of manufacturing work.[144]

In 1929, the Bosch board of management decided to start producing refrigerators. This marked the company's entry into electrical household appliances. There were already several manufacturers in the field, but their low production volumes made the models they produced correspondingly expensive. Here the company's experience in the automotive market was a clear benefit. Bosch was confident that the small, inexpensive, mass-produced refrigerator it intended to build would be a market success. However, designing a new fridge was rather more complicated than making a machine for cutting hair. Not only did it call for costly trialing with a variety of cooling agents, but designers would also have to decide between the compression and absorption principles. Moreover, the company had to ensure that this appliance also came up to the high quality standards for which Bosch was known. It took four years to make the Bosch refrigerator ready for the market. It was a small, drum-shaped model with a 60-liter capacity.[145] When the refrigerator was first presented at the Leipzig trade fair in early March 1933, it met with "practically unqualified approval" – as was proudly reported to the next meeting of the supervisory board. However, there was also criticism of its "hitherto uncustomary round shape."[146] Nor did the drum shape, as it turned out, ever become customary in refrigerator design. Nowadays, the model presented in 1933 would more probably be taken for a washing machine or a dryer. Another lesson Bosch had to learn was that this market obeyed different rules than the automotive business. Moreover, since there was considerable demand for larger refrigerator models, the company very soon began producing 90-liter and 120-liter versions.[147] With refrigerators and hair trimmers, Bosch was manufacturing for a broader customer base than was the case for automotive technology. A different marketing strategy was needed. However, quality was not to be compromised, even though Bosch had little experience as yet in the manufacture of household appliances. After all, who was going to seek advice in a Bosch workshop if the Bosch refrigerator at home was refusing to work properly?

By the time the Great Depression set in, Robert Bosch AG had not made much progress with its diversification program. Hair trimmers and power tools, though well enough accepted, had done nothing to alter the company's dependence on the automotive market. Since demand for ignition systems, generators, and electric starters picked up strongly in the two years preceding the crisis, Bosch may no longer have felt it urgent to find new fields of business. Things changed when, with the onset of the Great Depression, the automotive market collapsed. In 1930, a special investigative office named BTH3 was set up

Ad for first Bosch refrigerator (1933)

which reported directly to the corporate engineering department. This office was tasked with conducting initial studies to clarify what new products Bosch might well take up in the future. In the throes of economic crisis, spending a lot of time on development was the last thing the company needed. Instead, it decided to fall back on the groundwork done by other companies. The way forward for Bosch was a strategy of acquisitions.[148]

Ten years after BTH3 was created, it presented a report listing items that had been considered but not incorporated into the Bosch production program. These included office machinery, electric clocks, vacuum cleaners, washing machines, ironing machines, and dishwashers, as well as mufflers, piston rings, gaskets, and brake linings. There were also items which were initially included in the Bosch product portfolio but later taken out again. These included carburetors, hydraulic shock absorbers, and record players. Some of these products had been removed from the portfolio by agreement with other companies. Production of record players, started in 1932, had proved unprofitable as a result of the tough price competition in this market, and manufacture of gasoline pumps had been stopped since development of the gas-station network had come to a halt. Altogether, BTH3 examined more than 10,000 offers and proposals between 1930 and 1940.[149]

After Robert Bosch had set about purchasing ABMC in the U.S. in the autumn of 1929, management at Bosch once again considered going into radio production. ABMC had a large radio division, and following the merger with RBMC it contributed this to the new Bosch subsidiary, United American Bosch. The path to a transfer of know-how was now open, and Bosch soon identified an attractive takeover target: Ideal-Werke AG, a Berlin-based company specializing in wireless telephony. Hermann Fellmeth, the member of the Bosch board of management accountable for sales, had had his attention drawn to this company by an acquaintance. Established at the end of 1923, Ideal-Werke AG was more a dealer in radios than a radio manufacturer. In 1929, 65 percent of its sales were generated outside Germany. Its product range included headphones, which, if they were especially outstanding, were marked with a quality seal in the shape of a blue spot. Accordingly, many customers were already calling the company *Blaupunkt* – which Ideal-Werke AG had registered as a brand name.[150]

Talks with Alfred Daeschner, a co-owner and managing director of Ideal, were promising so far as Bosch was concerned. Daeschner was prepared to sell, but there was a problem: the Telefunken manufacturing license. Telefunken had gathered its patents in the field of radio and vacuum tube technology into a pool, and would issue licenses only to companies that accepted strict conditions. One of those conditions was that a licensee could only be taken over with Telefunken's consent. Since Telefunken also had agreements with the major U.S. and British manufacturers, no company in Germany could make radios without a license from Telefunken. And there was a distinct possibility that Ideal would lose its license in the event of a Bosch takeover, since Bosch now had a stake in one of Telefunken's competitors in the field of television.[151] For this reason, Bosch and Ideal agreed on a concealed purchase deal. Through a newly established Liechtenstein company, Daeschner and his partner Heinrich Colden transferred the Ideal holding company (also domiciled in Liechtenstein) to a Swiss asset-management company that only a few people knew belonged to Bosch. In formal terms, the transaction did not infringe the Telefunken contract. Ideal-Werke AG had not in fact changed ownership, only its holding company had. The deal was signed on October 16, 1930.[152] Robert Bosch AG then disclosed in its 1930 annual report that production of radio components had begun – but not where or by whom.[153] Clearly the board of management was none too sure of itself. Telefunken must soon have found out how Bosch had contrived to produce radio components without first requesting a manufacturing license. But it was only in the annual report for 1933 that Bosch publicly acknowledged its subsidiary in Berlin-Hohenschönhausen.[154]

A year before taking over Ideal, Bosch had been involved in setting up a television company based in Berlin, Fernseh AG (FESE). When FESE came into existence on July 3, 1929, television was a purely mechanical process. A year later, a physicist named Manfred von Ardenne, working in his laboratory in Berlin-Lichterfelde, carried out the first fully electronic television transmission. Von Ardenne's sponsor was the entrepreneur and television pioneer Siegmund Loewe, who was also behind the founding of FESE.[155] As well as his company Radio AG D. S. Loewe, other parties with a stake in FESE were on the one hand the British company Baird Television Ltd., then Europe's leading television developer, and on the other hand Bosch and Zeiss-Ikon as financially weighty partners from the industrial sector. Each of the four held a quarter of the share capital.[156] Bosch had already approached Baird Television Ltd. before the founding of FESE, but to no avail. Only in association with Loewe did the Stuttgart company succeed in gaining entry into the new field of television.[157] With its partnership in FESE and the takeover of Ideal-Werke AG, Bosch now had a double toehold in telecommunications engineering.

In the autumn of 1932, Robert Bosch decided to acquire Junkers & Co. GmbH of Dessau. This was the first acquisition of a company from outside the electrical engineering industry. The inventor and entrepreneur Hugo Junkers, who came from the engine-building industry (for gas-powered engines), had set up the company in 1895 – long before his famous aircraft plant. Junkers & Co. GmbH (almost universally referred to by the abbreviations "Ico" or "Jco") was the market leader in gas-fired water heaters.[158] At the end of the 1920s, Bosch and Junkers became involved in a dispute over patents. Bosch had filed for a patent for a gas safety valve, but exploitation of this invention was barred by a patent held by Junkers, whom Bosch now threatened with a nullity suit. Bosch also claimed that Junkers had to take out a license under the Bosch patent, which for the renowned gas-appliance producer was a real slap in the face. However, in December 1931, Hugo Junkers bowed to Bosch's demands. Given the acute financial plight the Junkers group was in, he no doubt wanted to avoid costly litigation. Meanwhile, with its patented safety valve selling well, Bosch was beginning to acquire a liking for the gas-appliance business, and entertained the idea of making a takeover bid for Junkers & Co.[159] The Great Depression had affected the Junkers group badly, and Hugo Junkers was in a tight spot. His production of gas-powered engines and his research establishment had accumulated such heavy losses that he was forced to file for bankruptcy in March 1932. This also affected the financially sound Junkers & Co. GmbH, since Hugo Junkers was the sole proprietor of his companies. There now began a tussle over the debtor's assets.

With the Henschel group trying to take over the Junkers aircraft plant, Bosch decided to buy the heating systems business of Junkers & Co. as soon as possible.[160] On November 4, 1932, Bosch acquired Junkers & Co. GmbH for 2.6 million reichsmarks.[161] The proceeds enabled Hugo Junkers to rescue his aircraft plant and his engine plant. Subsequently, in the autumn of 1933 the National Socialist authorities forced him to surrender 51 percent of the share capital of Junkers Flugzeugwerk AG. In 1935, following the death of Hugo Junkers, the rest of the family-owned stake in the Junkers aircraft and engine plants was sold by his widow.[162]

At Bosch, other takeovers took place during the Great Depression. In 1932, a majority shareholding in Eugen Bauer GmbH was acquired. This was a manufacturer of film projectors in Stuttgart-Untertürkheim, even then known generally as "Kino-Bauer." The deal was set up by a friend of Robert Bosch's, the entrepreneur Julius Faber. Faber owned shares in Eugen Bauer GmbH and sat at the same time on the supervisory board of Bosch. By another account, before the takeover Bosch had refused Eugen Bauer GmbH a loan. At the time, the company (founded by the mechanic Eugen Bauer in 1905) had an export ratio of 75–80 percent and required more capital. As with Ideal-Werke, this takeover was not made public until later, in this case in 1934.[163]

The purchase of Junkers & Co. GmbH in November 1932 marked the end of this phase of expansion at Bosch. Since 1928, Bosch had been investing large sums in equity interests and takeovers: Lavalette in Paris and C.A.V.-Bosch in London, then Ideal-Werke, "Kino-Bauer," Junkers & Co. GmbH, and notably ABMC in New York. Most of the takeovers were financed by the company itself. Clearly, Bosch once again commanded sufficient liquidity only a few years after the 1926 crisis. There was one exception. The purchase of ABMC meant resorting to the banks for loans, though there was no need for a capital increase. Bosch capital stock had stood at 30 million reichsmarks since 1924. The expansion of 1928–32 had turned Bosch into a conglomerate, yet Robert Bosch was not an industrial group builder along the lines of Friedrich Flick or Günther Quandt. He was not on the lookout for profitable investments, nor was he trying to form a horizontally structured trust or a vertically integrated concern. However, Bosch did on several occasions take over smaller competitors, examples being Nuremberg's Noris Zünd-Licht AG, Unterberg & Helmle, Westfälische Metall-Industrie AG, and Scintilla AG in Solothurn (Switzerland).[164] Noris Zünd-Licht AG, which in the main made electrical equipment for the motorcycle producer Zündapp, was taken over by Bosch in 1930, but the investment was meant to be kept secret. For such delicate cases Bosch used a secret asset-management company, Südinteressen GmbH. At the end of 1932, this company owned 89.66 percent of the share capital of Noris Zünd-Licht

AG.[165] The takeover of Eugen Bauer GmbH in 1932 also made use of the services of Südinteressen GmbH.[166] After they had been taken over, the new subsidiaries remained discrete entities and continued to operate quite independently in their respective fields of business. Most of the companies taken over during this period no longer exist today, while the rest became part of Robert Bosch GmbH.[167]

II Bosch in the Third Reich (1933–1945)

1 The Bosch Group in the economic upswing of National Socialism (1933–1939)

The development of the enterprise and its subsidiaries

Despite what the National Socialists later alleged, it was not the policies brought in by Hitler that first overcame the Great Depression in Germany.[1] This emerges from (among other sources) the annual report of Robert Bosch AG for 1932, which said that at Bosch "the downward movement halted" as early as August 1932, and from November of the same year there was "evidence of improvement."[2] In the labor market, however, it was only during 1933 that a change in the economic climate became unmistakable. Hitler gave himself four months before the first law promoting direct job-creation measures (the so-called "Reinhardt Program" of early June 1933) came into force.[3] The new regime attached greater priority to promoting the automotive industry. A law promulgated on April 10, 1933, waived motor-vehicle tax for newly registered passenger cars and motorcycles.[4] Like the freeway [Autobahn] program launched not long afterward, the vehicle-tax change was designed to boost job creation as well as serving armament and propaganda purposes.[5]

There were two reasons why German automobile production would surely have increased strongly after 1933 even without such help: an improving economic climate and the demand that had built up during the Great Depression. With such help, however, what resulted was a genuine upswing – the likes of which the industry had not seen before.[6] At the start of 1933, there were some 561,000 passenger cars in Germany. By the beginning of 1939, the figure had risen to some 1,305,000. And motorcycle and scooter numbers had risen nearly as much.[7]

Not surprisingly, when the automotive industry boomed after 1933, suppliers also benefited. Bosch achieved huge sales increases with its automotive equipment. As a result, the consequences of the Great Depression were quickly overcome. While the company did not have the policies of the new regime to thank for seeing it through the crisis, its subsequent rapid growth was very likely due to those policies. Military demand did not at first play a big part in this connection. As far as passenger cars were concerned, the requirements of the armed forces had little relevance for the vehicle market in the years leading up to the war. With trucks and motorcycles, things were very different.[8] In its annual report for 1933, Robert Bosch AG had impressive figures to present. Headcount was up from 8,332 to 11,235, sales showed an increase of a quarter over the previous year, and net profit was more than half as high again.[9] Approval of Hitler's motorization program was as strong at Bosch as it was throughout the automotive industry. It was by no means necessary to be a National Socialist to regard the Weimar Republic's high levels of motor-vehicle taxation as ridiculous. Robert Bosch himself had repeatedly deplored its shackling effect. He summed up his arguments in an article published in February 1933 on the occasion of the Berlin Motor Show. The article was entitled "Das Auto für das ganze Volk" ["Automobiles are for everyone"].[10]

The boom continued through the ensuing years. In 1934 alone, sales rose by nearly 60 percent and headcount by some 30 percent. At the start of 1936, Bosch employed twice as many blue-collar and white-collar associates as at the start of 1933, and by the outbreak of war in 1939, nearly three times as many.[11] The company's annual reports show profits rising steeply. However, from 1935, profits no longer grew as fast as sales. It can nonetheless be assumed that, from the mid-1930s onward, the formation of hidden reserves meant that actual profits were markedly higher than the net profits shown in annual reports.[12] Reports by Deutsche Revisions- und Treuhand AG (DRT), which audited the annual accounts of Robert Bosch GmbH (as it had then become) from 1940, provide evidence of this.[13] These high profits allowed the company to avoid any capital increase despite such strong growth. From 1924 to 1941, its capital stock stood at 30 million reichsmarks. Only then was it increased to 48 million reichsmarks.[14] Bosch was able to increase its sales and profits so dramatically because the company occupied a dominant position in the German market for key vehicle components. With no need to fear the competition, Bosch could dictate its own prices in the marketplace. Even later, under war-economy conditions, this remained the case. In a report submitted after auditing the 1940 financial statements of Robert Bosch GmbH, DRT pointed out that nearly all the company's manufactured products were price-protected proprietary articles. The report stated: "Bosch therefore stipulates catalogue prices for its products that apply across the board, right down to the last customer."[15]

Even during the Third Reich, the stated aim of Bosch corporate policy was "to continue, come what may, to hold and defend our to some extent monopolistic position as an automotive equipment supplier in Germany."[16] And as a survey of market share in 1938 shows, the company undoubtedly succeeded in this. In generators, starters, and ignition devices, 75 percent of

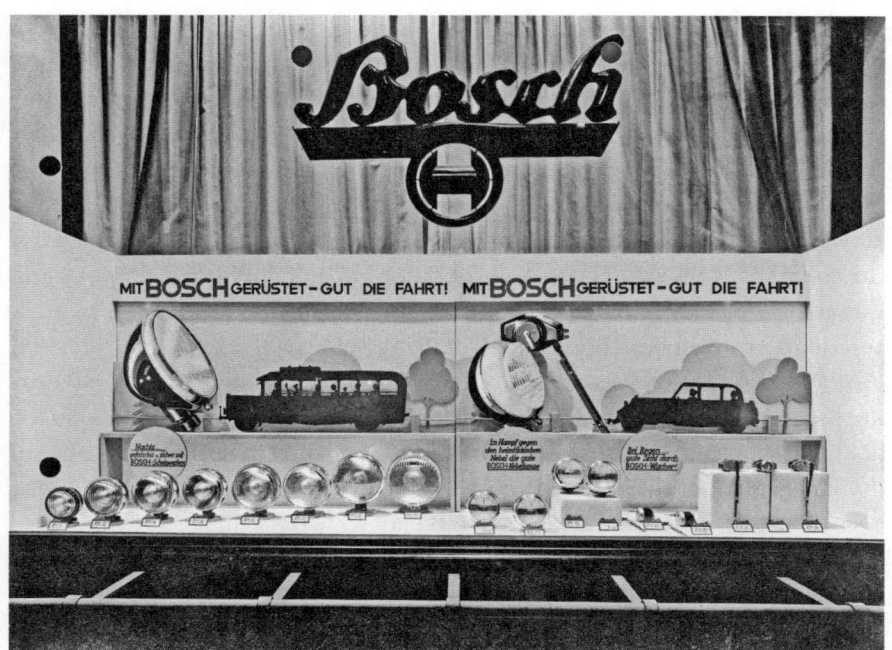

Window display in Berlin sales office (1934)

sales in Germany fell to Bosch. The figure for spark plugs and magnetos for stationary engines was 70 percent, for ignition distributors and contact breakers 65 percent, and for fuel-injection pumps 60 percent.[17] The company's strong growth in the period from 1933 to 1939 depended very strongly on domestic business, with export business failing to keep pace. While more than half of Bosch's sales were accounted for by exports in 1932, by 1934 the export share had fallen to 22 percent. In the last prewar year, it was down to as little as 11.6 percent.[18] This was a trend that must have worried the board of management. The 1936 annual report, for instance, pointed out that "the current ratio of domestic to foreign sales calls for much stronger growth in exports."[19]

One of the company's strengths during the Third Reich was a high degree of personal continuity on the board of management. Unlike during the 1920s, it was spared any major changes until the death of Robert Bosch himself in 1942. The National Socialists' assumption of power did not result in any changes at the top. Corporate and business policy continued to be determined by the three full members of the board of management, namely Hans Walz,

Hermann Fellmeth, and Karl Martell Wild, and the deputy members Guido Gutmann, Max Rall, and Erich Carl Rassbach. Walz was the actual head of the company, Robert Bosch having retired from day-to-day operations to assume chairmanship of the supervisory board (see below). When the "Work Order Act" of January 20, 1934, required the company to appoint what it termed a *Betriebsführer* (factory leader), Walz assumed the position. In practice, this in no way led to changes in top management. Not even the 1937 transformation of the company from an AG (stock corporation) to a GmbH (close corporation) was associated with a management reshuffle.[20]

Apart from Robert Bosch, the company was headed by a total of seven men (Walz, Wild, Fellmeth, Rassbach, Gutmann, Rall, and Ernst Durst) during the Third Reich. With the exception of Durst, all had been appointed to the board of management in the 1920s or even earlier. Durst, who joined the board of management of the GmbH in 1937, had joined Bosch in 1904 and had long been a works manager. The seven were all experienced, dyed-in-the-wool Bosch associates. They had known each other for many years, were thoroughly familiar with the company, and their loyalty to Robert Bosch was beyond reproach. During the Third Reich, there were no major disagreements among them. The senior management of the company over this period must be seen as a highly coherent group, almost as thick as thieves. For them there was no question but that they should speak with one voice, whether in the business or the political sphere.

By contrast, the company's workforce – its *Gefolgschaft*, to use the language of the "Work Order Act," now also in use at Bosch – had yet to forge bonds. The percentage of dyed-in-the-wool Bosch associates shrank steadily in a workforce that expanded rapidly in the years after 1933. The workforce was becoming younger. In September 1936, the average age of Bosch associates was 32 among blue-collar workers, 36 among their white-collar colleagues. On average, the former had been employed at Bosch for six years while the latter had eleven years of Bosch service.[21] The percentage of women declined, even though there were bottlenecks in the labor market as the economy began to improve from the mid-1930s. Furthermore, female associates were increasingly being used for unskilled tasks. The percentage of unskilled female workers went up while that of semiskilled female workers fell sharply. Bosch had no skilled female shop-floor workers at that time.[22]

Table 11 Composition of Bosch blue-collar workers in percentages (1933–38)[23]

Year (annual average)	Skilled workers (male)	Semiskilled workers (male)	Unskilled workers (male)	Semiskilled workers (female)	Unskilled workers (female)
1933	27.1	29.1	6.5	27.5	9.8
1936	25.0	36.2	7.3	17.0	14.5
1938	23.1	37.8	7.6	18.8	12.7

Despite its growing need for suitable associates, Bosch hesitated to build plants at new locations. Two new plants were set up to meet demand from the *Wehrmacht* – and in connection with these, Bosch had to comply with strategic site specifications – but otherwise, until war broke out, production was concentrated in Stuttgart. So Bosch recruited whatever skilled labor it required on its home ground, namely the mid-Neckar region. At the start of June 1936, some 60 percent of Bosch associates were living in Stuttgart, while a further 25 percent had their homes within 15 km of the city.[24] From the mid-1930s, it became increasingly difficult to find skilled workers within this region. As a result, the percentage of skilled workers fell, while that of unskilled associates rose. Nonetheless, despite an overstretched labor market in the latter half of the 1930s, the company still contrived to attract large numbers of skilled workers. That it attracted any at all was likely due on the one hand to mounting efforts to steer labor to areas of need. Being important to the automotive and the armaments industries, Bosch likely received preferential treatment in this respect. On the other hand, many skilled workers likely also switched to Bosch because of the good wages it paid. In October 1937, average hourly wages for Bosch workers were 39 percent above the standard wage, while average piecework rates were 28 percent higher. A skilled worker at Bosch earned 1.20 reichsmarks an hour, which put him a full 62 percent above the standard wage.[25]

Management had a real job on their hands to integrate the large number of newly hired workers into the culture of the company. Newcomers felt no particular loyalty to the company, so they will no doubt have been more susceptible to the watchwords of the German Labor Front [*Deutsche Arbeitsfront* or DAF] and the National Socialist German Workers' Party [*Nationalsozialistische Deutsche Arbeiterpartei* or NSDAP] than seasoned Bosch associates. Accordingly, management at Bosch heightened their efforts to stress "Bosch values" and persuade new associates to adopt them as part of their identity. This came across particularly clearly when the company celebrated its 50th anniversary in September 1936. The book published to mark the occasion, as well as mentioning Bosch's pioneering achievements in the field of engineering, made much of "Bosch spirit," the personality of Robert Bosch, and the Swabian character of the business he had founded.[26]

For any engineering company, the sort of rapid growth that Bosch experienced as a result of the post-1933 boom in the automotive industry holds risks. A report issued by BTH3, the investigative office tasked with identifying new products and product areas, stated: "When the economy is strong, technological progress is inevitably held up somewhat. Customer demand will force development departments to prioritize the solving of day-to-day problems, while plants have no choice but to reject anything that disturbs current production flow."[27] So far as automotive technology was concerned, Bosch's first imperative at that time was to push ahead with its most important innovation of the 1920s, the diesel injection pump, further developing it for use in passenger cars. In 1936, Daimler-Benz and Hanomag launched the first models using this technology. However, it was only after the Second World War that the diesel-powered passenger car made its breakthrough. Other new products such as the inertia starter, a high-speed wiper, and a high-beam headlight for freeway driving were not highly rated as inventions.[28]

At a meeting of the Bosch board of management held on June 8, 1938, future strategy was discussed. All present believed the automotive industry was going to see a second boom in the next few years.[29] Only eleven days previously, Hitler had laid the foundation stone for a new automobile plant on a greenfield site in the heathlands of Lower Saxony near Fallersleben [now a district of Wolfsburg]. Here the *Volkswagen* ["people's car"] designed by Ferdinand Porsche was to be mass-produced under the name of the "KdF car" – after the National Socialist organization *Kraft durch Freude* ["Strength through joy"].[30] Bosch had developed the electrical equipment for the "KdF car," and now expected to receive large orders for generators, starters, and ignition systems for the new vehicle.[31] To fulfill them, 750 new associates were to be taken on by mid-1940.[32] However, managers also feared that the expected boom in the automotive industry could overstretch the company. If Bosch wished to retain its leading market position as a supplier of automotive equipment, major investment was going to be needed. Nor was it certain that the company would find enough suitable workers. There was also a risk of so large an increase in size impairing the company's reputation for quality. In the end, it was Hans Walz who won through with his insistence "that we must, whatever the circumstances, maintain our current standing [as a leading supplier of automotive equipment]."[33] Against this backdrop, the board of management actually considered abandoning the production of power tools, domestic appliances, radios, and refrigerators which had begun in the early 1930s. But in the end, the company was reluctant to return to a total dependence on the automotive industry.[34] The course was thus set for further expansion. Walz told the meeting that annual investments of between 3 and 5 million reichsmarks would be needed over the next ten years.[35] The additional capacity required could no longer be accommodated on the Stuttgart and Feuerbach sites. The state planning authorities had already notified Bosch management that any extension of the Feuerbach plant would no longer receive their permission and that "the manufacturing sites in Stuttgart would need to be relocated outside the city over the next 10 to 15 years."[36] So the meeting approved construction of two new plants, each employing 1,500 associates – one in Renningen (near Leonberg, to the west of Stuttgart) and the other in Crailsheim (to the northeast of Stuttgart).[37]

In fact, the expectations voiced at the time failed to materialize. As early as 1939, the number of new passenger-car registrations in Germany began to fall as a result of a shortage of skilled workers and raw materials. By this time, raw materials and equipment required for the production of trucks for the army took priority. War made the market for passenger cars virtually a thing of the past.[38] One wonders, indeed, why in June 1938 a man of the caliber of Hans Walz was still assuming the automotive industry would keep on growing – at a time when Bosch regional subsidiaries had already been concealed in order to avert their expropriation in case of war.[39] It may be that Walz and his management colleagues could not imagine that the automotive plant intended to produce the "KdF car," whose establishment had been accompanied by so much propaganda, would simply be abandoned unfinished when war broke out. Or were they perhaps expecting that war might yet be avoided?

The Bosch Group that had emerged from the takeovers of the years between 1930 and 1932 expanded further in the years up to 1939. The additions were no longer on the same scale as during the Great Depression, but Bosch continued to expand. Again, certain investments were made secretly. In 1934, the company bought an 18 percent holding in one of its most important customers, the Frankfurt automaker Adler-Werke (or Adler Werke vorm. H. Kleyer AG to give it its full name). In return, Adler-Werke signed an agreement making Bosch its exclusive supplier. Acquiring a holding in this company was a delicate matter, since other major customers such as Opel and Daimler-Benz were competitors of Adler-Werke. So it was done through Bosch's secret asset-management company, Südinteressen GmbH.[40] A year later, through a similarly disguised share purchase, Bosch bought a majority holding in its Swiss rival Scintilla AG, then having to undergo reconstruction after sustaining severe capital losses. The disguised takeover was performed through the Guhl Bank in Zurich and became public knowledge only in 1954.[41] In September 1937, Bosch took over the ore-mining company Metallerzbergbau Westmark GmbH. In the context of Hitler's Four-Year Plan (1936–40), the purpose of this transaction was for Bosch to become involved in ore extraction in the Hunsrück mountains.[42] The previous owners had had to sell the company because, being of Jewish origin, they no longer qualified for government grants to sink further mines.[43] Metallerzbergbau Westmark GmbH, with a mere 220 employees at the end of 1938, subsequently played a negligible part within the Bosch Group. Also in 1937, Askania-Werke, the biggest rival of Junkers in gas-appliance production, was subsumed into Junkers & Co. GmbH.[44] The amalgamation of Eisemann-Werke AG with Robert Bosch GmbH in the same year was largely a technicality, particularly since part of that company continued to operate as Eisemann GmbH.[45]

It was a different story with the gradual takeover of Fernseh AG (FESE). In the case of this company, initially set up as a research operation only, Bosch's holding rose from 25 percent to 37.5 percent over the course of 1935. The British shareholder Baird Television Ltd. withdrew at that time, the reason being that the German authorities were no longer prepared to let large orders in the new field of television technology go to a company that was in part foreign-owned.[46] Subsequently, in 1938, Radio AS D. S. Loewe had to sell its 25 percent holding in FESE to the other two major shareholders, Robert Bosch GmbH and Zeiss Ikon AG. A year later, Zeiss Ikon ceded its shares in the now seriously indebted company to Bosch. As we will see later, Bosch played a dubious role in ousting Loewe from FESE.[47] Taking over FESE put Bosch in a strong position in the new field of television, with only Telefunken above it. FESE, with some 400 associates when war broke out, built the world's first outside broadcasting van as well as the first "Ikonoskop" camera.[48] At the Berlin Radio and Television Show in August 1938, it presented the DE 7 miniature television receiver with built-in radio. In the same year, Blaupunkt and FESE began production of the E 1 standard receiver (dubbed the *Volksfernseher* or "people's television"), the first mass-produced television appliance. The E 1 had been developed by five companies acting together in association with the national post office and the national broadcasting company.[49]

The companies that Bosch had taken over during the Great Depression (Junkers & Co. GmbH, Eugen Bauer GmbH, and Ideal-Werke AG) were now operated as subsidiaries. They all managed to increase production substantially between 1933 and 1938 – each in its own way, of course. At Junkers & Co., development of gas-fired heating appliance production was strongly linked to house building, which started to decline in 1936 as rearmament gained speed.

However, the company offset this decline with growing international sales. In 1937, export business accounted for 44 percent of output.[50] Following the take-over of Askania-Werke in October 1937, Junkers & Co. added stoves and ovens to its product range. Business in Germany rocketed, with the result that exports accounted for only 27 percent of the company's production by 1938.[51] Eugen Bauer GmbH, by contrast, was able to sell around half its reference-tone projectors abroad. Despite trade barriers, "Kino-Bauer" brought in substantial amounts of foreign currency. This was after the company had undergone an adjustment crisis in the mid-1930s that required additional capital of 2 million reichsmarks.[52]

Table 12 Bosch Group headcount inside Germany (1936–38)[53]

Year*	Robert Bosch AG/GmbH	Subsidiaries	Total	Share accounted for by subsidiaries
1936	18,292	3,984	22,276	17.9%
1937	19,772	4,543	24,315	18.7%
1938	23,233	7,200	30,433	23.7%

* As of December 31 each year.

Ideal-Werke grew rapidly as a result both of the economic upswing and of the regime's propaganda. To promote the spread of radio ownership, the Reich Propaganda Ministry had a *Volksempfänger* ("people's receiver") developed. This was an inexpensive appliance that Germany's radio companies were forced to produce to a uniform design. Ideal-Werke also built the *Volksempfänger*, which soon became a bestseller.[54] However, Ideal also marked itself out as a top brand. With products such as its gramophone, it was better represented in the high-end sector than most of its competitors. Soon, the capacity of its Berlin-Hohenschönhausen plant was no longer sufficient. The company built a new factory in the Wilmersdorf district of the city and moved into it in September 1936. Two years later, a further facility in Berlin-Kreuzberg was put into operation. As business grew, the company's share capital was increased: from 1.5 million reichsmarks in 1933 to 10 million reichsmarks in December 1938. On December 16, 1938, the company changed its name and its legal form. The old Ideal-Werke AG became Blaupunkt GmbH.[55] Ideal/Blaupunkt accounted for some 10 percent of domestic sales in the German radio-appliance industry in 1938. And in the export market, its share was close to 15 percent.[56]

Outside Germany, Bosch entered only one new partnership between 1933 and 1939. This was MABO S. A., founded in Milan in 1935. MABO was a sales company set up jointly by S. A. per il Commercio dei Materiali Bosch on the one hand, and Magneti Marelli on the other. Fifty percent of the capital stock of the latter company was owned by Fiat.[57] In Britain and France, Bosch met with reverses in these years – reverses that had considerable repercussions for its entire international business involvement. The Bosch Group withdrew from the U.K. company C.A.V.-Bosch Ltd. in May 1937. The holding was sold to the Birmingham-based Lucas Group, which had set up the company in partnership with Bosch and owned a majority of the share capital.[58] Lucas later stated that it had bought Bosch's 49 percent stake in C.A.V.-Bosch Ltd. because of the upcoming war.[59] Like Bosch itself, C.A.V.-Bosch also worked for the military – in this case mainly for the Royal Air Force. That may have been why the German authorities compelled Bosch to give up its holding in the British company. Equally, however, it may have been that C.A.V.-Bosch could not expect to receive orders from the British armed forces as long as it was partly owned by Bosch.[60]

In France, the Great Depression did not take effect until 1932, although it then lasted longer than in Germany. When the depression hit, the Bosch subsidiary Lavalette-Bosch had to dismiss 100 of its workforce of 720. Granted, in 1935 it was able to take on 120 new workers, but subsequently Lavalette-Bosch suffered the consequences of mounting tension between Germany and France. The number of German employees at Lavalette-Bosch had to be pared down, and in 1937 and 1938 the last German workers left the company. According to Heuss, this happened "in order not to damage the French company. Armaments were now becoming increasingly important for the economy in France as well".[61] The company was now called simply "Lavalette," although 60 percent of its share capital remained in the hands of a holding company that Bosch, because of the risk of war, had placed temporarily in the hands of a Dutch business partner, the Mendelssohn Bank in Amsterdam.[62]

Despite the difficult economic situation existing in the U.S., the Bosch subsidiary there, United American Bosch Company (UABC), was able to boost its sales substantially.[63] Around half the figure was accounted for by radio appliances. In fact, though, this part of the business made a loss, probably owing to cut-throat price competition in the U.S. radio market, and was given up in 1937. Of the Big Three in Detroit, only Ford was supplied by UABC. The company occupied a stronger market position as a supplier for agricultural machinery. It also did a lot of trading beyond its U.S. base, reaching into other countries of North, Central, and South America that could not be supplied directly from Stuttgart. After the heavy losses of the Great Depression, UABC was once again able to earn big profits. However, it was still in no position to distribute dividends.[64]

The Bosch Group benefitted from the annexations of 1938 and 1939 to a limited extent only. In Austria, no new stakes in companies were acquired after March 1938, and nor were any new permanent establishments set up. All that happened was that the existing dealer network and the sales facility in Vienna were integrated into the domestic set-up. A similar thing occurred in connection with the Bosch dealerships in the *Sudetenland*, which under the Munich Agreement of September 1938 was separated from Czechoslovakia and tacked on to the German Reich. In the part of Czechoslovakia that became the Reich Protectorate of Bohemia and Moravia after Hitler's crushing of the country in March 1939, the Bosch Group had already had two subsidiaries for some time. Robert Bosch GmbH possessed a sizeable sales company in Prague, and Ideal-Werke had set up Ideal Radio AG, Prague, at the beginning of 1933. Under regulations existing in Czechoslovakia before 1938, Ideal Radio AG was not allowed to trade as a German company.[65] In December 1938, it was taken into the direct ownership of Robert Bosch GmbH, which ceded it to its Blaupunkt subsidiary two years later. In January 1940, Bosch also acquired the sales company Robert Bosch GmbH Prag.[66] With these transactions, as a report by the legal adviser Karl Eugen Thomä states, "expansion of the group within Greater Germany was finally rounded off and structured in a functional manner."[67]

In other words, in the neighboring territories annexed by Germany, Bosch did not take advantage of the new power relations to gain market shares there, whether through takeovers or by setting up new subsidiaries. Nor would that sort of expansion have made any sense so far as the company was concerned. With no native competition in the field of automotive equipment, Bosch had long been market leader in those countries. It was different in the Far East. Following the Japanese invasion of China, Bosch was able to establish a number of new bases there.[68]

Unlike in 1914, the start of the Second World War did not plunge Bosch into crisis. One crucial reason for this was the limited size of the company's export business. In 1938, only 11.6 percent of sales were generated outside Germany, compared with 88.7 percent in 1913.[69] However, in the years preceding 1939, the company was also very much more involved in rearmament than had been the case before 1914, since motorization had become much more widespread. Bosch now had a far broader product range, including ignition devices and injection pumps for aircraft engines.[70] So while headcount did of course decrease with the outbreak of war as a result of conscription, sales in the first year of the war went up – although only when the subsidiary producing for the

Luftwaffe, namely Dreilinden Maschinenbau GmbH (DLMG), is included.[71] The loss of deliveries to the U.K. and overseas was made up for by sales in southern and southeastern Europe, and after the May 1940 armistice, Bosch sold more in the occupied countries of western Europe than it had before they were occupied. Major adjustment problems within the Bosch Group were experienced only by Blaupunkt GmbH, which had to slash its radio-appliance production.[72]

The transformation of Robert Bosch AG into a GmbH

On December 10, 1937, the annual general meeting (shareholders' meeting) of Robert Bosch AG resolved to transform the company into a GmbH, i. e. to give up the legal status of the company as an *Aktiengesellschaft* (stock corporation or public limited company) and to take on a new one as *Gesellschaft mit beschränkter Haftung* (close corporation or private limited company). On a formal level, the capital stock of 30 million reichsmarks was now known as *Stammkapital* instead of *Aktienkapital*, the board of management was now a *Geschäftsführung* instead of a *Vorstand*, and the proprietor was now a *Gesellschafter* instead of an *Aktionär*. At the same time, Robert Bosch, having previously chaired the supervisory board, now moved to the board of management, of which he became chairman and on which he sat in the future as shareholder with sole right of signature. What seems at first glance a mere legal formality[73] was in fact closely connected with Robert Bosch's efforts to settle his inheritance. At the same time, it was a reaction to a change in stock-corporation law.

Robert Bosch had converted his company from a sole proprietorship into an AG or stock corporation in 1917. During the course of the 1920s, he had increasingly come to regret giving the then members of the board of management generous holdings. Granted, they were not at liberty to sell those share packages as they wished, but the issue of inheritance had been left out of account in 1917. This meant a possibility had been created of such holdings falling into the hands of people quite unconnected with the company. The years 1919 to 1925 had seen the deaths of three board members who held shares in Robert Bosch AG: Heinrich Kempter, Gottlob Honold, and Ernst Ulmer. As a result, a substantial portion of the capital stock passed into the ownership of people who had nothing to do with the company.[74] Moreover, the dismissal of Hugo Borst in 1926 meant the company's shareholders even included a man with whom Robert Bosch had fallen out completely.[75] This development prompted the company founder to begin buying back minority interests. How much money he spent on this is not known, but the total purchase price must surely have exceeded the shares' face value of 14.7 million reichsmarks. As a result, Robert Bosch's view of how the AG had been established underwent a change. According to Heuss, he now maintained that the company had been converted into a stock corporation virtually without his consent – a contention which is simply not true. Bosch is also alleged to have said: "All I know is that the hour of the founding [of the AG] was one of the hardest in my life."[76]

In the meantime, the 1917 decision had ceased even to be appropriate to Bosch's family situation. At the time, the founder of the company had not anticipated having more children. This prospect had changed as a result of his second marriage. Since the birth of his son Robert Bosch Jr. in 1928, a male heir had once again existed (Bosch had never considered his daughters as potentially succeeding to the company), and three years later a grandson, Georg Zundel, came along. Bosch's comments quoted above suggest that by the time he made them (in 1930), he had already decided to alter the company's legal form. For a number of reasons, the transformation did not take place until seven years later. First, there were probably shareholders who, keen to retain their holdings, would not vote for the change. Until 1934, it was impossible to carry out a compulsory squeeze-out of minority interests in return for compensation.[77] Second, the repercussions of the Great Depression pushed the transformation plans into the background. Third, from the autumn of 1931, it became increasingly apparent that German corporation law was going to be amended by fresh legislation. New provisions governing the management structure of large companies and transformation of stock corporations looked likely to be introduced.[78] After lengthy preparatory work, the new stock corporation act was eventually adopted on January 30, 1937. Its provisions may well have constituted a further motive for Robert Bosch's decision to go ahead with changing his company into a GmbH.

The stock corporation act of 1937 was not shaped by National Socialist ideology. Early drafts dated from the Weimar years, and in terms of its substantive content, it survived largely unchanged in the postwar Federal Republic.[79] In addition to new provisions dealing with publication requirements, accounting, and auditing, the law laid down that stock corporations (AGs) could be transformed if a resolution to that effect was approved by 75 percent of the capital represented at the shareholders' meeting.[80] This enabled Robert Bosch to push the change through even against recalcitrant minority shareholders. There was a further reason why it now seemed advisable to convert Robert Bosch AG into a GmbH. The new act contained provisions that did not suit the company's existing management structure. The revised law strengthened the rights of the board of management of stock corporations, whereas the supervisory board of such companies could no longer actively manage affairs but only monitor the way the business was run. Like many other supervisory board chairmen of the time, Robert Bosch had directed corporate policy. Although the founder had withdrawn from the day-to-day running of affairs, he wished to retain the possibility of influencing how those affairs were directed. However, as the legal adviser Paul Scheuing put it, the provisions of the new stock corporation act meant that Robert Bosch "could not continue as chairman of the supervisory board while still exercising the same managerial function as before."[81] Following the conversion into a GmbH, Scheuing took over the chair of the supervisory board while Robert Bosch, at the age of 75, became chairman of the board of management as well as managing director with sole right of signature. And he held this position until his death in 1942.

It was soon being speculated that Robert Bosch's purpose in performing the conversion had been to protect his company from possible interference by the National Socialist regime.[82] This interpretation misses the true motives. Also, conversion was very much what the authorities expected, although this was certainly not what prompted Robert Bosch to take the step. The National Socialists were trying to discourage stock corporations, but the move was directed against anonymous stock corporations, not against "family AGs." That a company such as Robert Bosch AG relinquished the status of a stock corporation received favorable comment in the conformist press.[83] The fact was, however, by converting the company into a GmbH, Robert Bosch wished to avert the kind of fragmentation of shares that had been possible while the company was still an AG. Paul Scheuing made no secret of the fact that the founder's legacy was also at issue here. As he stressed, "the GmbH structure will offer more possibilities than the AG of binding and holding together share ownership, even in cases of inheritance. In this way, the existence of the company and its continued adherence to the guidelines of Mr. Bosch will be assured as far as possible."[84]

2 "Corporate community" versus "people's community": Bosch, the NSDAP, and the National Socialist regime

Robert Bosch AG after the National Socialist assumption of power

National Socialism flew in the face of all Robert Bosch stood for. The same revulsion for the regime was felt by Hans Walz, the most important senior-management figure at Robert Bosch AG, as well as by other close colleagues of the founder. For Robert Bosch and his entourage, democracy, justice, and international understanding were sacrosanct. Bosch and Walz belonged to what in the United States was known as the Anti-Defamation League.[1] Not unnaturally, a workforce of some 8,000 also included a number of National Socialists. There had been a National Socialist factory cell organization at Bosch since 1931.[2] However, it cannot have been a large one, and at senior management level National Socialists were not represented at all. After the war's end, Walz rightly pointed out that "before 1933 not one [member of senior management] had been an NSDAP member or even a sympathizer."[3] Hitler's appointment as chancellor on January 30, 1933, was not welcomed by Robert Bosch and his circle. However, they were sure the new government would not last long. Developments, they felt, would move inexorably toward a European entente.[4] It was an expectation to which Bosch and Walz clung for some time after 1933. Only in a lengthy process of disillusionment did their aversion to National Socialism turn into open hatred of Hitler and his regime. Initially, it was not things such as the regime's motorization program that made Robert Bosch go so far as to place certain hopes in the new government. He actually believed he could persuade Hitler of the need for detente with France, notifying the new chancellor's economic adviser, Wilhelm Keppler, in February 1933 that he would be glad "to have a talk with Mr. Hitler about our foreign policy."[5]

By contrast, the National Socialist assumption of power in Württemberg in March 1933 posed a direct threat to Bosch. That was when, under pressure from the NSDAP, the state parliament elected *Gauleiter* Wilhelm Murr as president of Württemberg. Following the *Gleichschaltung* [forced coordination] of Württemberg, in effect Murr ruled the state as *Reichsstatthalter* [Reich governor].[6] Within a short time, several thousand Communists,

Social Democrats, and other opposition elements were interned in "protective-custody camps," as the regime called its newly built concentration camps.[7] It was common knowledge in Stuttgart that Robert Bosch and his company were a thorn in Murr's side. For him, it was intolerable that the National Socialists lacked any influence in one of Württemberg's largest companies, and so he had Robert Bosch investigated.[8] Given the spate of arrests in the first months of 1933, Hans Walz and the board of management began to fear for Robert Bosch's safety. After the war, Walz wrote that the party leadership was also considering "taking Mr. Bosch into protective custody – a move which prompted me to seek help in Berlin."[9] Robert Bosch withdrew to his Mooseurach estate in Upper Bavaria for a few weeks. He told his friend Georg Escherich that as a result of "worry and concern about our political circumstances [I have] suffered a further episode of cardiac dilation."[10] On April 12, 1933, he wrote to Frank Rümelin, secretary general of the Franco-German Study Committee in Paris, saying that it was "entirely plausible that one of my friends will manage to get me interned in a concentration camp, if only for a short while."[11] By mid-May, it was clear that Murr and his henchmen were not going to proceed against Robert Bosch.[12] It is most unlikely, in fact, that Murr ever intended to have Robert Bosch arrested. It would not have helped his standing even within his own party to incarcerate Württemberg's most popular entrepreneur in a concentration camp. Moreover, he was likely able to see for himself that Hitler was not going to want relations between the new government and German industry put at risk by any mere *Gauleiter's* lust for power. Apparently, however, Murr felt that a little intimidation could do no harm, and those around Robert Bosch did indeed experience the situation as threatening. Even when the original fears proved groundless, people remained on their guard. They still believed it might one day be necessary to whisk Bosch away into Switzerland, and clandestine preparations were made for this purpose. Willy Schloßstein and Paul Hahn arranged for a temporary residence to be set up on the Swiss shore of Lake Constance – a possibility that still existed as late as August 1944.[13]

In Berlin, meanwhile, Keppler was trying hard to bring about the consultation with Hitler that Bosch had requested in February 1933. He succeeded in arranging an audience of around half an hour, which took place at the Chancellery in Berlin on September 22, 1933. Robert Bosch was still hoping to win Hitler round for an entente with France, but at the interview the dictator accepted none of his suggestions.[14] Bosch, though disappointed, did not give up hope.[15] No doubt as a token of goodwill, he donated 100,000 reichsmarks to one of Hitler's pet projects – building a "House of German Art" in

Hans Walz (1933)

Munich. He joined Friedrich Flick, Gustav Krupp von Bohlen und Halbach, Wilhelm von Opel, Carl Friedrich von Siemens, and other industrialists as one of the new exhibition building's "foundation-stone donors."[16]

In Stuttgart, the Bosch board of management found itself subjected to further pressures as early as the spring of 1933. As Walz wrote after the war, the board had been "urgently advised at that time that, to avert dangers immediately threatening the company, at least some of the senior executives should seek formal party membership."[17] Walz and Karl Martell Wild, the two most influential board members, then applied to join the NSDAP. They were joined by the head of human resources, Otto Debatin, and in May 1933 Robert Bosch's private secretary Willy Schloßstein also put in an application for NSDAP membership. Walz and Wild were accepted into the party with retrospective effect from May 1. Debatin and Schloßstein also received their membership cards.[18] Hermann Fellmeth, the third full member of the board of management after Walz and Wild, did not request admittance to the NSDAP, which may have had to do with his being responsible for international business.[19] The three deputy members of the board of management (Guido Guttmann, Max Rall, and Erich Carl Rassbach) likewise did not join the party.[20] Persuading

Robert Bosch to join the party was so hopeless a prospect that not even the *Gauleiter's* office attempted it.[21]

Some explanation is required as to why members of the board of management of a company known for keeping its distance to the NSDAP should have applied to join that party only months after Hitler's assumption of power. This is particularly true for Walz, a man of firm principles based on ethical and religious values. Walz and Wild underwent no change of heart in early 1933. Even after joining the party, Walz still remained a member of the German counterpart of the Anti-Defamation League until its dissolution in the autumn of that year. The explanation for his joining the NSDAP thus seems to have been that no one wished to give the *Gauleiter's* office an excuse for appointing a die-hard National Socialist to the board. Murr was known to be simply waiting for an opportunity to boost the influence of the party machine at Robert Bosch AG. Berlin would probably not have stood in his way. To that extent, the risk here was more real than the fear of Robert Bosch being arrested. The Bosch management could not imagine allowing influential positions within the company to be filled by a puppet from the *Gauleiter's* office or any other fervent National Socialist. Furthermore – in contrast to Daimler-Benz, for instance – there were no politically motivated board appointments at Bosch, nor any attempts to use National Socialist associates to forge contacts with the regime.[22]

However, any expectation that having several members of the board of management join the party might shield Robert Bosch AG politically soon proved illusory. Also, by adopting this stratagem Bosch management became ensnared in mounting levels of contradiction. A few years later, Walz joined the SS in the belief that this would give him more weight than mere membership in the NSDAP.[23] By his own account he was accepted into the SS "around 1935."[24] At the time, Walz still thought that by taking this step he could protect the company from political interference.[25]

At least one of the Bosch directors who applied for NSDAP membership in 1933, namely Otto Debatin, will doubtless have found this an easier step to take than Hans Walz. In an article for the April 25, 1933, issue of *Bosch-Zünder* he had extolled the "historical mission of the National Socialist movement," proclaiming that the party strove to create a "truly classless people's community [*Volksgemeinschaft*]."[26] Unlike Walz, Debatin was an opportunist. Even in 1918, when developing a plan for an in-house newspaper at Bosch, he had already known what phrases would go down well.[27] He also differed from Walz in looking after his own interests above all else. If he was to keep his job as head of human resources he was sooner or later going to have to join the NSDAP anyway. He may well have thought his advantage lay in making it sooner.[28] Debatin remained loyal to his management colleagues, making his human resources policies accord with company principles. But he also had excellent relations with the National Socialist worker representatives.[29]

Party membership was certainly not a requirement for a career at Bosch – yet neither was it a hindrance, as the example of Ernst Durst shows. In 1937, Durst became a deputy member of the board of management. He had belonged to the NSDAP since May 1933, but without being an active member.[30] A confidential report drawn up in April 1947 by Otto Henne, head of the staff office [*Angestelltenbüro*], lists a total of 39 "eminent persons" in the Bosch Group whom the human resources department deemed to have been tainted by National Socialism in the years 1933–45.[31] Topping the list is Friedrich Menzel, the head of development. He was an NSDAP member from 1931 onward, and was regarded as Murr's "eyes and ears" at Bosch.[32] Since he had Murr's backing, management was unable to move against him – until eventually he himself handed them a cast-iron excuse for giving him the sack. In October 1941, Menzel was arrested for test-driving a company car while drunk.[33]

Only a rough guess can be made at how large a percentage of the Bosch workforce were members of the NSDAP. After the war, the board of management and the works council offered differing estimates.[34] A mean value between the two will surely not be far wrong, namely just under 19 percent. As to subsidiary companies, with the exception of Trillke-Werke there are no surviving records of the prevalence of NSDAP membership among their workforces.[35] The head of engineering at Blaupunkt, Paul Goerz, may not have been an NSDAP member but he was a *Reichskultursenator* and obviously had close ties to Goebbels.[36]

Even in the Third Reich, human resources policy at Bosch continued to be guided by traditional company principles. A person's politics were considered a private matter, not to be taken into account in decisions about hiring and firing. During the Third Reich Bosch did not give anyone notice of dismissal on political grounds. Nor did the company ever, on its own initiative, sack people for so-called "racist" reasons. This is detailed elsewhere in the present volume.[37] When in the spring of 1933 Friedrich Schulz – once a Bosch engineer, now the leader of the NSDAP's factory cell organization for the Stuttgart district [*Gau*] and district head of the newly instituted German Labor Front [*Deutsche Arbeitsfront* or DAF] – called for the dismissal of 30 Communist associates, human resources refused.[38] Clearly, in this case some dismissals were in fact made.[39] But in a series of cases Bosch appointed associates hostile to the regime – people who had lost their jobs for political reasons or suffered imprisonment in a concentration camp. In total there were approximately 30 such individuals.[40] This "apolitical" approach to human resources matters was subsequently corroborated by the works-council chairman Eugen Eberle. His testimony is especially credible in this context since he was involved in fierce disputes with the board of management after the war and since he remained a convinced Marxist throughout. In his memoirs, he wrote of the postwar period: "It was a tricky job, shift supervisors and foremen were only interested in good work. No one, it seemed to me, took any interest in what people's politics had been."[41]

Financial contributions to the NSDAP and its various subsidiary organizations were none too lavish, judging from later declarations. A list drawn up by Debatin after the end of hostilities shows that the total amount paid to the party by the company between 1933 and 1945 was 553,000 reichsmarks. That was less than "donations to churches and Jews," which over the same period came to 600,000 reichsmarks, or "general donations" totaling 900,000 reichsmarks. However, Debatin's list does contain gaps for certain years.[42]

Even at Bosch, some occasions were celebrated in conformity with the rituals laid down by the National Socialist regime, one example being the inauguration of the "labor struggle" on March 21, 1934.[43] Where in-house matters were concerned, on the other hand, the company kept to its own traditions as far as possible. The company was loath to let National Socialist organizations tell it how to manage its own affairs. In clashes with the DAF, Hans Walz would argue that Bosch "could lay claim to being a forerunner of National Socialism in a social-policy sense."[44] However, party officials were well aware of what this really meant. In the company's welfare provisions they recognized the "Bosch spirit" that refused to fit in with the National Socialists' *Volksgemeinschaft* or "people's community." An official of the *Nationalsozialistische Betriebszellenorganisation* [NSBO, National Socialist factory cell organization] informed Walz pedantically in December 1937 that "it would be wrong to compare 'Bosch community' with 'people's community.'"[45] Walz did not disagree. In all likelihood, he saw things similarly, albeit for completely different reasons. For the Bosch management, it was a question of preserving the former (i. e., the *Bosch-Gemeinschaft*) even under the conditions of the latter (i. e., the *Volksgemeinschaft*).

Clashes and compromises with the NSDAP

The summer of 1935 saw the beginnings of a further conflict between Bosch and the party machine. This time it concerned a book-publishing company [Deutsche Verlagsanstalt or DVA] and a newspaper-publishing company [Stuttgarter Zeitungsverlag or SZV]. Robert Bosch owned 63 percent of the share capital of DVA, to which SZV also belonged along with two newspapers, the *Stuttgarter Neues Tagblatt* and the *Württemberger Zeitung*.[46] Robert Bosch's press ownership had long been a source of irritation for the Gauleiter's office, which saw the *Stuttgarter Neues Tagblatt* as a "shitty little democrat rag."[47] In April 1935, the president of the national press association, Max Amman, had a number of decrees enacted that enabled him to close down undesirable newspapers at any time. After that, the *Stuttgarter Neues Tagblatt* and the *Württemberger Zeitung* had to toe the regime's political line. Through an intermediary, Amman put pressure on Robert Bosch to cede a 50 percent stake in SZV to an NSDAP-owned company.[48] Since Bosch was not prepared to do so, Hermann Göring sent for him at the start of 1936 and threatened him with confiscation without compensation and (allegedly) "protective custody" as well. Faced with these threats, Robert Bosch let SZV go.[49]

In these early years of the National Socialist regime, both Bosch and Walz expected great things of Hjalmar Schacht, who was made national minister of economic affairs at the end of July 1934. Bosch had known Schacht since the time of the First World War. He respected the man, though he did not share his political views.[50] Schacht saw his role in Hitler's government as the patron of private enterprise and foreign trade. For management at Bosch, he was now their number one contact within the regime.[51] At company headquarters on Militärstraße, the hope was that his economic expertise would prevail over the NSDAP's claims to power.[52]

Tensions between Robert Bosch AG and the Stuttgart *Gauleiter's* office escalated on September 23, 1936, when the company celebrated its 50-year anniversary and Robert Bosch's 75th birthday. The book published to mark the occasion lacked the panegyrics to the regime that had become customary, if not de rigueur.[53] Consequently, the party representatives invited to attend the anniversary celebrations in the Stuttgart civic center declined the invitation. Undeterred by their action, Hjalmar Schacht delivered the ceremonial speech. Walz followed up by addressing the 8,000 guests and associates. His speech was as lacking in political deference as the anniversary publication.[54] In consequence, the *Gauleiter's* office launched an investigation against Walz and Debatin that concluded with a sharp reprimand.[55]

Ceremony to mark the company's 50th anniversary (1936)
(front row, from left: Bosch family, Hjalmar Schacht, Hans Walz)

There was a further clash in the autumn of 1937. An anonymous article (the author was in fact Rudolf Rohrbach, the *Gauleiter's* head of engineering) claimed that Robert Bosch AG, in return for a donation to Stuttgart Polytechnic, had requested honorary doctorates for four of its directors. The company's board of management rejected this as libelous and demanded right of reply. The affair escalated when Walz insisted that Rohrbach name his source. This turned out to be no less a person than the president of the Polytechnic, Wilhelm Stortz. Stortz then had to own up to having been taken in by a false declaration (made on oath) by the president of the Württemberg Chamber of Commerce and Industry, Fritz Kiehn. The "Bosch affair" ended in disgrace so far as the *Gauleiter's* office was concerned. Kiehn himself, an NSDAP "veteran" and a *Sturmbannführer* in the SS, had to answer before the district court [*Gaugericht*].[56]

By this time, Hans Walz belonged to a "study group" that Wilhelm Keppler had established in 1932 to advise Hitler on economic matters. The group had since become known unofficially as *Freundeskreis Reichsführer SS* – that is to say, "Himmler's Friendship Circle."[57] Keppler's nephew Fritz Kranefuß, who ran the group from 1934 onward, was aide-de-camp to the head of the SS,

Heinrich Himmler, and had transformed what was originally an advisory body into a funding society for Himmler's private passions. "Himmler's Friendship Circle" comprised not only prominent industrialists and bankers but also top civil servants and SS officers.[58] Members from the world of business (or their companies) were expected to donate generously to a special account set up by Himmler. Most industrialists and bankers who belonged to the "friendship circle" saw their membership as providing a kind of political "environmental protection." It did not entail belonging to the SS. However, business members who had enrolled in the SS were awarded an honorary officer's rank. Walz eventually rose to *Hauptsturmführer*, or captain.[59] Businessmen bearing such an honorary officer's rank did not perform active service with the SS. The donations to Himmler expected of Walz as a member of the group were transferred by Robert Bosch GmbH. His membership cost the company 25,000 reichsmarks a year.[60]

Walz himself later denied having already belonged to the Keppler group. And indeed, everything indicates that he joined only after the group had come under the patronage of Himmler, and that he was accepted because he was a well-known industrialist already enrolled in the SS.[61] Like his entry into the SS, Walz may well have regarded belonging to "Himmler's Friendship Circle" as a political precaution. He evidently believed he could play off one party organization against another. Indeed, in the conflict surrounding the company's 50-year anniversary and the book published to mark the occasion, he did so with some success.[62]

Robert Bosch AG or GmbH was not the only company to adopt such ruses. Other management boards, too, sought to take advantage of rivalries, spats, and power struggles inside the National Socialist regime. In this, they were acting in accordance with the logic of a power system characterized by competing institutions and a high degree of patronage. Management at Bosch, for example, soon recognized what possibilities were available to them when, in 1936 and 1937, Robert Bosch and his circle came into closer contact with an SS officer named Gottlob Berger. Berger revered Robert Bosch. His father, like Robert Bosch, came from Albeck, and the two of them had done their military service together in Ulm. For his part, Robert Bosch looked upon Berger not as an SS officer but as the son of an old comrade. Those around him regarded Berger as trustworthy – despite knowing that, as special superintendent of the SA high command in Stuttgart, he had acted ruthlessly in the city in the spring of 1933 and was partly responsible for the mass arrests carried out at that time. Interest in establishing a link with Berger clearly triumphed over scruple. In June 1937, when various NSDAP departments were making life difficult for the *Boschhof* (Robert Bosch's farm in Mooseurach, in Upper Bavaria), Berger offered to use his influence to sort matters out, which he managed to do. In return, from then on Bosch paid him, through a secret account, a monthly fee of 700 reichsmarks.[63] To those around Robert Bosch it made sense to use the man as a political intermediary, not only because of Berger's loyalty to "father Bosch." Berger was also a sworn enemy of *Gauleiter* Murr, whom he blamed for the fact that in 1933 he [Berger] had been forced out of the SA high command in Stuttgart.[64]

As late as the summer of 1935, Robert Bosch still hoped for a Franco-German entente. As a token of this hope, he invited some French first-world-war veterans to a meeting with associates in his company who had been wounded in the war.[65] However, during the course of 1936 it became increasingly clear to Bosch and Hans Walz that Hitler was planning a war of aggression. In October 1936, Hitler put Hermann Göring in charge of the Four-Year Plan, giving him general powers of attorney. Unlike Schacht, whom he then forced out of office as minister of economic affairs, Göring drove rearmament forward without regard for cost or the stability of the currency.[66] This turn of affairs incensed Robert Bosch. In September 1936, he tried to warn Werner von Blomberg, the Minister of War, of the dangers of an arms build-up, but without success. His action may have seemed naïve, and von Blomberg rebuffed him smartly, but Bosch refused to sit idly by while a war of aggression was being prepared.[67]

On a different front, the Bosch board of management was endeavoring to reach a "truce" with the *Gauleiter's* office and the DAF. The clash over the 1936 anniversary had shown that skirmishing with the *Gauleiter's* office was not in the company's interests.[68] Robert Bosch GmbH now signed up for the "productivity war [*Leistungskampf*] of German industry," and in the spring of 1939 the DAF was able to conduct its first training course within the company.[69] Presumably it was also due to the changed situation that, at its meeting of June 1, 1938, the board of management appointed Karl Hugo Bühler as its *Abwehrbeauftragter*, or counter-intelligence officer. Bühler had previously worked at the infamous "Silver Hotel" on Dorotheenstraße, Stuttgart's Gestapo headquarters. In no way had Robert Bosch GmbH been obliged to appoint Bühler. The company had spontaneously nominated him for the post. He had been recommended to Walz by Albrecht Fischer and Paul Hahn, both of whom had Robert Bosch's trust. Nor was Bühler a "professional" Gestapo man. Together with the press office of the Ministry of Internal Affairs, he had first been transferred to the regional police department and subsequently, together with this, absorbed into the Gestapo.[70] Walz was confident that Bühler would be loyal in his dealings with the board of management and that his good connections with the Gestapo might come in handy. Others distrusted

Bühler, however, and saw him as a risk. After the war, Debatin wrote, "I opposed this appointment of an ex-Gestapo man earnestly and stubbornly, but I failed to get through to Mr. Walz, who was keen to have him."[71]

The "Sudeten crisis" of September 1938 brought the risk of war almost within touching distance, further increasing Robert Bosch's bitterness toward Hitler.[72] According to the memoirs of Felix Olpp, who worked in the founder's private secretariat, Bosch told intimates in a discussion at the time, speaking in his native Swabian dialect: "Gents, the fellow is a criminal."[73] At the height of the crisis, 40 associates of Joseph Lucas Ltd., the Birmingham-based company with which Bosch had worked closely right up until 1937, sent a letter addressed "to all our friends in the Bosch organization."[74] A total of 54 Bosch associates replied, professing "the need for honest, amicable collaboration between our peoples."[75] While Walz and Schloßstein undertook yet another international trip in July 1939, during the course of which they voiced their fears to Bosch's London contact, Reinhard Schairer, and to the Amsterdam banker Fritz Mannheimer, ordnance production proceeded apace at the Bosch Group as well.[76] In August, Robert Bosch withdrew with his family to their Wespental hunting lodge, but at the start of the war, on September 1, 1939, he was back in Stuttgart. Together with Walz, Schloßstein, and Olpp, he listened to Hitler's speech on the radio. When Hitler boasted of having spent 80 billion reichsmarks on arms, Bosch reportedly said, "Right, now at least we know where we stand."[77]

Between "model company" and "state within the state": Bosch under wartime totalitarianism

In the first few years of the war, the "truce" between the *Gauleiter's* office and the Bosch board of management held. Both the party and the German Labor Front (DAF) were anxious to stay on good terms with a company that was so crucial to the war effort. Robert Bosch GmbH strove for its part to obtain the accolade "National Socialist Model Enterprise," which it had previously shunned. This distinction was conferred on the company by the DAF on May 1, 1942, by which time it had been granted to 20 companies in Württemberg alone.[78] Apparently, the title of "wartime model enterprise" was granted to Robert Bosch GmbH even without the company having applied for it.[79] These titles were accompanied by honors bestowed on Robert Bosch personally. From Wilhelm Murr he received the "War-Service Cross, 1st Class," and on his 80th birthday on September 23, 1941, Bosch was decorated by the DAF head Robert Ley as a "Pioneer of Labor."[80]

All the same, the National Socialist honors heaped upon Robert Bosch, culminating in the shameless spectacle of his funeral with national honors,[81] showed that the regime had no intention of altering the status of the company after the demise of its founder. As early as the mid-1930s, it had been speculated among senior management at Bosch that *Reichsstatthalter* Murr planned to take the company under NSDAP control following Bosch's death and run it as a "party enterprise."[82] The rumor, peddled by Gottlob Berger, was not necessarily taken seriously.[83] Even at Bosch, they must have known full well that Hitler was not going to take action against private enterprise, and that he would certainly not have put a *Gauleiter* in charge of a company so important to the war effort. Yet in the circle around Robert Bosch the rumor proved persistent, and was frequently alluded to in the denazification trials that followed the war.[84] Much the same applies to Murr's boasting. Heuss tells how in the summer of 1942, the Stuttgart *Gauleiter* and *Reichsstatthalter* Wilhelm Murr said he would "no longer tolerate Bosch acting as though it were a state within the state."[85] However, no action followed.

Meanwhile, Hans Walz had maneuvered himself into a completely absurd situation. On the one hand, he was supporting Carl Friedrich Goerdeler's resistance plans and secretly financing attempts by persecuted Jews to leave the country. At the same time, he was an SS officer sitting down with the very men who were persecuting them. How he dealt with the contradictions of his role on a day-to-day basis is touched on by Ulrich von Hassell in a report of an encounter with Bosch and Walz in August 1939: "Walz was summoned out of the room to a meeting with some SS people. He came back wearing the SS badge in his buttonhole that he had swiftly inserted for the meeting, only to voice his vehement disapproval of the policies of the Hitler government, and how disastrous they were."[86] Walz now faced the dilemma that leaving the SS could lead to disadvantages greater than if he had never joined in the first place. Unlike when he entered the organization in 1935, membership now was also a question of camouflaging the conspiratorial links established by Goerdeler. In July 1942, Walz was due to be made *Wehrwirtschaftsführer* ["wartime economy manager"] – a somewhat meaningless title awarded to most heads of large arms companies. Objection was raised to the conferral of this title by Ernst Kaltenbrunner, head of the security police (SiPo) and security service (SD), who had made certain enquiries. After instigating disciplinary proceedings against Walz, Kaltenbrunner notified Himmler that as recently as 1937, Walz had conducted a "lively private correspondence with Jews" and also that he had "strong church affiliations."[87] However, Himmler instructed the SS judges to adjourn their disciplinary proceedings until the war was over and gave orders for all objections to

Walz's appointment as "wartime economy manager" to be dropped.[88] In both cases, Gottlob Berger, having in the meantime been promoted to head of the SS main administrative office, had once again taken a hand.[89] As for Walz, he continued to sidestep the issue of resigning his SS membership. Nonetheless, his attendance at meetings of the "Friendship Circle" became less and less frequent until eventually he was no longer invited.[90] No perceptible advantage came of Walz's links with the SS. It was different with the Gottlob Berger connection, but that had not come about through the SS.

In the spring of 1943, Walz once again clashed with the *Gauleiter's* office. The head of the NSDAP party chancellery, Martin Bormann, had formed a banking committee to which several economic advisors to Gauleiters' offices belonged. The committee was intended to give *Gauleiters'* offices more influence over the banking business.[91] In Württemberg, the economic adviser to the *Gauleiter's* office was a man named Walther Reihle. He and the undersecretary of state Karl Wilhelm Waldmann were keen to bring about a merger between Handels- und Gewerbebank Heilbronn, a regional private bank with a long tradition, and Württembergische Bank. Handels- und Gewerbebank Heilbronn was headed by Erwin Bohner, who was close to Robert Bosch. Walz tried to block the plan. As it was, the *Gauleiter's* economic advisers were quickly reined in by Walther Funk, the national minister of economic affairs. Because of the increasing damage from air raids, all efforts to reorganize the banking business had to be postponed.[92]

On July 17, 1943, Walz spoke to a group of journalists whom the national Ministry of Propaganda had sent on a tour of various companies. In what became known as his "Feuerbach address,"[93] he was once again openly critical of the regime. Managers at Bosch, he told them, regarded the dirigisme of the war economy as stifling output – indeed, almost as shackling private enterprise. Walz's bold criticism of the war economy very accurately reflected developments, and this not only at Bosch:

"If we were inclined to leniency, we might say that our plant is characterized today by a forced growth in manufacturing capacity that is attributable to the central planning and armaments boom that have been with us since 1935 or 1936. However, this economic growth and its consequences for our company have been altogether of a more negative, rather than positive, nature. Without rearmament and without a war, we would, as far as anyone can judge, have developed perhaps not at breakneck speed, as has been the case, but better and more soundly."[94]

Reihle, the Stuttgart *Gauleiter's* economic adviser, left the room during the speech, firing off threats.[95] A few months later, after the manager of the Stuttgart branch of Deutsche Bank, Hermann Köhler, had been executed for comments critical of the regime, Reihle announced that Walz would be one of the next to "climb the scaffold."[96] However, unlike the situation following the 1936 anniversary, not even an investigation was instigated on this occasion.

The atmosphere of terror that characterized the National Socialist state was felt at Bosch, too. In a number of instances, it led to associates being executed. If members of the Bosch workforce were denounced to the Gestapo as "enemies of the state" or "defeatist," their fate was sealed. This applied especially to foreign forced laborers, but even regular associates were affected. A canteen employee at the Feuerbach plant, Christian Elsässer, was denounced by a colleague in the autumn of 1943 for saying "he'd rather look Italian POWs in the arse than you Nazis in the face." For that remark, Elsässer was summoned before the *Volksgerichtshof* [People's Court] in Berlin, condemned to death, and hanged on July 20, 1944. At Bosch, the human resources department reacted by releasing the informer for call-up.[97] Two blue-collar workers, Anton Hummler and Max Wagner, were arrested in September 1943 after being denounced by a Gestapo informer. Both belonged to a Communist resistance group, though this could not be proved in court. Hummler had helped some Russian forced laborers at the Trillke plant in Hildesheim, and, like Wagner in Stuttgart, had listened to radio broadcasts from abroad. Sentenced to death for acts preparatory to high treason and assisting the enemy, the two were hanged in Brandenburg Penitentiary on September 25, 1944.[98] At the French Bosch subsidiary Lavalette, some dozen associates were arrested by the Gestapo in 1943 and 1944. According to witness accounts, none of them returned.[99]

3   Bosch and the Jews

Jews and people of Jewish descent at Robert Bosch AG and GmbH

Both Robert Bosch and Hans Walz were consistent in their rejection of anti-semitism. For Walz, this was in line with his understanding of the Christian faith. For Bosch, religious equality and tolerance were basic humanitarian values. For both men, the principles of justice and the rule of law ruled out any discrimination against Jews. The two men had been members of the German equivalent of the Anti-Defamation League since 1926.[1] However, it was only when the extent of National Socialist tyranny became clear that the "Jewish question" became a matter of central concern to them. As early as May 1933, Walz protested to Hitler's economics adviser, Wilhelm Keppler, about anti-Jewish persecution.[2] Robert Bosch had no wish to benefit from the unfairness meted out to Jews. He even instructed associates not to take advantage of Jews in their dreadful plight.[3] Those in his circle went further, giving positive assistance to Jews suffering persecution. This not only took courage. It called for a fundamental stance that was far from common in the German business world. Seen in this light, the conduct of the Bosch circle provides a standard by which others must be judged, an example of what businesspeople in the Third Reich could achieve for Jews and people of Jewish descent if only they made up their minds to do so.

How the workforce of Robert Bosch AG and GmbH behaved toward Jews is hard to assess, given that only few people on the payroll were of Jewish origin. As one conflict surrounding a Jewish engineer reveals, attitudes toward Jewish exclusion varied widely.[4] On the other hand, senior management at Bosch was clearly immune to the prevalent racial ideology. This is particularly remarkable in that antisemitism was widespread even before 1933, also among the business class. This is not to say that all those who had risen to senior management positions at Bosch were morally better people than in other companies. However, it does show how profound an effect a corporate culture can have, even in the circumstances of the Third Reich, and how it can be shaped by dominant personalities. Because Robert Bosch and Hans Walz absolutely opposed discrimination against Jews, and because only people who enjoyed their full confidence were appointed to the board, a clear consensus existed within the company's senior management. At Bosch, antisemitic smear campaigns were not a way to get ahead. On the contrary. And these management attitudes had a certain effect on careerists and associates who were unsure of their opinions. They knew they would be wise to stick to the code of conduct. That, presumably, explains why a man like Otto Debatin, who was known to take his cue from whatever seemed to work to his own best advantage, behaved protectively toward Jewish colleagues.[5] Hugo Bühler, who in 1938 became "counter-intelligence officer" at Robert Bosch GmbH, is unlikely to have sprung to the defense of Jews in his former jobs with the local police and with the Gestapo. Yet at Bosch he took part in a number of relief actions.[6] Debatin and Bühler occupied key positions in human resources. It was usually there that the fates of associates suffering persecution or denunciation were decided, not at board level. So it was hugely important that such crucial office-holders – who were not, like Robert Bosch and Hans Walz, guided by moral principles – should follow company policy. Naturally, it also has to be said that Robert Bosch GmbH had only a small number of Jewish associates or associates of Jewish descent, none of whom held senior managerial rank. And since almost all cases were exceptional, human resource managers could intervene in a more targeted fashion than would have been possible in a large company with many employees of Jewish origin.

It is impossible to establish how many Jewish blue- and white-collar associates and apprentices Robert Bosch GmbH employed at the start of the Third Reich. The company did not keep any record of the religious affiliation of its employees. A "List of Jews and people of Jewish descent on the payroll of Robert Bosch GmbH over the past 12 years" was drawn up in September 1945. It includes only two "full Jews" working on the shop floor, one a technician and the other an apprentice. It further records two technical managers of sales offices presumed to be of Jewish origin and eight Jews formerly working at Bosch agencies. The number of "half-Jews" was slightly larger.[7] The September 1945 list uses the terms "Jew" and "half-Jew" as defined in the Nuremberg Laws. These were based on genealogy, not on religious affiliation. This makes it difficult for the following account to avoid the use of terms that match the categories of contemporary sources, since persecution targeted all whom the race laws deemed *Juden* or *Halbjuden*.

In June 1933, the city of Stuttgart had 416,522 inhabitants, 4,876 of whom were Jews.[8] Most of the latter are likely to have worked in the services sector, with only a small number in electrical engineering.[9] The few Jews demonstrably employed at Bosch in the Third Reich remained with the company as late as the immediate prewar years. One was Georg Einstein, who completed an apprenticeship as a technician between 1935 and 1938. After that he is thought to have emigrated to England.[10] The Jewish technician Julius Landauer, despite suffering acts of hostility from National Socialist workmates, stayed on at Bosch until February 1939. Only the backing of human resources made this possible. He then left by mutual agreement.[11] Bosch subsequently tried to get him a job at the Netherlands agency, but to no avail, since the border had already been closed to Jews. Landauer returned to Bosch after the war.[12] Debatin is said to have told the National Socialist head of development Friedrich Menzel in 1935 that "the Jew Landauer was indispensable to the company and anyway he [Debatin] was not against Jews."[13] In another version, Debatin's remark is said to have concerned someone else of the same name, the managing director of the Bosch subsidiary Eugen Bauer GmbH, Fritz Landauer. Forced to emigrate, Fritz Landauer subsequently settled in the U.S.[14] Both Landauers clearly had the support of human resources management.

No dismissals on so-called "racial" grounds were made in Bosch sales establishments, either. Two very different cases involving Jewish associates working in this field are documented. The technical manager of the Stuttgart sales office, Mosso Johanan, was a Greek unable to show "proof of Aryan ancestry." Debatin claims to have asked him to "procure from Greece in one way or another some kind of proof of the sort required." Johanan came back with evidence that the Gestapo were at least unable to disprove.[15] The technical manager of the Frankfurt sales office, Hans Breitbart, was a "full Jew" according to the race laws, but disputed the description. When in August 1938 he was asked to report to the German Army District Command, which involved furnishing evidence of descent, he took his own life.[16] Of the eight Jews who demonstrably worked for Bosch in its agencies, two – Max Eisenmann and Willy Bendit – emigrated. A Jewish agent in Sofia died as early as 1933. Another, in Warsaw, was dismissed for (according to the company) "unsatisfactory work." Walter Heusel, a further Bosch representative of Jewish origin working in Poland, continued to work for Bosch as an agent after the war, but in Bavaria. Also employed by Bosch throughout the war years were agents of Jewish descent in Zagreb, Casablanca, and Bombay.[17] However, other parts of the Bosch Group harbored different attitudes toward Jewish representatives. Junkers & Co. GmbH informed a business associate in February 1938 that it had been working for some considerable time on "the question of transferring our agencies into Aryan hands" and was currently redoubling its efforts.[18]

Most of the 25 "half-Jews" named in the list drawn up in September 1945 had joined the company only during the war – and most of those were pressed into service. In the autumn of 1944, some 15 "half-Jews" were employed at Bosch.[19] That was when Himmler gave orders that "half-Jews," "persons of mixed race" [*Mischlinge*], and "Jewish-related persons" [*jüdisch Versippte*] were to be removed from the weapons industry and handed over to forced labor building roads and military installations.[20] To protect associates of "half-Jewish" origin from such a fate, the company came up with what may well have been a unique solution. For "half-Jews" and "Jewish-related persons," a workshop was set up that traded independently under the name "Sicht- und Zerlegebetrieb für Autoersatzteile" [Inspection and Disassembly Workshop for Automotive Parts]. The Inspection and Disassembly Workshop did not count as an arms operation for two reasons: it was not a legal entity of Robert Bosch GmbH, and it occupied separate premises. Here a total of between 30 and 40 associates worked. As well as "half-Jews" and "Jewish-related persons," nearly all of whom had previously had office jobs, they included forced laborers from a number of countries. In the ghostly setting of a room in the ruins of the light works in Feuerbach, these people spent the final months of the war dismantling and sorting parts from vehicles salvaged from the German army and captured from the Allied forces.[21]

The workshop remained in existence until the war's end and saved the "half-Jews" employed there from a dreadful fate. Among them were two associates of the company who had come to Bosch as commercial apprentices: Kurt Löwenstein and Fritz Nast-Kolb. Others included the bookseller Konrad Wittwer, who had been assigned to Bosch by the Labor Office at the beginning of February 1945, the wife of the ex-associate Julius Landauer who had left the company in 1939, the theologian Hansrudolph Hauth,[22] and Friedrich Haarburger, the son of an industrialist.[23] In addition to them, a list drawn up after the war names ten other Bosch associates in the "half-Jew" and "Jewish-related persons" categories who would otherwise have been interned in a forced-labor camp.[24] The Inspection and Disassembly Workshop had been set up not conspiratorially but with the permission of the Stuttgart Gestapo and by arrangement with the authorities organizing forced labor on roads. Working in conjunction with the counter-intelligence officer Hugo Bühler, Ernst Rogowski, a Bosch executive with general power of attorney and later Bosch board member, had achieved this through prolonged negotiations.[25] It may have made some difference that the Inspection and Disassembly Workshop was able to supply urgently needed spares for army vehicles. Moreover, Bühler's good connections at Gestapo headquarters in Stuttgart's Dorotheenstraße will certainly have helped the proposal to win acceptance there.[26]

Jewish forced laborers were not used at Robert Bosch GmbH, although the authorities had offered the company this option.[27] Jews pressed into service and Jewish concentration-camp prisoners did in fact perform forced labor at the Blaupunkt and Siling-Werke subsidiaries. We will return to this subject in greater detail later.[28]

"For the sake of justice and humanity":
how the Bosch circle helped Jews

Around the mid-1930s, Walz intensified his contacts with Jewish organizations. Through Friedrich Jaffé, a journalist on the *Stuttgarter Neues Tagblatt*, he got in touch with Leo Baeck, the president of the "National Agency
for German Jews" [*Reichsvertretung der Deutschen Juden*]. During the clash
over the *Gleichschaltung* of the *Stuttgarter Neues Tagblatt*, those contacts
became closer. Walz, Albrecht Fischer, and Willy Schloßstein were now in
close touch with the agency's Leo Baeck, Otto Hirsch, and Cora Berliner.[29]
A key figure in the assistance that the Bosch circle provided for Jews was
Karl Adler, the founder and for many years the principal of Stuttgart's New
Conservatory of Music. Adler was a prominent figure in the city's musical
world. As a musical educator he was as successful as he was revered.[30] However, even before the National Socialists came to power he had been subject
to malicious slander because of his Jewish origin. In March 1933, he was
beaten up in broad daylight, and a few months later the New Conservatory
had to shut down. Adler continued to work in the Jewish community.
During the pogrom of November 9, 1938 [*Reichskristallnacht*], he was
arrested. On his release he was forced to agree to cease all cultural activity
and assume the directorship of the *Jüdische Mittelstelle*, a welfare center
which, operating under the supervision of the Gestapo and the security
service (SD), was responsible for overseeing the emigration of Württemberg's Jews.

   Adler's new task was unimaginably difficult, especially as Jewish bank
accounts had been frozen by then, and most countries were unwilling to admit more German Jews.[31] In November 1938, with Adler still in prison, Hans
Walz had arranged for a middleman to bring Adler's wife a substantial sum
of money. Subsequently, Adler's work at the welfare center was supported by
regular payments from Robert Bosch GmbH. These were made in the strict-
est confidence and secrecy. The funds came from a company account named
Welfare II [*Wohlfahrtskonto II*]. The same account furnished aid to the group
around Leo Baeck, who was now a personal friend of Robert Bosch himself.
Other funds were transferred to a private account held by Robert Bosch at
the Amsterdam branch of the Mendelssohn & Co. Bank. Fritz Mannheimer,
the manager of Mendelssohn Amsterdam (and also closely acquainted with
Robert Bosch) regularly made substantial payments from this account to
Jewish aid committees in the Netherlands. The committees used the money
to support Jews who had left Germany, no doubt enabling many of them to

emigrate overseas. In all, some 300,000 Dutch guilders were withdrawn from this account.[32]

In Stuttgart, the Jewish welfare center was able to use the Bosch donations to fund relief actions that would not have been possible otherwise. The money was administered in a special secret fund at the *Mittelstelle*, which Adler used for assistance in particularly urgent cases.[33] Eventually, at the end of 1940, Adler himself was able to emigrate to America. Under his successor, Alfred Marx, it soon became impossible to carry out relief actions. In October 1941, Jewish emigration was finally prohibited, and only weeks later, on December 1, deportations began in Stuttgart.[34] In the years 1938–40, Bosch aided the emigration of persecuted and imprisoned Jews with a sum verging on 1.2 million reichsmarks all in all.[35]

Together with around a thousand other Württemberg Jews, in late November 1941 the Stuttgart industrial chemist Martha Haarburger was told to report to an assembly camp on Stuttgart's Killesberg for subsequent "evacuation" to the east (i. e., to the *Reichskommissariat Ostland*) – specifically to Riga (Latvia).[36] Haarburger may well have suspected what fate awaited such "evacuees." Few survived, in fact. Most died in mass shootings.[37] In her distress, she turned to Hans Walz.[38] Walz first had Haarburger admitted to the new Robert Bosch Hospital, where she was examined and declared unfit to travel. He then gave her a job in the Bosch research department. Again, Bühler's Gestapo contacts proved helpful (Bühler was the counter-intelligence officer).[39] Haarburger could be kept safe from deportation until 1943. Then the *Reichssicherheitshauptamt* [Reich Main Security Office] took up the Haarburger case. Walz and Bühler were summoned to Berlin. They tried to involve Gottlob Berger, the high-ranking SS officer (he was an *Obergruppenführer*) who had helped the Bosch circle repeatedly, but this cut no ice with Adolf Eichmann, who was in charge of Jewish affairs at the Reich Main Security Office. He gave orders for Haarburger to be deported on the next transport to Auschwitz. Walz managed at the last minute to have her assigned to a transport bound for Theresienstadt. As a result, Martha Haarburger was saved from certain death in the gas chamber, but her fate remained unclear. Of the approximately 140,000 internees held in the Theresienstadt concentration camp and ghetto, only some 17,000 lived to see the day of their release. Those who died there included Martha Haarburger's mother as well as the revered Stuttgart physician Marga Wolf, for whom Walz had intervened in vain. Wolf had been deported despite the company's having requested her services for the medical care of forced laborers. Martha Haarburger survived the war to head the Hippokrates publishing house founded by Robert Bosch.[40]

When Walz was arrested after the war, both Karl Adler (in the meantime a professor at Yeshiva University in New York) and Leo Baeck interceded on his behalf. Subsequently, Adler persuaded the Yad Vashem World Center for Holocaust Research in Jerusalem to award him the honorary title "Righteous Among The Nations." This was the highest honor that the state of Israel conferred on Gentiles, awarded exclusively to people who in the Third Reich had selflessly risked their lives to save Jews.[41] For Walz, resistance to Hitler was not the reason he had helped Jews. He had acted, he later told Karl Adler, "for the sake of justice and humanity."[42]

"Aryanizations": acquiring equity interests and real estate from Jewish ownership

Robert Bosch and Hans Walz were clear about what they thought of the "Aryanization" of companies and other assets from Jewish ownership. Both men were determined not to profit from it. According to Olpp, Robert Bosch said "he refused to enrich himself at the cost of the misfortune of Jews."[43] However, it was a different matter when it came to the question of how to react when offered real estate, companies, or equity interests by Jewish owners who urgently needed to sell but were having trouble finding a buyer who would pay them a fair price. In a number of instances, Bosch did acquire property formerly owned by Jews. And because they were subject to restitution after the war, such purchases are very well documented.

Two formerly Jewish-owned buildings acquired by Bosch were an apartment block with storage facilities at 8 Affalterstraße in Stuttgart-Feuerbach and business premises at 102a Büchsenstraße in the city itself. These were evidently sold to the company by common consent.[44] The files relating to postwar restitution also contain the names of Max and Otto Rosenfeld, proprietors of the cigar shop at 75 Rotebühlstraße where Robert Bosch had had his first workshop.[45] Robert Bosch AG had bought Max Rosenfeld's house at 63 Herdweg in July 1937. As later established by the Jewish Restitution Successor Organization (JRSO), there was no repossession involved here. The Rosenfelds had had to declare bankruptcy in 1926 and surrender title to their real estate to the Mendelssohn Bank in Amsterdam and to the Amsterdamsche Bank as collateral for loans. So in reality Bosch had purchased the building from Mendelssohn Amsterdam, the manager of which was Fritz Mannheimer, a close Stuttgart acquaintance of Robert Bosch and very likely also of the Rosenfelds.[46] In another case, a building at 35 Breitscheidstraße (formerly Militärstraße) was restored to Ilse Weinberg, *née* Rosenfeld, whose whole family had been killed in concentration camps. Robert Bosch GmbH had bought the house from the German government in January 1943. It had been stolen from its owners by the tax authorities.[47]

In June 1939, the Jewish industrialist Richard Heilner, former president of Deutsche Linoleumwerke, sold his villa at 94 Herdweg in Stuttgart to Robert Bosch GmbH for 385,000 reichsmarks. Heilner knew Robert Bosch well.[48] The money he was due to receive from the sale was confiscated by the authorities. In 1942, Heilner was deported to Theresienstadt. He survived the concentration camp and on his return to Stuttgart initiated restitution proceedings against Robert Bosch GmbH for aggravated dispossession. His attorneys maintained that the purchase price had been against good morals. And indeed, it had been lower than the price put on it by a 1939 valuation.[49] At Bosch, however, Alfred Knoerzer recalled that Heilner had approached him at the time and said that "he would rather have Bosch buy the property than someone else". When Knoerzer mentioned this to him, Heilner had no recollection of having said this. Unlike his legal team, however, he took the view that Robert Bosch GmbH had behaved correctly. He had not asked a higher price at the time for fear that, if he did, the authorities would not let the sale to Bosch go ahead.[50] In this restitution case too, then, a solution was reached in the form of a mutually agreed settlement.[51] In other cases of Bosch acquiring Jewish real estate during the National Socialist period, it has become impossible to establish the circumstances in which the purchases took place and whether a fair price was paid.[52] Nor can any precise details be given concerning the privately owned real estate purchased by the Bosch board member Hermann Fellmeth, who acquired two Jewish-owned buildings in Stuttgart.[53]

As early as the spring of 1934, two Jewish families, the Gutensteins and the Lerchenthals, sold their holdings in the publishing house Stuttgarter Zeitungsverlag to the Frankfurt banker Alwin Steffan. As majority owner of the publishing house, Robert Bosch had right of first refusal, but did not exercise it at the time. However, in November of that year he bought from Steffan the shares that the two families had sold to the banker. Why Steffan withdrew and whether he had simply purchased the Stuttgarter Zeitungsverlag holdings on Bosch's behalf can no longer be established.[54]

Through Reichskreditgesellschaft, a nationally owned major bank in Berlin, Bosch obtained two formerly Jewish-owned companies. In March 1937, on the recommendation of this bank, Bosch acquired the Berlin carpet company Feibisch & Co. AG (later known as Teppichwerke Berlin-Treptow).[55] The Jewish owners of the company urgently needed to emigrate. Following the occupation of Poland, Willy Schloßstein, the head of Robert Bosch's private secretariat, approached Reichskreditgesellschaft to inquire whether Feibisch & Co.

could acquire carpet companies in Lodz. In 1950, a settlement was reached between Bosch and the former proprietors of Teppichwerke Berlin-Treptow.[56] Reichskreditgesellschaft also negotiated the sale to Bosch of another company whose owners had to emigrate because of their Jewish origin: the Robert Koch jewelry business in Frankfurt am Main. After the war, Bosch sold the building in order to compensate the former owners.[57]

In 1938, Bosch's trust administration company Vermögensverwaltung Bosch GmbH (VVB) took over substantial Jewish-owned blocks of shares in two insurance companies, Victoria zu Berlin Allgemeine Versicherungs AG and Victoria Feuer-Versicherungs AG. According to Schloßstein's later account, a Jewish broker or banker drew VVB's attention to these holdings. As they consisted of registered shares, their origin was in no doubt.[58] According to Felix Olpp's very different account, the Jewish shareholders had appointed Kurt Hamann, the director of Victoria, as their fiduciary with instructions to find a buyer who was not a National Socialist. Hamann had sold the holdings to Bosch on condition that the shares should not be sold on, except in an emergency, and that they certainly should not be traded on the stock exchange.[59] Approximately 90 percent of these Victoria shares, worth a total face value of some 220,000 reichsmarks, were owned by the Jewish Landau family. After the war, members of the family filed restitution claims. They settled for the comparatively small sum of 10,000 reichsmarks. With regard to the other Jewish-owned Victoria shares, in 1951 the Jewish Restitution Successor Organization waived restitution claims against payment of 6,000 reichsmarks. The holding, which later rose steeply in value, remained with the Bosch heirs.[60]

On two occasions, Robert Bosch GmbH took over formerly Jewish-owned equity interests in companies that were then absorbed into the Bosch Group. These were Metallerzbergbau Westmark GmbH (1937) and the television company FESE (1938). Mention has already been made (see p. 162 above) of the circumstances of the former purchase, in so far as they can be reconstructed from the documents. After the war, Bosch settled with the former owners in return for payment of 50,000 German marks.[61] In the case of FESE, 37.5 percent of the share capital had been in the possession of Robert Bosch AG since the withdrawal of the British partner Baird Television Ltd. in 1935. Other major shareholders were Zeiss Ikon AG, also with 37.5 percent, and Radio AG D. S. Loewe (whose owner, Siegmund Loewe, was classified under the Nuremberg Laws as a "person of mixed blood, grade 1"), with a holding of 25 percent.[62] The Bosch Group representatives at FESE, Erich Carl Rassbach and Paul Goerz, were intent on ousting Radio AG D. S. Loewe from the television development company.[63] For them, it was clearly decisive that Loewe had been moving closer to the Bosch rival Telefunken since 1932. Goerz and Rassbach can hardly be accused of antisemitism (with the former having a "non-Aryan" spouse and the latter clinging to his American citizenship). However, there are reports that Goerz said several times that he would not work with a Jewish company.[64] He used the political situation to force Loewe into a corner. In November 1937, Loewe learned from Goerz that Bosch and Zeiss-Ikon were now determined "to squeeze our company out of Fernseh A. G."[65] The two major shareholders announced their intention of carrying out a 50 percent capital increase, bringing the total to 1.5 million reichsmarks. If Loewe refused to participate (as seemed likely, given its financial situation), FESE was to go into liquidation. Loewe protested against this attempt at blackmail, but had to bow out in the end. It sold its FESE holding to Bosch and Zeiss-Ikon, who took half each.[66] In this entire transaction, the Bosch Group representatives undoubtedly based their strategy on the political environment. As a "non-Aryan" company, Loewe was unlikely to be able to keep pace for much longer.[67] Goerz took advantage of Loewe's inability to defend himself as a result of the Nuremberg Laws. So here, there can be no question of any "Aryanization by consent."

After the war, Loewe-Opta AG filed restitution proceedings against Robert Bosch GmbH and FESE. However, these turned out to be more controversial and drawn-out than other such proceedings faced by Bosch.[68] In this case Bosch's legal counsel was Baron Reinhard von Godin. The baron doggedly contested the competence of the Berlin compensation authority, with the result that the dispute dragged on. The case was still unresolved as late as 1962, when Siegmund Loewe died. Not until the Loewe heirs had sold their company to Philips did a solution begin to emerge. Philips wished to end the legal battle, so on January 14, 1965, a settlement was reached, with Bosch agreeing to pay Loewe-Opta AG the sum of 1.5 million German marks.[69] This payment also concluded the only documented "Aryanization" case in which Robert Bosch GmbH acted against the will and interests of the seller.

4 Involvement in rearmament
and arms production in the Second World War

Bosch and rearmament

For the armaments planners at the *Heereswaffenamt* [Army Procurement Office] and the Air Ministry, Bosch was a company of central importance. There was no doubt in their minds that the war they were working toward would be decided by motorized ordnance. Rather than fight a war of attrition, as in the First World War, they were looking to capture extensive areas rapidly with fighter aircraft, tanks, and combined infantry and armor. The new mobile form of warfare called for high-performance engines with ignition systems that could be relied on.

As the market leader in automotive technology and one of the largest manufacturers of ignition systems for aircraft engines, Bosch was given arms contracts almost as a matter of course. The company had no need to solicit orders – but neither could it turn them down. The armed forces would never have tolerated the resultant shortfall in supply for air force and army. Refusal would in all likelihood have led to compulsory intervention by the national authorities, as happened in connection with the expropriated Junkers-Flug-zeugwerk AG.[1] This would likely also have meant that compulsory licensing and government loans would have been used to build up parallel production programs at Bosch's competitors. The Stuttgart company had no choice. It had to accept that the military authorities, which were already "inclined to look unfavorably on 'the monopolistic market position of Bosch'," might be prepared to "foist upon us as a second manufacturing operation some licensee whom we might find deeply embarrassing for reasons of product quality."[2] The Bosch board of management was determined to preserve the company's independence under all circumstances, and there was also, not unnaturally, much interest in preserving its market position over the long term. Robert Bosch himself may have taken an anti-war stance, but this did not mean that the board were going to rule out any involvement in the arms industry, particularly since in the early days of the National Socialist dictatorship no one expected Hitler's rule to last.[3] Contrary to what some sources reported later, Bosch's participation in the arms build-up assumed tangible form as early as the summer of 1934. That was when the company agreed to build Dreilindenwerk, a new plant to meet *Luftwaffe* needs.[4] Bosch's Berlin agency appointed a former department head at the Army Procurement Office, the retired major general Walter Knoblauch, to conduct the relevant negotiations with the authorities responsible for arms procurement.[5] Unlike in the First World War, Bosch seems to have refused to "have a hand in developing pure weapons technology such as electric detonators for bombs and other explosive devices, etc."[6] However, Bosch was not required to produce bomb detonators. Plenty of other companies could do that.

In general terms, it is virtually impossible to establish which of a supplier's products go into armaments and which do not. Certainly, the ignition systems for aircraft engines Bosch produced were purely for weapons use, and for these a separate subsidiary was formed: Dreilinden Maschinenbau GmbH (DLMG) in Kleinmachnow, near Berlin. Similarly, the subsidiary Elektro- und Feinmechanische Industrie GmbH (the later Trillke-Werke) was set up in Hildesheim a few years later to produce generators, starters, and ignition systems for army vehicles. The following account focuses on these two subsidiaries, for it is in this context that the conduct of the Bosch Group toward its military customers can best be understood. However, it is important to remember that Bosch carried out increasing numbers of army contracts in its home plants in Stuttgart. Until war broke out, most supplies for military use were in any case manufactured in Stuttgart. The new plants were still under construction.

Robert Bosch would have preferred to avoid building new plants for arms production. In his view, the work of constructing the Dreilinden plant, which initially went ahead without government funding, was a needless financial burden. In a letter written to the *Boschhof* manager Walther Mauk on December 22, 1933, he complained, "At the request of the War Ministry we are having to build a back-up factory in Berlin in case Stuttgart falls into enemy hands. It's going to cost some 3 million marks."[7] Building a plant in Hildesheim ran counter to his principle of producing only in places where a precision-engineering industry already existed. However, the founder was aware that there was no alternative to erecting new arms factories if his life's work was to survive. Consequently, the aforementioned letter to Mauk also pointed out that "I am prepared to make all kinds of sacrifices" and "first and foremost it benefits our associates that the plant should continue to exist."[8] And while attitudes toward the National Socialist regime grew more and more critical in the circle around Robert Bosch, the company's participation in arms production took on a momentum of its own. As preparations for war increased, the Bosch Group became steadily more involved in the arms economy. Once the fighting was under way, plants operated by Robert Bosch GmbH could only work to capacity if they produced for the armed forces. In 1940, 67 percent of sales were accounted for by contracts for the armed forces, 18.7 percent related to "civilian supplies important to the war effort," and the remaining 14.3 percent went abroad.[9] In the case of army contracts, the vast majority of supplies went to other companies – Daimler-Benz, for instance – rather than directly to military agencies and other authorities.[10]

The members of the Bosch board of management were aware of the disadvantages of relying so heavily on a single source of demand – namely, the military. They rejected mounting government regulation in the context of the war economy, convinced that without the arms build-up and the war the company would have developed "better and more soundly," as Walz put it in his Feuerbach address of July 1943.[11] However, Bosch had no alternative.

Emergence and early years of Dreilinden Maschinenbau GmbH

Bosch had built ignition devices for several manufacturers of aircraft engines, including BMW, as early as the time of the First World War.[12] As civil aviation emerged in Germany in the 1920s, this line of business was developed further. In the context of the secret arms build-up that took place during the Weimar Republic, aircraft ignition systems were also manufactured for the military.[13] Following the assumption of power by the National Socialists, the newly established Air Ministry ordered Bosch to build a back-up plant [*Ausweichwerk*] near Berlin for the manufacture of ignition systems and other electrical equipment for aircraft.[14] Because of its proximity to France, Stuttgart was deemed particularly at risk in the event of war. The Berlin region, however, was already home to a number of aircraft-engine plants, and the intention was to create an air force hub there.[15] At the talks with the Air Ministry that began in the spring of 1934, Bosch was represented by the deputy board member Erich Rassbach and the retired major general Walter Knoblauch.[16]

The agreement to set up a back-up plant was signed as early as August 16 and September 3, 1934. In it, Bosch undertook to erect such a plant near Berlin within seven months for the purpose of manufacturing magnetos, starters, and generators for aircraft engines as well as other aircraft-engine equipment previously produced in Stuttgart. The company expressed readiness to fund the project from its own resources and have the Air Ministry supervise construction.[17] The site had already been decided: a wooded plot covering approximately 10 hectares in Kleinmachnow, just beyond the Berlin city limits. Since the location lay within the forest district of Dreilinden, the name Dreilinden was given to the new plant.[18] Construction of the back-up plant was not exactly welcomed at Bosch. However, there is no indication that the company opposed the project, let alone an extension of its manufacturing operations for *Luftwaffe* purposes. It was customary at the time, in connection with such capital expenditure, for the government to relieve companies of any financial risk, and not even Bosch declined the opportunity to hedge the risk. After all, the new plant would be wholly dependent on the arms economy. The Air Ministry said it was prepared to make a "fair settlement" should it fail to exploit capacity to the full.[19]

The Bosch management had previously avoided building plants outside the Stuttgart region, particularly since there were few other locations where a similarly extensive pool of suitable employees was already present. But in Berlin it very definitely was, so the company likely had little difficulty in agreeing to the location suggested. Berlin at the time was the undisputed capital of the electrical-engineering industry in Germany.[20] Furthermore, having taken over Ideal-Werke (later Blaupunkt), Bosch already had a subsidiary in Berlin. This company could supply the new plant in Dreilinden, and the new connection would be to its advantage. However, were the arms boom to continue, the location would inevitably become problematic. In such a case, given the high concentration of electrical-engineering companies in Berlin, the labor market would be drained.

On October 8, 1934, a meeting was held at the Air Ministry to outline a construction plan for the Dreilinden plant. The ministry put forward a draft based entirely on protection against possible air raids. Like many Third Reich arms factories, the new plant was to be built in woodland and comprise a number of smallish buildings that "from the air would look more like a housing development."[21] Bosch was reluctant to accept the Air Ministry's architectural suggestions, deeming the construction of several "miniature facilities" scattered among trees to be "totally uneconomical."[22] The company's representatives eventually held out for a few larger assembly shops, but basically the Air Ministry got its way. It was hardly a harmonious construction project, but the clashes were not due to any underlying stratagem of delay on Bosch's part.[23] Dreilindenwerk duly went into operation in August 1935.[24] The new plant was headed by Paul Vogelsang, the former commercial manager of the Feuerbach Metallwerk, and the engineer Heinrich Walchenbach.[25] A core of associates from Stuttgart accompanied them to Kleinmachnow. The start-up phase was concluded in December 1936 when the plant was spun off as a close corporation or private limited company. Vogelsang and Walchenbach became man-

Dreilinden Maschinenbau GmbH, Kleinmachnow, near Berlin

aging directors of the new Dreilinden Maschinenbau GmbH (DLMG). In the articles of association dated December 8, 1936, Bosch transferred capital stock of 5 million reichsmarks and the plant premises in Kleinmachnow to the new subsidiary.

While Dreilinden was in its start-up phase, the Third Reich's drive to create an air force assumed entirely new dimensions. Clandestine at first, in 1935 the *Luftwaffe* threw off its disguise. Thanks to an ambitious program (known as "IRG 38"), it was to achieve "war readiness" within only a few years. For building aircraft engines alone, the plan was to employ 60,000 persons.[26] In February 1937, a mere three months after the establishment of DLMG, a new Daimler-Benz aircraft-engine plant at Genshagen went into production. This plant was within 10 miles of Kleinmachnow. Aircraft-engine production also underwent substantial expansion at Brandenburgische Motorenwerke in the Berlin suburb of Spandau, which lay within 20 miles of Kleinmachnow. The government had taken over this company from Siemens and sold it to BMW in 1939. And there were other aircraft-engine plants in the Berlin region. This very rapid growth in capacity of the industry (not only around Berlin) called for correspondingly large production increases on the part of suppliers.

This was all the more true for Bosch, since it had come up with an important technical innovation in 1937. In some seven years of development work, the company had created a gasoline injection system for aircraft engines and readied it for production. Aircraft engines with gasoline direct injection boasted greater performance and were safer than conventional carburetor engines. So direct injection soon became the predominant technology employed in Germany. Bosch had developed gasoline direct injection in conjunction with Daimler-Benz AG, and from November 1937 the first mass-produced aircraft engine to use gasoline injection, the DB 601, came off the production lines at the Daimler-Benz plants in Genshagen and Berlin-Marienfelde.[27] Since the Bosch subsidiary at Kleinmachnow produced the injection pumps and injection lines for Daimler-Benz 600 series aircraft engines, its importance to the Air Ministry was now even greater.[28]

Table 13 Sales of DLMG (1937–41)[29]

Year	1937	1938	1939	1940	1941
RM (millions)	13.5	15.4	27.1	44.0	66.6

It was not long before DLMG received fresh manufacturing targets that far surpassed its physical capacity.[30] The company now needed additional premises, new machine tools, and a dramatically increased workforce. However, by now there were few suitable workers left in the Berlin labor market. Production also remained dependent on supplies from Stuttgart.[31] Even when war broke out, DLMG was still unable to meet the Air Ministry's supply demands. A major row ensued. Erich Carl Rassbach and Hermann Bauer were summoned to the ministry, where they were met by an irate Wolfram Eisenlohr, head of the Air Armament Trials Center. According to Bauer's account, Eisenlohr made no bones about the possible consequences for Bosch: "This is tantamount to sabotage! I'll give you six months. If the plant is not fulfilling its targets by then, there'll be trouble."[32] Protesting that Bosch was being accused of "bad faith," Bauer said he was prepared to have a task force of engineers, technicians, and 100 workers sent to Kleinmachnow from Stuttgart immediately.[33] Bosch launched a massive expansion program for Dreilinden. This was chiefly financed by government loans.[34] All in all, the number of aircraft magnetos and special magnetos produced by the Bosch Group rose more than tenfold in the period 1933–40 – from 4,335 to 48,230.[35] In gasoline direct-injection pumps for aircraft engines, the Bosch Group had a market share of some 35 percent. In total, between 1937 and 1945 Bosch and DLMG manufactured around 148,000 of these direct-injection pumps. Apart from the V-12 engines of the Daimler-Benz 600 series, BMW aircraft engines were also fitted with Bosch injection technology. In 1941, BMW switched to Deckel injection pumps for its aircraft engines. Junkers equipped its aircraft engines with its own injection systems.[36]

Building the Dreilinden plant brought another Bosch subsidiary into the Air Ministry's sights. This was Ideal-Werke (later renamed Blaupunkt). Back in the summer of 1935, talks had begun concerning a "second domestic plant belonging to Bosch" – with clear reference to Dreilinden. This second plant was to be constructed in the vicinity of the new Ideal-Werke site in Berlin-Wilmersdorf.[37] As with Dreilinden, the parties disagreed over the architectural plans. The Bosch Group representatives, Goerz and Knoblauch, reached an understanding with the Air Ministry that they should wait "until the Dreilinden capacity question is sorted out."[38] Clearly, this was about working in conjunction with Dreilinden to supply aircraft electrics for *Luftwaffe* needs – in the area of radio technology, for instance. Following proclamation of the Four-Year Plan, the accelerated pace of the arms build-up allowed for no further delay. Ideal-Werke built an additional plant in Berlin-Kreuzberg, which went into production in 1938.[39] The Dreilinden link became crucial for Blaupunkt when the radio-set market collapsed with the outbreak of war. However, the company also benefited from this development over the long term. For the radio-set manufacturer Blaupunkt, aircraft electrics offered an entry into the production of high-frequency instruments and hence into an area in which significant technological advances were made during the war.[40]

From Elektro- und Feinmechanische Industrie GmbH to Trillke-Werke GmbH

The accelerating arms build-up under the Four-Year Plan also brought an increase in the army's requirements for Bosch products. In the spring of 1937, the Army Procurement Office insisted that an additional back-up plant be built for the purpose of securing supplies of electrical-engineering equipment for the army's automobiles, trucks, high speed tractors, and tanks.[41] Air raids were too big a risk for manufacturing of these items to remain concentrated in Stuttgart. Moreover, in the company's home plants shortages of labor and space made further expansion of capacity impossible. Yet from June 1937, the Army Procurement Office expected a tripling of the previously anticipated requirement for generators, ignition systems, and other kinds of automotive electrical equipment.[42] As to location, all that Bosch had been told by the people responsible for armaments planning was this: the new plant must be built east of the River Weser and north of a line between Kassel and Leipzig.[43] Unlike DLMG, this plant did not come into being as part of a regional network of customers and suppliers. The search for a suitable site was thus a lengthy one, which began in the spring of 1937. According to Manfred Overesch, a total of nearly 20 sites in northern Germany were considered. Finally, at a meeting held in Stuttgart on October 17, 1937, the choice fell on Hildesheim.[44] The project held little appeal for the Bosch board of management. After the war, Otto Debatin wrote that Bosch was "dead against" the idea of building this plant.[45] The relevant minutes that survive from 1937–38 contain no evidence of this.[46] However, the Stuttgart camp did have reservations about the Hildesheim location, since there was no local precision-engineering or electrical-engineering industry. Stuttgart, apparently, took the view that the local workforce was made up "solely of blacksmiths."[47] Development of the new plant was financed differently than had been the case with DLMG. Under the "Montan-Schema," the army would commission a private-sector company under a joint framework agreement to build an arms factory at government expense. That plant would then belong to an army-owned limited-liability company named Verwertungsgesellschaft für Montaninteressen GmbH (subsequently referred to as Montan GmbH). Under a further agreement, the plant would be leased by Montan GmbH either to the private-sector company originally commissioned or to a sales company set up by the latter. The lessee undertook to furnish the manufacturing facility with the appropriate expertise and oversee its operations. Under the "Montan-Schema" the government removed all economic risk from the company's shoulders. It could then ask it to produce items that were necessary to the war effort but were otherwise non-essential or uneconomical.[48]

The new plant in Hildesheim was planned from the outset to be an army-owned operation developed on the "Montan-Schema" model.[49] However, the joint framework agreement with the Army Supreme Command was concluded only on November 2/December 20, 1938.[50] A year earlier, on December 18, 1937, Bosch had established a subsidiary to operate the plant, namely Elektro- und Feinmechanische Industrie GmbH (ELFI). Headquartered in Hildesheim and furnished with capital stock of 50,000 reichsmarks, ELFI began leasing the plant site and equipment in November 1938 from the army-owned Montan GmbH.[51] Two heads of department from the Stuttgart home plant – Max Clostermeyer and Hermann Bauer – were appointed managing directors of ELFI. A short time later, Bauer was replaced by Carl Martin Dolezalek, who then became technical director of the plant, while Clostermeyer remained commercial director.[52] Like Dreilinden, the new plant in

Hildesheim was built in a wooded area to protect it from air raids. For this purpose, Montan GmbH was able to purchase from the city of Hildesheim an approximately 42-hectare plot on a wooded ridge about 7.5 kilometers from the city center. Bosch was able to get most of its own architectural ideas accepted. The industrial part was designed on the basis of plans drawn up in Stuttgart, both in regard to the requirements of manufacturing technology and in regard to style. By 1942 an office and communal-facilities block had been completed as well as five large sheds, covering a total built-up area of some 28,000 square meters.[53] The plant management was more than happy with the result. Dolezalek even thought the red-brick buildings in the forest outside Hildesheim made up "one of the loveliest industrial complexes ever built."[54] Recruitment remained a central problem, however. As technicians from Hildesheim's artisanal labor force were not going to be sufficient to meet the new factory's needs, an apprentice workshop and a retraining department were opened in downtown Hildesheim.[55] In November 1938, ELFI had only 68 associates – 12 of them apprentices. By the end of 1939, headcount had risen to 534, including 35 apprentices.[56] Most of the newly appointed associates had been assigned to the plant by the employment office, having been transferred from industries of lesser importance to the war effort.[57] The number of NSDAP members was higher among male associates, but lower overall than in the parent company.[58]

On the outbreak of war, ELFI was supplying only Bosch plants in Stuttgart and Feuerbach, where its components were then assembled into systems. Not until the autumn of 1942, four years after the laying of the foundation stone, was construction of the Hildesheim plant finally completed.[59] In the meantime, the manufacturing plan originally agreed had become obsolete. As early as January 31, 1940, Clostermeyer visited Stuttgart to ask for fresh specifications more appropriate to wartime requirements. At Bosch – not at the Army Procurement Office – the manufacturing plan was now changed. ELFI was in the future "to restrict itself to equipment needed for [the engines of] special army vehicles (armored cars, high speed tractors, radio cars, and the like)."[60] Not many months later the Army Procurement Office was urging accelerated manufacturing for "rapid-response units."[61] In a subsequent phase of construction, the Hildesheim plant was specifically adapted to produce generators, electric starters, inertia starters, and magnetos for tanks, tracked artillery prime movers, and heavy trucks. Orders for these products increased substantially following the attack on the Soviet Union.[62] On December 23, 1942, ELFI was renamed, having repeatedly been confused with similar-sounding companies and makes.[63] From then on it was named Trillke-Werke GmbH for a small stream, the Trillkebach, that flowed nearby.[64]

As a result of the "Adolf Hitler Tank Program" of 1943, production at Trillke-Werke underwent a further boost. All new "Panther" and "Tiger" combat tanks were fitted with Bosch ignition systems, electric starters, generators, and headlights. At the same time, Bosch continued to make generators and starters for the Class IV tank. The Hildesheim plant now gained additional strategic importance. To achieve higher volumes, manufacturing of electrical equipment for tanks was concentrated on one site. Stuttgart was out of the question because of the air-raid risk. So in 1943 much of the machinery in the Feuerbach light works was moved to Hildesheim, including the special machines used to make electrical equipment for tank regiments. Trillke-Werke GmbH was now the sole manufacturer of electrical equipment for the army's tanks.[65] Unlike the plants in Stuttgart and Feuerbach, and thanks to the cover provided by the Hildesheim Forest, Trillke-Werke remained undamaged until the war's end.

Concealing operations outside Germany

After the experience of the First World War, Robert Bosch felt it advisable to transfer his company's operations outside Germany to non-German ownership. That way, should war break out again, they could not be confiscated as German assets. Initially, the acquiring entities were companies in Switzerland and the Netherlands that formed part of the Bosch Group without this being apparent to people from outside the company. Later, the Bosch subsidiaries outside Germany were sold to banks in the Netherlands and Sweden. These were "concealed" or disguised purchases in that Robert Bosch GmbH was secretly granted a right of repurchase. To understand these highly complex transactions, which can only be outlined briefly here, it is necessary to cast a quick eye over the distribution of Bosch's assets outside Germany before 1936.

In 1930, Bosch transferred its holdings in the non-German subsidiaries set up in Scandinavia, Belgium, Spain, and Argentina after the First World War to Industria Kontor AG, a newly-established Swiss holding company.[66] A second Bosch Group holding company was set up in Switzerland a year later. This was Robertina AG, which took over a share package from Robert Bosch AG and operated as a sort of foreign-exchange institute for the non-German subsidiaries.[67] The two Swiss companies also took over a share package from Bosch's holdings (which totaled some 82 percent) in United American Bosch Corporation (UABC), subsequently renamed American Bosch Corporation (ABC). Bosch's remaining UABC shares were in the hands of N. V. Administratiekontoor voor Internationale Belegging (Nakib), an Amsterdam holding company that Bosch had taken over following the collapse of Danatbank in 1931, as well as in the hands of the Amsterdam subsidiary of the Mendelssohn Bank and of the Stuttgart company Eisemann.[68]

With the risk of a new war looming, Walz and Bosch decided to hand the company's European non-German subsidiaries over to Mendelssohn in Amsterdam as well. It is clear from a note written later by Bosch's private secretary, Schloßstein, that this decision was taken in October 1936. This was after Walz had attended a meeting in Berlin at which leading representatives of German industry had been instructed by Hermann Göring to borrow against their companies' non-German assets and make the resultant foreign exchange available to the German government.[69] The board of management of Robert Bosch AG agreed that the non-German subsidiaries should now "be sold off properly and rendered wholly independent of Germany in terms of equity as well as politically, with the foreign exchange generated being handed over to the Reichsbank." If war did occur, they felt there would be less risk of confiscation, and "once all risk of war had passed, suitable ways would have to be found to recover the holdings."[70]

Fritz Mannheimer, the head of the Mendelssohn subsidiary in Amsterdam, agreed to include a secret additional clause granting Bosch right of repurchase of the blocks of shares the bank had acquired. On April 6 and 7, 1937, the agreement between Bosch and Mendelssohn was signed. The bank paid Bosch 3.88 million Dutch guilders (5.29 million reichsmarks) for the non-German subsidiaries and took over Nakib as the holding company for them. Of the purchase price, some 2.7 million Dutch guilders in foreign exchange went to the Reichsbank, which showed its appreciation with a bonus of 500,000 reichsmarks. Mannheimer received 100,000 U.S. dollars from Bosch as his commission fee.[71] Robert Bosch AG had good business relations with Mendelssohn & Co. in Berlin, then Germany's largest private bank, as well as with its Amsterdam subsidiary.[72] Between Robert Bosch and Fritz Mannheimer, there was also a personal connection. The banker had grown up in Stuttgart, close to the Bosch manufacturing facilities and headquarters. During the 1920s, Mannheimer had amassed a huge fortune as a result of some high-risk speculative transactions.[73] At Bosch, of course, a very different business style was cultivated. Mannheimer nonetheless enjoyed the trust of Robert Bosch and Hans Walz. He had repeatedly done Bosch good service, notably in connection with the activities leading to the purchase of ABMC, the predecessor company of UABC.[74]

On August 9, 1939, in circumstances that have never been satisfactorily revealed, Fritz Mannheimer died at his villa near Paris. He had run up large debts, and his lavish lifestyle was evidently financed partly by the capital of the bank. After he had failed to place two loans for the French government, Mendelssohn's Amsterdam subsidiary became insolvent. The day after Mannheimer's death, the bank filed for bankruptcy.[75] According to a report by the company's legal adviser Karl Eugen Thomä, the fateful news from Amsterdam "fell like a bolt from the blue" at Bosch.[76] After all, nearly all the attempts to conceal the Bosch Group's non-German subsidiaries rested on agreements with Mannheimer or with Mendelssohn Amsterdam. When war broke out, however, the bank's collapse turned out to be to Bosch's advantage in at least one respect. The Dutch courts, investigating the books and ledgers of Mendelssohn Amsterdam, were able to confirm that Bosch had sold off its holdings outside Germany. The non-German subsidiaries were subsequently removed from the Allies' black lists.[77] Of course, this was possible only because the secret repurchase clause remained undiscovered.

At Bosch, there now began a frantic search for a buyer for the non-German subsidiaries that had hitherto been parked in Amsterdam. With Waldemar von Oppenheim (the owner of the Sal. Oppenheim bank in Cologne) acting as intermediary, the Stockholms Enskilda Bank (SEB), Scandinavia's largest financial institute, was persuaded to look at the deal. It proved fruitful in this connection that Carl Goerdeler had strong links with the Wallenberg family, who owned SEB. He also managed to obtain the consent of Walther Funk, Germany's Minister of Economic Affairs, to the projected transaction.[78] As early as December 5, 1939, Bosch and SEB reached agreement regarding the takeover of eight non-German subsidiaries. A few days later, a holding company set up by SEB, A.B. Planeten, purchased those non-German subsidiaries from the bankrupt estate of the Amsterdam branch of the Mendelssohn Bank for the equivalent of some 2.3 million reichsmarks. Subsequently, Industria Kontor AG, Robertina AG, and two other holding companies were transferred to A.B. Planeten. A secret additional agreement to the bill of sale entitled Bosch to repurchase the holdings taken over by SEB or A.B. Planeten.[79] In return, Bosch enabled SEB to cede German securities with a face value of some 1.3 million U.S. dollars to Deutsche Golddiskontbank without making any loss. It did this by paying the price differential to its Swedish business partner.[80] In July 1940, following lengthy negotiations, the SEB Group also acquired the shares in Bosch's U.S. company (now trading as American Bosch Corporation or ABC). It paid some 2.94 million U.S. dollars (7.35 million reichsmarks) for the shares, which had previously been held in Amsterdam by Nakib, and represented 77.2 percent of ABC's capital stock. As with the European non-German companies, SEB granted Robert Bosch GmbH a right of repurchase in this case as well. In return, with a further additional payment

Bosch bought from SEB German securities worth a nominal 3.6 million U.S. dollars.[81] Not all the non-German holdings in the hands of Nakib in Amsterdam were acquired by the SEB Group. Paris now being under German occupation, the Lavalette holding was repurchased by Bosch. So were the two Bosch companies in Prague and the shares in MABO in Milan.[82] In all, 13 non-German Bosch companies passed into the hands of the SEB Group.[83] The fact that Bosch consigned these companies to Swedish ownership despite Hitler dominating most of Europe says a great deal about the expectations of Bosch management at the time. Clearly they did not expect a swift end to the war, nor a certain Axis victory.

When the United States entered the war on December 8, 1941, SEB came under pressure for having bought shares in ABC. The U.S. authorities assumed that the bills of sale were simply concealment and that in reality ABC was still controlled by Bosch. When they tried to obtain further information about the ABC transactions from Sweden's Riksbank and from SEB, the Wallenbergs denied that a repurchase option existed.[84] Even so, the structure of previous years was now too awkward for them. SEB urged Stuttgart to cancel the secret additional agreement. Accordingly, by April 1942 the arrangement had been changed in such a way that Bosch no longer had an option to repurchase its majority stake in ABC.[85] In the meantime, the American authorities had made further inquiries. The ABC case had high priority for the U.S., since military interests were also involved. If it was a Swedish company, ABC could not be used for equipping the American armed forces. However, as a confiscated enemy asset it could. The U.S. Department of Justice soon had unambiguous evidence of a close link between Bosch and ABC.[86] In contrast to SEB, the American authorities were clearly in the driving seat here. Not only could they lean on the ABC head office in New York and the plant in Springfield. They could also exert pressure on the bank where the ABC shares were deposited – namely, the New York Trust Co.[87] On May 18, 1942, despite all the protestations of SEB and the Swedish government, the U.S. government confiscated ABC as an enemy asset and handed it over to the Office of Alien Property Custodian to administer.[88]

SEB was now determined to ditch the Bosch non-German companies.[89] However, the relevant transactions were not completed until August 1943. Bosch bought back the non-German holdings through a company owned by two directors of the Swedish Bosch subsidiary Robo.[90] Since SEB was coming under heavy pressure from across the Atlantic to sell its ABC shares to an American buyer, Bosch was keen to repurchase these certificates, too, although they were no longer covered by a repurchase option. On May 19, 1943, Carl Goerdeler informed Jacob Wallenberg that Bosch had placed the amount needed to repurchase ABC with a Swiss bank, Basler Handelsbank. The amount was in foreign currency plus some 5.7 million Swiss francs in gold. Goerdeler, Knoerzer, and Thomä had successfully negotiated with the Reichsbank for Bosch to buy this gold, claiming that it was to be used as collateral for a loan from the Swiss bank to SEB.[91] However, at the time the Reichsbank had very few gold reserves left from the period before 1938. The vast majority of the gold in its vaults came from the central banks of occupied countries that had been plundered in defiance of international law or from the confiscation of private assets and other sanctions imposed by the National Socialist regime. From July 1943 there was also the gold robbed by the SS from its concentration-camp victims and recast at Degussa.[92] The provenance of the gold that Bosch bought from the Reichsbank in March 1943 can no longer be established. However, in all probability it was not gold that the Reichsbank had acquired legitimately. It is possible, though not certain, that people at Bosch knew where the Reichsbank had sourced its gold. Goerdeler at least, given his international contacts, may well have had information in this regard.[93] Wallenberg soon sensed to his alarm that this might be suspect gold. In December 1943, he made enquiries regarding where the gold came from. His recommendation was that the ingots should be sold and bonds bought instead.[94] Six months later, Basler Handelsbank sold the "Bosch gold" to Schweizerische Nationalbank. With the proceeds, Bosch bought respectable Swiss-government bonds and Swiss medium-term bonds.[95]

In any case, given the way the war was going the projected repurchase of the ABC shares can only have been about minimizing SEB's losses. Since its confiscation, ABC had been a U.S. corporation, and there could be no doubt it would stay that way. The former Bosch subsidiary was playing an important role in American war production. In each of the years 1943, 1944, and 1945, ABC received excellence awards from both army and navy.[96] For SEB, the end result of its dealings with Bosch was deeply disappointing. The bank had to write off the ABC shares it had acquired. In America, ABC remained confiscated alien property. It was expropriated, and in 1948 it was sold to the investment company Arma. The accounts of SEB were frozen by the U.S. authorities and Jacob and Marcus Wallenberg arraigned as collaborators.[97] Bosch had failed in its attempt to conceal its non-German holdings. The belief that the non-German companies could be preserved from seizure by being sold in neutral countries with a repurchase clause proved to be a false hope. To all extents and purposes, ABC had been lost as early as 1942. The non-German companies parked in Sweden with Robo were later seized. So was the holding in Ateliers Lavalette. The assets in Switzerland were frozen.

For the second time within three decades, Bosch had lost its entire international portfolio.

Integration into Germany's wartime economy

After the war began, there was increasing pressure on Bosch to find suitable workers and locations for larger and larger military orders. This was particularly true with regard to manufacture of aircraft-engine parts and related equipment. DLMG in Kleinmachnow was unable to keep pace with the new Air Ministry targets. So in addition to Blaupunkt, another Bosch subsidiary, Junkers & Co. GmbH, began producing goods for DLMG in Dessau.[98] Moreover, two new plants constructed in Germany in 1939 and 1940 were directed to support the efforts of the air force.

The Bosch board of management had decided to build these two new plants (in Crailsheim and in Renningen) just before the war. They were originally intended to supply the civilian automotive market.[99] The company had begun building the Crailsheim plant in the spring of 1939, opening an apprentice and retraining workshop.[100] However, the hopes associated with it locally were soon dampened. A major development had been planned, but this was suspended. War was expected to break out imminently, and the project was deferred for the duration.[101] Building a new plant for the civilian automotive market no longer made sense. Apart from the apprentice and retraining workshop, all that came into existence in Crailsheim was an offshoot of the Bosch plant in Stuttgart, which then operated to meet military requirements.[102]

Instead, from about mid-1939 Bosch looked for a location where additional manufacturing capacity to meet Air Ministry orders could be erected quickly. It was found in Bamberg, where on September 29, 1939, Bosch was able to take over the premises of the former Stadler metal-goods factory. In February 1941, the new facility (called "Außenwerk 1") began producing spark plugs for aircraft engines.[103] Even though new premises had been erected on the former Stadler site, production at Bamberg soon reached capacity. Parts of production had to be relocated to disused weaving mills in Zeil and Forchheim. Headcount at the Bamberg plant rose from 580 in December 1940 to 3,116 in December 1944.[104] To keep its existence concealed, the plant was renamed "Opus GmbH" on May 1, 1944.[105]

Bosch built a further "branch operation" in Alsace in the autumn of 1940. After the capitulation of France, Alsace had been placed under German civil administration and effectively annexed. The border had not been

Reichsberufswettbewerb [Reich vocational competition] at Bosch (1940)

redrawn by peace treaty, so under international law the region still belonged to France. Nonetheless, Alsatian companies whose proprietors lived in or had taken refuge in other parts of France were seized by the German authorities. One of those companies was Manurhin (Manufacture de Machines du Haut-Rhin) in Bourtzwiller (or Burzweiler as the Germans called it), a suburb of Mulhouse (which had now been rechristened Mülhausen).[106] Having reported interest in Manurhin as early as the summer of 1940, Bosch was able to move into the plant in September of that year.[107] Sundgau Maschinenbau GmbH, a subsidiary of Robert Bosch GmbH founded on October 7, 1940, rented the Manurhin plant. Purchase was impossible, since transfers of ownership were to occur only following a peace treaty with France. However, Sundgau Maschinenbau GmbH was granted right of first refusal.[108]

Bosch was by no means the only German company expanding into Alsace during these years. For instance, a branch of Manurhin was taken over by Deutsche Waffen- und Munitionsfabriken AG, part of the Quandt Group.[109] It was easier to find qualified labor in Alsace than in pre-1938 Germany. And most Alsatians spoke and understood German. However, investments in Alsace made sense only on the assumption that the Third Reich was going to win the war. Only then would the region become part of Germany. The establishment of this new plant in occupied Alsace thus stood in stark contrast to Robert Bosch's commitment to Franco-German entente. Here was a case where the company ranked its own principles below the priorities of the war economy. Hoping to relieve some of the burden on DLMG, Bosch set up a special production line for gasoline injection pumps at Sundgau Maschinenbau GmbH. However, the shortage of building materials meant that extension of the plant could not be completed until 1943.[110] In contrast to all other Bosch Group locations, the Mulhouse plant was able to go on operating with the original workforce until the autumn of 1943, since it was only then that Alsatians could be drafted into the German armed forces.[111]

Following the occupation of France, Bosch also became majority owner of Ateliers de Construction Lavalette in St. Ouen, near Paris. The company had never entirely given up the Lavalette shares it had held since 1928. It had only assigned them to Nakib in Amsterdam, with a secret repurchase option.[112] Now, besides buying back its former holding in Lavalette, Bosch also took over a majority share in the company and reinstalled Friedrich Gönnenwein as manager. Manufacturing operations hardly changed. Before occupation, Lavalette had filled orders for the French army. Now it did so for the *Wehrmacht*.[113]

The Manurhin production facility in Mulhouse-Bourtzwiller was the only new plant in German-occupied areas that Bosch took over. After the war, Walz claimed that he and his colleagues had not wished to profit from the occupation.[114] The fact is that Bosch cannot have had any interest in further expansion, since the existing network of its non-German companies already covered the "Greater Germany" of the Third Reich quite adequately. In France, any takeovers would only have competed with Bosch's own subsidiary, Lavalette. Moreover, Bosch had long had subsidiaries of its own in Belgium, the Netherlands, and Denmark. The fact that Bosch constructed no new plants in the occupied areas of eastern Europe no doubt had to do with the company's specific location requirements. But Bosch had already invested heavily in setting up new plants in Kleinmachnow, Hildesheim, Bamberg, and Mulhouse. It also needed to make financial provisions to repurchase its concealed non-German subsidiaries, notably ABC in the United States. It was here, rather than in the East, that the company had vital interests at stake. Even so, the Bosch Service franchise was already represented in the East. It existed in occupied Poland, and it was present in the Protectorate of Bohemia and Moravia. In the Baltic countries and the occupied areas of the Soviet Union, new Bosch Service operations were set up to service German army vehicles – the so-called BDK-Werke ["Bosch Service K plants"] that sprang up in Riga, Tallinn, Vilnius, Minsk, and elsewhere.[115] Bosch associates who were employed in the BDK-Werke or traveled there for inspection purposes will certainly have learned of the crimes that the SS and the *Wehrmacht* committed in those regions. Whether they passed on such information back to Stuttgart cannot, of course, be proved. If they had, they would have done so behind closed doors.

As arms orders increased, Robert Bosch GmbH sales also went up, growing by some 70 percent over the course of the war. However, headcount (excluding subsidiaries) rose by only some 6 percent between 1939 and 1943.[116] The only reason why the drafting into the army of some 6,100 blue- and white-collar associates did not bring about a complete breakdown was the enlistment of foreign forced labor and temporary workers at the new locations.[117] As a result of the growing number of subsidiaries and their rapidly growing output of armaments, Bosch Group headcount rose by some 36 percent between 1940 and 1943.[118] The percentage of export business in the sales of Robert Bosch GmbH fell (as it had in the First World War) to a new low. It even dipped below 10 percent in 1939 and 1941.[119]

Table 14 Bosch Group headcount (1940–44)[120]

Year	1940	1941	1943	end of 1944
Headcount	33,700	39,600	46,000	39,963

At the subsidiary company Blaupunkt, 84 percent of its 1941 sales were already accounted for by armaments orders.[121] Blaupunkt now played an important role in high-frequency research. It developed apparatus for the army such as the "Korfu" radiolocation device, and as a member of the "Rotterdam Association" it undertook radar research.[122] After it was damaged by an air raid at the beginning of March 1943, parts of the production and the development department of the Blaupunkt plant in Berlin-Wilmersdorf were moved to Reichenberg, in what was now called *Sudetengau* ["Sudeten district"]. Further relocations to Munich and Vienna followed. Subsequently, headcount rose from 1,426 in June 1943 to some 3,800 in April 1945. Sales went up by 55 percent in the 1944 fiscal year.[123]

Blaupunkt's sister company FESE was actually even more deeply involved in developing new technologies and devices for the armed forces. Among these were high-resolution television images for air reconnaissance.[124] FESE was commissioned by the German post office to develop a "seeing bomb" – an electronic weapon that would enable German bomber squadrons to hit targets from a long distance by remote control, using a television image.[125] These armaments contracts from the national post office helped FESE to catch up with its rival Telefunken in television technology.[126] In automotive technology, the Bosch Group was the market leader, but not in television. This sort of thing thus improved its competitive position in relation to companies such as Telefunken. To protect its plant from air raids, in 1943 FESE was moved to Tanvald (Tannwald in German) in northern Bohemia and later to Taufkirchen in Bavaria. Meanwhile the *Luftwaffe*, trialing its "seeing bomb" in Peenemünde, realized that the technology was not ready for deployment. The project benefited FESE nonetheless. From 1943, it was able to mass-produce two devices developed for the glide bomb: the "Tonne" television camera and the "Seedorf" universal receiver.[127] However, FESE's triumphs brought problems for Bosch. The Air Ministry decided it wanted a slice of the television subsidiary. When Bosch refused, a serious clash resulted. In the end, the Air Ministry was obliged to abandon its ambitions to own part of FESE, as Bosch received support from two members of the government: not only from Wilhelm Ohnesorge, who headed the *Reichspost*, but also from Albert Speer, the minister responsible for armaments and war production.[128]

Bosch also sat on the arms committees and other bodies that Speer had set up for all areas of production in the wartime economy.[129] Nonetheless, in early March 1943 the company came under enormous pressure from Speer. Taking the view that Bosch's production capacity was going to fall short, the minister addressed a demand to the Bosch board of management that was in fact more like an order: "Using all the resources and funds at its disposal, Bosch will undertake immediately a comprehensive extension of its output potential, building a great part of that new capacity in the eastern part of the Reich." Speer warned that other companies would be called in, using Bosch patents, if the company were unable to comply.[130] Bosch promptly began to scour what was now called simply "the East" for a site for a new plant in which it could start manufacturing magnetos, generators, starters, and other items essential to the war effort. The decision eventually fell on Langenbielau (now Bielawa) in Lower Silesia, where two companies – Christian Dierig AG (then Germany's largest textile manufacturer) and Suckert AG – were obliged to vacate their plants for Bosch to move in.[131] Allegedly, the *Gauleiter* of Lower Silesia, Klaus Hanke, who was friendly with Speer, pushed the decision through in the face of Bosch's objections.[132] In fact, other companies were building back-up plants and new manufacturing facilities in Lower Silesia at the time. The region was deemed so unlikely to be bombed that it was dubbed "the Reich's air-raid shelter."[133] At Bosch, people were not exactly happy to be told to build a new plant in "the East." However, with Speer's threat hanging over the company, construction proceeded apace. On May 29, 1943, Bosch established a separate subsidiary for the purpose: Siling-Werke GmbH.[134] The managing director was Theodor Baumann, the plant manager Alfred Brack.[135]

It was not possible to set up new Bosch manufacturing facilities using only textile workers from the Dierig plant and other local companies. Accordingly, a large number of Bosch workers had to be relocated to Langenbielau from the home plants in Stuttgart. By April 1944, nearly 800 former Bosch associates, together with 590 non-German civilian workers (most of whom may well have worked for Bosch in Stuttgart previously), were employed at the Langenbielau plant.[136] Up until the spring of 1944, more than 400 railroad cars transported machinery and tools from Stuttgart to the new Siling-Werke in Lower Silesia.[137] It soon became clear that Speer's orders could not be carried out in the time expected.[138] Baumann, the plant's managing director, was hoping to receive support from the *Gauleiter*'s office in Wrcolaw (Breslau). In addition to non-German forced laborers, concentration-camp internees were now also assigned to Siling-Werke.[139] However, this did not solve the problems. In the autumn of 1943, some manufacturing equipment from the Feuerbach light works, originally meant to be moved to Langenbielau, was instead relocated to Trillke-Werke in Hildesheim.[140] At a meeting presided over by Speer in October 1943, the Bosch board member Hermann Bauer was forced to concede that the rebuilding work in Langenbielau was making slow progress because Bosch had been assigned the lower priority of "grade 2 construction."[141] When Bauer went on to report problems connected with other relocation plans, *Generalluftzeugmeister* Erhard Milch lost his temper. Raising a hand menacingly, he is said to have retorted: "If through your obstinacy you jeopardize the air-armament effort, you will not get off with a fine of 20,000 marks. It will cost you your head."[142] Here we see the true face of Speer's "armaments miracle." For reasons of air-raid protection, Bosch was forced into accepting relocation to a place that lacked the requisite manpower and building materials. To solve this, forced labor was assigned. And when things continued to falter, threats of capital punishment were flung around.

The last year of the war

On February 21, 1944, the Bosch plants in Feuerbach were severely damaged by an Allied air raid. Further substantial bomb damage was inflicted on the main plant in Stuttgart and on plants in Feuerbach by air raids on July 26 and 29, 1944, September 10 and 12, 1944, October 20, 1944, and January 28, 1945.[143] Because of air raids, more and more manufacturing facilities had been moved from Stuttgart and Feuerbach since the autumn of 1943. At the beginning of 1944, Bosch was instructed to house some of its production facilities underground, in a railroad tunnel near Bruttig, a small community on the River Mosel. An underground Bosch plant was meant to go into operation there in May 1944. However, two months later only a small production operation had been relocated there.[144] The tunnel having been enlarged by inmates of the Natzweiler concentration camp under SS supervision, some 150 workers from Feuerbach and Bamberg were transferred to Bruttig.[145] For this subterranean operation, Bosch set up another subsidiary: WIDU GmbH, based in Cochem.[146] For reasons of concealment, the company name chosen arose from a combination of the surnames of the two Bosch board members Wild and Durst. Air raids were also the reason for plans to put some of DLMG's production underground – in a mine in occupied Lorraine. Here, too, Bosch set up a separate company for the purpose, calling it ROWA, a name derived from Rogowski and Walz. The Armaments Ministry's Fighter Command gave DLMG/ROWA the use of the "Rothe Erde" mine in Audun-le-Tiche (Deutsch-Oth as it was called), but because of the way the war was going the plan had to be abandoned in August 1944.[147] In the summer of 1943, DLMG had moved part of its injection-pump production to Flugmotorenwerke Ostmark in Brno. Other manufacturing operations were transferred to a textiles factory in Boletice nad Labem (Politz an der Elbe) in northern Bohemia in July 1944.[148]

In Berlin, after an air raid had damaged its Wilmersdorf plant, Blaupunkt moved a production operation involving 150 personnel (most of them probably forced labor) into the catacombs (now converted into bunkers) beneath the Olympic stadium. This temporary facility was known as "Alma 1."[149] Junkers & Co. moved part of its manufacturing operations from Dessau to Asch and Roßbach in *Sudetenland*.[150] In Bamberg, Bosch's "Branch Operation 1" moved part of its production into the underground cellars beneath the local breweries.[151] Even in Stuttgart, a start was made at relocating certain facilities underground. Bosch manufacturing operations were transferred to the Pioneer Tunnel in Stuttgart-Mühlhausen and the Unterer Grund mine in Feuerbach,

Spark-plug assembly in a spinning mill in Brühl, near Esslingen (1942)

among other places.[152] In 1944, Robert Bosch GmbH transferred not only several thousand files to the salt mines in Heilbronn and Kochendorf for storage, but also a large number of paintings from the Bosch family collection and various items belonging to senior associates in the company or their friends and acquaintances.[153]

Above ground, plants belonging to Robert Bosch GmbH were moved out of danger to a total of 74 locations.[154] Württemberg's many textiles businesses were an obvious choice of temporary home. As early as June 1941, Bosch had relocated one manufacturing operation to the premises of Ulrich Gminder GmbH, a textiles company in Reutlingen.[155] In the last years of the war, more than 100 further temporary homes were found. In Tailfingen in the Swabian Jura alone, 18 companies lent Bosch accommodation during this period – for tool-making and producing machine parts, among other things, or simply for storing materials. Facilities were also re-housed in inns, schools, banks, and penitentiaries. Even Tübingen University was used.[156] Only a few relocation sites, such as those in Giengen and Reutlingen, were retained by Bosch after the war.[157]

These relocations led to further changes in the composition of the workforce. To an ever-greater extent, Bosch was obliged to train new workers and take on unskilled labor. The level of qualification among its staff declined accordingly. Where 23.1 percent of the personnel on the company's payroll had been skilled workers in 1939, by 1943 this figure was down to 19.4 percent. And in contrast to the First World War, the number of women employed at Bosch rose only slightly between 1939 and 1945.[158] However, in the final years of the war, as a result of the relocations that had been made, a new category of worker, described as *Fremde Arbeitskräfte*, appears in Bosch personnel statistics.[159] This refers to employees "on loan" from the companies where Bosch found temporary premises, and who worked for Bosch at these new sites. Because of the numerous relocations to Württemberg textiles companies, Robert Bosch GmbH had 5,861 such "non-Bosch workers" on its payroll by the end of 1944. By this time, the Bosch Group as a whole employed a total of 7,616 blue-collar and white-collar staff from the companies where its operations were temporarily housed.[160] Apart from forced laborers from other countries, these "non-Bosch workers" constituted the only labor reserve on which Bosch could draw during the war years. Redeployment of women into arms production was no longer possible to the same extent as in the First World War, since large-scale industry – and that included Bosch – already employed many more women than had been the case then.[161]

Training new or non-Bosch personnel was done initially in training workshops. These were the first things Bosch set up at all its major new locations. Some indication of the form such training took can be gleaned from the report *Unsere Betriebsgesellschaft* ["Our staff and management"], published in 1941. According to this report, individual courses were delivered by two to three instructors to each group of 15–30 trainees. Instruction followed a fixed teaching plan. This began with three weeks of basic training, including practical instruction at machines and vises as well as in "micrometer skills." Next came a period of vocational training lasting between six and twelve weeks, with instruction in how to read technical drawings and theoretical grounding in operations, materials, and machinery. Trainees (both men and women) finished off with a four-week probationary period in which to familiarize themselves with the operations carried out in their particular workplace. This phase was also known as the "crunch time" [*Krisenzeit*]. In it, trainees received the support of shift supervisors, adjusters, and calculators.[162] Under this scheme, Bosch trained not only women draftees but also non-German forced laborers and temporary workers at the relocation sites.

Shortly after the Allied landing in Normandy, Bosch had to begin reversing its relocation program. In June 1944, immediately prior to the liberation of Paris, the company withdrew from its Lavalette subsidiary in the city. It became necessary to vacate the Sundgau Maschinenbau GmbH plant in Mulhouse at the beginning of September 1944.[163] Where associates and equipment from there came back across the Rhine, they were absorbed into the engineering works in Giengen an der Brenz.[164] Siling-Werke in Langenbielau had to be abandoned in January 1945.[165] Once Hildesheim had been occupied by American troops on April 7, 1945, the only large sites remaining to the Bosch Group were its premises in and around Berlin and Stuttgart.[166] The DLMG plant in Kleinmachnow was occupied by Soviet troops on April 24 and dismantled shortly afterwards. So were Blaupunkt's Berlin plants. FESE escaped dismantling at first because the Soviet military was interested in its weapons technology.[167] A hard fate befell the DLMG managers Paul Vogelgsang and Heinrich Walchenbach. Both men were interned in camps and given long prison sentences. Vogelgsang was freed after five years. Walchenbach died in the NKVD internment camp in Buchenwald in 1947.[168]

In Stuttgart, with French troops approaching from one side and American troops from the other, Reich Governor Murr declared the city a fortress. In line with Hitler's "Nero Decree," he was determined not to allow the city to fall into enemy hands in a state of less than total ruin. A number of Stuttgart businessmen saw it as their duty to save their city from Hitler's and Murr's scorched-earth scenario. Alfred Knoerzer, Wilhem Haspel (chief executive officer of Daimler-Benz AG), and Otto Fahr (of Werner & Pfleiderer) were able to convince the Lord Mayor, Karl Strölin, of the need to surrender. The Lord Mayor persuaded Murr not to blow up the supply grid [i. e., for electricity, gas, water, and the like] but simply to disconnect it. And on April 10, Strölin made secret contact with the French army and let it be known that he would give up the city without a struggle. On April 21, French troops were able to take Stuttgart with negligible resistance. Murr had fled several days before. He went into hiding, living under a false name in a mountain hut in Austria's Vorarlberg region. After being captured there, he took his own life.[169]

When Bosch took stock of affairs after the war's end, the situation that presented itself was appalling. Of the 6,143 blue-collar and white-collar associates who had been drafted, 1,365 were reported killed. The actual number of dead was probably much higher.[170] The Mulhouse and Langenbielau plants had to be written off. So did DLMG and much of the equipment at Blaupunkt GmbH and FESE. The partially destroyed Junkers & Co. plant in Dessau lay in the Soviet zone of occupation. Only the facilities of Trillke-Werke in Hildesheim remained intact, and they now took over some of Blaupunkt's production from Berlin.[171] The Bosch plants in Stuttgart and Feuerbach had suffered major air-raid damage. Something like a third of buildings and installations were ruined, a further third were badly damaged, and some 4,000 machine tools had been lost. The company put its war damage (excluding

Bombed light works in Feuerbach (1944)

capital losses and subsidiaries) at some 97 million reichsmarks. 42 million reichsmarks of that total were due to bombing and 15 million reichsmarks to relocation costs.[172] It was a heavy loss, but by no means an insurmountable one. The war damage corresponded approximately to the sales figure for 1935 or the hidden reserves of 1940.[173] Most of the machinery in the home plants in Stuttgart and Feuerbach had been preserved, also as a result of relocation programs. And in any case, the company had not lost its know-how. What weighed much heavier than the damage to facilities was that all non-German assets were gone. Also, all export markets remained closed to the company for the foreseeable future.

5 Beyond the bounds of the "Bosch community": forced labor

The Third Reich war economy was kept afloat by a total of 13.5 million non-German civilian laborers, prisoners of war (POWs), and concentration-camp inmates. Some 90 percent of these have to be deemed forced laborers, since they could neither quit their jobs nor influence their deployment.[1] While there were still voluntarily recruited non-German workers at first, notably from countries allied to the Reich, from 1942 at the latest all *Fremdarbeiter* were employed against their will. In the armaments industry, forced labor started with assignment of POWs. As the fighting went on, fast-growing numbers of civilians from occupied countries joined them. These civilian workers – male and female – subsequently accounted for more than 60 percent of all forced labor. From the autumn of 1942, Hitler ordered concentration-camp inmates to be set to work in armaments companies.[2] Forced labor was in clear contravention of international law. Under the 1907 Hague Convention respecting the Laws and Customs of War on Land, civilians could not be made to work abroad, nor POWs obliged to do jobs that had any "connection with the operations of the war."[3]

Treatment of forced laborers followed the precepts of National Socialist racist ideology. French POWs and civilian workers from western Europe (*Westarbeiter* or "West workers") came under less coercion and were better fed than Polish forced laborers. These in turn received better treatment than so-called "East workers" from the Soviet Union (*Ostarbeiter*; they had "OST" marked on their clothing). "East workers" and Soviet POWs, along with concentration-camp inmates, were at the bottom of the heap. Whereas POWs were accommodated in camps (*Stammlager* or "stalags") under army supervision, non-German civilians occupied camps for which the relevant employer was responsible. Some "West workers" might be quartered with private landlords. Concentration-camp inmates lived in purpose-built *Außenlagern* [subcamps] close to where they worked. As detainees, they remained at the mercy of the SS, even while deployed as forced labor. The authorities dictated that civilian workers from France or the Netherlands should normally receive a gross wage comparable to that of their German counterparts. However, fixed deductions were made for board and lodging.[4] "East workers," on the other hand, received only a wage from which, after all deductions (including a separate "East worker levy"), no more than about 30 pfennigs a day remained.[5] In the case of POWs, most of the pay went to the "stalag" administration. Here, too, there were substantial differences. Concentration-camp inmates received no wages at all.[6]

German companies had a vital interest in using forced labor. This was because, as the war went on, more and more of their core workforce were drafted into the military. Without forced labor, no industrial enterprise would have been able to maintain its level of output, let alone increase it.[7] The extent to which companies benefited in business terms from the relatively low wages paid to forced labor is a matter of historical dispute. Lower pay among such personnel, in addition to the poorer conditions they lived and worked in, also meant they were less productive than the core workforce.[8] But the decisive advantage from the company's point of view was quite simple: forced labor was the only manpower resource available to them on this scale.

All these considerations also applied to Robert Bosch GmbH. During the war years, something like one-quarter of its core workforce was drafted. The company would have been unable to meet the rapidly rising demand for armaments with such reduced manpower. The Bosch board of management would undoubtedly have preferred to retain its full core workforce than accept forced laborers, but it had no choice. Other companies usually had forced laborers assigned to them by employment offices or recruited them from that source. With Bosch, however – a particularly important armaments company – the situation was different. From mid-1940, the armaments command responsible for Bosch would ask for a monthly statement of requirements. This had to be explained both to the armaments command and to the employment office.[9] At Bosch, all matters concerning the use of forced labor were concentrated in one department. The person chosen to head it was the deputy counter-intelligence officer Heinrich Luckau.

What the Bosch board of management thought of using forced labor cannot be deduced from the documents that have come down to us from the war years. Much the same is true for other companies as well. Any contemporary statements by senior executives on the issue are very rare. Depositions made after the war in the context of denazification proceedings are not a reliable source. They all serve the purpose of self-justification and are uniquely designed to minimize guilt. Walz claimed after the war that the Bosch board of management had protested at having forced labor imposed upon it. This, he said, was because "the usually unskilled foreign workers [were] no real substitute for the German skilled or semi-skilled personnel who had been drafted into the military." However, it had been "impossible in the long run to avoid using labor from abroad."[10] In other words, the Bosch board of management regarded the deployment of POWs and non-German civilian labor chiefly from the point of view of qualification rather than in terms of any infringement of international law or as a crime against humanity. After the war, Walz was surely aware that such an infringement had in fact taken place. This is the only possible explanation for the peculiar justification put forward in his statement of July 1947: "The company was told that these were voluntary workers. In our eyes, therefore, all labor from abroad (POWs excepted) was voluntary."[11] This line of reasoning is so completely implausible that we are tempted to believe Walz simply made it up to salve his own conscience. Of course he will have known that hundreds of thousands of young Polish and Ukrainian women did not voluntarily undertake the train journey in freight cars to Germany in order to find work. Debatin went one better, claiming after the war that "jobless people from Paris" had worked for Bosch of their own accord during the war years.[12]

In his postwar statements, Walz also claimed that the Bosch board of management expected forced laborers to be treated and looked after in line with the "Bosch spirit": "I gave instructions that associates should as far as possible receive an excess rather than a dearth of care, particularly as regarded food distribution. Foreign workers were to be subject to the same treatment as Germans – for reasons of common decency as much as for business reasons. After all, only persons who are well treated, properly fed, and content can be expected to do good work."[13] The reasoning here matches the principles of Robert Bosch so closely that this cannot simply be dismissed as retrospective justification. Walz may well have had this intention. Whether he also acted on it is another matter. As it was, the Bosch board of management had only limited influence over how POWs and non-German civilian workers were treated. Human resource directors, plant managers, even the relevant shift supervisors had more. A key figure in this context was Heinrich Luckau, the man responsible for labor deployment. Others were Otto Debatin as director of human resources and Hugo Bühler as counter-intelligence officer. Yet not even they could control the atmosphere surrounding a forced laborer's everyday life. This atmosphere was characterized and driven by a hierarchy which derived its justification from a racist ideology. This "pecking order," in turn, which made life so difficult if not impossible for "East workers" and Soviet POWs – but for Jewish concentration-camp inmates in particular – was a fact of life under the National Socialist regime. No company could rise above that. Yet some scope existed. Instances of abuse against forced laborers within a company could be tolerated or punished. Standards of catering could be humane or inhumane. Violations could be reported to the Gestapo or they could not. Within these limits, the question is whether Bosch remained true to its own principles in connection with the use of forced labor or whether it instead betrayed them.

Only approximations can be given regarding the growth and extent of forced labor at Bosch. No figures at all are available for the main plant in Stuttgart or for certain of the subsidiaries. Nor did Bosch record non-German civilian workers separately in its human resource statistics. Lists giving the names of forced laborers are available only for the Feuerbach plants and for Trillke-Werke, Siling-Werke, and Junkers & Co.[14] At Bosch, too, use of forced labor began with POWs, who arrived in Stuttgart in group shipments from early November 1939.[15] Larger numbers of POWs were deployed after the armistice on the Western Front. In fact, shortage of space made it difficult to accommodate them in Stuttgart.[16] From March 1941, Bosch also had non-German civilian workers assigned to it.[17] As we know from a report "concerning our efforts to acquire foreign workers," drawn up by Otto Debatin in June 1941, the human resources department was at that time especially keen to receive a contingent of Italian workers. As citizens of a friendly country, they possessed a certain special status.[18] Deployment of civilian workers from occupied parts of the Soviet Union began in the autumn of 1941. A year later (in November 1942), Debatin reported that there were already 3,200 non-German workers on the Bosch payroll, including 1,400 "East workers" of both genders. However, it is unclear whether these figures relate to the company as a whole or only to the Stuttgart and Feuerbach plants.[19] According to the human resource statistics of Robert Bosch GmbH, at the end of 1942 the number of POWs stood at 715.[20] At a meeting at Bank der deutschen Luftfahrt on November 19, 1942, Alfred Knoerzer, a Bosch executive who held general power of attorney, announced that Robert Bosch GmbH needed 6 million reichsmarks of investment funds to build huts for 7,000 POWs and civilian workers.[21]

There is a further reason why the total number of forced laborers at Bosch is so hard to ascertain. From 1943, the relocation of manufacturing operations meant that an increasing percentage of them no longer appeared in the headcount statistics of the Feuerbach and Stuttgart plants. The number cited by Knoerzer in November 1942 was never reached there. A headcount report dating from the end of November 1944 tells us that 2,885 forced laborers were employed in the Bosch plants in Stuttgart and Feuerbach. Of these, 470 were POWs, 639 "East workers," and 1,776 other non-German civilian workers.[22] A realistic idea of the extent of forced labor at these locations can only be gained if the available lists of names on the headcount listings of the Feuerbach plants are evaluated. According to this source, 6,451 POWs and non-German civilian workers were employed in Feuerbach alone. In 1943–44, 261 of these were transferred to Siling-Werke in Langenbielau.[23] At the time, forced laborers also included detainees who were obliged to work for Bosch.[24] From as early as the spring of 1939, inmates of the Ludwigsburg penitentiary had worked for the company. During the war, various Bosch subsidiaries had prisoners in the Celle (ELFI/Trillke-Werke), Brandenburg an der Havel (DLMG), and Jauer (Siling-Werke) penitentiaries working in their manufacturing operations. It can be assumed that no fewer than 1,000 prisoners in all worked for the Bosch Group during the war years.[25]

There is no indication that concentration-camp inmates were assigned to the Bosch plants in Stuttgart and Feuerbach. After the war, Walz stated that he had "decisively rejected forced employment of interned Jews and concentration-camp detainees."[26] Heinrich Luckau wrote to Karl Martell Wild in 1947: "A few times we were offered Jewish women." However, these offers were not acted upon and "Jewish women were declined." Provisions for employing Jews included separate accommodation, segregated workplaces, and special catering arrangements. Luckau does not say whether the forced labor of Jewish women was declined because the human resources department rejected such discrimination or because providing separate accommodation and segregated workplaces would have cost too much. His letter can be interpreted both ways.[27]

The Kleinmachnow and Hildesheim subsidiaries suffered even greater labor shortages after the outbreak of war than Robert Bosch GmbH. Unlike the parent company, they had been set up only a few years previously and had no core workforce. ELFI was already employing 59 French POWs at the end of 1940. By 1945, the number of forced laborers working there had risen to 1,871 – 46 percent of the workforce. A surviving list of names indicates that there were 2,711 forced laborers at ELFI and at Trillke-Werke during the war. They included 963 "East workers," 439 French, 363 Poles, and 31 people from India. Altogether, male and female non-German workers from 21 countries were employed there.[28] At DLMG, too, there was a massive increase in forced labor during 1942. In May 1943, a total of 1,668 forced laborers from the Soviet Union, France, the Netherlands, Belgium, Croatia, Hungary, and Italy were employed there.[29] In September 1944, some 800 Polish women from the Ravensbrück concentration camp were assigned to the company. Most had been deported since the start of the Warsaw Uprising. This was not the first instance of detainees being assigned to a Bosch Group company, but it was by far the largest contingent. To house the Polish women, an extension to the concentration camp (an *Außenlager* or subcamp) was built in Klein-machnow. Like Ravensbrück itself, it was also run by the SS.[30] An insurance document shows that DLMG had 2,591 non-German forced laborers in

March 1945. They came from 15 countries and included some 1,100 men and women from Poland (including the group from the Ravensbrück concentration camp), 467 civilians from the Soviet Union, plus 335 Belgian, 190 French, and 112 Dutch nationals.[31] Large numbers of forced laborers also worked at Blaupunkt, Junkers & Co., Siling-Werke, and Sundgau Maschinenbau GmbH. For Blaupunkt, no figures are available. For Junkers & Co., evaluation of a list drawn up for the Dessau plant after the war's end gives a total of 909.[32]

So far as the Bosch Group is concerned, the lack of available data means that a grand total of forced laborers can only be estimated. However, there are some reliable pointers. One is the only headcount report for the entire Bosch Group that still survives from this period, which documents the status as per the end of 1944. And we also have data handed down for individual companies or plants for the period September 1944 to April 1945.[33] For the Stuttgart and Feuerbach plants and for four subsidiary companies (DLMG, Trillke-Werke, Siling-Werke, and Sundgau Maschinenbau GmbH) we have headcount records as well as data concerning numbers of forced laborers employed over the same period. The subtotal for these companies and plants is 8,860 forced laborers, as against a total workforce of 27,119. While certain atypical features can be ascertained for these plants and companies, these anomalies cancel each other out to a certain extent. Due to the relocation of operations, forced labor in Stuttgart and Feuerbach accounted for less than 20 percent of the workforce at the end of 1944. On the other hand, the figure exceeded 50 percent in the new armaments companies DLMG and Trillke-Werke. This gives us an average forced-labor figure of 32.7 percent. If this is applied to the total Bosch Group headcount at the end of 1944, we arrive at a figure of some 13,000 forced laborers. For the entire duration of hostilities, the number must of course be set much higher. If we include penitentiary inmates, there is reason to suppose that at least 20,000 forced laborers were used in the Bosch Group over the course of the war.

Table 15 Forced labor in the companies of the Bosch Group*

Company, location	Headcount Dec. 1944[34]	Forced laborers 1944–45 (month/year)	Percentage of forced laborers 1944–45	Total forced laborers 1939–45
Robert Bosch GmbH	20,282			
– Stuttgart and Feuerbach plants	15,658	2,885[35] (Nov 1944)	18.4%	
– Feuerbach plant only	9,232			6,190[36]
Dreilinden Maschinenbau GmbH, Kleinmachnow (DLMG)	4,303	2,591[37] (Mar 1945)	60.2%	
ELFI and Trillke-Werke GmbH, Hildesheim	3,874	2,019[38] (Sep 1944)	52.1%	2,711[39]
Siling-Werke GmbH, Langenbielau	2,450	885[40] (Apr 1944)	36.1%	1,292[41]
Sundgau Maschinenbau GmbH, Giengen	834	480[42]	57.6%	
Junkers & Co. GmbH, Dessau	3,315			909[43]
Blaupunkt-Werke GmbH, Berlin	3,802			
Blaupunkt, Kommando Groß-Rosen		200[44] (Dec 1944)		
WIDU GmbH		50[45]		
Other Bosch Group companies	1,103			
Total: Bosch Group	39,963			

* as evidenced by sources, not including penitentiary inmates

This number is markedly higher than previously reported. Yet when looked at more closely, it is not so very different, since it relates not only to Robert Bosch GmbH or to the Stuttgart and Feuerbach locations but to the Bosch Group as a whole. Walz, looking back after the war, put the number of forced laborers at Bosch at around 5,000.[46] As a snapshot of the situation within Robert Bosch GmbH, his figure was not too far off. The company, remember, comprised not only the plants in Stuttgart and Feuerbach with their roughly 2,900 forced laborers (as recorded statistically in November 1944) but two other plants: Crailsheim, where around one-third of the roughly 1,000 associates were POWs and non-German civilian workers, and Bamberg, where in 1944 a further 600 forced laborers were employed.[47] Scholtyseck puts the number of forced laborers working at Bosch in 1944 at 3,553, basing his assumption on the reported headcount at the Stuttgart and Feuerbach plants.[48] However, we must also bear in mind that the numbers for Stuttgart and Feuerbach in 1944 do not give the full picture for Robert Bosch GmbH at the time. By that time, a number of back-up plants had been built and manufacturing operations relocated due to the risk of air raids. A lot more forced labor was deployed in the armaments factories of the newly established subsidiaries than in the home plants. The true scale of forced labor at Bosch was revealed only when Angela Martin's book about the deployment of concentration-camp inmates at DLMG and Manfred Overesch and Stefan A. Oyen's research into Trillke-Werke were published.[49]

At the end of 1944, some 33 percent of Bosch Group headcount were forced laborers as compared to (in August 1944) some 25 percent across German industry as a whole.[50] But at DLMG and at Trillke-Werke, forced labor accounted for more than half the workforce by that time. At Siling-Werke (built in 1943), the figure was not quite so high. This was because of Albert Speer's insistence that Bosch relocate a large number of core associates from Stuttgart to Langenbielau. To these, the company was able to add many workers on loan from the local textiles industry. At the Mulhouse-Bourtzwiller operation of Sundgau Maschinenbau GmbH, it was not until the autumn of 1943 that deployment of forced labor attained more substantial dimensions. The reason for this was that the original Alsatian workforce was at first protected against being drafted into the German armed forces. In 1944, with the Allied front advancing, the German workforce and non-German forced laborers fell back across the Rhine to Giengen, leaving the original Alsatian workforce behind. As a result, the percentage of forced labor in Giengen was relatively high at the end of 1944.

Concentration-camp inmates were deployed at three Bosch Group companies altogether: Blaupunkt GmbH, Siling-Werke, and DLMG. They likely numbered around 1,200 in all. Exploiting such victims of the National Socialist regime stood in particularly stark contrast to the principles of Bosch senior executives and the members of the "Bosch circle." There is hard evidence to show that some 800 Polish women from the Ravensbrück concentration camp were assigned to DLMG (as mentioned above) and 200 inmates from the camp at Groß-Rosen to Blaupunkt. Others went to Siling-Werke in Langenbielau. How many concentration-camp inmates worked at Siling-Werke altogether cannot be established from the documents handed down. In April 1944, the number was 74, but by the end of 1944 this had likely risen sharply with the extension of the Langenbielau plant.[51] Jewish women liable for compulsory service had worked at Blaupunkt in 1941–43. Most of these had subsequently suffered deportation.[52] In 1943, Blaupunkt established a miniature production operation in the Groß-Rosen concentration camp in Lower Silesia. Some 200 Groß-Rosen inmates attached to the "Blaupunkt Commando" were made to manufacture condensers in a hut rented from the SS-run company Deutsche Erd- und Steinwerke GmbH.[53] The workforce in Stuttgart may have known nothing about this "Blaupunkt Commando." However, this was certainly not true of the forced-labor deployments in Langenbielau and Kleinmachnow. Built by Bosch associates from Stuttgart, Siling-Werke received deployments of inmates from the Langenbielau subcamp, which was erected specifically for the industrial enterprises relocated to Langenbielau.[54] The aforementioned deployment of 800 Polish women from the Ravensbrück concentration camp will certainly not have passed unnoticed in Stuttgart. For DLMG, the large number of additional hands meant a strengthening of personnel that could not have been achieved otherwise. In June 1944, plans had been laid to move part of DLMG's production to a mine near Audun-le-Tiche (Deutsch-Oth as it was called) in occupied Lorraine. Approximately 800 to 1,000 inmates from Natzweiler concentration camp were to have been deployed there. Bosch associates made several site inspections, when board and lodging for inmates were among the subjects discussed.[55] With the Allies advancing rapidly through France, the relocation to Audun-le-Tiche never happened.[56] The fact that the operation was concealed as "ROWA GmbH" shows how deeply the contradictions at Bosch could run at the time. The abbreviation "ROWA" stood for Ernst Rogowski and Hans Walz. In Stuttgart, Rogowski and Walz were committed to protecting associates of Jewish descent. Yet in Audun-le-Tiche, as part of a project that bore their names, arrangements were being made to accommodate concentration-camp inmates. A similar deployment was proposed in connection with another relocation project – namely, WIDU GmbH. Plans drawn up in April 1944 called for a workforce of 2,000, including 1,000 "foreigners, POWs, and detainees."[57] Here, too, the course the war was taking meant that this deployment of concentration-camp inmates did not come about.[58]

Most accounts of how the Bosch Group treated forced labor date from the postwar years. For the most part compiled by board members, former plant managers, or individual camp commandants for the purpose of reducing sentences in denazification courts, these do not give an objective picture. Walz, for instance, stated after the war that he had kept himself informed "about the satisfactory condition of the camps and whether inmates were content." French POWs in particular had often "spontaneously expressed contentment and gratitude."[59] The point was made repeatedly during denazification trials that "following the collapse there were no complaints from any quarter."[60]

French POWs at Bosch (1942)

A different picture emerges from a report on morale drawn up in Vienna in September 1942 by the office responsible for examining foreign mail. Based on intercepted letters from non-German forced laborers, the report described conditions at Bosch in Stuttgart as "particularly bad."[61] After the war, former forced laborers, most of them having by then returned to their native countries, had little opportunity to tell of their deployment in Germany. It was usually left to members of works councils to point the finger in denazification proceedings. In the Walz trial, the works-council chairman Eugen Eberle said that "people were reported to the Gestapo and sent to concentration camps."[62] It was also pointed out that forced laborers were barred from using shelters during air raids.[63] On the other hand, there is evidence that the Bosch air-raid shelters on the Siegelberg had a separate entrance for "East workers" and POWs.[64]

Some of the accounts written after the war are mutually inconsistent. They can be ranked in order of reliability only on the basis of context. For instance, a witness put up by the works council said that Soviet POWs in the Stuttgart-Mühlhausen facility were given potato peelings to eat instead of potatoes.[65] Another witness alleged that the works canteen at Mühlhausen was particu-

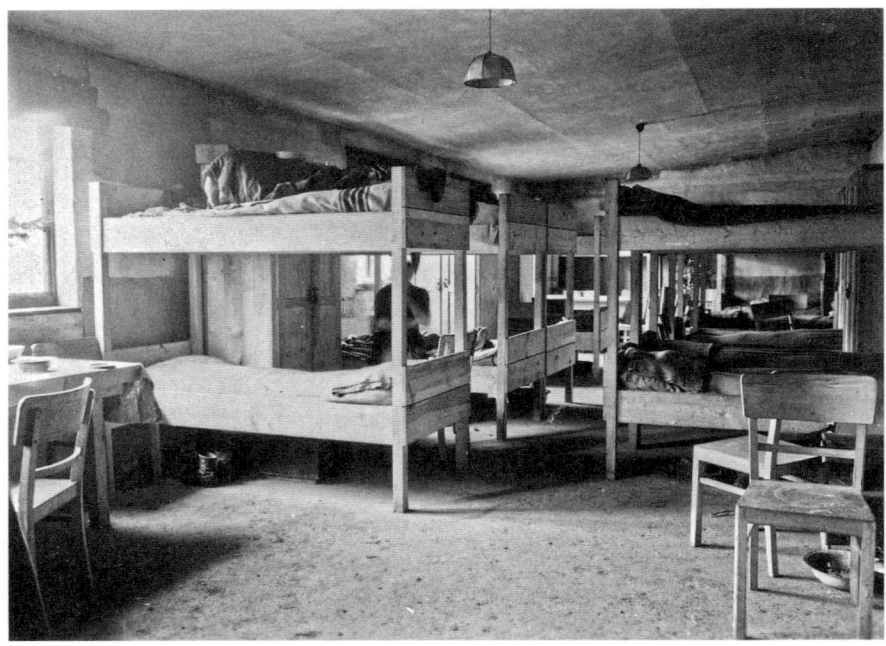

The "Russian camp" (1944)

larly known for feeding Soviet POWs better than the rules laid down.[66] Both claims may be true. We simply do not know. After the war, a Russian woman who had worked as a supervisor at a camp for female "East workers" in Weilimdorf made positive reference to the fact that the camp had four washrooms for a thousand inmates.[67] Hardly model conditions, one would think. However, another statement made after the war stressed that the management of the Feuerbach light works had been at pains to treat "foreigners as associates of equal value." Reference was made in this connection to (among other things) "West workers" enjoying equal access to plant catering facilities and distribution of work clothing. Not that this was anything out of the ordinary.[68] The same applied to the secondhand clothing collection for which the Bosch human resources management appealed in November 1942 to replace the tattered garb of the "largely quite inadequately equipped male and female workers from the East."[69] Previously the German Ministry of Economic Affairs had itself made such a collection.[70]

The reports from Bosch subsidiary companies all reveal how deeply the forced labor system was imbued with National Socialist racist ideology. "West

Forced laborers in the kitchen of the "Russian camp" in Weilimdorf-Schützenhaus

workers" not only earned considerably more than "East workers." Unlike the latter, they also enjoyed freedom of movement outside the camp. Some even had private lodgings. The companies concerned had not designed this inhuman regime. It had been imposed on them by the authorities. Yet the persons responsible within those companies were not unaffected by it – and that was also the case at Bosch. Vivid descriptions of the impressions of one "West worker" can be found in the letters that a Dutch forced laborer at DLMG, Henk de Koning, wrote to his family. We have to remember that these letters were subject to censorship. Nonetheless, they show that the writer was not badly fed and could go into Berlin with workmates.[71] Other Dutch as well as Belgian and French civilian workers worked on a non-voluntary basis in German armaments factories. But unlike Soviet POWs, they were not undernourished. A different picture emerges from the interviews that Angela Martin and Ewa Czerwiakowski conducted among Polish women who had been brought to Kleinmachnow from the Ravensbrück concentration camp in September 1944. Coming from the hell of Ravensbrück, these women experienced forced labor at DLMG as an improvement – often as a deliverance. Yet the food, apparently, was "very poor" ("At noon there was soup made from well-stewed leaves, occasionally three potatoes, still in their skins").[72] Mostly very young, the women had to work 12-hour days. At weekends the only outing was a roll call with exercises in the woods, with every error being punished by the SS guards' whips.[73] Of the plant's shift supervisors and machine setters these female forced workers had a range of memories. Alfreda Gorączko, then 17, had the following to say in retrospect: "It all depends on the character of the individual, I think. It's got nothing to do with their being a member of the party."[74]

There were also big differences between conditions in the various Bosch subsidiaries. At Trillke-Werke in Hildesheim, forced laborers seem not to have been systematically assaulted. Also, their accommodation was later described as exemplary. Overesch attests that Bosch "had here succeeded in activating the social tradition associated with the company."[75] Naturally, other accounts paint the situation in different colors.[76] What we should assume is that, as Oyen and Overesch write in an article about forced labor at Trillke-Werke, the "Bosch spirit" applied purely to the German part of the workforce, and that accommodation arrangements met only minimum standards.[77] For the forced laborers concerned, their deployment at Trillke-Werke was undoubtedly not Overesch's "relative success story," but for the company it probably was.[78] The plant manager Max Clostermeyer was able to report to the supervisory board on November 6, 1942, that "the performance of foreigners is satisfactory on the whole. Men achieve 80–85 percent of German output, women equal German output."[79] Karl Josef Fricke, involved in training forced labor at Trillke-Werke at the time, could corroborate this, particularly with regard to female "East workers." The Ukrainians among them "did exceptional work," he reported.[80] Another reason why performance in Hildesheim was relatively good may well have been that production there was less demanding than at DLMG, say. Also, having been built only a few years previously, Trillke-Werke incorporated state-of-the-art production technology.

By contrast, at Siling-Werke in Langenbielau, terror reigned. Here, under the difficult conditions of the autumn of 1943, Speer had ordered a new, large-scale industrial operation to be constructed. The Bosch subsidiary in Langenbielau saw serious abuse of concentration-camp inmates and non-German civilian workers. After the war, the former plant management and six other Siling-Werke employees were accused of "failing to observe the most basic requirements of humane treatment."[81] Subsequent investigation showed the worst bullies to have been Gotthilf Hundt, the head of the factory cell organization, together with Richard Nitsche, the cell operations foreman, and the

Ceremony at Siling-Werke in Langenbielau (Bielawa)

shift supervisor Wilhelm Herzlieb. The plant manager, Theodor Baumann, keen to stay on good terms with the Gauleiter's office in Wrocław in order to have their backing in the difficult task of building the new plant, knew about the acts of violence but did nothing. Conditions at Siling-Werke were bad. We know this from what happened to the Jewish concentration-camp inmate Albert Adler, whose fate emerges from the Langenbielau denazification-trial files. Adler had asked a female workmate to contact his mother-in-law in Berlin and request that she bring him food. After a food parcel and some money had reached him in this way, Hundt caught him in possession of them. Hundt and a colleague then took him to a compressor room and beat him so badly that Adler could no longer walk. Witness statements suggest that he died the next day.[82] In the autumn of 1947, Hundt was sentenced to seven years' labor camp, Nitsche to three and a half years.[83]

It is difficult to tell how much was known in Stuttgart about conditions in Langenbielau. Walz and Debatin later said the first they had heard of them was after the war.[84] However, the works-council chairman Eugen Eberle claimed to have heard quite soon after the Langenbielau plant opened that "Jews who worked there were treated so badly that they stooped to pick up any apple core they could find."[85] What Eberle meant, of course, is that they were starving. A contingent of over 1,000 associates from Stuttgart helped to set up Siling-Werke, so it can safely be assumed that conditions in Langenbielau were discussed among the Stuttgart workforce. Management is unlikely to have known nothing. Yet there may have been a reluctance to know too much. After the war, Hundt, Nitsche, and their accomplices were sacked. Debatin deemed it "advisable that the company should also dismiss Baumann; otherwise there might be accusations that it had not been seen to take the physical maltreatment of half-starved Jewish concentration-camp inmates seriously."[86] At the time, Baumann was no longer working for Bosch anyway, i. e., no longer for Siling-Werke. In October 1947, the Stuttgart denazification court handling the Langenbielau case sentenced him to four years' labor camp. However, two years later the verdict was quashed by ministerial decree, and in a fresh hearing before a higher-level court in Stuttgart, Baumann was acquitted. On July 1, 1951, he was reinstated at Bosch as technical plant manager in Hildesheim.[87]

In the Langenbielau trial, the court in question, in Stuttgart-Feuerbach, was concerned to portray the reported offenses as special cases.[88] But things were not that simple. The forced labor system of the National Socialist era included certain unlegislated areas emanating from the racist ideology that underpinned it. Hundt, Nitsche, and Herzlieb were typical so-called "situational perpetrators" who were lured into their crimes rather than seeking them out. In a different situation – in Stuttgart, say – they may have acted quite differently and as a consequence may not have attracted any attention at all. In Langenbielau, however, they had no reason to expect legal punishment, and braced by the racist mindset of the day they chose to exploit their positions of relative power in a thoroughly sadistic manner. How much depended on "the character of the individual" was something that a Polish detainee, Jan Pankiewicz, also experienced. Pankiewicz did forced labor for Blaupunkt in the Groß-Rosen concentration camp. Deployment to the Blaupunkt Commando (also known as the Schyndler or Schindler Commando) was an enviable fate for Groß-Rosen inmates, given the murderous circumstances of camp life. Admittedly, it meant a 12-hour working day, but "conditions were still relatively tolerable," as Pankiewicz wrote later. So far as detainees were concerned, the crucial factor was how people behaved at "NCO" level. This one would hit you, that one not. In the commando, Blaupunkt was represented by two shift supervisors, both of whom lived outside the concentration camp. They were no exception, as Pankiewicz recalls: "One supervisor was a brute. The other was different, showing a friendly manner toward detainees."[89]

In no Bosch Group company did the rules laid down by the National Socialist regime regarding deployment of forced labor allow non-German employees to be treated in a way that would have accorded with the "Bosch spirit." Bosch had no influence so far as those rules were concerned. Nonetheless, key figures in the field of "enforced foreign labor" – Heinrich Luckau, Otto Debatin, Hugo Bühler – were by no means free of thinking in National Socialist categories. In dealing with "West workers," there were certain standards that one felt compelled to observe. On the other hand, repressive action was taken against "East workers," even where it would have been entirely possible to do otherwise. These could expect neither sympathy nor backing, and clearly people felt no inhibitions about denouncing them. Debatin arranged to have a document posted on the bulletin board of the Feuerbach plant on August 11, 1942, describing as unfounded certain complaints made by "female East workers" [*Ostarbeiterinnen*]. His wording leaves no doubt that in his mind these people did not form part of the "Bosch community" since they did not belong to the "national community" or *Volksgemeinschaft*. His document read: "Would Germany's women and girls, one wonders, have it so good in political Russia? And how our German POWs are treated in Russia, no one knows. We appeal to all thinking members of staff: please ensure that you for your part do not let your German good-naturedness cause you to lose your sense of dignity."[90] According to a statement by Otto Fischer in Debatin's denazification hearing, the head of human resources was not alone in taking this stance. Some ill feeling existed among the core workforce concerning the "excessively generous" treatment meted out to "foreign workers."[91] Again, forced laborers from abroad were evidently seen as alien to the "Bosch community."

As we have seen, the company's counter-intelligence officer, Hugo Bühler, enjoyed good contacts with the Gestapo. In numerous instances, he used these to save Jews and "half-Jews" from deportation. For "East workers," however, he showed less consideration. Ten such women, arrested by the Gestapo for "industrial sabotage" and dispatched to a labor camp, received no support from either Bühler or Debatin.[92] In a letter written after the war to Karl Martell Wild, Debatin reported a hideous crime: "Only the four hanged Russians may not rise from the dead. Sole responsibility for the case lay of course in the hands of Dr. Bühler. The Gestapo had appointed him during the war as counter-intelligence officer for Bosch. It was he who filed the report on the Russians. I myself was only just able to prevent the execution from going ahead as announced in our Pfostenwäldle camp with the assembled workmates looking on."[93] Because of their position in the company, Debatin and Bühler held many fates in their hands. In their dealings with "East workers" both fell short of observing the standards of treatment meted out to "West workers." Certainly they did not adhere to the principles that at Bosch applied to German associates – including those of Jewish origin.

Statistics drawn up in mid-1943 regarding the output of forced labor in the Bosch plants in Stuttgart reflect the same hierarchy based on the National Socialists' racist ideology. Italian and Hungarian workers came almost up to the level of the core workforce. Dutch, French, and even Polish civilian work-ers reached a level of about 80 percent. Russian civilian workers, on the other hand, reached only 73 percent, while Russian POWs, at 53 percent, lay far be-low the German norm.[94] All values (with the exception of those ascribed to Italian and Hungarian workers) were well inferior to those scored by "foreign workers" at Trillke-Werke in November 1942. However, they approximated the levels indicated by other studies of the period, particularly for the heavy in-dustry of the Rhine-Westphalia region.[95] When we consider the principle championed by Bosch that well-fed, contented workers were also productive workers, then these data suggest that at Bosch, forced laborers fared no better than at most other large companies. This is particularly true of Russian POWs. In the case of many "West workers," apart from the fact that they worked un-der compulsion there was little to choose between them and the core work-force. They ranked lower, but they were not otherwise deemed inferior. For "East workers," on the other hand, treatment varied enormously. Some saw a minimum standard respected, others suffered arbitrary acts of violence and denunciations. In the case of concentration-camp inmates, there were no lim-its to such barbarity. The social entitlement that was one of the distinguishing characteristics of the "Bosch community" did not apply to non-German forced labor. With regard to "West workers," the company and its subsidiaries at least did not violate their own principles. But where concentration-camp inmates, "East workers," and Russian POWs were concerned, they did.

Until the year 2000, Bosch provided no form of compensation for former forced laborers.[96] The company declined all responsibility. It took the view that forced labor in the Third Reich, having been imposed by sovereign decree, could not be used to justify claims under private law.[97] However, in 1998 and 1999 the behavior of business in the Third Reich became a matter of extensive public debate. With class actions being filed in the United States against Ger-man companies, Bosch took an early part in the efforts of German industry to set up a compensation scheme for the benefit of former forced laborers. From within the Bosch family itself, top management at Bosch was requested to cast a critical eye over its own National Socialist past. In December 1998, Ise Bosch, a granddaughter of the company founder, wrote to Marcus Bierich, the chair-man of the Bosch supervisory board. Acknowledging that she felt in part per-sonally responsible for whatever had happened, she asked him to look into the role the company had played under the National Socialists.[98] Together with Manfred Gentz (Daimler-Benz AG) and Michael Jansen (Degussa AG), Tilman Todenhöfer, the deputy chairman of the Bosch board of management, was among those who launched the talks that led to a fund being set up to compen-sate forced-labor victims, the *Stiftungsinitiative der Deutschen Wirtschaft*.[99]

For the negotiations in the German Federal Chancellery in Berlin, Hans L. Merkle, the influential honorary chairman of Robert Bosch GmbH, proposed a formulation to be used as a working preamble for any agreement of the parties present, namely, that "using forced labor [implied] no moral guilt but certainly a material obligation on the part of German business."[100] However, the intergovernmental treaty between the Federal Republic of Germany and the United States concerning the ensuing "Remembrance, Responsibility, and Future" foundation finally did state that having used forced labor engendered a "moral responsibility on the part of German business."[101] Once the foundation was set up, Bosch paid a proportionate contribution into the compensation fund.

6   The Bosch circle and resistance to Hitler

Between 1934 and 1936, Robert Bosch hired three respected Stuttgart citizens as advisers: Albrecht Fischer, Paul Hahn, and Theodor Bäuerle. These men, all of whom had lost their old jobs, were a major influence on the founder in his final years. Together with Hans Walz and Willy Schloßstein (head of Robert Bosch's private secretariat), they ultimately constituted a tightly-knit group that became known as the "Bosch circle." Albrecht Fischer, taken on as economic-policy adviser in 1934, played a particularly important role. This experienced and very widely connected official had been a member of the center-right *Deutsche Volkspartei* [German People's Party]. In the Weimar Republic, he had made a name for himself as chief executive of the regional employers' association in the metalworking industry as well as of the Union of Württemberg Employers' Associations.[1] In 1935, it was Fischer who recommended that Paul Hahn, a retired police commissioner, should also be made a Bosch adviser. Hahn's biography had been erratic, to say the least. He had begun his professional career as a teacher, illustrator, and fine artist. Then, at the start of 1919, having been given the command of the newly commissioned security squads, he played a key role in suppressing the Spartacist uprising in Stuttgart. He was subsequently made chief of police, though a difference of opinion with Württemberg's minister of the interior obliged him to resign after only a few years. He found temporary employment with a Stuttgart company as a designer of steel furniture. Before Bosch took him on, however, he had been out of work.[2] Hahn still had good connections with the police. But when Robert Bosch hired him, the thought likely uppermost in his mind was that Hahn's organizational skills made him the right man to oversee construction of the homeopathic hospital that Robert Bosch endowed in 1936 to mark his company's 50-year anniversary.[3]

A year after Hahn had joined the company, an educational thinker named Theodor Bäuerle was taken on as the third adviser. Bäuerle had started out as an elementary school teacher before becoming deeply interested in educational reform. In 1918, he founded the Stuttgart Society for the Promotion of Adult Education, which he ran as managing director until its disbandment. Robert Bosch supported the society financially and was its first chairman. When the NSDAP's district director of education tried to oust Bäuerle from the management of the society, Bosch withheld his financial backing and suggested the society should disband. This it subsequently did. Bosch then hired Bäuerle as adviser for occupational and vocational education.[4] Much uncertainty surrounds what Bäuerle and Fischer actually did as Bosch advisers. Bäuerle had no office of his own at Robert Bosch GmbH headquarters. To mark the founder's 80th birthday, he presented a biography of Robert Bosch that the subject dismissed as "gushing."[5]

The Bosch circle assumed greater definition when Carl Goerdeler joined it at the beginning of 1937. Goerdeler, also hired by Bosch as an adviser, was someone of a different caliber. He also differed in character from Fischer, Hahn, and Bäuerle. A former lord mayor of Leipzig, for several years he had also held national office as price-monitoring commissioner. His cast of mind and political views did not really match those of the people around Robert Bosch. Goerdeler was a national-conservative civil servant of the Prussian school. Repudiating the parliamentary system of the Weimar Republic, he wished to see Germany recover its great-power status. Moreover, in his exposé *Das Ziel* [The Goal] written in late 1941, he advocated Jewish expatriation.[6] Unlike Bosch, Goerdeler had initially welcomed Hitler's assumption of power, but then shunned National Socialism due to subsequent events. For example, he resigned as mayor of Leipzig because, in his absence, the city council [on November 9, 1936] had had the Mendelssohn Memorial torn down [the renowned nineteenth-century composer Felix Mendelssohn Bartholdy had Jewish roots]. By this time, Goerdeler was already in touch with Fried. Krupp AG, where he was offered a position on the board of management. However, Krupp did not want Goerdeler on its board without Hitler's consent. Hitler would not give it, so in March 1937 Krupp withdrew the offer.[7]

Goerdeler contacted Bosch in the summer of 1936. Walz promptly traveled to Leipzig and conversed with him at length. There is unlikely to have been talk of sweeping away National Socialist rule at this first meeting, as Walz claimed after the war.[8] However, in their rejection of Hitler the two men will have found common ground. A memorandum that Goerdeler drew up in late 1937 and left with a friend in New York condemns the Hitler dictatorship as a system of lawlessness, corruption, and moral decay.[9] Following his resignation as mayor of Leipzig in April 1937, Goerdeler signed an advisory contract with Robert Bosch GmbH. People often say he was hired as a financial adviser, but that is not so. Nor would it have made any sense. Goerdeler was contracted to establish and cultivate contacts with authorities and businesses at home and abroad.[10] He did in fact use his contacts in Berlin partly in the business interests of the Stuttgart company. However, only once was he involved in actual transactions. That was in connection with the sale of Bosch's non-German subsidiaries to the Swedish bank SEB Group.[11] Goerdeler had no office in Stuttgart but visited the city at intervals to report – once or twice a month, apparently. On these occasions, he also held discussions with Robert Bosch, Walz, Fischer, Bäuerle, and others.[12]

Initially, Goerdeler worked for Bosch above all as a sort of special envoy. Between June 1937 and August 1939 he made 12 trips abroad, mostly to Britain but also to France and Italy, Switzerland, the United States, and the Middle East.[13] Later statements all confirm that Goerdeler undertook these trips not for business reasons but to warn people in the countries concerned of Hitler's intentions. However, Goerdeler's mission was unsuccessful. He managed to hold confidential discussions with many influential personalities, but that was all. Outside Germany, his warnings caused mainly irritation. People were unsure what to make of a Prussian conservative agitating so vehemently against his country's government. As one British government representative told him, he was committing treason.[14] Goerdeler's views on the role Germany should play in Europe hardly helped him in his mission, and imagining that his connections would enable him to sway the governments of Britain and France was more than slightly out of touch with reality. Amazingly, the German authorities suspected nothing. Until the last moment, they thought Goerdeler was doing business for Bosch in Zurich, Amsterdam, Stockholm – wherever it might be. Each of his foreign trips was sanctioned unreservedly. For his part, Goerdeler reported fully on his travels, sending copies to the War Economics Directorate, to Hjalmar Schacht, and even to Hermann Göring.[15]

Part of his job involved cultivating contacts with the Reich authorities. Using this as cover, Goerdeler held confidential talks with opponents of the Hitler regime on his visits to Berlin. These included the Army Chief of Staff, General Ludwig Beck, and other members of Berlin's illustrious *Mittwochsgesellschaft* [Wednesday Society], a private club of 16 men, distinguished scholars, diplomats, physicians, and others, who met every two weeks to discuss matters related to their areas of expertise. Beck opposed Hitler's war plans. A group of leading officers had formed around him, determined to prevent Hitler from going to war. With Beck's consent, Goerdeler expanded this group of officers to include a civilian wing that several members of the Wednesday Society then joined. Beck took a critical attitude to the preparations being made for war, and in August 1938 he had to resign. A month later, during the "Sudeten crisis", with war a likely prospect, Beck and his fellow conspirators resolved to take Hitler prisoner. But when the Western powers buckled and Hitler triumphed with his Munich Agreement, the plan came to nothing.[16]

Carl Friedrich
Goerdeler (1943)

It is likely that Goerdeler informed Walz, Fischer, and Bäuerle of his resistance activities in the Beck group at an early stage. He was scarcely a model of discretion, and could hardly have taken his plans forward without someone at Bosch knowing. Who at Bosch did know is hard to say. After the war many people claimed to have been among them, but those genuinely in on the secret will have had a mutual interest in ensuring that their numbers did not proliferate. The knowledge will certainly have extended to the members of the "Bosch circle": Albrecht Fischer, Paul Hahn, Theodor Bäuerle, and Willy Schloßstein. Within the company, initiates will have included Hans Walz, of course, and also Alfred Knoerzer, the man responsible for making payments to Goerdeler, but not Hermann Fellmeth, Karl Eugen Thomä, or Otto Debatin. Schloßstein wrote after the war that he had informed Robert Bosch of the link to the resistance movement in the military in October 1939.[17] Schloßstein's reflections are not a particularly reliable source, but on the whole the founder himself may be assumed to have been generally aware of these activities, if not of their details. Clearly he was now hoping, with mounting impatience, that the dictator would be removed. Eva Madelung, Bosch's youngest daughter, recalls how in private her father would say, "It beats me why no one bumps the fellow off."[18] Two things are worth noting here. One is the way the men of the Bosch circle unreservedly approved plans for the coup. The other is the conspiratorial energy they put into shielding Goerdeler's activities. It would not have occurred to any of them to back away from this risky connection or to attempt to play a double game.

The swift military successes at the start of the war were a setback for the resistance group around Beck and Goerdeler. Hitler now stood at the height of his power and popularity, and the generals who had warned him against going to war had to endure his scorn. After the armistice in the west, Goerdeler used his contacts abroad for new peace efforts. In the spring of 1941, he and Friedrich Wilhelm Siegmund-Schultze, a theologian who had the ear of colleagues in the Church of England, drew up a peace plan. Among other things, it provided for a Germany returned to its 1914 borders plus the territories annexed in 1938.[19] The plan even reached the London Foreign Office, where Foreign Secretary Anthony Eden declared it "quite unacceptable."[20]

Goerdeler remained pivotal to the resistance activities of the Bosch circle in the ensuing years. Neither Walz nor Fischer had resistance contacts of their own. The active contribution of both men lay in their support for Goerdeler. This was not confined to organizational services or to money (which was what made Goerdeler's activities possible and which amounted, in total, to some 540,000 reichsmarks).[21] The conspiratorial discussions that Goerdeler held at Bosch headquarters turned also on assessing anti-Hitler resistance among the military, attitudes abroad, and the ethical justification for tyrannicide.[22] That Goerdeler had plotted with top officers no doubt greatly strengthened the determination of his accessories in Stuttgart. The Bosch circle, too, was clearly aware that only the armed forces could carry out a coup. However, in contrast to Goerdeler, Hans Walz and other members of the Bosch circle had huge misgivings regarding the army top brass and the so-called "spirit of Potsdam," the notion of a military state. Walz put it to Goerdeler that he should not include officers in any future government.[23] As the fighting dragged on, it became clear that the resistance group around Beck and Goerdeler was not making any progress toward its objective. The Bosch circle began to lose patience. They had never really trusted the military anyway, and it now was the military they blamed.[24]

On June 8, 1942, Bäuerle was arrested. A theologian belonging to the *Bekennende Kirche* [Confessing Church], whom Bosch had supported with a scholarship, had named him during interrogation. Walz, Schloßstein, and Marianne Weber (Bäuerle's secretary, who also did secretarial work for Goerdeler) wasted no time in hiding Bäuerle's papers. To free Bäuerle, Walz once again called on the services of Gottlob Berger. Berger, now in charge of the SS head office, still saw himself in the role of protector of Robert Bosch GmbH. He contrived to obtain Bäuerle's release after eleven days' detention.[25]

In the autumn of 1942, Walz pursued a separate initiative to inform foreign agencies of the aims and activities of the German resistance. On a trip to Switzerland, he spoke in detail with an industrialist, Conrad Bareiss, about plans for the post-Hitler period. Bareiss passed the information to the American consul in Bern, Maurice Altaffer, who then met with Walz in December 1942.[26] Walz was taking a big risk here, since all German security and secret-service personnel in Switzerland had their informers.[27] Nor was Walz particularly careful when, in his Feuerbach address of July 1943, he attacked the National Socialist war-economy system.[28] Had the authorities investigated him they might easily have stumbled across Goerdeler's conspiratorial activities. Goerdeler, who was constantly compiling cabinet lists for the government he planned to lead in the future, had put down Walz as minister of economic affairs without telling him first. When Walz found out, he had his name removed from the list. This may later have saved his life. Scholtyseck conjectures that Walz had begun to doubt the usefulness of a coup by this time, deeming it more sensible to await an Allied victory than to take as yet incalculable chances beforehand.[29]

In May 1943, Goerdeler traveled to Stockholm to negotiate the repurchase of American Bosch Company (ABC). He took advantage of the visit to ask Bosch's business partners there, the bankers Jacob and Marcus Wallenberg of SEB (whom he knew well), to get a message to the British government. The message was in fact a 26-point memorandum. Among Goerdeler's requests were that Allied air raids should be suspended during the forthcoming coup and that the plan to demand an unconditional surrender on Germany's part should be dropped. Marcus Wallenberg knew Churchill's private secretary, Desmond Morton, and told him what Goerdeler was proposing. Morton's answer was unambiguous. As in 1941, London found Goerdeler's ideas went beyond what it was prepared to accept.[30] The Allies had long since decided to pursue the war until Germany surrendered unconditionally. Through the Wallenbergs, Goerdeler repeatedly urged the British government to spare the cities of Berlin, Leipzig, and Stuttgart, as centers of anti-Hitler resistance, from any bombardment.[31] Again, this hardly suggests that Goerdeler was realistic when it came to assessing the influence he had. Yet this did not prevent the stubborn persistence of the myth that Stuttgart had escaped air attack before July 20, 1944, on account of its resistance to Hitler. There was huge readiness to point out that the heaviest air raids had taken place on July 25–26 and September 12.[32] In reality, the Allied bomber commands will certainly not have made allowance for German resistance activity. In any case, Stuttgart was bombed almost 20 times before July 20, 1944, and the Bosch plants in Feuerbach had suffered heavy air-raid damage on February 21, 1944.[33]

In the days and weeks prior to July 20, 1944, the mood among the members of the Bosch circle was tense. Goerdeler had paid a final visit to Stuttgart in mid-June. Paul Hahn had learned from him then that "the move against Hitler was imminent."[34] Clearly Bäuerle was also in the picture, as were two former centrist politicians then living in Stuttgart, Eugen Bolz and Joseph Ersing, as well as the theologian Helmut Thielicke. On the other hand, Walz and Fischer were not.[35] Knoerzer met with Goerdeler in Berlin as late as July 12. Five days later Goerdeler was already on the run. An arrest warrant had been issued against him. The Bosch circle had prepared an escape route into Switzerland for just such an eventuality. Paul Hahn spent several days waiting for Goerdeler on Lake Constance. Goerdeler, however, had decided to make a dash for Sweden via his West Prussian homeland.[36] When news of the failed July 20 attempt on Hitler's life reached Stuttgart, the members of the Bosch circle realized their own lives were in danger. Albrecht Fischer was arrested in the night of July 20–21. Goerdeler had made him the plotters' political adviser for "military district V" (Stuttgart). Schloßstein, apparently acting with the assistance of the counter-intelligence officer Bühler, destroyed the documents that Goerdeler had left behind on Militärstraße.[37] The Gestapo, looking for Goerdeler, made a thorough search of the Wespental hunting lodge. Bäuerle, Fellmeth, Knoerzer, and Olpp were interrogated. On August 4, Paul Hahn was arrested. Hans Walz, on the other hand, was not touched – less, we should assume, as a result of "divine providence," as he later claimed, than because his name did not appear on any of Goerdeler's numerous cabinet lists. Being an SS officer might also have protected him.[38]

Goerdeler himself was arrested in West Prussia on August 12. Fischer, Hahn, and the others who had helped Goerdeler could now expect their lives to depend on what he admitted under interrogation. Fischer and Hahn were in fact incriminated by Goerdeler.[39] Schloßstein was arrested on the basis of notes made by Goerdeler (who had wanted him as Württemberg's minister of economic affairs). With Fischer and Hahn, Schloßstein was taken to the *Reichssicherheitshauptamt* in Berlin. Walz promptly turned to SS *Obergruppenführer* Gottlob Berger, who secured Schloßstein's release. Albrecht Fischer was arraigned before the *Volksgerichtshof* [People's Court]. His trial took place on January 12, 1945, under the notorious Roland Freisler. Nicknamed *Blutrichter* or "the Blood Judge," Freisler had already handed down several thousand death sentences. He acquitted Fischer but condemned his co-defendant Reinhold Frank to death – although both men had faced similar charges.[40] Undoubtedly, Fischer owed his acquittal, and with it his life, to the intervention of

Gottlob Berger, whose services Walz had once again called upon. After the war, Berger bragged about how he had pleaded with Hitler personally on behalf of Fischer, Hahn, Schloßstein, and another man from Württemberg, the theologian and later politician Eugen Gerstenmaier.[41] This may well have been one of Berger's many fabrications in which he repeatedly portrayed himself as a hero. He will not have been able to influence Hitler. However, it seems correct to assume, as Scholtyseck does, that Berger did indeed intervene, whether indirectly through Himmler or by contacting Freisler direct.[42] Certainly, Freisler took the hint from SS headquarters. This might also have become apparent in the Paul Hahn trial. But Freisler was denied the opportunity to try Hahn. Only hours before the case was due to begin on February 3, 1945, he was killed in an air raid. His replacement as presiding judge was a man from Reutlingen, near Stuttgart, who adjourned proceedings in the case of Hahn. At a later date, Hahn was sentenced to three years' imprisonment.[43]

Carl Goerdeler was executed in Berlin-Plötzensee on February 2, 1945. His Bosch circle accomplices all survived.[44] Schloßstein was certain that without Berger's help the entire Bosch board of management would have faced execution.[45] That is, we should assume, an exaggeration, but for Fischer, Hahn, and Schloßstein it is quite true. It may also have been Berger's doing that further proceedings – against Walz, for instance – were not instituted. As it was, the men of the Bosch circle saw themselves deeply indebted to a convicted war criminal: in 1949, Berger was sentenced by the International Military Tribunal at Nuremberg to 25 years' imprisonment. Robert Bosch GmbH expressed its gratitude to Berger after the war and stood by him in various ways until his death in 1975.[46]

The Bosch circle was one of the few instances of entrepreneurs participating in anti-Hitler resistance. Even if no one in Stuttgart apart from Goerdeler was involved in planning the July 20 assassination attempt, the conspiracy that was organized there was clearly an act of political resistance rather than of simple protest.[47] Admittedly, only a small group was involved, not the company as a whole, and within that group only Walz can properly be described as an entrepreneur.

The fact that this resistance emerged had a lot to do with Goerdeler himself. However, that alone is insufficient explanation. The specific situation at Bosch, the sharp clashes with regime representatives that had pre-dated Goerdeler's appearance on the scene, repudiation of a war of aggression, and the example of feisty obstinacy set by Robert Bosch himself – these things were clearly contributing factors. Scholtyseck interprets the Bosch circle as a form of "liberal resistance," since most of its members held liberal attitudes and had formerly belonged to liberal political parties.[48] Yet the common de-

Albrecht Fischer before the *Volksgerichtshof* (January 1945)

nominator that led to the emergence of the circle was not liberal politics but the fact that its members worked at Bosch. Goerdeler was a national conservative advocate of the Prussian-German authoritarian state. In his case, any liberalism was economic at best. In different circumstances he would no doubt have met with deep distrust at Bosch. But across political and ideological divides, there was a common conviction that Hitler had to be resisted. In the case of the Bosch circle, belonging to the group engendered a momentum of its own, without which the behavior of these men is hard to explain. Individuals like Theodor Bäuerle and Willy Schloßstein were not born conspirators. On their own, they would have been unlikely to join the resistance. Belonging to the Bosch circle and being in close touch with Goerdeler made them throw caution to the winds and become part of the plot. Remaining aloof would have meant betraying the others.

7 Death and legacy of Robert Bosch

Robert Bosch celebrated his 75th birthday on September 23, 1936. The celebrations were combined with those for the company's 50-year anniversary, brought forward in his honor. For him, the occasion was also marked by the fulfillment of a long-cherished dream – the setting up of Stiftung Homöopathisches Krankenhaus Stuttgart [Stuttgart Homeopathic Hospital Foundation].[1] Robert Bosch had arranged for the company to donate 3.25 million reichsmarks for the project, giving his adviser Paul Hahn the job of overseeing construction. On April 28, 1940, Germany's largest and most modern homeopathic hospital opened its doors on Hahnemannstraße in the city's Pragsattel district. Robert Bosch's inaugural address to the hospital staff was at the same time a catalogue of his own business principles: "All tasks are important, even the most modest."; "We should all strive to improve on the status quo."; "We must all work for the good

Inauguration of Robert Bosch Hospital (1940)

Gate of the Feuerbach plant on Robert Bosch's 80th birthday (1941)

of the whole, and neither for the benefit nor at the cost of individual persons.";
"Make every effort, therefore, to win the trust of the many."[2]

The founder's 80th birthday on September 23, 1941, was celebrated under very different circumstances. The National Socialist regime bent over backwards to pay court to Robert Bosch. He was awarded the title "Pioneer of Labor" that Hitler had introduced only the year before as the highest honor that could be conferred on an entrepreneur. It had been conferred only four times until then.[3] Out of consideration for the founder, his birthday celebrations were held not in Stuttgart but in Baden-Baden. In Stuttgart itself, the day was marked with a concert by the company's own orchestra in the city's concert hall, the *Liederhalle*, at which Lord Mayor Karl Strölin made a speech.[4] Robert Ley, head of the German Labor Front [*Deutsche Arbeitsfront* or DAF], traveled with Gauleiter Murr to the Brenner's Park Hotel in Baden-Baden, where he bestowed the "Pioneer of Labor" title on Robert Bosch. The birthday guests included Carl Goerdeler, Hjalmar Schacht, and Paul Reusch.[5] A few weeks after his 80th birthday, Robert Bosch gave a moving speech to thank his workforce for their congratulations.[6] It was to be his last major public appearance.

State funeral for Robert Bosch (March 18, 1942)

On March 4, 1942, Bosch asked Theodor Heuss to write his biography. He wrote: "Thank you very much for sending me your biography of Justus von Liebig. I find it excellent, and the purpose of this letter is to ask whether you would be interested in taking the time to write a biography of myself."[7] To which Heuss replied two days later: "For the time being, without beating about the bush, my answer in principle is simply: yes."[8] Heuss had already edited a book about Robert Bosch in 1931 to mark the founder's 70th birthday.[9] The two had known each other since 1917, having first come together through Ernst Jäckh and Friedrich Naumann.[10] Subsequently, Bosch had given financial support to the *Deutsche Hochschule für Politik* [German Academy for Politics] in Berlin, where Heuss taught. In 1933, Heuss had lost his teaching post and his seat in parliament. During the Third Reich he wrote mainly biographies and biographical articles, although in the end he could publish only under a pseudonym.[11]

Bosch was now suffering from an ear infection that he was unable to shake off. Only days after writing his letter to Heuss, the eardrum burst. As late as March 9, he was still going into his office. Complaining of impaired balance and recurrent pain, he nonetheless had Schloßstein report on the latest reflections concerning the wording of certain passages in his will. In the early morning of March 12, 1942, Robert Bosch died in Stuttgart's Marienhospital.[12]

The members of his family and the senior management of the company had to stand aside while the National Socialist regime usurped the grief at Robert Bosch's death for its own ends. Hitler ordered a state funeral for March 18. On the evening before the funeral, a ceremony was held at the company, where eight senior shift supervisors bore the coffin through the works site to the lobby of the sales building. Hans Walz, Paul Scheuing (chairman of the supervisory board), and Alfred Weißenborn (*Hauptbetriebsobmann* [senior shop steward]) all delivered orations.[13] The next day, in the König Karl hall of the State Museum of Industry (now known as the Baden-Württemberg Haus der Wirtschaft), the state funeral for Robert Bosch took place. The national government was represented by the Minister for Economic Affairs, Walther Funk, who gave a speech hailing Robert Bosch as a national hero. Then, in front of the whirring cameras of the newsreel propaganda machine, the *Deutsche Wochenschau*, Funk gave a Hitler salute and laid a wreath from the dictator on the coffin.[14] After the state funeral, the coffin was taken to the crematorium at the Pragfriedhof cemetery, where a large crowd was already waiting. Inside the crematorium, Hans Walz and Hermann Bücher gave brief addresses. Ten days later, on March 28, the urn containing Robert Bosch's ashes was interred in a tomb of honor at Stuttgart's Waldfriedhof cemetery.[15]

The family found the stage-managed nature of the state funeral humiliating.[16] Margarete Bosch later left Stuttgart, together with her children. At first she shared a house with her son in Pfronten, where Robert Bosch Jr. was completing an apprenticeship in order to escape being drafted into an anti-aircraft unit. His sister Eva lived on the Bosch estate (the *Boschhof*) and attended school in Icking. Both children spent the last year of the war at the *Boschhof*, together with their mother.[17] Meanwhile, Theodor Heuss had begun work on the Robert Bosch biography. He had the support not only of Friedrich Schildberger but also of Otto Debatin, Otto Fischer, and Hugo Borst. The book was published after the war. However, it was written during the war's last years – mostly in Heidelberg, where Heuss and his wife were living at the time, but in part at the *Boschhof*, where for a number of weeks his wife tutored Eva Bosch and other children.[18] Robert Bosch GmbH secured a deferment from the military for Theodor Heuss, later the first president of the Federal Republic of Germany, on the grounds that he was "performing academic work."[19]

The legacy: a family company – with reservations

Robert Bosch had spent much of the period 1935–38 sorting out what he would leave to posterity, and how. He had drawn up six wills one after another – the latest on May 31, 1938. In addition, there were three sets of guidelines for the executors, two for the trust administration company Vermögensverwaltung Bosch GmbH (VVB), and one for Robert Bosch GmbH. The individual versions do not differ greatly. Core components appear in sometimes identical words in both will and guidelines.

Robert Bosch's central concern was that his company should continue to be run in his spirit after his death. It was for this reason that he had set up VVB in the early 1920s. His repeated offers to sell VVB his shares in the company are more likely to have been declarations of intent.[20] However, clashes surrounded the capital holdings in the stock corporation Robert Bosch AG owned by former board members or heirs of deceased board members. These spats had the effect of increasing Robert Bosch's determination not to expose his life's work to the risk of his own heirs falling out or proving incapable of running the company. He backed the "VVB option," since after his first son died there was no male heir to whom he might have assigned ownership of the company.[21] Quite soon after meeting his second wife, Robert Bosch set about altering the arrangements for succession. In August 1927, five months before the birth of his second son, Robert Bosch Jr., he added a confidential addendum to the VVB guidelines, providing for greater involvement on the part of the heirs. The heirs were to hold 40 percent of the share capital of VVB. If they included a male heir particularly suited to running the company, following a probationary period the shareholders of VVB were to cede between 18 and 31 percent of the shares to him, giving him as "family director" the majority holding.[22]

In his last will and testament of May 31, 1938, Bosch appointed his closest family members in legal line of succession as his heirs. At the same time he arranged how the will was to be executed, naming as his executors [*Testamentsvollstrecker* or TV] the seven other VVB shareholders: Erwin Bohner, Hermann Fellmeth, Arthur Leinss, Paul Scheuing, Richard Stribeck, Hans Walz, and Karl Martell Wild. Fellmeth, Walz, and Wild belonged to the group of executors as representatives of the company, while Leinss represented the family (his adoptive mother, Helene Leinss, *née* Kayser, being a sister of the founder's first wife Anna).[23] The executors (it was further stipulated), who were always to be VVB shareholders, were "expected to ensure that the business activities of Robert Bosch GmbH are carried out and carried on in a manner reflective of my wishes, i. e., of my spirit and will," and were given the task of securing for the company a "strong and meaningful development."[24] At a later date, the executors were to decide by a three-quarters majority whether the founder's shares in Robert Bosch GmbH should be transferred to VVB in accordance with Robert Bosch's last sale offer of July 13, 1935. If the executors should decide against this "VVB option," the will left open the possibility that, on expiry of their mandate, the executors should allow the shares to pass to the heirs of Robert Bosch. This was the "TV option."

In addition to the executors, the "family director" was to play a key role. Bosch was very keen for a male descendant to come to occupy what he called a "leadership position" [*Führerstellung*] at Robert Bosch GmbH – provided that the person concerned turned out to be up to the job.[25] His suitability was something the shareholders of VVB were to decide on once the candidate had completed a probationary period, as defined more fully in the VVB guidelines.[26] A letter sent by Robert Bosch to his son in January 1939 suggests that he saw Robert Bosch Jr. as such a future family director.[27]

As the rules stood, the Bosch children did not enjoy free disposal of their inheritance during the execution period. They were mere legatees. The executors were required to decide not later than 30 years after Robert Bosch's death whether the shares he had bequeathed to Robert Bosch GmbH should be purchased by VVB (the "VVB option") or whether they (the executors or *Testamentsvollstrecker*) should manage those shares until their mandate expired, at which point the shares were to pass to the heirs (the "TV option"). In other words, the executors were not only to exercise an owner's rights of disposal over Robert Bosch GmbH, but also to determine – to determine alone – where in the future that ownership should lie – with the founder's descendants or with VVB. Since the executors were also shareholders of VVB, this was tantamount to judging one's own case. Moreover, in their capacity as shareholders of VVB it was their job to rule on the suitability of the son, a grandson, or a son-in-law to become family director, thus entitling him to receive the majority shareholding in VVB, which would in turn, if the "VVB option" were taken, hold the capital majority in Robert Bosch GmbH.

Granted, following the death of Robert Bosch more than 70 percent of the original investment in VVB was owned by the community of heirs, comprising the founder's four children.[28] With that majority, together with the consent of the other shareholders (i. e., the seven executors), the children could have dissolved VVB. There was indeed such a plan shortly after the founder's death, when the hospital that he had built was in need of more funds. In light of this, Robert Bosch's children were determined to wind up VVB, take over its shares in Robert Bosch GmbH, and assign part of the proceeds to Stiftung Homöopathisches Krankenhaus. The executors backed them. Walz and Schloßstein submitted a request to the Treasury in Berlin on July 30, 1943, for the tax due on the transaction (calculated by the inland-revenue office responsible at some 9.8 million reichsmarks) to be waived.[29] Their request explained that, following the birth of his second son and his grandson, Robert Bosch had "abandoned the plan to leave all his shares in the company to VVB." Instead, he had "bequeathed the shares to his four children, which had of course involved his making special provision for the transitional period, until such time as the education of his presumed successor was complete. This was done by stretching the execution period, which was not to exceed 30 years, during which the shares would be administered accordingly."[30] The Stuttgart Tax Office for Corporations turned down the request for tax relief, which marked the beginning of lengthy negotiations. Carl Goerdeler having complained to the Treasury in June 1944, the tax burden was reduced to a one-off payment of 1.5 million reichsmarks.[31] In October 1944, VVB declared that it was prepared to pay such a sum, but in the confusion of the war's final months, the dissolution of the VVB no longer came about.[32]

III Adaptation and change between economic boom and economic crises (1945–1983)

The period between the immediate postwar years and the early 1980s was one of great upheaval for Bosch – a pivotal phase of crucial importance in the history of the company. Robert Bosch himself was now dead, but his stamp and legacy were still omnipresent and tangible, whereas the style of the non-family managers who succeeded him was slow to make its presence felt. When it did, though, it quickly assumed a formative force of its own. And not least, these pivotal years between 1950 and 1982 (from the start of the "economic miracle" to the end of the second oil-price shock) are also significant for Bosch history, in that this was the era in which many of today's senior executives, as young engineers and members of the lower and middle tiers of management, acquired their first professional experience and their early corporate socialization. The company faced three huge challenges. The first was legal, with the changeover from family-based shareowner structures and the creation of a new corporate constitution. The second was technological, with the advent and rapid integration of electronics in automotive engineering, coupled with a simultaneous revolution in manufacturing methods and organization. The final challenge was economic, with the end of the "economic miracle" and the start of the "long-drawn-out 1970s" with the oil-price shock, stagflation, and the emergence of green politics. In addition, once the company had come through the Allied policy of deconcentration, there was pressure to internationalize and to return to pre-war markets. Each factor on its own involved considerable risks, and failure in any of them could have meant a serious threat to the company's financial viability, independence, or ability to compete. Taken together, they represented a massive accumulation of risk that could imperil Bosch's very livelihood or at least put the company in a decidedly precarious position for many years to come. The following chapters examine more fully how the company saw those challenges in the first place, and how it then overcame them through a complex process of adaptation and change.

1 Reconstruction in the shadow of Allied decartelization policy and disagreements within the company

At the war's end and in the early postwar years, Bosch was in a far more fragile position than is often assumed. The task of rebuilding the company's damaged and destroyed factories and putting its manufacturing and sales operations back on their feet was overshadowed not only by the uncertainties of Germany's economic and monetary situation (repressed inflation, a flourishing black market, and a food crisis) but also by other potential sources of conflict, both external and internal. There was considerable turnover in corporate leadership – in the Bosch board of management, in the supervisory board, and in the group of executors. Some of these comings and goings were age-related, others sprang from the denazification process and from political strains. And the situation was no less troubled for the employee representatives when it came to reconstituting the works council and reappointing union spokesmen. As a result, industrial relations were marked by considerable conflicts. In what Walz once called "the interregnum, the terrible interregnum" from the death of the founder until one of his descendants could take over, Bosch was plagued by shifting, ill-defined corporate-governance structures. On top of all this came the deconcentration and decartelization measures pursued by the French, American, and British occupying forces. For years, these measures cast a mantle of uncertainty over how much economic and technical potential Bosch was going to be able to deploy as it sought to re-enter the national and international marketplace of the postwar period. It was not until 1952 that a series of radical changes began to give the company more stable management structures and put an end to internal squabbling.

Continuities and breaks with the past: the struggle for positions of power within the company

At the start of September 1945, as a precautionary measure, the board of management was expanded by six members. Of these six, three were full members of the board: Alfred Knoerzer was accountable for finance and human re-

Members of the Bosch board of management, 1948–49. From left: Alfred Knoerzer,
Otto Fischer, Walter Lippart

sources, Max Dipper for engineering, and Ernst Rogowski for sales. The other
three were associate or deputy members: Walter Lippart assumed responsibility for technical sales, and Otto Fischer and Hermann Bauer were joint heads
of manufacturing, Fischer for commercial and Bauer for technical issues.[1] The
incumbent members of the board of management, namely Karl Martell Wild,
Hans Walz, Erich Rassbach, and Hermann Fellmeth, had indicated their consent in writing to this formation of a ten-member board, but despite what at
first glance seems a major upheaval there cannot be said to have been any major changes in senior management. Each of the new members of the board of
management had worked for Bosch in a senior position for decades. However,
in late autumn, the situation took a completely different turn. At the beginning of October, the military government removed Fellmeth and Walz from
office on grounds of Nazi involvement. Walz himself was arrested and interned. The man who had been the company's most senior management figure
since the death of Robert Bosch was thus unavailable to make decisions until
the beginning of July 1948, after his denazification tribunal had pronounced
its final ruling. Wild and Rassbach resigned their management posts voluntarily, and to make matters worse, a further 65 Bosch executives were sacked
by order of the military government – including Knoerzer.[2] Albrecht Fischer
now became the new chairman of the supervisory board, and to assist him the
Americans installed an acting board of management. This was headed by

Martin Steins as "general manager," and also included Otto Fischer, Walter Lippart, and Ernst Rogowski. However, a fierce struggle for power soon broke out among the new members of the board, with intrigues, denunciation, accusations of misleading the authorities, and other shenanigans. Not until March 1947, nearly eighteen months later, did the supervisory board manage, by dismissing Steins and Rogowski, to draw a line under the episode. With Otto Fischer at human resources, Walter Lippart at engineering, Fritz Honold at sales, and Alfred Knoerzer at finance (his political rehabilitation was complete by April 1946, and despite obvious ill-feeling between him and Otto Fischer, his appointment followed in May), a new board of management was now in place that could at last give its full attention to the urgent task of running the company.[3]

But the real center of power at Bosch at this time was still the seven-man group of executors [*Testamentsvollstrecker* or TV]. This group comprised Walz, Fellmeth, and Wild, as well as four other senior executives: Arthur Leinss, Willy Schloßstein, Erwin Bohner, and Richard Stribeck – the latter two occupying seats on the supervisory board at the same time. When the group of executors convened on October 30, 1945, for its first meeting after the war, it already lacked Stribeck and Walz, although Margarete Bosch and her then 17-year-old son Robert Bosch Jr. were present as guests.[4] The group resumed its examination of the very complicated inheritance and probate affairs that the executors had begun to address after the founder's death in 1942.[5] The main problem the executors had to wrestle with in late 1945 and early 1946 was this: the tax authorities, assuming a rate of 300 percent for Robert Bosch GmbH shares (soon afterwards the rate rose to 450 percent), presented a demand for hefty inheritance and property tax payments that were more than the family heirs could afford to pay.[6] At the end of 1946, therefore, the executors even considered dissolving the trust administration company Vermögensverwaltung Bosch GmbH or VVB. All that prevented this drastic step from being taken was the fact that the military government had confiscated all the tax files of Robert Bosch GmbH, compounding the difficulty the executors already had in properly fulfilling their office.[7] The executors did indeed, in May and June 1948, hand over some of the remaining VVB shares still held by Robert Bosch GmbH (amounting to 2.72 million reichsmarks, i. e., 5.66 percent) to the heirs, pursuing a course already set, but they stopped short of dissolving VVB altogether. In the meantime, future relations between the board of management and the executors were quickly becoming the focus of discussion. This had not been a problem at first, with Walz, Fellmeth, and Wild having feet in both camps, but with the removal of Fellmeth and Wild and the arrest and internment of Walz, an entirely new situation had arisen. The executors, citing their obligations toward Robert Bosch and his heirs, argued that they would now have to "look after things more" in the future:[8] "By virtue of his shareholding, [Robert] Bosch had been director and sole owner of the company. Following his demise, the executors should now assume that role, the purpose being to select from among [Robert] Bosch's descendants suitable successors within the meaning of the guidelines. Until such time as that objective has been achieved, the group of executors, if need be in consultation with the heirs, but with explicit power to act without their participation or consent, should be alone in having the final word in all fundamental company matters."[9] It was not surprising that the executors' interpretation met with dissent within the new board of management.[10] That dissent turned to conflict in November 1948, when Walz once more took a hand in the company's fate.

Following his arrest in October 1945, Walz had promptly set about moving heaven and earth to regain his freedom. From his prison base he had countless high-ranking figures intervene on his behalf with the U.S. authorities, but without success.[11] Initially, Walz was interned on the grounds of his role on the supervisory board of Dresdner Bank, but then also because of his membership in the SS, or rather the *Freundeskreis Reichsführer SS*, as well as his appointment as *Wehrwirtschaftsführer* in 1944. Walz himself deemed it a crying injustice, especially since he was the only member of the former Bosch senior management to be called to account politically.[12] During his time in custody,

Walz not only wrote dozens of increasingly desperate petitions for his release. He also wrote a series of memoranda about "12 years under the Nazi yoke" as well as "My part in the Goerdeler campaign," in which he virtually took credit for being the true nucleus of the former resistance cell.[13] In many other respects, too, Walz's attempts at political exoneration used the same arguments that other German businessmen had during their terms of imprisonment and denazification. The point of the very substantial sums paid out to party agencies had simply, he claimed, been to shield the company from attack by other party agencies and to defend it against the threat of being handed over to a state commissioner. As a member of the supervisory board of Dresdner Bank he had not, he said, had detailed knowledge of the business dealings of its board of management. And not least, he alleged, Bosch had resisted the allocation of non-German labor, since only with difficulty could such labor be trained in the precision-engineering tasks required. And in any case, "all non-German labor was voluntary."[14]

Not until September 1947 was Walz released from internment. By then he was 64, and the former Bosch manager's odyssey through a variety of prisons and camps as well as his countless interrogations and fruitless protestations of innocence had taken a great physical and mental toll. It was quite possibly only now that the psychological pressure of the National Socialist period made itself felt. Moreover, the spring of 1948 brought both his hearing before the *Spruchkammer* and his official denazification trial, in which Walz appeared as a main offender (group 1). Walz enlisted Bosch's help to defend himself, presenting a whole host of witnesses – from a joint declaration signed by 538 associates to 100 individual testimonials from various prominent figures in church and state. These did in fact enable him to persuade the trial court judge of the groundlessness of the charges leveled against him. These charges had mainly been brought by Eugen Eberle, then chairman of the Bosch central works council, concerning Walz's responsibility for abuses at Siling-Werke in Langenbielau (Bielawa).[15] In June 1948, Walz was exonerated and acquitted, and thus formally rehabilitated politically. However, the man who had once been Robert Bosch's closest and most trusted associate had undergone a character change. He had become more domineering, more arrogant in his behavior, even high-handed. At the same time, recurring health problems meant that he was more and more frequently absent from the company.

Within weeks of the conclusion of his denazification proceedings, Walz called a meeting of the executors. One item on the agenda was "Settling the legal status of Messrs. Fellmeth, Walz, and Wild within the supervisory board of Robert Bosch GmbH".[16] Robert Bosch had, Walz said, voiced "the desire and intention that those directors who had contributed the most to building up the company and who are fit to be pillars and guardians of the Bosch tradition should, on retiring from the board of management, […] move over to the supervisory board, creating a close link with the board of management and allowing the younger generation, while acting on their own responsibility, to do so under the guidance of former members of the board of management."[17] Walz saw not only himself, but also Fellmeth and Wild, as such "pillars of the Bosch tradition," and Walz now demanded that these three should band together organizationally in the form of a working committee. "The three gentlemen having now been politically re-established, it is our duty to fulfill the intentions of Mr. Bosch."[18] In the final analysis, this meant concentrating powers within the group of executors in the hands of these three individuals. Albrecht Fischer, the former chairman of the supervisory board, now had to cede this position to Walz, but above all, the incumbent members of the board of management had to accept substantial curbs on their powers. Wild was granted a special position, as later was Walz, "in that he may at his own discretion become involved in the day-to-day management of RB GmbH, i. e., in dealing with all business transactions and issues, and that he may have people report to him, issue instructions, declare individual actions or decisions as subject to his prior or subsequent approval, and so on." Citing Robert Bosch's motto to the effect that "the eye of the master never rests but keeps critical watch over the company," Walz said that they too had something similar in mind.[19]

Arthur Leinss was the only person to voice misgivings about Walz's plans. Walz, however, brushed such reservations aside on the grounds that it was "the express intention of Mr. Bosch that matters should be dealt with as he, Walz, proposed." Indeed, he went on, the whole matter would have been settled along these lines long since, but for the improper dismissals ordered by the Americans. In his view, once Fellmeth, Walz, and Wild had been exonerated, the right course for the members of the board of management would have been spontaneously "to place themselves at those gentlemen's disposal. But Fräulein Bosch [editor's note: Margarete Bosch, one of Robert Bosch's two daughters from his first marriage] (for instance) had felt it would be intolerable if people such as Mr. Walz should return to office."[20] Yet what the Bosch family may have said was "beside the point for the present. In our view it is the will of Mr. Bosch that counts. It is vital that we do our job in accordance with his spirit and intentions."[21] That ended the discussion, and the matter was indeed resolved as Walz proposed.

The debate succinctly illustrates Walz's behavior and style, and until he resigned all his positions at Bosch at the end of March 1963, it was to be a recurrent theme through the further evolution of the company's management and decision-making bodies. It was not simply that Walz claimed to be the only member of the group of executors who knew how the wishes of Robert Bosch were to be interpreted and implemented. It was also typical of the man that he was already thinking about the future institutional continuity of that controlling, monitoring, and decision-making body. Not until October 1952 did the question of controlling and decision-making powers and hence the whole complex relationship between the group of executors, the supervisory board, and the board of management return to the Bosch agenda. The occasion was the new law relating to corporate governance, the Works Council Constitution Act [*Betriebsverfassungsgesetz*] that came into effect in November of that year. The supervisory board of Robert Bosch GmbH as it was then constituted possessed substantially greater powers under the shareholders' agreement (corporate constitution) than the new law allowed. However, Walz felt he needed to do something, given that employee representatives would be elected to the supervisory board in the future. In other words, the supervisory board could no longer continue in its current form, notably in view of what would in the future be the legally inadmissible special position occupied by Walz and Wild.[22] The new supervisory board would possess only monitoring and control powers and would no longer be allowed to involve itself directly in management affairs. As Walz saw things, the only way for himself and Wild to retain their special position and powers was to step down from the supervisory board and, equipped with all the special rights and functions flowing from Robert Bosch's will, return to the board of management.[23] So it was that Wild (now 70) and Walz (just one year younger) re-joined the board of management on November 5, 1952. When Wild died only a few days later (on November 20), Walz assumed sole chairmanship. Early in December, at a meeting of the group of executors held very soon after Wild's death, Walz also had all special rights formally transferred to himself, to the extent that "supreme leadership of Robert Bosch GmbH should now be exercised and the position that Robert Bosch had once occupied within the company should in the future be filled by Mr. Walz alone, who also assumes responsibility for all business fields, including the entire technical field."[24] To justify this action, Walz again drew on his large store of declarations, resolutions, desiderata, and reflections uttered by Robert Bosch, declaring that the latter had personally harbored and expressed the intention of making him, Hans Walz, *Generaldirektor*.[25]

The mere fact that the members of the board of management were presented with a *fait accompli* led to tensions among senior executives. However, actual conflict broke out over the question of who should replace Wild in the group of executors. From the ranks of the board of management, Otto Fischer and Alfred Knoerzer had been proposed, but Walz rejected both out of hand.

In Fischer's case, he did so with reference to his belonging to the family, having married Margarete Bosch [editor's note: Robert Bosch's daughter from his first marriage] on September 13, 1952. Knoerzer was rejected on the grounds that, as a member of the board of management, he could not at the same time serve as an executor, since that would make him effectively his own supervisor. Only in his own case did Walz see an exception as being adequately justified. When Albrecht Fischer and Leinss nonetheless insisted on Knoerzer's appointment, Walz announced that he would "most resolutely oppose" any such nomination. During the time when the three men [i. e., Walz, Fellmeth, and Wild] had been out in the cold, Walz alleged, Knoerzer had campaigned against their return and sought to reduce their influence within the company, "in gross violation" of the wishes of the founder. He had even taken part in an "attempted palace revolution" that spring. Walz claimed to know that Fischer's wife, Dr. Fischer-Bosch, had visited various individuals, vigorously lobbying for Knoerzer's election. Yet she had no right at all, he said, "to meddle in matters concerning the company and the executors. She is neither capable of saying nor entitled to say anything whatsoever about questions of the succession and the work of the executors. That is just what Mr. Bosch wished expressly to achieve with his testamentary provisions, namely that the heirs of his first marriage should be given no influence over the company and the executors of his will."[26] Walz further stated that "Mr. Robert Bosch talked to me about the most private matters. Laying aside all false modesty, I declare that I am the most important of the executors. As such I must have a colleague who is acceptable to me, not one who is unacceptable. [...] When it comes to the last will and testament of Mr. Bosch I will not stand for any nonsense. I feel responsible toward Mr. Bosch, and should I meet him in another world I want to be able to say that I performed the task he set me and did so correctly."[27]

Conflicts with the works council

As was the case in other companies, the postwar Bosch works council was made up of members who had been active in the Social Democratic and Communist parties prior to the seizure of power by the NSDAP. Whereas in Stuttgart it was SPD-oriented works-council members under the chairmanship of Willy Boetzer who were in the majority, the Feuerbach works council under Eugen Eberle was firmly in the hands of Communists. And the two groups were fierce enemies.[28] Works-council business had little trade-union input as yet, being still very much governed by party-political issues, and Eberle wasted no time in creating a smoothly functioning cell of like-minded representatives in Feuerbach that gave him a solid power base both in Feuerbach and company-wide. With a collapsing currency, a flourishing black market, and a national food crisis, the most urgent problem facing works councils and management alike was how to find enough to eat for a fast-expanding workforce. The "food crisis" lasted from 1945 to 1948, and for three years large sections of postwar society staged repeated "wildcat" hunger strikes and demonstrations against the rationing policies of both the military government and the German authorities. At Bosch, such a strike was called on September 5, 1947.[29] Meanwhile, a motley workforce structure had also developed – long-standing Bosch associates, war returnees, and above all hundreds of refugees (at the end of 1946, Bosch employed around 1,150 displaced persons). All these needed to be molded into a new Bosch workforce, and this then had to be given a sense of belonging. However, the main problem for Bosch, the one that dominated all others, was denazification, which carved deep rifts between management and workforce representatives and determined the lines of conflict into the 1950s.[30]

In late 1950 and early 1951, wage disputes began to dominate the picture more and more. However, the way employees were organized had meanwhile shifted very much toward union affiliation and factory-wide or industry-wide negotiations.[31] Strike ballots regarding a new wage agreement were held throughout the Württemberg metalworking industries, with the Bosch workforces in Stuttgart (75 percent) and Feuerbach (87 percent) also signaling a readiness to strike. Only at the eleventh hour did the IG Metall metalworkers' union and the employers' association manage to reach a settlement. The member of the Bosch board of management responsible for industrial relations was Otto Fischer, who nonetheless expressed "sadness" that so many Bosch associates, in being prepared to strike "against their own workplace," had "failed to show the Bosch spirit" of mutual toleration and pulling together for the good of all that had been so widely invoked.[32] "Cooperation or class struggle" is how Fischer had described the fateful question of the future relationship between employees and employers at Bosch, and the intensive debate about codetermination and the Works Council Constitution Act that began around the same time whipped the waves even higher. Subsequently, labor relations within Bosch became less tense, as did relations between works council and Bosch board of management. In June 1952, new work rules were signed, and following the works-council elections of May 1953, management noted with relief that no communist-party candidates had stood in Stuttgart, while in Feuerbach only some 6 works-council members out of a total of 25 were affiliated to the KPD, meaning that "there is now no Communist majority on the works council in Feuerbach either".[33]

Signing the new labor regulations with (from left) Bosch board members Bauer and Fischer, works-council chairmen Boetzer (Stuttgart) and Frank (Feuerbach), and works-council members Müller and Grieshaber (June 19, 1952)

The constraints of Allied antitrust legislation: Bosch and its "deconcentration case" (1947–1952)

The immediate postwar years also presented Bosch with a problem of a quite different kind, one that became more and more urgent. On February 12, 1947, the American military government passed Law no. 56, forbidding "excessive concentration in the German economy." It was coupled with another piece of legislation to the same effect, Law no. 78, enacted by the British occupying power.[34] It was around this time that an initial phase of the break-up, deconcentration, and antitrust policy pursued by the British, American, and French military governments in their respective zones of occupation immediately after the end of the war reached its climax. The policy was aimed mainly at the heavy-industrial groups of the iron and steel sectors, the chemicals industry in the shape of IG Farben, and the banks, but Bosch was also affected. Following capitulation, German industrial companies – including Bosch headquarters in Stuttgart and various Bosch plants – had received visits from innumerable intelligence teams of technical experts – the American Field Investigation Agency, Technical (or FIAT) being one example. Such teams confiscated papers and patent documents, conducted interrogations,

Works assembly (1961)

and inspected manufacturing facilities in order to give themselves a precise picture of Bosch's product and manufacturing expertise.[35] Such "intellectual reparations," however, were of little value to competitors in Britain or the U.S., since they comprised only the expertise that had been written down. The papers did not include the essential know-how shared by the company's engineers and technicians. Without this, the information was of little use.[36] A more painful imposition so far as Bosch was concerned was a decree issued by the French military government in November 1946. This ordered the relocation of machine tools, equipment, raw materials, and semi-finished and finished products from Reutlingen in the South Württemberg section of the French zone of occupation to Homburg, in the Saarland. Despite protests by the Bosch board of management, items began to be moved at the beginning of December. For a long time the board of management was led to believe that Bosch still co-owned the plant, partly in order to provide technical assistance to put the Saar protectorate back on its feet. But then, one year on, the French used deconcentration legislation to justify the whole operation retrospectively.[37] All the same, Bosch later received compensation for loss of assets, and over the medium term it gained a further advantage. Through the permanent establishment that was soon trading in the Saar as "Feintechnik AG," it renewed contact with Lavalette, its former long-standing joint venture partner in France.[38]

When in March 1947 Law no. 56 and Law no. 78 came into effect, Bosch did in fact brace itself for a thorough examination.[39] Not that anyone believed that the antitrust provisions were going to pose any great threat to the company. The intention of the law, as Albrecht Fischer put it to the group of executors on March 17, 1947, was "to rule out any conglomeration of companies for arms-manufacturing purposes."[40] However, it soon became clear that the American antitrust experts in the military government took a very different view of Bosch. A report by the Decartelization Branch named Bosch as a monopolist of the same caliber as IG Farben, Flick, and Siemens, and toward the end of 1947 evidence was piling up that the military-government departments responsible were already considering whether and to what extent the Stuttgart and Feuerbach plants could be forcibly separated.[41] Suddenly, concern about a break-up of Bosch, whether violent or arbitrary, loomed large. What was crucial, according to an internal memorandum written during August 1947, was to defend the status of the parent company and, if possible, to steer it through the decartelization process without forfeiting a single one of its products.[42] The other subsidiaries were, it said, so far removed from the production focus of the parent company "that from a purely manufacturing point of view it would not matter, should it come to amputation, which one is sacrificed first."[43]

Following intensive discussions with military-government agencies as well as with the Württemberg-Baden Ministry of Economic Affairs, the Americans indicated that they would welcome deconcentration proposals coming from Bosch itself. They wished to see the law implemented by "consent decree" so far as possible, rather than imposed from above. And indeed, the Bosch board of management subsequently expressed a willingness to make a series of concessions in order to reach a compromise that would bring the whole matter to an end. Among its proposals was that Noris Zünd-Licht AG in Nuremberg should be sold off, as should its holding in Adlerwerke AG, Frankfurt. Eisemann AG was to be wound up, although the part of it belonging to its core field of business would be kept on, and finally Trillke-Werke in Hildesheim and Sundgau Maschinenbau GmbH in Giengen were to be dissolved as legally independent companies and would continue to be run as Bosch plants – something that was already happening de facto.[44] As a precaution, however, Bosch also secured the counsel of Dr. Rudolf Mueller, a well-known attorney familiar with U.S. antitrust law. This single legal adviser was soon to be joined by a whole host of attorneys – some of them American, British, and French. In the ensuing weeks and months, they looked into the finer points of both U.S. and German competition and antitrust legislation. How necessary this was came to light no later than the beginning of 1948, when the implementing regulations relating to Law no. 56 and Law no. 78 were enacted, introducing what in the future would be two different procedures: decartelization [*Entkartellierung*] and break-up or deconcentration [*Entflechtung*]. The clear terminological distinction was important. The latter procedure was (solely) about breaking down companies into economically independent units – decentralization, in effect. Decartelization, on the other hand, was about dismantling monopolies and cartels that restrained competition. The procedure used against Bosch was therefore primarily one of *Entflechtung* rather than *Entkartellierung*.

On March 25, 1948, the deconcentration commission at last arrived at its ruling in the Bosch affair. At the offices of the military government, it was formally handed over to Albrecht Fischer as chairman of the supervisory board and to Arthur Leinss as representative of the executors. It took the form of a "provisional decision and directive," and came as a shock to the Bosch management, since it exceeded their worst expectations. Bosch was accused of restraining and obstructing trade and commerce, among other things through provisions in its agreements with other companies, by instances of price-fixing, carving up market territories, allotting production quotas, suppressing technologies, and using restrictive patent and licensing practices. The company therefore (the directive went on) constituted an excessive concentration of economic power within the meaning of the law.[45] Consequently, the military government decreed a whole series of decartelization and deconcentration measures, including hiving off the Bosch plants in Mühlhausen and Bamberg, the subsidiaries in Hildesheim (Trillke and Blaupunkt), Taufkirchen (Fernseh GmbH), and Stuttgart-Untertürkheim (Eugen Bauer GmbH), among others, as well as the company's equity interests in Nuremberg (Noris) and Frankfurt (Adler). In addition, extensive conditions were attached to the use or licensing of industrial property rights and patents. Bosch was given 90 days to submit a timetable for implementing these measures. The board of management was especially concerned that separating off the Bamberg spark-plug plant and the Trillke factory in Hildesheim would substantially weaken Bosch's core field of business.[46] As a result, the board lodged an immediate objection, and requested a hearing. In an objection that ran to more than 100 pages, together with numerous appendices and witness statements, the company fundamentally questioned the validity of Law no. 56 and Law no. 78 in international and constitutional law, and issued a detailed rebuttal of the individual charges laid against it under antitrust law.[47] The objection was supported by a series of protestations from the works councils and workforces of the plants concerned, together with interventions on the part of the central works council as well as by local union representatives before the Decartelization Branch of the U.S. military government. It was also backed up by further legal opinions in which Bosch, using concrete examples, showed that numerous provisions of this piece of Allied legislation conflicted with the way U.S. antitrust law was administered in practice.[48] Eventually, in February 1949, an oral hearing was called.[49] It was clear from the outset that in lodging its objection and requesting the hearing Bosch was playing for time, hoping that the climate of Marshall Plan aid and considerations of reconstruction and integration with the West would bring about fundamental changes in Allied economic policy.[50]

On June 17, 1949, the "final decision and directive" was presented to Bosch. To its dismay, the board of management had to face the fact that very little had changed since the harsh terms of the provisional directive.[51] So Bosch promptly appealed the military government's ruling. Shortly thereafter, the appeals committee originally set up by the Allies was transformed into a court of appeal – which complicated the issue for Bosch, since things were now to be dealt with under U.S. (that is to say: Anglo-Saxon) law. On January 5, 1951, nearly four years after the deconcentration law came into effect, Bosch submitted its writ of appeal – a printed book comprising 134 pages with numerous statistical appendices and diagrams.[52] One of its arguments was that, in assessing Bosch's market position, the deconcentration commission had based its findings on obsolete market-share figures dating from 1938.[53] However, Bosch was now only half the size of its British competitor, Lucas, for instance, and in any case (the Bosch argument ran), "Bosch would never have been able to retain its position in the German economy or elsewhere and would certainly not be able to do so today if the company behaved toward its customers as if it had no competition to fear whatsoever."[54]

By this time, partly at Bosch's urging, the German government had also stepped in. Compared to the breaking up of the coal and steel sector and the heavy-industrial deconcentration policy of the Allied high commissioners – matters that from the autumn of 1950 dominated negotiations between the German federal government and the occupying powers – the Bosch case was somewhat marginal. Nonetheless, persistent intervention by the Bosch board of management succeeded in mobilizing assistance from the Federal Ministry of Economic Affairs in Bonn. Besides Bosch, several other German companies were in a similar position at this time (i. e., threatened with U.S. deconcentration measures), including Maschinenfabrik Augsburg-Nürnberg (MAN), Siemens & Halske, Degussa, and Vereinigte Glanzstoffwerke. However, it was beginning to look as if the other cases would no longer be prosecuted, which left Bosch as the only company still under threat from compulsory break-up under Law no. 56. According to a letter (formulated in advance by Bosch) from the Federal Minister of Economic Affairs Ludwig Erhard to Federal Chancellor Konrad Adenauer, the German federal government handed a memorandum to the economic advisers of the Allied High Commission on December 28, 1950, asking the commission to refrain from implementing the projected deconcentration measures or at least to postpone doing so until Germany had enacted its own antitrust or competition legislation.[55] The Bosch case (the memo suggested) should then be dealt with under German antitrust legislation.[56] "But the Americans," Knoerzer complained to the supervisory board in mid-June 1951, "are sticking obstinately to their plan to bring Bosch down. Tackling this problem is not only taking a lot of time, it is also costing a lot of money. So far, 450,000 German marks have been spent."[57] The unanimous feeling, however, was that a settlement should not be sought as things stood. Despite the risk involved, "the fight should go on."[58] At the end of December 1951, therefore, the German federal government sent a second memorandum to the Allied High Commission.[59]

At the same time, the Bosch board of management tried, by intervening directly and holding talks with the Allied High Commission, to find a way out of what had become a gridlocked situation. Knoerzer urged the American High Commissioner John J. McCloy to defer proceedings before the court of appeal (now set to begin on January 14, 1952) until a new German Act against Restraints on Competition came into force. McCloy gave no assurances and tried to lay much of the blame on Bosch ("the sole reason for the case's not yet being over is the objection lodged by Bosch and the legal questions to which it gives rise").[60] Nonetheless, there was a clear awareness on the American side that the deconcentration commission had over-reached itself with the one case left on its books, and that the Bosch deconcentration proceedings themselves, not to mention the measures threatened as a result, were politically no longer opportune. Before long, therefore, it was mainly a question of finding a sensible conclusion to the matter, one that would allow the Allied authorities to save public face. In January 1952, accordingly, intensive attempts to reach a settlement began in the Grand Hotel Petersberg, overlooking Bonn. On February 5, 1952, these talks ultimately led to a new "final determination and order."[61] This new ruling still described Bosch as a market-dominating, monopolistic group, but the measures now imposed on Bosch (or rather, voluntarily undertaken by Bosch as a result of the settlement) were significantly less severe. Bosch relinquished Noris Zünd-Licht AG, the Adlerwerke, Dreilinden Maschinenbau GmbH (lost in any case), and the Ideal-Werke in Berlin. This was almost precisely what Bosch had offered in the first settlement of 1947 – less, actually, since there was no longer any mention of shedding the Bamberg facility, the Hildesheim plant, or Eisemann AG. Only certain provisions concerning the granting of licenses remained.

In the end, Bosch got off lightly so far as decartelization was concerned, despite the long period of uncertainty. However, whether this was due to the way Knoerzer stood his ground (in contrast to the conciliatory stance adopted by Otto Fischer, as was later alleged by some of those involved) is hard to judge.[62] In any event, had proceedings indeed been deferred until Germany passed its own Act against Restraints on Competition, Bosch would have gained no advantage. Discussion of that law was long drawn out, not least because of the resistance of German industry. It was not until January 1, 1958, that the relevant piece of legislation took effect.[63] Misgivings about the patent provisions also turned out to be groundless. Nonetheless, so far as the Bosch managers most directly involved were concerned, the whole case remained an open wound until as late as the end of 1952. As Knoerzer wrote in his retrospective account in the *Bosch-Zünder*, "We are not happy with the outcome, since we still take the view that we were the victims of an obsolete law and of economic principles that, while they may be justified in America, can only cause harm in this form in Germany."[64] For five years, the Bosch board of management members Fischer and Knoerzer had done virtually nothing else but fight a running battle with the conditions imposed and legal papers issued by the deconcentration commission. Now that proceedings were over, the board of management could at last set about building up the corporate organization without having to fear the loss of facilities or subsidiaries.[65] Be that as it may, the Bosch deconcentration case had not so much an economic as a political dimension, falling as it did in the middle of an awkward phase when competition control was passing from the military government to the new West German government – and when all the associated problems were (so to speak) blamed on the Bosch case.

On the brink of a growth crisis: sales figures and corporate financing in a period of tumultuous expansion

Despite all setbacks, operational business had developed well since the war's end. Once the military regime had sanctioned resumption of manufacturing operations, the most urgent concern was bringing home the many parts of the company that had been moved elsewhere. Since Bosch plants were split up among the various zones of occupation, this task was made more complicated.[66] Direct and indirect war losses resulting from bomb damage, expropriation (notably of the five factories in the Soviet zone of occupation), and other instances of dismantling and requisition totaled more than 100 million reichsmarks. However, like other large companies across Germany, Bosch also managed to rapidly resume at least some of the manufacturing operations that were temporarily interrupted by the war's end. In Feuerbach, the first products began rolling off the lines before 1945 was over, and from January 1946 some 1,000 generators a month were being turned out. And before long, magnetos, ignition coils, spark plugs, and headlights were also being made once more. In September 1946, the first export order for Czechoslovakia was filled, and soon orders were also coming in from Belgium, the Netherlands, Austria, and especially Switzerland, from where several other European countries were supplied with Bosch products. Yet problems obtaining raw materials, elaborate export procedures, and a shortage of foreign exchange made such transactions laborious. Moreover, there were constant capacity problems as a result of the huge loss of machines (some 6,000 in number) and the threat of restitution demands. Until new machines could be acquired from the United States or from the German mechanical engineering industry, plants often had to improvise.[67]

The diagram on the following page shows the organizational structure of senior management on January 1, 1950. It follows a classic functional scheme. For all Knoerzer's skillful financial management, however, the financial situation at Bosch was tight. At the end of March 1951, the company found itself facing a short-term funding shortfall of 25.7 million German marks. And a 2-million-German-mark loan from the *Kreditanstalt für Wiederaufbau* [KfW: reconstruction credit institute] did not offer much help. In November and December 1952, therefore, Knoerzer spent almost a month in the United States talking with American banks and financial experts about possible loans. The results, however, were disappointing. Bosch's head of finance was given to understand that it would be years before Germany could once again raise private loans in the United States.[68] There was no capital market in the

Fig. 2 Organizational structure of senior management at Robert Bosch GmbH (1950)

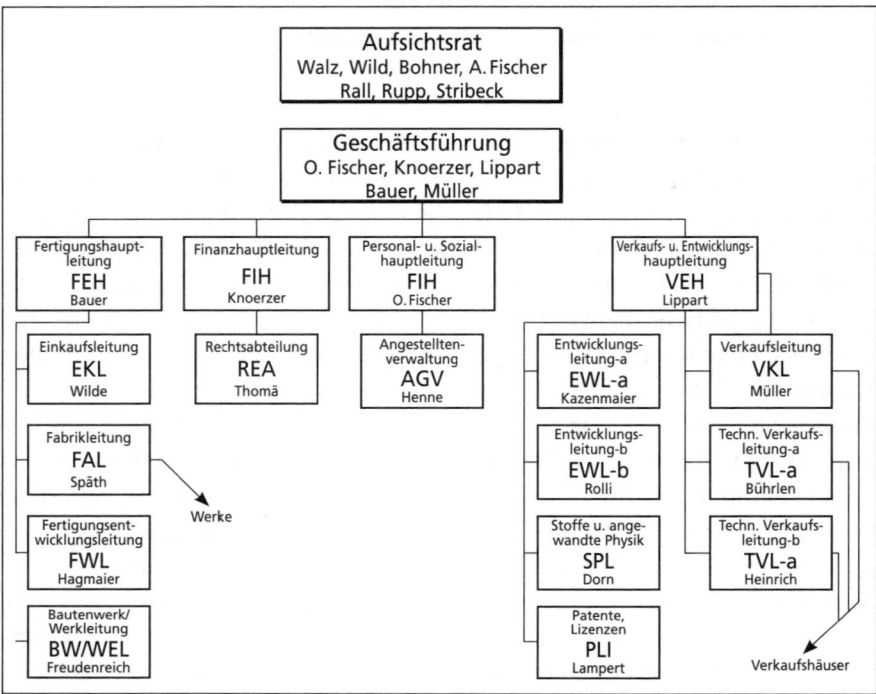

Source: *Bosch-Zünder* 1950/1, p. 6.

United States for foreign bonds, he was told. Knoerzer even turned to the World Bank, asking for a 10-million-dollar loan, but again met with refusal. "There is no question of Bosch raising loans in America – now or in the foreseeable future," he acknowledged soberly.[69] However, the trip had its good side. At a reception in New York, Knoerzer met the president of the German insurance company Allianz. This led to the prospect of Bosch receiving "several million on a long-term basis" from this source.[70] Ultimately, behind all these efforts lay a single question of principle – one that was clearly the subject of much controversy at board level. As Walz summed it up in May 1953, the question was "whether we should allow the tempo of the ever more urgent reconstruction of the company and development of its rationalization processes to be dictated by the financial resources available or instead raise additional funds to make more rapid progress."[71] The man now serving as chairman of the board of management was undoubtedly among those holding Bosch back in this connection. Walz felt committed to the traditional Bosch way of doing business – as he himself had formulated in 1936 on the occasion of the company's 50-year anniversary. "We are not," Walz had stressed, "collectors of blocks of shares, we have no talent for capitalism, we are entrepreneurs and manufacturers and wish to remain so. All we want is that the scope of our enterprise and the extent of our growth should keep pace with our own financial and leadership abilities. We would prefer to slow the process of expansion – indeed, to forgo expansion or additional business opportunities altogether – if there is any risk of our strength not being up to the appointed task, of our losing sight of our goal, or – heaven forbid – of our falling under the yoke of borrowed capital."[72]

In the early summer of 1953, however, an initial blow for freedom from something of a financial prison was delivered in the form of a bond of 20 million German marks, the first bond Bosch issued after the war. With a 98 percent issue price and paying 8 percent interest, the bond ran for between 5 and 15 years. In denominations of 5,000, 1,000, and 500 German marks, it was part-aimed from the outset at the small private investor. The bonds sold like hot cakes, being oversubscribed by several times. The modernization and extension investments that the company's plants (particularly in Feuerbach) so urgently needed could be made at last.[73] However, rapidly rising demand clearly exceeded this extension of manufacturing capacity. In consequence, Bosch mainly bought up existing factory premises from other companies at first, converting them to its needs. The company already had branch operations in Giengen, Bamberg, Hildesheim, and Berlin. These were joined by plants in Leinfelden, Waiblingen, Rutesheim, and Nuremberg, and other plants were added subsequently in Bühlertal, Blaichach, and Homburg. Only in the late 1950s did Bosch start building new facilities in Göttingen and Dillingen. These developments, coupled with the labor shortage in Germany, had resulted in a geographical decentralization of the company's manufacturing facilities. While some 72 percent of Bosch associates were employed in the Stuttgart and Feuerbach plants in 1954, that figure was down to 39 percent seven years later.[74]

The continuing need for capital expenditure made the next bond issue (this time for 30 million German marks) necessary as early as the summer of 1955. This time, however, the projected issue failed to receive the blessing of the Federal Ministry of Economic Affairs. Bosch tried again in the following spring, and after being blocked for a while by a twofold increase in the bank rate, the new Bosch bond issue was successfully placed in November 1956 – this time with a volume of 40 million German marks and paying 8 percent interest.[75] Further substantial capital requirements were expected for subsequent years, prompting fresh discussion between the group of executors and

The one-millionth Bosch diesel
injection pump (1950)

the board of management regarding the financial-policy principles of Robert
Bosch GmbH.[76] Debate centered on the ratio of non-current and current
liabilities to total assets Bosch could safely bear without compromising its
financial independence. It was eventually decided that liabilities must not
exceed 45 percent of operating capital – though in special circumstances
they would be allowed to temporarily exceed 50 percent. "However, if the
said limit is reached, a voluntary curb must be placed upon business expansion in order to preserve the company as an independent family-run enterprise in line with the intentions of Robert Bosch, as set out in the will, the
guidelines for the executors, and the shareholders' agreement. In this connection, measures shall be taken to ensure that the company's core area of
automotive equipment is promoted first and foremost, and that any necessary restrictions are put in place in other areas, whether at the main plant or
the subsidiaries."[77]

The sales figures leave no doubt as to how tempestuous the growth was
that brought Bosch to the brink of crisis. Between 1949 and 1955, average annual increases of 27.6 percent boosted sales revenue from 188 million to
757 million German marks. In December 1950, the pump works announced
production of its millionth injection pump. In September 1955, less than five

years later, the 2-million mark was reached. The year 1958, with sales of 1,153 million German marks, saw the company's sales pass the one-billion mark for the first time.

By 1952, Bosch already had market shares of over 90 percent in crucial sectors of the German automotive original-equipment business, namely in generators, injection pumps, ignition coils, and starters. In spark plugs, its share was over 70 percent. In this respect, the Allied deconcentration authorities were not so far wrong in their assessment of Bosch's market position.[78] In 1956, automotive equipment accounted for more than 70 percent of total sales at Bosch, but particularly the "cooling business" was really "hotting up," so to speak. Bosch refrigerators were selling extremely well both at home and abroad, soon accounting for some 20 percent of total sales. Germany was not only looking at a motoring wave. It was already riding a wave of electrification and modernization of household appliances. There could be no doubt that Bosch was well on the way to recovering its former market power.

2 From family-run business to foundation-owned company: the long march to a new Bosch constitution

During the 1960s, profound changes were made to the structure of the company, as well as to its character and its corporate governance. The story is a complex one, turning on material having not only to do with corporate law, but also with inheritance and tax law, and exhibiting a number of anomalies. It is also a story that has never been told in public before. The first thing to note is that the narrative is dictated from the outset by the last will and testament of Robert Bosch. It is by no means a straightforward narrative, with constant wrangling going on about what the founder actually meant by what he wrote. At the same time, the "constitutional principles" of the company were exposed to adaptation and change in order to make them comply with altered circumstances and to allow for as many contingencies as possible. The second thing is that Bosch did not simply cease to be a family-run business in order to become a foundation-owned company. Both elements were retained. Only the weighting changed. It became a company that bore some resemblance to a foundation – but with the family playing a role, albeit a subordinate one, as shareholder, controller, and active member of the board of management. Thirdly, this upheaval in the corporate governance of Bosch went on for much longer than a first glance might suggest. The subject first appeared on the agenda in the 1950s, when the question of succession arose and Robert Bosch Jr. joined the board of management. It came to a head between 1962 and 1964, culminating in the "grand settlement" [*die große Einigung*], as it was called. However, as will be shown, the subject remained acute into the 1970s, and even reared its head once again in the early 1980s. In truth, the consultations and mediations surrounding this upheaval constitute a process, one which is still going on today, with relations between company and family constantly being redefined. Fourthly, this process, together with the creation of a new corporate constitution, seemed to the outside world to evolve in an atmosphere of harmony. In other words, neither matter affected operational business. The workforce, even the upper tiers of management, were almost completely unaware of them, although important members of the board were directly involved, and very much so. Yet in reality the relevant negotiations were conducted in a way that left scars on members of both branches of the family and on Robert Bosch Jr. in particular. Fifthly and finally, there is a myth which needs to be dispelled. It is often still said that the great architect of the new Bosch constitution was Hans L. Merkle and that the credit for this fundamental renewal must go to him. But while Merkle was certainly involved, the real strong man, the real initiator, was the man who had replaced Hans Walz as chairman of the group of executors, namely Alfred Knoerzer.

Who decides what the will means?
Execution of the will, and the appointment of Robert Bosch Jr. to the board of management (1953–1964)

Despite holding very substantial de jure powers, Walz scarcely ever intervened at either operational or strategic level. De facto, it was Knoerzer who, as chief financial officer, ran the company's affairs. It is possible, too, that Walz's failing health meant that the intricate details of day-to-day management were more than he could cope with. Ultimately, however, he saw his true mission as being to update the "constitutional principles of Robert Bosch GmbH" and to ensure that one or other scion of the family succeeded Robert Bosch. In his will, Robert Bosch had stipulated that leadership of the company might pass to a family director if one of the male heirs showed suitable aptitude. There were two possible candidates for the post. First, Robert Bosch Jr. (born 1928), his son from his second marriage, and second, Georg Zundel (born 1931), the son of Paula Bosch (one of the two daughters from his first marriage) and her husband Georg Friedrich Zundel, who had died in 1948. Robert Bosch Jr., who stood in direct line of descent, took priority. In late 1952, then, the crucial question for Walz and the other executors was: when should the founder's son join the Bosch board of management? During the war, the son had served a three-year apprenticeship with Wetzer, a precision-engineering company in Pfronten. In the postwar years, he had studied electrical engineering at the Stuttgart Polytechnic, taking his final exams in the spring of 1953. Walz himself may have felt very much like a "son" to the founder, often referring to him as "Father Bosch." Now, with the founder's actual son having reached the age of 25, Walz had high hopes of the young man filling the gap – the "interregnum" – that had existed at the top of the company since the founder's death 10 years earlier. As the years sped by, he thus worried more and more about the young man and his state of health. For instance, one item on the agenda of the January 1952 meeting of the group of executors read: "Robert Bosch Jr.: driving and Africa trip." The founder's descendant "had his attention drawn to the general guideline" that he must avoid particular risks and unnecessary dangers. Otherwise he would be flouting his father's intentions.[1] A similarly worded appeal was addressed to Paula Zundel when Walz learned that young Zundel was planning a motorcycle trip to Greece via Yugoslavia.[2] Robert Bosch Jr. had indicated that he was prepared to take on his father's legacy and follow in his footsteps. When it came to legacy, mission, and authorization, he could refer to a moving letter that the founder had addressed to him in January 1939, when he was just 11 years old.

"My dearest boy," Robert Bosch had written, "I am of an age that does not offer me the prospect of living to see you take over the business I have been able to build up over the years [...]. I simply wish to say that it is very important to me that you should, one day, take over my business and continue it, and that you should, when that time comes, be well prepared for the task. It will not be easy, but this task, this ambitious aim, is the best thing I can leave you [...]. I believe that I can expect you, with your disposition and with the education that your good, wise mother is providing for you, to follow in my footsteps when the time arrives, and to continue my business [...]. You have the gifts that it takes, and you also have personality, the right personality for the task [...]. Above all, beware of the people who tell you not to listen to the "old fogies" around you. Pay heed instead to the old fogies, listen to what they say, for they will certainly have the company's best interests at heart and will give you the best advice. [...] The task of continuing my business, the task I want you to take on, is a heavy one [...]. [However] I trust you to be equal to it."[3]

If we are to understand further developments and the way Robert Bosch Jr. acted in subsequent years, it is vital that we should be aware of this letter and the primacy of the "TV option" that it undoubtedly expresses [editor's note: For a discussion of the "VVB option" and the "TV option," see the latter half of the chapter "Death and legacy of Robert Bosch" at the end of the second part of this book; see also the text below]. At the end of 1952, entirely in line with his father's intentions, Robert Bosch Jr. said that he wished, once his course of studies at the Stuttgart Polytechnic was finished, to pass through several departments at the company and see something of the world of business. And initially at least, he implicitly trusted the "old fogies," who did indeed surround him all the time.[4] Hans Walz, acting in concert with Knoerzer, Lippart, and Otto Fischer, proceeded to draw up a training program for the young man, detailing stages in particular plants and departments and including a lengthy stay in the United States.[5] Walz said he "felt under an obligation to ensure that, while he [Walz] was still at the helm, Mr.

Bosch Jr. should be able to grow into his task as his father's successor."[6] More than ever, Walz saw himself as the "standard-bearer of the Bosch tradition." As the eulogy marking his 70th birthday in March 1953 put it, it was he who "had looked most deeply into Robert Bosch's heart and mind."[7] Walz's near-religious understanding of his mission and of the Robert Bosch legacy and its imminent fulfillment came out with particular clarity in his speech at the "Herrenabend," the traditional year-end gathering of Bosch senior executives held on December 21, 1953. "I am one of the few men still living," Walz said, "whom Father Bosch repeatedly and solemnly charged with preparing the way for his son, provided – of course – the indispensable conditions for succession should be met. Therefore, given that men of advanced age are especially aware of the frailty of human existence, and given that the requirements laid down by the father with regard to his son have been successfully met, I am filled with an almost impatient striving to bring about the situation that the son was intended to inherit – and to do so without further ado."[8] In other words, despite qualms voiced by some of the other executors, Walz was keen for Robert Bosch Jr. to receive a seat on the Bosch board of management as soon as possible. The young man had officially been taken on by Robert Bosch GmbH as a trainee engineer on October 1, 1953. Following an introductory period lasting until the end of 1954, the plan was to promote him to the board of management and, at the same time, for him to replace Arthur Leinss (retiring on age grounds) in the group of executors [*Testamentsvollstrecker* or TV].[9] The executors agreed to allow the founder's son to sit in at their meetings (albeit not on a regular basis) in order to familiarize him with his future role.[10] With that decision, the executors were taking a further step toward the "TV option."

At a meeting of the group of executors held at the end of November 1954, Walz proposed that Robert Bosch Jr. should be appointed to full membership of the Bosch board of management with effect from December 21, initially without portfolio. His work in the company thus far, Walz said, had demonstrated "his suitability as family director." His critical judgment and rapid grasp of affairs had been impressive. In this respect, Walz suggested, he took after his father.[11] Other senior executives had felt the same. No one was in any doubt as to his ability to enter upon his father's inheritance one day. In particular, repeated stress was laid on his exceptional intelligence, his swift understanding and ability to put two and two together, his gift for fiercely logical thought, and his quick, clear judgment. Walz quoted at length from the subjective reports from the various departments in which the young man had worked, all of which sounded promising. The proposed appointment was eventually made official at the executors' meeting of December 15, 1954.

"Surrounded by old men"; meeting of the group of executors. *From left*: Ernst Rupp, Albrecht Fischer, Arthur Leinss, Robert Bosch Jr., Hans Walz, Max Dehn, Erwin Bohner, Alfred Knoerzer, Karl Schreiber (December 15, 1954)

With great ceremony, Walz sent news of the resolution to Robert Bosch Jr. "It is a great occasion for us when, as on this day, we can dub you knight, so to speak – a great occasion, indeed, since with it our work as executors attains one of its high points."[12] "Soon," Walz had said only the day before the meeting in his address to the members of senior management gathered in Stuttgart, "the Bosch Christmas message" would be proclaimed. Once more (that message would run) "the eye of a lord and master belonging to the Bosch line will keep watch within and over our company." It gave him "blissful satisfaction" to know that, as a result of this decision, "an aspiration very dear to the heart of Father Bosch would be brought closer to its final fulfillment."[13] All this shows how much hope all those concerned attached to Robert Bosch Jr.'s joining the board. However, the young man himself immediately made clear that he intended to place his own stamp on things. Reporting on the young man's reply to the executors, Walz wrote: "He said it was not the end of the matter that he should take his foreordained place. He also meant to form his own judgments on any problems that might arise. The confidence and support of the executors and board members would undoubtedly be of valuable assistance to him."[14]

Hans Walz in conversation with Robert Bosch Jr. (January 4, 1954)

First, however, a further induction period was set. This was to last until the spring of 1955. After that, the founder's son was to spend about a year in the United States, gathering experience. He did indeed visit dozens of companies in the U.S. between March and June 1955, including IBM, American Bosch, Hartford Machine Co., and General Motors, before Walz recalled him prematurely. In the meantime, he had been made a full member of the group of executors (instead of merely sitting in as a guest), and at last, on January 1, 1956, he joined the Bosch board of management, taking over as head of engineering and thus becoming the company's most senior development manager. Here, he continued to express his own opinions freely. In November 1956, for instance, he quite clearly stated "that in connection with forthcoming arms contracts the company should keep as low a profile as possible."[15] In engineering per se, he was also now setting his own agenda – introducing an organizational split between development of equipment for electrical motors and for electrical bodywork, ordering personnel changes in the development management of household appliances, and deepening co-operation between development on the one hand and sales and manufac-turing on the other.[16] However, to give Robert Bosch Jr. further managerial experience, it had been decided at the start of 1959 that, after concentrating on manufacturing for a while, he should take over the technical directorship of Eugen Bauer GmbH ("Kino-Bauer").[17]

What concerned Walz especially at this time, however, was the question (which had first arisen in 1952) of who should succeed the executors them-selves. What in particular had to be settled was "whether it can be deemed proper or even useful that, when a seat in the group of executors falls vacant, someone from the active senior management of Robert Bosch GmbH should more or less automatically be appointed."[18] In a 15-page, historically discur-sive memorandum, he concluded that at no time had automatic co-optation been intended, and that (as Walz himself had argued in 1952) the triumvirate of Fellmeth, Walz, and Wild had been a purely expedient arrangement. With Walz, Knoerzer, and Robert Bosch Jr., there were once again three active members of the board of management who at the same time belonged to the group of executors. The critical problem now was that Albrecht Fischer and Max Dehn were retiring from the latter body on grounds of age and ill health. In the event of a further by-election appointment of active members of the board of management, these would now suddenly number five, which would give them a majority in the shareholders' meeting.[19] Yet by its whole tendency and nature, Walz argued, the group of executors stood above both board of management and supervisory board at Robert Bosch GmbH. It was, he said, "the supreme authority of the company so long as, either alone or jointly with the family director, Robert Bosch Jr., it represents and performs owner-ship functions."[20] It also served "as court of appeal for such differences of opinion as might arise within the board of management." However, a super-ordinate appeal body could not be made up of persons from the level of au-thority lying below it. Otherwise, material and personal clashes of various kinds might result. That was why the laws governing both stock corporations and close corporations expressly forbade members of boards of management from sitting simultaneously on their own supervisory boards. A clear sepa-ration of levels of authority (he argued) was essential, "which clearly means that my question has to be answered in the negative." Moreover, even with a number of family directors present, there was a danger of factions forming. In short, "having active members of the board of management on the com-mittee of executors could distort the essence and nature of that body, even blow it apart [...]. The election of active members of the board of manage-ment to the group of executors of Robert Bosch GmbH [therefore] conflicts with the overall interests of the company."[21] In January 1957, Walz added a further supplement to the succession memo. In it, he distinguished between a "family director in the true sense" (someone, in other words, whom the founder's last will and testament entitled to be the sole representative of the interests of the shareholders of Robert Bosch GmbH) and "an as yet un-proven family director" who was still in the development and probation stage. This was clearly aimed at Robert Bosch Jr. One reason why the subject of succession loomed so large in the group of executors was that several members were about to retire on age grounds. Not counting Robert Bosch Jr., the average age of the executors was a little over seventy-two. Whatever happened, there was a need for young blood, which meant appointing successors.[22]

Walz was also working on a new version of the shareholders' agreement of Robert Bosch GmbH. The process took two years and was concluded only on March 12, 1958, at a formal ceremony attended by the family shareholders, the executors, and the members of the supervisory board and the board of management. Walz began his presentation by detailing the sense, purpose, and motives of the various alterations and additions.[23] He reminded his audience that the "constitution" of Bosch [its *Grundgesetz* or "basic law"] comprised three documents, namely: the will, the guidelines, and the shareholders' agreement. The founder himself had gone to a lot of trouble to make these documents logically consistent in order to ensure four things. First, after his death, he wanted his economic, social, and cultural objectives to continue to be pursued in his spirit and as laid down in his last will. Second, it was his wish that Robert Bosch GmbH should remain in existence for as many generations as possible, preferably as a family business. Third, male descendants or the husbands of female descendants should, if suitably qualified, be able to become family directors. Fourth, a family director should, if wholly suitable (a matter for the group of executors alone to decide), be appointed sole successor to Robert Bosch and hold 51 percent of the shares, thus becoming principal shareholder and owner in place of the group of executors. However, Walz contested that the situation in which the three documents were conceived had been changed so fundamentally by the war and its aftermath "that the will and the shareholders' agreement diverge widely at key points, so that fulfilling vital elements of the former, notably the continued existence of Robert Bosch GmbH and the possible appointment of a family director as sole successor, had been thrown into question or become frankly impossible."[24] So it was time to change the letter of the constitution, i. e., the shareholders' agreement, in order to bring it back into line with the meaning and spirit of the objectives voiced by the founder.[25]

It is not clear whether Robert Bosch Jr. knew what he was in for when, at the start of 1959, the group of executors decided that he should take over the technical directorship of Kino-Bauer as part of his induction program. It is equally unclear whether the executors deliberately assigned the young man to this sphere of responsibility. It soon emerged that the subsidiary had massive problems and was actually in serious need of reorganization. What *was* clear, on the other hand, and abundantly so, was that not just Walz but also the other executors were now very much less keen on Robert Bosch Jr. At some point in the spring of 1959, the group of executors (above all, Walz himself) changed their minds about their chosen policy in the matter of assigning the majority shareholding in Robert Bosch GmbH. They were clearly turning away from the "TV option" and back to the "VVB option." However, the distance already traveled down the road to the "TV option" made switching direction a complex matter. It especially sowed a great deal of strife in relations with the family shareholders – the more so since in principle the founder's will provided for (or rather suggested) three distinct options. The first was the gradual emergence of a capable descendant as family director, culminating in the assignment of 51 percent of the capital stock by the group of executors as trustees (the so-called "TV option"). The second was to waive such special assignment by the group of executors, which meant that the normal rules of inheritance would apply with regard to the company shares, with any unclaimed shares falling to VVB by default. The third, finally, was the deliberate strengthening of VVB through assignment of all Robert Bosch GmbH shares (preferred shares excepted), as a result of which VVB would hold 86.3 percent. This was the "VVB option."[26]

The executors undoubtedly had the right as well as the authority to change course in this way. A detailed legal opinion of March 1959 concerning the purpose of VVB and TV expressly confirmed that the founder had made it clear in his guidelines that "his idea should not be a rigid system of rules to be adhered to at all costs. On the contrary, he instructed his executors that, in dealing with specifics, they should always look for and adopt the solution of which it can be assumed in all good conscience that he himself would give it his approval, if he were aware of the facts and could appraise all the relevant circumstances."[27] The executors, then, must similarly decide whether in the circumstances the founder would have gone for the "VVB option" or the "TV option." Both options were designed to pave the way for competent descendants to assume leadership of the company. More or less the only difference was that the "TV option" would give the heirs direct ownership of Robert Bosch GmbH while the "VVB option" would give it to them indirectly through their direct participation in the trust administration com-

Hans L. Merkle (1958)

pany VVB. But there was a further difference, and it was crucial. The "TV option" implied that, from 1972 onward, there would be no chance of executors, advisors, or trustees influencing the company's future development [editor's note: In 1972, after a period of 30 years following the death of Robert Bosch, the will was due to expire; see the latter half of the chapter "Death and legacy of Robert Bosch" at the end of the second part of this book]. If the "VVB option" was followed, no time limit was placed on such potential influence. Be that as it may, a note written by Walz on April 7, 1959, and attached to the opinion reads: "With hindsight of course, knowing Mr. Bosch's way of thinking as I do, I can say that, were he alive today, in the interests of his company he would have given preference to the VVB option or to a similar option that takes account of current circumstances."[28] With that, the final verdict on the future suitability of Robert Bosch Jr. as family director and potential head of the company was delivered.

In the following months and years, there were also many lesser signs that the group of executors and the board of management saw Robert Bosch Jr. as

The double anniversary: 75th anniversary of the founding of the company and 100th anniversary of the birth of the founder, September 23, 1961. *From left*: Georg Zundel, Hellmut Bredereck, Robert Bosch Jr., Eva Bosch, Margarete Bosch, Theodor Heuss, Hildegard Walz, Hans Walz, Kurt Georg Kiesinger, Margarete Fischer-Bosch, Ludwig Erhard, Alfred Knoerzer, Paula Zundel, Ernst Rupp, Heinz Küppenbender, Hugo Rupf

something of an odd man out – certainly not as his father's replacement.[29] As early as in January 1959, Walz had commissioned a graphological report on him, as a result of which he (Walz) felt his mounting skepticism confirmed. Where the report described the founder's son as "knowing the limits of his ability" and possessing a "highly developed sense of organizational interrelations," Walz wrote a bold "no" in the margin.[30] Similarly, he underlined a passage in the report that talked of the subject's "plunging into a task with all guns blazing" and "making a mountain out of a molehill." The passage, incidentally, went on to say that "on occasions such as these he lacks the shrewd assistance of a younger Hans Walz, who was very good at advising Father Bosch in similar cases."[31] There was another reason why the position of Robert Bosch Jr. on the board of management had become awkward. Both the group of executors and the board of management had undergone certain changes of personnel. Walz still dominated both bodies. However, since October 1954 Knoerzer had also been a member of the group of executors. In fact, Knoerzer was soon to rise to become the real strong man at Bosch. It was Knoerzer, too,

Hans Walz giving the ceremonial
address, September 23, 1961

who in October 1958 had brought Hans L. Merkle to Bosch to succeed him as head of finance when he himself switched to the supervisory board and became its chairman.

In addition to Merkle, Robert Bosch Jr., and Max Frei (who had also joined in 1954), a further new board of management member was appointed to the group of executors in the shape of Eugen Hagmaier. This was after both Hermann Bauer (in June 1957) and Otto Fischer (in June 1960) had resigned on grounds of age.[32] Walz was soon full of praise for Merkle in particular. As the former said at a meeting of the group of executors held at the end of March 1960, "his [Merkle's] whole manner and bearing suggest someone who spent his formative years at Bosch." For that reason, as well as for his exceptional commercial and entrepreneurial skills (Walz continued), he was nominating Merkle as his successor in the group of executors.[33] In fact, the differences between Robert Bosch Jr. and Hans Merkle could hardly have been greater, not only in terms of their managerial prowess, but also in terms of their entire character.

However, despite these developments, the tensions within the group of executors persisted. In November 1960, they came out into the open, provoked by clashes between Walz and Otto Fischer (who accused Walz of increasingly conducting "secret diplomacy" without keeping the board of management informed). On July 1, 1960, after resigning his board of management seat and moving to the supervisory board, Otto Fischer had drawn up a memorandum entitled "Problems of the future business policy of Robert Bosch GmbH." The memo leveled serious accusations at Walz, who then replied to Fischer in harsh terms. But the real explosion occurred when three executors (Alfred Knoerzer, Albrecht Fischer, and Ernst Rupp) sent a letter to Walz which amounted to a formal reprimand of his behavior. They demanded that he "end this discord in a spirit of reconciliation. We should be glad to receive your prompt reassurance that you have successfully done so."[34] The letter also re-ignited the old conflict between Walz and Knoerzer, although only two years earlier Walz had himself proposed Knoerzer to succeed him in the chair of the group of executors in the event of his (Walz's) retirement.[35] Walz now laid the blame on Knoerzer for having instigated the letter, and accused the co-authors of disloyalty. In a sharp rejoinder, Knoerzer objected that Walz, too, as chairman of the board of management, had a responsibility toward the group of executors – "because if it were otherwise and even in the group of executors the decisions were all your own, your fellow-executors would simply be advisors and the group of executors a farce."[36] For a while, however, the mounting tensions and problems within and between the senior executive bodies at Bosch were upstaged by the celebrations marking the great double anniversary of September 1961.

In his speech before hundreds of guests from the worlds of commerce and public life, Walz invoked the thinking and values of Robert Bosch as well as the "spirit of unanimous, unswerving cooperation that is the common bond uniting the members of the board of management, executives and associates, and associates with one another, forming a single community unanimous in the desire to give its best." At the same time, he stressed the ubiquitous presence of the founder. "For us, Robert Bosch is not dead but intensely alive […]. Still today, 19 years after his passing, the tradition he handed down – his driving, guiding spirit – reigns over the teeming bustle of his entire enterprise."[37]

In December 1961, however, the question of the future role and destiny of the GmbH shares suddenly attained huge importance. Margarete Fischer-Bosch announced her intention of transferring her 14.083 percent of the company shares (then still held by the community of heirs) to VVB. There were conditions, however: VVB must become a charitable GmbH, and she herself must be given some say in its affairs. Converting VVB into a pure holding company for charitable purposes as well as the various options that should govern proprietary relations at Robert Bosch GmbH were issues that a working committee of the group of executors (comprising Walz, Knoerzer, and Rupp) had been wrestling with since the start of 1959. The object at that time had plainly been "to seek out legal ways and means of ensuring that the executors had the final word about what happened to the Robert Bosch Hospital."[38] That, however, implied a further prejudgment in favor of the "VVB option." The group of executors now found itself presented with an opportunity to contribute "all or part of the 86.3 percent stake in Robert Bosch GmbH to VVB, solely on the basis of their own decision. In their capacity as VVB shareholders, they could then go on steering the fate of Robert Bosch GmbH for what was an indeterminable period of time."[39] Clearly, though, tax reasons dictated that following the "VVB option" to the letter was a very costly, not to say unaffordable option. An appropriate way of modifying this solution had to be found. One solution would be to have the executors stay on after 1972 as an "administrative council" [*Verwaltungsrat*], safeguarding the Robert Bosch GmbH shareholder rights. However, such a body had to be set up as soon as possible, ideally involving the older shareholder generation (Margarete Fischer-Bosch and Paula Zundel), and with the full agreement of all shareholders.[40] Another potential solution was to transfer the Robert Bosch GmbH shares to VVB in trust for (say) a 30-year period. The executors saw this as a particularly advantageous solution if something transpired "to make the executors' job more difficult in future. In recent years the Bosch family members have approved the actions of the group of executors or at least accepted them more or less uncomplainingly."[41] However, the closer 1972 came, the greater became the risk of "the members of the family forming a solidarity collective with the aim of surviving, in opposition, well beyond the term of office of the executors and in this way securing as many rights of their own as possible to assert freely on their own account." For this reason (the recommendation from the executors went on) the literal "VVB option" laid down in the last will and testament should at some point be costed in detail. The intention was that, "should the owners oppose reasonable solutions put forward by the executors, the threat could still be raised of the original 'VVB option' being pursued with all the substantial expense that such a course would involve. If the shareholders were made fully aware of just how much value the 'VVB option' would devour, it would undoubtedly be easier to persuade them to join the group of executors in taking a sensible, less costly adjustment course."[42] The executors agreed that Robert Bosch Jr. might be persuaded to settle for the adjustment proposals discussed, but it was far from clear how the other members of the family (notably, Georg Zundel) would react.

What actually happened was that, also for Margarete Fischer-Bosch, tax considerations played the key role. Fischer-Bosch was presented with calculations showing that a direct transfer of Robert Bosch GmbH shares to VVB GmbH would be taxed so highly as to be impracticable. However, leaving the shares in their present ownership would involve heavy inheritance taxes in each subsequent case of death. For Fischer-Bosch alone, they would come to 11.5 million German marks. For all members of the family together, they would total as much as 94.1 million German marks, far exceeding available family assets. The company would have to step in, either directly or by paying higher dividends. The resources of Robert Bosch GmbH would in any case be depleted to an intolerable extent. The company might even go under.[43] All concerned were aware that time was short. Some sort of solution had to be found. Fischer-Bosch, now 73, was the eldest daughter and had no descendants herself. For her proposal to be implemented, three conditions would have to be met: equal and exclusive participation by the executors in VVB GmbH, recasting of the shareholders' agreement of VVB in the direction of not-for-profit status, and not least negotiations with the tax authorities aimed at achieving recognition of VVB's not-for-profit status. To cap everything, substantial financial funds also needed to be made available. The fact was, in return for the shares, Fischer-Bosch was owed the average notional share price for the last three financial years, payable to herself and her heirs in 30 equal annual installments with 3 percent interest until eventual redemption. But it was above all Fischer-Bosch's claim to rights of codetermination in VVB that gave the executors, and particularly Walz himself, the greatest headaches.[44] Walz had addressed the problem thoroughly in a separate report, referring somewhat brusquely to the founder's wish that female descendants should not occupy senior management positions. As Walz told the group of executors in June 1962: "The principle that family members standing outside Robert Bosch GmbH should not be allowed to dictate to management was something on which he brooked no opposition. Giving ground on this point could have ruinous consequences for the company."[45] In the end, Fischer-Bosch was given certain verbal reassurances, but without in any way altering the executors' position, either formally or in terms of substance. So it was not until November 1962 that Fischer-Bosch actually transferred her legacy claim against the community of heirs for transfer of the Robert Bosch GmbH shares to VVB, now recognized as a company having not-for-profit status.

The other problem then confronting the executors in relation to the family shareholders was this: Georg Zundel wished to act as an independent engineering adviser to Robert Bosch GmbH, in a position resembling that of a family director or what the minutes of the group of executors' meeting of June 28, 1962, call a "family director of a special kind" [*Familiendirektor eigener Art*]. Zundel had told the meeting of family members that, seeing himself as a scientist, he had no interest in a management job at Bosch. However, in the sphere of research and development he was keen to contribute his skills in an advisory capacity. Like Fischer-Bosch, he was prepared (or so at least the minutes of the meeting record) to assign his GmbH shares to VVB if the group of executors assured him that after a trial period he would be appointed a family director of this special kind.[46] However, it is not clear what Zundel actually said at the time. He later complained bitterly to Margarete Fischer-Bosch about the "terrible distortions" that Rupp (who took the minutes) had recorded.[47] He (Zundel) had never wished to become a "family director of a special kind" – if only because he was anxious not to stand in the way of Robert Bosch Jr.[48] Anyway, when in late June 1962 the executors came to discuss the Zundel case, Walz made it clear from the outset that provisions and rules laid down in the will meant that in no way could Zundel's wish be met. Moreover, only under very specific conditions could he "run for family director."[49]

In the meantime, the executors had made some progress with the possibilities of implementing the "VVB option" and clarifying matters of legal detail. They had commissioned a full opinion from the Cologne law firm of Ellscheid, Nussbaum, Hirtz. When it arrived at the end of February 1963, the report numbered 66 pages. Ellscheid, a professor of company law, was strikingly well-qualified, with credentials including managing the assets of Amélie Thyssen and sitting on the board of curators of the Fritz Thyssen Foundation.[50] The opinion gave unreserved backing to the executors' position and approach as well as to their preferred route of transferring the shares to a new, not-for-profit VVB. The version of the "TV option" that included appointing a family director and giving him the majority capital holding was discounted on tax grounds. On the other hand (the opinion stated), the chosen route of having Fischer-Bosch surrender her shares was viable on all counts. What made it particularly so was the fact that the shares received from her "turned out to have changed hands for substantially less than she (the testatrix) had intended."[51] Ellscheid further confirmed that the executors "might adopt the aforementioned modified 'VVB option' partly by right and partly as the authorized representatives of the legatee-shareholders, without even expressly asking the heirs for their permission." Nonetheless (the opinion went on), it would be inappropriate to take such momentous steps without obtaining their consent.[52] A crucial question, however, was whether VVB could perform its future business management role without putting its not-for-profit status at risk. For this reason, Ellscheid floated the idea of a "VVB 2" as seat of the management function alongside a "VVB 1" as seat of the charitable function. What he was suggesting, in other words, was separating the financial benefits arising from VVB's ownership of the company from the right to exercise the entrepreneurial powers that such ownership conferred. There had been no previous mention of distinguishing between the charitable and entrepreneurial ownership functions of the VVB. Only now did the idea arise. So in April 1963, the executors set up a four-man committee whose mission was to go through the opinion with the heirs and sound out the views of the family shareholders regarding its recommendations.[53] Subsequently, in individual discussions, the executors set about persuading the members of the family of the utility and significance of the future share-transfer arrangement. Both sides were aware of the significant financial sacrifices that the Bosch family was being asked to make in connection with transfer of their shares to VVB. All the same, the executors undoubtedly used the looming property-tax and inheritance-tax problems to exert pressure if their proposals looked like being rejected.[54]

When the executors swapped findings at their meeting in late May 1963, it became apparent that the family members were by no means of one mind. Knoerzer said of his discussions with Fischer-Bosch that she recognized the tax threat and was willing to accept the VVB solution. Paula Zundel was known to have formed no considered view of her own as yet, but was clearly worried about the severely reduced financial means she would be left with once the transfer had been made. And Georg Zundel, while agreeing that the transfer to VVB was necessary, would consent to it only on one condition: that the executors made sure that, from 1972 onward, he had a say in the future "VVB 2" – and that they confirmed as much in writing.[55] Finally, so far as Robert Bosch Jr. was concerned, lengthy debate unfolded during the meeting. He had not yet considered the matter in detail, he said, though he felt that the "VVB option" would be the correct one if it ensured a living link between the family and VVB. But nor could he disregard what the family might do after 1972, when the shares became free. However, what really mattered was "a guarantee of consistent management of RB GmbH over the long term. There is a high level of consensus among today's younger generation of family members, so I foresee no threat to consistent management of the company by the younger generation."[56]

That was not what the executors wished to hear, and Knoerzer immediately pointed out that under current tax legislation any free handover of Robert Bosch GmbH shares to individual family members was out of the question. It would also run counter to the principles of the founder's will. Robert Bosch Jr.

was asked to speak to the other members of the family "and to persuade them that for tax reasons there was simply no alternative to the V V B solution."[57] The central question raised by Robert Bosch Jr. in return was: how much weight would the members of the family carry as shareholders of "VVB 2," which would in the future be the real center of power and decision-making at Bosch? The fact was, with Georg Zundel and Gero Madelung [the husband of Robert Bosch Junior's sister Eva], there were two further family members who might accede. "The influence of the family should be kept as great as possible, but without its using V VB 2 to endanger the fundamentally consistent management of Robert Bosch GmbH," he argued.[58] However, a decision about this was blocked by the other executors with reference to the provisions set out by the founder concerning the quality and abilities of family directors. An obvious attempt was being made to apply the founder's strict rules of execution to "VVB 2" as well, and, not without justification, Robert Bosch Jr. queried this. The discussion ended without a resolution being passed. Then, in mid-October, a further step was taken in the direction of share-transfer. Paula Zundel, like Margarete Fischer-Bosch, was now prepared to assign her shares (representing almost 7 percent of the capital stock) to VVB, thus quitting the community of heirs.[59] VVB was now already in possession of 21.125 percent of the shares in Robert Bosch GmbH.

In the middle of these developments, Hans Walz resigned, not only as chairman of the board of management but also from the chair of the group of executors. Shortly before his 80th birthday, he announced to a meeting of the latter body that he was retiring on age grounds from all his positions with effect from March 31, 1963.[60] In recognition of his services to the company, the executors handed him a letter, signed by them all, appointing him honorary chairman of Bosch for life.[61] Knoerzer now took over the chair of the group of executors in Walz's place, thus becoming the new strong man at Bosch. However, he made clear from the outset that he would be holding the office for only two years and would then hand it on to Hans L. Merkle. Merkle, who was also to take over Walz's position as chairman of the board of management, would then from 1965 onward become overall head of Bosch, invested with supreme authority. But it was Knoerzer who, in November 1963, at one of his first meetings in the chair addressed the executors plainly in the matter of the "grand VVB solution" [*große VVB-Lösung*]. In 1972, he told the committee, "the will expires, giving the shareholders a completely free hand. If no settlement has been reached by then, the existence of the company will be in grave danger. The fact is, no descendant has so far shown the kind of suitability as family director that Mr. Bosch was talking about in his last will and testament. Robert Bosch Jr. cannot be expected to acquire such suitability in the future. Georg Zundel, having failed even to take the test, is out of the running. And in the case of Gero Madelung, who looks very impressive, the question is still entirely open. Only in 1966 will he decide whether he will stand for the position of family director apparent. For this reason, as well as for tax reasons, the executors are compelled to select the 'VVB option.' The executors would be contravening the clear intention of Robert Bosch if they allowed the last will and testament to expire without exhausting every possibility of persuading the members of the family to assign their company shares to VVB. So compromises must be accepted that nonetheless still take account of the founder's guiding principles. Under no circumstances must the fate of the company be allowed to lie in the hands of unsuitable people."[62]

Robert Bosch Jr. was not at that meeting of November 1963. It was Karl Eychmüller, chairman of the supervisory board of Wieland-Werke AG in Ulm and the man only recently appointed as the new representative of the family on the group of executors, who spoke for him and his relatives. Eychmüller made a passionate case for ensuring that any actions were taken in consensus with the family. Indeed, the big unknown for the executors was how they should react if the members of the family did in fact refuse to consent to the "split" VVB option [i. e., VVB 1 and VVB 2] – even, possibly, instituting legal proceedings in order to have the whole matter clarified by the courts. Eychmüller told of a discussion he had had with Robert Bosch Jr., Georg Zundel, and Gero Madelung. All the members of the family had recognized the need for and efficacy of the "VVB option." However, they attached conditions – on the one hand as to their further involvement, on the other as to the remuneration due on the shares to be surrendered. Moreover, Robert Bosch Jr. had told him (Eychmüller) that "he desired in his heart of hearts to work for the company and was keen to prove that he is indeed his father's son."[63] There had apparently been a number of meetings between him [Bosch] and the executors since the start of the year 1963. Bosch insisted, however, on keeping his seat on the Bosch board of management, refusing to be booted upstairs to the supervisory board. Neither would he be "fobbed off" by the offer of a fringe area at Bosch outside the board of management. So from the executors' standpoint a compromise was needed, and the intention of Knoerzer's proposal was to keep Bosch on the board of management with accountability for certain engineering operations [*ein Teilgebiet der Entwicklungshauptleitung*] as his own fiefdom but on condition that he could be dismissed immediately if not up to the job. He should also be included in the VVB advisory group [i. e., VVB 2] as a shareholder.[64] Giving Robert Bosch Jr. his own management sphere even though he was not a confirmed family

Hans L. Merkle in conversation with Robert Bosch Jr. at an end-of-year senior management meeting (December 1963)

director in fact ran counter to the strict rules governing that position. However, given that he bore the name Bosch, and since he had after all worked for the company for nine years now, an exception had to be made for him. The other executors concurred, and Merkle proposed placing Robert Bosch Jr. in charge of quality assurance, as a kind of stopgap area of responsibility. "In such a post he would be unable to slow the company's momentum," Merkle argued, "which is something we must particularly watch out for. Requirement: he would have to move aside if he did not fit in or shape up to the task."[65] The executors took the view that the best solution [for the son] would have been a seat on the supervisory board. But to that, Knoerzer was sure, Bosch would never agree. If he were to demand that of him, he would never be able to speak to the man again. "And then we would not get their shares, either – neither his nor his sister's."[66] In other words, Robert Bosch Jr. was completely ostracized by the executors in November 1963, notably by Knoerzer and Walz. A few days later he was told of the executors' decision regarding his future place in the company.

A compromise therefore appeared to have been found. As it happened, Robert Bosch Jr. had already written to Walz in confidence in January 1963 indicating that he (together with his sister Eva) was willing in principle to waive his claim to the office of family director, a willingness which he later confirmed in practice, as it were, in a letter to Knoerzer in April 1964.[67] In the end, it was this waiver that freed the way for the «enhanced VVB solution» to be implemented – the split option, in other words, with «VVB 1,» the future Robert Bosch Stiftung GmbH, to carry out the charitable functions, and with «VVB 2,» the future Robert Bosch Industriebeteiligung GmbH (RBIG), to carry out the entrepreneurial ownership functions. At the same time, Robert Bosch Jr. took it for granted that, as a full member of the board of management with his own area of accountability and as a fully authorized shareholder of the new RBIG, he would continue to play an active role in the company.

When on March 23, 1964, the executors gathered for their next meeting, the future make-up and corporate legal framework of Robert Bosch GmbH were nonetheless still unclear.[68] A whole army of attorneys and tax experts had pored over the details for months, trying to find a watertight legal and fiscal solution. And while the main lines were established, the core problem of the voluntary acquiescence of all members of the Bosch family still remained. And regardless of the waiver and the agreement of Robert Bosch Jr. and his sister Eva, opposition from the other branch of the family continued. Both Margarete Fischer-Bosch and Georg Zundel raised strong objections. Zundel in particular said repeatedly that he would consent to transfer his shares only on condition that he was given a say at Robert Bosch GmbH and included in the partnership group [i. e., RBIG] that was to form its new governing body. "Otherwise he would certainly not surrender his shares voluntarily, nor would he co-sign the requisite notarial document," as he once again told Eychmüller at a meeting at the end of March 1964.[69] However, the executors categorically rejected these demands. Only after prolonged negotiation did the two sides reach a compromise. Knoerzer promised Zundel a subsequent appointment to the supervisory board, knowing full well that the latter had no real say in the management of the company's affairs. And in accordance with Zundel's express wish, the minutes of the discussion noted his firm conviction that "he would have been appointed to the new governing body [i. e., RBIG] had his grandfather [i. e., Robert Bosch] still been alive."[70] This at last freed the way for the second branch of the family to assign their inherited shares in Robert Bosch GmbH to VVB. On April 23, 1964, the executors formally resolved to invite and to empower VVB to exercise the right bestowed upon it by the founder's will to purchase the shares of Robert Bosch GmbH still remaining in the estate.

On June 2, 1964, however, when the executors met with the members of the Bosch family for a final discussion of the agreements enshrining VVB [hitherto referred to as VVB 1] and RBIG [VVB 2], it quickly became clear that by no means all the family members' reservations had been dispelled. Substantial differences remained. Granted, the share-transfer arrangement and the separation of share ownership and voting rights were in principle accepted without challenge. The part that was called into question was the reduced role of the family, both in VVB and in RBIG. This came in for particular criticism from Margarete Fischer-Bosch. Why, she wanted to know, could the governing body RBIG not be enlarged from seven to nine persons, giving all members of the younger generation a say?[71] Knoerzer replied that, in the view of the executors (not including Robert Bosch Jr., it has to be said), this would constitute a flagrant violation of both will and guidelines. In accepting such a ruling, the executors would be excluding themselves from RBIG. The family members, for their part, were convinced that, "given today's circumstances, Robert Bosch would have thought and acted otherwise."[72] However, this family initiative was swiftly parried. The minutes continue: "There was no scope, in the present instance, for such an interpretation of the will, nor was there any need to deviate from the testator's instructions in any way whatsoever."[73] Further dramatic weeks were therefore to pass before, on June 26, 1964, the agreement between "VVB 2" (now renamed Robert Bosch Industriebeteiligung GmbH or RBIG) and the members of the Bosch family could finally be signed. So, too, could the extensive accompanying paperwork governing the transfer and certain details of company law. Only three-quarters of an hour before the notary-office deadline, however, Margarete Fischer-Bosch was joined by Paula Zundel and Georg Zundel in vetoing a paragraph stating that the family exonerated the executors for their previous actions. The family deemed such a clause unreasonable.[74] With the committee of executors refusing to compromise over appointing family members to the governing body [RBIG], the executors could not be granted the blanket exoneration they requested because "none of us is truly at ease with the present solution."[75]

In the end, things did turn out as planned. The shares owned by members of the family were assigned to VVB, which now held some 155 million German marks or 86 percent of the capital stock of Robert Bosch GmbH. At the same time, to keep its not-for-profit status, VVB waived the voting rights accruing to those shares.[76] Instead, the executors set up Robert Bosch Industriebeteiligung GmbH (RBIG), which acquired a total of 20 shares from VVB. Those shares were invested with the authoritative voting rights. The founder himself had always spoken of a VVB advisory group. But since the VVB no longer had any governance functions, the executors, acting on their own authority, founded the new governing body, RBIG. They established that the entrepreneurial ownership functions, and hence governing authority, should in future lie with this industrial trust. And as a legal basis they created a shareholders' agreement specifically for this body, supplemented by "Instructions of the shareholders of RBIG to the members of the Bosch board of management."[77] That completed the separation of the two ownership functions. The entrepreneurial governing authority derived from share ownership passed to a group of distinguished businessmen who were independent in their actions and who enjoyed equal rights. This "governing body" then assumed all rights and duties of the "executors' constitution" – that is to say, deciding jointly and acting entrepreneurially, constituting a body of members who, as well as enjoying equal rights, were unassailable in their status as trustee owners and self-perpetuating through co-optation.[78] The two pillars of the new RBIG constitution were collective decision-making by the shareholders and equal rights and duties in consultation and voting. This legal status also meant that shareholders might associate with each other freely, without fear of sanctions, and at the same time were inseparably bound together for an extensive period. The members of RBIG therefore saw themselves as owner-entrepreneurs in direct succession to Robert Bosch. They exercised discreetly and (so far as the outside world was concerned) invisibly the governing authority that accrued to ownership and carried out the entrepreneurial ownership functions. Yet the name subsequently chosen for the new governing body (with *Industrietreuhand* or "industrial trust" replacing *Industriebeteiligung* or "industrial holding") also indicated that the shareholders saw themselves as trustees of the last will and testament of Robert Bosch, as well as of the rights and duties originally assigned to the executors under that will. Despite this strong position of RBIG, the Bosch board of management was not constrained in its entrepreneurial actions. In fact it was free to develop the company's business activities as it chose. RBIG was not permitted to intervene in day-to-day operations. However, the strategic alignment of the company had to be cleared with RBIG before it was acted upon. Major projects also had to be submitted to RBIG in advance for examination and approval. Under the new Bosch constitution, important entrepreneurial decisions were thus controlled in differing but mutually complementary ways both by RBIG and by the supervisory board. However, it was clear from the outset that RBIG was going to be the real seat of governing authority and power at Bosch.

Now that the executors had done their job, their duties lapsed. As shareholders, however, they automatically became members of RBIG, thus preserving continuity of the ultimate decision-making and executive powers. The dual role originally assigned to VVB had, as planned, been split into a charitable function on the one hand and a directive function on the other.

The remaining shares (with a nominal value of some 25 million German marks or just under 14 percent of the capital stock) were held by members of the family. At the same time, the shareholders' agreement of Robert Bosch GmbH was amended and voting rights redefined. VVB now had no votes, RBIG held 60, and the family together held 10. At the end of 1964, following two capital increases (in 1960 and 1961) from company funds, the nominal capital stock totaled 180 million German marks. Shares in Robert Bosch GmbH were now distributed as follows [editor's note: see also the next chapter]: 281 shares (nominally worth 155.4 million German marks and representing 86.32 percent of the shares) were held by VVB, while all that remained in family hands were 38 preferred shares. However, at the insistence of Robert Bosch Jr., the agreement also provided for a family council. The purpose of this council was "to enable the family to continue to be involved in what happens to the company, to live alongside it, share its thinking, and give advice. It is also intended to form a bridge between company and family as regards training family members for a responsible position within Robert Bosch GmbH." The family council therefore had a purely advisory function. Meeting as a rule twice a year, it served to keep the family informed, to notify it of business developments and of important plans and undertakings of Robert Bosch GmbH, and lastly to foster "greater familiarity and a growth of trust" between members of the family, the shareholders of RBIG, and the members of the board of management.[79] Another decisive document, likewise concluded on June 26, 1964, was an agreement signed by the executors in their capacity as shareholder-partners in RBIG. This once again set out the thinking that had led them to decide in favor of the "split VVB option." In addition, the executors – Alfred Knoerzer, Hans L. Merkle, Robert Bosch Jr., Heinz Küppenbender, Hugo Rupf, Carl Wurster, and Ernst Rupp –undertook to continue to comply with the wishes of Robert Bosch when it came to the stipulations for the future leadership of Robert Bosch GmbH as set out in the last will and testament and the guidelines. The agreement also set out the rules for the co-optation of successors whenever members retired for age reasons.[80]

In June 1964, the workforce at all Bosch plants and subsidiaries were informed about the changes by special posters proclaiming "Bosch profits to be mainly for the public good in the future." Once a family-run business, Bosch was now a foundation-owned company – although VVB, despite its not-for-profit objectives, was not legally a *Stiftung* but a foundation-like entity. Furthermore, with the family remaining a minority shareholder, Bosch had not entirely lost its family-business character. Neither this complete separation of the two aspects of ownership nor the idea of having a charitable foundation on the one hand and a body of non-family members on the other had been originally foreseen, planned for, or intended by Robert Bosch. However, both the will and the guidelines offered enough indications for them to be interpreted in such a way as to point down the route agreed. It was not so of necessity. As late as December 1966, Walz laid emphasis on the "nature of RB GmbH as a family business," and in a separate memorandum he gave reasons for Robert Bosch having wished his company to "retain indefinitely the character of an independent, self-sufficient family business."[81] "Assiduously safeguarding this status of a family business, the financial independence of such a business, and its entrepreneurial freedom, is from the standpoint of Robert Bosch a rule of constitutive importance, a postulate that must form the guiding principle [...] governing all corporate policy."[82] His words evince not least the fact that and the extent to which the historical understanding of the nature of the company were also, in the minds of Bosch management, subject to change. For Walz was still stressing the family character of the company as an advantage – something adding positive value. Under Merkle's leadership over the course of the 1960s, however, the new model of the foundation-owned company became more attractive while the family business was increasingly seen as outmoded and inefficient. Particularly for large-scale enterprises structured as industrial groups, the format was actually deemed disadvantageous. Subsequently, the late 1980s and the 1990s saw a reversal in public opinion and a rediscovery of the family-business ideal.

Ultimately, the new "constitution" of the Bosch Group did not simply result from intensive discussions and negotiations between the executors and the family. It was also preceded by a meticulous process of consultation with the Federal Ministry of Finance and the Stuttgart tax authorities. The central concern was securing tax relief under the rules governing not-for-profit status. Here, the legal transaction conducted by the executors for the account and with the agreement of the heirs was a gift coupled with an obligation, performed partly in return for a compensation [a transaction known in German tax and estate law technically as *gemischte Schenkung*]. However, the compensation amounted to only the nominal value of the shares, which was many times less than their actual worth. Seen in this light, so far as the family was concerned this was indeed an endowment [*Stiftung*] – not legally, perhaps, but in economic terms. For the family, this was more than just a case of saying goodbye permanently to management and control. A substantial financial sacrifice was also required of them.[83] That they and in particular Robert Bosch Jr. were still prepared to subscribe to the compromise won the executors' respect, even though for the executors this was simply a question of fulfilling the wishes and intentions of the founder. The great achievement of the June 1964 agreement is to have found a seemingly impossible compromise between divergent demands, interests, and pressures.[84] The ultimate aim was to find a solution that would work, one that would both meet the requirements of the will and satisfy the desire of family and heirs to assume active responsibility – rather than simply taking the financial-settlement route. On the one hand, an efficient, adequate management structure had to be found for the company. On the other hand, the founder's undoubted charitable ambitions had to be satisfied. It followed that the new Bosch constitution by no means reflected the last will and testament to the letter. Nor could it have done. At no stage did the will envisage creating a minority shareholding for the family. Nonetheless, a solution was eventually found that was true to the spirit of the will, which was to give the company greater strength and make it more receptive to future developments – while at the same time ensuring that the family played an active part in its affairs, adhering to the founder's principles.[85]

The public announcement of the new corporate set-up also met with "an exceptionally positive echo," as the VVB shareholders noted at their meeting at the end of September 1964.[86] Comments in the press were thoroughly favorable, both within Germany and without, as they were in a number of letters addressed to VVB directly. The Bosch solution undoubtedly struck a nerve: for many family businesses, the question of how the business would survive a handover to the next generation was a worrying one. The actions taken by Bosch were widely seen as a recipe for success in dealing with the innumerable legal and fiscal problems to which succession gave rise. Bosch itself, on the other hand, tried hard to dispel such expectations. Advantageous though the arrangement turned out to be for Bosch in ensuing years, it was clear at the time that the Bosch solution would at best suit only a small number of family companies. Bosch was by no means a typical case. Not even in outline could the same solution be applied in other companies. Nor was the complex history of corporate reorganization at Bosch yet at an end, even after the seismic changes of 1964.

Robert Bosch Industrietreuhand KG and shareholder structure: further development of corporate governance at Bosch (1965–1982)

The agreed personnel changes on the Bosch board of management took effect on January 1, 1965. Robert Bosch Jr. became accountable for quality assurance (a newly created position), Klaus Alberts and Kurt Losten took over account-ability for technical and commercial sales, and Wilhelm Hofmann and Hans Bacher shared accountability for manufacturing.[87] The old guard on the board of management had finally been replaced by younger men. As announced, Knoerzer stepped down as a shareholder of RBIG and as chairman of the Bosch supervisory board in June 1967. His 75th birthday had been celebrated with great pomp in April. Before leaving, he drew up a detailed memorandum entitled "Business policy: a long-term view" [*Geschäftspolitik auf weite Sicht*], which contained words of caution for his RBIG colleagues.[88] "For some time now," Knoerzer wrote, "with developments proceeding as rapidly as they have done over the past few years, I have been concerned whether we shall be able to keep the character of a family business in the long term, or whether we shall at some stage be forced to borrow capital. My own view is that we have a duty to retain the present structure, as Mr. Bosch would have wished."[89] Knoerzer thus wanted RBIG to exercise greater restraint when it came to future capital expenditure, and argued that approval for such decisions needed a strong ma-jority within RBIG. In principle, this was a warning against the policy of mod-ernization, growth, and diversification freshly embarked on by Merkle. "The goal of gradually bringing our market share in products other than automo-tive equipment up to the level of the latter [...] is one I deem beyond reach, since the huge amount of capital this would require is more than can be met from our own resources plus a reasonable level of borrowing."[90] For Knoerzer, the underlying principle had to be that the expansion called for by the founder should remain in line with what financial potential the company was capable of generating for itself. True, the 1964 changes to corporate governance at Bosch had made it harder to convert the company into a stock corporation. But they had not made it impossible. In Knoerzer's thinking, a further major check was needed – as was indeed provided by subsequent amendment to the guidelines of RBIG.

In the spring of 1970, Robert Bosch Jr. told the RBIG shareholders that he and Eva Madelung wished to set up a separate charitable foundation from their various sources of income. Initially, he did not foresee any change in his responsibility as a member of the Bosch board of management. However, in November of that year he decided to resign from the board of management

Alfred Knoerzer's 75th birthday. From left: Alfred Knoerzer, Robert Bosch Jr.,
Hans L. Merkle (April 1967)

completely and move to the supervisory board.[91] There were three problems
here. First, Robert Bosch Jr. had to have the agreement of the RBIG shareholders for his foundation plans. Second, the question of the projected contribution of shares to the new foundation needed to be sorted out legally. But
finally (and most importantly) there was the matter of the founder's son remaining an RBIG shareholder, and thus continuing to belong to the company's most powerful supervisory and decision-making body. In June 1965,
the RBIG shareholders had set themselves rigid guidelines, largely along the
lines of the provisions that had governed the work of the group of executors.
Both sets of guidelines defined in detail the co-optation process (which was
to remain valid) as well as the criteria for suitability of candidates.[92] Accord-

ing to these provisions, the shareholders (i. e., RBIG) comprised a six-person "advisory group" including not more than two family directors, two members of the board of management, as well as one representative of the family who was not an actual family member and who played a purely advisory role. The fact of the matter was, the term "advisory group" had long since become misleading, if not invalid. The group was not merely advisory: as a body of shareholders, it wielded extensive rights. Nonetheless, those involved at the time continued to use the term, as a result of which it also appears in the documents from this time. So for all the protestations about keeping Bosch a family business, the family was accorded only a weak position from the outset. "A shareholder of the advisory group may not be a member of the Bosch family," the regulations stated, "an exception being family directors." To guarantee impartiality, shareholders were not permitted to be related, and women could not be RBIG shareholders on principle. Moreover, as soon as VVB had paid all it owed the Bosch family as a result of the 1964 agreement to buy their shares, the family's entitlement to send a representative to the RBIG shareholders' meeting came to an end. Shareholders might continue to consult family representatives as required, though any voice they had was only advisory.

However, the decisive issue was the detailed provisions governing the selection, powers, and position of any family director who was a member of RBIG. As had been the case with the executors, the advisory group alone had the right to make such an appointment. It was also for the advisory group to determine "how far it wishes to allow a family director to exercise the voting right arising out of the RB GmbH shares belonging to RBIG."[93] In March 1971, therefore, the RBIG shareholders (in the absence of Robert Bosch Jr.) discussed the consequences of the latter's resignation from the board of management. They concluded unanimously that he could no longer belong to the advisory group. They also decided, invoking the sorely tried principles of the founder, that the existing regulations did not allow any exceptional arrangements or amendments.[94] It was further resolved that Robert Bosch Jr. could replace Eychmüller (Eychmüller's mandate expiring in August 1972) on the advisory group as family representative. However, this too was only on condition that he retained his shares in the company and did not contribute them to his new foundation.[95] What no one admitted in so many words was that this was tantamount to demoting the founder's son to the position of a second-class RBIG shareholder with limited rights. His future role was indeed purely advisory, and as a result the family lost its vote in the deliberations of RBIG. The fact that he also based his desire to stay in the RBIG advisory group on things said in his father's last will remained without effect. In fact, it was rejected on the grounds that other passages in the will took precedence.[96]

On January 19, 1972, the founder's first daughter Margarete Fischer-Bosch died. Under the terms of her will, her remaining shares passed to Robert Bosch Stiftung GmbH, a charitable foundation which had been set up on June 3, 1969, as the successor organization to Vermögensverwaltung Bosch GmbH. The VVB had been essentially renamed, not least in order to give verbal expression to the organization's true task. At the same time, Georg Zundel was elected Fischer-Bosch's successor on the board of trustees of the Stiftung. Two years later, on August 22, 1974, the founder's second daughter, Paula Zundel, also died. Together with her share, the Stiftung now possessed some 90 percent (89.115 percent, to be precise) of the (non-voting) shares in Robert Bosch GmbH. The family still had 10.875 percent of the shares or 6 votes, while the remaining 0.01 percent (but carrying 60 votes) was held by RBIG. Four months before (on April 23, 1974), Hans Walz had died aged 91 – the person who, more than any other, had felt it his vocation to keep alive the achievements and spirit of the founder Robert Bosch.[97]

But there were two further developments in the second half of the 1970s that influenced how the corporate-governance structure of Bosch and the relationship between family and company evolved. The first was the advent of extended codetermination in the summer of 1976. The new parity of owner-entrepreneurs and employee representatives that this brought about on the supervisory board did not only concern the GmbH. It also affected RBIG as the true center of executive and decision-making power in the Bosch Group. As Bosch's legal department had forewarned back in February 1974, the provisions of the new codetermination laws would make "sweeping changes to current legislation, rendering important RB constitutional norms invalid."[98] There was another problem: various RBIG shareholders whose appointment dated back to the time of the group of executors had retired on grounds of age or were about to reach the 70-year age limit. At the end of 1974, Karl Klasen, former president of the *Bundesbank*, and Robert Holzach, a member of the board of management of Schweizerische Bankgesellschaft, were therefore elected to the RBIG shareholder group. As well as Merkle and another Bosch board of management member, Merkle's right-hand man Paul A. Stein, this group now comprised Hugo Rupf, board member of J. M. Voith GmbH, Angelo Hammelbacher, managing director of Salamander AG, and Heinz Küppenbender, chairman of the board of Carl Zeiss. Hammelbacher was succeeded in June 1976 by Peter Adolff, then managing director of the chemicals company Wacker Chemie and from October 1976 a member of the board of management of Allianz AG. In March 1976, to prevent external circumstances forcing a change in the tasks and functions of RBIG as the most important share-holder in Robert Bosch GmbH, the company form of RBIG was hastily changed into that of a *Kommanditgesellschaft,* or limited partnership. From June 23, 1976, the group of shareholders was known as Robert Bosch Industrietreuhand KG (abbreviated as RBIK).[99] In essence, the shareholders' agreement and guidelines of RBIG were adopted by the new limited partnership. The opportunity was also taken to renew the "Instructions of the shareholders of RBIG to the members of the Bosch board of management" dating from 1959. These instructions established the duty of board members not only to observe the principles and guidelines of corporate policy (from now on set out by RBIK) but also to submit to RBIK for its approval all business activities of major import.

The second major development concerned the need for fresh capital increases. Where not financed from company resources, these raised the question of the participation of family shareholders and their future dividend entitlement. The capital stock had already been increased (using internal resources) from 180 million German marks to 300 million German marks back in July 1968, and in July 1973 a further hike of 120 million German marks had brought it up to 420 million German marks. The next capital increase was due in May 1977. Comprising a mixture of company money and cash contributions, this would take the total to 680 million German marks. For years, the board of management had been asked by associates and customers alike how it proposed to fund the company's future growth. The fear was that the company's capital cover might at some point in time become inadequate, for unlike an *Aktiengesellschaft* the company could not raise new capital from outside sources. In the past, the company had always managed to satisfy its capital requirements from retained profits. Now, however, Bosch had reached the limits of that option. Another reason for choosing the mixed capital increase of 1977 was "to prove to the public and our associates that we too are capable of improving our capital stock by creating additional equity," as Merkle put it to the March 1977 RBIK meeting.[100] However, it was an open question whether and to what extent the family shareholders would also participate by making a contribution and receiving new shares in return.[101] The whole matter was further complicated by a corporation tax reform in January 1977. On the whole, the resultant discontinuation of double taxation for corporations had positive effects. However, for a few groups (including not-for-profit shareholders in corporations) it also meant clear disadvantages.[102] And for the family share-holders, there was a further crucial aspect. They needed to secure their dividend income, which they mainly used to pay their tax liabilities. Under the founder's will, it was the company's duty to distribute at least as much profit to the family shareholders as would enable them to maintain an appropriate standard of living. In 1977, Robert Bosch Jr. and his sister indicated their willingness to subscribe to a capital increase, but Georg Zundel set conditions. Zundel wished to "make use of only half his entitlement to take over a shareholding corresponding to his existing participation and to use the other half to allow the workforce to share in the financing and earnings of the company."[103] In essence, Zundel's request was a demand for the introduction of associate shares totaling 2.5 million German marks. This caused something of a stir among the RBIK shareholders while meeting with little enthusiasm on the works council, which had been told about it in confidence by Merkle through Richard Rau, the chairman of the central works council at Bosch. In that quarter, there was more interest in a new wage structure being introduced. Anyway, the sum was considered far too small for a sweeping program of wealth formation among staff. Nonetheless, the RBIK shareholders felt it necessary to promise Zundel in a non-notarial rider to examine his plan for workforce profit sharing.[104]

The three family shareholders did in the end participate in the capital increase. In July 1980, after the allocation of workforce shares had proved unworkable for fiscal and legal reasons, Zundel's outstanding shareholding was divided equally between Robert Bosch Jr. and Eva Madelung, securing this family share.[105] However, this did not alter Robert Bosch Jr.'s restricted voting right in RBIK.[106] Furthermore, in June 1978 Merkle had suggested that the circle of RBIK shareholders be widened. Disregarding Bosch, only the six remaining members had full voting rights, which in a borderline case might lead to a voting stalemate. In any event, such an additional appointment had to be from outside the family. April 1979 saw the election of Marcus Bierich, then chief financial officer at Allianz AG. At the same time, the RBIK meeting resolved that "the right of the Bosch family to send a representative to RBIK [had] expired."[107] On December 28, 1978, the company had paid the final installment of what it still owed from the company-share transfer of 1964, or more exactly of 1962–64. This was 16 years earlier than originally agreed. In other words, the company had bought out the family shareholders far sooner and at a far better rate than Knoerzer had predicted.[108] In mid-1982, Georg Zundel sold his entire remaining holding of preferred shares to RB Industrieanlagen GmbH. The family line stretching back to Paula Zundel, *née* Bosch, thus withdrew completely from the company and from the circle of family shareholders. The condition was that RB Industrieanlagen GmbH had to sell the shares on to Robert Bosch Jr., Eva Madelung, or Robert Bosch Stiftung GmbH within five years.[109] Finally, in July 1983 Robert Bosch Jr. and his sister set up Robert Bosch Familiengesellschaft, to which they contributed their remaining preferred shares. The two of them together still held nearly 8 percent of company shares.[110] This marked the provisional end of a difficult transitional period which may in part have been humiliating for the family, and in particular for Robert Bosch Jr.[111] Nonetheless, it resulted in stable corporate-governance structures at Bosch that were to prove their worth in ensuing years. The structures gave the company "all the advantages that result from being managed by a committed, responsible owner-entrepreneur: a high degree of internal and external independence, precisely defined accountability, short lines of decision, quick and clear decisions, no company-external interests on the part of those making such decisions, no fear of losing one's position when initiating unpopular measures, a corporate policy oriented to long-term goals, discretion, managers who speak with the same voice when addressing third parties, a lean organization, personal reliability, and respect for human values."[112]

Only one area of conflict remained, affecting Robert Bosch Stiftung GmbH and the family equally: namely, the annual distribution of profits and hence the company's dividend policy.[113] One of the peculiarities of the "Bosch constitution" was that the foundation received "only" dividends, as it were. Any entrepreneurial power of direction was exercised by RBIK, which the board of management and its chairman then executed. At the same time, however, there was a de facto feedback effect in that the ideas and plans of RBIK were very much worked out and strongly influenced by the executive, i. e., by the board of management and the executive management of individual divisions.[114] Under Walz and Knoerzer, a strong hierarchical structure had still prevailed. Not until Merkle became chairman of RBIG did it prove possible, through intensive personal discussions, to weave a subtler web of relations among members. Often that web was strengthened by amity, trust, and above all a sense of loyalty. Unconditional loyalty to the company was something that had shaped the character of Robert Bosch Jr. in particular. However, it had turned him from being crown prince with a conditional, will-based claim to sole proprietorship into the spokesperson of the founder's family in a foundation-owned company in which he lacked full voting rights.[115] Even after his exclusion from the governing body, he attended every meeting of RBIG and subsequently RBIK, yet he never really belonged by nature to this group of independent, experienced entrepreneurs. So the enabling of the new corporate constitution at Bosch and the withdrawal of his own claim to ownership may well have been his greatest disappointment in life – and at the same time his greatest achievement.[116] The central problem facing not only Robert Bosch Jr. and the members of the family but also the executors and later RBIK shareholders was the inherent contradiction manifest in the founder's last will and in the guidelines. On the one hand, Robert Bosch had established the dogma of preserving the character of the company as a family enterprise. On the other hand, he had also taken every conceivable measure to protect the company from the family – whether from an unsuitable scion taking control, from crippling disputes between or within different branches of the family, or from clashes over holdings and the threat of fragmented share ownership. This raised the question of how to interpret the last will and the guidelines, as well as the shareholders' agreement that was derived from them. But this was not simply a matter of interpretation. It was also about fulfilling the will of the founder.[117] However, the architect of the new "Bosch constitution" was not Merkle, as erroneously claimed many times since.[118] In fact, there were two architects, Knoerzer and Walz, even though in the years after 1965 Merkle played an ever greater role in implementing and exercising the new regulations and structures. There is also always, in principle, a certain gulf between constitutional law and constitutional practice, between law-making and legal practice. A permanent process of mutual balancing and sometimes also of modernization of legal norms is called for as a result. At Bosch this process was very powerfully driven forward by Walz in the postwar years. It continued under Knoerzer and Merkle, of course, but the direct link to the "constitutional principles of RB GmbH" inevitably became ever looser over time. Fewer and fewer actions and decisions could be traced back directly to the text of the will. Often they were justifications after the fact rather than interpretations of the last will and the guidelines, together with such practical instructions as might be derived from them. This was the case, for example, when the VVB solution, as a sort of permanent group of executors, received preference over retaining the company's family-business character. But it was also true of the foundation construction itself, as well as of the position and voting entitlement of the family director and family representative. The literal interpretation of the terms of the legacy was increasingly displaced by a more pragmatic approach that exploited the scope for action and for shaping policy and events that both the will and the guidelines allowed. Certainly, meetings of the executors and the later RBIK shareholder meetings were a kind of ongoing legal commentary on the documents underpinning the entire Bosch enterprise. This process of interpretation, adaptation, and implementation is indeed ceaseless. It remains a key ingredient of the "Bosch phenomenon." That said, the irreversible principles and values of Bosch business management have always been the backdrop behind every detail of interpretation of the constitutional cornerstones of the legacy of Robert Bosch. It was only in these decades of upheaval (the 1950s, 1960s, and 1970s) that these true Bosch principles and values crystallized out, as it were. The corporate aim is and always has been to achieve financial independence from banks and the capital markets by permanently reinvesting profits. This goes hand in hand with an obligation to further the common good and a practice of orienting to the long term. Finally, Bosch sets out to be an exemplary business enterprise, forever determined to take seriously its duties to all its business partners, also in a wider sense: to customers, suppliers, associates, society, and the environment as a whole – to make money, of course, but also to make a contribution toward cultural, civic, and ethical objectives.[119]

3 Corporate organization and corporate strategy between economic miracle and oil-price shock

Hans L. Merkle unquestionably defined Bosch corporate policy in the 1960s, 1970s, and 1980s. Soon after his appointment to the board of management as head of corporate finance in 1958, he set about modernizing the company's financial operations. He followed this up by continuing the reorganization of corporate structure – a process that had already begun before he came along. In the ensuing years, he drove forward the growth of the company, its diversification, and its globalization. In doing so, Merkle and Bosch were not much different from the other major companies in Germany at the time. All were going through similar transformation processes – albeit slightly later in most cases. And all were confronted by the financial and structural crises of the "long-drawn-out 1970s." After years of uninterrupted growth, German managers in general faced the challenge of guiding their companies through a volatile period of boom and bust. Surging upswing and crumbling demand switched places every three years. For many businessmen, grown accustomed to the high yields of the "economic miracle" years, this was quite a new experience. Two things distinguished Bosch from other companies here. In confronting change, Bosch was proactive instead of reactive. It was thus largely successful in avoiding crisis-driven swings and roundabouts and the resultant constraints in its freedom to act. And in Merkle it had a manager who, beyond corporate policy as such, saw himself as a "political entrepreneur." He both dictated the agenda in the field of economic policy and at the same time commented on it. The chairman of the Bosch board of management sat at the epicenter – *was* the epicenter – of the web of personal friendships and intersecting mandates among top bankers and industrialists that made up the essence of "Germany Inc." Even during his lifetime, nothing short of a myth accrued around the power and influence of Hans L. Merkle. The myth was further nourished by the specific leadership style he cultivated at Bosch. Merkle ruled with an iron hand, and considered it his birthright to have the last word on all matters of policy. And of course the myth was aided by the position of virtually unlimited power he had occupied since 1965, uniting in his person the chairmanships of the Bosch board of management and of RBIG.

Having said that, closer examination of Merkle's actual operations in the field of corporate policy often reveals a different, more nuanced picture. Here, though, one thing in particular must be borne in mind. The expanded board of management of the late 1970s, which comprised as many as 13 individuals, was complemented by the group (some 150 persons strong) of divisional, plant, or sales directors – in brief, the second tier of management. Together with such figures as Hans Bacher, Konrad Eckert, Paul Stein, or Kurt Schips, they, too, shaped internal corporate developments at Bosch to a far greater degree than the eyes of the outside world, fixed on Merkle alone, entirely appreciated.

Divisionalization, crisis strategies, and corporate management in the Merkle era

At the start of 1963, Bosch shed its old functional and horizontal corporate organization and began to develop decentralized groups devoted to individual product categories. It was a lengthy restructuring process. Talk of modernizing the way Bosch was organized had begun in 1953 and, following a series of further organizational developments, did not reach a provisional conclusion until the autumn of 1968, when divisional product groups were formed. According to a position paper issued in March 1953 by the corporate department for industrial administration, a paper critical of the way Bosch was organized, "the foundations [of this organization] stem essentially from the 1920s. We have now grown so large that we must ask ourselves whether our old organizational form still fits. There are times when we feel that our horizontal structure has resulted in red tape and a certain unwieldiness, to the detriment of initiative and responsibility."[1] Initially, however, Bosch did not progress beyond the early stages of decentralization and divisionalization. Only in the course of the year 1960, on the initiative of Hans Walz, was a fresh start made. "Our organization needs to become faster, more flexible, more effective, and less costly," he told the group of executors in May 1960. "Moreover, managers must be relieved of routine duties and given time for their real tasks of leadership and timely planning for the future."[2] In January 1961, to look more closely into the risks and opportunities of reorganization, a special working group for decentralization was set up. Meetings of the group were attended by an adviser from the Bruce Payne consultancy, whose services Bosch had been using frequently around this time. Eighteen meetings and one year later, in mid-March 1962, the working group presented its findings.[3] It suggested forming seven (later six) separate internal product groups – groups which differed widely in size and internal structure. Group A comprised the company's core business of automotive electrical equipment (subdivided into engine equipment and bodywork equipment), spread over 13 plants and 25 manufacturing sites. It was by far the largest, accounting at the time for some 600 million German marks of sales annually. Next, with more or less equal sales of some 300 million German marks each, came groups B (injection equipment, diesel pumps, and hydraulics, spread over 8 plants and 11 manufacturing sites) and H (household appliances) – except that the latter was hived off as an independent subsidiary shortly afterwards. Groups E (power tools), M (semifinished products), N (new products for industrial use, later industrial equipment), and K (condensers) accounted for sales of between 20 and 50 million German marks each and were spread between 2 and 4 plants only, which meant they were much smaller. Nonetheless, at the working-group meetings there was continuous and at times vigorous debate, notably about the many measures required if the empty organizational shells were to take on the kind of operational clout considered necessary, and this as quickly as possible.[4]

Fig. 3 Bosch corporate organization (1966)

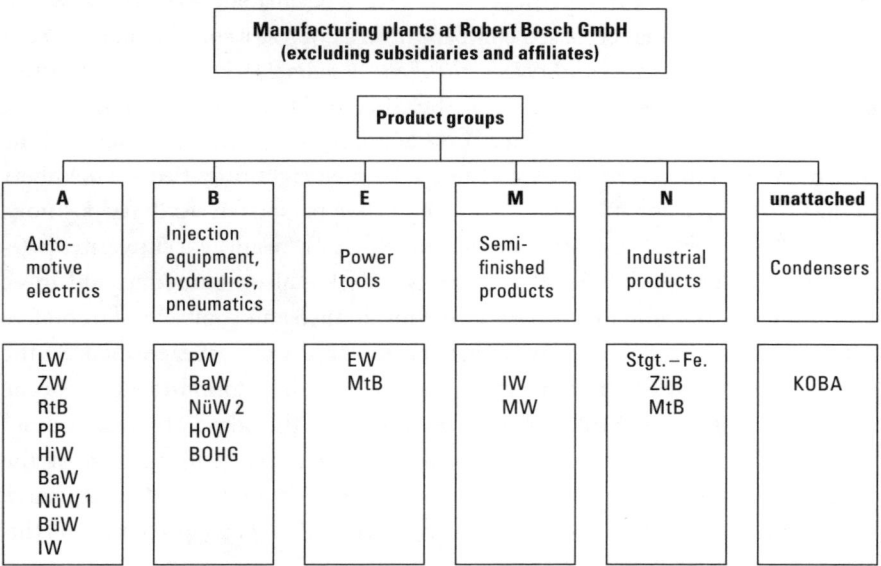

In the ensuing years, Merkle systematically created a leadership culture and an organizational structure designed to give it tangible expression. This structure was as complex as it was clear. Complex, since in addition to the Bosch board of management as the seat of executive power in a narrower sense, it featured other, sometimes expanded executive groups and committees. Clear, since it was tailored to suit his own understanding of corporate leadership as well as

his specific leadership style. The changes began in November 1965 with the introduction of group executive sectors [*Führungsbereiche*] to replace the old units
dedicated to purely functional management responsibility [*Hauptleitungen*].[5] As
chairman of the board of management and head of finance, Merkle was from
now on referred to as F1, while Robert Bosch Jr. (quality assurance) was F2 and
Karl Schreiber (human resources and social services) was F3. Klaus Alberts and
Hans Bacher were together responsible, as F4, for the core business area of automotive original equipment. F5 was Kurt Losten (marketing and sales), F6 Gustav Wagner (corporate research and development), and F7 Willi Hofmann (engineering, purchasing, and manufacturing). Rounding this off, there was Helmut
Ohr, who as F8 was briefly responsible for the subsidiary companies.[6] Not long
afterwards, in February 1967, the board of management for the first time drew
up a paper entitled "Business principles of Robert Bosch GmbH" ("*Geschäfts-
grundsätze der Robert Bosch GmbH*"). This was long before it became customary
to engage in discussions of corporate culture or values, let alone to draft mis-
sions or visions. The three main principles were performance (*Leistung*, which
also implied performance-based compensation as well as a social policy in keeping with the times), impartiality (*Sachlichkeit*; "Leadership by virtue of objective
conviction, only in exceptional cases by directive"), and trust (*Vertrauen*; "I
would rather lose money than trust").[7] In September 1971, Merkle expanded the
Bosch board of management by adding to the then eight fully-fledged members
of the board three deputy members, as well as two persons in auxiliary positions
termed "members of executive management." As a result, executive management at Bosch now comprised 13 persons.[8] Merkle also planned to add three
cross-functional group executive sectors (for finance and contracts, automotive
equipment, and human resources), but these groups were never formed. At the
same time, effective January 1, 1972, a "business policy committee" was to be
established with the task of preparing resolutions of the board of management.[9]
However, for one reason or another, this committee had still not met by the
middle of 1974. Not until June 1974 was there talk of its activation. Subsequently,
what were called "executive information meetings" (*Führungsinformationssit-
zungen* or FIS) did in fact take place.

Merkle had his own view of what running a company meant, as well as a
specific, even special understanding of himself as an entrepreneur. One sign of
this was that Anglicisms and American management-theory jargon never
passed his lips. No one at Bosch used the English terms "marketing" or "management." Instead, they spoke of *Verkauf* and *Geschäftsführung*. And under the
motto *Dienen und Führen* (i. e., leadership as an expression of service to the
company and to society at large) Merkle increasingly saw entrepreneurs as having more duties than rights, and as charged with the task of "finding answers to

the burning questions of the day, in particular of the last quarter of this century."[10] Merkle managed Bosch in decentralized fashion. In doing so, he always tried to draw a clear distinction between policy and strategy, between operational management and tactical leadership. He also differentiated precisely between the individual steps and phases of management decisions, from identifying a problem to implementing a solution and then to monitoring results.[11] However, Merkle always saw management, saw leadership [the German word *Führung* carries both meanings], as a moral category as well. Above all, his management style was founded on discretion. An atmosphere of virtually holy secrecy surrounded the Schillerhöhe [where Merkle had relocated the company's head office; see below]. Market share was not publicly talked of, nor was strategy. As for margin or profit, the words were most certainly never heard. No whiff of controversy, let alone conflict reached the outside world. When this rule was shattered in March 1979 and a business journal came out with three articles concerning internal matters at Bosch, there was quite a stir.[12] But Merkle's biggest upset was likely the sudden death of Hans Bacher, the board of management member responsible for automotive original equipment. Bacher, who died on October 30, 1982, had been a shining example to all engineers and technicians at Bosch. It was to Bacher, essentially, that the company owed the expansion of its core business. For a long time, nobody knew that Merkle had singled out Bacher to succeed him as chairman of the board of management. It was only in late September 1982, shortly before Bacher's death, that the human resources committee of RBIK had adopted a formal resolution to make Bacher the new chairman of the Bosch board of management effective June 1984.[13]

Merkle may have operated unobtrusively so far as internal affairs were concerned, but he cut a very prominent figure outside Bosch. His public image covered the whole spectrum from model industrialist adorning the covers of the business press (though he was never elected "manager of the year")[14] to adviser to the federal government. He also gave freely of his talents to various associations, organizations, and above all other companies' supervisory boards. He not only sat on such boards at Deutsche Bank, Allianz AG, BASF, Royal Dutch Shell, AKZO, Otto Wolff, Volkswagen, RWE, Continental, and Klöckner-Humboldt-Deutz (KHD); he also served Reemtsma, Bahlsen, Henkel, Wayss & Freitag, and Voith on similar bodies. Moreover, he occupied other advisory positions – for Warburg International, for instance, or for the international advisory board of Chase Manhattan Bank.[15] In addition, and fanning out to other companies via connections outside his own person, there were the many supervisory-board mandates and other positions held by outside members of the Bosch supervisory board, by RBIK shareholders, and by the members of Bosch's own international advisory committee (set up in

November 1981), on which five other top managers of major international concerns including Dunlop, Dow Chemical, and Sweden's Wallenberg Group also sat. If we include all this, we gain at least some idea of the dense and powerful web of influence that Hans L. Merkle wove in his work for Bosch.[16]

Also striking in this connection is the fact that, unlike Walz and Knoerzer, Merkle only rarely took his cue from the late founder. He played no part in further interpreting the will and guidelines of Robert Bosch, seldom even mentioning his legacy.[17] The company ceased to feel the need to justify current operations by citing the writings of Robert Bosch. The founder was very much less of an underlying presence than had formerly been the case. Yet there was no contradiction in Merkle's continued insistence that he stood in direct line of descent from Robert Bosch and had a solemn duty to preserve his legacy. This was especially true of the founder's knack for anticipating the future – his "nose for the imminent," as Merkle once termed it.[18] The only difference was that now he, Merkle, was placing his own unmistakable stamp on the company. One example of this was a further crucial development in how Bosch defined its leadership culture and organization. In April 1970, the company moved its head office out of central Stuttgart and relocated it to the Schillerhöhe [which, as the name implies, lies atop a lofty, even majestic, forested ridge] overlooking Gerlingen, just southwest of Stuttgart.[19] Simply putting this kind of clear geographical distance between administrative and manufacturing areas created a hierarchy of above and below – noticeable particularly when plant managers or works-council members were summoned to headquarters and had to make their way up to the Schillerhöhe. Outsiders and newcomers alike now faced additional hurdles. Not only did they have to try to "understand Bosch." They also had to solve such puzzles as "what makes the Schillerhöhe tick?" and how was one to behave "up there"? Robert Bosch Jr., as well as Bacher and Schreiber, were familiar figures on the shop floor because of their specific areas of responsibility. But associates now no longer came face to face with top management in the person of Merkle. The chairman, though, was all the more present in his lectures, speeches, and newspaper articles, which regularly graced the pages of the in-house journal, *Bosch-Zünder*. Whether staff in Feuerbach, Giengen, or Hildesheim actually understood such discourses is doubtful. These were abstract pieces in the main, intellectual constructs entitled "The art of prediction," "The demonic nature of power," or "Fault lines of present-day society." And they were written in a style peculiar to the man himself – a medley of meditations on financial theory, analysis of social policy, and economic facts and forecasts, sprinkled with philosophical asides and witticisms.[20] Today's reader can only guess what it all meant at the time and what the general public will have made of it.[21] Merkle's pronouncements echo a very different mindset, one of the 1960s and 1970s.

Hans L. Merkle (1988)

With Merkle, the whole question of corporate finance and earnings moved center-stage. When in April 1965 he presented the Bosch financial program for the coming fiscal year, this was entirely dominated by growth. It provided for record levels of capital expenditure (310 million German marks) and forecast an annual profit of 94 million German marks.[22] But then, in the autumn of 1965, the business sky darkened abruptly. In the statement of income, broken down by product areas, the first half-year showed red figures alongside such key Bosch products as injection pumps and household appliances. What especially troubled Merkle was that for the first time the company had suffered a perceptible reverse in its automotive-equipment business. Total inventories were growing twice as fast as planned, in September sales fell, and the profit situation took a turn for the worse. Merkle's reaction was swift. He radically amended corporate policy. Insiders were soon referring ironically tongue-in-cheek to the turnaround as the "October Revolution."[23] Various capital expenditure plans, notably in construction, were promptly cancelled, and capital expenditure as a whole was drastically reduced or extended over a longer period. All staffing requests pending before human resources departments were cancelled and action was taken to slash overheads instantly.[24] Overtime was forbidden, the higher categories of white-collar staff whose bonuses depended

on sales performance took a 10 percent salary reduction, and battle was declared in advance regarding the unions' next round of wage demands. However, it was made known explicitly that major job cuts were to be avoided.
Finally, in November 1965 Merkle put to the RBIG shareholders a full "Action
plan to make management leaner, adjust production, and bring down costs."[25]

Merkle's "crisis policy" caused a stir not only within the company but also
in public. For the first time, a major German company, in the midst of what appeared to be an unbroken "economic miracle," was preparing itself for an economic downturn.[26] But that was not all. In the eyes of the outside world, Bosch
appeared to be showing signs of weakness. "Global company in tight fix," ran
the headline in one newspaper at the end of October 1965 ("Weltfirma Bosch in
einer Klemme"). Senior management felt obliged to react by calling an immediate press conference. There was no question of finance being tight, they stressed.
Instead, this was about adjusting to new developments.[27] Other rumors surrounding a "crisis" in the household-appliance business and the launch of joint-
venture talks with Siemens gave rise to further speculation about the company's
health. However, no later than July 1966, when figures that were "as good as
ever" were published for the previous year, all these conjectures were shown to
be unfounded.[28] Sales of almost 3 billion German marks, profits totaling 90 million German marks (25 percent up on the previous year), and an equity ratio of
30 percent gave Bosch a better-than-average health report in the world of German big business. However, within the company Merkle continued to wage war
on cost inflation, reining in the divisions still further. Management accounting
was introduced everywhere, budgetary accounting was modernized to bring it
up to U.S. standards, and the associated profit orientation was made obliga-
tory.[29] Already existing rationalization measures in manufacturing were further
enhanced, and at the start of 1967 they were extended to administrative departments. As Merkle told an RBIG meeting in March 1967, "examining and analyz-
ing the entire company is expected to take five years."[30] In 1966–67, the economic slump Bosch had anticipated did in fact arrive. Although there was no
negative growth, there was a feeling in the German economy that the downturn
marked the end of the postwar boom. However, the downturn found Bosch in
good shape. Merkle's prompt strengthening of the company's manufacturing
efficiency, the radical reduction of its inventories, and its improved price competitiveness all stood it in good stead. Earlier than other companies, it was able
to boost its levels of capital expenditure once more. "If there were an 'Oscar' for
the smartest behavior in the crux year 1966, the winner would be Robert Bosch
GmbH of Stuttgart," wrote one newspaper retrospectively in July 1967, when
Bosch presented its 1966 financial statements.[31]

Fig. 4 Development of Bosch Group sales (1952–83):
consolidated global sales in millions of German marks *(left)* and as a percentage year-
on-year change *(right)*

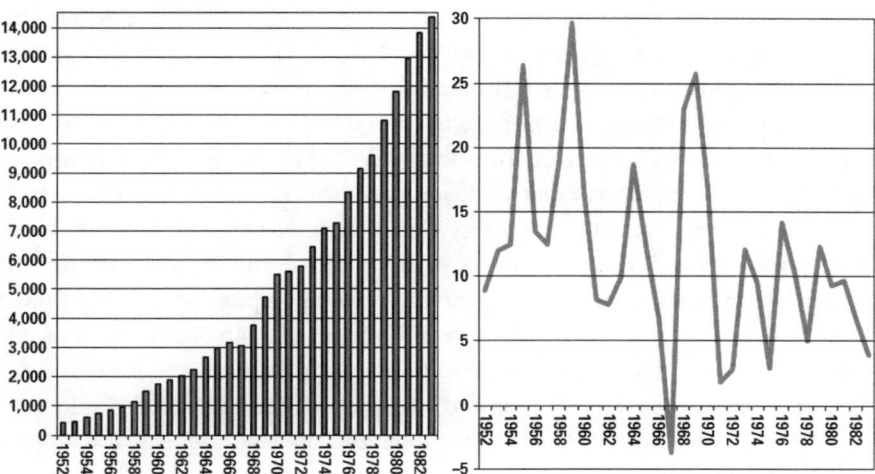

Source: Compiled and calculated from RBIK papers dated June 27, 1984, in RB 1 001 401

In the following years (the "long-drawn-out 1970s"), economic cycles fluc-
tuated frequently and violently, sorely trying the anticipatory abilities of Bosch
management. If we look at the development of company sales, there is a big
difference between the absolute figures and the year-on-year percentage increase. Seen absolutely, the figures for the core company alone, Robert Bosch
GmbH, passed the one billion mark in 1959 (1.13 billion German marks) to top
9 billion German marks in 1983. A glance at the year-on-year percentage rates
of increase, however, reveals a kind of temperature curve in the company's
business development – something with which Bosch management had to
struggle.

In February 1971, Merkle gave a talk to senior executives at headquarters.
Entitled "Business policy of the Bosch Group" (and published in the *Bosch-
Zünder* soon afterward), his talk aimed to prepare both management and shop
floor mentally for the next crisis.[32] In typical digressive style, he prefaced his
exposé with theoretical and philosophical considerations and remarks of a
generally sociological nature, ranging from Karl Marx through economic and
financial theory to organizational sociology. According to Merkle, Bosch corporate strategy (which at the time, at least, was never explicitly referred to as
such) might be said to comprise five main strands. The first was "dealing posi-

tively with economic fluctuation." Bosch, its chairman said, had already successfully anticipated a recession. Once again, Merkle said, "we find ourselves in stormy economic weather." Sales increases had been slowing since 1968 (dropping from 26 percent to 1.8 percent over the Bosch Group as a whole and even to minus 1.5 percent for Robert Bosch GmbH), while operating profits were sinking visibly. Consequently, and this was the second strand he wanted to identify, the spotlight was shifting to diversification, or rather to a business policy "deliberately aimed at spreading risk." The core field of automotive equipment, despite figures that were stagnant or even at times negative, continued to promise opportunities for real growth, "given that the share of Bosch parts per vehicle is rising." Nonetheless (he went on), in keeping with the policy of the founder, and in stark contrast to the contemporary policies of most U.S. conglomerates, diversification would be pursued to an ever-increasing degree. Thirdly, Bosch would continue to pursue globalization as a fundamental part of its business policy. It followed that the market, enhanced production conditions, global developments in technology, and geographical risk-spreading factors would require Bosch to invest more money outside Germany. Fourthly, Merkle made yet another explicit declaration of his faith in division-based corporate organization. Decentralization, he insisted, was the way to preserve freedom of decision coupled with a deepening sense of responsibility within the company. And finally, there was the principle of a sound financial policy based not on borrowing but on gaining ever greater independence. "A successful business policy is subject to a constant process of renewal." Such was Merkle's goal. However, the twin business-policy objectives specific to Bosch remained: the best possible use of economic resources coupled with making any profit not reinvested available for civic initiatives.

The subsequent economic crises, characterized by inflation, oil embargoes, and the associated energy-price explosion, were not long in coming, and left their mark on the earnings of individual divisions and product groups. Over the following period, therefore, various crisis-adjustment measures were introduced "to preserve and enhance the competitiveness of the Bosch Group." In February 1974, an eight-person committee was set up to draft proposals for simplifying Bosch's structure and cutting its costs. The committee shone a merciless light into every corner of the company, and in mid-July of that year presented a bulky report. The former "product groups" [*Produktgruppen*] had been operating explicitly as "business sectors" [*Unternehmensbereiche*] since the start of 1974, though their number and nomenclature had changed. The largest of these sectors (larger than ever) was Automotive Equipment [*Kraftfahrzeugausrüstung*] or K. This was split into eight divisions, which now included the once independently organized groups Hydraulics/Pneumatics (K6) and Diesel Injection Equipment (K5). There was also the NK [i. e., non-auto-motive] sector (as it was usually called), comprising other fields of business: household appliances, basic materials (condensers and plastics), producer goods (electronics, packaging machinery, and industrial equipment), and technical consumer goods (power tools and photo and film products).[33] The core point in the proposals was the dismissal of some 600 associates, mostly in administrative positions.[34] However, it soon became apparent that this alone was not going to be enough to restore profitability and preserve financial flex-ibility. In late July 1974, Merkle called a special meeting of the Bosch board of management, "since we now have numbers that give cause for concern."[35] What he meant was that in the past half year, sales and earnings had both shown dramatic falls of at least 20 percent and, in worst cases, of more than 40 percent. Sales of certain products had dropped by sums running into tens of millions of German marks. Black-and-white televisions, for instance, were down by 25.3 million German marks, while sales of the K-Jetronic mechanical injection system had shed 15.9 million German marks, those of metals prod-ucts 52 million German marks, and those of distributor pumps a massive 150 million German marks.[36] This called for radical restructuring, most nota-bly the dismissal of some 6,000 associates across the Bosch Group and the re-moval from production of "chronic" loss-makers – if necessary shutting down entire operating units or even locations. Bosch, Merkle told the meeting, must have the courage to divest unprofitable fields. "Proper preparation for the next crisis involves not over-exploiting the prior boom."[37] Large-scale dismissals and divestments now formed the core of the company's business policy, which undoubtedly marked something of a break with tradition. The 1973 oil-price shock was a catalyst that ushered in a harsher climate in Bosch corporate cul-ture. Even so, in the spring and summer of 1976 the company was able to pres-ent excellent financial statements with fresh increases in sales and earnings – despite the fact that, as Merkle pointed out at the relevant press conference, no major upswing was yet in sight. It was for Bosch, though. The company was riding "a wave of automotive demand."[38] In 1975, sales reached a new high of 4.57 billion German marks. The consolidated figure for the Bosch Group soared to as much as 7.28 billion German marks. And in 1976, both German and worldwide sales figures enjoyed double-digit rates of growth, rising to 5.37 and 8.32 billion German marks respectively. The figures for earnings and capi-tal expenditure in the financial program for 1977 were adjusted upward ac-cordingly. The growth in orders received between 1975 and 1976 underlined how Bosch had succeeded in breaking away from the general economic situa-tion in the manufacturing industry of the Federal Republic. The 1977 figures again revealed that a striking gap had opened up in Bosch's favor.[39]

The next crisis began in the second half of 1978 and, in conjunction with the second wave of oil-price hikes, led eventually to the great recession of 1980–82. This time, however, Bosch was hit sooner and harder than the board of management had expected. In January 1979, Merkle addressed an unusual document to all Bosch executives. In its preface, the document suggested that cutting costs was going to be particularly important in the coming year. Virtually all areas in which Bosch operated were now dealing with a global buyers' market "that will not permit us to base our selling prices on cost accounting. Instead, prices will be dictated by the market, and our costs must follow suit."[40] Attached was an "outline of costs and earnings." Close study of this was recommended since it "will serve not least to shake up received habits, ways of thinking, and prescriptions for action." In over seven pages, Bosch executives were urged to look critically at structures and modes of behavior as they related to a wide range of problem areas, all the way from organization, taking in locations, reporting, telephone conversations, and travel, to product fields, markets, and customers. They were also asked to review investment and divestment. The paper ended by urging its readers to examine "whether you have set aside enough time in your personal work schedule to think calmly about the tasks ahead and how to solve them. For 1979, devote even more time to reflection than you have before. The future of the Bosch Group depends on prompt, correct, systematic action, and that requires forethought."[41]

In the summer of 1980, the board of management assembled for a fresh crisis meeting.[42] The toolkit settled on this time did not diverge from the actions that had proved their worth in previous economic crises. Under Merkle, it was mainly earnings, headcount, and inventories that were used to direct and fine-tune the various divisions, and in these fields all Bosch management personnel worldwide were asked to take immediate action. However, in April 1981 the new income statements for product categories showed that the situation was not improving at all. If anything, it was growing worse. More than a third of product categories were making a loss, and new products especially, in which Bosch had placed high hopes of future sales and earnings, were showing negative results. The antilock braking system (ABS) had accumulated losses of some 120 million German marks, semiconductor ignition systems were also hemorrhaging money, and even glow plugs were in sharp decline.[43] Thus far, the Bosch board of management concluded in May 1981, they were not adapting fast enough. "The future of [Bosch] depends on our costing policy. We need to work with costs that will restore our competitive edge over our Japanese rivals."[44] Nonetheless, in 1982 the economic downturn continued undiminished. Sales increases declined from 9.7 percent (1981) to 6.6 percent. By

1983 they were even down to 3.9 percent, with business outside Germany suffering particularly as a result of the international recession. The plain fact was: not merely economic vicissitudes but also structural changes in supplier relationships were now affecting developments.

Monopoly of supply versus collective buying power: Bosch and terms of supply in the pre-López era

At Bosch, the economic situation in the automotive sector and its increasingly violent fluctuations dictated the overall course of business and the way the company developed. From the 1960s to the 1980s, the automotive industry shaped the entire German economy – indeed, the economy of all Europe – like few others. In this respect, too, the "long-drawn-out 1970s" are a pivotal phase, including not only two oil-price shocks, but above all the decline of the long-dominant American automotive industry and the simultaneous rise of its Japanese rivals – Toyota, Nissan, and Honda. For the German automotive industry and its suppliers, the main concern during this period was to avoid being crushed between these opposing forces. They needed to hold their own in the new tripartite market comprising Europe, the United States, and Japan. Worldwide, the automotive market was still largely confined to the traditional industrialized countries, where it was fast approaching saturation. Yet what was in one sense a crisis at the same time had the effect of catalyzing a fundamental shift in relations between original-equipment suppliers and their customers. Decades of a supply monopoly were first shaken up by an emergent "two-supplier approach," then by a growing tendency for automakers to manufacture their own equipment in-house, and finally by a new self-assurance of automakers who had discovered for themselves their collective buying power. It was an era that saw them telling suppliers what prices and costs they would accept.[45] Bosch reacted to these challenges in three ways: first by introducing innovations in its product range and its production engineering, second by extending the global reach of its industrial activities, and third by starting to radically rethink its own approach, seeking out new business opportunities in the wake of the energy crisis and in the fundamental changes this meant for the relationship between growth and the environment.

The technical innovations introduced by Bosch were the result of its core competencies in electronics and precision mechanics. In remarkably quick succession during the 1960s and 1970s, a great many technological milestones were developed and made ready for production. What distinguished Bosch in this connection was its ability not merely to come up with innovations but also to stick with them through long barren periods, even where no overnight, sweeping success was forthcoming. The company was also capable of taking expensive innovations involving high initial production costs and, in a complex and intensive development process, turning them into high-quality yet low-cost mass products. "If Bosch can do one thing, it is painstakingly cut costs on the factory floor. [...] We are not born masters of engineering, not by any means, but we can sniff out the developments that deserve priority, and we know where to go to get things."[46] A striking example of this was the distributor pump, which the then head of research Gustav Wagner brought back from the United States in 1963. Bosch produced it under license for years, consistently making a loss. But with the breakthrough of the diesel engine and electronic injection control, it became one of Bosch's biggest earners. There were few other phases in the history of the automobile where technological change was so dramatic. Cars now needed less maintenance, were longer-lived and more comfortable, and, thanks to the rapidly growing part played by electronics, increasingly sophisticated. Initially, the focus was on powertrain technology, turning successively to engine and transmission control, to emissions control (or "decontamination" [*Abgas-Entgiftung*], as it was then termed) using sensors and catalytic converters, and finally to electronic brake control.[47]

To make this clearer, let us once again cast a backward glance. In the course of the 1950s, as motorization in Germany caught up after the war, Bosch was able to recover a dominant position in the market sooner than expected. In 1955, the main customer for Bosch automotive equipment was Daimler-Benz, spending 35.9 million German marks and accounting for 16 percent of all Bosch original-equipment sales in the German market (224.12 million German marks). Other large customers were Volkswagen with 31.7 million German marks (14.1 percent) and Opel (12.4 percent). Interestingly, in the market for original equipment outside Germany, where at this time Bosch earned only 34 million German marks (a mere 13 percent of its total automotive original-equipment sales), it was Holden (i. e., GM Australia) that occupied first place with 9 million German marks (26.5 percent), followed by Volvo (7.5 million German marks) and Fiat (4.5 million German marks).[48] In 1962–63, after the legislature passed a law calling for the extent of concentration in the German economy to be scrutinized, Bosch was the subject of an investigation. The findings, presented in July 1963 in a wide-ranging, four-part report, revealed that Bosch's position as a supplier had become even stronger.[49] Barely ten years after the Allies had concluded their decartelization and deconcentration proceedings against Bosch, the company enjoyed market shares ranging from 20 to 97 percent in a whole series of product areas in automotive electrics. Particularly with such innovations as electronically controlled alternators, gasoline injection pumps (in series production from 1951), and diesel direct-injection pumps, Bosch had virtually the whole of the German market to itself. But also in starters, ignition systems, and spark and glow plugs, Bosch commanded market shares of 70 percent and more in Germany, between 20 and 40 percent in the EEC (as it was then called), and even a respectable 15 to 20 percent worldwide.[50] Nonetheless, the concentration study did not attribute excessive market power to Bosch. It saw Bosch more as competing internationally with the vast capital might of the large automotive groups, and (as was the case not only with Ford and GM but also, now, with Fiat and Toyota) facing additional competition from automakers' own in-house production of automotive equipment. It concluded: "The only way in which a producer of automotive electric and diesel equipment can remain independent of the giants of the automotive industry is by being so competitive that it can match quality and price to the ever-changing demands of the world market."[51]

However, at this point in time the whole original-equipment market was subject to capacity bottlenecks. Bosch *allocated* its products to automakers more than it sold them – and did so at prices that Stuttgart boosted by 8 to 10 percent annually. Yet by the mid-1960s at the latest, it was becoming obvious that the risks as well as the intensity of competition were on the rise. This was in addition to the collapses and insolvencies among many of the small automakers that had sprung up in the 1950s alongside major players such as Volkswagen and Daimler-Benz. Companies such as Borgward, Hanomag, Lloyd, and Goliath still, in 1960, accounted for some 22 million German marks' worth of sales at Bosch – some 10 percent of the entire original-equipment business. Shortly before the Borgward Group failed in the following year (1961), it still owed Bosch some 4 million German marks. The rapid concentration in the German automotive industry also had its repercussions for Bosch. In 1963, automotive original equipment accounted for 63 percent of all its automotive business in Germany. While these sales were the result of business with some 100 companies in all, in practice 90 percent was accounted for by the ten largest original-equipment customers, including Daimler-Benz, VW, Opel, Ford, and Klöckner-Humboldt-Deutz (KHD) – with 80 percent going to those five companies alone.[52] If only one of those companies withdrew its business, Bosch would be hard hit. The board of management therefore agreed unanimously that the company's position in the automotive sector had to be defended at all costs. The situation worsened in the autumn of 1969 as a result of the revaluation of the German mark. Of the 9 percent price hikes brought in as a result, Bosch was able to pass only a fraction on to customers. On top of everything, the automotive sector then went into recession, with growth rates declining steadily while downturns in the economic cycle followed one another in ever shorter and sharper succession.

Fig. 5 Business developments in Germany's automotive sector.
Year-on-year percentage change in automotive production* (1950–82)

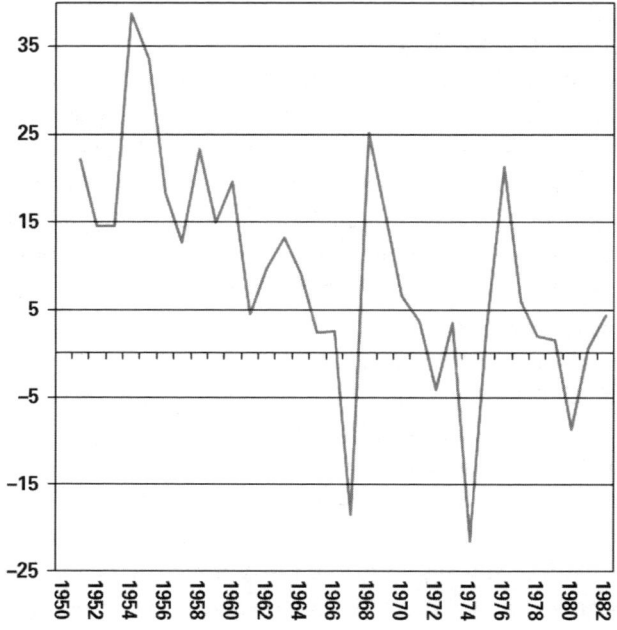

* Passenger cars, trucks, and buses
Sources: http://de.wikipedia.org/wiki/Wirtschaftszahlen_zum_Automobil#cite_note-OICA-1
and VDA annual reports from 1961 onward at http://www.vda.de/de/publikationen/
jahresberichte/index.html

While absolute numbers of automobiles produced in Germany almost doubled between 1960 (2.05 million) and 1982 (4.06 million), in relative terms growth continued to weaken. Above all, the relationship between the economic situation and the automotive-equipment business at Bosch became evident. Annual sales cycles in the automotive technology business sector moved up and down in parallel to numbers of vehicles produced – but with one important difference. From the early 1970s, sales slumps at automakers did not by any means herald equally negative sales developments in Bosch's supply business.[53] For 1977, for instance, the automotive industry expected at best insignificant increases in production. Bosch, on the other hand, anticipated major sales boosts in its automotive business, partly because of the boom in diesel injection and gasoline injection equipment. Moreover, Bosch benefited from its internal diversification, being able to supply a very wide range of products. In March 1974, for instance, while orders for distributors, headlights, and other lights plummeted, demand for heaters and above all diesel injection pumps remained brisk. The Bosch automotive-equipment business as a whole increased tenfold between 1960 (sales totaling 860 million German marks) and 1982 (sales of 8.6 billion German marks), bringing in substantial earnings even in periods of recession. As automakers recorded losses, Bosch continued to chalk up handsome profits. However, this made it more difficult to find acceptance for future price hikes, and this in turn made Bosch pursue a more cautious price policy.[54]

By the mid-1970s at the latest, the Bosch board of management went on the offensive in the original-equipment business. One contributory factor was that, after years of sometimes heavy initial losses, sales of gasoline injection equipment in particular were now booming swiftly. From some 100,000 units in the late 1960s, the number of injection systems produced annually had risen to almost a million by the early 1980s. Diesel products (distributor pumps in particular) and gasoline injection systems were both major areas and drivers of growth. Over the seven-year period from 1975 to 1981, sales almost doubled from 1.127 billion to 2.18 billion German marks in the case of diesel products, and in the case of gasoline injection systems tripled from 211 million to 595 million German marks.[55] In addition, the antilock braking system was to go into series production from 1978. Between October 1978 and June 1983, Bosch supplied around 250,000 first-generation and second-generation ABS systems to Daimler-Benz, BMW, and Audi. From the perspective of Bosch as an automotive supplier, no sooner had automakers freed themselves from dependence on particular components than they became dependent on systems instead. Indeed, as Merkle explained to the RBIK shareholders in March 1979, in the second half of the 1970s relations between Bosch and its largest original-equipment customers were "a contest played out between ourselves and a handful of major automakers as to who is going to be the systems leader in the progressive introduction of electronics into automobiles. It goes without saying that we are doing all we can to continue supplying not merely electric and electronic components for internal-combustion engines and the vehicles fitted with them, but instead complete systems. The policy pursued by the development departments of some leading producers of engines and vehicles runs counter to ours. With certain exceptions, their aim is not necessarily to shed Bosch as their supplier but certainly to become independent of Bosch in terms of future development."[56]

Even in the early 1980s, major customers such as Daimler-Benz still depended to a great extent on mechanical systems. Bosch, on the other hand, had taken on the challenge of introducing electronics into the automotive realm as early as the start of the 1960s, incorporating high-performance semiconductors into the electronic controls of generators and employing electronic ignition systems. And 1970 saw the inauguration of its new engineering center for automotive electrics in Schwieberdingen, just northwest of Stuttgart, not only creating a corporate research and development center but at the same time elevating systems thinking to become the guiding principle behind all future development work. In other words, Bosch possessed important knowledge and experience in systems technology at a substantially earlier stage than most of its major customers.[57] However, competitive circumstances had tightened up generally, with Bosch's share of supply in automotive original equipment now coming more frequently under attack. The process of concentration sweeping through the international automotive industry gained even greater momentum in the second half of the 1970s, increasing "the risk that automakers would further emancipate themselves from suppliers" – as Merkle stressed at one meeting of the Bosch board of management.[58] And little had changed regarding Bosch's risky dependence on a handful of major customers. Daimler-Benz, Volkswagen, Opel, Ford, and KHD were still, in 1972, its "Big Five" original-equipment customers. Business with them generated sales worth 1.12 billion German marks (some 80 percent of all its automotive-equipment business), with more than half that figure (namely, 792 million German marks) accounted for by Daimler-Benz and VW alone.[59] Not until a decade later did things look different, with the share of the ten biggest customers in the automotive business down by over half (to 43 percent) and Daimler-Benz and VW (still Bosch's biggest original-equipment customers, with combined sales revenue of 2.3 billion German marks) accounting for only 26.7 percent of all automotive technology sales. Just as customers were about to discover and flex their collective buying power, Bosch had significantly reduced its reliance on only a few major customers. Now Ford and Opel were joined on the list of the "Big Ten" by such substantial new customers as BMW, Renault, Fiat, Volvo, and Peugeot/Citroën/Talbot. However, at the end of 1981 (just as at the end of 1971), the automotive sector still accounted for between 50 and 60 percent of total Bosch Group sales, and the original-equipment business remained the essential "constant" of Bosch manufacturing operations, as well as the essential generator of profits.

In the mid-1970s, however, one single major customer, Daimler-Benz, became the focus of concern, confronting Bosch with an automaker-related problem of a quite different kind. During 1974, Middle Eastern oil-producing countries began making offers for stakes in major German companies. OPEC countries throughout the world were keen to invest their oil-sale profits, which were estimated at between 300 and 600 billion German marks. In the period January to October 1974 alone, financial investments coming in from the Middle East totaled some 45 billion German marks. This was more than the market value, at the time, of all publicly traded shares of German stock corporations. As well as Krupp and Gutehoffnungshütte, Daimler-Benz had now also become a target for Middle Eastern investors. In January 1975, intensive and somewhat frantic discussions were launched at the Federal Ministry of Economic Affairs as to how this "foreign infiltration" of the German economy might be halted, possibly through a law requiring non-domestic shareholdings to be registered.[60] Along with representatives of the Federal Association of German Industry and the banks, Merkle was involved in these discussions from the outset. After the Quandt Group had sold its 14 percent holding in Daimler-Benz to the Sheikhdom of Kuwait, and the Flick Group had contemplated putting most of its large block of Daimler-Benz shares (in excess of 39 percent) on the market, Deutsche Bank stepped in as purchaser. In doing so, it forestalled the Shah of Persia and prevented one of Germany's largest automakers from falling into Middle Eastern hands, as well as the loss of technological know-how that it was feared this would bring. However, Deutsche Bank wished to offload some of the majority Daimler-Benz shareholding it now held, and in April 1975 it began talks with a number of friendly companies. These included Bosch, and Merkle was prepared (for more elevated reasons of national economic policy as well as for narrower reasons of business policy) to take a stake, "since there were grounds for believing that in the event of a Persian penetration of Daimler-Benz there might be unwelcome relocations of technology and capacity."[61] On the table was a package worth 75 million German marks or about 1 percent of the nominal capital of Daimler-Benz, but at the same time Deutsche Bank was offering Merkle a seat on the Daimler-Benz supervisory board. Declining the offer on the grounds that he already possessed such a mandate at Volkswagen, Merkle proposed Hans Bacher as the Bosch representative instead.[62]

On no account did Merkle want the stake in Daimler-Benz to be seen as a sign of some deeper relationship – if only for the sake of Bosch's other original-equipment customers, among whom (at BMW and Volvo especially) there was already substantial concern that Daimler-Benz might in future receive preferential treatment in matters of supply. The actual share purchase by Bosch did not take place until December 1975. Deutsche Bank laboriously cobbled together a complex, multi-level arrangement involving participation in another company (Mercedes Automobil Holding AG), with various sub-participations. At the end of this complex process, Merkle suddenly found himself looking at a Bosch holding of 115 million German marks.[63] By 1981, after capital increases, Bosch owned 1.58 percent of Daimler-Benz. In view of the excellent earnings situation of the automotive group (with sales almost three times those of Bosch and a margin twice as high), this was not a bad financial investment – quite apart from the highly unusual and surely unique situation whereby Bosch, as a supplier, sat on the supervisory boards of its two largest customers.

Meanwhile, to boost the company's clout and better coordinate its core business operations, a four-person group of senior Bosch managers had been created. The group comprised Hans Bacher, the man with overall responsibility for the automotive sector, Konrad Eckert and Hermann Scholl as line managers for the six automotive technology divisions,[64] and Peter Rose, responsible for relations with original-equipment customers. But not least, it was Hans L. Merkle who played a key role in cultivating business relationships with automotive companies. Merkle had regular meetings with his counterparts not only at Daimler-Benz, Volkswagen, Opel, and Ford, but also at Renault and Peugeot. He was befriended and close with Pehr Gyllenhammar, chairman of the board of management of Volvo. Eberhard von Kuenheim, who was elected chairman of the BMW board of management in 1970, had once served a several-year apprenticeship at Bosch. All the major figures in the automotive world, from Giovanni Agnelli to Henry Ford II, called at Merkle's Schillerhöhe office. But almost more important were their regular invitations to the Bosch hunting lodge at Pfronten in Bavaria's Allgäu region, where on long walks Merkle would discuss original-equipment pricing policies and tell his guests about new Bosch products and technological advances. But Merkle himself also made frequent trips to Detroit and Tokyo. He gained great authority from being a member of the board of the German Automotive Industry Association (*Verband der deutschen Automobilindustrie* or VDA) and from presiding over its "Parts and Accessories Producer Group." With 224 member companies, the latter represented the interests of Germany's automotive-supply industry in its dealings with politicians and automakers. In regular situation analyses, close exchanges of information about the latest developments in engineering and research, and assessments of the broader political and economic climate, Merkle sought to lay down the "rules of engagement" both within the supplier industry ("we are caught up in a veritable war of extermination") and between suppliers and their customers. This he contrived to do in a way that benefited all involved.[65] Whether in the clash over abolishing resale price maintenance or in the notorious "spare parts dispute," an argument about labeling original spare parts that raged between automakers, automotive suppliers, and spare-parts dealers,[66] Merkle sought to mediate and broker a settlement. This was particularly true with respect to the concern that the German automotive industry and its suppliers might fall and be crushed between the two fronts of the U.S. and Japan, where all sectoral structures were undergoing transformation. In this respect, Merkle issued a warning at a VDA producer group meeting held in November 1977: "In the longer term, it cannot be ruled out that competition from the Japanese and American automotive industries, already evident in other markets, will reach the German market as well."[67]

For Bosch, albeit for the most part under different circumstances, what now began to dominate supplier relations (and this to an increasing extent) was the old problem of allocating materials and synchronizing its own manufacturing operations with those of its customers. This is a recurrent theme in the history of the original-equipment business at Bosch. More and more frequently, automakers were making sudden changes to their call orders and projected figures, which tested Bosch's production engineers and plant managers to the limits of their adaptability. In November 1973, at the height of the first oil-price shock, the situation was particularly inscrutable. Domestic sales had been in marked decline for some time, but demand from outside Germany was still rising. Of 1.01 million vehicles originally planned, Opel abruptly cancelled 170,000 (no less than 17 percent), with far-reaching consequences for production at automotive suppliers and a greater scheduling risk for Bosch. For the first time in the company's history, Merkle was unable to draw up a provisional financial program "because our largest customer group, the automotive industry, has entered a period of uncertainty as regards its production planning."[68] Even for the first quarter of 1974, automakers gave their suppliers production-plan figures that were far too optimistic, only to reduce them all the more radically and unexpectedly as the year went on. On the other hand, toward the end of 1977 Bosch found itself facing starkly increased demand for mechanical and electronic gasoline-injection systems for the coming year. Rather than the 700,000 units originally planned, the company was now asked to produce almost 850,000 units. This necessitated a swift expansion of manufacturing capacity with correspondingly greater levels of investment (in the order of millions of German marks).[69] As the Bosch management had been forced to concede in May 1976: "Automakers have trained their suppliers well in the matter of adjusting their supplies up and down in short order. Reason enough for us to do even better in this direction than before."[70]

Particularly the second oil-price shock of 1979–80 prompted a rapid shift in supply structures and relations between suppliers and their customers. In March 1977, Bosch had reached agreement with Volkswagen that it would be VW's sole supplier of diesel equipment worldwide, producing 800,000 units. However, as early as July Bosch learned that its quota had been reduced to 80 percent in favor of its British rival CAV, whose price for diesel injection pumps was 10 percent lower. What chiefly irritated Bosch in this connection was that the supply problems that CAV experienced later, and the consequent postponements in the sale of the new Golf diesel, were publicly blamed on Bosch. Stuttgart also looked on critically as, in the spring of 1978, close contacts between Volkswagen and Siemens in the area of electronic engine management led eventually to a development alliance. Moreover, the press reported at the time that VW was collaborating with the U.S. company Fairchild on a project to develop a breakerless transistorized ignition device "to undermine the market-dominant position of Germany's largest producer of automotive electrics."[71] The first major turning point came in the spring of 1979, when Volkswagen announced the development and production of its own gasoline injection system as a "step in the direction of achieving independence from Bosch," which is how the then chairman of the VW board of management, Toni Schmücker, described it in a letter to Merkle. In intensive talks with the Volkswagen board of management, Merkle tried to persuade VW to abandon any such intention, stating baldly that "as a member of the VW supervisory board as well as a supplier to VW" he regarded "the commencement of such in-house production as a mistake."[72] In fact, events soon sounded the all-clear. But where Bosch had once imposed price increases of between 8 and 10 percent, all that remained now were increases of between 2 and 2.5 percent – and that often only after laborious negotiations. "VW still threatens to buy automotive equipment in Japan if we do not offer the same terms with regard to price, quality, and security of supply," Merkle told the RBIK meeting at the end of November 1980.[73] Then, in December 1980, the second turning point came. For the first time, VW chief Schmücker demanded that Bosch lower the prices of some of its parts by as much as 20 percent. With Japanese automobiles being imported into Europe and America in rapidly increasing numbers and production figures at Bosch's biggest customers declining, and this with a lower share of Bosch equipment per vehicle, the cards in the automotive-supply business were being reshuffled. Bosch's response was "more Bosch per vehicle" and, above all, further innovations through increased international sharing of Bosch know-how.[74]

The challenge of re-entering the U.S. market: stages and problems of the second phase of internationalization

The return of Bosch to automotive-supply markets outside Germany was by no means straightforward. After the end of the second World War, Bosch found itself largely excluded from the markets of the traditional industrialized countries. Its former sales offices and manufacturing sites for automotive equip-

Manufacture of spark plugs, injection nozzles, and injection pumps at MICO (1961)

ment in the U.S. and Europe had been destroyed, confiscated, or lost for other reasons. In addition, even exporting from Germany to those countries was very much harder for Bosch in the immediate postwar years than it had been before. Only in Switzerland was Bosch able to buy back its majority holding in Scintilla AG in Solothurn and resume manufacturing of its own spark plugs, generators, and other products there. To make up for these losses at least in part, the company decided at a very early stage to first of all open up markets on the fringes of the world economy. A start was made in 1951, when Bosch concluded a licensing agreement with the Indian company Motor Industries Co. (MICO), which had been set up in the same year. In 1953–54, Bosch took a 49 percent direct holding in the Bangalore company, it having become clear in the meantime that an automotive industry was about to be built up in India with the aid of Daimler-Benz. By 1961, the holding had grown by degrees to reach 57.5 percent.[75] Meanwhile, February 1954 had seen the founding of Robert Bosch Pty. Ltd. in Australia – again, initially as a joint venture with a regional company manufacturing under license. However, two years later Bosch took over majority control.

November 1954 brought the launch of Robert Bosch do Brasil, which from the outset traded under that name as a separate entity. Robert Bosch do Brasil developed rapidly into the largest and fastest-growing regional subsidiary of the Bosch Group.[76] Industrialization was just beginning in Brazil, and since it had been prohibited by law since 1953 for Brazilians to purchase vehicles manufactured outside the country, the Bosch board of management expected the automotive industry to grow rapidly. As an automotive-equipment supplier producing locally, Bosch was now ready to participate in this growth. Soon after, moreover, V W and Daimler-Benz began establishing their own manufacturing capacities there.[77] By the end of the 1970s, Bosch was indeed to occupy a dominant market position in Brazil. As regards diesel business, it was virtually the sole supplier, and in automotive electrics the company enjoyed a 40 percent market share. Up to this time, at least, it had been able to prevent incursion by its longstanding arch-rival, the British company Lucas Ltd.[78] In addition to this involvement in Brazil, there was also the renewal (in one case) and initial conclusion (in the other) of license agreements for diesel injection systems with two Japanese companies. These were Nippondenso, a Toyota subsidiary, and Diesel Kiki, majority-owned by Isuzu Motors Company. Since the relevant license fees could not be transferred outside Japan, Bosch converted them into shares and soon had minority holdings of nearly 10 percent in each company.

Bosch's investments in markets outside Germany increased rapidly in the ensuing years, with the emphasis initially on re-establishing sales companies, coupled with building up a robust customer-service organization. In 1960, Bosch already had 11 sales offices and companies, either wholly or partly owned – in Italy, France, the U.K., Portugal, Denmark, and Sweden, among other European countries, as well as in Argentina, Canada, and the United States.[79] By 1967, Bosch had invested more than 400 million German marks outside Germany since the German currency reform in 1948 [when the *Deutsche Mark* (DM) replaced the *Reichsmark*]. Most of this (worth 230 million German marks) was in the EEC or EFTA, while 83 million German marks fell to the Americas and 52.7 million to Asia and Oceania.[80] Within a few years, in other words, Bosch was once again present in the main international markets, also through the presentation of its products at the major industrial trade fairs worldwide.

As early as the spring of 1969, Merkle introduced a fresh wave of Bosch investments outside Germany. In the following year alone, 60 million German marks flowed into new manufacturing locations in Argentina, Brazil, Mexico,

Shah Reza Pahlavi (*center, in uniform*) and Ludwig Erhard, German minister of economic affairs (*right*), at the Bosch stand at the opening of the German Industrial Exhibition in Tehran on October 4, 1960

and India.[81] The aim was to build on Bosch's good market position in these regions and other parts of the world while continuing to hold back with manufacturing facilities of its own in the rest of Europe. In 1966, to coordinate and above all to support the financing requirements of Bosch companies outside Germany, Bosch had founded Robert Bosch Internationale Beteiligung AG, headquartered in Zurich.[82] Its task was to make international sources of finance available. At the beginning of 1971, the new company was reorganized as part of a re-arrangement of the international investment portfolio for business-policy and especially tax reasons. This reorganization of Robert Bosch Internationale Beteiligung AG transformed it into an independently operating executive holding company with its own advisory staff and its own management.[83] The fact was, Bosch was now generating sales of 2.17 billion German marks (or 42.2 percent of total sales) through its companies outside Germany. Close to 25,000 associates worked for Bosch outside Germany, and with few exceptions all its affiliates were profitable. In 1973, they brought in earnings of 44.3 million German marks – around 15 percent of total earnings. By far the greater part of that sum was earned in Brazil, with the Swiss company Scintilla coming in second.[84]

Despite all Bosch's success in expanding its business outside Germany through sales and production facilities in Latin America, India, and even Australia, the company had difficulty in repositioning itself in the various European markets, and even greater difficulty in winning back a strong position in the U.S. automotive-supply market. Because of the strong position occupied by Lucas, the U.K. had never played a big role so far as Bosch was concerned, although the automotive industry was still strong there.[85] France, where Bosch had traditionally had a good position, proved to be a hard market to penetrate. Initially, in 1950 the company operated through two sales agencies. In 1958, it acquired a minority stakeholding in Lavalette, a company with which it had cooperated back in the 1930s.[86] In 1961, Bosch acquired a majority interest in SAVEM, which one year on was trading as Robert Bosch (France) S. A., owing to Bosch having reacquired its full rights to use its own name in the French market in that year. Also in 1962, initially with the collaboration of the French automotive supplier Labinal S. A., Bosch set up its own plant with production facilities in Saint-Ouen. In 1966, this was followed by a second plant in Rodez. In 1970, the company rethought its strategy for the French market. The background to this was that the French automotive-supply industry was in a general state of turmoil as a result of concentration and takeover plans. The automotive supplier SEV Marchal was up for sale, and Bosch had signaled interest in purchasing a stake in it. However, Bosch was keen to avoid anything that was going to bring it into conflict with the French authorities, with such powerful original-equipment customers as Peugeot and Renault, or with its own licensees.[87] In mid-June 1970, therefore, Merkle traveled to see Valéry Giscard d'Estaing, who at that time was France's Minister of Economy and Finance. Disregarding the historically loaded semantics of the title, he laid before him the *Bosch-Generalplan Frankreich*. Among other things, this foresaw a 30 percent Bosch holding in SEV Marchal.[88] Starting in the summer of 1976, Bosch stepped up its attempts to secure substantial market shares in the automotive electric and electronics segments of the French original-equipment market. The opportunities were good. While electronics were gaining ground in the automotive industries of Germany and the U.K., France still lagged behind. In addition to operating plants of its own, Bosch now focused increasingly on an alliance with the Société Financière d'Equipement Automobile (FEA). This was not an automotive supplier as such but a holding company that included various automotive suppliers. To prevent penetration by other, rival groups (chiefly Lucas/Thomson, Delco, and Motorola), Bosch bought a 35 percent holding and, together with Ferodo (later renamed Valeo and the holder of

65 percent of the shares), took over the industrial leadership of FEA.[89] The operations of the Bosch Group in France were now gathered in seven locations, employed 4,700 people, and generated sales totaling 1.3 billion French francs (equivalent to some 770 million German marks), and this with earnings which were genuinely encouraging.[90]

Merkle's expansion of Bosch operations outside Germany from the mid-1960s onward included a plan to establish plants in Spain. The reasons for going to Spain were obvious. There was a larger pool of labor in Spain than in Germany, and wage levels were lower. So it made more sense to take manufacturing sites to the workforce than to bring fresh guest workers into Germany to operate production facilities there. But above all, Merkle had learned from the then chairman of Volkswagen's board of management, Heinrich Nordhoff, that the Wolfsburg company was itself planning to start automotive production in Spain. The Spanish automotive-equipment market, with plenty of catching up to do, offered corresponding opportunities for growth. In July 1967, Bosch began producing automotive electrical equipment in the country, having first acquired a 50 percent holding in Constructora Electrica Española S. A. in Madrid for this purpose. This company was subsequently renamed Robert Bosch Española (RBES). After Switzerland, France (2), Sweden, Australia, Brazil, India, and Mexico, Bosch now had nine manufacturing sites outside Germany. However, the great expectations with regard to sales and earnings in Spain failed to materialize. In 1973, for instance, RBES was the only Bosch company in Europe to make a loss (of 1.23 million German marks). Then, in the spring of 1977, there suddenly arose an opportunity to acquire a direct interest in Fábrica Española Magneto S. A. (FEMSA), Bosch's main rival in Spain. With a workforce of some 1,100, RBES was recording sales of just under 100 million German marks. On the other hand, FEMSA, with 8,400 workers, had sales of 390 million German marks – nearly four times as much. However, FEMSA was in a liquidity crisis and facing financing difficulties. Even the immediately apparent risks were substantial. Both RBES and FEMSA were operating without profit. The former was already looking at a loss of 2–3 million German marks for 1977 alone. Not until 1980 at the earliest could a positive result be expected – not counting any reorganization costs that might have to be incurred in the meantime. According to Merkle, who had visited FEMSA in February 1978 to gain a picture for himself, the company was "overmanned," "overtooled," and "overstocked."[91] But that was not all. As was already the case in France, industrial policy was high on the political agenda in Spain, particularly when it came to the automotive industry, which was regarded as strategic. In the years that followed, Bosch was to become hopelessly entangled in this web of interests woven by Spain's family shareholders, the Madrid government, and not least the self-assured workforce and the country's strike-happy socialist trade unions. For the Stuttgart company, FEMSA came to resemble a bottomless pit. The complicated history of the FEMSA involvement and the company's Spanish business would trouble the Bosch board of management on an almost weekly basis until well into the 1980s. It cannot be told again here in detail.[92] At the end of 1983, after countless negotiations, dismissals, strikes, shop-floor disturbances, and two failed restructuring plans, the books eventually recorded a "cash-effective outlay by Robert Bosch for FEMSA in the period 1978 to 1983 of approximately 500 million German marks."[93]

From the beginning of the 1970s, the Bosch board of management's focus, so far as international operations were concerned, turned more and more toward southeast Asia,[94] as well as toward their main target, the United States. This was where the real challenge lay, the greatest challenge of all. In the immediate postwar years, after the confiscation of Bosch operations and properties in the U.S. and the loss of trademark and brand-name rights resulting from the Second World War, Bosch was left empty-handed. In 1952, an initial "name agreement" was concluded between Bosch and American Bosch to govern use of brand names, and in 1953 Robert Bosch Corporation was founded in New York City. This was a sales subsidiary, on the basis of which a network of sales offices was built up over the years. Under the terms of the name agreement, Bosch could trade in the U.S. only as "Robert Bosch" or "Bosch in Germany." However, Bosch management in Stuttgart continued to cultivate close relations to AMBAC, the successor company of American Bosch. In April 1966, for instance, members of Bosch management visited the U.S. to examine "what legal and business opportunities for cooperation exist between us and American Bosch regarding our long-term interests in the United States."[95] When it came to getting a foot in the door of America's major automakers as an original-equipment supplier, those opportunities were virtually non-existent, whether because of in-house production or because of such supplier subsidiaries as Delco-Remy. However, Volkswagen and Daimler-Benz had made successful export inroads into the U.S. early on, and their presence offered Bosch the possibility of providing local maintenance services. But the greatest opportunity was presented by the transition from carburetor to injection technology and the growing U.S. diesel market (with its demand for appropriate injection equipment). This was a gateway that Bosch exploited determinedly from the second half of the 1960s.[96] By the end of the decade, Bosch had developed a "U.S. plan." At the start of the 1970s, it moved this plan forward, it now being the company's top priority so far as its non-German operations were concerned. Achieving it, as the board of management was well aware, would call for a commitment of funds totaling as much as 100 million German marks.[97] An initial step was taken in 1973–74, when a factory was built in Charleston, South Carolina, to produce injection equipment for diesel engines. At this time, the American subsidiary, RBUS, with sales equivalent to 206.5 million German marks, was already earning profits of 3.38 million German marks. A further step was taken in the summer of 1975. On June 11, Merkle received a letter from the Borg-Warner management, offering to reopen cooperation talks that had stalled five years before.[98] Intensive negotiations followed, leading in February 1976 to the idea that the two suppliers should cooperate closely in certain areas. The Americans further suggested that Bosch take a 10 percent stake in Borg-Warner. Borg-Warner had sales equating to 4.45 billion German marks and a widely diversified product portfolio organized in a total of 75 divisions. Only some 38 percent were devoted to automotive equipment, and here the Americans concentrated mainly on non-electronic drivetrain products such as clutches and transmissions. Twenty-three percent of its sales were in the field of industrial equipment, 20 percent in air-conditioning, and 17 percent in various chemicals products. For Bosch this meant potential for cooperation and exchange of experience in the fields of hydraulics and pneumatics. But above all, a stake in the company, which was expected to cost some 100 million German marks, offered the prospect of a stronger presence in the U.S. market.[99]

From an engineering point of view, Borg-Warner was not an ideal partner. The structures of the American original-equipment market were moving into other areas, and especially into gasoline and diesel injection. As a result, the cooperation with Borg-Warner never progressed beyond a financial investment. Bendix would have been a far more interesting joint-venture partner, but here talks stretching over years had seen no solid outcome.[100] So the board of management agreed unanimously that Bosch needed to adopt a more aggressive strategy in the United States. It had to boost both its operational and its financial involvement in the country by building up the original-equipment side of its business, expanding its sales base, and entering new product areas outside the automotive industry.[101] However, at least in the short time proposed, this seemed an impossible target to attain through organic growth alone. It would take further acquisitions and investments. A document drawn up in November 1979 and headed "Current state of U.S. acquisition plans" listed (across the divisions) 21 projects and companies that had received serious consideration. In some instances, steps had already been taken.[102] For the Bosch board of management, there was no time to lose. As Merkle announced at a meeting of the board of management in November 1980, "The allocation of U.S. markets will have been completed by the mid-1980s. The next few years will decide what role Bosch will play in the American market."[103]

One problem in particular had to be finally resolved – and this with all possible speed. This was the re-acquisition of Bosch's trademark rights. Both name and trademark rights remained in the possession of American Bosch Corp. (AMBAC), although certain concessions had been achieved since the "name agreement" of 1952. Since 1960 and 1964 respectively, use of the name "Bosch" for power tools and household appliances had once again been permitted in the U.S. without qualification.[104] However, the agreement with AMBAC expired at the end of November 1972, with the option to prolong it for five years at a time if not terminated a year before expiry. By the autumn of 1971 at the latest, therefore, Bosch had to decide "whether we are prepared to accept the present situation for the period after November 1972, whether we cancel and allow an unregulated situation to arise, or whether we wish to try to negotiate a fresh settlement."[105] Bosch chose the third option, but negotiations dragged on for ten years. In the meantime, AMBAC had been taken over by the U.S. conglomerate United Technologies (UTC), which now became Bosch's opposite number in the negotiations regarding repurchase of the Bosch trademark. However, talks broke down in 1981, since UTC was asking too high a price (55 million dollars). At this, Bosch terminated the agreement within the period allowed. One reason for its doing so was to improve its own position in the face of increasing activity by AMBAC (i. e., UTC) in markets outside the United States. The Americans responded by filing charges in a U.S. court, and proceedings began in the autumn of 1982. Soon afterwards, however, United Technologies showed a new readiness to negotiate, and in February 1983 an out-of-court settlement was reached. UTC waived the right to use the "American Bosch" trademark worldwide with immediate effect and from 1988, at the latest, also the "Bosch" trademark which it had acquired. For its part, and in return for a compensation payment, Bosch was allowed to use its trademark without any restriction in the future.[106] Bosch, in the U.S., was Bosch again. After a 40-year interruption, the company was once again, in the world's largest automotive market, able to call itself by its own name and use the "Bosch" trademark unconditionally. Its operations there, which by now accounted for sales worth the equivalent of 800 million German marks and employed 2,300 associates, could advance from strength to strength. And while buying back the trademark rights came at a price, costing 24.85 million dollars (the equivalent of 70 million German marks), it meant that for Bosch the postwar era was finally over. A major step had been taken toward the objective Merkle had set in the mid-1970s for the following decade: that of restoring Bosch to the position it had occupied in the U.S. at the beginning of the century.

All in all, the internationalization of Bosch had made substantial progress in the 1960s and 1970s. Business outside Germany was becoming more and more important within the Bosch Group. In 1971, its share of total sales had stood at 42.2 percent. By the end of 1982, it accounted for nearly 55 percent of total sales. One visible sign of this was that the 1972 financial year saw the first accounts published for the "Bosch Group Worldwide." France, Italy, and Sweden were the most important markets outside Germany, but the U.S. was already in fourth place. Strictly speaking, with its many production facilities abroad, Bosch had been a "multinational" company since the mid-1960s. Merkle, though, positively loathed the term. By the end of the decade, it had become the subject of a politically loaded debate, also in Germany, given the wide range of activities on the part of giant U.S. industrial groups that were coming in for ever-increasing public criticism. To prevent Bosch from being dragged into this debate and being tarred with the same brush as these U.S. multinationals, the board of management sent out a directive (accompanied by human-resources and social-policy guidelines) to the Bosch Group's regional subsidiaries in November 1981. The directive contained this appeal: "As a global enterprise, we come in for heightened scrutiny from public administrations, political organizations, churches, labor unions, and not least the media."[107] As a result, it said, Bosch was reiterating its existing guidelines. These were that the human-resources and social policies of its regional subsidiaries should echo the principles of the parent company. Terms of employment must therefore comply with the laws and wage agreements of the countries concerned. "Where it is in the interests of the company and its associates, we are not afraid of breaking new corporate and social-policy ground."[108] A further key principle of human-resources and social policy (the directive went on) was equality of opportunity. Every action taken had to conform to strict legality. Long before the terms became common parlance in Germany, Bosch thus committed itself to business ethics and codes of corporate governance. Actually, why this was done so explicitly was in part because there had recently been wage disputes and labor clashes at MICO in India, forcing the company to admit in June 1981 that "implementation of the principles of Bosch human-resources and social policy [had been] less than adequate at MICO and elsewhere."[109]

The "greener automobile": aspects of an environmental history of Bosch

In the Bosch annual report, environmental protection first emerged as a distinct concern in 1970. The publication listed a whole series of environmental-protection measures, ranging from noise reduction in the workplace to a greater focus on materials research.[110] Galvanized by the energy crisis and the oil-price shock, the topic soon came to dominate Bosch corporate policy. There had been signs of the increasing significance of environmental protection since the early 1960s, above all in the legislative sphere. In the United States, for example, the Motor Vehicle Air Pollution Control Act had come into force in 1965. This was to be followed in December 1970 by the Clean Air Act and the establishment of the U.S. Environmental Protection Agency (EPA). In 1971, the international anti-nuclear, peace, and environmental-protection organization Greenpeace was founded in Vancouver, Canada. However, the real beginning of international environmental policy is considered to have been in Stockholm in 1972, with that year's first global UN conference on the subject of the environment.[111] The publication of the Club of Rome report *The Limits to Growth*, also in 1972, finally spread concern among the wider public. The study warned that, if humanity continued to pursue its current lifestyle as well as its current use of resources, in 50 or 100 years' time it would face a dramatic worsening of the conditions under which it lived. *The Limits to Growth* caused worldwide consternation. It kicked off serious scientific debate on the subject of "sustainable development." In Germany, the first sector to respond to the warning was the chemicals industry. But it was not long before the automotive industry, and thus also its supply arm, came in for criticism as potential polluters. The motor vehicle mutated, as it were. As an energy user, "Germany's pet" was now a polluter. How did Bosch react? To what extent did the company not only develop an awareness of the crisis facing the industrialized world but also begin to acquire "green" expertise? Let us be clear about one thing from the start: there is no seamless line connecting this early awareness of the need for greater environmental protection with today's "green strategy" as practiced by Bosch. Merkle's perception of the problems surrounding energy and the environment was typical of the reactions felt in boardrooms across Germany.

Tucked away in a talk entitled "Feedback control in corporate planning" that Merkle gave to the annual conference of the national association of the coal-mining industry in late October 1972 are the beginnings, at least, of a debate about *The Limits to Growth*.[112] Merkle's verdict was ambivalent. On the one hand, he criticized the categorical, black-and-white statements made in the book, which he said "could [therefore] become the bible for the enemies of growth." Yet elsewhere he praised the study for "giving us food for thought." In his view, minimizing or rather optimizing deployment of raw materials and energy on grounds of their scarcity opened up a whole new field for entrepreneurial decision-making "that shows foresight precisely where it seems in the short term to thwart or even damage the company's interests."[113] Such remarks may seem progressive, but when it came to the question of what it would cost the company, Merkle's position was crystal-clear. The "polluter pays principle" now being bandied about was only an illusion, he said. "It is not the producer who pollutes the environment who should [then] bear the costs for undoing such damage." Such costs had to be reflected in the price of the product, he insisted. That was tantamount to externalizing them and shifting them onto the consumer. Moreover, whenever an opportunity presented itself, Merkle condemned the "mounting attacks in the press and in the public sphere on the internal-combustion engine" and the automobile. "This newly aroused energy-awareness," he told a board meeting in November 1973, "is lending fresh impetus to the old propaganda against the motor vehicle."[114] By this time, some economists had made more progress than Merkle in the question of dealing with environmental issues, even if they still fell far short of concepts such as material streams, resource conservation, and industrial metabolism that were to emerge in the 1990s with "industrial ecology."[115]

Actually, from the early 1970s Bosch was as concerned as any other company to present the public with a detailed account of the expenses incurred in connection with measures to protect the environment. A summary published in 1974 tells us that over the previous ten years the Bosch Group had spent in excess of 100 million German marks on such measures. Investment in environmental protection accounted for 3 percent of total capital expenditure. However, most of this amount was not capital expenditure as such, but instead the operating costs of environmental protection, i. e., expenses arising from measures relating to waste disposal, air purification, and noise abatement at manufacturing sites, most of which were statutory.[116] In fact, these meticulously assembled figures never reached the public. "The experiment of including a paragraph in this year's annual report dealing with [the company's] achievements in the field of environmental protection has misfired," reads a note of July 6, 1973: "A poll of the various divisions and corporate departments yielded such paltry facts and figures that publication would not have made sense."[117] Nonetheless, in the meantime a series of articles on "contributions to environmental protection" made at Bosch had appeared in the *Bosch-Zünder*. They showed that environmental protection was in fact practiced – initially through in-house measures.[118] A "new broom" of enhanced procedures not only fostered conservation but at the same time permanently improved conditions at the Bosch workplace. There was mounting recognition right across the German economy that environmental protection was a management responsibility. At Bosch, the start of this process can even be dated precisely. At a management meeting on July 6, 1972, a Bosch engineer gave a detailed presentation entitled "Developmental trends in the field of environmental protection."[119] Following a thorough description of the current situation and an outlook on future trends, he noted that Bosch had a clear need to catch up, particularly when it came to developing more eco-friendly technologies.

This appeal to awareness of environmental problems did not fall on deaf ears. On January 15, 1973, the board of management issued its own environmental-protection directive.[120] Staff were urged to comply with all legal requirements. An officer charged with responsibility for environmental protection was appointed at each manufacturing location. Reference was made to the favorable treatment offered in-house as an incentive for investments in environmental protection. And initial steps were taken toward compulsory recording of waste. Clearly, therefore, environmental protection was seen chiefly as a problem of health and safety and of avoiding pollution at the end of the manufacturing process and the chain of value creation. It was not yet considered something integral to that process and to the products which resulted, as gradually became the case throughout German industry during the course of the 1980s. Accordingly, huge efforts were made in the next few years to bring manufacturing processes into line with modern environmental-protection principles. Regular audiometric inspections were carried out in factories to monitor noise levels. Methods were developed for disposing of copper baths contaminated with cyanide while at the same time recycling the copper. Other improvements concerned recovering lead from the sludge left behind after battery production. Hardening shops introduced salt-free nitriding for steel components. Eco-friendly methods were devised for paint shops. Extensive replacement and modernization measures were undertaken with regard to air-conditioning equipment on the shop floor, coupled with installation of heat-recovery units.[121] Environmental protection now formed a regular item on the agenda at the Bosch Group rationalization conferences held each year. In June 1975, for instance, one such conference looked at workplace noise abatement.[122]

By the end of the 1970s, there had been a radical rethink at Bosch, leading to a much more proactive approach to environmental and energy problems. This became apparent at the meeting of the board of management in mid-November 1979, when members discussed the ideas and proposals regarding new business opportunities that each of the divisions had been invited to present.[123] The meeting examined the potential opportunities for new products, business models, and methods arising from changes in the global economy and society as a whole as a result of the energy crisis and the oil embargo. It came up with a broad but nonetheless fascinating medley. Proposals ranged from increased use of lightweight and hence energy-saving plastics and other high-performance polymers, through R&D projects designed to make engines more energy-efficient, to using electronically controlled ignition systems and new injection technologies to cut fuel consumption. Others included developing sensors and chips as "systems to standardize driving behavior." For instance, the Diesel Systems division said that the energy situation and emissions regulations "are generally good for our line of business." It cited examples such as diesel exhaust-gas treatment to remove particulates, the use of alternative fuels for spark-ignition and diesel engines (which would require a wide variety of specialized technologies and devices), as well as technologies devoted to mixture formation in gas-powered vehicles. At the same time, the corporate engineering department was giving a lot of thought to energy-saving household appliances. Cooking and refrigerating were the biggest energy consumers in the home, and here new insulation materials using polyurethane foam made huge savings possible. However, the greatest scope for energy saving lay in television sets, which with the old cathode-ray tube technology still used 380 watts. By using integrated circuits and new cathode-ray tube technologies, energy consumption could be cut to just 75 to 90 watts, and in this innovation process Blaupunkt was seen to be playing a leading role.[124]

Research departments at Bosch had in fact been busy with alternative ways of generating power since the late 1950s – notably down the electrochemical route.[125] The dream of vehicles with no gear shifts and no exhaust, electrically driven with the aid of fuel cells, was nothing new. However, it had been revived in the 1960s by intensive research and development efforts in the United States.[126] Virtually every major industrial concern in the U.S., from Union Carbide through General Electric and Esso to the giants of the automotive industry (GM especially), was working on the fuel cell, as a Bosch engineer reported back to Stuttgart in October 1961 after a four-week visit to the United States.[127] In the spring of 1967, Bosch engineers stepped up their own development work on an experimental electric vehicle. The engine and transmission were removed from a small mass-produced gasoline-powered automobile and replaced by an electrical powertrain made by Bosch. The engineers looked into providing continuous, low-loss electronic control of drive-motor power by means of a "power pedal." They also studied and developed the recuperation of braking energy, and tried replacing ordinary lead batteries with the promising new zinc-air batteries. By this point, a fully-fledged if somewhat loose development consortium embracing Daimler-Benz, the Bölkow engineering company, the Varta battery group, Bayer, MAN, VW, BMW, and KHD (even the utility company RWE had shown great interest in joining in), had come together under the overall leadership of Bosch.[128] At the same time, Bosch launched a further development project for an electric bus using a hybrid drive. Originating in the U.S., a veritable mania for building electric vehicles spilled over into Europe. "Ford builds electric automobile," "Industry sees big future for little electric cars," "Will the automobile of the future be electric?" – under these and similar headlines the trade journals as well as the daily press published article after article about a seemingly imminent revolution in automotive powertrain technology. Above all, the question these articles increasingly asked was whether Germany's automakers and automotive suppliers were not lagging behind, with a lot of technological ground to make up for.[129]

Before long, however, Bosch engineers were returning from their U.S. trips with less fervent reports and more equivocal accounts of what was happening across the Atlantic. In May 1968, a stir was created when news broke that the development of electric automobiles in America had been put on ice for the time being, since the batteries developed so far were not up to the job.[130] Bosch, though, stayed on the lookout for possible joint-venture partners in the U.S., in connection with fuel cells as well as with hybrid drive technology. And in Germany, simply because of the risk of Daimler-Benz collaborating in the future with such rivals as Siemens or AEG, Bosch felt obliged to go on exploring electrical powertrain technology, even increasing the resources devoted to this objective.[131] In the meantime, the company had assembled considerable expertise and developed a fully functional electronic impulse control system that made low-loss conversion (of power into motion) and continuous speed regulation possible. In 1974, this system was also installed in two electric buses in Mönchengladbach. However, insuperable technical difficulties emerged and technological blind alleys were encountered. The batteries were too heavy and their range much too small, and as far as fuel cells were concerned, the available systems simply did not deliver enough power.[132] The dream of an exhaust-free or at least low-exhaust power source remained unfulfilled. On the bright side, between 1968 and 1973 Bosch had put only some 9 million German marks into fuel-cell and electric-drive research. By the mid-1970s, attitudes to alternative forms of energy had become generally circumspect.

Nonetheless, it was the automobile – and with it Bosch's core field of business – that remained at the center of efforts to develop and introduce more eco-friendly technologies. Over the decades, the trigger and driver of this concern was environmental legislation. Originating in the U.S. in the late 1960s, such legislation spread to Europe and West Germany after a certain delay. Essentially this was about setting ever-lower emissions limits, gradually reducing the lead content of fuel, and altering the combustion process while at the same time cutting fuel consumption. Ever since 1967, Bosch had had a solution for making the exhaust caused by spark-ignition engines cleaner. This was the electronically controlled system of gasoline injection that the company marketed under the brand name D-Jetronic. When the state of California slapped the first mandatory limits on exhaust emissions in the same year,

Volkswagen was able to respond (and remain competitive) by swiftly installing the new control technology in the many cars it was then exporting to the United States. Automotive electronics became the crucial enabler for auto-makers seeking to meet the lower consumption and emissions targets set by legislators. Bosch, with its extensive experience and know-how, was virtually predestined to occupy pole position as a supplier not merely of sensors and injection nozzles but also, and above all, of complex electronic systems for measuring and controlling fuel injection and ignition. Vehicles fitted with the new Bosch Jetronic systems had no difficulty complying with the increasingly stringent emissions regulations brought in across the U.S. after 1970.[133] Even though other original-equipment manufacturers were putting together electronics expertise of their own, at this point in time Bosch was years ahead, with an ultimately unassailable lead. America's fuel-economy legislation prompted a reappraisal in the automotive industry, with the focus now turning to smaller engines and greater use of fuel-injection systems and electronics. As early as 1964, Bosch had begun conducting intensive research into ignition systems. Its engineers employed electronics to control the moment of ignition, and developed a breakerless transistorized ignition system, which underwent further refinement in the years that followed. This system enabled the moment of ignition to be optimized for each and every engine, and to be precisely adhered to throughout the engine's lifetime, which was also decisive for reducing emissions. In 1969, moreover, Bosch had begun work on lambda control for catalytic exhaust-gas treatment. The core of this system was the lambda sensor, which could ascertain how much free oxygen the exhaust gases contained. On the basis of feedback from the sensor, the injection electronics were able to set the air-fuel ratio at the stoichiometric mixture, which ensured optimum exhaust-gas treatment in the catalytic converter. The net result was a significant reduction in exhaust-gas pollutants.[134]

Series production of this system began only during the course of 1976, but for a long time before that there had been huge interest in the new Bosch exhaust-gas treatment process. In the autumn of 1972, for instance, Bosch engineers were invited to give a presentation on the subject to the U.S. Academy of Science. Shortly after that, two of the Big Three automakers, GM and Ford, announced their "medium- and long-term interest in Bosch injection systems on the basis of Bosch's designs and the experience the company has gathered in meeting U.S. emissions regulations and reducing gasoline consumption," as noted with satisfaction at a board of management meeting in late November 1973.[135] "Development Goal: Environmental Protection" was the headline above an interview that the then head engineer of Bosch's Automotive Technology business sector, Richard Zechnall, gave to the business weekly

Wirtschaftswoche in the autumn of 1971.[136] At the end of 1973, the board of management gathered all the various R&D strands relating to automotive environmental protection under a catchy slogan. It was at the above-mentioned meeting of November 19, 1973, that the "3S" program was born, the expression having been coined not by Merkle but by Hans Bacher, the board of management member responsible for the automotive technology business. The minutes of that meeting record that the chief points of emphasis in the company's future operations would be, "first, developing a safe [*sicher*], clean [*sauber*], and economical [*sparsam*] scenario for individual mobility; second, developing the electric vehicle; and third, investigating the scope for cutting energy consumption in the household – heating systems included."[137] The "3S" program was neither a systematically elaborated strategic concept nor was it (to echo broader corporate-policy measures being adopted in other areas) a wider "plan for the environment." It was a catchphrase (and a slogan to be used only in-house, initially) denoting the very broad spectrum of research, development, and manufacturing operations being carried out in the various automotive divisions. The fact was, Bosch now saw itself as a specialist in fuel economy and driving safety, as well as an expert in mixture formation, optimized ignition, and exhaust-gas treatment. When the program was first briefly presented to the public in the 1973 annual report and then at greater length in November 1974, a total of 31 different projects could be pointed to – projects tackling economy [*Sparsamkeit*] and cleanliness [*Sauberkeit*], but above all both active and passive safety [*Sicherheit*] in automotive transportation.[138]

However, it was not until 1975 that the company put its reservations aside and propagated the "3S" slogan to positive public-relations effect as the global development goal of not just one Bosch area of activity but of corporate policy as a whole. Its reluctance to do so had also been due to its desire not to irritate its original-equipment customers. A press release issued in May 1975 proclaimed that every division of the Bosch Group aimed "to turn out products and systems that meet market needs, are eco-friendly, and have a high degree of reliability and utility value."[139] Moreover, Bosch engineers were now in demand as expert witnesses at hearings of the Environmental Protection Agency (EPA). One such instance was when, in January 1975, the U.S. automotive industry asked for a postponement of the emissions limits proposed for 1977 and a full moratorium for 1978. Bosch engineers reported on their Jetronic systems and the performance, costs, and milestones of what was known as the "RB exhaust-gas plan."[140] Clean-air legislation in the automotive sphere gave Bosch a massive development boost. The company benefited enormously from regulations to cut emissions limits and fuel consumption. At a presentation to the Chrysler board in Detroit on January 7, 1981, Hans Bacher proclaimed: "Our basic development strategy was already drawn up in the early seventies under the headings 'clean, safe, economical.' Today there is no question that fuel economy is predominant."[141] However, there were also repercussions, leading to fresh challenges, notably the complicated EPA provisions – such as, for instance, voluntary declaration of a spare part which influences emissions as equal in value to an original spare part. According to the provisions of the Clean Air Act, such an emissions-relevant part would then require its manufacturer to accept a guarantee of a full five years.[142] And ultimately Bosch engineers found themselves up against a growing technical dilemma. As Bacher explained in a talk at the Feuerbach plant in the autumn of 1981: "Cutting fuel consumption and at the same time lowering emissions are incompatible aims. Physics tells us that cutting emissions beyond certain limits involves using more fuel."[143]

So by the early 1980s, Bosch could already look back on considerable technical achievements in the "battle for the greener automobile."[144] In a matter of years, the engineering and manufacturing units involved had built up a strong basis of sophisticated environmental expertise. However, Bosch's involvement in this sphere had little to do with idealism. To a far greater extent, it had to do with the inevitable way things were going, and how Bosch should position itself within these potential future business fields. Its various business activities relating to the environment were soberly assessed and costed, and wherever a particular technical or commercial blind alley loomed, the corresponding projects were promptly wound up. Much of this expertise and accumulated knowledge of the many ins and outs around energy, the environment, society, and engineering was lost or forgotten in ensuing years as oil prices fell and the automotive industry enjoyed a fresh sales boom. Nonetheless, it was to a great extent Bosch that promptly explored technical solutions to the problems raised by environmental legislation in the U.S. and Germany and, as a supplier, with its innovations of the 1960s and 1970s, that virtually drove forward progress in the "ecological revolution in automotive technology." Bosch did not wait until its original-equipment customers came up with requests. As Bacher proclaimed in a speech in Feuerbach on October 28, 1981: "There are currently 370 million automobiles in operation on the world's roads. Seventeen percent of them are fitted with Bosch products. Not a bad starting position! The products we have developed over the last 15 years – and that in timely fashion! – have earned respect the world over […]. As I see it, the greatest risk is that, with major changes having taken place in product development in automotive equipment over the last few years and others just beginning in manufacturing, we shall adapt too slowly or fall short entirely."[145] In environmental protection, too, there were fresh challenges ahead. A report issued at the end of November 1983 on the current business situation warned: "Our automotive divisions are preparing for stricter emissions regulations in Europe and the introduction of unleaded gasoline on January 1, 1986, and are thus intensifying their research and development. [...] However, the consequences of the imminent legislation as regards increasing our capacity cannot begin to be assessed. No automaker has so far put any viable plans in place."[146] Due to misunderstandings and the trading of accusations between the federal government and the German automotive industry, the "emissions debate" had in the meantime become politically charged, and this in increasing measure. In the years to follow, this debate was set to reach its peak.

4 Between Americanization and Japanization: manufacturing organization and work environment

Manufacturing organization in times of postwar reconstruction, capacity bottlenecks, and labor shortages

When it came to role models for manufacturing organization, the first country West Germany turned to was the United States. In the years following the currency reform, German businesspeople made the pilgrimage across the Atlantic in their hordes. Having spent many years in isolation, they now went on painstaking inspection tours of U.S. companies, seeking to catch up with the latest developments in industrial engineering. Aware that a serious gap had opened up technologically, they were determined to close it.[1] In the spring of 1949, one of the people Bosch sent to the U.S. was its chief engineer, Albert Kilgus. He took a long list of detailed technical questions with him, such as: "Do they have household appliances using ultrasound technology?" Between April and June, Kilgus visited a whole series of major companies including General Motors, Philco, Auto Lite, Bendix, General Electric, Westinghouse, and McDougal. The reports he subsequently sent back to Stuttgart, addressed to the then head of manufacturing, Hermann Bauer, dealt initially with questions of refrigerator manufacturing and cooling technology. Later reports contained information about the manufacturing of alternators and starters. But Bosch engineers were also interested in finding out how American machine-tool technology had progressed.[2] The next major wave of U.S. trips by Bosch engineers followed in the spring and summer of 1951. This time the visitors were in no doubt about the conclusions to be drawn from what they had seen. "If we are serious about making up at least some of the ground we have lost to the Americans, this is what we must do: greatly standardize our designs, adapt our designs to rational production processes, transfer more of our manufacturing to dedicated assembly lines while equipping those lines with the latest special-purpose machinery, and cut work in progress and inventories."[3] All these matters were to shape the rationalization processes introduced at Bosch in the years that followed.

The many visits made by Bosch engineers to the U.S., which continued for some years to come, show how much time and effort went into gathering know-how. This know-how then had to be put into practice and adapted to Bosch's own manufacturing structures. However, the learning process resulting from the U.S. trips had to do not only with manufacturing engineering and organization in a narrower sense, but also with other, more far-reaching concerns. For example, in December 1955 Bosch managers returned from a study trip to America with the latest findings from the new and flourishing field of "operations research."[4] At the Chesapeake and Ohio Railroad Company, they studied the processes employed there for cost recording and cost accounting. And at IBM and Remington Rand, they had their first look at how staff used electronic calculators. Not until 1960 did these industrial-engineering study trips to the U.S. by Bosch engineers (trips motivated by "technology gaps" and the need for "know-how influx") largely come to an end. In their place, the company now made intensive efforts of its own to take manufacturing organization and rationalization further, concentrating on developing a specifically "Bosch method" of organizing manufacturing operations.

In the Bosch plants, there were still deficits in manufacturing organization as well as a great need for rationalization. Starting in 1952, plant managers and engineers responsible for operations scheduling in all affiliated companies met regularly to exchange information in the field of manufacturing. From April 1956 onward, these occasions became the large in-house "Bosch rationalization conferences" held half-yearly.[5] In the early 1950s, Bosch as a whole was feeling the negative effects of a manufacturing program that was highly fragmented, and tending to become even more so. The huge influx of orders caused by the boom in the automotive industry accompanying the postwar "economic miracle" (in alternators and starters, to take two examples) hit plants that "have always, up to now, operated at full stretch."[6] The corporate department in charge of business administration [*Leitung für Wirtschaftlichkeit und Organisation* or WOL] thus began conducting thorough annual operational analyses containing detailed "economic-efficiency indicators."[7] By the late 1950s, it was clear that the system of technical planning figures and product plans introduced immediately after the war had proved its worth. Above all, a comparison of the 1950 figures with those for 1958–59 showed the impressive progress that Bosch had made in the meantime. Delivery volumes had more than doubled, rising from 35.7 million to 78.1 million units. Net production value had nearly quadrupled, from 138 million to 535 million German marks. And labor productivity (measured as net production value per hour worked) had shot up by 169 per cent from 5.48 German marks in 1950 to 9.25 German marks in 1959. Productivity, in other words, had increased nearly twofold. What in 1950 had taken Bosch workers 100 hours to do, they could now, nine years later, do in 56 hours. Wages accounted for 18.8 percent of the total manufacturing cost of all Bosch products, while sales had positively rocketed from 215 million to 933 million German marks. In 1950, in other words, each person employed had generated sales of 13,957 German marks, whereas by 1958 that figure had risen to 36,198 German marks.[8] In 1960, Bosch manufacturing experts were thus able to report: "In industrial engineering, the huge lead that the Americans possessed ten years ago is dwindling. We have not only caught up with such giant companies as Ford; in some instances we have overtaken them. Delco-Remy is still ahead of us in industrial engineering as a whole, but these days it is less in ideas than in use of resources [...]. In all companies visited, associates were working not faster, but in fact more slowly than our own. Workstation design, too, was with certain exceptions no better than at Bosch. As a result of consistent work in this sphere, we have a chance of outpacing the Americans within a couple of years. The only advantage that our American competitors still have over us is that for specialist tasks they can draw on largely specialized companies. We, too, should try to exploit such opportunities more and more. For our own 'Bosch method' – which combines workstation design and mechanization with maximum economic efficiency – we could then have our own experts at our disposal."[9]

So far as recruiting properly qualified associates was concerned, it was first and foremost a matter of rethinking the company's program of social benefits. As Walz put it in July 1958, Bosch had once been able to "draw good people from all over Germany" by paying good money and offering favorable working conditions (the eight-hour working day, free Saturday afternoons), as well as by "guaranteeing other pioneering social benefits." But this advantage had largely disappeared by now.[10] In the board of management's view, all that remained in terms of "exerting power of attraction" was "gradually, year by year, enhancing our bonus scheme." The plan was to distribute this bonus half-yearly in future in the hope of slowing the high rate of turnover (some 21 percent among wage earners alone) in the workforce. Accordingly, in March 1959 Otto Fischer (the board of management member then carrying the human-resources portfolio) presented more than 30 pages of "proposals to secure an industrious workforce," all taking a similar line.[11] Bosch should once again (Fischer suggested) attract potential employees with new optional social benefits ranging from supplementary health insurance to housebuilding loans.[12] Fischer's proposals were subsequently adopted. Total payments under the bonus scheme rose from 4.1 million German marks in 1955 to 21.1 million in 1960 – constituting an average of 434 German marks per associate and marking a deliberate shift in the voluntary social benefits that Bosch provided.

Assembly-line work: wiper production (1951)

The second key component of the Bosch-specific "manufacturing model" (on top of this modernization of Bosch's social-benefits program) was a fundamental change in workstation design and manufacturing processes. Bosch had been experimenting since 1956 with the "work factor system," a method of rationalization that focused on motion studies and labor optimization using simple means. The individual work steps were meticulously analyzed to "eradicate unnecessary movements."[13] All this was in the tradition of earlier rationalization processes introduced at Bosch. However, the end of the 1950s signaled the beginning of an entirely new developmental phase in manufacturing organization and industrial engineering at Bosch, which was to extend over the following decades. The company enlisted the services of the U.S. management consultancy Bruce Payne, and implemented the (likewise U.S.) "methods-time measurement" (MTM) process.[14] The main feature of this process was to establish a standard data system whereby any manual task could be broken down into the work stages and basic movements that its performance required. Each of those work stages was then allotted a time measurement unit, determined in advance.[15] The advantage over ordinary time studies was that tasks could be analyzed before they were actually performed on the shop floor. Using MTM as a time-management and workstation-design system thus made it possible to rationalize manufacturing processes substantially. "Working times established by MTM," the consulting engineers promised, "are entirely fair for both workers and the company. Workers are allotted a time that in normal circumstances they can achieve day in, day out. The company can rest easy in the knowledge that the wage paid will result in the requisite piece number, i. e., that its labor costs will come out right."[16] The method had its limitations, though. Process-dependent machine times and tasks involving an extended cycle could not be assessed by MTM.

Bosch and Vorwerk & Co. were the first companies in Germany to use MTM successfully. They were its demonstrators, in effect.[17] As early as in the spring of 1957, an essay in the *Harvard Business Review* entitled "Steps in Long-Range Planning" had caught the attention of Bosch engineers. Its author was the managing director of Bruce Payne, and two years later, in 1959 (three years prior to the foundation of the German MTM association in October 1962), the Bosch board of management asked the Bruce Payne engineers to conduct a similar investigation of manufacturing organization at Bosch. The briefing document defined ambitious aims for the project: "How can Bosch assure itself of being the most effective manufacturer in its line of products in the Common Market?" read one. Another was "How can Bosch double its production in the next 5 years without more operators?"[18] A total of four consulting engineers traveled to Stuttgart, and in an initial assessment of the situation they concluded that Bosch lacked up-to-date industrial engineering.[19] The U.S. advisers officially commenced work at Bosch at the beginning of March 1960. By as early as the end of June, visible and measurable interim improvements could be announced, not only in prime costs, direct labor costs, and workforce numbers, but also in identifying and tracing weak points of the manufacturing process itself.[20] Manual work still accounted for some 30 percent of total manufacturing time at Bosch – even 90 percent in certain product areas. MTM thus offered considerable potential for rationalization, and the ambitious goal of doubling productivity within five years proved to be entirely realistic. The board hoped that MTM and the principles of industrial engineering would be introduced at all Bosch plants and subsidiaries by the end of 1962.

However, it was not just workstation design that the engineers from Bruce Payne examined closely; they also took a hard look at Bosch's entire accounting system from cost control to the costing system.[21] And it was with genuine vehemence that Payne exhorted the board in July 1961 to undertake an urgently necessary "modernization of our cost accounting and investment analysis." Here, such terms as "direct costing," "marginal income,"

New workplace design following adoption of MTM methods (1964)

"cash flow," and "return on investment" played a key role. These terms were already familiar to management at Bosch, but the company was still a long way from applying them in regular business practice.[22] However, the work-force initially had mixed feelings about the introduction of MTM and the associated reforms in operations scheduling and manufacturing organiza-tion. In German, so it was rumored, MTM stood for *mehr tun müssen* ["more work"]. Yet the initial skepticism soon gave way to a less prejudiced verdict, and in April 1961 those in charge of production were able to announce that at the light works [*Lichtwerk*] in Feuerbach, training of technical personnel in using MTM was virtually complete. Plant management and shift supervisors attended various introductory courses. Later on, machine-setters received instruction in the meaning and purpose of MTM methods. As a result, the *Lichtwerk* was the first Bosch plant to complete the main points of MTM training and implementation. One report stated: "The MTM mindset has already become deeply rooted in the operations scheduling department."[23] From now on, it continued, no major project would be approved without first having been subject to an MTM analysis to find its best possible design and economic efficiency.

At the end of June 1962, the board of management took stock of the pro-gress made so far in introducing MTM. It found that certain expectations had been exceeded by a large margin. Economies of 21.6 million German marks could be expected by the end of the year, some as a result of the roughly 700 jobs that had been shed in the course of the changes. To some extent these were offset by introductory costs of 4 million German marks and other items of expenditure totaling 11.6 million, but the bottom line was that the net savings were substantial. However, the key effect of bringing in MTM lay not in any temporary reduction of expenditure but in the lasting innovative stimulus given to industrial engineering and rationalization at Bosch. MTM was not a short-term cost-cutting measure, but instead a permanent process of production reorganization. As more and more new workstations were designed from the outset along MTM lines, the less immediately apparent its benefits became.[24] Talks between the board of management and the central works council on the subject of the introduction of MTM opened in March 1962, with a works agreement being reached shortly afterward. The talks concerned the right to inspect MTM analyses, but repercussions on the pay system were a bigger issue, partly as a result of changes in wage grades. A second, supplementary works agreement relating to MTM was to follow in February 1964. Among other things, this provided for an "MTM bonus" of 1.5 percent of salary to be paid out as a share of the company's productivity gains. Two additional issues were how to render the process of setting piece rates more transparent for works council and associates and how to ease the transition from the old system to the more rigid MTM procedure.[25]

Efforts by engineers to develop the Bosch-specific production system further continued undiminished in ensuing years, not least because the labor-market situation remained critical. At the same time, the workforce was becoming increasingly diverse. It was in 1959 that the first Italian migrant workers arrived at Bosch – 102 of them, mostly from Sicily.[26] In December 1955, the West German federal government had signed an initial recruitment agreement with Italy, the main aim of which was to procure seasonal labor for agriculture. In 1959, however, there were for the first time more job vacancies in West Germany than people unemployed. This was the signal for industry to start employing more and more jobseekers from Italy.[27] Further recruitment agreements followed with Spain and Greece in 1960, with Turkey in 1961, and with Morocco, Portugal, Tunisia, and Yugoslavia in subsequent years. Contracts of employment for workers from abroad were originally limited to one year, which is why such persons were usually termed *Gastarbeiter* or "guest workers." At the insistence of employers, those contracts were first extended and then eventually awarded without time limit. And in increasing numbers, family members followed in the footsteps of the workers. By 1973, migrant-worker numbers had risen to some 2.5 million. Then, in reaction to the first oil-price crisis and the ensuing recession, the West German government called a halt to recruitment. A total of some 14 million immigrant workers had entered West Germany by 1973, with some

Signing the industrial agreement concerning MTM. From left: board members Eugen
Hagmeier and Karl Schreiber with central works council members Friedrich Frank
and Hans Moestel (February 5, 1964)

2.5 million remaining permanently.[28] At the end of 1960, Bosch was already
employing 2,462 workers from the recruitment countries around the Medi-
terranean. Ten years later, the number had risen to nearly 19,000, accounting
for 26 percent of all blue-collar workers and some 17 percent of all employees.[29] The number of migrant workers at Bosch reached an initial peak at the
beginning of May 1970, when it stood at 20,536. In the next two years, it was
markedly lower before climbing back to exceed 20,000 during the course of
1973. The absolute high-point came at the beginning of December 1973, with
21,301 migrant workers or 35 percent of the company's blue-collar workforce.
The recruitment ban imposed by the government made itself felt at that
point, and within two years (i. e., by early December 1975) the number of
"guest workers" at Bosch was down to 14,428 – although they still constituted
an even higher percentage of the total Bosch workforce than had been the
case in 1970.[30]

Because of its migrant workers, for a time Bosch found itself facing demands for which no preparation had been made. For instance, no one had really considered that the Italian workers recruited might have no knowledge of
German. Not even the work rules had been translated. With regard to their
accommodation, the Italian workers had different ideas from their employer.
Bosch wanted to house them in private dwellings, but the first "guest workers"
preferred communal accommodation, where they could be together with their
countrymen.[31]

The Greek associate Konstantina Margaritou at a coil winder in the Feuerbach plant (1972)

Italian interpreter (1961)

In a second wave in the early 1960s, it was mainly Greeks who came to Bosch. The number of Italian workers soon declined as the employment situation in their own country improved. In 1967, Greeks formed by far the largest contingent (some 50 percent) of migrant workers at Bosch, and while their share of the total Bosch workforce declined over the next ten years, they still remained the largest non-German ethnic group.[32] The Greek migrant workforce was quite different in structure from the first wave of "guest workers," who had mainly come from Italy on their own. From Greece, entire families and even whole sections of village communities moved to West Germany in a process of "chain migration." Here, the female contingent was far larger than in labor migrations from other countries. It included many unmarried women who could find no paid work at home, where they were expected to do unpaid work on family farms.[33] At Bosch, the overall percentage of women among migrant workers now increased – reaching some 53 percent in 1970.[34] Over the ensuing decade, the numbers of Greek, Italian, and Spanish workers declined, while those of Turkish and (to a lesser extent) Yugoslav workers continued to rise. In the early 1970s, something like 12 percent of "guest workers" had five or more years' service at Bosch behind them, which in the view of the human-resources department indicated "that despite the steep rate of turnover, particularly among migrant workers, a 'core' of approximately 12 percent of the immigrant workforce is forming."[35] Within the Bosch Group, the Feuerbach plant of Robert Bosch GmbH and the Blaupunkt plants had the highest percentages of migrant workers. In the autumn of 1974, some 46 percent of the Feuerbach workforce – and as much as 80 percent on the production line – came from recruitment countries. This share was particularly high in the *Lichtwerk*, including the Rutesheim sub-plant. As early as 1970, more than half those employed there were "guest workers."[36] The likely explanation is that in the *Lichtwerk* (more than in other plants) relatively simple operations were also carried out – the sheet-metal work done in the pressroom, for instance.[37] At Rutesheim, regulators and governors were mass-produced in large numbers.

Table 16 Migrant workers in Bosch Group plants in Germany (1960–76)[38]

Date	Italian	Greek	Spanish	Yugo-slav	Turkish	other	total	percentage of total workforce
31 Dec 1960							2,462	5
01 Aug 1967	1,541	3,949	755	221	889	513	7,868	16
01 Aug 1970	3,495	8,338	1,108	1,629	3,615	920	19,105	26
01 Jan 1976	1,807	5,239	578	1,762	4,443	746	14,575	30

According to Gerhard Sautter (who chaired the works council in Feuerbach for many years), employment of immigrant labor at Bosch turned out well, although that was hardly the company's own doing. Management had at first taken the view that giving "guest workers" a job and somewhere to live was all that was needed. Nonetheless, it was amazing "how quickly people settled in and got on with their work."[39] As time went on, language courses were organized – not just for the immigrants but for German associates as well. Sautter, in whose department many Greek women were then working, took Greek lessons himself.[40] Bosch issued information sheets in the languages of the recruiting countries, and associates with a migrant-worker background also sat on the works council. Good Bosch wages and the company's high level of social benefits may well have eased the transition for migrant workers. Language, after all, was not the only change. They also had to get used to technical standards, and adapt to the experience of working in a large industrial company, given that most of them had previously worked in agriculture. To what extent migrant workers saw themselves as true *Boschler* and identified with the culture of the company are not matters that can be gauged in any general way. Given that turnover rates were higher than among German associates, few will have felt a particular loyalty to the company. However, it is likely that the "core" of migrant workers with five or more years' Bosch service identified with the company more. The only culture clash to emerge was when Bosch refused to set aside prayer rooms for Turkish associates on the grounds that other employees did not have access to similar facilities. It was a Bosch business principle that religious observance should not play any role at work.[41]

Employing "guest workers" at Bosch (as throughout the German economy) differed fundamentally from earlier forms of labor relations with non-Germans, notably the forced-labor system imposed in the Second World War. Migrant workers enjoyed equal rights in West Germany. The principle of "equal pay for equal work" applied to them just as it did to everyone else, and employers did not discriminate against them. As the news journal *Der Spiegel* wrote in October 1964, "Migrant workers come not as second-class citizens who are being exploited, but instead as well paid, properly recruited friends."[42] For all that, such "friends" hardly found themselves in a rose garden. Their jobs generally required a low level of qualification and earned them a correspondingly low wage. Often they were required to do work which their German counterparts were no longer willing to do. In addition to this "ethnic underclassing," they found it difficult to integrate. Although for the most part they adapted to the demands of their new workplace and environment, they were never fully accepted. They lived in hostels where conditions were substandard, and they kept to themselves. In this respect, Bosch was no different from anyplace else. There was "a good atmosphere" between Germans and migrant workers, but that was all.[43] For management and works council alike it was a major challenge to bring workers from a range of countries together with their German colleagues to form a workforce characterized by stability and by loyalty to the company. Indeed, the early years were characterized by obstacles. When works managers were asked at their May 1960 meeting about their experiences with Italian workers on the shop floor, a mixed picture emerged. "The Italians do very good piecework, which we welcome," some said. "Their quality is no worse than that of our German associates, i. e., 50 percent good, 25 percent average, and 25 percent below average."[44] There were occasions when relations between German and migrant workers broke down. On one occasion in 1971, groups of German and Turkish workers at the Göttingen plant clashed, to the point of exchanging blows. A Turkish worker accused the shift supervisors there of behaving like "medieval slave-drivers," directing his accusation not only to the union, but also to the senior shift supervisor, apparently assuming that management would not condone such behavior.[45] In fact, Bosch management took a public stand in support of migrant workers. On March 11, 1965, the mass-circulation newspaper *Bild* carried the banner headline

"Company chiefs unhappy with foreign workers: 'No more Italians!'." Karl Schreiber of the Bosch board of management wrote a strong letter of complaint to the publisher Axel Springer that same day.[46] Next morning, Bosch issued a press release condemning all publications "whose blanket judgments also disparage our migrant workers."[47] However, when in 1973 the number of migrant workers at Bosch topped 20,000, Hans L. Merkle voiced serious misgivings. At the board of management meeting of September 24, 1973, he described the mounting numbers of "guest workers" as "resulting from the extreme strain on our resources that is becoming evident in many areas." He saw this as foreshadowing "the threat of growing political instability in our country."[48]

The "guest workers" were an important factor for Bosch, particularly the women workers from Greece, Yugoslavia, and Turkey. As a 1970 analysis by the human-resources department puts it, they operated at "workplaces with low labor-value rankings." Such jobs were deemed women's work, and for such jobs "the German labor market [offered] almost exclusively migrant women workers."[49] Against this background it becomes clear why Bosch employed particularly large numbers of Greek migrant workers. The many women among them made it possible to fill jobs in the low-wage range, jobs for which no German women would have applied and that would otherwise have to have been filled by men – whose pay would have been around 30 percent higher, even where "guest workers" were concerned.[50] Among the Greeks employed at Bosch in 1970, women accounted for 55 percent. Among Yugoslavs and Turks the proportion was even higher (71 percent and 59 percent respectively), but the absolute numbers were not as high as among Greeks.[51] The wage-cost advantages that Bosch enjoyed by employing the mainly young women who came from the recruitment countries meant that the company (in the view of its human-resources department) could accept the "disruption" caused by the "high fertility rate" among these women workers.[52] A further advantage flowed from the fact that, like the German economy as a whole, Bosch was able to use the employment of migrant labor as a cushion against cyclical fluctuations. In boom times it could be increased. During recessions (such as those of 1967 and 1973–74) it could be allowed to shrink. The pool of migrant labor particularly benefited locations where above-average numbers of "guest workers" were employed. Without such workers, manufacturing operations at such locations could never have been so productive, and a lot of production would have had to have been relocated. So far as Bosch was concerned, this was especially true of Feuerbach. In Sautter's estimation, without migrant labor the Feuerbach plant "could not have developed [as it did]."[53]

The Bosch central works council in 1961, the year of the 75th anniversary.
Standing (from left): Friedrich Schweikhardt, Otto Harrer, Wilhelm Frey, Willy
Boetzer, Franz Ehrlich, Hans Moestel, Fritz Grieshaber, Friedrich-Karl Ehlers, Albert
Riehle, Oswald Todtenberg, Ernst Bode, Richard Rau.
Seated (from left): Eugen Blankenhorn, Christian Stauch, Karl Woerner, Friedrich
Frank, Hans Vetter, Peter Leikauf, Hugo Stadelmann.

As the "economic-miracle years" continued, employers and employees increasingly found themselves in dispute over how the wealth generated should be distributed. The first strikes hit German industry in the early 1960s. The biggest was the wage dispute in Baden-Württemberg in the spring of 1963, which lasted for two weeks, with some 350,000 metalworkers taking part. Following the intervention of Ludwig Erhard, then minister of economic affairs in the West German federal government, it eventually ended with wage increases totaling 5 percent. What made the industrial action so significant was that it was the sharpest postwar clash between the two sides. For the first time since the Weimar Republic, employers reacted with general lockouts wherever the workers downed tools. The Bosch plants also found themselves in the thick of this dispute. On April 18, 1963, following the breakdown of wage talks, 85 percent of the unionized associates at Feuerbach voted for industrial action. The Feuerbach plant was actually one of the centers of the strategic strike action organized by the metalworkers' union IG Metall. In addition to the 14,000 Feuerbach associates, the lockout drew another 8,000 Bosch associates into the struggle. Despite these developments, the dispute remained peaceful and controlled. A report drawn up by the "industrial-action committee" specially formed by the corporate department for human resources and social services (*Zentrale Personal- und Sozialhauptleitung*) concluded that "no Communist activity of any substance was observed."[54] And when the industrial action was over, Bosch made up for the loss of earnings resulting from the lockout by offering both what it termed "plant staff" [*Werksangestellte*] and blue-collar workers, unionized and non-unionized alike, a one-off special payment or, on request, an advance against wages to tide the recipient over.

Unspectacular though the outcome of the industrial dispute was at Bosch, in the latter half of the 1960s there were unmistakable signs that the end of the "economic-miracle years" was imminent. This in turn ramped up the tension in industrial relations at Bosch. In February 1966, for instance, wage negotiations in the metalworking industry once again broke down when, the unions having demanded 9 percent, the employers came back with an offer of 5.5 percent. There was a ballot, and the Bosch human-resources department, expecting demonstrations, set up another industrial-action committee as a precaution. In addition, an unusual decision was taken. A letter from plant and departmental heads was sent to the private addresses of all Bosch blue-collar workers.[55] In any event, at the last minute (and only by a whisker) strike action was averted when the two sides reached agreement. Wages for 1966 were raised by 6 percent and for 1967 by a further 5 percent. In return, the union accepted a postponement of the final phase of the program to reduce working hours. As far as the board of management was concerned, however, the net result was a substantially higher wage bill. As was pointed out to associates, the pay increases far exceeded the savings made through rationalization, posing a growing threat to the company's competitiveness. And where jobs had been temporarily shed at Bosch in 1957 and 1962, in 1966 and 1967 there now followed wholesale dismissals and workforce reductions, which were to be typical of the crisis decade of the 1970s.

A fresh phase of rationalization was ushered in at Bosch during the second half of the 1960s. The key phrase here was "value engineering." Where previously only manufacturing had been considered, this new method also included development and sales. All rationalization ideas were already taken into account during the initial phase of a product's development – in other words, before the first design draft.[56] The idea of value engineering was also one that Bosch engineers had brought back from their U.S. trips in the fall of 1963, when it was not only new manufacturing technology that was being looked at but also the latest developments in manufacturing management.[57]

Fig. 6 Development of the Bosch Group workforce (1950–83)

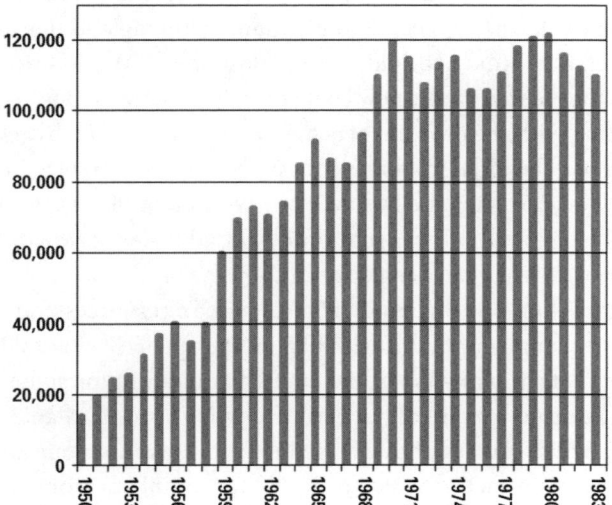

Value engineering had been developed at General Electric in 1947 to cut purchasing costs and had afterward spread quickly right across U.S. industry. One of the core principles of the new rationalization philosophy was: "It is not the cost of purchased materials that is the problem, but achieving the lowest costs for the functions that the customer wishes to see in a product."[58] Traditionally, cost reductions were component-oriented, with a focus on lower raw-materials costs and cheaper methods of manufacture. Value engineering, on the other hand, focused on function. Costs were seen in relation to the function of the particular product. It called for a change from a price-driven mindset to one driven by function and cost. So far as implementation in the Bosch production system was concerned, it was not simply the great opportunities that became clear, but also the problems that were going to arise. In an unparalleled tour de force, the new method was put in place at Bosch in the ensuing years.

Structural adjustment policies, rationalization strategies, and labor conflicts in the 1970s

A new strategy now emerged, whose bywords were decreased vertical integration and streamlined product portfolios as a result of fewer models and variants. The strategy saw itself as one of rationalization and made no bones about its intention. Its two pillars demanded a rethink on the part of management and workforce once again. Addressing the rationalization conference in early June 1970, Hans Bacher appealed to his manufacturing and development engineers for such a rethink: "The old, cozy philosophy of 'We do things best on our own' needs to give way to this new concept."[59] The fact was, Bosch engineers had been wrestling with the problem of achieving rationalization by reducing model numbers since the first in-house rationalization conference in April 1956.[60] However, it was not until the business policy briefing of 1973 that this task was properly taken in hand, when Bacher and Konrad Eckert gave a detailed presentation of the work that had been done in this regard.

Having a lot of models tied up a lot of human resources and capital. "Anyone walking through our plants with half an eye open," Bacher told the meeting, "will notice that, in many areas, products that account for some 30 percent of our sales take up 70 percent of the manufacturing space available. Much of that space is filled with a mass of underused machines turning out 'dead models' – which are never in fact allowed to die."[61] The numbers from the automotive technology business sector alone spoke for themselves. The range of Bosch components comprised more than 150,000 individual items. Six hundred and fifty starter models had been released for production. And for Daimler-Benz alone, the company manufactured 133 combinations of injection pumps and regulators.[62] The reality of life in the automotive divisions' development departments is shown by the following example. Each year, 1,200 customer requests for changes were received for in-line pumps for diesel engines alone. In other words, some five such requests needed to be dealt with every day, each request involving a modification to an existing in-line pump. Ultimately, this profusion of models was the result of market demands: the market created product differentiation, and this had repercussions for suppliers. In addition, technological progress increased the speed at which products changed. The result was more and more phases in which old and new products overlapped, thus increasing the number of models still further. Finally, a policy of rationalization in small steps only made things worse.[63] Bacher's conclusion was that rationalization at Bosch had to take a great leap forward and reduce this profusion of models "before the market forces us to." The solutions were selection (including the pooling of manufacturing of a particular product outside Germany), modular concepts, and procurement from outside the company. All these solutions were things Bosch systematically took on board in the ensuing years. "In the beginning was and is the market. The market dictates what we do," is how Bacher summed up matters at the 24th rationalization conference in late October 1976. "We need to improve our aim. Missing the mark is not something we can afford to do too often – either in terms of time or money."[64]

However, important rationalization effects resulted to an ever-increasing extent also from greater use of electronic data processing. Even in the early 1960s, Bosch engineers had noticed on their U.S. trips how electronic data processing and numerically controlled machine tools were being deployed in industrial engineering, offering "American companies any number of opportunities for rationalization."[65] From the mid-1970s, European industry, too, used NC and CNC machine tools on a large scale.[66] Soon pilot projects for computer-aided job preparation in tool design and computer-aided generation of "flow charts," parts management, and optimization of materials supply and materials flow were also being launched at Bosch. Order and delivery planning were also being organized with the help of computers, and everywhere at Bosch computerization was transforming process engineering generally. Between 1971 and 1981, annual data-processing costs rose from just under 50 million German marks to 140 million. As a result, Bosch itself was transformed. What had once been a merely "knowledge-based enterprise" became in addition an "IT-based industry." This had huge consequences so far as organizational structures and in-house process flow were concerned, both administratively and in terms of manufacturing. It often also met with some initially considerable resistance from the shift supervisors, who traditionally formed the backbone of the manufacturing process.[67] Quite obviously, the manufacturing organization and the production system were again facing a major upheaval. The trend was toward greater flexibility, unmanned production, and new industrial structures.[68]

Meanwhile, relations between employers' associations and the unions had become increasingly strained and conflict-laden. As early as the autumn of 1970, in the run-up to the collective bargaining round, wildcat strikes broke out across the metalworking industry. At the end of September, they reached Bosch, too, and in the months that followed they flared up there repeatedly.[69] In the autumn of 1971, the conflict finally crystallized into an official strike movement, with the employers once again threatening lockouts.[70] And two years later, a fresh wave of wildcat strikes convulsed the metalworking industry of North Rhine-Westphalia. The purpose of these was to underline the demands of unions and works councils not just for wage rises but also for a more humane working environment. That autumn the labor struggle engulfed Bosch as well. For nearly two weeks (from October 16 to October 24, 1973) the associates at the Feuerbach plant came out on strike. Here, too, higher wages were only ostensibly the reason for the dispute. It was far more (at least, this was how members of the works council and union representatives saw it) about combating the ever-increasing division of labor, pressure to deliver results, and noise and heat at the workplace, coupled with constantly tighter standard times and task times – all leading to "intolerable circumstances in the realm of piecework."[71] As some of those involved recalled later, it was "a revolt against the assembly line, a call for more humane working conditions, and for less worry and vulnerability."[72] For his part, Merkle's main concerns were customer relations and security of supply. "Bosch on its own must not be allowed to bring the automotive industry to a halt," he warned when the pay dispute was discussed by the board of management.[73] Consequently, an amicable settlement with the works council was reached relatively quickly. Under the terms of the new wage agreement *Lohnrahmen II* [or "wage framework II"], tasks were to be made more varied, allowing assembly-line workers to move up into higher wage grades. Furthermore, minimum recreational periods and restroom times were agreed in connection with piecework, repetitive work, and assembly-line work.

The year 1973 also saw the first serious thinking about additional manufacturing capacity and sites outside Germany. At the time, Portugal and Spain in particular appeared to be very promising low-wage countries. However, the first principle of location strategy was that no existing assembly lines or other production facilities should be relocated outside the country.[74] So for the time being, Bosch concentrated on modernizing its existing plants and manufacturing sites.[75] But workforce numbers were going down. Between 1974 and 1975 alone, they dropped from 115,171 to 105,553 – i. e., by 8.3 percent. The reductions were indeed drastic. Overtime was halved between 1973 and 1976, while for roughly 20,000 Bosch associates, short-time work soared from 4,575 to 265,550 man-days over the same period.[76] The drop in workforce numbers went almost unnoticed outside the company, but inside the company the lines of conflict between members of the works council and members of the board of management grew more and more pronounced. Particularly in September 1977, in the run-up to the annual collective-bargaining round, talks took place between Merkle and the chairman of the central works council at Bosch, Richard Rau. The big questions were the raising of the MTM bonus and the redrafting of pay scales (the demand for a "Bosch wage").[77] Merkle successfully persuaded the works council that a special in-house scale was not a good idea, but by the spring of 1978 relations had again become icy. Talks between the employers and unions broke down, and from March 15 to April 5 the Bosch workforce joined colleagues in the metalworking industry in staging a three-week strike for improved wage agreements. The dispute also led for the first time to a substantial polarization of the Bosch workforce, notably between wage earners and salaried staff. Fewer than one-third of the latter voted to strike, and as "scabs" they had virtually to run the gauntlet in order to reach work during the strike.[78] Once again the employers' association had reacted with a "defensive lockout," inflaming the conflict even more.[79] Some 13,600 Bosch associates were involved – 9,600 strikers plus around 4,000 victims of the lockout.

From the spring of 1981, fresh lines of conflict formed between works council and management. On the one hand, the employee representatives were keen to link company bonuses to pay increases. On the other, management wanted to talk about developing a whole "new RB remuneration system" designed primarily to make pay scales more flexible. In addition, in late 1981 and mid-1982, against a background of fresh downturns and the imminent second oil-price shock, further action was taken to adjust staffing levels. In fact, outright dismissals on a major scale were considered.[80] On top of this, in June 1983, the board of management first announced a reduction in voluntary social benefits.[81] This was widely seen as a "pointer from Bosch," to quote the headline in the *Handelsblatt* newspaper – "and this from the board of a company that has a great social tradition and that can certainly not be accused of dismantling social standards."[82]

An already tense atmosphere was placed under further strain by Merkle's stance on extended codetermination and the new Works Council Constitution Act. Since the early 1970s, no other topic had stirred up so much emotion on both sides of the employer-employee divide.[83] Even before the new Works Council Constitution Act came into force in January 1972, the board of management voiced serious doubts about the constitutional legality of certain of its provisions. It saw them as paving the way for a future politicization of the company's workforce.[84] However, the board was even more concerned by a law that the West German federal parliament passed on May 4, 1976. The extended Codetermination Law, which came into effect at the beginning of July of that year and applied to all German corporations employing more than 2,000 persons, gave union or workforce representatives an (almost) equal number of seats and votes on supervisory boards. To get around this, immediate consideration was given to changing the legal structure of Robert Bosch GmbH. One possibility was conversion into a partnership limited by shares. The greatest cause for concern was the new position of director of industrial relations on the board of management.[85] Finally, at a board of management meeting held in early May 1977, the idea was floated that Bosch might join a cross-industry group and lodge a complaint of unconstitutionality against the Codetermination Law. The employers' associations had already launched a campaign to this effect.[86] Bosch soon found a number of like-minded companies (Bayer, Braun, Daimler-Benz, Linde, Hoechst, Röhm, Varta, and Roederstein), and on June 29, 1977, only one day before the time limit for appeal expired, a total of 9 companies and 29 employers' associations lodged their constitutional complaint. The fact that Bosch was among them, and that it had "in consequence thrown the weight of the world-renowned Bosch name behind a cause that we, as the elected employee representatives, have no choice but to reject" met with the works council's fury and "deep disappointment."[87] The board felt obliged to respond immediately with a detailed explanation of the management's position. A letter to the works council stated that the management's aim was not "to stop the law but rather to create conditions that will allow the law to be applied in a way that is fair to companies." The signatories were attempting (the letter said) to forestall the tensions and friction that otherwise might arise in connection with its practical implementation.[88]

The fact was, the members of the Bosch board of management saw the codetermination issue in a far less ideological light than was the case, for instance, with the Confederation of German Employers' Associations and its president, Otto Esser, who saw codetermination as being categorically at odds with free collective bargaining.[89] But they also rejected the arguments that came from the union side, one example being the allegedly well-substantiated theory that free collective bargaining was a confrontational model while codetermination was a cooperative model.[90] Whatever the rhetoric on both sides, the members of the Bosch board of management were motivated, no less than were their comrades-in-arms, by a desire to defend employers' interests. This was a power issue affecting industrial relations right across the Federal Republic of Germany. Not until March 1979 did the tedious disputes over employee codetermination reach an end. All told, the dispute stretched over nearly two decades, having begun with the bill first submitted by the German Trade Union Confederation [*Deutscher Gewerkschaftsbund*] in 1962. It was in March 1979, three years after the Codetermination Law had been passed, that the Federal Constitutional Court established its constitutionality. The law was to become one of the major sociopolitical projects of the Federal Republic of Germany, as well as a cornerstone of its economic and social order.

From the standpoint of employees and trade unions, however, the practical implementation of the Codetermination Law looked anything but encouraging to start with. What they saw in a great many companies was a clear weakening of supervisory boards as a result of amendments to articles of incorporation and changes to rules of procedure. Often, the work done by supervisory board members was "drawn under the veil of an exaggerated duty to observe secrecy."[91] Merkle himself practiced a model of industrial codetermination that was all his own. He and Richard Rau, the chairman of the Bosch central works council, enjoyed a special relationship of trust from the outset. Rau had joined Bosch during the war as an apprentice technician. He was elected a member of the works council in 1953, chaired the works council at the Feuerbach plant from 1962, and moved on to his position as chairman of the central works council in 1967. He had also been a member of the Stuttgart city council as well as a member of the board of the metalworking union IG Metall for many years, and thus had good connections both as a politician and as a trade unionist. So Rau pulled union strings, Merkle exploited his contacts with employers' associations, and ultimately both were concerned above all with the interests of Bosch.[92] Even before the introduction of extended codetermination, "King Richard" (as Rau came to be known) had been vice-chairman of the much smaller supervisory board that existed at Bosch before extended codetermination, and there had been close and regular contacts between him and Merkle since that time. Looking back, Rau for one felt that those contacts had eventually ripened into a personal friendship. "On the basis of this friendship, I profited of course immensely from him. Wherever I failed to achieve something (in my official talks with the board of management), here was the button I could press, so to speak. And very much to my advantage."[93] When Rau and Merkle met up at the Schillerhöhe, the conversation would often last for two or three hours. And much of what they talked about was entirely private, as well as informal. Not least, Merkle wanted to know what kind of atmosphere reigned at work: "Here he was always very eager for information. He'd always ask, 'How are things looking down there?'"[94]

The close relationship between Rau and Merkle again proved of great worth to Bosch in the early 1980s, when manufacturing processes underwent further major change, and a new manufacturing model began to emerge at Bosch. This time, the role model Bosch turned to was no longer the U.S., but Japan, where the electrical and automotive industries were streaking ahead. The secret of the country's success was the "Toyota model" of flexible manufacturing. Through license agreements with Nippondenso and Diesel Kiki, Bosch had enjoyed close links with the Japanese automotive-supply industry since the early 1950s. More recently, since the second half of the 1960s, Bosch engineers had been making regular trips to Japan. Their reports provide insight – in fast-forward mode – not only into the extraordinarily swift development of the sector there but also into the rapid change taking place back at Bosch in management's awareness of things Japanese. For instance, summing up their impressions of a study trip to Japan in the spring of 1964, Bosch engineers wrote that, despite Japan's leading position in the Far East, there was "still no reason to suppose that our own markets might be put seriously at risk as a result."[95] Following further visits in 1968 and 1969, it was again noted that the general level of industrial engineering "is well below ours. Less mechanization coupled with much manual work, all workers paid by the hour [...]. Product maturity of Japanese automakers and automotive-supply companies lies some two years behind the U.S. and Germany, in the field of manufacturing processes some three years."[96] Actually, the number of automobiles produced and exported by Japanese industry more than doubled between 1966 and 1968 alone, and one glance at the numbers reveals that a serious competitor was emerging. At the start of 1970, the Swedish journalist Håkan Hedberg caused a stir with a book about what he called "the Japanese challenge." The book was read assiduously at Bosch, confirming the impressions that Bosch engineers themselves formed on subsequent study trips in the early part of the 1970s.[97] Hans Bacher was clearly much impressed by Japan's huge investment in rationalization, as well as by the rapid work-rate, the industriousness, the loyalty, and the sheer ambition of the Japanese people. Finally, in 1974, and above all in 1976, Bosch engineers paid visits to their licensee Nippondenso. Their main aim was to "compare manufacturing technologies, giving special attention to mechanization and automation." They spent weeks studying their host's industrial engineering and workstation design. Among the things that particularly struck them was the evident automation of assembly lines featuring high piece numbers.[98]

In December 1979, to mark the recently celebrated 25-year anniversary of the license agreement and the 30th anniversary of Nippondenso as a company, Merkle visited Japan to see for himself what was happening there. Like his engineers before him, he came back with the impression that conditions for the planned assault on the European machine-tool and automotive markets were "optimal."[99] Soon afterward, the massive "Japan shock" hit the German automotive industry. Major automakers including VW and Daimler-Benz faced a huge export drive by the Japanese, which caused the market share of Japanese automobiles in Germany to soar to 13 percent by the end of 1980.[100] Everywhere, people turned their attention to Japanese management and manufacturing methods and tried to integrate both into their own approach.

A group of Bosch managers paid another visit to Nippondenso at the beginning of December 1980. This time their aim was to study the Toyota and *kanban* system "in the context of industrial engineering, planning, and control, materials planning and materials supply, and use of IT with a view to its applicability at Bosch."[101] Since 1971, when the Japanese company had begun introducing the *kanban* system, Nippondenso had been able to reduce its overall inventories from 77 percent to 25 percent of the manufacturing cost of a month's production. That meant a growth in productivity of 12 to 13 percent annually.[102] *Kanban* was a materials-flow-based information, production, and control system (somewhat off-handedly abbreviated by Bosch engineers as "MIPS"). It was designed to assemble all products at all stages of production in synch with their sale, thus minimizing inventory between those stages. Materials flow and hence inventories formed an integral part of production sched-

New, fully automatic assembly line for air-conditioning fan motors at the Bühl plant (1985)

uling. Inventory therefore took absolute priority when it came to measuring the progress of rationalization. There was every reason to introduce this production concept (tailored to the specific circumstances of German plants) at Bosch without delay.[103] It was hoped that *kanban* would provide the answer to the obvious changes in the marketplace. Innovation times for new products were becoming shorter, which left less and less time to exploit engineering advances. Purchasers were announcing their requirements at short notice, and international competition was forcing prices down. At the same time, consumers were becoming increasingly quality-conscious. Given these circumstances, *kanban* made it possible to square the circle, so to speak. Greater flexibility led to reduced inventories, better quality, improved observance of deadlines, and lower costs. The choice of pilot locations in which the new production system could be developed and tested fell to the Bühl/Bühlertal plant (BüW) for mass production (fan motors) and the Homberg 2 plant (HoW2) for one-off production (hydraulics). On matters relating to materials supply and call orders, Daimler-Benz was also involved from the outset. The newly established "flexible manufacturing and *kanban*" team first met on April 10, 1981.[104]

Implementing the Japanese manufacturing philosophy meant breaking with the approach to production that Bosch had used before, as well as with its practice. Specifically, it called for shorter re-equipping times and a turning away from batch production. In other words, it meant turning the whole production process on its head. Even the quality system previously employed at Bosch had to be fundamentally rethought, in close consultation with suppliers. *Kanban* could work only if uninterrupted, defect-free production was guaranteed. "Designing a different kind of plant organization will mean a radical departure from existing structures," reads one internal memo.[105] "Production technology is in the middle of a revolution," is how Hans Bacher put it in October 1982, addressing executives at the beginning of the 26th rationalization conference on the subject of the imminent changes. "Engineering in our factories will change beyond recognition. Nor will the change be confined to 'a revolution on the factory floor.' It amounts to a reorganization of the entire manufacturing process. It will ultimately touch all our associates, affecting what is demanded of them and challenging both their adaptability and their willingness to learn."[106] However, this radical flexibilization of manufacturing and the application of the principle that "the market alone determines the scope and timing of supply" soon ran into trouble. There were legal problems, wage-agreement headaches, and a certain amount of conflict with the existing Bosch pay system.[107] The new manufacturing concept called for a higher level of qualification, which meant more jobs for workers with the right skills at the expense of unskilled and semiskilled workers. Indeed, with commercial and technical spheres in the workplace increasingly overlapping, it was becoming clear that production personnel training had to be more interdisciplinary. Clearly, then, all plans and general concepts to do with recasting "manufacturing as an integrated system" were going to require the early involvement of the works council. Unlike in Japan, when it came to implementing the *kanban* system in Germany, social-policy considerations affected what technologies could be applied, as well as the profitability that was actually achieved. Nonetheless, a new and forward-looking "manufacturing concept for the 1980s" quickly crystallized out at Bosch. The autumn 1983 manufacturing conference took as its motto "Controlled flexible manufacturing" [*Beherrschte flexible Fertigung*].[108] A fresh phase in the history of the Bosch production system was about to open. The company stood on the threshold of a progressive evolution of industrial engineering, "the likes of which [had] not been seen in the last 30 years."[109]

5 The phase of "indiscriminate diversification": strategic alliances and the move into new areas of business

In the late 1950s, Bosch revived a policy it had first pursued back in the 1920s: buying up interests in other companies and diversifying into new fields of business. The aim was still the same: to reduce the company's heavy reliance on the automotive-supply business and to avoid the associated economic ups and downs of this business. As was already pointed out, in the early 1950s nearly 80 percent of total sales came from the automotive sector. This was the main pillar of the company's sales. Only just over 20 percent was accounted for by other fields of business. In its search for a second pillar, the company turned its attention to the consumer sector. Given the West German market's considerable need to catch up in domestic equipment – refrigerators, washing machines, and gas-fired boilers – Bosch initially moved into household appliances. The company also resumed its traditional association with power tools, an area that grew very rapidly in a period of reconstruction and a rising consumer society. In addition, Bosch developed its consumer-electronics business, which at the time comprised movie cameras, car radios, television sets, and radio-gramophones. Here the company was represented by a whole series of subsidiaries and a range of brands from Kino-Bauer to Blaupunkt. However, following a short-lived heyday in the 1960s, the entire consumer-electronics business plunged into crisis, and the 1970s saw an intensive search for alliances in this sector, both in Germany and the rest of Europe. In its search for a third pillar, the company turned to the capital goods industry, looking at new fields of business with a promising future – packaging machinery, hydraulic systems, and industrial equipment.[1] Finally, Bosch played a role in the major reorganization of structural and industrial policy on which the West German federal government, the big banks, and business itself increasingly focused throughout the "long-drawn-out 1970s." During this crisis-ridden decade, a whole series of industrial sectors underwent major change in the Federal Republic. A radical upheaval transformed the economic landscape of German industry, from textiles to the automotive sector to consumer electronics all the way to defense and aviation.[2] Robert Bosch GmbH and Merkle (who in this regard particularly saw himself as a *political* entrepreneur) found themselves occupying center stage in these developments. Bosch owned shares in Daimler-Benz, Gerling Insurance, and Allianz AG, albeit with minority holdings of under 5 percent in each.[3] Above all, however, Bosch was involved in the tedious, time-consuming political attempts to restructure Messerschmitt-Bölkow-Blohm (MBB), as well as in the crisis surrounding AEG. This latter involvement coincided with the company's entry into what was then deemed the very promising field of information and communications technology – the "great coup" of Merkle's diversification strategy. The challenge, however, was twofold. On the one hand, the company had to manage these varied and often at the same time hectic operations and integrate them into its overall corporate policy. On the other hand, the managers concerned had to learn to come to terms with businesses which were as disparate as they could be, each addressing a distinct market and having its own specific competitive situation. There is no doubt that, in this phase of its existence, Bosch was operating at the very edge of its financial and, above all, its managerial capabilities.

The Bosch-Siemens alliance in the household-appliances business

One of the first areas of manufacturing that Bosch resumed immediately after the war's end was aimed at the household. In 1952, the company premiered a food processor. This was followed in 1956 by the Bosch freezer and in 1958 by the first Bosch washing machine. The market had a lot of catching up to do, and business flourished accordingly. Between 1950 and 1964, annual sales in this area rocketed from 20 million to more than 350 million German marks. Over the same period, the share of Bosch sales accounted for by the household-appliances business rose from just under 10 percent to 21 percent. However, as early as 1960–61 (still well within the "economic-miracle years"), the outlook clouded over. A confidential memo from the sales department warned that the refrigerator market, for instance, would be saturated within ten years. Unit sales, which in 1961 stood at 800,000 a year, were at risk of falling to roughly half that figure.[4] Consequently, talks with Siemens opened in November 1963 on the subject of a "pool agreement for household appliances." The two companies had been on cordial terms for decades, and the household-appliances business offered an opportunity to revive their old ties.[5] Both operated in the field of electrical household appliances (including radio and television), where they generated annual sales of some 1.2 billion German marks between them. Bosch focused more on refrigeration, Siemens more on washing machines. The aim was to optimize manufacturing output at both companies and to make better use of their respective sales organizations. The projected collaboration thus encompassed development as well as production, and even extended to things such as joint investment planning. When it came to sales operations, however, the partners would still enjoy absolute freedom. Above all, the independence of their brands was to remain intact.[6] In the spring of 1964, the negotiations began to take on more concrete form. There was no time to lose, for despite strong sales growth, earnings from the household-appliances business were not as high as they might have been. Moreover, although the major U.S. consumer-goods producers had made little impact on European markets up to then, profound changes could be expected soon.[7]

However, the real problem facing the projected alliance with Siemens lay elsewhere. It was to find "an acceptable form of cooperation in light of the Act against Restraints on Competition" without having to take the further step (which though legally watertight neither party saw as desirable) of actually merging the two companies' household-appliances interests. A preliminary agreement was signed by Bosch and Siemens in late May 1965. It set out the key features of the new alliance, with general managers appointed by joint agreement and a shareholder's committee comprising an equal number of representatives from each company.[8] However, in December of the same year, the Federal Cartel Authority raised objections to the draft agreements. It took particular exception to the application by Bosch and Siemens for a specialization cartel and to the pooling of profits. In a long letter sent in mid-January 1966, Bosch management tried to change the Federal Cartel Authority's collective mind. The letter explained that the purpose of the proposed joint venture was precisely to enhance the competitiveness of the electrical goods sector as a bulwark against the concentration process going on in the rest of Germany and throughout Europe.[9] Eventually, in March 1966, the two companies called a press conference to announce their joint venture for household appliances and radio and TV sets. The news commanded an exceptional level of attention in the business press at the time, and not only because of the unusual way in which the alliance was constructed. Here were two giants of the electrical industry, Bosch and Siemens, joining together while at the same time continuing to compete. "The process," one major newspaper commented, "is revolutionary for German circumstances if only because of the individualism that characterized the two companies' respective founders."[10] Yet only a few days later (far sooner than the Bosch board of management had expected), the Federal Cartel Authority told the two companies that the projected joint venture agreement did not constitute a merger (requiring neither notification nor approval), but was instead a cartel (and as such inadmissible). The authority therefore expected that the agreement would not be concluded and certainly not put into practice.[11] In fact, however, Bosch and Siemens had already signed. Nonetheless, they indicated to the cartel authority that they would not operate the agreement "to the detriment of the competition act" until the matter had been resolved. "Antitrust proceedings against Bosch-Siemens," proclaimed a headline in the *Frankfurter Allgemeine Zeitung* in mid-April 1966. The Federal Cartel Authority had indeed instituted proceedings against both companies for breach of administrative rules, even though precise legal clarification of the whole issue between the companies and the antitrust authorities was still pending.[12]

Why did the case cause such a stir? With effect from January 1965, the Act against Restraints on Competition had been amended for the first time. The originally narrow definition of abuse of market power was dropped in favor of a more general clause, and a political debate had begun over such questions as "Is our competition law up to the tasks we shall be facing in the future?"[13] In the end, Bosch and Siemens backed away from open conflict with the Federal Cartel Authority. Taking their lead from the authority's pronouncements on corporate law and antitrust law, they now considered two alternatives to the joint-venture solution. Either Bosch and Siemens should acquire 50 percent stakes in each other's household-appliances operations, or they should together (acting on a fifty-fifty basis) establish a holding company to buy up both.[14] Following protracted negotiations (some of which took place in Brussels before European antitrust authorities), the Federal Cartel Authority finally reached a settlement with the two companies in December 1966.[15] Accepting the economic objectives of the agreement, the authority nonetheless made it a condition that the term *Interessengemeinschaft* or "joint venture" should be avoided – lest "the Bosch-Siemens agreement lead to use of an *Interessengemeinschaft* model as a cover for inadmissible cartels."[16] The new label was therefore "Bosch-Siemens Hausgerätegemeinschaft" (BSHG). The organization operated as a holding company with a centralized management team and, in order to comply with a further condition imposed by the Federal Cartel Authority, with an obligation to maintain its legal and corporate structure for a period of 30 years. From a purely legal standpoint, the new company was neither a cartel nor a joint venture but a "group based on contracts" [*Vertragskonzern*]. The relevant agreements were signed on February 9, 1967, and with retrospective effect from January 1 of that year, BSHG was established with a capital stock of 1 million German marks.

Meanwhile, much had changed not only in the household-appliances market but also in other business areas where Bosch and Siemens were active. They now faced increased price pressure as a result of "Italian throwaway prices," a veritable collapse in prices in certain areas (a Bosch refrigerator that cost 514 German marks in 1957 cost only 258 ten years later), growing competition, technical developments, and the dreaded signs of market saturation that came from shrinking unit-sales figures.[17] Despite all these problems, the joint household-appliances operation run by Bosch and Siemens was by all means successful in the ensuing years. Still operating at a loss in 1968, despite a significant increase in sales to 423.1 million German marks, the joint venture's business then boomed until the early 1980s, reaching almost 3 billion German marks, with profits rising concomitantly.[18] Only between 1974 and 1975 was there a brief dip, although this was made up swiftly in the next few years, partly as a result of increased exports, which constituted some 30 percent of total sales. There was some initial friction in the joint management of a company with a workforce of 12,800 distributed over four production locations (Berlin, Dillingen, Giengen, and Traunreut). But otherwise BSHG developed satisfactorily for both parties as a "good way of satisfying the need to form larger entities in the household-appliances business."[19]

The Blaupunkt crisis and attempts to reorganize the German consumer-electronics industry

The Bosch consumer-electronics business, chiefly comprising Fernseh GmbH (FESE) and the Blaupunkt (BPWG) plants in Berlin, had been relocated and re-established after the war's end. Bosch had resumed production of car radios in the new Blaupunkt plant in Hildesheim in 1949. In 1951, it began turning out television receivers at its Darmstadt site, subsequently transferring production to Blaupunkt in Hildesheim. Well behind in radio and television engineering because of the war, Bosch quickly made up lost ground. By 1954, when TV was introduced in the Federal Republic and other European countries, and with R&D departments already working on the color-television receiver, the company was among the top suppliers in the booming consumer-electronics market.[20] Subsequently, sales at Blaupunkt and FESE quickly soared – from 31 million German marks (Blaupunkt) and 2.2 million German marks (FESE) in 1952 to 320 million and 33 million respectively in 1965.[21]

First, however, Bosch had to deal with a legacy from the National Socialist era. It concerned restitution of the FESE shares bought from Loewe in 1938. What had made the whole matter resurface after all this time was evidently not a reimbursement claim by Loewe but the action for infringement of patents that Bosch (in the shape of FESE) brought against Loewe in 1959. The consumer-electronics company Loewe, now operating from the Franconian city of Kronach (in northern Bavaria), had since 1953 been exploiting industrial property rights belonging to FESE to build and market domestic television sets. A license agreement relating to those rights had been sent to Loewe but not in fact signed, so Bosch filed a suit against Loewe before the regional court in Düsseldorf. However, the suit was suspended when Loewe stated that, as the former parent company of FESE, it was entitled to make free use of the patents.[22] Bosch vehemently contested this. It further argued that, when Loewe sold its FESE shares to Bosch and Zeiss-Ikon, it had not lost any assets but simply restructured them. Nor had there been any loss of assets so far as Loewe's shareholders were concerned, since the shares in their company had been restored to them after the war.[23] Not until November 1964 did reimbursement proceedings (Loewe Opta AG v. Robert Bosch GmbH and Fernseh GmbH) open before the regional court in Berlin. The matter was finally settled by compromise in January 1965. Bosch paid Loewe 1.5 million German marks by way of compensation for its reimbursement claims. At the same time, Loewe paid Bosch 375,000 German marks in license fees. The net result was that 1.125 million German marks passed from Stuttgart to Berlin and then on to Kronach, and both companies agreed to end a dispute that, off and on, had lasted for years. Only now was Bosch able, operationally speaking, to draw a line under the National Socialist past.

Meanwhile, the entire West German consumer-electronics market was in a state of flux. The end of the boom looked imminent, and when even Grundig (then the largest group in German consumer electronics) indicated a willingness to enter merger agreements or sell off assets, the Bosch board of management began to give consideration to ideas relating to the reorganization and restructuring of the entire consumer-electronics industry. In June 1967, in the context of the talks with Siemens about an alliance in white goods (washing machines and refrigerators), initial ideas were drawn up for a Bosch-Siemens partnership to include Grundig with its radio, tape-recorder, and TV business ("brown goods"). The initiative for this "brown alliance" came from Siemens, to whom Grundig, as a major customer for components, was of "crucial importance." For Siemens, it was imperative that Grundig be prevented from forming a rapprochement with Philips or one of the powerful American consumer-electronics groups of the time, such as RCA.[24] For Bosch, too, a brown-goods alliance presented both direct and indirect strategic advantages, partly because Siemens could not make the alliance work without Bosch. However, for the Stuttgart company the *sine qua non* of any alliance was that Siemens should abandon its plans to move into automotive equipment.[25] But the negotiations dragged on, without producing any tangible results.

Blaupunkt's business prospects began to darken at the start of 1970. Having overestimated demand for color TV sets, the company suffered a considerable setback, while the car-radio market saw increasing activity by non-German (notably Japanese) competitors, whose products were of comparable quality. In the first half of the 1970s, therefore, Blaupunkt stayed in the red, and only with difficulty was it able to regain profitability in the years that followed. And while Blaupunkt sales rose steadily to reach 1.15 billion German marks in 1977,[26] a rude awakening followed in the autumn of 1978. With the Bosch movie-camera business also having made a loss and showing a need for restructuring, Blaupunkt, and with it the entire brown-goods business at Bosch, slid into a severe crisis. The reasons for this were many and varied. For all its engineering skill, Blaupunkt was too small to compete on its own in the color TV business. Capturing a serious share of the market would have required massive investment on the part of Bosch management. By rights, the only course open to the subsidiary was to exit the field completely. However, as one of the managers involved recalled later, "such a dramatic retreat was not an option for the board of management at that time. This was back in the days when one simply didn't do things like that, at least not at Bosch."[27] As for earning money, Blaupunkt did this the way it had always done: with car radios. But here, too, there were huge problems with growing competition and slumps in revenues. There were also quality problems with electronic components, and a generally "belated use of electronics" in car radios.[28] Only from 1981 onward was the car-radio program likely to be capable of competing with Philips and Grundig. In hi-fi, too, Blaupunkt had entered the field far too late. As early as March 1978, the board of management tried to assess whether, given the clear advances made by other manufacturers (especially the Japanese), Blaupunkt still had adequate market opportunities in the video-recorder business.[29] There were tensions in corporate culture as well ("Blaupunkt and the [consumer-electronics] business were still suspect to many of the old guard at Bosch").[30] And not least, there were difficulties within management itself – difficulties that were to come to a head in the spring of 1979 with the resignation of Rudolf Scharpff, the member of the Bosch board of management responsible for Blaupunkt.

In the spring of 1978, however, Merkle was unwilling to make a quick decision regarding the future direction and focus of the product portfolio and the market positioning of the Blaupunkt subsidiary. In consequence, at the end of that year Blaupunkt recorded a loss of 50 million German marks.

Hectic restructuring plans followed, as well as talks with various companies, including Telefunken, the consumer-electronics arm of AEG. The object of the talks with AEG-Telefunken was either an alliance or (taking the bull by the horns, as it were) an actual buyout of Telefunken by Bosch (or rather Blaupunkt).[31] Apart from Grundig and Philips GmbH, all the country's consumer-electronics producers were in the red, and talks were being held everywhere in the search for a remedy. Again, Bosch (i. e., Blaupunkt) found itself at the center of the restructuring efforts of an entire sector, although the general principle was "first and foremost, let's put our own house in order."[32] Accordingly, the consultancy company McKinsey was asked to work out solutions for Blaupunkt in connection with product strategy, process flow, and structural simplification.[33] But 1979 closed with the Blaupunkt financial statements showing yet another loss of 50 million German marks.[34] Only radical staff cuts of 2,000, pruning the total workforce to 11,000, would (it was hoped) bring about a change. "We do not expect to end the loss-making situation at Blaupunkt before 1981–82," Merkle told the RBIK shareholders in late June 1979.[35] As it turned out, the cuts had to be twice as drastic, with 4,000 associates losing their jobs. Further major deficits were recorded in 1980 and 1981, though the losses did begin to come down. Nonetheless, it soon emerged that other mistakes had been made. In video-recording technology, the Japanese VHS system had a head start in the market. But in January 1978, as a technical standard for their own product design, Blaupunkt managers had opted for a European alternative – the Philips Video 2000 system. At the same time, they had become embroiled in an avoidable licensing dispute with BASF about recording methods, and having spent a large sum on development, they had begun making their own video camera for the home-movie market. Only at the last minute did Bosch contrive to wrest the helm around, so to speak. In July 1981, it concluded a joint-venture agreement with the Japanese electronics group Matsushita to produce video recorders using the VHS system. VHS looked like becoming the fastest-growing market segment in the consumer-electronics business.[36]

At the same time, the Bosch board of management had been trying, through countless fresh alliance negotiations, to prevent Blaupunkt from becoming increasingly isolated. Regroupings within the German and European consumer-electronics sector had led to ever greater concentration and more and more joint-venture deals – notably the one concluded in the meantime between Grundig and Philips. In the autumn of 1978, talks had begun with AEG-Telefunken regarding collaboration or a merger, but this avenue had closed as early as mid-October of that year, following a change of strategy at the top of AEG. As Merkle wrote to the head of Siemens, Bernhard Plettner, in this regard: "The chance, by merging Blaupunkt and Telefunken, of attaining what I consider to be the right degree of size for international competition, has now gone, yet I feel some relief that a leadership burden of exceptional weight has been removed from our shoulders (to say nothing of the financial commitment)."[37] Max Grundig's somewhat bizarre plans to create a pan-European consumer-electronics company were blocked by the Federal Cartel Authority in 1983, whereupon AEG promptly sold Telefunken to the French Thompson-Brandt Group. In a countermove, Philips increased its existing shareholding in Grundig. These were the changes that shaped the future of the consumer-electronics industry in Germany. For the time being, Bosch and Blaupunkt were left empty-handed.[38]

Strategic investments and political machinations: Bosch, MBB, and restructuring in the arms and aviation industries

In April 1975, Bosch was offered shares in the Messerschmitt-Bölkow-Blohm defense and aviation group (MBB). The Blohm family wished to sell their 25 percent stake. They had already sold part to the Bavarian state and Siemens, and wanted Bosch to be involved as well.[39] The offer concerned a roughly 10 percent stake, worth 25 million German marks. The Schillerhöhe was not averse. The feeling at Bosch was that the company could benefit from the association in terms of engineering and technology. But there were conditions: the others must "agree amicably. Talks with Siemens called for."[40] Meanwhile other interested parties had appeared, keen to have a say in any rearrangement of the corporate structure of MBB. Bosch found itself being drawn into negotiations that were increasingly being dominated by political players. The city of Hamburg, which acquired the above-mentioned Blohm holding at the end of 1976, now for its part offered Bosch some of its MBB shares. Siemens and Thyssen also became involved. Jointly with another partner, SNIAS (Aérospatiale), they had for tax purposes put their combined holdings, totaling 25.6 percent, into an affiliated company [*Schachtelgesellschaft*] called Fides GmbH. They were now prepared to welcome Bosch, together with the stake it would acquire from Hamburg, into the fold. Bosch itself was "interested in strengthening the influence of the industrial partners in MBB [as opposed to the political influence exerted mainly by the Bavarian state]."[41] MBB had meanwhile become Germany's leading aerospace group, with annual sales in excess of 1.5 billion German marks. Of those sales, 65 percent came from aircraft production, 20.5 percent from defense technology, and somewhat less than 10 percent from space exploration and transport engineering. The ownership situation, too, was complicated, with 25.6 percent being held by industry through the aforesaid Fides GmbH, 20.25 by the city of Hamburg, 1.8 percent still by the Blohm family, 16.3 percent by Professor Willy Messerschmitt, and 13.42 percent by his fellow-founder, Dr. Ludwig Bölkow. In addition, the Bavarian state owned 13.73 percent, either directly or indirectly through Bayerische Landesanstalt für Aufbaufinanzierung, and at the end of 1976 Boeing, which was clearly going to be a U.S. rival to the Airbus project, held a further 8.9 percent.[42] At a board of management meeting in December 1976, therefore, Merkle moved that participation in MBB should be turned down. Bosch, he said, should concentrate instead on talks relating to a stake in a U.S. company, Borg-Warner – talks which were being held at the same time. Furthermore, he added, negotiations up to this point had shown that "immediate and continued access to technologies developed by MBB is not guaranteed, nor is cooperation with the other industrial partners, notably Siemens and Thyssen, going to be possible in the manner expected."[43]

Nonetheless, negotiations resumed as early as March 1977. Two things had changed. First, the city of Hamburg was now prepared to unconditionally sell around half the shares it had purchased from the Blohm family to industrial buyers. Second, the thought of an interim holding company (Fides II) had come into play, in which Allianz, Bosch, and another partner might each own one-third. Given the right coordination of the industrial companies involved in the two holding companies, the management of MBB by industrial enterprises that Merkle, too, was striving for (not least for reasons of regulatory policy [What is the business of the state, what is the business of business?]) seemed within reach. Also, there were clear indications, from both Bavaria and Hamburg as well as from the federal government, that such an "industrial" solution would find approval. However, the talks subsequently launched by the industrial side (under the joint leadership of Siemens and Allianz) about how the new shareholder structure for MBB was to be implemented proved highly complex. Above all, they kept taking surprising turns. Bosch clearly held back, leaving the initiative to others. "We are conducting these negotiations calmly," Paul Stein noted toward the end of July 1977. "If agreement is reached on reasonable terms, we would welcome it. If on the other hand no agreement is to be had on a sensible basis, that too we would accept with the same calm."[44] The problem was that there was by no means consensus among the companies involved. Only Bosch and Allianz sang in tune. Merkle and Klaus Götte, a member of the Allianz board of management, corresponded and spoke on the phone repeatedly to make sure they stayed that way. Siemens, on the other hand, pursuing its own interests, absolutely refused to let a potential third partner, MTU, board the same Fides II boat as Bosch and Allianz.

Following prolonged and repeatedly faltering negotiations, things finally began to move in June 1978. Allianz established another holding company, ABM Beteiligungs GmbH [i. e., Allianz Bosch MTU Beteiligungs GmbH], to accommodate the MBB shares that it, Bosch, and MTU wished to purchase. The other holding company, Fides I, and Siemens together took over the Boeing holding of 8.9 percent with the proviso that they should transfer this to ABM later. Now, however, the 16.3 percent shareholding owned by Willy Messerschmitt, who died shortly later in September 1978, was suddenly up for grabs. This provoked a fresh tussle between Bavaria and the industry partners. "In the chokehold of the state: financial and management poker games over MBB," ran the headline above one article in the business press as it tackled the industrial and political drama that was the rearrangement of Germany's aerospace industry.[45] "Opposed to any extension of the influence of industry, the Bavarian governor is fighting to enlarge the state's share," Paul Stein told a board meeting in mid-October 1978.[46] And the governor in question, Franz Josef Strauß, did indeed get his way. On December 20, Merkle received a phone call from Strauß telling him that the MBB shares reserved for Bosch would now be going to the Nuremberg defense company Diehl. Stuttgart was out of the running. "Telling the whole long story of Bosch's non-participation in MBB would take more time than the matter is worth," Merkle wrote to [Siemens's] Plettner subsequently.[47] Over and over again, he went on, Bosch had been approached – most recently by the federal government, which had backed the idea of an industrial majority. "Our answer was the same all along. In principle we would participate, but only if all existing shareholders welcomed our joining the circle – and on condition that our holding was no larger than those of your own company and of Thyssen. And provided, finally, that certain tax prerequisites were met. When the two states [Länder] came on the scene, there was a further proviso: no voting-right commitment where this might undermine vital corporate decisions. Our stance made it clear from the outset that we had no wish to be pushed around. However, if all parties deemed it useful, we were willing to collaborate."[48]

But the Bosch-free phase of the MBB story was short-lived. In the summer of 1979, it emerged that the shareholder structure desired by Strauß (with Diehl, Flick, and Krupp participating) was not going to come about. Partly at the suggestion of Thyssen, the old tripartite model of Allianz, Bosch, and MTU as participants was looked at once again. On November 29, 1979, Bosch thus acquired a 50 percent holding in ABM, which then took over the

12.15 percent holding in MBB pre-financed by loans taken out by Allianz and Bosch and held temporarily by Fides I. As a result, Bosch too was now an indirect shareholder in MBB. Its investment in the 7.5 percent stake had so far cost it less than 38 million German marks altogether. Yet the company was not really happy. When it took a stake in MBB, Bosch had no inkling that it would be sucked into a maelstrom of "political machinations" relating to structural and economic policy. Engineering and corporate strategic interests soon lost the upper hand to the kind of responsibility for industrial policy that Merkle believed was incumbent on a political entrepreneur. And in the end, this sense of responsibility was his main motivation in seeing the deal through.

Moving into telecommunications technology: Bosch and the AEG crisis

In February 1979, Hans Bacher gave his fellow board of management members a presentation entitled "Telecommunications products – business opportunities for Bosch."[49] His talk listed a number of trends that were to become hugely important at Bosch. They included the increasing volume of information, the mounting pace of developments in electronics and its applications, and how IT markets (telecommunications, office technology, data processing, measurement and control technology, and so on) were merging or overlapping. At the same time, Bacher told his colleagues how the telecommunications and office-technology markets were both splitting internally into one for mass products and one for systems and solutions addressing specific applications. He further touched on how the division of labor between manufacturers of components and those of systems in this field was losing importance as a result. In Germany, four big companies shared this fast-growing telecommunications market and dominated developments in the field. They were Siemens, Standard Elektrik Lorenz (SEL), AEG-Telefunken with its Telefonbau und Normalzeit Lehner & Co. (T&N), and the Dutch electronics company Philips with its German subsidiary, Tekade. The chances of Bosch getting into this market with telephone networks, telex and data-transfer networks, and telephony on its own were deemed small. Entry was only possible by means of an acquisition, despite Bosch's existing jumping-off points: radios, cable TV sets, VDUs, videotext equipment, and telecommunications equipment for drivers.

Technically and structurally, however, the telecommunications field was in upheaval. Hardly had the transition been made from electro-mechanical to electronic telecommunications systems than the rapid development of micro-electronics led to a further burst of innovation. The shift from analog to digital paved the way for the integration of a whole range of telecommunications technologies.[50] But there was one major player in the telecommunications and electronics markets that had been in deep crisis since the mid-1970s: AEG-Telefunken. Following the failure of its attempts to expand into consumer goods manufacturing, a fiasco in the field of nuclear energy, and huge losses in computer technology, this long-established company found itself saddled with a huge burden of debt. It owed some 4 billion German marks in all.[51] In 1979, the efforts by Walter Cipa (who had been appointed chairman of the board of management in 1976) to turn the company around failed. As Merkle told his own board at their late-November meeting, the banks involved (notably Dresdner Bank) then appealed to German industry on political and general economic grounds to join them in a solidarity campaign in support of AEG. The aim was to find a private-enterprise solution.[52] Following a capital reduction and subsequent capital increase, the banks and insurance companies were to put up 1.8 billion German marks, while industry for its part was to put up loans against borrower's note totaling as much as 400 million German marks. Considerations of regulatory policy prompted Bosch to contribute 17.5 million German marks.[53] Moreover, it was Merkle who in February 1980 installed Heinz Dürr as chairman of the AEG board of management.

It soon became apparent that AEG could not survive without reorganization. In March 1981, Dürr made Bosch the following offer: AEG would contribute its participation in T&N to a new company, in which Bosch would have a 50 percent stake.[54] Bosch's investment in T&N would be coupled with the development of a communications technology business concept to which AEG would contribute its long-distance telephony and cable engineering business. However, the question of industrial leadership was left open. Bosch was required to put up some 470 million German marks in funding, but the 50 percent holding in T&N, combined with the prospect of eventually taking over the company, were things Bosch management found extremely attractive. With some 19,000 employees, annual sales of some 1.4 billion German marks, and generating profits year on year, the company was also the jewel in the crown of AEG's engineering operations. With the automotive business promising only stagnation and shrinkage, Bosch could now build up a new product area, as Merkle explained to RBIK shareholders in March 1981. Here was the "rare chance of creating a new and hugely promising area of operations, securing jobs while shutting out other undesirable interested parties at home and abroad, and increasing the earnings power of Bosch." The whole project was felt to hold promise for the future and to represent a great step forward, particularly since Siemens, too, was willing to support the initiative, as we know from the minutes of the same meeting.[55]

By the beginning of August, negotiations had at last reached the point where the *Stuttgarter Zeitung* could report the imminent "betrothal of two electrical giants," which also had the blessing of the antitrust authorities.[56] There were no actual agreements ready to be signed as yet, but in the meantime Bosch had persuaded AEG to accept two things. First, Bosch was to have clear industrial leadership of the T&N participation (to be controlled by a holding company). Second, via a spin-off, AEG was to grant Bosch a minority shareholding in its long-distance telephony and cable engineering business.[57] Merkle assured the RBIK shareholders that it was the joint aim of AEG and Bosch "not only for Bosch to replace AEG, but also to secure sustained cooperation between AEG, Bosch, and T&N by binding them together in a corporate alliance that might one day form the nucleus of a far larger company concerning itself with telecommunications in the broadest sense."[58] In fact, the whole deal was also about the future of AEG generally, and it was not long before there was talk of Bosch taking an even greater share. Further fuel was added to this speculation when the U.S. company ITT, through its German subsidiary SEL, signaled its interest in joining the "AEG poker game" as a player interested in a possible takeover. In the summer of 1981, the *Stuttgarter Nachrichten* wondered, "how far can Merkle go if he is to avoid entwining his own interests so closely with AEG that Bosch is also sucked in."[59] And indeed, the negotiations in September 1981 regarding a "Bosch model" made it perfectly clear that Merkle was interested only in AEG's "jewel in the crown" – namely, communications technology. Under the Bosch model, AEG transferred its T&N shares to an intermediate holding company, in which Bosch had a roughly 76 percent stake. Buying further shares would give it a majority shareholding in T&N. AEG sold off its long-distance telephony and cable engineering business, which in the future was to trade as AEG-Telefunken Nachrichtentechnik GmbH (ATN), and in which Bosch would be granted a shareholding of up to 20 percent. Bosch further acquired a minority interest in Olympia Werke AG, and with AEG and Mannesmann jointly founded Telematik Systemplanungs GmbH, which operated in the marketplace as a provider of systems solutions. Bosch deemed these moves essential, particularly as a way of securing its cooperation with AEG against infiltration by third parties, who might appear out of the blue, as it were, as major new AEG shareholders.[60] This increased Bosch's capital outlay to some 495 million German marks, in which connection Merkle explained that "our financial input rests purely on our own corporate-policy objective. It is not some kind of 'restructuring contribution' for the benefit of AEG."[61]

At the end of September, Merkle put the whole matter before RBIK for a final decision. AEG's situation had worsened in the meantime, and a swift, successful conclusion of the negotiations with Bosch played a key role in its bid for survival.[62] For Bosch this offered great opportunities – but also risks. A dossier put together especially for the purpose explained once again that the telecommunications project "brings RB closer to the goal of being less reliant on the automotive-equipment business, which is unlikely to deliver significant growth any longer."[63] Bosch's investment, the alliance agreement, and the Telematik company itself gave rise to a close-knit web of association involving Bosch, AEG, T&N – and Mannesmann as well, which Merkle saw as a desirable partner chiefly because of its experience in process plant engineering and in data processing, as gathered through its subsidiary, Kienzle Apparate GmbH. The four of them together possessed substantial expertise in the fields of telecommunications, data processing, computer engineering, and office technology.[64]

Fig. 7 Cross-ownership in the Telematik consortium (as of the end of 1981)

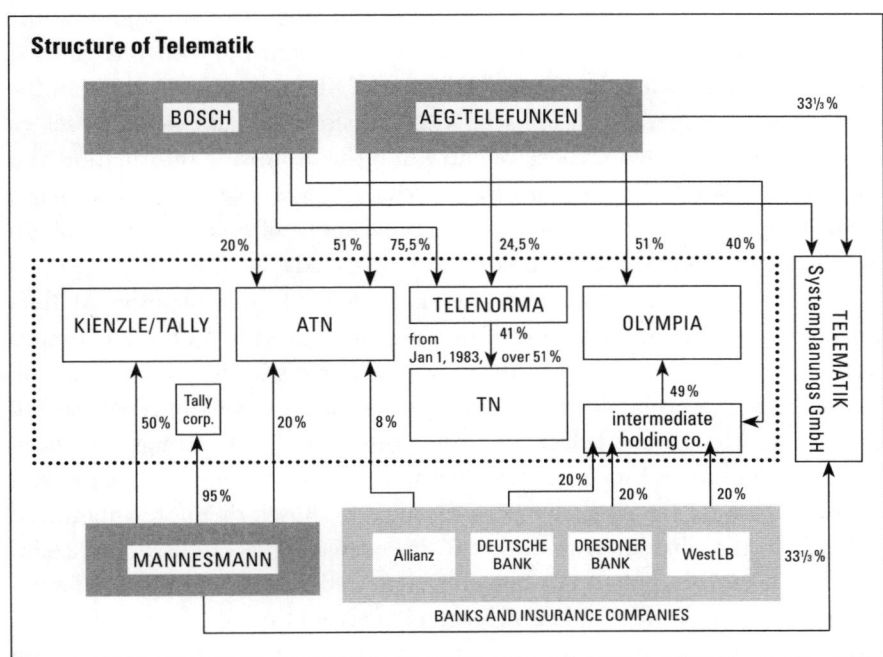

The consortium was forecast to make annual sales of nearly 4.3 billion German marks, which according to the Bosch board of management would give it a central position in the rapidly growing information and communications technology market of the future. It was not without rivals, however. Other large groups were realigning strategically, including Philips Kommunikations Industrie AG, under the umbrella of which the Dutch electrical group had gathered its various telecommunications activities in Germany in January 1982, and Siemens's *Kommunikationstechnik* division. Bosch expected its existing activities in telecommunications to provide additional synergy effects. But this tougher competition also meant unpredictable risks, as well as the danger that a strong international competitor might enter the field. And there were other risks specific to AEG. The big question concerning the RBIK shareholders was: "What will happen if AEG's situation continues to go from bad to worse?"[65] However, Merkle had taken precautions. He had secured from the consortium banks adequate declarations that they would continue to support AEG in the following year. This was a condition of what he himself dubbed the "Bosch deal."[66] Furthermore, in the event of both infiltration by third parties and insolvency and bankruptcy proceedings being instituted against AEG, there was extensive contractual provision for Bosch to have purchase options in relation to the remaining shares in ATN and T&N.[67] "Not a three-way mega-merger, more an ingenious alliance," ran the headline in *Handelsblatt* on December 4, 1981, when news finally came through that the relevant telecommunications contracts had been signed and that Telenorma Beteiligungsgesellschaft had been established.[68] The undoubted winner in the agreements now reached was Bosch. AEG's misfortune had enabled Bosch to make a comparatively inexpensive entry into the promising information and communications technology sphere, in which it was able to act as a major competitor from the start. The business press spoke of Bosch setting out "in new directions" and bursting "boldly" into new fields.[69]

However, over the summer of 1982 AEG ran into fresh difficulties. Matters worsened rapidly, and in August of that year they came to a dramatic head.[70] AEG was insolvent and had to file a petition for institution of composition proceedings to avert bankruptcy. As a legally separate company, ATN was not directly affected. Nonetheless, now that insolvency proceedings had been instituted, Bosch and its other two partners Mannesmann and Allianz were entitled to ask for the AEG shares to be called in. Bosch therefore announced publicly, in the autumn of 1982, that it was exercising its confiscation, exclusion, and takeover rights. AEG, however, contested this, leaving open "whether it was taking a positive stand or merely had to accept this against its will."[71] On January 1, 1983, the confiscation of AEG shares laid down in the consortium agreements finally took effect. Bosch demanded that the AEG board enter into immediate negotiations regarding details. Again the AEG managers tried to play for time, with the result that Paul Stein openly threatened on behalf of the Bosch board of management "to settle the matters of principle touching on the interests of ATN in some other fashion."[72] The situation was inflamed still further when Dürr used the platform of the AEG annual general meeting to criticize the confiscation of shares retrospectively and speak of inflexible action against AEG's will.[73] In the end, Dürr did in fact succeed in taking advantage of the share-confiscation situation to force Bosch, Mannesmann, and Allianz into talks regarding what AEG called "compensation" [*Entschädigung*] and Bosch called "payment" [*Vergütung*]. The dispute about how the AEG shares should be valued dragged on for eighteen months. The respective expert opinions placed the value as lying somewhere between 247 million and 1.2 billion German marks, depending on the client. The dispute finally ended in the autumn of 1984. "The three partners [had to pay] the ousted majority shareholder" a further 650 million German marks, with most of the obligation falling to Bosch.[74] Getting into the new business field of communications and information technology had thus cost Bosch roughly 1 billion German marks on balance, substantially more than originally planned. More importantly, telecommunications had yet to prove its ability to deliver the earnings that Bosch expected.

In retrospect, the end-result of Bosch's diversification efforts has to be seen in an ambivalent light. They tied up substantial financial resources and management capacity, and proved ultimately to be only a modest source of profit. Above all, they saw Merkle taking on ever greater entrepreneurial risks. In December 1981, while the great AEG-ATN coup was still being wound up, the U.S. company Sperry Vickers put its hydraulics division and its 19 manufacturing locations worldwide up for sale. Merkle spotted a major opportunity to attain an internationally leading position in hydraulics in one go, while also gaining a foothold in the U.S. market for aviation hydraulics.[75] However, the proposed purchase price (and therefore the medium-term financial commitment) was in the region of 1 billion German marks. Moreover, as Merkle learned during exploratory talks in New York, there were big risks. In Europe, Vickers was hemorrhaging money and needed urgent restructuring. In the U.S., on the other hand, its business was profitable. So the board was split in its views about the project (which incidentally soon came to be referred to simply as "V"). Skepticism was clearly voiced, not only as to whether Bosch management was up to the necessary restructuring and development of the Vickers concern but also with regard to the financial burden involved – not to speak of any problems that antitrust legislation might pose.[76] Acquisition would not only reduce earnings in the Bosch Group markedly for some time to come, but also block any major capital expenditure and investment plans in the years ahead. Yet Merkle, seeing this as "the last chance of our becoming a globally important hydraulics manufacturer," pushed ahead with the talks. The expectation was that within three to five years the Vickers European operation could be knocked into shape as well – to the point where good growth and earnings prospects could be counted on. Early in February 1982, a special meeting of the board of management was convened. The opportunities and risks of the acquisition were extensively reviewed, and a decision was made to open purchase negotiations.[77] However, in July 1982 these negotiations fell through – fortunately for Bosch, as it turned out. The move would no doubt have overstretched the company both financially and in terms of available expertise.

Initial conclusions

Looking back over this whole pivotal period of the company's history, it becomes clear that Bosch, compared with other companies (notably automakers and automotive suppliers), emerged relatively unscathed from the "long-drawn-out 1970s" – the crisis-laden decade that saw an explosion in oil prices, recurrent recession, and stagflation. The new Bosch constitution and decentralized organization had proved their worth, coalescing to form a strong, self-assured corporate culture. Leadership methods and financial management had been modernized with the emergence of improved planning and reporting procedures, Bosch bond issues, and annual press conferences to present the financial statements. The company had passed through an upheaval in supplier relations affecting the entire automotive industry to emerge stronger than ever. Bosch did not simply benefit from the advent of electronics and the "environmental-policy revolution" that swept through the sector, but also used its own engineering experience and systems know-how to drive these developments forward. And not least, Bosch mastered the far-reaching changes in manufacturing organization and technology, as well as the automation and enhanced flexibility this involved, without any major tension and conflicts with its workforce. Sales of 1.7 billion German marks in 1960 had by 1983 soared to 14.3 billion German marks, while headcount had grown from 71,000 associates to 110,000. Hans L. Merkle's untiring efforts to anticipate economic trends had brought some success in the years since 1965, although even Bosch had to admit that its track record in this respect was patchy. After all, not even at the Schillerhöhe was there anyone capable of forecasting precisely how economic cycles would play out.

Moreover, toward the end of Merkle's term of office as chairman of the Bosch board of management there were a whole host of steps half taken and problems as yet unsolved. At Blaupunkt, Photokino (the Bosch film-projector and camera division), and other companies in the consumer-electronics sector, at the Spanish FEMSA subsidiary, and in individual product areas in the automotive sector, Bosch was making losses, and it was going to cost hundreds of millions of German marks to put things right. And while internationalization had made substantial progress, most notably with the company's successful return to the U.S. market, the expansion of original-equipment operations entailed considerable risks, especially in the United States. Radical shake-ups and dynamic changes were still pitted against forces of continuity and inertia. A look at the way sales were spread over the Bosch business sectors shows little movement between the late 1950s and the early 1980s. In 1958, the automotive sector accounted for some 70 percent of sales. Still almost 60 percent in 1975, the figure was to stay on this level for years to come. The share of the house-hold-appliances business (around 22 percent) likewise remained more or less constant. So there was little question of any reduced dependence on the auto-motive business, particularly if we look more closely at the earnings situation for individual product categories. The statement of income for 1963 showed that 90 percent of total Bosch profit had been earned by automotive electrics, not including injection equipment.[1] Nearly 20 years later, nothing had changed. Merkle's strategy of freeing Bosch from the "dangerous monoculture of the automotive supplier" had failed for the time being. Actually, it had never really taken root in the company at all. Because for as long as it remained customary at Bosch to refer to all product areas lying outside the company's core field of business as "non-automotive" (a practice that managers working in those areas had always found demeaning), nothing *would* change. Such condescension was part of the corporate culture. Bosch was basically a supplier to the auto-motive industry with certain "add-ons" – fringe areas, in other words. In 1981, 15 years after Merkle had proclaimed the principle of "spreading the risk" and elevated diversification to the status of a cornerstone of corporate policy, Bosch was still fundamentally a producer of "diesel pumps, injection nozzles, K-Jetronic systems, and starters." These four products alone, from the two divisions Diesel Systems and Starter Motors and Generators, were responsible for profits of 495.4 million German marks, or 74 percent of total Bosch earnings. The automotive business sector, with its 47 product categories, brought in a total profit of 678.5 million German marks before tax, which, when all was said and done, made it the sole generator of earnings. The "non-automotive" divisions, with their 59 product categories, made a total loss of 9.2 million German marks. Not even the pro rata inclusion of Bosch's household-appliances busi-ness, now organized as BSHG, changes the picture in any way.[2] That was pre-sumably the reason why Merkle drove the company so forcibly into telecom-munications and information technology in 1981–82. Yet despite every insistence to the contrary, this entry into a new market smacks not so much of a deliberate and considered move as of a desperate attempt to break out of a difficult situation. None of these stabs at diversification altered the fact that Bosch was inexorably on the way to becoming the largest and most influential automotive supplier in the world. Its continuing livelihood depended on its innovative strength in this field. However, we must immediately add a qualification. No matter how important engineering achievements and innovation were and are at Bosch, the company owes its special position in the global marketplace to its culture. It is only because of this distinctive corporate culture, which Bosch has constantly reinvented and lived by, that the company has been able, over and over again, to scale new peaks of technological achievement.[3] The corporate culture has thus always been a distinctive mixture of transformation and continuity. Bosch at the beginning of the 1980s was neither a foundation-owned company nor an overgrown family-run concern. Nor was it a multinational. As the then human-resources chief Ulrich Mertz put it: "We are a modern, very large industrial enterprise with old-fashioned small-business structures. People may laugh, but that's the way it is."[4]

IV Bosch and the challenges of globalization (1984–2012)

A decade that had brought two oil-price shocks was followed by several years of worldwide economic recovery, accompanied and encouraged by a sales boom in the automotive industry. At Bosch, this marked the start of a fresh phase of growth. But there were further economic and structural crises to follow. In the two particularly recessionary years of 1993 and 2001, German industry as a whole had to battle with declining competitiveness and some considerable collapses in earnings. Bosch, too, forfeited much of its special status at this time, becoming increasingly mired in structural and economic problems of a general nature. Recession and restructuring, weak earnings, debates about Germany's future as an industrial location, increased relocation of manufacturing facilities, the search for new growth opportunities, the ceaseless struggle with loss-making product categories – all these things characterized the daily round of business at Bosch. And there was a further problem to deal with. Weak growth and earnings were no longer restricted solely to its non-automotive businesses. Now, as a result of globalization, Bosch's core automotive supply business faced substantial problems.

Three distinguished entrepreneurs left their mark on Bosch during these difficult years of adjustment and renewal: Marcus Bierich, Hermann Scholl, and Franz Fehrenbach. Each had a different leadership style, yet as regards corporate policy and the culture of the company all three stood in many ways for continuity. They also all faced periods of recession that, albeit of varying length, ran particularly deep. Bierich had to deal with the fierce disputes with works councils and workforce that accompanied the recession of 1993 – disputes which both sides experienced as traumatic. Scholl faced the challenge of the rapid collapse of the world economy in 2000 and 2001, following a stock-market crash and terrorist attacks. And in 2008 and 2009, Fehrenbach had to steer the company through the financial and economic crisis following the failure of Lehman Brothers. These challenges and the concomitant changes in the competitive environment were central to the corporate-policy activities of all three men. But it was above all Bierich and Scholl who saw themselves as operating in a "post-Merkle phase." During this period, which lasted well into the 1990s, the chairman "emeritus" of the board of management continued to pull levers in the background, casting a long and persistent shadow over everyday business operations and decisions. His two successors were plagued by the irksome and thankless task of repeatedly having to report declining sales, job cuts, and cutbacks in company welfare services, as well as earnings that remained obstinately below expectations and indeed budget. At the same time, they had to steer the Bosch group of companies through the stormy waters of economic fluctuation and structural change, ensuring that they suffered as little fundamental harm as possible. Pursuing the grand strategic lines of internationalization and globalization, stronger external growth, and diversification through acquisition remained the order of the day, but putting them into practice was incomparably harder than it had been in the 1970s and 1980s. Nonetheless, Bosch did much to renew itself in this period. It introduced new leadership and management methods, reshaped its organization, and changed its approach to manufacturing. Not least, it conducted an internal debate about its corporate culture. Much of what Bierich and Scholl planted during these years they had to let others harvest. In the end, the process of reflecting on the corporate culture that had shaped Bosch, while at the same time promoting a cultural change designed to kick-start modernization, resulted in a Bosch-specific response to fresh challenges. Ultimately, once these years of upheaval were over, Bosch had regained much of its special status, which is evident in many different respects.

1 Radical change and continuity in the shadow of economic turbulence (1984–1993)

"Bosch is unstoppable":
the dynamics of growth and a new leadership culture

When Marcus Bierich took office as the new chair of the Bosch board of management in July 1984, the second oil-price shock was already a thing of the past. The world economy had taken a turn for the better. The automotive industry was setting new sales records, and profits at Bosch were rising accordingly. The 1983 sales figure, 16 billion German marks, shot up to 31.8 billion by 1990. Sales thus virtually doubled in only seven years. Bierich, who had studied mathematics and philosophy, was 58 years old at the time of his appointment, so there was no real change of generation at the top of the company. But he brought with him years of management experience as head of finance at Mannesmann and at Allianz. Above all, Bierich already knew Bosch well, having been a member of the RBIK shareholder group (the company's supreme governing and decision-making body) since 1978. For this reason, the new chair of the board of management, who like his predecessor became known as F1 [*Führungskreis 1*] for short, made no changes in the distribution of powers. There were twelve board members – seven full members and five members with full power of attorney, or deputy members. They included such long-serving Bosch executives as Paul Stein, who as F2 was in charge of legal and tax affairs (and whose place was taken by Karl Gutbrod in 1987), Peter Rose, responsible as F3 for human resources and social services, and Kurt Schips (F6), coordinator for the communications technology division. But above all, Bierich knew that the core area of automotive engineering and supply, with its ten individual operational divisions, was in the best possible hands with the experienced executives Konrad Eckert and Hermann Scholl. Nor, for the present, did Bierich make any changes in corporate organization, which had by now become a complex affair. Unlike most of the country's major companies, Bosch had no management levels equivalent to business sectors. Instead, it had a jumble of 24 divisions located in Germany and 44 regional subsidiaries located worldwide. This was held together, after a fashion, by a bewilderingly decentralized network of relations and responsibilities, and controlled and

Marcus Bierich (1984)

steered by monthly "executive information meetings" [*Führungsinformations-sitzungen* or FIS], as they were called.

Bierich did, however, introduce a new management culture at Bosch. Whereas Merkle was hardly ever seen in person, not even by people working at corporate HQ, Bierich cultivated a visible presence. He made a habit of meeting his colleagues at the Schillerhöhe face to face.[1] Bierich was approachable – and as some of his close associates were soon saying, this was a "veritable surge of motivation."[2] His relaxed conversational manner was something that colleagues at Bosch, often unnerved by the authoritarian atmosphere of the Merkle years, had first to get used to. Unlike Merkle, Bierich placed greater faith in dialogue than in memos and "top-down" directives. So in the autumn of 1984, prior to the half-yearly "business policy briefing" [*Geschäftspolitische Information* or GPI], colleagues on the Bosch board and other members of senior management were stunned to have Bierich ask them, by way of preparation for his speech about business-policy objectives, for proposals as to issues and points to be addressed. The new F1 saw himself less as a chairman presiding over his board-member colleagues than as a facilitator fielding their views. A quite different kind of internal communication grew to be the norm at Bosch – the chief was no longer a patriarch, but instead a team player. This was true not only at board level, but also in dealings between the board on the one hand and other tiers of senior executives on the other. The full significance of the change became apparent in the fall of 1985, when the first "seminar for executive management" [*LD-Seminar*] was held. Granted, with the said "executive information meetings," "business policy briefings," and year-end conferences there were already sessions at which senior Bosch executives met. But as Bierich explained in his inaugural speech at the seminar, "we lack an occasion when, away from the everyday world of work, we can sit down together and have time for personal exchanges as well as for discussions of higher matters."[3] Having laid down the principles governing future Bosch corporate policy, Bierich threw proceedings open to the floor – something that in Merkle's day would have been unthinkable.

The very way in which corporate policy was defined ("Who formulates it and who oversees it? With whom is it discussed?") as well as the terms in which the company's objectives were set out ("serving our customers but also our associates and the wider community, including our duty to protect the environment") differed markedly from things that Bosch managers had previously heard from the board. Moreover, Bierich proclaimed a change in corporate planning. Previously, Bosch had used a planning process that covered one year plus two preview years. It was derived from the business plans of individual units, but the findings were never fed back to the divisions. "That means we do not have any platform for a joint discussion of our corporate objectives and of how each division with its individual targets fits in to the overall targets of the group."[4] From now on, that would be changing in favor of a longer-term planning horizon. First, Bierich presented a detailed review of the period 1972 to 1985. He coupled this with statements taking stock of the present situation and looking forward to the next financial year, 1986. The company's sales and earnings, broken down by region, operating area, product category, and relevant growth and profit criteria, were all universally satisfactory. There were fluctuations, of course. For instance, return on sales varied between 5 and 11 percent, depending on product group. Nonetheless, as Bierich summed up, "our objective for the future must be to emulate the positive developments of the past. We wish to remain an enterprise characterized by growth. However, in line with what has long been our corporate policy, size alone is not what we are after. Our objectives are performance and competitiveness."[5]

So the fundamental thrust of corporate policy did not change under Bierich. The new F1 placed his faith in continuity. Corporate policy was still about extending business operations into countries outside Germany and into regions outside Europe (internationalization), creating an international manufacturing and development network (globalization), developing new product areas (notably in capital goods and communications technology), cutting costs, and improving quality. With respect to business fields, this meant continuing the shift of emphasis within the company's core activities already started or proposed by Merkle. "Our position as a leading supplier of automotive original equipment," Bierich told the LD-Seminar, "may be at even greater risk in the future than was the case in the past. There are three reasons for this. First, our greatest rival Nippondenso is plainly growing faster than we are. There is every indication that we must adjust to a more aggressive approach in our main markets in the U.S. and Europe. Nippondenso's strength lies in cost and quality advantages. Second, we must expect new competitors to emerge from the electronics industry. Those competitors have their own electronics expertise, and our customers in the automotive industry are contributing to that development, partly for reasons of basic purchasing strategy. Finally, we can assume that the automotive industry will step up its current efforts to extend backward vertical integration. In Germany, this particularly applies to Daimler-Benz and VW with their recently acquired subsidiaries. But it is also true of GM and Ford, which are traditionally self-sufficient."[6] The great strategic objective of Bosch corporate policy was therefore to balance the product portfolio in a way that spread risk – which meant nurturing other areas of activity that could together rival automotive technology in terms of market attractiveness, competitive position, and volume of sales. "So it is a question of building up and strengthening our communications technology and capital goods businesses in such a way that together they match automotive in volume and positioning."[7] For Bierich, too, the overriding principle of Bosch corporate and finance policy was preserving independence, which meant "covering our total capital requirement by means of internal funding."[8] It therefore looked as if investment would be flowing less into the automotive sector in the future and (while still respecting the company's traditionally strict financial policy) more into restructuring the various areas of operations and efficient portfolio management. Here Bierich had valuable experience to contribute from his time at Mannesmann.

In mid-October 1985, Bierich gave *Industriemagazin* his first interview as the new Bosch CEO. The Stuttgart company's new culture of openness and communication was now displayed to the outside world. "Bosch is unstoppable," the title read, referring not only to the company's continued growth but also to the new dynamism driving it forward.[9] The boom undoubtedly made Bierich's early years as F1 easier. When in 1985 he presented the results of the first financial year of his term of office, he could report above-average growth rates in all business areas – but mainly in automotive technology. In the following years, too, percentage growth rates in this area at times reached double figures, on the back of record sales of the ABS antilock braking system and of diesel and gasoline injection systems. The picture was one of tumultuous growth, with a veritable explosion of profits in 1984 (showing a surplus for the year of 446 million German marks, compared with 242 million in the year

Marcus Bierich and Hans L. Merkle (1986)

before) and again in 1987 (surplus for the year: 825 million German marks).[10] Bosch was more successful than ever before. "Marcus Bierich gets Bosch moving," ran a headline in *Die Welt* in early July 1988. The occasion was the annual press conference, and the newspaper drew attention to a livelier pace of investment.[11] Moreover, the Bosch chief utilized the opportunity to plunge into the political debate about Germany's competitiveness as a manufacturing location. With labor costs of 32.67 German marks an hour (as compared to 5.32 German marks in Portugal, for instance), Bierich made no secret of the fact that the Federal Republic of Germany, despite large-scale series production and stringent rationalization, was no longer competitive. Bosch would therefore increasingly have simple items produced outside Germany, relocating certain assembly lines to countries where labor was less costly.[12] The company redoubled its efforts to globalize its manufacturing network. The new strategy had in part been prompted by the experience of labor struggles at the Stuttgart plants in May and June 1984, which had led to difficulties and interruptions of supply to certain major original-equipment customers. "For the purpose of enhancing security of supply," the board of management therefore resolved that Bosch would create up to 4,500 jobs outside Germany in the second half of 1984.[13]

Over the course of 1987, Bierich set about restructuring the organization of the Bosch Group, which had remained largely untouched for more than two decades. Above the operational areas and divisions, four new business sectors were created. These were: firstly, Automotive Equipment (with divisions responsible for ABS, braking, and displays; automotive lighting; gasoline injection and ignition; wipers and motors; diesel injection; semiconductors and electronic control units; starters and generators; and automotive aftermarket); secondly, Communications Technology (with the Electronics division as well as the subsidiary companies Blaupunkt, Telenorma, ANT Nachrichtentechnik GmbH, Teldix, and BTS); thirdly, Consumer Goods (with the Power Tools division as well as the subsidiary companies Bosch und Siemens Hausgeräte GmbH, Junkers, and Feierabend GmbH); and, finally, Capital Goods (with the divisions Industrial Equipment, Packaging Machinery, Plastics and Metal Products, and Hydraulics and Pneumatics). Bierich tackled another necessary task in rejuvenating the board of management. On July 1, 1990, he made a number of new appointments, including promoting Clemens Börsig (then 41 years of age and already heading the corporate department for business administration) to sit with his elders. And greater use was made of management consultants such as McKinsey to support both operational and strategic measures.

In 1988, 1989, and (bolstered by the exceptional upturn that followed German reunification) again in 1990, Bosch enjoyed above-average sales and earnings. Yet dark clouds were gathering on the economic horizon. For instance, the steady rise of the German mark against the U.S. dollar began to cause problems. Also, in a Bosch-dominated market for automotive electrics, the company's competitor Siemens sounded the attack in the second half of the 1980s and met the company head-on. Only with difficulty had Bierich prevented the company's Munich rival from taking over Pierburg, Germany's second-largest producer of carburetors. In the spring of 1988, however, Siemens did acquire the majority holding in the U.S. automotive supplier Bendix Electronics. This move catapulted Siemens into the top league of automotive electronics companies, where it now ranked third after Bosch and Nippondenso.[14] Even before this takeover, Bierich had warned of difficulties ahead. In his examination of future corporate policy at the GPI meeting of December 1987, he had spoken not only of mounting uncertainties facing the world economy (the stock-market crash in the autumn of that year had seemed almost to announce such developments). He had also warned of "serious structural shifts in the international automotive industry" threatening the profit situation of Bosch's original-equipment customers and hence also the company's own earning opportunities.[15] The aggressive ascent of Japanese and Korean automakers in the global market coincided with the downturn in the economic cycle governing the automotive industry (now reckoned at five years). As a result, the Bosch board of management found itself facing the combined effect of both cyclical and structural problems. Together, these problems called for a review of previous economic planning at Bosch, coupled with the adoption of long-term adjustment measures. That was clear at a glance, not least from the unmistakable fact that the company's pace of growth was weakening. There were fluctuations, but it was declining from year to year. Where sales had once grown 15 percent year on year, by 1993 this figure was negative, at minus 5.3 percent. This was the first drop in sales since 1967, and marked a new low.

It was Bosch's core field of business, automotive technology, that was worst hit by this weak growth. Between 1989 and 1993, this business sector had to endure a five-year stagnation phase, with annual sales averaging 15.5 billion German marks. Even so, top managers in the sector oozed a customary self-confidence. In April 1987, for example, Hansjörg Manger, member of the board of management, addressed the supervisory board at Bosch on the subject of "international developments in the automotive industry and their repercussions for [Bosch]." There, he referred to the growing trend (regardless of the number of vehicles produced) for ever-higher densities of equipment with complex systems designed to improve what Bosch called the "3S" – *Sicherheit* [safety], *Sauberkeit* [cleanliness], and *Sparsamkeit* [economy]. In other words, "over recent years our share of what goes into automotive products has gone up very steeply."[16]

As ever, Bosch was well ahead of the competition, able repeatedly to offer solutions to complex problems in particularly sensitive areas of automotive engineering. Exceptional process engineering, a wide range of technological expertise, and close cooperation with automakers (members of the Bosch board of management traditionally sat on the supervisory boards of Daimler-Benz [Bierich], VW [Merkle], and Porsche [Eckert]) ensured that Bosch had a clear advantage. For the time being, nobody at Bosch saw the situation changing, particularly since with mobile communications, electronic brake control systems, and electric power steering the company had promising new products and design ideas in the development pipeline. At the end of June 1989, reporting to the supervisory board on "past achievements and future tasks in the automotive sector," Eckert took much the same line. Bosch, he said, was particularly experienced at combining electrical, electronic, precision-engineering, hydraulic, and pneumatic technologies. This gave it a competitive edge, even if electronic components were gaining in significance.[17] Systems engineering too, of which Bosch had a better grasp than its rivals, was becoming increasingly important. So from an engineering viewpoint Bosch expected no threat. On the contrary, the outlook appeared to be excellent.

Fig. 8 Development of sales in the Bosch Group (1983–93): sales in millions of German marks (*left*) and as a percentage year-on-year change (*right*)

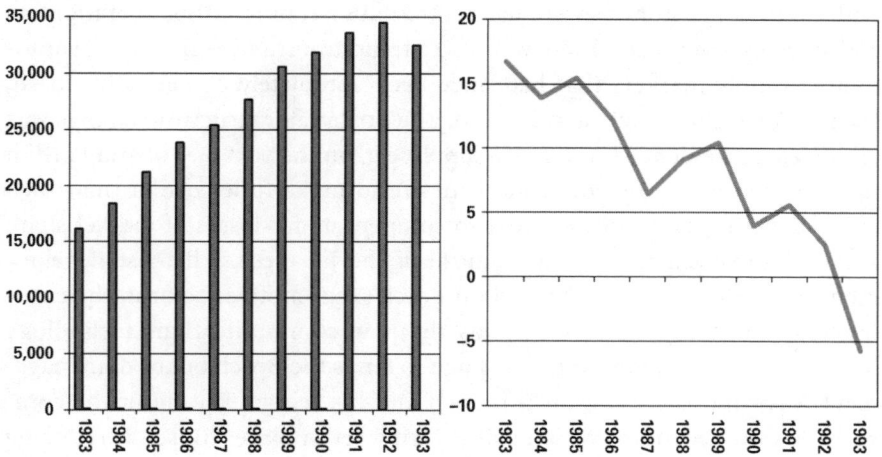

Source: Compiled and calculated from figures in annual reports

As late as the summer of 1990, Bosch managers in the automotive divisions continued to regard the prospects of their business sector as rosy. For them, product planning geared to market requirements (in part initiated by Bosch, ahead of the market, but in part lent extra impetus by such external developments as emissions legislation and safety-consciousness) was the key to success, and had been for 20 years now.[18] Equipment for eco-friendly automotive powertrain systems was still a major growth area. Moreover, the potential of safety technology based on systems such as ABS and the TCS traction control system, chassis systems control, four-wheel drive, and automatic vehicle dynamics control was by no means exhausted. However, it was not so much engineering as other factors (quality, price, customer behavior) that were going to weigh far more heavily in years to come. In other words, managers in the automotive sector at Bosch were slow to recognize the radical changes that had taken place in markets and customer expectations. "In previous years," Eckert had said in April 1987, "most of our automotive customers were German companies that often worked with Bosch in an enviably uncomplicated way. Important customers invested all over the world and Bosch followed, all over the world."[19] The first major (European) challenges posed to Bosch automotive managers came from French, Swedish, and Italian original-equipment customers – later from U.S. automakers as well. The problem now looming came from aggressive international investments by

Japanese and Korean automakers, with whom such managers would be forced to do business in the future. At the same time, their major German and European customers were using international purchasing operations as a way of reducing costs. There was also a trend toward liberalization of auto-motive-supply markets that had once been completely or partially closed, such as Australia, Brazil, and Mexico. The final major structural change was an increased tendency toward self-supply, e.g. on the part of GM and Ford in the U.S., motivated by automakers' desire to make fuller use of their own manufacturing capacities in order to compensate for losses of market share and declining vehicle sales over those of the Japanese. All these develop-ments were to have a huge impact on Bosch's automotive sector in the ensu-ing years. Initially, however, it was the new communications technology business sector that moved center stage so far as the Bosch board of manage-ment was concerned; not until Bierich and his reorganization of the com-pany was the second pillar of business truly set in place. "Bosch is reducing its dependence on the automobile," ran the strategic message (yet again) that the company now promoted in its public relations work.

When the Berlin Wall came down on November 9, 1989, Bosch did not particularly see the event as offering fresh business opportunities. Signifi-cantly, the *Bosch-Zünder* began its next issue with an article about the com-pany's involvement in France. Only on page 4 was there an article by Adolf Ahnefeld, the company's chief economist, about growth opportunities in East Germany and other Comecon countries.[20] Over the following months, to meet existing demand in East Germany, agreements were signed with local companies and licenses granted. The board did not expect formal re-unification. Its members assumed that there would still be a customs barrier between the two parts of the country and that Bosch would need to set up its entire production program in East Germany as well if it was to retain a pres-ence in that market.[21] That was hardly a lucrative prospect. After the first free election to the *Volkskammer* (the East German parliament) on March 18, 1990, Bosch had to rethink its plans. Various major customers, including Daimler-Benz and VW, were urging it to follow them into East Germany with a joint venture.[22] On the day after the election, the Bosch board of man-agement met to discuss "East Germany: a location for automotive produc-tion." For "reasons of market strategy," a presence in East Germany was now deemed necessary.[23] In conjunction with a local partner, a new manufactur-ing facility for headlights, wipers, and starters was to be set up in the Eise-nach region.[24] Bosch had a particular partner in mind. It was the state-owned combine Fahrzeugelektrik Ruhla. This headlight specialist had already shown great interest in cooperating with Bosch and signed a supply agreement with VW before the wall came down. A joint-venture agreement with Fahrzeugelektrik Ruhla was rapidly concluded. However, when reunification came shortly thereafter, joint-venture companies in the former East Germany were robbed of their strategic significance. Bosch could now supply all products direct from its plants in the west to the new *Länder* in the east. It nonetheless did build a new plant in Eisenach, and its ANT subsidiary acquired radio-link equipment production from Robotron Telekom GmbH, based in Radeberg. The Eisenach plant, as Hermann Scholl recalled, was established "more as a result of patriotic feeling than from any economic necessity."[25] It turned out to be a success story nonetheless, and today Robert Bosch Fahrzeugelektrik Eisenach GmbH is the Bosch Group's lead plant for a number of devices, including low-pressure sensors.

From ray of hope to quagmire:
development of the communications technology business

From the time of Marcus Bierich's appointment as chairman of the board of management, the communications technology business underwent massive expansion with the aid of substantial investment and continuous reorganization. During this time, Bosch was constantly on the lookout for strategic alliances and suitable partners. Initially, the board's hopes lay in a close strategic partnership with Mannesmann. At the end of 1984, the two companies' combined activities in information and communications technology amounted to seven companies and divisions, with total sales of 4.7 billion German marks and a headcount of nearly 37,000. These companies ranged from Telefonbau & Normalzeit (TN), Kienzle Apparate GmbH, and ANT Nachrichtentechnik GmbH, across the two Bosch divisions of Electronics and TV sets, to Blaupunkt and Teldix GmbH. However, it was not only their business activities that were somewhat fragmented, but also their ownership structure. At TN, Bosch held some 30 percent of the shares but controlled 51 percent of voting rights, while at ANT Bosch and Mannesmann each owned 41 percent of the equity capital, with Allianz holding the remaining 18 percent. And at Blaupunkt, Siemens was indirectly involved through the 25 percent holding that BSHG owned in that company. The other companies and divisions were wholly owned by either Mannesmann or Bosch. When in December 1984, after many joint meetings, the Bosch and Mannesmann "telecommunications consortium" strategy commission presented its findings, it was clear that the two companies were in agreement so far as the key strands of future developments were concerned. In the wake of the digitalization of transmission and switching technology, an international market for integrated information and telecommunications technology was rapidly emerging. On the one hand, this market offered above-average growth opportunities. On the other, it was characterized by tough international competition.[26] However, there was substantial disagreement as to how the two companies' activities should be pooled and organized. The Bosch proposal was to gradually merge – in three separate phases – the particularly close operational spheres of TN and Kienzle on the one hand and ANT, the Bosch electronics division, and Teldix on the other. The two companies thus created would be run under the umbrella of a joint marketing and holding company. The Mannesmann plan provided for the immediate establishment of a single company with three business sectors.

At the same time, both Bosch and Mannesmann were putting out feelers for other strategic partners. In January 1985, for instance, Bierich asked the McKinsey consultancy to make a thorough study of the telecommunications business at Bosch. McKinsey was to examine two options, the first being expansion (say, by introducing products relating to office automation or office communications), and the second being the possibility of further strategic partnerships and acquisitions – jointly with the Allianz Group.[27] Robert Bosch GmbH (the consultant was briefed) "wishes in the medium or long term to complement its automotive-supply business by developing its communications-technology business internationally. It wants to give this business an enduring foundation by moving into office automation [...]. [Bosch] is setting its sights high here: second place after Siemens in the German telecoms business and a strong international presence in telecoms and office automation."[28] The company already had its eye set on a whole series of potential investments and alliances: Kienzle, Nixdorf, Philips, ITT/SEL, AT&T, DEC, Wang, and other U.S. companies. It was particularly keen to have the "RB/Nixdorf model" considered, and in the ensuing weeks and months there were indeed intensive talks and negotiations with Heinz Nixdorf, whose own attitude was open-minded.[29] However, these plans fell through as early as May 1985 (in the end, most of the Nixdorf ordinary shares were acquired by Siemens on October 1, 1990). For the rest of the 1980s, the merry-go-round of potential strategic partnerships and communications technology alliances went on spinning, with more and more interested parties climbing aboard – not only Bosch and Philips but also Siemens, IBM, ITT, Ericsson, and Olivetti. At the same time, Bosch considered taking over Kienzle and/or Triumph-Adler.[30] Moreover, in the autumn of 1986, the emergence of a new European communications giant, Eurotel, caused a stir. Eurotel grew out of the merger between the French company CGE and the Stuttgart-based company Standard Electric Lorenz (SEL), which had been sold by the crisis-plagued ITT group. A veritable love-tussle over an additional interest in Eurotel of some 25 percent began, involving Siemens, Daimler-Benz, Mannesmann, and Bosch. Siemens and Bosch in particular had repeatedly tried – and failed – to prise SEL out of the ITT group of companies. However, none of these potentially promising openings produced any tangible results for Bosch. But time was increasingly running out. New major players were now jockeying for position in the promising growth market of communications technology. As early as May 1985, managers in Stuttgart had realized that "Bosch's telecoms business [is] too small as it stands to have any long-term chance of holding its own against the large integrated enterprises and consortia presently emerging."[31]

Nonetheless, the Bosch board of management persisted with the internal expansion and engineering and organizational reinforcement of its existing activities in the communications business. At Blaupunkt, for instance, intensive work began in the early 1980s on prototypes in three areas: vehicle navigation (with the market launch of the "TravelPilot" planned for the end of 1988), the integration of CDs into car radios, and the use of key codes to prevent theft. In late 1985, it also entered an alliance with Grundig to produce color TVs and car radios, and applied to the antitrust authorities for approval. Blaupunkt further embarked on a comprehensive restructuring of its manufacturing operations. Production of color TVs was phased out and that of car radios pooled in the Hildesheim plant, while Blaupunkt's "telecommunications products" unit (monitors, displays, satellite receivers, pay-TV, BTX systems, and other information and video systems) underwent expansion. But even with this reorganization and a reduction of the workforce, Blaupunkt found itself deep in the red again. In the autumn of 1987, Bosch and Mannesmann agreed to end their alliance, and for a "high price" Bosch bought the remaining roughly 41 percent of shares in ANT Nachrichtentechnik GmbH. As Bierich explained to the November RBIK meeting, the purchase gave Bosch the industrial leadership as well as full freedom of action in restructuring its telecommunications interests. It also pushed sales in telecommunications up to nearly 6 billion German marks – a sales volume that made its activities in this area interesting for international alliances.[32]

At TN, too, Bosch was now sole shareholder, so that at last operations, including marketing and R&D, could be meaningfully allocated to individual units (for instance, Teldix became part of TN). On January 1, 1988, mobile communications (which at Bosch had for some time meant anything to do with communications technology in and around the automobile, i. e., car radios, systems for positioning, navigation, and driver information, taxi radios, and car telephones) was established as a separate division, known as MC. In essence, the new division amalgamated Blaupunkt and what had been the electronics division. Given its interface function between automotive and communications technology, it was deemed particularly important.[33] Actually, on closer examination it was mostly a mere lumping together of existing operations in the sense of "old wine in a new bottle."[34] When Bierich addressed Bosch management at the GPI meeting just before Christmas 1987, he openly admitted that the establishment and development of the mobile communications division "will place great demands on our ability to innovate and to invest. We shall need to make major preparations in terms of technologies, products, and markets and survive a long dry period before any profitable business emerges here. In doing so, we must be aware of the risks involved and anticipate setbacks."[35]

On July 1, 1989, following further reorganization of the still somewhat unwieldy business units and divisions, Bierich finally set up a business sector C (Communications Technology), also known as "Bosch Telecom." Into this sector, Bosch crammed all its multifarious communications-technology operations (which now included an 80 percent holding in the leading French producer of private communications systems, Jeumont Schneider Telecom S. A.). Three core operating areas, now constituted as separate divisions, made up the new business sector: first, Mobile Communications Technology (MC), with (as we have seen) the business units mobile radio, broadband communications, medical technology, vehicle antennas as well as traffic guidance and information systems, and, finally, car radio and consumer electronics (this division accounted for the lion's share of total C sales, namely some 42 percent); second, the new Private Communications Technology division (TN) with Telenorma at its heart and the business areas private communications systems, information systems, and security systems (together accounting for some 34 percent of sales); and third, Public Communications Technology (AN), in which the activities of ANT were pooled, i. e., multiplex technology, microwave radio, telecommunications cabling, space and satellite technology, public transmission technology, and navigation devices for land, air, and sea transport (the latter being the defense operations of the former Teldix), and where 24 percent of C sales were generated.[36]

At last, some structural discipline had been brought into Bosch's wide range of communications technology operations. Individual business units could now be more intelligently allocated, and over the longer term the aim was to bring traditionally independent companies together under common leadership and a uniform nomenclature within the Bosch Group. Further benefits were "the support for a multi-brand policy through association with Bosch Telecom" and "the creation of conditions that would allow synergies with other areas of activity at Bosch."[37] However, conferring independence on the C business, with or without partners (something that had been successfully practiced at BSHG, for instance), was more than they dared to undertake at the Schillerhöhe. And coordinating all three divisions was a truly Herculean task, particularly given the dominance of the automotive business sector. Communications technology was still part of the "non-automotive world" at Bosch and, like those responsible for Blaupunkt back in the 1970s, its chief executive on the 12-person board of management sat virtually alone, facing the five executives from automotive. At the Schillerhöhe, automotive "ruled." Granted, the new business sector was headed by Kurt Schips, 61, a member of the enlarged board since January 1972 and very much an old hand at Bosch. He had joined the company in 1952 as an engineer in the patents department. In the 1960s, he had become technical director of what was then Bosch Elektronik und Photokino GmbH. And he had then been placed in charge of all patents and licensing affairs at Bosch. But managing the new C business sector posed its own challenges, and they were daunting. In Germany, Europe, and all over the world communications markets were emerging, and the potential players in those markets were jockeying for position. Governments were gradually deregulating mobile communications, glass-fiber and ISDN technologies were revolutionizing data transfer, and integrated, PC-based workplace and office-communications systems were coming onto the scene. But none of this made its way into business policy briefings or supervisory-board meetings. Instead, audiences were treated to generalized descriptions of work in the various (nearly two dozen of them) fields of operation, and were showered with invariably optimistic forecasts.[38] In many areas of communications and information technology, Schips said, Bosch had already grown large enough to survive in an increasingly international marketplace. And no other area would show such potential for growth in the years to come. In Germany, according to Schips, Bosch had already achieved a leading market position, second only to Siemens. Schips's strategic plan was all about expanding the business in Europe, opening up other new fields of business, and focusing on the development of services. No in-depth analysis of competitive structures, no careful appraisal of differing speeds or specific patterns of innovation in the industry, no detailed estimate of profit potential and market opportunities – none of this was ever touched on.

At the same time, there was nothing in the organizational, financial, or staffing structure of the new C business sector (so highly prized as Bosch's "second pillar") to suggest that it would be a success story. The board of man-

agement hesitated far too long before reorganizing its structures and investing serious money. The solutions proposed by Mannesmann or Nixdorf (for
an independently trading, jointly managed subsidiary) would undoubtedly
have had better luck. But finding someone to direct the operational and strategic interests of such a company would have required the courage to bring
in a well-known managerial figure from outside – a leader with experience of
the international communications industry.[39] As it was, when Schips retired
from the board on age grounds at the end of June 1989, he was replaced by
another engineer from within the company. Herbert Weber, who had come
to Bosch from ANT/AEG in 1984, was now appointed chief executive for the
communications sector. Aged 55, the new board member was from the outset
intended to be an interim manager only, to serve until June 1994. The reason
given said it all: restructuring was imminent, and "this sector is shrinking,
not just in size but in its need for leadership."[40] And later on, the practice of
clinging to individually attractive technologies and engineering products
such as cellular telephones was to further delay a swift exit from communications technology. In the summer of 1988, as a key player in the new field of
information and communications, Bosch and a consortium that the company had formed with Philips had bid successfully for a GSM cellular network license. And in January 1989, in partnership with Allianz, it planned to
establish a GSM network-operating company, not least in order to be able to
shoulder the requisite investment costs estimated at 2.8 billion German
marks.[41]

Outwardly, therefore, everything seemed to be developing successfully.
In March 1991, at a CeBIT press conference in Hanover, Herbert Weber reported increased sales (7.3 billion German marks), a growing workforce
(40,700 associates), and above all a massive increase in capital expenditure.
The latter totaled nearly a billion German marks in 1990, including 625 million German marks for R&D at Bosch Telecom alone.[42] With the establishment of communications infrastructure in the new *Bundesländer* of former
East Germany as well as card telephones for the Post Office and the new in-
tercity express trains, business in Germany was booming. And outside Germany as well, developments looked promising. Bosch was setting up a new
telephone network in Thailand, ANT was supplying Egyptian Railways with
a modern, solar-powered telecommunications system, and Bosch was supplying the Swiss Post Office with digital splitters to serve increased numbers
of subscribers. For Weber, it was clear that Bosch Telecom was going to be
improving its market position mightily. New strategic considerations about
international alliances or acquisitions were intended to contribute to this
expansion. In June 1991, for instance, at a presentation at the Schillerhöhe,

the Morgan Stanley investment bank set out some ideas regarding partnerships between Bosch on the one hand and Canada's Northern Telecom (NT) or Sweden's Ericsson on the other. A note in the archives reads: "Owing to its engineering expertise, NT is undoubtedly the preferred option. In the case of Ericsson, it is doubtful whether it can survive in the top group of telecommunications providers for long."[43] In many respects, the remark speaks volumes about how Bosch saw others at the time, as well as how it saw itself. At around the same time, the company contemplated a joint communications-technology venture with Philips. Talks were also held with General Electric regarding possible collaboration in the area of mobile telephony. And in March 1990, negotiations with another Canadian company, Novatel Communications Ltd., concerning a nearly 150-million-mark deal for a 50 percent shareholding almost reached the signing stage.[44] However, the deal never materialized.

As a result, despite all the company's activity in the communications technology field (activity that stretched back more than ten years, and that had been transformed many times since its beginnings in information technology and consumer electronics), the impression deepened that this whole business sector was still half-baked. Not only in the public eye but also in the eyes of its own associates, the C sector seemed to have no clear idea of where it was heading. Individual units coexisted, with little sense of belonging to a whole. Constant reorganization in an increasingly complex market environment brought growing risks. And with the product structure remaining heterogeneous, R&D costs soared without being focused. Meanwhile, the key question remained unanswered: what was the core technology around which the sector was to evolve in the future?

Looking ahead, let us finish telling the story of the communications technology sector at Bosch in this present chapter, even though the farewell dragged on beyond 2000, well into the chairmanship of Hermann Scholl, Bierich's successor at the head of the Bosch board of management. The years up until 1992 saw continuous growth, but this was comparatively weak given the low level from which it started. Between 1983 and 1992, total sales in the C sector nearly doubled – from 4.5 billion German marks to something over 8 billion German marks. But then, in the mid-1990s, came the collapse. With a loss of 286 million German marks in 1995, the sector became the biggest loss-maker in the Bosch Group.

Back in July 1993, there had once again been a change in the management of the sector. Herbert Weber had been replaced by Friedrich Schiefer, who had also been made the new deputy chair of the board of management. Schiefer had worked for McKinsey before switching careers and joining the Munich-

Fig. 9 Sales and development of sales in the communications technology business sector (1983–99): Sales in billions of German marks (*left*) and as a percentage year-on-year change (*right*)

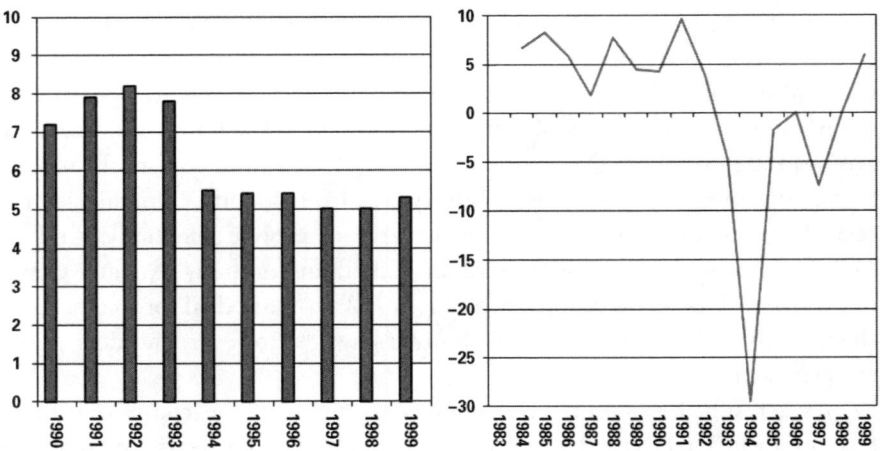

Source: Compiled and calculated from figures given in annual reports

based insurance company Allianz. There he rose rapidly to become financial director and right-hand man to the then head of Allianz, Wolfgang Schieren. He subsequently moved to Bosch, where in January 1992 he was appointed to the board and was initially responsible for the company's North American business. Schiefer's appointment to the C business sector meant that one of Germany's most capable managers of the day was taking over this difficult area. Yet he too was primarily a finance specialist, and so lacked the necessary market know-how and engineering experience. With great élan, Schiefer immediately set about shaking up communications technology at Bosch, working at great speed and implementing a reorganization policy that bore the McKinsey stamp. His goal, he told the RBIK shareholders in November 1994, was a "fundamental reorientation," one of his objectives being to restore the sector's profitability. "What we must do," he said, "is build on our engineering strengths, boost sales in product segments that can be expanded, eliminate product weaknesses in individual segments, and intensify our business efforts internationally. At the same time, costs must be cut in a way that will last [...]. To place the C sector on a solid footing, sales must be doubled to reach 10 billion German marks by the year 2000."[45] Or again, speaking to the supervisory board: "We need to become larger. [The sector] has to grow from being a national systems provider to being a global provider of products and

From left: Friedrich Schiefer, Marcus Bierich, Hermann Scholl (1993)

subsystems [...] In other words, in our core areas we must strive to reach a position comparable to Ericsson's."[46] A further aim was to occupy "a leading position among medium-sized suppliers." At the same time, he deemed it essential to decide which areas no longer fitted the company.[47] "We are offering too broad a range; we need to focus" – which also meant laying off 2,000 associates. Despite this, Schiefer vehemently denied all rumors that Bosch would eventually be withdrawing from communications technology altogether. Here at last was a detailed, no-holds-barred analysis of the communications technology business. Among both supervisory board members and RBIK shareholders, there was general agreement that reorganization and reorientation, though late in coming, were not too late. The situation was, they felt, not unlike the early years in the optical and consumer electronics industries. Nonetheless, the future held "promise" for the C sector.[48]

In addition to pooling ANT's manufacturing operations (which among other things meant shutting down the Schwäbisch Hall plant), certain mobile-communications activities, including car radios, indicator systems, and navigation and driver-information systems, were moved back into the automotive business sector as the new K7 division. The former radio-technology division (based in Berlin and Wolfenbüttel) was spun off from Robert Bosch GmbH and transferred to Telenorma GmbH. In addition, ANT Nachrich-

tentechnik GmbH in Backnang and Bosch Telecom Öffentliche Vermitt-
lungstechnik GmbH in Eschborn were likewise merged with Telenorma
GmbH, which at the same time was renamed Bosch Telecom GmbH. However, these measures meant nothing more than an annual saving of 4 million
German marks in administrative costs. The broad product portfolio and the
variety of markets and technologies with which business sector C had to
struggle remained unchanged. Blaupunkt was still one of the main areas
needing attention, as well as a major loss-maker. In 1992, this subsidiary
recorded the biggest loss in its history – 79 million German marks. Even
between 1985 and 1991, Blaupunkt's losses, which Bosch had to shoulder, had
run into a nine-figure sum. Yet the parent company went on pouring money
into Blaupunkt, investing not only in what were held to be promising technologies but also in manufacturing facilities outside Germany, as well as in
development capacity. Nonetheless, the core business of Blaupunkt was still
the classic car radio. Here, the market was stagnant, R&D costs remained
high, and the prices charged by foreign competitors were low. Despite the
closure of the Herne plant (which made car speaker systems), repeated reorganization plans, and long-term efforts to strengthen competitiveness, there
was a key question that still awaited an answer in the mid-1990s: "Will Bosch
go on supporting Blaupunkt?"[49]

Given this situation, it was especially tragic that on May 31, 1996, only
three years after becoming head of the C sector, Friedrich Schiefer quite unexpectedly died. The figures for 1996 and 1997 were just beginning to show
signs of recovery, as well as some signs (if only minor) that the restructuring
measures that he had introduced were beginning to bear fruit. Private-com-
munications systems (the largest business unit, generating sales of around
1.1 billion German marks) was expected to break even. An appreciably improved result was even forecast for broadband communications, once engineering innovations had been introduced. And other business units, such as
public switching systems and traffic-guidance technology, looked similarly
positive.[50] However, the two largest units, land mobile radio (LMR) and terminal equipment, continued to make major losses. Moreover, an incomplete
product portfolio, aggressive competition, and an absence of digital technology meant that sales and market share were on the wane. The mobile-tele-
phone business was heavily dependent on outside suppliers, given the low
level of in-house production. Consequently, Bosch now began producing its
own wireless telephones, and likewise considered making mobile telephones
built to GSM standards. However, this would have called for substantial outlay, which communications technology managers at Bosch were reluctant to
underwrite.

Meanwhile, the public and private communications-networks divisions accounted for 66 percent of total sales in the C business sector, and thus the lion's share of business. The high contribution of service functions (assembly and maintenance) as well as rental business meant that the business with private networks stood out radically from other divisions at Bosch.[51] "Future development of the communications technology business sector needs to be monitored carefully. In this connection, consideration must be given both to opportunities for working with third parties in certain areas and to the necessity of cutting loose from individual businesses," runs the summary of the discussion of this problem area at the RBIK meeting of March 20, 1997.[52] Before 1996 was out, the Bosch board of management did indeed make a start on divesting, shutting down, and selling individual product areas and production departments in communications technology. Yet that year alone once again brought an operating loss of between 200 and 250 million German marks. In 1998, the business sector told an unsuspecting management board that there would be a further heavy loss – a new nine-figure record. This disastrous situation served only to accelerate Bosch's long-drawn-out withdrawal from a sphere in which it had once had high hopes. First to go was the consumer-electronics product area (color TVs, video recorders, camcorders) in the K7 division. At the same time, the satellite-networks product area was sold to General Electric. After numerous unsuccessful attempts to turn it around, Teldix GmbH (i. e., Bosch's defense and space arm, which with sales of under 100 million German marks had always constituted a fringe area) had already been sold off to a U.S. defense-technology company in mid-1995. The spring of 1997 saw the sale of a major loss-maker, the LMR or non-public radio networks business unit, to Motorola. This was despite sales of between 350 and 400 million German marks and a workforce that at times topped 2,000.[53] In November 1998, Bosch sold its holding in Signalbau Huber AG, which it had purchased as recently as 1992 for some 100 million German marks, originally to develop its telematics operational field. The sale now netted only 16 million German marks. Finally, the autumn of 1998 saw a dramatic worsening of the situation in the public-networks division. In addition, Bosch had long since begun pulling out of a series of regions because of the considerable upfront investments needed for marketing operations. But now there were signs that "a turnaround of public networks under its own steam will not be possible – at least not for the foreseeable future," as the board of management was forced to admit to the RBIK shareholders.[54] In the private networks division, too, things were going from bad to worse. Neither division had adapted as it should to the increasing globalization of business, to tough price competition, and to a rapidly changing market situation.

Bosch's position in European markets was weak, its market presence beyond Europe insignificant. The core business of the communications technology business sector, with 3.3 billion German marks' worth of sales and some 11,500 associates, thus found itself in deep trouble. In the spring of 1999, a U.S. investment bank was asked to look for buyers.[55]

Not that the competition showed much interest. Only Marconi plc, the British company evolved from GEC, declared its willingness to buy the public networks division. As for the private networks division, not a single industrial investor came forward. Only the U.S. venture-capital company Kohlberg Kravis Roberts & Co. (KKR) made an offer. And it was with difficulty that the two divisions could eventually be sold off in November 1999. In that month, the sole major unit left on Bosch's "for sale" list was terminal equipment, with sales of nearly 1 billion German marks and a workforce of 1,700. As highly in-tegrated semiconductors had become available, the markets for car telephones and mobile telephones had grown very fast – the former since the mid-1980s, the latter since the early 1990s. In each case, however, Bosch had failed to gain a foothold by developing and manufacturing its own devices. In the meantime, Nokia had conquered both, with sales of 35 million devices. Bosch, with only 3.2 million devices sold and a market share of 2.5 percent, was fighting a losing battle. Only shortly before, the Stuttgart company had invested heavily in building a new plant in Denmark. Clearly, the board of management found it particularly hard to part company with its mobile telephone business and the revolutionary innovation it stood for in communications technology. The buyer eventually found this time, in the spring of 2000, was Siemens.[56]

When the board gave a "state of play" report to the RBIK meeting about the winding-up and reorientation of the communications technology busi-ness sector at the end of November 2000, all that remained of what had once (after automotive) been the second-largest sector at Bosch were a few rudi-mentary business units: space technology, broadband networks, and security systems. After very nearly 20 years, Bosch's excursion into communications technology had finally met its end. With it, another dream died – that of a business sector that would at some time in the future equal automotive. From the vantage point of the present, the memory of this development may well still cause pain. For a historian to analyze it in retrospect is likely to seem superfluous. Yet failure, too, brings experience and offers learning processes that have been and still are of value in facing what is now the second or third wave of transformation in communications and information technology. In this particular case, however, the company paid a high price for these things.

Bosch in the three major economic regions of the 1980s:
Europe – USA – Japan

Bosch had greatly expanded its business operations outside Germany in the 1970s. Direct investments outside Germany had also shown a marked increase. With 48 non-German companies in which the company directly (or indirectly, through the Zurich-based Robert Bosch Internationale Beteiligungen AG) held a majority interest, the Bosch Group was represented on all five continents. Now known as "regional subsidiaries" [*Regionalgesellschaften*] and usually referred to internally by the abbreviated company name (RB) coupled with a country code (such as TR for Turkey), these non-German companies employed some 37 percent of all Bosch Group associates by 1980. Ten years earlier, the figure had been less than half that – some 18 percent.[57] New factories had been built in Bursa (Turkey, 1973), Charleston (USA, 1973), Penang (Malaysia, 1973), Tienen (Belgium, 1974), and Brits (South Africa, 1976), among other places. The Bosch Group also had manufacturing operations in France, Austria (Friedmann & Maier AG), Sweden, Switzerland (Scintilla AG), and Spain (FEMSA), as well as farther afield: Argentina, Brazil, Mexico, Australia, and India (MICO).[58] But despite this global presence, by far the largest part of non-German business was in western Europe. At the start of the 1980s, the regional companies in the Americas, Asia, Australia, and Africa together accounted for only some 18 percent of Bosch Group sales worldwide. Bosch's biggest market outside Germany was France, where in 1983 Robert Bosch (France) S. A. became the largest German employer.[59]

In the largest automotive market in the world, the United States, Bosch was comparatively poorly represented. The company could not even begin to resume the role there that it had played before the Second World War – let alone before the First. The market was dominated by the U.S. automotive giants General Motors, Ford, and Chrysler, with whom Bosch had not yet been able to resume business relations. The "Big Three" had their vehicles equipped by American suppliers, and their market power meant they could virtually dictate the terms on which they did business with those suppliers. Some of the major suppliers actually belonged to the automakers or had once been part of them.

Back in the 1970s, the Bosch board of management had decided that it would no longer tolerate such a weak presence in the U.S. market (which at the time accounted for only some 3 percent of its global sales). In 1977, Hans L. Merkle declared the expansion of the U.S. business a major objective.[60]

The Schillerhöhe was well aware that Bosch's strong presence in western Europe was insufficient to give it "global player" status in the industry. The company's own history was evidence enough. The triumph of its U.S. business before the First World War was not simply a vivid memory. It was also, much as had been the case in the 1920s, a marker for the position aimed at internationally. Merkle, too, made it a corporate objective to restore the reputation that Bosch had enjoyed in the U.S. in the early years of the 20th century.[61]

Repeating the pattern set back then, Bosch did not move to the United States in the wake of its major German customers. The company had set its sights primarily on the major U.S. automakers. Bosch even beat VW and Daimler-Benz to the draw when it came to setting up its own manufacturing facility in the country. The foundation stone for a plant to make diesel injection equipment was laid in Charleston, South Carolina, as early as 1973. Four years later, the plant employed more than 800 people. Bosch further expanded its U.S. presence by purchasing Lehr Instrument Corp. and acquiring equity interests in Borg-Warner Corp. and American Microsystems Inc.[62] In 1983, as we have already seen, Bosch was able to buy back the U.S. name and trademark rights that had gone to American Bosch (AMBAC) after the Second World War, and had subsequently passed into the possession of United Technologies. However, Bosch was not interested in its former Springfield plant, which United Technologies then closed in 1986.[63] In that same year, Bosch built a research and development center in Farmington Hills, near Detroit – the first of its kind that the Bosch Group had set up outside Germany. To boost its manufacturing potential, it built a further plant in Anderson, South Carolina. Following this expansion, the Bosch Group reorganized its U.S. operations, bringing them together to form Robert Bosch Corporation.

Bosch expected great things of its U.S. business. A number of states in the U.S. had brought in emissions regulations, which meant that automakers were now forced to feature injection systems which reduced pollutants. Bosch was the technology leader in this field. And in 1977, orders for lambda sensors for Ford and Chrysler models allowed the company to become an original-equipment supplier for the "Big Three" once again, for the first time since the war.[64] Five years later, it was able to conclude a sole-supply agreement for gasoline injection systems for several General Motors models. At the same time, Bosch equipped the U.S. versions of German automakers' models – notably the "Rabbit," the American version of Volkswagen's new "Golf." As a result, Bosch was indeed able to benefit from the upswing in the American automotive market that followed the oil-price shock of 1979–80. By 1984, the U.S. was the largest

Manufacturing at the Charleston plant (1983)

non-German market for Bosch products, ahead of France, Italy, and Brazil. Around 10 percent of Bosch Group sales worldwide were now accounted for by the North American business.[65]

In the latter half of the 1980s, however, this expansion of U.S. business hit the barriers, and new circumstances even led to setbacks. Japanese automakers appeared to be unstoppable as they made inroads into the American automotive market, capturing a greater and greater share of the market from the "Big Three" with an unprecedented price challenge and, more importantly, with better engineering and higher quality. Bosch could not do business with the plants that Japanese automakers had set up in the U.S., since such plants dealt only with the many Japanese suppliers that had followed Toyota, Honda, and other producers. What damaged Bosch most was that General Motors, Ford, and Chrysler, under price pressure from their Japanese rivals, passed this pressure on to their own suppliers. As a manufacturer of technically sophisticated and high-priced goods, Bosch found itself in a difficult position.

Stuttgart was forced to concede that certain innovative, high-end Bosch products, much in demand "at home," sold less well in America. This was particularly true of ABS, which proved less attractive to American drivers because of existing speed limits. Not until 1988 (ten years after its market launch in Germany) was the system also fitted in General Motors automobiles. In 1990, ABS featured in 15 percent of all passenger cars produced in the U.S. – a figure only slightly lower than in western Europe (16 percent) but still very much lower than in West Germany (34 percent). By contrast, in the same year, 70 percent of new automobiles in the U.S. were fitted with gasoline injection systems, whereas in Germany the figure was only 57 percent.[66] One thing that particularly affected Bosch was that Americans had strong reservations about the diesel engine. Since U.S. producers barely invested in this technology, all the Charleston plant produced was in-line pumps for heavy trucks. The fact that a diesel-powered passenger car consumed less fuel than its gasoline-powered equivalent played virtually no role at all in the U.S., where gasoline was so cheap. Not even the oil-price shocks of 1973–74 and 1979–80 changed matters. Diesel engines had a poor image in America, and it stuck. People associated them with sluggish and foul-smelling utility vehicles.

Moreover, when the oil price fell dramatically in 1986, U.S. demand for low-consumption Bosch fuel-injection systems declined further. Less expensively equipped "gas guzzlers" enjoyed a resurgence. A year later, the U.S. dollar also collapsed, pushing the exchange rate below two German marks. For U.S. customers, German products were now significantly more expensive. Not even Bosch could escape the repercussions of the low exchange rate. The company produced in the U.S., but its Charleston and Anderson plants were supplied from Europe. The blow was even harder for German automakers doing business in America. VW terminated its U.S. production entirely in 1988. For Bosch, the American market now became what Marcus Bierich called a "battlefield."[67]

Table 17 Sales structure of the Bosch Group (1980–95), in percentage figures[68]

	1980	1985	1990	1995
Europe	81.6	76.2	83.3	80.0
North, Central, and South America	11.2	16.7	10.6	13.5
Asia, Africa, Australia	7.2	7.1	6.1	6.5

In the second half of the 1980s, the company enjoyed substantial sales increases both in Germany and throughout western Europe. As a result, the percentage of Bosch Group sales generated in the Americas fell markedly. In

1990, it was lower than ten years previously, although it increased again subsequently. Indeed, between 1985 and 1990, business in the Americas shrank in absolute terms as well.[69] France now replaced the U.S. once again as Bosch's largest market outside Germany.[70] Since the share of sales generated in Asia, Africa, and Australia in the 1980s was also down as a whole, at the end of the decade Bosch's international business was even more heavily weighted in favor of Europe than had been the case previously. Moreover, the share of total Bosch Group headcount accounted for by associates in the regional companies was lower than in 1980.[71] "As regards global presence, much remains to be done," was the verdict of Hans Konradin Herdt, a business journalist writing in *Börsen-Zeitung* in July 1993, following the Robert Bosch GmbH annual press conference.[72] Granted, so far as headcount was concerned Bosch now had a broader global footprint, but that was only because labor-intensive manufacturing operations had been expanded considerably in certain emerging countries. Brazil, for instance, had the largest number of Bosch associates outside Germany. In second place was India, where the MICO subsidiary in Bangalore (Motor Industries Co. Ltd.) produced – among other things – spark plugs and diesel injection pumps for the local market.[73]

The sales figures also fail to show that Bosch had achieved notable success in Japan, whose companies had been producing more automobiles than those of any other country since 1980. True to the *keiretsu* principle, the Japanese automotive industry worked almost exclusively with local suppliers. Consequently, the European and American automotive-supply industries stood little or no chance of doing original-equipment business in Japan. Even in 1992, the Bosch Group's direct involvement in automotive engineering in Japan was still bringing in sales of only 30 million German marks.[74] But for many years, Japan's automotive suppliers had been operating under licenses from Bosch. The Bosch name had been well-known in the country since 1911, when the company opened its first Japanese sales office. As already mentioned, particularly important licensees were Nippondenso (later Denso), Japan's largest supplier, and Diesel Kiki Co. Ltd., which had been founded by Tokyo Jidosha Kogyo (today's Isuzu Motors Ltd.) and Mitsubishi Heavy Industries. Diesel Kiki had been supplying the Japanese automotive industry with Bosch diesel equipment since 1939. At Nippondenso, as at Diesel Kiki, Bosch also acquired an equity interest. However, with the steep rise of the major Japanese automakers in the 1960s and 1970s, this license strategy lost some of its importance. The stronger such companies as Toyota, Honda, and Nissan became, the more their suppliers set up development operations of their own, and the less they relied on licenses from non-Japanese suppliers. Bosch therefore switched to a fresh strategy, seeking to gain a foothold in the Japanese market

Inaugurating the Yokohama Engineering Center (1992)

through joint ventures. Companies set up in collaboration with Japanese partners could supply the Japanese automotive industry directly, which non-Japanese equippers were prevented from doing. At the same time, they could give
Bosch access to the innovations and industrial engineering of the major Japanese producers. Addressing a GPI meeting later, Friedrich Scholl, a member of
the Bosch board of management, adopted a well-known English motto for this
Japanese plan: "If you can't beat them, join them."[75]

Important milestones in this development included the "Technical Liaison Committee" meetings attended by Bosch and Nippondenso (later Denso)
managers annually from 1971, and the establishment of a subsidiary in Tokyo,
Robert Bosch (Japan) Ltd., in 1972. The Japanese subsidiary sold power tools,
Blaupunkt car radios, Junkers gas-fired heating systems, and other non-automotive items. But it was above all the closer contacts it facilitated with Japanese automakers that paved the way for joint ventures in the field of automotive engineering. Only a year later, Bosch was able to announce its first
joint-venture agreement in Japan. Together with Nissan Diesel Motor Co. and
Diesel Kiki Co., the Stuttgart company set up Japan Electronic Control Systems Co., Ltd. With Bosch holding a one-third equity interest, the purpose of
the new company was to manufacture and sell electronically controlled gasoline injection systems.[76] Moreover, the Japanese automotive industry showed

interest in ABS before U.S. automakers did. Accordingly, in 1984, Bosch and Nippon Air Brake Co. Ltd. (NABCO) set up the joint venture Nippon ABS Ltd. Six years later, Bosch was able to increase the equity interest it held in Diesel Kiki. At this juncture, Diesel Kiki changed its name to Zexel Corporation. The establishment of an engineering center for development and calibration in Yokohama in 1992 allowed Bosch to move even closer to the Japanese automotive industry in these areas as well. It now became possible to display and demonstrate new developments and products in the country instantly. Finally, in April 1999, this period of Bosch involvement in Japan culminated in the acquisition of a majority shareholding in Zexel Corporation.[77]

Like Bosch's adaptation of Japanese models in industrial engineering, its new strategy of alliances in Japan was the appropriate answer to a challenge that, in the 1980s, prompted almost hysterical reactions in the industrialized countries of the West. "Japan's automotive invasion – Europe going to the dogs," screamed a headline in one German news periodical, and there were predictions that the future of the automotive industry was going to be "Japanese and American."[78] The U.S. and Japanese automotive industries did indeed command substantial shares of other markets at the time, while neither in the U.S. nor in Japan could their European rivals capture more than 5 percent.[79] Among suppliers, however, the picture was a different one. In this sector, neither American nor Japanese companies could dislodge Bosch in Europe. Yet international competition had sharpened in the automotive supply industry too, and Bosch was to feel the full effect of this in the years after 1990.

Kaizen auf schwäbisch: CIP and lean production in Bosch manufacturing

The Japanese *kanban* ["signboard"] system was introduced into manufacturing organization at Bosch – as well as at other German companies – in the early 1980s, and in the 1990s the "Japanization" of manufacturing processes continued apace. To be able to compete with their Japanese rivals, European and American automakers began a new era of productivity improvements involving cost cuts and price reductions. The result was a considerable upheaval in the automotive-supply sphere. The strain this placed on earnings in its automotive business sector forced Bosch to undertake far-reaching reorganization and restructuring processes – both externally, in terms of manufacturing locations and location structures, and internally, in terms of manufacturing processes. For years, the secret of Bosch's success had been its highly developed expertise in precision engineering. Tolerances in the region of one-thousandth of a millimeter were quite normal for Bosch, and in its large-scale series manufacturing operations, such tolerances were managed quite routinely. Moreover, each time Bosch doubled its production volumes of injection systems, its manufacturing unit costs dropped by 20 percent. "Predatory pricing by competitors was something the people in Stuttgart could therefore rebuff easily, without putting their profit margins in danger."[80] That had been the situation in the 1980s. However, times had changed. Developments from outside the company changed manufacturing at Bosch radically. These developments included outsourcing (reducing backward vertical integration), global sourcing (internationalizing purchasing operations), just-in-time approaches to manufacturing (synchronizing delivery of parts with their assembly), single sourcing (buying from only one supplier), and modular sourcing (buying in system components). The tried and tested toolkit used to survive periods of recession was no longer enough on its own to meet the new challenges these developments brought. The company required a completely fresh approach. At the heart of that renewal stood the twin concepts of the "continuous improvement process" (*kaizen* in Japanese) and "lean production" – as advocated (at the latest) in the bestselling book *The Machine that Changed the World* (1990). Written by three MIT scientists – James P. Womack, Daniel T. Jones, and Daniel Roos – the book preached the Japanese system of production, holding it up as a model for European and U.S. manufacturing companies.

A production philosophy guided by customers' individual engineering requirements had once been among Bosch's great strengths. Now, though, it was increasingly proving to be a disadvantage, also in terms of cost. Furthermore, the purely internal training received by the company's manufacturing specialists and the virtual exclusion of lateral entrants both from the company's own engineering departments and from outside companies had bred a certain isolation. One result was that Bosch was now slow to spot new trends. Particularly when products were rolled out, there were glaring quality problems.[81] In the early 1990s, the Bosch manufacturing specialists themselves realized that all was not well, as the following analysis shows: "[We need to] reverse what has now become an excessive division of labor in the non-productive sphere. Instead, associates should perform a wider range of tasks on their own. In this way, the number of interfaces will be reduced, as will delays resulting from waiting for work processes structured in a great many successive steps to be completed."[82] Internal analyses showed that, by and large, manufacturing operations themselves were rationally organized and cost-effective. However, it was in the time taken by development projects that weaknesses were chiefly identified. To quote one internal memo: "Often, in connection with customer projects, agreed deadlines cannot be adhered to. To keep customers happy, expensive special measures are tolerated. And when new and less costly products are introduced to supersede existing designs, these time delays mean any rationalization gain is lost."[83] No longer-term, strategic production planning existed yet at Bosch. In the automotive business sector, products were not planned; they simply "happened" – through the traditional process of close collaboration with individual major customers. Most of the efficiency issues had their roots in the interfaces between Bosch divisions and business units, i. e., in the processes of internal collaboration. This was hardly surprising, given the rapid increase in individual decisions that was bound to arise given Bosch's range of products and variety of customers. In short, there were many starting-points at Bosch for the improvement measures that underlay Japan's whole approach to production.

One central factor, the importance of quality, was not new. The concept of total quality management (TQM) that flowed from it had moved into the foreground of manufacturing thinking in the 1980s. But for the Bosch board of management it helped to propagate a new awareness of quality, for which the company founder could be invoked as a pioneer. Indeed, the founder's own words were quoted at the beginning of the "12 basic principles of quality" that were drawn up in 1989: "Given goodwill, careful consideration, and thorough trials, only the best that can be manufactured with the help of the finest technological aids and the choicest raw materials is good enough to bear the name 'Bosch.'" [84] "Bosch work" was quality work. And that was the watchword Hansjörg Manger attempted to impress upon his senior management colleagues in his detailed address ("The importance of quality") at the annual business policy briefing in December of that year.[85] Manger reminded his listeners that a new structure of quality assurance had governed Bosch manufacturing since 1982. This structure was subsequently complemented by statistical process control (SPC). Between them, they provided the basis for consistent application of one idea: quality must not be the result of a process of correction, but instead must be right from the very start. In the spring of 1991, a new and powerful impetus to change in Bosch's manufacturing processes arrived from Japan. Unlike the highly innovation-oriented procedure common in western industrialized countries, *kaizen* (dubbed "continuous improvement process" or CIP) was based on incremental improvements. Wherever possible, these were to be introduced immediately, using existing resources, with no new or only minimal capital expenditure. It was a question of exploiting available, tried and tested expertise. The improvements were carried out at the point where jobs were performed or value added, involving the staff who were affected.[86] The object was to bring about a rethinking process in the workplace. CIP aimed to cultivate a stronger sense of identification, boost commitment, and persuade associates to take more ownership. At the same time, it set out to improve collaboration (group work). In other words, it was mainly about "the willingness to go the extra mile."[87] The expectation was that this combination of innovation and continuous improvement would add to result, not only quantitatively but also qualitatively. CIP would help spot potential for cutting out activities that did not add value, as well as for eliminating waste generally (including "unnecessary movements by associates"). It would increase efficiency and reduce costs by constantly improving processes. Even the manufacturing specialists conceded that these elements and tools were not, at root, new to Bosch. What was new was "the strategic goal common to similar programs that had characterized Japanese companies for years, notably to improve quality and productivity."[88]

Putting CIP into practice at Bosch was itself a step-by-step process, starting with lectures by one of the authors of the MIT study as well as by the head of the Kaizen Institute in Brussels. Above all, there were information and training events. In the period up to November 1991, special CIP teams held between two and four pilot seminars in all the German plants belonging to the automotive business sector. There were 41 such seminars altogether, carrying out a total of 95 pilot projects. A second phase saw pilot workshops set up on the premises of the communications technology business sector. And in a third phase it was planned to transfer the CIP measures to the remaining manufacturing locations. An initial evaluation of the pilot projects was unequivocal. Manpower savings worth millions of German marks went hand in hand with an almost equally high potential for reductions in inventories. In addition, CIP was not only about the potential for improved performance but also about ways of reducing workload, which – in theory at least – made CIP more acceptable to associates. To give some examples: an improved materials flow in P-pump housing production at the Homburg plant cut processing times and work in process by some 45 percent, the reorganization of wiper-arm assembly at the Eisenach plant reduced floor space requirements by 40 percent, and the redesign of the assembly line for TCS control units at the Ansbach auxiliary plant made it possible to cut work in process on components by 80 percent and standard times by 15 percent.[89] Consistent implementation of CIP had far-reaching repercussions. As well as calling for a change in labor organization, it also required a switch from the usual piecework to a pay system based on time and bonuses. What for management had been complex, inflexible work and pay structures were now broken up, and a total of three separate teams now devoted all their attention to developing labor and remuneration systems appropriate to CIP. The result was the specifically Bosch concept of "team-oriented production" in conjunction with team pay based on bonuses. But in December 1991, with the first pilot schemes being introduced to try out this system, there was still some way to go.

Five years later, in June 1996, the board made an interim assessment of the new manufacturing concept. It was clear that further progress had been made.[90] CIP was now embedded at Bosch on a worldwide basis. Special CIP coordinators and CIP promoters looked after the process locally, making sure that the relevant activities were indeed sustained continuously. Divisions and regional companies largely managed their own improvement projects, and most of the topics monitored had their particular divisional and locational points of emphasis. In order to improve entire production flows – from raw-materials or components storage to packaging or dispatch of the finished product – and individual parts of that flow, the manufacturing analysis method had meanwhile been evolved. It had been used to great effect in many plants both at home and abroad. Manufacturing analysis also enabled new manufacturing lines to be laid out in a way that reduced costs. In the case of assembly lines, initial studies showed that manufacturing analysis made it possible to cut capital expenditure by as much as 10–20 percent.[91] Moreover, a start had been made at introducing CIP not only in manufacturing-related work but also in administrative departments. Here, a key development went by the name of "policy deployment." This process took the strategic and operational targets of a division or plant and defined what they meant for the various levels and functions. At the same time (and with the collaboration of those concerned), the measures needed to achieve those targets were derived and coordinated. By tracking performance and showing the current degree of target fulfillment in individual departments, these targets were visualized. Using policy deployment and this visualization, a division could then focus its resources on achieving its overriding objectives. At the same time, associates were given far more responsibility for getting their tasks done.[92] "More than five years ago," one Bosch manager summed up, "we embarked on a journey [with CIP] that in fact has no end. CIP is designed to be open-ended. It tends to keep on developing, added to by whatever points of emphasis are called for at the time. We have made good progress, certainly, but in many places there is still catching-up to do, and signs of weariness are appearing here and there [...]. What is crucial as regards the future is that the process of change set in motion by CIP is taken further and does not lose impetus."[93]

The impetus had clearly not been lost when Hermann Scholl addressed the GPI meeting in December 1997. Scholl was able to report numerous instances of "continuous improvement." There was the productivity drive in spark plugs at the Bamberg plant, where following substantial improvements in manufacturing it was now possible to turn out 1.1 million units per working day on just 17 lines instead of the 20 previously required. It had also been possible to reduce the throughput times for mass-production of sensor elements for the new planar lambda sensor from 22 to 16 working days. And the new CIP for reducing complexity had shown great potential, completely convincing members of the board of management.[94] So far as associates were concerned, work had been enriched – considerably in some instances – and interdisciplinary collaboration had been improved. Crucially, none of the associates whose jobs had become superfluous because of CIP were dismissed if at all possible, but offered appropriate new employment instead. The board knew full well that, without such a prospect, associates would not be prepared to give sufficient commitment to CIP projects, let alone take initiatives that might undermine or eliminate their own jobs. The eventual goal was to create, through CIP, a corporate culture in which each associate played an active part, each and every day, in designing and carrying out improvements in his or her sphere of operations. This was going to place a permanent question mark against current systems, processes, and modes of behavior in every sphere and at every level. CIP, the board saw, had brought Bosch a big step closer to that goal.

Further measures to reorganize and fine-tune the production system at Bosch were taken in the years that followed. There were still plenty of weaknesses in the company's manufacturing processes. A large part of its resources (both hardware and personnel) was tied up in "fire fighting." Above all, this was about solving engineering problems affecting projects that were already in production, so that customer deadlines could be met. Many top-class Bosch engineers were kept busy with such jobs instead of devoting their time and skills to innovations.[95] "Design to cost," "design to manufacturability," and "standardization" – such were the new philosophies and watchwords of international management in the late 1990s. All of them (senior executives were told) "must be given far greater priority at Bosch."[96] Customer-specific product development and the order-handling process that went with it were, in many instances, too lengthy and too bureaucratic, and went hand in hand with a failure to meet quality targets. For the Thomas Group management consultants hired by Bosch, it was clear that the various "resource steering committees" set up to plan and allocate resources had to be given a substantially greater degree of autonomy if "simultaneous engineering" (i. e., the simultaneous ramp-up of new product generations worldwide) was to work at Bosch. Consequently, customer-oriented product teams were set up. Their brief was to achieve consensus among the relevant specialist departments, whose reactions to new ideas and measures to improve processes were frequently hostile and characterized by comments such as "not standard Bosch practice," or "out of synch with the directives and norms of Bosch policy," or "that will not work because [and here it seemed only English would do] 'it will never be accepted by our automotive sector'."[97]

This was the period when in other German industrial companies, too, "change management" was the big thing in management methodology. Soon after the turn of the 21st century, a new form of production organization eventually emerged at Bosch. This was the "Bosch Production System" (BPS). Once again, familiar principles such as just-in-time, flow, flexibility, delivery reliability, and standardization were combined to provide the "foundation for the worldwide, consistent implementation of uniform principles aimed at low-cost, zero-defect production and 100 percent on-time delivery."[98] The Bosch Production System was above all the response to yet further changes in customer behavior and the competitive environment as well as to new production systems introduced by automakers. Global overcapacity and stiffer competition forced companies to define what made them special and therefore to offer greater choice. At the same time, original-equipment customers' call orders and planning had become extremely short-term and, above all, unpredictable. Large-scale series production decreased. Manufacture of smaller batches coupled with faster throughput times was more in demand. This called on the one hand for stable and transparent processes worldwide and on the other for better coordination of product creation and production-system planning. However, over the course of time each plant had devised and developed its own principles of production, procedures, and methods. While it was to be expected that the manufacturing facilities would develop in this way, from the point of view of the production system as a whole this required constant course correction. Plants were therefore compared with each other, using standardized audit catalogues, and attempts made to align and improve processes further. To plan, produce, assemble, and transport the right part in the right quantity at the right moment – that, in a nutshell, was what the Bosch Production System wanted to achieve.

So-called "time-to-market" (TTM) programs were designed and implemented or further "internalized." These had three purposes. They sought to improve product-creation processes, to make sure that rollouts were soundly managed, and to rule out the need for constant reworking. "Bringing in BPS is a process of change lasting several years, and it must largely be done on our own," remarked one Bosch management board member during his presentation at a management board retreat session in May 2001.[99] Individual plants and divisions had assessment concepts for measuring "TTM maturity levels." "One-piece-flow" organization and reassessments of "value flow," "value-flow design," and a string of newly developed "BPS principles" – the new terms and phrases just kept on coming.[100] At first glance, the term "Bosch Production System" itself gave the impression of an entirely unique, self-contained concept with fully thought-out methods and tools for manufacturing products of the same high quality as had been developed during the 1960s. In fact, it was not only terminologically that Bosch took its lead from the new systems of production already introduced at automakers. And so far as associates were concerned, the new production methods ultimately often meant more stress and a heavier workload. For instance, one of the new manufacturing or assembly concepts within BPS was called *chaku-chaku*[101] – a version of conveyor-belt or series production (and the labor involved) in which all the workstations associated with production of a particular item are juxtaposed according to the product departmentalization principle, so that the paths between them are as short as possible. It also involves work at several machines. Usually a single person works at several pieces of equipment, feeding in material and taking out a processed product. For the rest, the stations work independently, without the worker intervening. In practice, five workers (say) operated ten machines in three overlapping flow circles. For the individual, this meant using three machines in 40 seconds while constantly moving in a circle. There were only "stand and go" workstations here; buffer inventories were frowned upon; items were passed from hand to hand.[102] Secondary operations such as fetching materials or topping-up assembly containers were not deemed "value-adding," and so were delegated to "milk runners," as they were called.

The great clash of 1993

In the United States, the long-established and firmly entrenched structures that characterized relationships between automakers and their suppliers began to shift during the 1980s. The reason was stiff price competition in the market. In Europe, on the other hand, suppliers had still been able to meet cost increases by raising their prices. Moreover, the mood in the German economy, following reunification and with the European Single Market imminent, was one of buoyant optimism. Bosch also benefited from the special economic circumstances following reunification. As a European company par excellence (more than 80 percent of its total sales were generated in western Europe), it expected EU-wide deregulation to offer major opportunities and faster growth in its own business. However, during the course of 1990, it became obvious that growth within the Bosch Group was slowing down significantly. In the view of the Bosch board of management, the automotive industry, concerned for its own profits and keen to secure its own future, had adopted an exceptionally tough price policy at the expense of its suppliers. The major automakers were endeavoring, sometimes with draconian measures, to reduce costs. To this end they were shedding jobs, shifting production to countries where labor was cheap, and using their market muscle to put suppliers under pressure. In automotive production at the time, suppliers already contributed some 65 percent of value added, so the largest scope for economies lay in this area. For suppliers, the price of their products now became the key competitive factor. Offering state-of-the-art technology was no longer enough. Now, they also had to offer markdowns. As a result, a process of concentration began within the supplier industry as a whole, since many companies, particularly small and medium-sized ones, could not survive such shrinking margins for long.[103]

In retrospect, the change is often mentioned in the same breath as the López effect, the program of cost cutting through process improvements practiced in no-nonsense and even ruthless manner by José Ignacio López, from 1988 head of purchasing for General Motors Europe, later (from 1992) for General Motors in Detroit, then (from 1993) for Volkswagen. But López was merely the figurehead for a widespread process of change. In the end, the shrinking margins that so harmed the automotive-supply industry at the time were the result of increased international competition, intensified by the recession of 1992–93. Yet Bosch found itself in a relatively good position here. As one of the world's largest automotive suppliers, the company wielded considerable negotiating muscle. It was also a systems supplier, so crossing the Stuttgart company off their lists was less easy for automakers than was the case with smaller competitors. Even so, Bosch found itself under pressure from at least three sides. First, it was known for particularly high-quality products – which also came with a high price tag. During the boom of the preceding years, there had been little attempt on the part of the company to reduce its own costs. The market, after all, could take higher prices. But now, with price competition stiffening, Bosch was at a disadvantage compared with many rivals. The kinds of price reduction that its customers were demanding were something the company had never contemplated before. Second, international competition among suppliers was also on the increase. For Bosch, the high wage costs at its German plants were now a detrimental factor.

Third, and most importantly, Bosch was under threat from a fresh competitor in its own home market. Having bought a majority stake in Bendix

Electronics from AlliedSignal in 1988, Siemens had set about expanding in the field of automotive engineering. In automotive electronics, it was now seen as the third-largest producer worldwide after Bosch and Denso.[104] At Bosch, the new rival was taken very seriously. Not only did Siemens possess great financial strength. It also had excellent contacts with BMW and Daimler-Benz. And the new challenger made its purpose very clear. "The industry needs a second Bosch," was the message from Munich.[105] And indeed, Bosch gained the impression that the major automakers were not averse to this increased involvement of Siemens in automotive engineering. At the beginning of 1991, for instance, Bosch failed to better Siemens in connection with an offer to BMW for engine-management systems that in its own [Bosch's] view was "highly attractive."[106] Following long-established procedure, the engineering sales management at Bosch proposed that talks be scheduled between members of the Bosch and BMW boards of management.[107] Talks were agreed, but BMW refused to budge.

At meetings of the RBIK shareholders, Merkle had been making dire predictions since November 1990. Bierich was less drastic, but still talked of a subdued outlook for the future. In Merkle's view, sales growth and profits of the kind seen in recent years were frankly unlikely for the foreseeable future. Bosch, he said, had to make "every effort" to adjust to the new situation.[108] Financial planning and capital expenditure budgets were scaled down substantially, and an extensive cost-cutting program totaling one billion German marks was adopted.[109] Here, particular attention was paid to one area of structural costs – namely, personnel expenses for administrative associates, as well as to depreciation and other operating expenses, adding up to some 36 percent of total structural costs. To quote the minutes of the April 9, 1991, RBIK meeting, "It is not out of the question that, in the interests of securing the long-term future of the company, even deeper cuts will need to be made in these areas. As well as across-the-board solutions that bring about quick results, there will also be a need to make and carry out deliberate, flexibly controlled decisions specific to individual operating units. In this connection, there must be no shrinking from measures that have not been accepted at [Bosch] in the past. The shareholders declare this to be their firm opinion."[110]

"Bosch preparing to face years of slow growth," ran the headline in *Börsen-Zeitung* above its report of the annual press conference given by Bierich at the beginning of July 1991.[111] Referring to the high level of costs in Germany and to wage increases, Bierich announced a strengthening of Bosch's international manufacturing operations, sparking a fresh debate about Germany as a business location. Bierich had taken the Bosch subsidiary Blaupunkt as an example to demonstrate publicly what he believed was the manifestly questionable nature of recent wage settlements. The metal-workers union had demanded that those settlements include a social compo-nent for the lower income brackets. This increased wages in those brackets by as much as 12 percent. For Bierich, the logical consequence of this was that more production was relocated outside Germany and jobs "at home" were lost. "The union's wage policy is destroying jobs in Germany," the Bosch chairman was quoted as saying.[112] These were fighting words of a kind not heard from the Schillerhöhe before. But above all, Bierich made no bones about the dramatic drop in earnings and other growing problems. The press had a field day. "Fin de siècle. The cozy world of Bosch is coming apart at the seams," was the sensational headline that *Manager Magazin* put above a piece published only days later. In bald terms, the article portrayed the crisis in the two core business fields of automotive and communications tech-nology.[113] "New competitors are making the one-time monopolist vulnera-ble [...]. Even Swabia's distinguished global enterprise, with its proud reputa-tion as the indispensable supplier of quality products to the automotive industry, must now stoop to pick up the coins its customers toss its way."[114] Not only *Manager Magazin* speculated that more needed to change at Bosch than simply the figures. Bierich himself was now having thoughts about the whole structure of the organization and how to recruit a suitable younger generation of managers. He wanted to see more willingness to take risks, greater entrepreneurial freedom, and a change in the organizational struc-ture "which is allegedly highly decentralized but in fact stymied by a close-knit system of reporting and controlling that fosters red tape and a risk-averse mentality."[115] The intriguing question journalists were now asking was "What can survive of the old Bosch spirit?"[116] – and there were doubtless many voices inside the company asking the same thing.

Indeed, the outlook had worsened considerably, especially in the automo-tive technology business sector. At the GPI conference of June 1991, Hermann Scholl gave both external and internal reasons for the problems with profit-ability. They ranged from the weak dollar to the fact that there was still room for rationalization.[117] "We are currently in a critical situation in the automotive business sector," Scholl warned. "The business environment is hostile and we failed to take sufficient precautions in good time. There is no lack of ideas as to where we need to go from here. But we have to do more. We need to get on and transform those ideas into action. And we must be quick about it. That is the most difficult part, and it still lies ahead of us."[118]

For far too long, automotive managers and executives at Bosch had clung to past engineering successes: to such groundbreaking systems as gasoline injection, the lambda sensor, the ABS antilock braking system, the TCS traction control system, and electronic airbag deployment ("all products that we were the first in the world to produce in series"). They had clung obstinately to the fact that "in former times our German customers were prepared to pay [...] relatively high prices for our new-generation products."[119] Only gradually had they become aware of and begun to react to profound changes in the automotive-supply industry. One instance of those changes was the reduction in backward vertical integration among automakers, as a consequence of which many former tier-one suppliers had been demoted to the second tier. As a supplier of systems and modules, Bosch found itself forced into the role of a prime contractor. And while it was clear that this would have far-reaching consequences with regard to accountability for development, purchasing, and quality, the precise nature of those consequences was still completely unclear. At the same time, original-equipment customers were trying to break down complex systems such as gasoline injection into their component parts, to put individual parts out to tender worldwide, and to award the contract to the lowest bidder.[120]

In November 1992, Merkle reported to the RBIK meeting about his meetings with top executives in the German automotive industry. His report painted a grave picture of the business situation faced by Bosch's major customers.[121] Bosch had already had to concede reductions of more than 2 percent in negotiations with original-equipment customers for the current business year. Now these customers were asking their suppliers to make further price concessions of 5 percent for the following year – and 5 percent for each of the following five years as well. And when Hansjörg Manger, the board member responsible for original-equipment sales, reported in June 1993 to the Bosch supervisory board about "our customers' altered purchasing behavior," the situation had "worsened dramatically."[122] The simple formula now facing original-equipment suppliers (Bosch included) was: "German suppliers must bid foreigners' prices." The subject mentioned most often in this connection was the purchasing behavior of VW – since GM's chief buyer José Ignacio López had moved to Wolfsburg, this was increasingly resembling the procedure that had made him notorious at Opel. Volkswagen's "corporate sourcing committee," which met each Friday under the chairmanship of the head of purchasing, made all its decisions on the basis of a "bidder list" drawn up for the occasion. "In the days before each of these Friday purchasing meetings, the remaining bidders are confronted with target prices that have again been lowered, as well as with different supply shares. They are then given a minimal amount of time (often only an hour) to respond to demands for further concessions. Deliberate indiscretions, i. e., leaks regarding lower bids submitted by competitors, are all part of the procedure. As the to-ing and fro-ing continues, bids go down and down, and the other terms and conditions also become more favorable for Volkswagen."[123] As Manger summarized: "We're learning the hard way – but we're learning a lot. The weeding-out of the supply industry is in full swing."[124]

In the second half of 1992, the bottom fell out of the European automotive market. Bosch sustained a loss of 190.7 million German marks in this six-month period alone. The operating result for 1992 fell to 218.2 million German marks as a result.[125] That brought it down to 29 percent of its 1990 level.[126] For 1993, the VDA (Germany's automotive-industry association) forecast a double-digit drop in new registrations coupled with lower prices in the used-car market. And when the German federal government announced a hike in mineral-oil tax, reality surpassed even the gloomiest forecasts.[127] In January 1993, therefore, the Bosch board of management notified the works councils of new economy measures and further cuts in pay, personnel expenses, and fringe benefits. At a special session of the works councils' economic committee, attempts were made by the board to explain to employee representatives that the company faced a prolonged adjustment process, at the end of which costs had to have been brought down by 25 percent.[128] During March, however, it became clear that attempts to reach agreement with the works councils regarding what was to be done were getting nowhere. On March 25, the Bosch board of management presented the RBIK meeting with a package of measures that, from a works-council and associate perspective, were catastrophic. The union-negotiated 3 percent pay rise for non-exempt associates was to be completely offset against payments over and above union rates, exempt associates (i. e., those with individual contracts) were asked to forgo 3 percent of income, and three internal agreements [Betriebsvereinbarungen] were to be cancelled: one concerning supplements for two-shift and three-shift operation, another concerning meal prices, and a third concerning anniversary leave.[129] Taken together, these meant a short-term saving of 120 million German marks. However, this was only a fraction of the total restructuring package. The intention, over a two-year period, was to make cost cuts in the automotive business sector of some 2 billion German marks – including some drastic structural changes at the old-established Feuerbach location. For members of the Bosch works councils, this was going too far. In a sharply worded statement by the combined works council, the "unilaterally resolved removals and reductions of social benefits as well as cancellations of internal agreements" were roundly condemned.[130] "This way of going about things [the statement says] constitutes a break with the social tradition that has evolved historically at Bosch. It abandons the kind of cooperation with the inhouse representatives of employee interests that has been the rule up to now."[131] At the beginning of April, there was a memorable demonstration by some 11,000

Demonstration outside the Schillerhöhe headquarters (April 1993)

Bosch associates in the form of a march converging on the Schillerhöhe from several directions simultaneously. The rally held outside headquarters marked the culmination of a wave of protest against the company's sweeping program of cost cuts, with the chairman of the central works council, Ludwig Vogt, demanding its complete retraction.[132]

Quite obviously, the mutual trust that had held sway between the central works council and the board of management had been shaken to its core. The relationship had reached rock bottom. Not since 1920 had there in all likelihood been a confrontation at Bosch that had had similarly traumatic repercussions on both sides. Yet the great clash of the spring of 1993 was at the same time a turning-point. In future crises, the board would be much quicker to inform and consult employee representatives. And more precise calculations would be made beforehand as to how cost-cutting measures were actually going to affect individuals. Above all, management would avoid such inflexible job cuts. The fact was, one of the things executives learned from the recession was that the company's actions had led to a loss of know-how, which was then missing when the upturn came.[133] To quote Alfred Löckle, who later became chairman of the central works council: "As soon as the last lot quit with their hefty severance payments, the first of the new lot had to be taken on. There simply weren't enough to stem the tide."[134] Not least, it soon became clear that the adjustment measures had cost huge sums (hundreds of millions of German marks) in compensation payments, severance payments, and early-retirement schemes. But there was another sense in which the great clash was a turning point. It marked what one might call the last manifestation of the Merkle policy of iron-fisted, radical job-cutting measures.[135] Undoubtedly, the levers pulled in the background by the honorary chairman of the Bosch Group had in fact helped bring about the confrontation, not without causing some collateral damage to the board of management.[136]

Toward the end of May 1993, Bierich reported on the current business situation to Bosch executives assembled at the GPI conference. By this time, some 12,000 associates had already left the company with severance payments or had taken early retirement (sometimes because they had been threatened with dismissal), while a further 23,000 were working shorter hours. Since "the end of the current economic downturn is not yet in sight," he said, a further reduction of nearly 20,000 associates was now planned. The Bosch board of management saw this recession as differing from the economic crises of the mid-1970s and early 1980s. This time "we are dealing with a fundamental process of structural adaptation to a changed environment. The purpose of that adaptation is to recover the international competitiveness we have currently lost."[137] It was beginning to look as if, for the first time in its postwar history, Bosch was going to have to accept an operating loss as well as the steepest drop in sales since 1968. Granted, with its traditional nose for future economic developments, Bosch had stepped in earlier than most other companies to counter a downward slide. It had cut costs, made rationalizations, and reduced its workforce. However, in its manufacturing operations Bosch was a slave to its customers' call orders, and could not slow its own output before their orders came in. Bierich explicitly defended the savage cost cuts, notably the workforce reductions at locations with a long tradition behind them and the brutal slashing of in-house social benefits that had led to such opposition. The measures had been necessary, he explained, and "it would have been wrong to duck conflict. Only through what we did were we able to bring about the kind of rethinking needed to change our system of fringe benefits."[138] It was his firm conviction that Bosch would emerge from the current crisis stronger than before.

From left: Tilman Todenhöfer, Günter Bensinger, and Marcus Bierich at a conference of members of Bosch works councils (1993)

Bierich's report not only sounded like a farewell speech. It actually *was* the last time he addressed his executives as chairman of the Bosch board of management. In late March 1993, Merkle had made two announcements to those present at a crucial meeting of the RBIK shareholders. On June 17, having turned 80 on January 1, he himself would be retiring from RBIK. And on June 30, one year before both his term of office and his contract expired, Marcus Bierich would be stepping down as chairman of the board of management. He would become chairman of the supervisory board at the same time as taking over the chair of RBIK.[139] Bierich was succeeded by Hermann Scholl, with Friedrich Schiefer being appointed vice-chairman of the board of management – a position that had not existed before. At the same time, the number of board members and directors with full power of attorney was reduced from fourteen to ten. Bierich was not the only one to resign. The director of industrial relations was also replaced. In January 1988, the man who had served as human-resources director for many years, Peter Rose, had resigned on age grounds in favor of Günter Bensinger. Bensinger was now singled out as scapegoat for the escalation of hostilities, and on August 1, 1993, he was obliged to make way for Tilman Todenhöfer.

It would be hard to persuade Bosch associates (both wage earners and salaried staff) of the need for cuts "unless such measures also involve[d] the upper levels of management," Merkle advised. "It follows that the board of management, too, must be tightened up and a new management generation introduced."[140] We can only speculate about the precise circumstances of Bierich's resignation and the reasons behind it. What is certain is that it was the culmination of many factors. For one thing, there was what Merkle considered the excessively feeble and so far unsuccessful crisis management practiced by the Bosch board of management. But there was also the mounting and (to the senior management team at least) quite obvious personal ill-feeling between Bierich and Merkle, to the point of outright breakdown of relations. The inner tensions had become too great over time and Bierich's position within the company had progressively weakened. This had often led to difficult decision-making processes.[141] Moreover, the recession and its inevitable cutbacks and clashes had affected Bierich personally more than he allowed to show. A growing number of his Bosch colleagues were no longer willing to ignore that, as a financial expert brought in from outside the company, Bierich had little understanding of the automotive sector and hence of Bosch's core business field, while with the venture into communications technology he was frankly unsuccessful. Lastly, for Bierich himself it may well have played a role that he now had no doubt that he was incurably ill.[142] On June 24, 1993, Bierich faced the press for the last time as Bosch CEO to present the financial statements for the previous business year (1992) and comment on the outlook for the months ahead. A meager sales increase of some 2.5 percent could still be announced, along with positive (if dwindling) earnings. But at the same time Bierich delivered a gloomy review of the current year, with reduced capital expenditure, collapsing sales, a costs crisis, more job cuts, and other consequences of the recession that Bosch would have to combat. And in 1993, the company did in fact suffer its first drop in sales for years. The domestic market fell by some 8 percent, and worldwide Bosch Group sales by some 6 percent – with automotive technology suffering even more than communications.[143] In its operating result, Bosch sustained a loss of some 650 million German marks.[144] The figure included the costs arising out of what was termed a "workforce adjustment" [*Personalanpassung*]. Without this item, the operating result might not have been negative.[145] The published statement of income of Robert Bosch GmbH for 1993 showed a "result of ordinary business activity" of 716 million German marks and net earnings of 60 million German marks. On the subject of operating result, the annual report commented laconically: "The pressure on our earnings continued. Operating result declined further and was negative."[146]

Bierich's years at Bosch did not end when he stepped down as chairman of the board of management in June 1993. With his assumption of the chairmanship of the supervisory board and RBIK, the Bierich era flowed into a second phase, which lasted until the beginning of the new century. That era stood for openness, collective leadership, internal renewal, and structural change. The man made his mark in many ways, though these "are no longer always associated with his person."[147] That his chairmanship was on the one hand associated with the company's unfortunate involvement in the field of communications technology, and on the other closely bound up with the conflict and crisis of 1993, was nothing short of tragic.

Upheaval at old-established locations: labor relations and labor conflicts

For the Bosch workforce, the repeated restructuring drives of the 1990s meant a period of constant unrest and pressure. This restructuring was always accompanied by fresh waves of cost cuts, the reorganization of manufacturing sites, the relocation or even closing of assembly lines, and the rollout of complex manufacturing schemes, increasingly putting to the test a tradition of industrial relations that relied largely on consensus. A glance at the development of headcount between 1983 and 2001 gives an initial impression of the radical shifts in the size and structure of the workforce.

Fig. 10 Bosch Group headcount within Germany and without (1983–2001)[148]

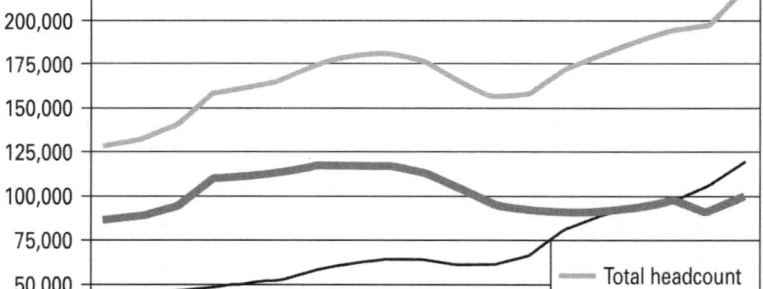

Total Bosch Group headcount grew by 70 percent over this period, from just under 130,000 in 1983 to 218,000 in 2001. But there was clearly also fluctuation, and some massive reductions in workforce in crisis periods (e.g. by 23,000 or 12.7 percent between 1991 and 1994). The workforce-reduction measures began sooner in Germany (1990–91) than in other countries, extended over a longer period (until 1996), and involved deeper cuts in total. Workforce expansion was thus achieved at the expense of those employed in Germany. In 1983, twice as many Bosch associates worked in German plants as worked in plants outside the country. In 1998, with around 94,000 in Germany and the same outside Germany, numbers were roughly equal. After that date, internationalization and globalization ensured that there were more Bosch associates outside Germany than within. This trend was observable in all large companies in Germany. Among associates in Germany, it was women who were affected most by the restructuring measures of the 1990s. In 1980, female employment at Bosch in Germany (not including subsidiaries) stood at 36 percent. By 1990, it was down to 29 percent (30 percent if subsidiary companies are included). In 2000, only 23 percent of the workforce (Bosch plus subsidiaries) were women – that is to say, 9 percentage points fewer than in the mid-1950s.[149]

Nonetheless, given the employment situation at original-equipment customers, Bosch associates were in a relatively good position. At companies such as GM, Ford, and Chrysler, followed by Fiat and Peugeot and eventually by VW, BMW, and Daimler-Benz, dismissals and shorter working hours were on the agenda long before workforce reductions set in at Feuerbach, Bamberg, and Nuremberg. Even Japanese automakers shed jobs and provisionally closed some of their plants outside Japan.

Before the great clash of 1993, therefore, we have to go back several years to find serious clashes between works councils and board of management at Bosch. In 1984, nationwide industrial action by the metalworkers' union IG Metall to support its demand for a 35-hour working week had also led to strikes and protests at Feuerbach and other Bosch locations. These took place against a background of bitter infighting among labor representatives at Bosch. The 1984 struggle was conducted with enormous vehemence by both employers and employees. When workers were called out at Bosch in Reutlingen, management retaliated by locking out associates in Feuerbach. When supply problems arose, white-collar workers were ordered to assembly lines – which further exacerbated tensions within the workforce.[150] Only after seven weeks, following the so-called *Leber-Kompromiss* (named for the mediator Georg Leber), was the conflict resolved in July 1984. A period of comparative calm followed. In 1988, Richard Rau stood down as chairman of the central works council at Bosch, making way for Ludwig Vogt, who for many years had been a member of the works council at the Bamberg plant. At that time, Bamberg was Bosch's second largest manufacturing location in Germany after Feuerbach.

Works assembly with Richard Rau, the chairman of the central works council (1985)

Starting in 1990, the Bosch employee representatives found themselves working in increasingly difficult times. There were more and more recruitment freezes, coupled with major changes at a series of plants. There were changes, too, in the federal government's labor-market policy and social-welfare legislation. One change involved an amendment to section 116 of the Law for the Promotion of Employment Measures [*Arbeitsförderungsgesetz*]. This had the effect (negative, as unions saw it) of making industrial action more difficult. In the future, if non-striking enterprises were affected by a strike elsewhere, the state would no longer pay short-time allowances. Meanwhile, the Bosch board of management found itself dealing (on the union side) with Walter Riester. Riester was the district head of IG Metall in Stuttgart, and in the spring of 1992 he had negotiated a 5.4 percent wage and salary increase with effect from April 1992, with a further 3 percent to follow from April 1993, plus improved fringe benefits.[151] Under the circumstances, the verdict of the Bosch board of management was that a more favorable wage settlement for the company could not have been achieved at that time. As in 1984, a strike would have made it very difficult for the company to meet its delivery obligations. The extended lifetime of the deal "does remove some of the tension from the distribution struggle and gives us a sound basis for costing."[152] At the same time, the members of the Bosch works councils were devoting most of their attention to internal agreements [*Betriebsvereinbarungen*], notably with regard to the expected (or feared) effects of the continuous improvement process (CIP). The central works council demanded an undertaking that "nobody will be laid off and nobody will be worse off as a result of the introduction and application of CIP."[153] Initially, the board declined. It did this for two reasons. Not only would the effects of CIP be difficult to distinguish from those of other measures, but also any concessions made would severely restrict management's freedom of action. Even so, executives knew full well that open resistance by the central works council and by local works councils would make CIP considerably harder to introduce. But in the autumn of 1992, while the issue of CIP was still being negotiated, the board decided that the extra month's salary (13th salary) agreed with the union for 1992 would be offset against payments under the work bonus scheme, which was not part of the collectively bargained wage agreement. The decision sparked massive unrest and indignation among large sections of the workforce. "Associates," one letter to Bierich noted, "learned only from the notice-board that part of their hard-earned 13th salary is being stopped. This action may be correct in strictly legal terms, but in moral terms it is dubious. It raises the question of how serious management is about *kaizen* and CIP and *Lernstatt* (to cite only a few catchwords). It seems they are only interested in these things when there is a possible management advantage. As we see it, it is unthinkable that anyone serious about a new leadership style should behave in this way as regards the 13th salary! Or does management think this sort of trick is going to motivate the workforce to do any more than work to rule? We hardly think so. If you want *kaizen*, you must stick to the ethical rules. That is something the founder himself thought important. His slogan 'I would rather lose money than trust' demonstrates this all too clearly [...]."[154]

Relations between the central works council and the board of management had been badly damaged by the great clash of the spring of 1993, but matters were inflamed further only months later. In October 1993, the board of management announced that the Feuerbach light works [*Lichtwerk*] would be closed on April 1, 1994. Since 1988, there had been talk at board level about restructuring the facility as part of the rethinking of the Bosch Group's location strategy. The profit situation of the alternators assembled in the light works had long given cause for concern, so it was planned to move alternator manufacturing to a lower-cost location outside Germany. At the same time, light-metal casting at Feuerbach was to be discontinued. It was also planned to shift sales, development, and administration of the lighting technology division from Feuerbach to Reutlingen. In return, and in order to take some of the pressure off the Schwieberdingen engineering center, the executive management of the starters division plus their associated departments were to move to Feuerbach to kick off the conversion of the Feuerbach plant into an automotive engineering location.[155]

Taken together, these changes would make the old-established Feuerbach location more important, though at the same time there would be a marked reduction in headcount and a shift in the ratio of salaried staff to wage earners from 1 : 3 to 1 : 1.8. In the spring of 1993, this package of measures received increased attention, and the restructuring of the Feuerbach plant was driven forward. The pump works and the light works were merged into a single unit and given a uniform plant management comprising three operating areas: diesel injection pumps, alternators, and ABS. Manufacturing of compact alternators was discontinued in Feuerbach and concentrated at two new locations outside Germany: the plant inaugurated in Cardiff, Wales, in 1991, and the plant in Treto, Spain.[156] Not least, the reason Bosch built a new plant in the U.K. was that Britain did not require a legal system of employee representation to be established. In the process of setting up the factory in Cardiff, therefore, Bosch was able to stage a "beauty contest" among the four unions that qualified. The relevant single-union agreement was awarded to the EETPU (the Electrical, Electronic, Telecommunications, and Plumbing Union), which for its part entered into a no-strike agreement.[157] Shortly afterward, Bosch built a plant in the Czech Republic for the large-scale production of diesel injection pumps. Over the long term, this was to employ over 5,000 workers. The closure of the light works came as a real shock to the workforce. There was enormous uncertainty. Nobody knew what was coming next or where they would be working in the future. Some die-hard Bosch associates decided to accept the offer of severance pay. Many migrant workers went back to their own countries. Those who stayed were assigned to the pump works, where fortunately the diesel boom had led to an expansion in production of distributor pumps. However, as one of the female associates affected was to remember in later years, "the working climate in the pump works was quite different from that in the light works. Many of us found it hard to integrate. At the pump works, they seemed to think that the relocation of the light works was our fault, and that we had come here to the pump works to take their jobs. There were lots of conflicts."[158]

But other Bosch locations were affected, too. At the start of the 1990s, the company had manufacturing operations at 17 locations in Germany and 15 in other countries, with the Bosch plants in Germany (still) on average substantially larger than those elsewhere. So it was that an internal retreat session in March 1993 discussed a wide range of measures, from disbanding the old Blaichach site and the Bühlertal site over the long term, through closure of the

Göttingen facility, to reshuffling assembly lines between the Ansbach and Nuremberg plants in order to focus operations there. In October 1993, it was announced that the Schwäbisch Hall plant (with 400 associates) would close.[159] And to quote the minutes of a board of management retreat session in December 1993: "To adjust to the structural decline in employment, job cuts and a reduction in headcount will continue through 1994."[160] At this point, social compensation plans were under negotiation at nine Bosch locations. And a whole package of further location-policy and employment-policy measures was already being implemented. These included changes in terms of employment in order to preserve jobs, reduction of collectively agreed rest periods (the "Steinkühler break" named for the IG-Metall chairman Franz Steinkühler), further-training measures during periods in which working hours were reduced, and the formation of so-called core locations. "The worktime models currently under discussion (part-time arrangements, annual working times, etc.) are to be examined for suitability at Bosch. Our aim here remains that of securing a location-specific agreement with the relevant works council."[161]

Only gradually did relations between board of management and central works council find their way back to a trustworthy footing. Smaller warning strikes and demonstrations were still held occasionally. In February 1995, for instance, attempts to relax the rules governing weekend work led to industrial action. But at the latest from the *Bündnis für Arbeit* ("alliance for employment") debate in the spring of 1996, with workforce reduction halted, both sides tried once again to make a joint effort to preserve Bosch's competitiveness. In mid-April 1996, Tilman Todenhöfer presented a catalogue of measures to the supervisory board. The catalogue was a program that the board of management and the central works council had already discussed at a special joint meeting in late March "as a key sign of their determination to solve problems together."[162] Todenhöfer explained to the supervisory board that the current "alliance for employment" campaigns did not, from Bosch's point of view, seem adequately to meet the company's real needs, as regards either timing or content. What was required, he said, was "for everyone to be prepared to take a critical look at all aspects of the old system." Arguments like "such-and-such won't work, given current operating conditions" or "we downed tools over this once already, fighting for this benefit even at the expense of more pay" were no longer admissible in that form.[163] It was felt that greater (and faster) success could be achieved as a result of "Bosch-related actions and measures," notably from cutting overtime. In addition, there was the "cautious" reintroduction of Saturday as a normal working day. "The reduction of overtime will only create new jobs," Todenhöfer claimed, "if it goes hand in hand with the flexible inclusion of Saturdays in shiftwork models as normal working days." A third point was flexible working times, coupled with promotion of partial retirement schemes and not least with bringing down what he described as a "far too large" number of days lost through sickness at Bosch. "The Robert Bosch Alliance for Employment Scheme," the presentation concluded, "will succeed only if we allow locations (with their very different needs) adequate freedom of action. Individual sites must reduce costs further, and they will know best where particular working-time models make most sense for them."[164]

The board proposed that the starting-gun for a Bosch-specific implementation of the "alliance for employment" program should be an appeal launched jointly with the central works council – which is what actually happened. By the summer of 1996, more than 100 working-time models had been agreed with works councils at many different locations, with the aid of which working times could be made more flexible locally and machine running-times extended accordingly.[165] The spectrum ranged from using part-time workers at the Bühl plant through introducing "working-time accounts" [Arbeitszeitkonten] (which recorded numbers of hours worked) all the way to work bonus schemes that factored in absenteeism. But no matter how much control this gave Bosch over internal problems relating to workforce development, over cyclical fluctuations, and over the constraints of structural adjustment, management still found itself paralyzed and all such efforts frustrated by developments on the level of labor and social policy. Among these was the amendment of the Works Council Constitution Act [Betriebsverfassungsgesetz] in the summer of 2001.[166]

A second major recessionary period announced itself even before 1999 was out. A new balance of power and of interests in industrial relations had been achieved at Bosch in the meantime, and the recession was to put it to the test. From the outset it was clear that management was trying explicitly not to repeat the mistakes of 1993. Talks with the central works council began promptly regarding a works agreement to secure jobs during cyclical fluctuations and a five-point program for making working time more flexible.[167] At a supervisory-board meeting held at the end of November 2001 (when the crisis was at its peak), the board of management confirmed that, unlike in 1993, it would first exploit all the opportunities for countermeasures offered by existing agreements in order to keep associates on board for as long as possible.[168] There would be no repetition of the error of cutting jobs at great cost and then not having enough skilled associates available when the upswing came. However, neither unions nor management at Bosch could avoid the very controversial debate that followed soon afterward: should people work longer hours without compensation in order to improve the competitiveness of Germany as an industrial location? One of the chief reasons why they could not circumvent the debate was that Franz Fehrenbach, who from July 2003 chaired the Bosch board of management, had been among those instigating it.[169] The years since have seen a number of additional works agreements. In 2002, for instance, there was one concerning the introduction of working-time accounts in order to secure jobs. And in 2007, a further agreement concerned a program to set up new manufacturing lines for diesel-injection technology at Feuerbach.[170]

2 Into the digital age

Technical strengths: research, development, and innovation

Even in the 1970s and 1980s, it was automotive engineering that had a decisive influence on the evolution of the Bosch Group, despite the breadth of the Bosch product range. Just as in the times of the founder, the future of the enterprise depended on its ability to innovate and to assert itself as the technological leader in this particular field. Granted, the transition to electronics and to microelectronics meant that the company had to satisfy radically different requirements. Unable to sustain its market position in the automotive sphere by producing individual components and devices, the company increasingly became a systems supplier. While the first-generation Bosch electronic gasoline-injection system (the Bosch D-Jetronic that went into series production in 1967) still comprised individual components, integrated circuits were developed for the second generation (the L-Jetronic). And the ABS antilock braking system that debuted in 1978 marked the breakthrough into digital technology.[1] This quantum leap called for enormous investment in research and development as well as substantial expertise in semiconductors, in open-loop and closed-loop control technology, and in materials research.

To organize its R&D work, Bosch traditionally employed a three-way split into basic research, advance engineering, and product development. Even after a separate development sector was set up in the late 1950s, this pattern was retained. When the company was given its present divisional structure in 1965, a special corporate sector was set up for research, materials, and process engineering (*Zentralbereich Forschung, Stoffe und Verfahren* or FSV). It was responsible for cross-divisional projects in areas such as semiconductor technology or materials research. This also gave it a certain autonomy vis-à-vis product development. Establishment of a separate research institute in Berlin (also in 1965) served the same purpose.

The creation of engineering centers toward the end of the 1960s significantly expanded Bosch's R&D capacity. The engineering center for research (*das Technische Zentrum Forschung*), subsequently relocated to the Schillerhöhe together with headquarters, and the engineering center for automotive electrical systems (*das Technische Zentrum Autoelektrik*) in Schwieberdingen, on the north-western outskirts of Stuttgart, were both built in 1968. Here the company was following a contemporary trend. German industry had already more than doubled its R&D spending between 1961 and 1965.[2] The Schwieberdingen facility was designed to "help the company demonstrate its systems capabilities in automotive technology."[3] Schwieberdingen is still the Bosch Group's largest engineering location.

The organizational structure of R&D went through several changes in the decades that followed. In 1972, the corporate FSV sector was itself divided in two (research and process engineering) – only to be recentralized a few years later. Research, process engineering, advance engineering, and product development were now pooled in a corporate sector for engineering (*Zentralbereich Technik*). In 1983 however, this gave way to a less centralized structure, the transition to microelectronics having proceeded faster in the divisions than at the corporate level. In the years between 1985 and 1990, this technological change was accompanied by a further jump in R&D expenditure. For the first time, this expenditure exceeded 6 percent of the company's total sales. The business sector that benefited the most from this spending was of course the automotive technology sector. Its share of R&D expenditure in 1989 was 52 percent, which more or less equaled the sector's share of sales. On the other hand, the 35 percent share enjoyed by communications technology was far higher than its share of sales. The consumer goods and capital goods business sectors received 4 percent and 9 percent of R&D outlay respectively.[4]

Since 1994, research and advance engineering have been reunited in a corporate sector. Despite the repeated changes outlined above, R&D at Bosch has always shown a remarkable consistency of direction. Walter Kaiser drew attention to this in his book *Bosch and the Automobile, 1950–2003: A Review*, first published in 2004: "Although Bosch altered the organizational structure of its research again and again, it experienced neither the flights of research-policy fancy nor the cultural revolutions that research departments in other companies had to face. New knowledge at Bosch was always knowledge that was close to application."[5] A further feature of R&D at Bosch was and is the low level of government funding involved. The substantial amounts invested in this area were always largely self-financed.

Given the strongly pronounced technical orientation of the company, it is hardly surprising that most of its innovations have been technology-driven. As a result, they were distinguished by top-quality engineering. This cost a lot, and high prices were something else Bosch was known for. Not infrequently, new systems were so expensive that at first only limited numbers of them sold. Only after several years and significant price reductions did such products become competitive and establish themselves in the market. Orientation to customer and market demands was not Bosch's strong point. The board knew this, and executives were always having to admit that the company was slow to offer the technologies the market was demanding.[6] This was particularly true of the communications technology business sector built up during the 1980s. Here (in certain areas, at least) demand came direct from end consumers and developed in shorter cycles than was the case in automotive technology.

Bosch also had a reputation for requiring long development times and for taking its time when transferring technical innovations to series production. As the McKinsey consultancy company pointed out in 1988, the high demands placed on its own products could mean that the company spent too much time on advance engineering and product development. The McKinsey study also suggested that the unusually close relationship between R&D and application was not without its problems. It led to deficiencies in the company's basic research and in its networking with academic institutions and universities.[7] Moreover, for a long time R&D departments at Bosch focused on Germany. As late as 1988, only 8 percent of R&D associates worked outside the country.[8] Not until the 1990s did the company realize that making this work more international offered additional growth opportunities. New engineering centers then sprang up in Farmington Hills, Palo Alto, and Pittsburgh in the U.S. and Yokohama in Japan.

The innovations of previous decades illustrated one of the company's strengths: its ability to allocate large numbers of highly qualified experts to work on strategically important developments and to drive them forward. It could also, after launching new products in the market, survive prolonged loss-making periods while making constant improvements. Here the advantages of a strongly application-driven approach were evident, as were those of being a non-listed company. The board was able to heavily subsidize promising projects without being punished for it by the capital market. Some of the most successful Bosch innovations were developments of systems that other companies had invented. Two examples were the ABS antilock braking system and the "common rail" diesel injection system. In both cases, development had begun elsewhere but Bosch had successfully brought it to fruition and launched the products in the market.[9] The company was not afraid to spend money here, and it took some heavy risks. Its market position as a technology leader in the automotive field could be sustained only with a steady stream of fresh innovations. As a supplier, Bosch was even more obliged to constantly innovate than other companies. Conversely, its innovative power gave it a significant advantage over smaller rivals that operated in the same field but were barely able to afford their own R&D facilities. This explains why Bosch was constantly on the lookout for models that would help it spot future trends promptly and break fresh technological ground at an early stage. In 1979, for instance, a research sub-committee of three scientists was formed to advise the company in connection with long-term R&D projects.[10] Beginning in 1993, special focal points, so-called "TOP" projects, were set up and given special budgets to identify new product and business areas.[11]

The clearest evidence of this innovation focus is to be found in R&D spending, which increased faster than sales from the 1980s. And despite the recession and the profit crunch of the 1990s, Bosch consistently remained committed to this policy. In fact, the board urged its researchers to come up with more home-grown products, and expanded the company's engineering capacities for the purpose.[12] At the end of the 1990s, Bosch employed a total of 16,300 scientists, engineers, and technicians in R&D projects across the globe. Ten years earlier, the number had been 12,600.[13] In Abstatt, north of Stuttgart, Bosch built a new and spacious engineering center, which started its work in 2004. By 2010, the company was employing 34,000 associates in R&D worldwide, and R&D expenditure accounted for over 8 percent of total sales.[14] This is partly because in the automotive industry, the trend is for an ever-increasing amount of R&D work to be delegated to suppliers, which in turn is because a great many of the advances in automotive engineering are now being made in the supplier sector, notably with respect to electronically controlled systems. In other words, suppliers make investments to develop products from which their original-equipment customers reap most of the benefit. This is particularly true in the case of Bosch. The Bosch Group's R&D cost ratio, already well above average for the German automotive-supply industry, exceeds even that of other large R&D-intensive enterprises such as Siemens and BMW.[15] In 2011, Bosch filed the largest number of patent applications of any company in Germany.

Fig. 11 Bosch Group R&D cost ratio (1985–2010)

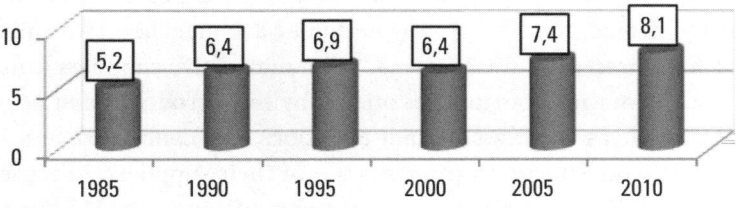

Source: Robert Bosch GmbH, annual reports

Development and acceptance of electronically controlled gasoline injection

Automotive electronics became established at Bosch during the 1960s, and was taken very much further during the following decade. For a long time, it was the guiding theme of the company's technological ambitions and efforts. In particular, electronically controlled engine-management and vehicle-dynamics systems formed the basis of the strong growth that Bosch subsequently achieved in the 1980s.

The earliest developments in the area of automotive electronics took place in the United States, where the transistor effect had been discovered. Bendix Corp. filed a patent application for the first electronic gasoline-injection system in 1957.[16] Two years later, advance engineering at Bosch began to look into this technology. However, it was not until 1967 that the company was able to present an electronic gasoline-injection system, the D-Jetronic, at the International Motor Show in Frankfurt. D-Jetronic (the "D" stands for the *Druck* or "pressure" that controlled fuel metering in the system) was based on transistors of a kind that Bosch was not itself making at the time. The electronic control units or ECUs used in the system were developed at Bosch and initially produced at Blaupunkt. The advantage of D-Jetronic over the carburetor system was that the electronic control of the injection nozzle allowed the composition of the engine's air-fuel mixture to be calibrated with great precision. This made it possible to reduce pollutant emissions. However, the first-generation systems were unreliable, susceptible as they were to malfunction and failure, and most automakers refused to take the risk of fitting them as standard equipment. Large-scale series production thus being out of the question, the electronic gasoline-injection system remained a very expensive product.[17]

The first automaker to step up to the plate was VW, which from the summer of 1967 fitted the U.S. version of its 1600 TL/TLE with D-Jetronic as standard equipment. It was prompted to do so by developments in the United States. For new passenger cars from the model year 1968, California had introduced stricter emissions limits, and other states were expected to follow suit. Without D-Jetronic, the VW 1600 would not have met the new limits and could not have been sold in California.[18] For automotive suppliers, this was the first inkling of the opportunities offered by the introduction of pollution controls. So far as cutting pollutant emissions was concerned, automakers were heavily dependent on the expertise of their suppliers. Because of the patents it held, Bendix Corp. was in a strong position in the U.S., as a result of which Bosch felt almost "locked out" of this market. The two companies therefore concluded a cross-license agreement for electronic gasoline-injection systems, with Bendix supplying the U.S. market and Bosch the European. In Europe, it was chiefly makers of high-end automobiles such as Volvo, Saab, Citroën, and Daimler-Benz that went over to fitting certain models with D-Jetronic, word having got around that electronic injection technology increased engine performance.[19] Bosch now decided to invest further in electronics and built its own semiconductor plant in Reutlingen, which went into operation in 1970.

However, with D-Jetronic still so unreliable there were repeated setbacks. Meanwhile, Bosch had developed an improved electronic gasoline-injection system. L-Jetronic, as it was called, was based on a new generation of high-performance components – integrated circuits. At the same time, a mechanical injection system known as K-Jetronic was developed. Both systems came onto the market in 1973. Parallel developments of this kind were not unusual, since they allowed a certain spreading of risks. Yet only rarely during the company's history did two rival systems compete with such stubborn persistence as L-Jetronic and K-Jetronic. "A neck-and-neck race continued for years within Bosch," Kaiser tells us.[20] It virtually split the company's experts into two camps. The electronics specialists around Hermann Scholl, who had been in charge of the development of the D-Jetronic system, faced off against the supporters of mechanical injection grouped around Konrad Eckert, the board member responsible for both diesel and gasoline injection. It was also a face-off between different approaches within the company. Eckert, a mechanical engineer by training, stood for precision mechanics. For him, the number-one priority was a product that never broke down. Scholl, with a background in electrical engineering, was in no doubt that the future belonged to electronics. And he wanted Bosch to be among the frontrunners when this leap of technology came.

At first, L-Jetronic lagged behind its rival K-Jetronic. Mechanical gasoline injection worked more reliably. With the D-Jetronic systems fitted to certain Mercedes models having broken down repeatedly, this reliability was particularly appreciated at Daimler-Benz.[21] Indeed, for a time it even looked as if electronic gasoline injection would be ousted from the market. However, it did then prove possible to bring down costs and hence prices for electronic systems. By contrast, with the demands made of exhaust-gas treatment rising, K-Jetronic systems had to be upgraded electronically, and so became more and more expensive.[22] In the shape of the lambda sensor, Bosch came up with a revolutionary innovation in the area of exhaust-gas treatment. Volvo fitted this technology from 1976 in models destined for sale in the United States. A year later, a major order was placed by Ford, and eventually nearly every automaker represented in the U.S. market fitted lambda sensors made either

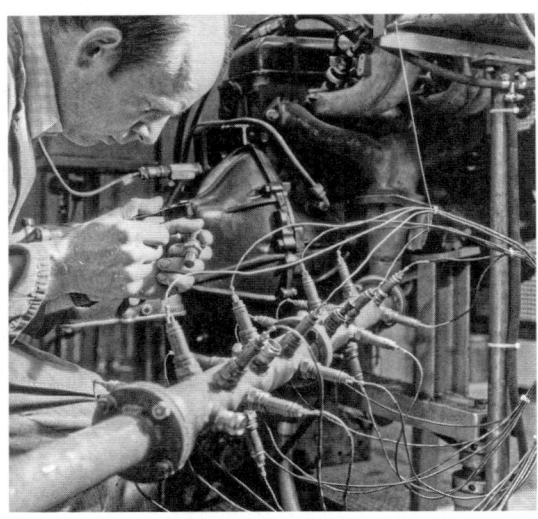

Testing a lambda sensor (1975)

by Bosch or by other suppliers able to copy the technology quickly enough. On the basis of information from the lambda sensor about the oxygen content of the exhaust emissions, the injection system knows how much fuel has to be injected into the engine to produce an exhaust gas composition perfectly attuned to its subsequent treatment in the catalytic converter. Thanks to this sensor, vehicles equipped with electronic gasoline injection could be fitted with what was then the most advanced development in exhaust-treatment technology, the three-way catalytic converter.[23]

Electronic gasoline injection swung back into favor once Bosch succeeded (in 1979) in launching a new engine management system called Motronic, which combined electronic gasoline injection with electronically controlled ignition. Motronic had been developed in the automotive electrics division, which was responsible for ignition. Within the board of management, this division fell under the accountability of Hermann Scholl. The new digital technology gained acceptance in connection with ignition devices because it made lower exhaust values possible. Electronically controlled ignition could be coupled with electronic gasoline injection but not with a mechanical system. Spotting an opportunity of promoting electronic gasoline injection through the back door, as it were (and thus achieving what was not to be had directly), Scholl gave the automotive electrics division the brief of developing a digitally controlled system that combined gasoline injection and ignition. Recalling the episode later, he described this as opening up "a second front." He could not sit idly by "while we lost our chance of making progress in electronics."[24]

Motronic, which went into production in 1979, used a unified, microprocessor-based electronic control for both ignition and fuel injection. The system made it possible to control three things at the same time: exhaust emissions, fuel consumption, and engine performance.[25] Scholl's development engineers had worked closely with BMW on this innovation, since its preferred partner for other projects, Daimler-Benz, was unwilling to drop either the K-Jetronic system or its electronically upgraded version, the KE-Jetronic. In 1979, BMW fitted its new 732i model with Motronic. However, that was not the end of the rivalry between the two gasoline injection systems. Scholl described this later in an address marking the 40th anniversary of electronic gasoline injection: "The fierce internal wrangling at Bosch between KE-Jetronic and Motronic continued for several years. The automotive electrics division and the diesel and gasoline systems division fought over each customer project, sometimes with aggressive pricing that was not covered by cost accounting."[26] But in the end Motronic proved the superior system, and the conflict between the two camps in Bosch's automotive business sector was defused organizationally by merging the KE-Jetronic, L-Jetronic, Motronic, and ignition units to form a new division.

It took time, but eventually Motronic became a major earner at Bosch. The principle of the system, controlling ignition and injection digitally by means of a central microprocessor, became generally accepted in automotive engineering. Of course, success of this kind was not something the developers of Motronic had either planned or foreseen. Their efforts were not geared at setting an international standard, nor had they worked on the system because the market demanded it. They had been concerned to seize an opportunity to gain acceptance within their own company for a technology they firmly believed in. For them, Motronic had initially been a side step, a detour, a means to an end, never an end in itself. It was their way of achieving their objective. If electronic gasoline injection had trumped its mechanical rival at Bosch at an earlier point in time, a system such as Motronic would not have been developed until later – possibly too late. As so often in the history of engineering, the "round-about way" led to even greater success than had been originally desired.

Vehicle dynamics systems and navigation devices

In addition to Motronic, Bosch also came up with innovations in the area of brake control systems that played an important role in establishing automotive electronics as a standard technology. The two landmark achievements in this field were the ABS antilock braking system [*Antiblockiersystem*] and the

ESP electronic stability program [*Elektronisches Stabilitätsprogramm*]. Again, the development period had begun long before, and again, other companies had pioneered the technologies concerned. The basic principle of ABS (preventing a vehicle's wheels from locking when the brakes are applied) was something engineers had been looking at back in the 1920s. As early as 1928, a Berlin engineer named Karl Wessel had been granted a patent for a mechanical braking-force regulator for automotive vehicles, which he then offered to Bosch. Preferring to develop a system itself, eight years later Bosch was granted a patent for a "lock-braking preventer." However, the Second World War broke out and the device never reached the production line.[27] The development of vehicle dynamics systems was at that time dictated by aircraft construction. U.S. and British companies had made some important inventions in this field, but the limitations of electrical engineering were such that these could not be transferred to road vehicles.[28] Furthermore, automakers showed little interest in brake control systems in the postwar period. Their products were selling like hot cakes even without such systems. But once semiconductor technology had become established, more sophisticated electronically controlled braking systems were developed on the back of it during the 1960s. A pioneering role in developing such systems was played by the Heidelberg company Teldix (today's Rockwell Collins Deutschland), a jointly owned subsidiary of Telefunken and Bendix Corp. that (among other things) produced electrical equipment for military aircraft.[29] In 1964, Teldix entered an alliance with Daimler-Benz to develop an electronic braking system for passenger cars. A similar project was also started a year later at Bosch. For Bosch, the field of braking technology was a formidable challenge at the time. With no prior expertise, it nonetheless began developing its own lock-braking preventer. As to what induced the company to do so, Bosch appears to have received some indication from Daimler-Benz that no one was really sure whether Teldix would be able to mass-produce its ABS when the time came.[30] So once again it was clearly a case of a technological push, not a demand-driven development.[31] Still, Bosch will doubtless have had its sights on its preferred customer in neighboring Untertürkheim from the outset.

In 1970 Teldix, in collaboration with Daimler-Benz, was the first company to test an electronic brake force regulator with independent regulation of individual wheels.[32] As Teldix was ahead of Bosch (which had not begun preliminary development work on ABS until 1969) at that time, Daimler-Benz opted for the Teldix ABS as the system it wished to take into series production. However, preparations had to be broken off when it emerged that this initial version of ABS did not satisfy the safety requirements. The parties involved began to doubt whether a safe system was going to be pos-

Testing vehicles with (*right*) and without (*left*) ABS at Daimler-Benz (1978)

sible at all, given the technology available at the time (with electronics still at the analog stage). When tests exposed further defects and ABS threatened to fall into disrepute because other producers had started to market technically immature systems for heavy trucks, work on the first generation of the anti-lock braking system, the Teldix ABS, was halted in December 1974. The decision was likely initiated by Daimler-Benz, even if all four companies involved (Bosch, Daimler-Benz, AEG, and Teldix) took it together.[33]

Bosch then re-started its efforts in ABS development. There were other reasons why the company was particularly interested in taking ABS development further. In 1973, through the mediation of Daimler-Benz, the Stuttgart company had acquired the 50 percent holding in Teldix previously owned by Bendix Corp. In this connection, it was the Teldix ABS development engineers that constituted the real value of the deal so far as Bosch was concerned. Moreover, ABS was the perfect match for the "3S" program that Bosch announced in November of that year. Jointly with Daimler-Benz, Bosch was keen to embark on a tour de force, using new digital technology and between 50 and 70 engineers to get ABS ready for series production within a few years. The instigator of this ambitious project was Hans Bacher, chief of the automotive technology business sector. The person accountable for the project itself was Hermann Scholl. Bosch developed the components and undertook the system design at the engineering center in Schwieberdingen. Fitting it into a vehicle was the responsibility of Daimler-Benz, as was testing the system as a whole. To bring ABS expertise under one roof, the automotive operations of Teldix were merged with Robert Bosch GmbH in 1975. Bosch also seconded additional associates from its other divisions to help develop "ABS 2," as it was dubbed. New electrical and hydraulic components, as well as a digital electronic control unit (ECU), had to be developed, and here Bosch was able to draw on synergy effects from its development of the electronic fuel-injection system. No expense was spared for this tour de force. Total expenditure for developing ABS, expressed as German marks, "ran into nine-digit figures."[34]

Accordingly, a production-ready ABS was presented in October 1978. In the end, digital electronics had proved to be crucial for its development, since the system could not work perfectly without it. Daimler-Benz could now offer its Mercedes S-class automobiles with ABS fitted as optional equipment. However, this triumph was overshadowed by news later described by Daimler-Benz as the "ABS trauma." Even before the Stuttgart press conference announcing the coup, the daily *Süddeutsche Zeitung* reported that BMW would similarly be offering its series 7 models with Bosch-developed ABS. Daimler-Benz felt deceived, since its development partner Bosch had assured it a head start of one year. For its part, Bosch claimed that Daimler-Benz was to have begun series production in the spring of 1978. The subsequent delay did not constitute a reason for breaking assurances already given in Teldix GmbH agreements with BMW and Porsche, under which series production was to begin a year later – that is to say, in the spring of 1979.[35] Following malfunctions of D-Jetronic systems in Mercedes models, there was already ill feeling at Daimler-Benz against Bosch, its "purveyor to the royal court" [*Hoflieferant*]. The "ABS trauma" again clouded relations between the two companies, though it did not keep them from collaborating on other development projects in the field of vehicle dynamics.

ABS was the first electronic brake control system. By preventing wheels from locking up during braking, it removed one of drivers' main fears, and made a clear improvement in driving safety possible. It was also feted in the media. Bosch, Daimler-Benz, Teldix, and others were awarded a major prize by *Bild-Zeitung*.[36] However, such accolade was not reflected in unit sales. The high development costs of ABS meant that it came at the hefty price of 2,500 German marks. Initially, unit sales lay well below expectations. In 1979, Daimler-Benz fitted ABS in a mere 5,000 automobiles.[37] Granted, ABS was available only as optional equipment for the premium segment – namely, for the Mercedes-Benz S class and later for the BMW series 7. But even among the well-heeled purchasers of these models, few were prepared to pay so much extra for what was still considered an obscure system. Yet for the producers, Bosch and Daimler-Benz, the retail price did not even cover costs. As a result, the heavy development costs of ABS were now compounded by sales losses of as much as 30 million German marks a year.[38] Bosch was able to offset these with its Motronic profits, but even so, given the capital invested, there could be no certainty that ABS would be a long-term business success.

Gradually, volume sales began to show a clear upward trend. ABS proved itself on the road, it became better known year by year, and increasing numbers of drivers were now prepared to pay a substantial price for the system. As sales went up, manufacturing costs per unit came down. At the same time, Bosch worked at reducing the latter by making engineering adjustments. From 1983, ABS sold at a profit, and two years later the upfront investments had been paid off. By then, and for some time to come, ABS was among the biggest earners in the Bosch product portfolio. Production and sales kept on setting new records, and in 1986 the million figure was reached and passed. In 1988, the price dropped to 1,400 marks, resulting in a further boom. ABS could now be featured as standard equipment for middle-class vehicles. By 1990, a quarter of the passenger cars made in West Germany were fitted with ABS. At the same time, manufacturing capacity had to be increased. Bosch built new plants in Immenstadt and Ansbach to make ABS components, while at the Reutlingen plant assembly of integrated circuits was further expanded. Teldix GmbH had already been taken over completely in 1981. Between 1983 and 1988, Bosch invested an approximate total of 850 million German marks in property, plant, and equipment for ABS production. The investment had soon paid for itself. By 1995, the number of ABS systems produced by the company for passenger cars totaled 20 million.[39] One reason why ABS became a business triumph on this scale for Bosch was that the engineering advance bought at such expense was one that rivals could in practice never make up. For the first six years, there was no competition at all. Only then did Teves start marketing its own electronic antilock braking system. Lucas Girling, Honda, and other producers followed, but Bosch remained the undisputed world-market leader with a share estimated at 60–80 percent. Even after the turn of the century, that share still lay at 35 percent.[40]

Before ABS became a commercial success, Bosch had already begun to develop further innovations in the field of vehicle dynamics. Together with Daimler-Benz, it began work on a TCS traction control system that used electronically controlled braking to prevent drive wheels from spinning when setting off or accelerating. The project was able to draw on preliminary work done by Daimler-Benz and experience gathered during the development of ABS, but it was not until 1986 that a version of TCS was ready for series production. It was now offered as an add-on to ABS (the ABS/TCS system).[41]

In the early 1980s, work also began at Bosch on a vehicle dynamics system that had to do not with "longitudinal dynamics" (like ABS) but with "lateral dynamics," and that would prevent a vehicle from skidding as a result of lateral forces. The project was launched with a team of some 50 associates. They initially developed a rear-axle steering system, but from 1983 they concentrated on a fresh approach suggested by Konrad Eckert, the board member with project accountability. This approach proposed utilizing ABS and TCS sensors to stabilize a vehicle laterally by braking individual wheels.[42] As with ABS and TCS, Bosch again worked closely with Daimler-Benz on this task. The two companies agreed to have the new system ready for series production by mid-1995. To optimize coordination between their respective teams, in 1992 a joint project unit was set up in Schwieberdingen. Extensive trials were carried out at the proving ground in Arjeplog, Sweden, where extreme winter temperatures and the remoteness of the site provided ideal conditions. There, the new VDC vehicle-dynamics control system, based on ABS and TCS technology, was presented in March 1994. Three years later it was renamed the ESP electronic stability program. When VDC went into series production for the S-class Mercedes in the summer of 1995, the development engineers from Bosch and Daimler-Benz had achieved their ambitious goal. The two companies were now building the world's first system of this kind.

Like ABS, ESP was not at first a business success. Following eighteen months in which Daimler-Benz offered the innovation on an exclusive basis, it was also installed by BMW and VW/Audi. Even so, Bosch had still produced fewer than 90,000 ESP systems by the end of 1997.[43] Before they would buy the new system, the customers who bought the premium vehicles produced by Daimler-Benz and BMW still needed to be convinced that it was worth the extra money. This was more difficult than with ABS, since ESP prevented skidding, a phenomenon that occurred less frequently than wheel-lock during braking. Then, practically overnight, ESP found itself in the limelight. The reason for this was an unexpected, indeed unwelcome event that provided one of the most spectacular object lessons in automobile history. In an attempt to enter the compact class, Daimler-Benz had launched a new model, the A class. In Sweden on October 21, 1997, this strategy hit the rails when an A class vehicle driven by the motoring journalist Robert Collin failed the so-called "elk test" (or "moose test") – a double lane-change that simulates the evasive action that has to be taken if an elk (or moose) wanders onto the road. When the Mercedes A class took this test, it keeled over. Collin's report on the incident in the Swedish specialist periodical *Teknikens Värld* opened the floodgates for a wave of negative publicity for Daimler-Benz. The A class was now sarcastically nicknamed *Vältklasse* ("rollover class"), and the German periodical *Auto Bild* published a photomontage of a skidding A class in free flight. Overnight, the phrase "elk test" was suddenly on everyone's lips.[44]

Daimler-Benz had to temporarily suspend sales of its A class, announcing that it would be fitting all vehicles of this type with ESP. Ironically, two years earlier, Daimler-Benz had been the first automaker in the world to market a system that would prevent skidding and rolling over even during elk test-style driving maneuvers. But because of its high price (in excess of 1,700 German marks), ESP had been reserved for premium automobiles. To save the A class, the Daimler-Benz CEO Jürgen Schrempp and the man in charge of his passenger-car sector, Jürgen Hubbert, had ESP fitted as standard equipment in the compact car at no extra cost. According to Daimler-Benz estimates, the modification cost the company some 100 million marks a year. In the press, the decision initially met with criticism. *Der Spiegel* called it an "electronic crutch" and a "logistical suicide mission," aimed solely at putting off the fateful decision to cease production of the A class entirely.[45] But if anyone was justified in speaking of a "logistical suicide mission," it was Bosch. Daimler-Benz pressed Bosch to supply 250,000 ESP systems for its A class vehicles, instead of the 60,000 systems already ordered for 1998. And if possible, it wanted them in the first quarter of the year. Normally, Bosch would have been unable to increase production so dramatically before August 1998, but the Schillerhöhe was aware of the pressure its neighbor, development partner, and preferred customer was under. It likely also realized that the elk-test disaster offered an opportunity to promote ESP. If it succeeded in saving the A class by fitting ESP, sooner or later other automakers would be unable to avoid fitting their compact and medium-sized vehicles with the system as standard equipment. ESP would become the industry standard through customer demand.

Bosch thus responded with a crash program to boost ESP production by as much as possible within a short timeframe. The program was headed by Hermann Scholl, who had meanwhile become chairman of the board of management. By putting other plans on hold and by trimming release times, the company contrived to increase supplies as Daimler-Benz had requested, though doubtless not actually expected.[46] Equipped with ESP, the Mercedes-Benz A class vehicles passed every elk test, and over the next two years

Daimler-Benz fitted all its models, from premium to compact, with this feature as standard equipment. By the autumn of 1999, Bosch had made its millionth ESP system. ABS had taken 10 years to reach this point. Even so, ESP could not yet be looked upon as self-sustaining, or even as a sure-fire success. As the in-house newspaper *Bosch-Zünder* reported, the elk-test debate had narrowed the image of ESP – "as if all ESP does is prevent vehicles from overturning in elk tests, and not much more."[47] The advantages of ESP were still difficult to convey. Many drivers, when ordering optional equipment, would opt for air-conditioning rather than for vehicle-dynamics control. The task became easier when Bosch opened its new test track in Boxberg in 1998, having designed this facility especially for testing systems such as ESP.[48] In Boxberg, large numbers of customers and journalists could be persuaded of the advantages of such systems. Although competitors such as Teves (ITT Automotive Europe) and Kelsey-Hayes had launched similar systems, unit sales of Bosch ESP systems rose steeply over the next few years. In part, this was because vehicle-dynamics control systems found more rapid acceptance in Europe (Bosch's home market) than in the U.S. or Japan.[49] By the spring of 2001, Bosch had already produced 3 million ESP systems. By 2005, 72 percent of the passenger cars produced in Germany and 44 percent of those produced in western Europe as a whole were fitted with ESP. In North America and Japan, the corresponding figures were just 21 percent and 15 percent respectively.[50]

But even without the notorious elk test of October 1997, ESP would have been accepted by the market, because it enhances driving safety and can save lives. Yet despite the huge volume of publicity, it took about ten years for ESP to become standard in Europe. What this makes clear is that, unlike consumer goods, systems of this kind gain market acceptance only when they have proved their worth over a substantial period of time. If there is one thing the companies that manufacture such systems need, it is stamina. Nowadays, electronic vehicle-dynamics control systems are mandated for newly registered vehicles in the European Union, in the U.S., and in Japan.

These triumphs in the field of automotive electronics should not obscure the fact that some Bosch innovations did not win acceptance. There were occasions when new products failed. In fact, looking back over the period 1973–2003, Hermann Scholl summed up: "The result of our multi-year innovation drive [is] to some extent sobering."[51] Scholl counted no fewer than 16 product areas that had been discontinued. They included only three from the automotive sector (magnetos for two-stroke engines, air brakes for heavy trucks, and headlights). All the rest were in non-automotive technology, and most of these were in communications technology. Here, too, it was clear that Bosch's technical strength lay overwhelmingly in the automotive sector. In terms of the company's innovative strength, the sector's significance was even greater than its sales suggested.

Unlike the automotive sector, other Bosch Group business sectors occasionally failed to spot trends in time. This was the case with video recorders, video cameras, and cell phones.[52] In communications technology, unlike automotive technology, Bosch clearly lacked the feeling for the core technologies of the future.[53] That said, products frequently had to be discontinued not because Bosch was behind technologically or had bet on the wrong technology in the first place but for other reasons: either costs were too high and the company could not compete in price terms, or the relevant product was deemed too complex to succeed in the market concerned. Bosch did best where its level of development expenditure put it so far ahead that rivals had trouble catching up. But while this was possible in the case of electronic engine management systems, which comprised several hundred components made from specially processed materials, it was not attainable in communications technology or consumer goods, where the competition could usually make up for lost ground quickly. One example that illustrates this is the development of navigation devices for passenger cars by the Bosch subsidiary Blaupunkt.

Back in the 1970s, Blaupunkt had worked with an institute of RWTH Aachen University to develop a "driver guidance and information system" (*Autofahrer-Leit- und Informationssystem* or ALI). The idea behind this system was that induction strips under the road surface would provide drivers with information about their chosen route. However, fitting out all the major routes in the country with induction strips was completely unrealistic, since it would have required astronomic levels of spending by the public authorities responsible for road construction. When this investment failed to materialize, the ALI project had to be terminated.[54] Having learned their lesson, developers began work on a stand-alone navigation system that used sensors to register driving direction and that compared this information with digital street maps. In 1983, under the name "Electronic Traffic Pilot for Drivers" (*Elektronischer Verkehrslotse für Autofahrer* or EVA), Blaupunkt was able to premiere such a system. But EVA never reached the market because it was felt that digitizing all West Germany's street maps would be too complicated.[55] This, too, can be described as a technology-driven invention.

When Blaupunkt introduced TravelPilot IDS in 1989, it was its third generation of navigation devices to enjoy a technological lead. As with EVA, the far more compact TravelPilot IDS used sensors to calculate the position of the vehicle, and compared this information with digital maps. This enabled it to compute the distance to the destination, but not as yet to show a route. In to-

day's currency, TravelPilot IDS cost the tidy sum of 4,500 euros. Of the navigation devices available in the market at the time, this one featured the highest
performance, but no more than 10,000 units were ever bought.[56] In the 1990s,
the market underwent a transformation as a result of GPS technology becoming available for civilian use. Satellite-controlled GPS devices caught on, costs
came down, and with them prices. But after pulling out of a project with
Daimler-Benz, Blaupunkt fell back and had eventually to content itself with a
modest share of the market.

3 From restructuring to change: the process of renewal in the 1990s (1993–2003)

Corporate governance and corporate organization

For Hermann Scholl, appointment as chairman of the Bosch board of management on July 1, 1993, could hardly have come at a more unfortunate time. His first official duties included presenting the annual report for "the year of catastrophe, 1993," at the same time as announcing further cost-saving measures. "Shock at Bosch: 800 million [German marks] down, 6,000 jobs gone", ran the *Bild-Zeitung* headline. There were several reasons why it was not Friedrich Schiefer (as Bierich, the retiring chairman, would have preferred) who was crowned the new head of Bosch, but Scholl. Topping the list, no doubt, was that Hermann Scholl was a "Bosch product" – the first, in fact, to rise through the ranks to become chairman since Hans Walz. Scholl had been with the company since 1962. A member of the board of management since 1975, he had far-reaching accountability for the company's main business sector of automotive technology. He knew Bosch, its manufacturing locations, its products, and its customers inside out. Above all, Bosch associates knew him. Scholl was also strongly influenced by Merkle and by his style of leadership and business policy. In other words, with Scholl in the saddle, the reins were once again drawn more tightly at Bosch, and the Schillerhöhe resumed its policy of control by central directive. In the view of Hans L. Merkle, Peter Adolff, and Robert Holzach, who comprised the human-resources committee at RBIK (which had the last word on Bierich's successor), this was the kind of leadership style that was needed to lead the company out of crisis, given the difficult restructuring phase Bosch faced. From Bierich (67 years of age) to Scholl (58) was hardly a "radical generational leap" (as the *Börsen-Zeitung* and other publications noted and Bierich himself said). Certainly, Scholl did not see himself as representing a new generation but very much as following in his predecessors' footsteps.[1] Aged 54, Schiefer (the new deputy chairman of the board of management), was also not much younger. The board now had only 10 rather than the previous 14 members, yet it could scarcely be called an appreciably younger assembly. Tilman Todenhöfer (human resources and social services, legal affairs, taxes, auditing, and public relations) and Clemens Börsig (commercial affairs and coordination of certain industrial technology and consumer goods divisions) operated as close advisers to Scholl (who at the same time was accountable for the coordination of the automotive technology business sector) and Schiefer (who coordinated the communications business sector). Completing this senior management team were the four long-serving automotive-sector executives Hansjörg Manger, Hermann Eisele, Heiner Gutberlet, and Hubert Zimmerer, as well as Wolfgang Hugo for sales organization and the aftermarket business and Rainer Hahn, now accountable for industrial technology and power tools. Scholl's initial priority, therefore, was continuity – in terms of both staffing and structure. Both externally and with regard to the internal organizational structure of the Bosch Group with its four business sectors and many subordinate divisions, regional companies, and subsidiaries, everything was to remain as it was for the time being. During this initial phase, Scholl, Schiefer, Todenhöfer, and Börsig formed a close-knit leadership quartet – supplemented by Bierich, who as RBIK chairman presided over the real center of power at Bosch.

But three years later, during the course of 1996, the organization of company leadership began to change discernibly. In 1993, there had still been much to suggest that Scholl simply represented a resumption or revival of Merkle's policy and leadership by other means. Now, however, a new, distinct leadership style emerged. The first sign was the introduction of what was called an "LD-Forum" [forum for *Leitende Direktoren* or senior executives], which took place annually over several days, complementing the half-yearly GPI gatherings [*Geschäftspolitische Information* or business policy briefing]. The latter (as Scholl explained in his introductory address to the LD-Forum) had permitted little or no real dialogue between executives and board of management – if only because of the structure of the program, which was mainly designed to keep people up to date. The hope was that the LD-Forum would give senior executives more opportunity to exchange views and contribute their own ideas and experience to the development of the Bosch Group. So it was not only the top leadership tiers of divisions and subsidiaries located in Germany who were invited, but all who belonged to those tiers worldwide.[2] Not long afterward, partly because of Schiefer's death and Börsig's departure in March 1997, Scholl reshuffled the board of management. The well-established leadership duo of Scholl and Todenhöfer invited a series of new, younger managers to join the board. By late 1997, only Gutberlet and Hahn were left of the 1993 leadership team. At the same time, Scholl set about changing the way the company was organized internally. The basic structure of the company with its divisions and regional subsidiaries (each of which

Hermann Scholl (2011)

was assigned to one particular group executive sector) had existed for some 30 years. This organization, broken down as it was according to industrial sector, had been by all means effective. It took its cue from the market, so to speak, and allowed especially divisions and business units to focus on the major competitors in each individual area. However, the volume of the company's business had increased more than tenfold over the same period, and the number of individual operating units had grown considerably. It was becoming clear that the members of the executive management of the divisions and regional companies very much took their lead from the group executive sector responsible for them. Important decisions were prepared first and foremost bilaterally, i. e., in consultation between the particular operating unit and the board member accountable. At the same time, however, they also had to be cleared with many other group executive sectors with responsibility for corporate functions.[3] Where decisions had to be taken at management-board level, these were in turn delegated to the executive management of individual operating units for execution. In short, the whole process was highly byzantine and inflexible. It called for extremely elaborate information flows, which themselves had to overcome numerous obstacles as they passed from department to department.

This now changed. From now on, the executive management of divisions and regional companies were directly involved in decisions made by the board of management, even attending the relevant board meetings on occasion. "The new arrangement will free up a substantial amount of time for members of the board of management, giving them more time to discuss questions of a more fundamental nature as well as enabling them to do so more often," or so it was hoped.[4] Before, this had been possible only at special retreat sessions of the board members – which normally, however, took place only twice a year.[5] One outcome of the new arrangement was that young executives began to carry greater weight within the board of management. From July 1999, in the persons of the deputy board members Franz Fehrenbach, Wolfgang Chur, Siegfried Dais, and Bernd Bohr (the "four young braves," as they were dubbed), a different generation received seats and votes on the expanded board. "It was clear to all of us," Fehrenbach recalled later, "that we had to find a counterbalance for our strong engineering orientation and rethink our culture, so that the company still had a chance of attracting talented young people in the future."[6] It was only after this opening-up, undertaken deliberately by Scholl with a view to his successors, that a radical generational change came about in the leadership of the company. Finally, over the course of the year 2001, Scholl also transformed the external organizational structure of the Bosch Group. Following the almost complete sale of the communications technology divisions, the corresponding business sector was wound up. That left only three main sectors: firstly, Automotive Technology (which until 2001 was referred to as Automotive Equipment), with its eight divisions (many of them regrouped): Gasoline Systems, Diesel Systems, Chassis Systems (i. e., including brake systems), Energy Systems, Body Electronics, Car Multimedia (now incorporating Blaupunkt GmbH), Automotive Electronics, and Automotive Aftermarket; secondly, the Industrial Technology business sector (Packaging Technology, Hydraulics, etc.); and thirdly the newly formed Consumer Goods and Building Technology business sector with the divisions Power Tools, Thermotechnology, Household Appliances (BSHG), Security Systems, and Broadband Communications (i. e., what was left under the roof of Bosch Telecom GmbH).

Before we go on to consider the corporate policy of the Scholl-Todenhöfer years in greater detail, let us look briefly at sales figures and growth over this period. What strikes us here is how quickly Bosch recovered from the 1993 crisis. Between 1993 and 2003, sales rose from the equivalent of 16.6 billion euros to 36.4 billion euros. Profits also rose, from 218 million euros to more than 1 billion euros in 2003.[7] However, it is also evident that this growth was by no means smooth. There were considerable drops in 1999 and particularly (following the first major recession of the new century) in 2001 and 2002. What is clear above all is that the growth rates, which were at times sizable, owed little to internal growth. They came mainly from external growth and resulted from major acquisitions.

Fig. 12 Bosch Group sales (1993–2003): sales in millions of euros (*left*) and as a percentage year-on-year change (*right*)

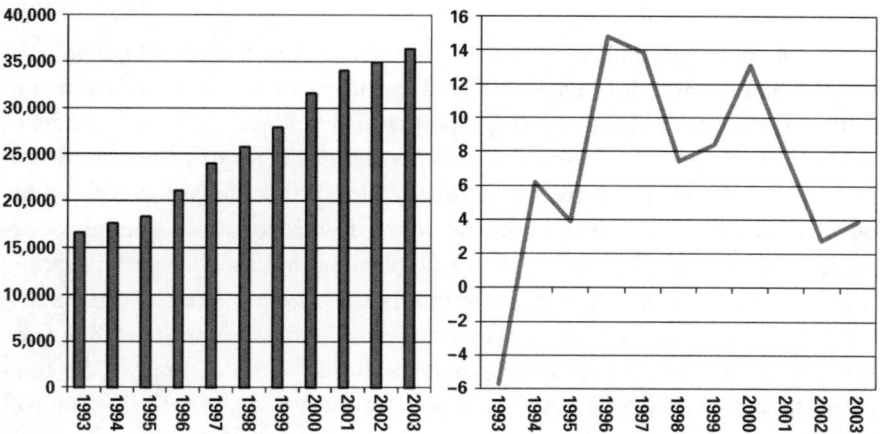

Source: Compiled and calculated from data in annual reports

On taking office in July 1993, Hermann Scholl got rapidly to work on the urgent tasks of restructuring, and continued his predecessor's cost-cutting policies with iron determination. Toward the end of September 1993, at a joint meeting of the board of management and senior executives, he presented a no-holds-barred analysis of the company's present position, warning his executives that there were more lean years ahead, during which operating units had to be turned around fast.[8] "At Bosch," he said, "we tend to blame a bad result mainly on a cyclical market decline. In doing so, we overlook the structural problems that we have had for some years now. They were obscured at first by a favorable market situation in the late 1980s and by the special economic circumstances of German reunification, but the current recession has only thrown a harsher light on those difficulties."[9] Scholl cited three main problem areas in this connection. In the first place, benchmarking studies had shown that costs at Bosch were 30 percent too high on average. Second, even when the economy was normal, too many products were posting heavy losses. Third, the effects of international price competition had been underestimated. "We knew what the problems were, but we didn't tackle them consistently enough."[10] Scholl then made a number of fundamental observations and points. They clearly showed where he intended to set a new tone in the future, and how. One point was the problem of over-investment in management methods and tools. He meant to make planning less bureaucratic. Highly differentiated though planning processes were at Bosch, they were often based on illusory premises.

"I sometimes feel that we bypass or simply ignore plans that we have elaborately developed and carefully put in place. There can be no other explanation for much that goes on here."[11]

Another recurring theme was the problem of associate development, the sorely belated search for highly qualified executives, and the lack of women in senior management. "Not one single woman is employed in the three tiers of management represented here, and this hardly speaks for us."[12] Finally, Scholl highlighted the need for creativity, for the ability to innovate, and for thorough, systematic, long-term planning coupled with consistent pursuit of research and advance engineering.[13] In an interview with the *Stuttgarter Zeitung* toward the end of October 1993, when journalists suggested that it had taken the U.S. automotive industry ten years to get back on its feet and asked how he was getting on with his recovery process at Bosch, he said simply, "We can't afford to take so long."[14] Bosch was, he said, in the process of shedding unprofitable fringe operations. The restructuring of its divisions and a considerable streamlining of its organization would be completed by the end of the following year. Moreover, the company was working hard on manufacturing new products at drastically reduced cost.[15]

As expected, the figures for the 1993 financial year that Scholl presented at the annual press conference in June 1994 were very poor. Yet he could also report better provisional figures for the current year (1994). It was too early, of course, to draw conclusions about the structural measures that had been introduced. Nor did the new figures indicate that the company had finally turned the corner as far as sales and costs were concerned. Instead, they were mainly due to economic recovery having set in sooner than expected.[16] The downward slide in earnings had been halted and, in the shape of vehicle dynamics control, Bosch had an innovative new product in the development pipeline that promised to achieve the same kind of market penetration as ABS within the foreseeable future, and thus to provide a massive boost to sales and earnings. However, as early as 1995, and then again in 1996, Bosch suffered setbacks. Ambitious sales and earnings targets had to be trimmed substantially.[17] Scholl gave several reasons for this. One was the unfavorable parity of the German mark to the U.S. dollar and thus unplanned changes in the exchange rate, but above all there was the need to set up provisions for losses (arising from supply commitments) amounting to hundreds of millions of German marks – "an amount that goes up from year to year, since original-equipment customers in the automotive sector make annual price reductions a precondition for long-term contracts."[18] Finally, the wage settlement of 1995 weighed down on result with unplanned additional personnel expenses of some 100 million German marks. Seeing few growth opportuni-

Annual press conference (1994)

ties in traditional markets and in such production regions as western Europe, North America, and Japan, the Bosch board of management increasingly placed its hopes on expansion in developing countries and emerging markets. Increased internationalization and globalization coupled with a hugely increased presence in southeast Asia, China, India, South America, and eastern Europe now became a core element of Scholl's business strategy.[19] However, this depended on a successful restructuring of Bosch's core field of business.

Crisis and reorganization: the automotive technology business sector and the perennial problem with loss-making products

At the end of 1996, a close analysis of the development of earnings showed that earnings structure (i. e., the source of operating result) had changed, and fundamentally so. Nine years earlier (at the end of 1987), the profit and loss statements for product categories still showed the usual picture. At just under one billion German marks, the automotive technology business sector accounted for nearly 100 percent of positive operating result, with ABS, L- and K-Jetronic systems, starters, and diesel distribution pumps as the largest sales drivers and profit earners.[20] On the other hand, the communications technology business sector (at only 52 million German marks) hardly counted at all, while the industrial technology (minus 49 million German marks) and consumer goods (minus 38 million German marks) sectors were in the red. In terms of operating margin (i. e., operating result as a percentage of sales), automotive technology and communications technology were more or less equal. Losses from product categories with negative operating results totaled some 600 million German marks, but these were very much more than made up for by earnings from the automotive business. Eight years on (in 1995), the picture had changed dramatically. The negative result from loss-making products had doubled to 1.3 billion German marks, while the positive operating result of the automotive technology business sector now totaled only 380 million German marks, one-third of its 1987 level.[21] The communications technology business sector (whose earnings had slumped to minus 286 million German marks) was now generating huge losses, while the consumer goods sector, having doubled its sales, had in absolute terms generated nearly as much profit as the automotive sector (i. e., 304 million German marks, including 140 million German marks from the power tools division alone, plus 87 million German marks from thermotechnology and 77 million German marks from BSH). Even the industrial technology sector (with an operating result of 7 million German marks) was in the black.

The biggest earners at Bosch were still ABS, together with so-called helix-controlled diesel distribution pumps and in-line diesel pumps. The biggest loss-makers, on the other hand, were time-controlled diesel distribution pumps, new products from the car multimedia division (including navigation systems), as well as common-rail diesel systems – chiefly because of their considerably longer development times and unexpectedly high upfront costs. Breaking down operating result by country of origin brings us even closer to the real problem. If operating result originating in Germany is compared with the result of all regional companies, the figures show that some 80 percent of operating result across the business sectors was "made in Germany" in the period 1988–90. That is to say, it was due to sales of products manufactured mainly in German plants. By 1995, the ratio was completely different. Profits from regional companies had doubled in absolute terms and were now higher than those of the divisions "at home."[22]

Eliminating loss-making product areas while at the same time promoting product categories with greater potential for growth and profit were therefore focal points of Scholl's business policy. In a company such as Bosch, with its wide variety of products and regions, there was never going to be an ideal situation with no loss-making areas. However, "in the Bosch Group both the number and the extent of loss-making areas are clearly excessive," as Scholl lamented at the GPI conference in December 1997. "The great danger when a situation is so far out of kilter is that there is increased pressure to earn even more in areas which are already profitable. This puts the long-term competitiveness of those areas at risk. Our aim must be to bring our company to the point where it is we ourselves who decide where to absorb short-term losses for the sake of long-term gain. And we must all do everything in our power to avoid having losses thrust upon us by external developments, whether in the form of competition or through altered business conditions."[23] There were indeed many instances of the board having had to take heavy initial losses over a large number of years in order to create a secure, future-proof position in the marketplace for new products or whole new areas of operation. The diesel distributor pump was one such product. Others were gasoline injection, the anti-lock braking system, and vehicle dynamics control. Even the new unit-injector and common-rail high-pressure diesel injection systems were still (in the latter half of the 1990s) making heavy losses. "Nonetheless," Scholl stated with conviction, "in a few years' time they will form the core of our future diesel business."[24]

Much of the future course of product engineering in the automotive business sector was thus determined from the outset. At its heart were the divisions for automotive electrics (ABS and chassis systems, as well as safety systems) and diesel systems (i. e., injection systems for diesel engines). As early as June 1994, Scholl told the RBIK shareholders that Bosch needed to become a systems supplier (brakes and ABS) in order to secure its competitiveness. For this purpose, he said, it needed to collaborate with, or possibly acquire, a brake manufacturer.[25] The company's chief competitor, ITT Automotive/Teves, was already a systems supplier, so it made sense to enter into talks with Lucas Industries. The British company was a reputable supplier of braking systems with a strong market position in Europe. The idea was to set up a joint-venture company limited to Europe and the United States. Bosch would have the industrial leadership, with Lucas contributing its brake operations and the Stuttgart company its ABS operations.[26] As concerns its diesel business, Bosch was counting on diesel-powered automobiles gaining further public acceptance and hence on expanded production of such electronic diesel-injection systems as common rail. The diesel systems division was still felt to have excellent market prospects. However, it was important to prevent the kind of development seen in the gasoline-injection market, where original-equipment customers had bent over backwards to help Siemens become a direct competitor to Bosch in order to counter the market leader's dominance.[27] There was also a challenge in the sphere of manufacturing engineering to be overcome – one that Bosch increasingly faced. This was the demand for modules, i. e., physical building blocks of sometimes functionally independent components intended to replace or complement systems as functional entities.[28] One internal problem for Bosch in this connection was the traditional product demarcation between divisions, which was of necessity giving way to cross-divisional collaboration with jointly established programs and priorities. Moreover, the trend toward modules frequently involved invitations to tender for what were called "planning competitions" [*Konzeptwettbewerbe*]. All bidders for a particular part or a particular function were asked by automakers to put forward ideas for its future design. The consequence was a substantial increase in development costs, partly because different versions of the function profile called for discussion and planning with the other partners involved in developing the module. Above all, however, such "planning competitions" raised a crucial question: how was Bosch to prevent its own know-how from being leaked to rivals when it submitted its ideas?

In April 1996, Scholl then offered a clear signal in this direction. The talks with Lucas having come to nothing, Bosch took over the entire hydraulic brake business of the U.S. AlliedSignal group. The production range it had bought covered all the key elements of a traditional automotive-braking program: disc and drum brakes, brake boosters, and brake master cylinders, all manufactured in a total of 14 plants employing some 11,000 people in the U.S. and Europe. The acquisition enabled Bosch to offer its automotive-industry customers complete braking systems (ranging from brake actuation through ABS to wheel brakes) for all classes of vehicle. As a result of the takeover, Bosch rounded out its know-how in the field of electronic brake control (ABS, traction control, and ESP) with additional expertise in the field of conventional braking systems.[29] Contacts with AlliedSignal went back to the mid-1980s, when the U.S. company had taken over the crisis-hit Bosch rival Bendix and itself approached Bosch with proposals for an alliance.[30] Talks dragged on intermittently, but it was not until *Manager Magazin* reported in February 1988 that Siemens and AlliedSignal were planning to set up a joint-venture company producing electronic systems for the automotive industry that the topic once again became a business-strategy priority for Bosch.[31] After an internal study had weighed up the pros and cons of an alliance with AlliedSignal, talks reopened at the beginning of 1990. However, a further six years were to pass before negotiations reached a successful conclusion.[32] The purchase price was a massive 1.5 billion U.S. dollars (the equivalent, at the time, of 2.2 billion German marks). Moreover, it had become public knowledge prematurely. It was the most expensive acquisition on record at Bosch.[33] But the prospects were irresistible. The takeover stood to give Bosch a leading position internationally as a brake producer, and offered an excellent opportunity to become a systems supplier to Ford and Chrysler, as well as to compete with Teves. All misgivings faded to nothing, particularly since the decision had already been taken against collaborating in a joint-venture company ("AlliedSignal's short-term, result-based mindset and the inconsistency of product strategy that goes with it could well make it a difficult, somewhat unpredictable business partner"[34]). Financially, the deal also seemed realistic and worth backing (two-thirds of the money to come from Bosch's own resources, one-third from U.S. dollar loans). Besides, it had the blessing of the antitrust authorities.[35]

However, the great expectations in the AlliedSignal acquisition (its brake business at the time was already deeply in debt) soon gave way to a more sober assessment, and in the end came to nothing. From a strictly commercial point of view, the takeover had seemed to make strategic sense.[36] Yet for Bosch, the brake business turned out to be something of a headache. A team of consultants from Arthur Andersen was called in. With their help, the Bosch project group looked at the brake business and visited AlliedSignal's various manufacturing plants. But restructuring costs incurred through plant closures on grounds of surplus capacity, the enormous R&D outlay, and a substantial need for further investment soon pushed expenditure well above the level originally planned.[37] Bosch's new braking venture lost more and more money, notably in the foundation brakes business (included in the deal), and in the end, despite many attempts at restructuring and turnaround, it had to be sold off piece by piece between 2009 and 2012.

For a while, though, Scholl could present improved figures for the automotive sector in the period following the AlliedSignal deal. In 1997, for the first time in years, the sector again recorded double-digit sales increases. These continued (albeit with major fluctuations) until the turn of the century. From the equivalent of some 10 billion euros in 1994, automotive technology sales more than doubled to top 20 billion euros by 2000. With a few exceptions, Bosch was able to maintain or even boost its market shares. Taking advantage of the fresh opportunities that opened up for non-Asian companies in the wake of the partial disintegration of traditional *keiretsu* supplier relations in Japan and the *chaebol* in Korea, it had strengthened its position in those two countries. As Scholl told the LD-Forum in June 1998, "[the automotive business sector] has grown more strongly than the supplier industry as a whole, with the result that its competitive position is much improved."[38] Nonetheless, on closer inspection, the profit situation in Bosch's automotive sector was "out of synch" with its sales growth and enhanced market position, as Scholl admitted to the RBIK meeting five months later.[39] Progress was being made with the turnaround of operational areas that were in deficit. However, the newly developed products in many fields of business, such as direct injection (whether gasoline or diesel) and navigation systems, placed a considerable burden on overall result. This was in addition to the massive losses in the brake business. The contribution made by the automotive sector to Bosch Group sales (formerly 55 percent) had risen to an average of 65 percent, even topping 70 percent on occasion. Bosch's dependence on the automotive industry was once again greater than ever – and this at a time when, through rapid concentration in the automotive industry, but especially through the large-scale merger of Daimler and Chrysler, the market environment was changing dramatically. Between 1980 and 1999, the number of major automakers halved to 16.[40]

The environment was changing on the competitor side as well. New competitors had emerged, including the major original-equipment suppliers Delphi and Visteon. Spun off from the GM and Ford groups respectively, these two now had to fend for themselves in a free market. They were also expanding increasingly in the direction of Europe, where not only Bosch but also such powerful suppliers as Siemens, Lucas, Valeo, and Magna were already jostling for position. At least Bosch had contrived to reduce its dependence on a small number of major customers. At the start of the 1980s, the ten largest original-equipment customers still made up 43 percent of Bosch's automotive sector sales, but by 1994 their share had fallen to 36.6 percent. Daimler and VW, traditionally Bosch's two biggest customers, who in 1981 had accounted for 26.7 percent of the company's sales, now contributed only 14 percent.[41] But all was not rosy. The guest speaker addressing Bosch senior executives at the LD-Forum in September 1999 did not mince his words: "[Bosch customers] no longer see themselves as beholden to your technology and are no longer going to accept an arrogance born of technological superiority."[42] As board members registered with concern, many major customers were now "seeking systematically to reduce our market shares, which are in most cases large."[43] This was not something that had existed in the 1970s and 1980s, at least not in this form.

Fig. 13 Sales of the Bosch Group's automotive technology sector (1990–2003): sales in billions of euros (*left*) and as a year-on-year percentage change (*right*)

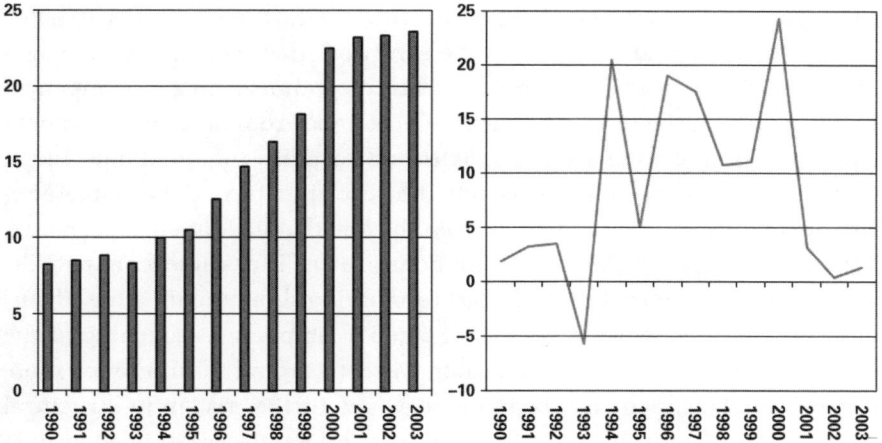

Source: Compiled and calculated from data in annual reports

This situation, plus a persistently unsatisfactory profit situation (which rising sales obscured), did not bode well for the years ahead.[44] A glance at the product-class profit and loss statement for 2000 also revealed that, despite many improvements and successful elimination of loss-making items, little had changed in principle compared with 1995. In fact, Bosch's efforts at managing this profit and loss situation (which was unsatisfactory in the eyes of the board) showed "startling continuity."[45] Total losses from product categories with negative operating results still came to around 700 million euros. However, the automotive sector had once again doubled its positive operating result to 398 million euros. And at 332 million euros, the consumer goods and building technology business sector had likewise strongly boosted both its absolute and its relative share in total earnings. The industrial technology business sector, with almost 50 million euros, was also contributing to Bosch's improved profit structure. On the one hand, the results of what had previously been heavily loss-making product categories had thus been markedly improved (the number of loss-making areas had itself been halved). On the other hand, high-earning, high-selling products were losing some of their potency (not least as a consequence of technological change in the area of diesel direct injection and measures to enhance profits for brakes). The chief "headaches," as before, were common rail, gasoline direct injection, brakes, and navigation systems, which were together responsible for nearly

70 percent of all losses, while the biggest earnings came from diesel injection pumps.[46] Yet despite all the restructuring measures that had meanwhile been either launched or successfully carried out in the core business area of automotive technology, and despite all the hard work that the board of management had put into instilling a new sense of optimism in the company,[47] events following the terrorist attacks of September 2001 and the subsequent global recession caused a setback. Sales and earnings collapsed once more, though unlike in 1993 Bosch avoided falling back into the red. But something else distinguished this fresh crisis from the one that had hit eight years earlier. This time the problems were not homegrown. They came from outside. To that extent the board could do little or nothing about them.[48] One advantage was that the company had anticipated a temporary weakening of the global economic situation, despite actual events. From the autumn of 2000, therefore, the company had begun to slow any further rise in its structural costs. And, unlike in 1993, the board also (as we have seen) decided against shedding jobs when the recession came. Lastly, with regard to the financial situation and its own liquidity, Robert Bosch GmbH was able (as publicly traded companies in particular were not) to absorb a temporary fall in its annual net profit quite calmly. Because of the way it was set up under company law, it did not have to distribute high dividends, so there was no need for it to fall back on reserves. But although even Bosch had less room for financing growth and acquisitions as a result of the crisis, it was precisely this period that saw two major takeovers intended to further reduce the Bosch Group's dependence on the automotive-supply business.[49]

Diesel injection systems and the diesel boom

The return to rapid growth in both sales and profit in the years around 2000 was due chiefly to the performance of the diesel systems division. Diesel engineering had long been considered one of the company's strong points, and since Germany supplied nearly half the global diesel-vehicle market, it was also considered a strength of the German automotive industry as a whole. In 1994, only 24 percent of the passenger cars produced in Europe were fitted with diesel engines. By 2004, this figure had doubled to 48 percent.[50] Bosch itself had made a decisive contribution to this boom. The new common-rail and unit-injector high-pressure diesel injection systems for passenger cars that the company premiered in 1997 and 1998 respectively not only improved torque and overall performance, but also made engines run smoothly and reduced fuel consumption and pollutant emissions. The result was a transformation in the image of the diesel engine, which found expression in sharply increased sales figures.

Development of such high-pressure diesel injection systems was another lengthy and by no means straightforward process. The unstoppable advance of electronics suggested that diesel distribution pumps would be replaced in the foreseeable future by a new and higher-performance technology. So in the mid-1970s, Bosch began work on an accumulator-injection system for passenger cars which came to be known as common rail. Up to then, direct injection had been used only in diesel-powered commercial vehicles, not in the fast-running engines fitted in passenger cars. Common rail was based on a completely new principle, separating the generation of pressure from the injection itself. This allowed the moment of injection to be flexibly selected. It also allowed for high injection pressures, which further reduced pollutant emissions. The principle itself was familiar, but had been thought technically too demanding to ever be readied for series production. In 1978, therefore, Bosch suspended work in this area. Advance engineering now turned its attention to a different kind of high-pressure diesel injection system, the unit injector. Unlike common rail, this system operated with separate injection pumps for each cylinder. The injection process was controlled electronically using solenoid valves, which meant that it could be made more regular. The system made it possible to reach substantially higher pressures (up to 2,050 bar) than could be attained with common rail. Emissions values were thus a further point in this technology's favor. Writing in the *Bosch-Zünder* in 1987, Max Straubel attested to common-rail technology's "grave disadvantages" and "major engineering problems." The directly controlled unit-injector system, on the other hand, was "a technology worth pursuing."[51] Having acquired a 49 percent holding in Diesel Technology Company in the U.S., Bosch bought in enough expertise to enable it at last, in 1994, to take the high-pressure unit-injector system into series production.[52] Bosch was the first automotive supplier in the world to offer this innovation, giving the company the status of technology leader. However, the system could not yet be fitted in passenger cars, only in commercial vehicles. The first truck producer to equip an entire model range with the unit-injector system as standard equipment was Volvo.

Meanwhile, common-rail technology had also made significant progress – though not at Bosch. While Bosch had opted for the unit-injector system, Elasis (an engineering company belonging to the Fiat Group) had in 1993 succeeded in developing and patenting a common-rail system. In fact, common rail, as Herman Scholl pointed out later, had "been in the offing for a while."[53] Fortunately for Bosch, Elasis (i. e., Fiat) was disinclined to manufacture the common-rail system itself. Instead, it turned to Bosch. Clearly, Fiat doubted its ability to make such a technically sophisticated system ready for series production. Trial runs had repeatedly presented problems. Even the Bosch engineers initially doubted whether it would be possible to series-produce the common-rail system to their company's customary high standards. So it was not until 1994, when a second automaker, Daimler-Benz, showed interest in the technology, that Bosch decided to acquire the patents. The common-rail system was then further developed at Bosch in collaboration with Daimler-Benz. This proved a bigger challenge than anyone had expected, since the system was far from mature. The work was done at Tecnologie Diesel Italia in Bari, a company created especially for the purpose, the Fiat Group having received subsidies from the Italian government on condition that the project was carried out in the structurally weak Mezzogiorno region of southern Italy. Bosch acquired the entire Elasis team of common-rail development engineers, headed by Mario Ricco. With the Bosch board member Hermann Eisele in overall command, the team set about developing a common-rail system that satisfied the requirement for extremely high precision. For three years, these engineers and technicians overcame difficulty after difficulty until at last, in 1997, series production of common rail could begin at the Bamberg plant.[54]

In parallel to the work on common rail, further development work was done at Bosch on the unit-injector system. The original intention had been to offer the unit injector for commercial vehicles only. This intention was quickly abandoned when VW decided to collaborate with Bosch's British rival, Lucas, on developing a unit-injector system for passenger cars. Having VW turn to Lucas was something that Bosch was determined to prevent. With a major effort and investments totaling 160 million German marks, the Stuttgart company succeeded in developing the unit injector to the point where, by mid-1998, series production of these systems for VW's Passat TDI model could be started at the Rommelsbach and Rodez plants. VW was soon fitting other models with this high-pressure diesel-injection technology, and Lucas dropped out of the race.[55]

Common rail had entered series production a year earlier. So automakers could now choose which of Bosch's diesel injection systems they wanted to fit into their vehicles – much as had been the case in the 1970s with gasoline injection systems. It was agreed with Fiat and Daimler-Benz that the first models (from October 1997) equipped with common rail should be the Alfa Romeo 156 and the Mercedes C 220 CDI.[56] While unit-injector systems were now supplied solely to VW, other automakers including BMW, Audi, and Peugeot were soon opting for common rail. However, as with electronic gasoline-injection systems in the early years, a number of problems presented themselves. As Scholl had to admit at the GPI conference of December 1998, the new high-pressure diesel injection systems presented "major engineering difficulties." These led to vexation on the part of important customers as well as to temporary cutbacks in production.[57]

Buyers of automobiles were nonetheless impressed by the new systems. In 1998 alone, the share of diesel-powered vehicles among new registrations in Germany climbed from 14.8 to 17.6 percent.[58] And with the same thing happening throughout western Europe, the order books at Bosch's diesel systems division filled up. While other parts of Bosch's automotive sector stagnated or even shrank, diesel systems took on 4,000 new associates in 1998 alone, as sales rose by 17 percent.[59] The success it enjoyed in this area took Bosch by surprise. Demand for high-pressure diesel injection systems far exceeded in-house planning figures.[60] Further quality problems resulted, as did disgruntlement among major customers. For instance, when it proved impossible to deliver enough unit-injector systems to VW, relations between the two companies soured for a while.[61] Furthermore, the situation led to high additional costs at Bosch, which ate into the contribution margins featured in the planning figures.[62]

Bosch had now also begun manufacturing common-rail systems at its plants in Bursa (Turkey) and Charleston (USA). By 1999, Bosch had already turned out its millionth common-rail system. By 2002, the figure stood at a full ten million – even though strong competitors such as Delphi, Denso, and Siemens Automotive had since moved into the field and were capturing a share of the common-rail market. Siemens and Peugeot had also developed piezo injection nozzles, which made even more precise fuel metering possible, and gave these two competitors – for a while, at least – a technological lead. In August 2000, an article in the *Financial Times Deutschland*, headed "Virtual monopolist Bosch under pressure on diesel front," quoted a top VW manager as saying that he fully welcomed the way Bosch's rivals had mounted an assault on the market leader's common-rail business. The man had allegedly added "off the record" that the Bosch monopoly in diesel systems was actually "a case for the EU Commission."[63]

Piezo inline injectors also featured in a third common-rail generation that Bosch debuted in 2003. In the years that followed, injection pressures in common-rail systems were further increased. In the first generation, these had measured some 1,300 bar. Now pressures of 2,000 bar and more were possible. Such high pressures had previously been the decisive advantage of the unit-injector system. With common rail capable of matching these pressures, the unit-injector systems lost their decisive advantage. In 2005, VW, the sole remaining customer for the unit injector, thus decided to abandon the unit injector and switch to common rail. Bosch had no choice but to discontinue production of this once lucrative product. Four plants had to be restructured, which affected several thousand associates.[64] To a greater extent than had been the case with ABS or ESP, the development of high-pressure diesel injection systems at Bosch was influenced by the decisions of other companies. Had Fiat not offered Stuttgart its common-rail patents and Daimler-Benz not shown interest in the common-rail system, Bosch might never have become technological leader in this field. And without pressure from VW, the company might never have developed a unit injector for passenger cars. Since engineering such technically demanding injection systems involves extraordinarily high levels of investment, it seems inevitable that what tipped the balance for Bosch was its being able to count on large sales volumes. However, this also increased its dependence on the decisions of individual major customers, and this can lead to heavy costs and heavy burdens in extreme cases, such as when VW switched from unit injector to common rail.

Table 18 Diesel-powered vehicles as a percentage of new passenger-car registrations in Germany, France, and Europe (1995–2010)[65]

	1995	2000	2005	2010
Germany	15	33	43	42
France	46	52	69	70
Europe (prior to 2005 western Europe)	22	33	50	51

The diesel boom continues. Diesel Systems, with its more than 50,000 associates, is the largest business division at Bosch. In today's Germany, nearly every second new registration is a diesel-powered vehicle. In 1997, the figure was just one in six. Without the common-rail and unit-injector high-pressure diesel injection systems, this development would have been impossible. They transformed the entire image of the diesel engine "from foul-smelling clunker to high-tech marvel," as the periodical *Auto Bild* put it.[66] Diesel was no longer associated with clouds of black smoke and a noisy, mechanical knocking. It now stood for a dynamic driving experience and low pollutant emissions. Not even the debate about the unhealthy effect of soot particles in diesel exhaust did anything to slow the boom. But technical advances are only one part of the story. Demand for diesel was also boosted by a radical change in the market for new cars. Only some 40 percent of new registrations are accounted for by individual customers nowadays. The other 60 percent go to companies, particularly leasing companies. And for people who lease cars instead of buying, the prime concern is running costs, and these are lower with diesel. The higher cost of purchasing diesel-powered vehicles is for them of secondary importance. However, the diesel boom has not been a worldwide phenomenon. Even within Europe, there are big differences in the popularity of diesel. Taxation plays a role here, of course, but so do driving habits and even culture. Austria, Belgium, and France have long had the highest percentages of diesel-powered vehicles in Europe, while Ireland, Sweden, Denmark, and Switzerland have the lowest.[67] In the United States, diesel-powered vehicles still account for no more than 2 percent of new passenger-car registrations.[68] Gasoline is still very cheap there, as a result of which few filling stations sell diesel. Moreover, the image of the diesel engine in that country still remains largely unchanged.

A fresh phase of diversification: acquisition of Rexroth and Buderus

At the end of 1990, the industrial technology business sector (with its four principal divisions: Hydraulics and Pneumatics, Industrial Equipment, Plastic and Metal Products, and Packaging Machinery) employed some 12,500 associates. It had been growing slowly but surely since the 1980s, in part as a result of minor acquisitions in France and the United States. However, 1990 marked the start of a prolonged period of stagnation. This field of operations was extremely heterogeneous, dealing with a wide range of products and operating in many different markets and competitive situations. In automotive hydraulics, the majority of customers were automakers with whom Bosch collaborated to develop systems solutions for complex hydraulic functions.[69] Automotive hydraulics was a bulk business in which the tone was set by high-volume suppliers such as the German and European market leader, Mannesmann-Rexroth, although even here Bosch occupied second place. In industrial hydraulics, on the other hand, demand from a hugely diverse customer set meant that the range of products was wide.

For its part, Industrial Equipment targeted an enormous variety of market segments relating to manufacturing automation. In the area of control electronics, for instance, machine-tool manufacturing was the focus of the business, accounting for 80 percent of sales. This Bosch division supplied complete assembly lines as well as special-purpose machinery to customer specifications. Here, too, Bosch was among the market leaders, despite competing with many small to medium-sized companies who were often highly specialized suppliers, some of them with more advantageous cost structures. The same was true of the Plastic and Metal Products division, which mainly turned out items for use in automobile manufacturing. The competitive situation in Germany was characterized by more than 1,000 small and medium-sized plastics processing companies, and Bosch's own market position was still largely aimed at the German market, with individual locations scattered across western Europe. A different situation was addressed by the Packaging Machinery division, which produced machines for filling and packaging foodstuffs and beverages as well as pharmaceuticals and industrial chemicals. Here, 80 percent of sales were generated outside Germany, with regional companies and joint ventures in countries including Japan, Brazil, India, and the United States.

Fig. 14 Sales in the Bosch Group's industrial technology business sector (1983–2003): sales in billions of euros (*left*) and as a percentage year-on-year change (*right*)

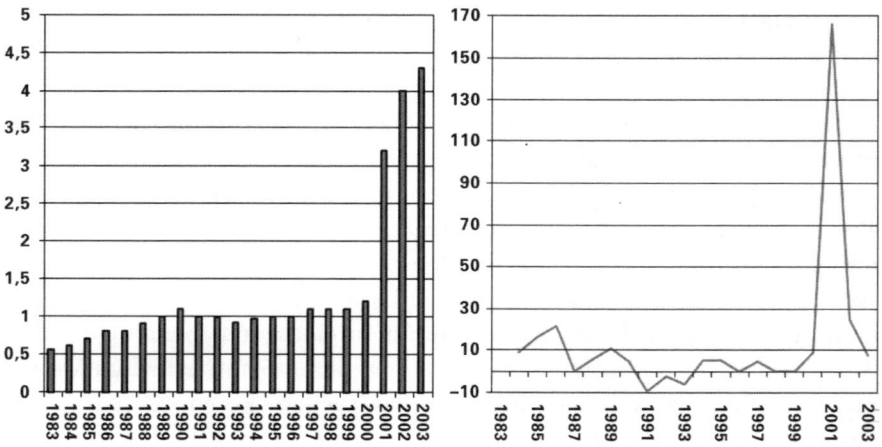

Source: Compiled and calculated from data in annual reports

All these business fields in the industrial technology business sector were seen as promising growth areas, but in most cases the board of management had to concede that their earnings situation was deteriorating and sometimes even negative. However, these business fields were considered part of the Bosch tradition, so extensive turnaround and restructuring measures were carried out in an attempt to bring them back up to strength. On April 1, 1996 (some 25 years after their organizational separation), the Industrial Equipment and Hydraulics and Pneumatics divisions were merged to form the Automation Technology division, which by this time employed only 4,600 associates.[70] Then, in June 1997, serious consideration (prompted by major earnings difficulties) was given to spinning off or selling the Packaging Machinery division, or contributing it to a joint venture with another company.[71] This had to do with both engineering and market strategy. The increasing integration of electronic control engineering into components of hydraulic drive and valve technology played a role, as did overlapping of customers and regional organizations, as well as customer demands for systems competence. But Bosch's market positioning was still, as it had always been, concentrated on Germany and western Europe. Expansion of business operations outside Germany (notably in South America and Asia) was thus considered a necessity, together with a streamlining of the product portfolio.

In the spring of 2000, following its takeover and dismantling by Vodafone, Mannesmann put its subsidiary Atecs up for sale (which combined such industrial operations as VDO, Rexroth, and Demag-Krauss-Maffei). This handed Bosch the chance of acquiring its once greatest rival, joining the big fish in the capital goods and industrial technology pool, and becoming a global player – all at the same time. In addition, this fresh plunge in the direction of diversification would reduce the company's over-dependence on the automotive supply business. Forming a consortium with Siemens AG (the Munich company was particularly interested in acquiring VDO), Bosch became involved in a 9.6 billion-euro bid for the Mannesmann subsidiary, competing with rivals such as ThyssenKrupp.[72] With regard to the antitrust authorities, Bosch and Siemens felt on the safe side. After intricate negotiations and several changes of financial plans, Bosch eventually paid Mannesmann 2.7 billion euros for Atecs's Rexroth AG operations, to which its own Automation Technology division was contributed. Bosch Rexroth AG (as the combined subsidiary was renamed) was staffed by 22,000 associates and run by a separate, functionally structured board comprising three former Rexroth executives and two from Bosch.[73] Annual sales leapt from 1.2 billion to 4.2 billion euros, putting the new company in an important position in key market segments, lending it technological leadership, and leading to its rising profitability. This gave the industrial technology business sector far greater weight in the Bosch Group, with its share of total sales rising from 4 to 12 percent. However, though operational integration proceeded swiftly and successfully during 2001, the merger itself was an altogether trickier and more prolonged process. This was due not least to differences in corporate culture.[74]

Assembly of wind-turbine gearboxes
at Bosch Rexroth AG (2001)

The second major coup of Scholl's diversification and M&A activities occurred almost at the same time. In May 2001, the decision was taken to buy
Buderus AG, thereby expanding the thermotechnology division of the consumer goods business sector (though the process was not in fact completed
until 2003). On balance, this business sector had always developed successfully, standing out from the mid-1980s onward with robust growth rates that at
times exceeded those of the automotive sector. The twenty years spanning the
period 1983 to 2003 had seen sales rocket from the equivalent of just under
1 billion euros to more than 8 billion euros.

Traditionally, the consumer goods sector with its divisions Thermotechnology (Junkers), Household Appliances (BSHG), and Power Tools averaged
something over 20 percent of Bosch Group sales, a substantial share. Above
all, BSHG (still run jointly with Siemens) continued to provide a model of success in this regard. With annual sales increases of between 8 and 11 percent,
with transferred profits nearly doubling between 1986 and 1991, and a total
workforce of 24,000 associates, the subsidiary was in good shape at the start of
the 1990s.

Despite concentration, globalization, and strategic alliances in an ever-
harsher competitive environment, BSHG was the undisputed market leader
in Germany. In western Europe it came in second, behind the Swedish Elec-

Fig. 15 Sales in the Bosch Group consumer goods business sector (1983–2003): sales in billions of euros (*left*) and as a percentage year-on-year change (*right*)

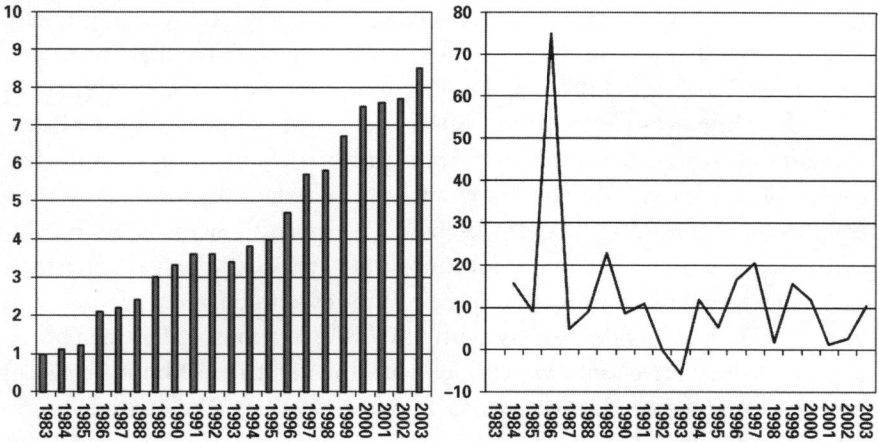

Source: Compiled and calculated from data in annual reports

trolux Group but ahead of Philips/Bauknecht. And in a markedly oligopolistic global white-goods market, it occupied what it considered an outstanding fifth place behind its competitors from the U.S. (Whirlpool, GE/Hotpoint) and Japan (Matsushita).[75] As early as the mid-1980s, BSHG had entered a new phase of internationalization, in which its aim was to systematically move away from being a German exporter to becoming a European household-appliance company with an international engineering, marketing, and sales network. An important step in this direction was the takeover of two Spanish companies in 1989. After that, BSHG looked increasingly toward southeastern Europe, where it collaborated with Turkish companies through licensing agreements. At the same time, it concluded strategic alliances with Matsushita in Japan, GE/Hotpoint in the U.S., and other partners in India and Egypt.

All the while, the BSHG management had continued, in terms of both corporate law and corporate strategy, to act as an intermediary between the two parent companies Siemens and Bosch, which in many other industrial sectors outside the household-appliance sphere were tough competitors. BSHG had successfully exploited this intermediary position to its strategic advantage, and above all enjoyed considerable entrepreneurial freedom. As a joint venture selling brands with a long tradition, BSHG faced a constant challenge on two fronts. On the one hand, it had to "operationally" integrate two different corporate cultures to form its own corporate identity. On the other hand, it needed to cultivate the specific identities of each brand name and communicate them in a way that was credible to the outside world.[76] In the history and corporate cultures of Bosch and Siemens we find many differences, granted, but also some striking similarities. The latter did much to facilitate constructive partnership within BSHG, and was therefore among the factors contributing to the company's success. Both Bosch and Siemens were long-established German industrial enterprises, with roots in electrical engineering and electronics. How they saw themselves was to a great extent determined by their larger-than-life founders, Robert Bosch and Werner von Siemens. Both companies shared a permanent quest for innovation and technological leadership, and both were guardedly discreet in their dealings with business partners and the general public. In other words, with BSHG the relationship between brand image and innovative ambition chimed with the identities of both its parent companies and matched its customers' high expectations. The exalted reputation of the Bosch and Siemens brands constituted a fundamental competitive advantage – not only domestically but also in the global household-appliance market.[77]

Like the other markets in which Bosch operated, this market had also been characterized by radical changes in the competitive landscape since the early 1990s. There had been a host of mergers, takeovers, and strategic alliances. Above all, Japanese and Korean producers of household appliances had aggressively been making inroads into this market. In some cases, BSHG had adapted to these changes earlier than its parent companies. It had now reached a size, market position, and global presence that enabled it not only to survive but also to grow and gain additional market share, even in a harsher competitive climate of increased concentration. And while lean year followed lean year throughout the 1990s, with output falling and prices declining, these things hit its larger competitors (Electrolux, for instance) much harder. During those years, however, BSHG (which had now changed its name to BSH Bosch und Siemens Hausgeräte GmbH) had successfully improved its position in the U.S. market, and above all in China, with its own regional manufacturing subsidiaries. It was still the only major household-appliance company offering two internationally established brands that stood for both quality and innovation. As a result, the company was ranked third globally behind Whirlpool and Electrolux by 2003. Its strategy was to be the European market leader with a globalized premium sector, and with both sales and profit figures rising significantly yet again after 2000, there was no doubt that this was the right one.[78]

By contrast, the thermotechnology division, with Junkers as its chief brand and subsidiary, was far more national in its focus (although since the late 1980s various smaller takeovers in Portugal, the U.K., and France had helped to bring in a degree of internationalization here as well). Following some radical restructuring and job cuts in 1999 and 2000, sales and operating result began to rise once again, with sales of nearly 900 million euros being generated by 5,200 associates in 2000.[79] The market for hot-water generation, heating, and ventilation was itself changing as a result of various developments. The use of renewable energy sources was becoming increasingly important, the replacement and modernization business accounted for a large share of sales, and concentration was continuing apace. However, the thermotechnology division (i. e., Bosch Thermotechnik or TT) already had two strong and at the same time internationally oriented competitors in its home market, namely Vaillant and Viessmann. But above all, the European market leader, Buderus AG, was a German company as well. During the 1990s, Bosch had dropped back to fifth place among the European manufacturers of heating systems. Buderus, with sales approaching 1.8 billion euros (1.2 billion euros of which was generated by its heating systems business) and a workforce of 9,600, was substantially larger than Bosch TT. When, in the spring of 2001, it became clear that the principal Buderus shareholders were ready to sell, Bosch was suddenly presented with a huge opportunity to step straight into the position of European market leader. However, this was a position with continued strong emphasis on the German market, where Buderus would give it direct access to an army of heating engineers and fitters, and hence to channels of distribution which up to then had been largely closed to Bosch.[80]

In principle, therefore, the decision to buy Buderus was quickly made. The actual transaction, with the acquisition of Buderus shares following in several stages, turned out to be intricate and prolonged. Gradually, Bosch picked up Buderus shares on the stock exchange and bought blocks from the company's wide assortment of major shareholders (they included the construction company Bilfinger & Berger, Commerzbank, Deutsche Bank, and the Arnhold & S. Bleichroeder Fund). By the end of 2003, Bosch had spent around a billion euros and owned the majority stakeholding in Buderus. The hope was that a range of further transactions would enable Bosch to bring its long-term financial requirement down to some 400 million euros.[81] But finance was only one problem. It was already becoming apparent that the Buderus board would oppose any change of industrial orientation. Indeed, because of differences in corporate cultures and the mere fact that the diminutive Bosch TT was swallowing a giant competitor, management at Buderus adopted a profoundly defensive stance.[82] "Surely all this involves a great many unknowns?," one RBIK shareholder noted in the margin of the relevant document. "The Buderus board does not support this takeover, and this makes for a less than auspicious start!"[83]

The executives of Bosch's thermotechnology division had therefore to field a series of critical questions about the acquisition and integration process, as well as about the draft industrial plan they had presented. One answer read: "On top of achieving sales synergies through expansion of our own portfolio and increased internationalization, in particular [it will be] possible to achieve cost synergies in connection with purchasing, manufacturing, engineering, and customer service."[84] Together with the Rexroth purchase, this acquisition was undoubtedly a tour de force on Bosch's part, and this not only financially. When the Bosch TT management once again reported on the state of integration with Buderus, the formal process of acquisition was in fact complete, but the legal merger of Bosch TT and Buderus Heiztechnik was still ongoing. This was not to be completed until 2004. Meanwhile, the market prospects as a whole were not exactly rosy. So far as the important German market was concerned, the next ten years were expected to produce only limited growth in the heating and hot-water market. The anticipated figure was a mere 1.5 percent – and this during an extended period of concentration.[85] The Buderus acquisition thus served mainly to help Bosch survive a time of oligopolistic market pressures and strong predatory competition. Not least, it helped "bring better balance to the Bosch Group's product portfolio."[86] Indeed, Scholl had already announced that the company's core concern, "in the interests of the wider Bosch Group," was to "reduce our reliance on the automotive sector."[87] And in fact, automotive technology's share of sales dropped back to just above 60 percent in 2002–03, while the share of its consumer goods business sector rose to 24 percent. In other words, Bosch's diversification policy was more sustained and above all more successful under Scholl than it had been under Merkle.

The rediscovery of values:
value-driven and values-based management

On July 1, 1999, the Bosch board of management underwent a marked rejuvenation. The new appointees were Bernd Bohr (b. 1956), Wolfgang Chur (b. 1947), and Franz Fehrenbach (b. 1949). They were made deputy members, while the former deputy members Stephan Rojahn and Gotthard Romberg rose to full membership. And with Tilman Todenhöfer, the board received a new vice-chairman.[88] Like most of their colleagues, the three new members had risen in-house and had spent their entire professional career with Bosch. Yet they (together with Siegfried Dais, b. 1948, who had been appointed to the board a year earlier) were frequently referred to as the "young braves."[89] The fact that men of their age who had already been with the company for two or more decades were so dubbed, even if ironically, says much about the way people thought at Bosch at the time.

The new members of the board of management, while not bringing in the breath of fresh air from outside that many observers had long thought necessary, were resolved to work for change. Wolfgang Chur had already struck a new note at a conference of vocational training managers in Bad Salzdetfurth in June 1999: "We need greater customer orientation, and that is no mere slogan [...] Bosch is widely considered to be too slow, too inflexible, too bureaucratic."[90] The company had focused too much on engineering, he went on, and as head of sales in the mobile communications division and before that in the power tools division, Chur doubtless knew what he was talking about. He further pointed out that he was pressing for change because the market demanded it. Increased competition and the so-called "López effect" left Bosch little choice. That was how Hermann Scholl himself saw things, and he had been in charge of business policy for the past six years. Many things that the "young braves" voiced openly and self-critically were charges that the media had been leveling at Bosch for years. Scholl might have seen this as an attack on his authority. The press had incessantly reproached him for being in thrall to the "Merkle system," powerless to break free. Yet Scholl knew all too well how many customers' perception of the Bosch name and image had worsened over the years. He had been forced to listen to the anger felt by some of the company's leading customers at quality problems in connection with the common-rail high-pressure diesel system, gasoline injection, and brakes. And he was aware that, in a climate of increased competition, Bosch could ill afford such damage to its reputation.[91] Yet there were positive examples in the field of customer relations – for instance, the production and supply of ESP for Daimler-Benz A-class vehicles in the spring of 1998.[92]

Against this background, the Bosch Group's LD-Forum of September 9–10, 1999, was a memorable occasion. Significantly, the watchword was "*Fokus Kunde* [customer first]." For two days, the reports of board members and other senior executives focused on customer dissatisfaction. Scholl summed up the principal insights, addressing weaknesses mercilessly: "We often miss agreed delivery deadlines and fail to supply the quality required. We react to perfectly fair demands in a way that is bureaucratic, arrogant, and dismissive. This is not true of each one of our operating units or of every associate having contact with customers – of course not. But it is true of too many of us."[93] Scholl went on to specify five "indispensable objectives" he wished to pursue as he led the company through a change process: "1. We want to sustain and extend our excellent competitive position in the field of engineering. 2. The Bosch brand must once again be universally associated with quality and reliability. 3. We intend to treat all our customers as partners, balancing their interests fairly with our own. 4. We mean to make the most efficient possible use of the resources available to us. 5. We want to achieve a decent operating result, one that will enable us to carry out the legacy of our founder – to keep our company financially independent, to enable its continued strong and meaningful development, and to place at the disposal of the Robert Bosch Stiftung the funds that it needs for its work."[94] Significantly and strikingly, for the first time in years here was a chairman of the board of management making explicit reference to the company founder. In fact, Scholl rounded off his address to the LD-Forum with two quotations from Robert Bosch: "Without some compelling reason, no one should take on a job that can be seen from the start to serve no purpose." And: "Entering into a contract without ulterior motives and honoring it conscientiously is an act of supreme business acumen."[95]

As the in-house newspaper *Bosch-Zünder* reported, the 200-plus executives attending the conference were "profoundly affected."[96] For many, it may well have been irritating, even disconcerting, to hear the board calling for a "perceptible change of culture at all levels and in all operating units" and naming "a service culture at Bosch" as the goal to be striven for.[97] "Customer focus" and "cultural change" were now the watchwords of the hour. In the *Bosch-Zünder*, associates described what they were doing for customers. Reporting on the Bosch exhibition at a BMW in-house trade fair, the newspaper wrote: "The product display alone was indicative of a more relaxed, one might almost say reinvigorated Bosch. No dry-as-dust commentaries on Bosch automotive divisions."[98] The Schillerhöhe was naturally aware that a change of culture was not going to sweep through the company in a single instant by virtue of a command from on high. So in September 1999, almost in parallel to the LD-Forum, a start was made at creating a mission statement whose catchy slogan would appeal to associates. To this end, Bosch asked Boston Consulting, Plaut Consulting, and the Thomas Group for advice.[99] The slogan selected was "BeQIK" – the association with the English word "quick" being of course no accident. What "QIK" meant was made clear by the graphic design within which the slogan was set. The letters stood for **Qualität** [quality], *Innovation* [innovation], and *Kundenorientierung* [customer orientation], while "Be" stood for *Betriebsergebnis* [operating result] and therefore appeared in black lettering (unlike "QIK," which was printed red).[100] Finding a subheading took slightly longer. Sixty executives were asked to choose from several proposals. They voted (by a large margin) for "Be Better. Be Bosch!" which in combination with "Be-QIK" yielded an alliteration. At the board meeting of October 4, 1999, a resolution was passed adopting the slogan plus subheading: "BeQIK – Be Better – Be Bosch."[101]

BeQIK was backed up by two initiatives. A "time to market" initiative coordinated by Bernd Bohr was designed to improve and accelerate production processes and shorten development times. A *Fokus Kunde* [customer first] initiative was designed to increase customer satisfaction in various ways, including closer customer contacts and enhanced reliability.[102] In a subsequent phase, associates were familiarized with the new model through a large number of seminars. A year later, Bohr saw himself as a kind of "traveling salesman for BeQIK."[103] For senior executives alone, between February and July 2000 there were as many as six seminars on the topic of "BeQIK: The courage to change." Written feedback suggested improvements, and these in turn indicated further shortcomings. There were reminders that a culture of open communication was needed and recommendations that the idea of "associate orientation" should also be cultivated. Participants also seem to have felt that too little was being said as to how these goals were to be achieved.[104] According to *Manager Magazin,* many Bosch associates were indifferent to the initiatives on the whole, tending to dismiss them as "the high-ups flying yet another new kite."[105]

In fact, for the most part BeQIK contained nothing new. Bosch had always been innovation-oriented, notably in automotive engineering. The company had been displaying this impressively for years. In the sphere of quality assurance it had proclaimed 12 guiding principles only a decade earlier. The continuous improvement process (CIP) launched in 1991 had pursued the same objective. Many associates had since made improvements both small and large in that context. Moreover, the board of management found it important to stress that CIP had not been replaced by BeQIK. CIP, it insisted, was "the foundation stone of the initiatives that have BeQIK as their goal."[106] Graphically, too, CIP was incorporated into the BeQIK presentation with the strapline "CIP leads step by step to BeQIK." Looked at in this way, the only new thing about BeQIK was the K [*Kundenorientierung*] for "customer focus." Up to that time, Bosch had tended to take the view that there was nothing wrong with customers waiting patiently until development work was completed. When that time came, they would get their products.[107] However, customer expectations had now changed, whether those customers were companies or private individuals. A seller was expected to give advice. A salesperson, instead of simply enumerating the features of a given product, was expected to help solve problems.

But with BeQIK, Bosch was also catching up with another trend. The German business world was becoming increasingly aware that it was operating in a communications-savvy, mass-consumption society. In such a society, striking catchphrases had an effect of their own. In what it said, BeQIK did not differ greatly from the mission statements being proffered by comparable companies at the time – one instance being the "Siemens Management System" ("Innovation," "Customer Focus," "Global Competitiveness"). Effect had to do with perception. Because the slogan was now an omnipresent logo at Bosch (in every plant, at every event, as a badge on the lapel of every important associate), it reinforced corporate identity. At the same time, it gave things a "modern" look, which was extremely important in an engineering company that had a slightly stand-offish public image. The younger members of the Bosch board were aware of the laws of the communications society, in which success also depends on generating attention. Wolfgang Chur put it in English in a report to the supervisory board in November 1999: "What gets attention, gets done."[108] When, at the annual press conference for the year 2000, Hermann Scholl said, "We are driving change, and we are managing it," he meant more than the restructuring of the Bosch business sectors taking place at that time or the Rexroth takeover. And his message was heard.[109] The newspaper *Die Zeit* praised the initiatives of the Bosch management as a "Swabian cultural revolution." There were, however, still critical articles in the press bemoaning a "reform backlog." [110] Scholl himself was forced to admit in the *Bosch-Zünder* that change had yet to reach the rigid hierarchies that were among the company's chief problems. "BeQIK is meant to facilitate decisions at the lowest level possible, but this isn't happening yet."[111]

Following the introduction of the BeQIK mission, the board of management began to address the subject of "values." The question was, what did "Be Bosch" really mean? Here, too, the company was following a contemporary trend. Employees in general were identifying less and less strongly with their companies. This being so, academics and management consultants alike felt that an important recipe for success (particularly in light of global competition for highly qualified workers) lay in a corporate culture that was positively perceived, "value-adding," and meaningful. Much later, a study by the Federal Republic's Ministry of Labor, published in 2008, was able for the first time to present empirical evidence of how corporate culture was a factor in a company's success.[112] However, what made this process special at Bosch was the thoroughness with which it examined the question of values and how it quite naturally related that question to the company's past. The board of management did not simply ask a communications agency or consultancy to produce a list of values. Instead, it withdrew behind closed doors (incidentally, in the house in Bad Teinach where Theodor Heuss had written his biography of Robert Bosch) and scrutinized the past.[113] It did not have far to look. Values permeated the history of the company in the form of the guiding principles of the founder. Heuss himself had cited them, and they had lost none of their relevance since, as Scholl had already pointed out at the September 1999 LD-Forum. The catalogue of basic values now drawn up began with trust, openness, fairness, and entrepreneurial thinking.[114] With the exception of "openness," this coincided entirely with the principles of Robert Bosch. When Scholl addressed the LD-Forum in December 2001 on the subject of "Be Bosch – Our values," he stressed that the company was already in possession of "strong values, values that were to a large extent shaped by our founder Robert Bosch." It was not the values that needed changing, Scholl insisted, but instead the way associates related to them. "We need to pay more attention to them."[115]

By now, the board of management had itself become aware that it lacked some of the founder's competence or at least confidence on the subject of values.[116] So it called in an ethics expert to advise. This was the Premonstratensian canon and management consultant, Father Augustinus, whose (aristocratic) name in civilian life was Augustinus Heinrich, Count Henckel von Donnersmarck. At the time, he and his consultancy company Unicorn were familiar figures in management circles throughout the German economy – at BMW, for instance. Father Augustinus had already impressed Bosch executives with his presentation at a GPI conference in June 1994. His recommendation now was that, rather than simply proclaiming "Bosch values" from on high, management should also find out how associates viewed those values and how their perception of the company related to them. Accordingly, in September 2001 Unicorn was commissioned to poll 126 Bosch associates (including 46 senior executives, but also members of works councils) on the subject of "values focus and cultural change."[117] What makes Unicorn's final report such a noteworthy document is that, unlike published statements, it reflects the unvarnished views of associates.

Unicorn found that a "positive basic attitude" existed at Bosch. BeQIK and "Bosch values" enjoyed a high degree of acceptance among the workforce. The associates polled were also sure the board really wanted the change that it was preaching. But the interviews showed something else as well. They showed that the values proclaimed and the mission aspired to did not match what was actually going on at the workplace. Interviewees spoke of a "penchant for detail" and a tendency, when mistakes were made, to apportion personal blame rather than analyze objectively. The general feeling was that Bosch possessed "outstanding specialist competence" but was over-inclined to stew in its own juice. "Management positions at Bosch are overwhelmingly held by Germans. There is little internationalism in evidence." Unicorn's report also showed that the initiative to re-establish Bosch values "awakens expectations among associates that not so much changes within the system but instead changes to the system are in the pipeline." Summing up, the report concluded: "Thus far, the experience of associates has been of a yawning gap between the postulates of change on the one hand and what they see in reality on the other." Unicorn recommended terminating the discussion on values and substantiating the values catalogue with a philosophy of leadership at the operational level.[118]

Changes in the parallelogram of forces in corporate governance

Ever since Robert Bosch Industriebeteiligung (RBIG) was set up in 1964, changing its name in 1976 to Robert Bosch Industrietreuhand (RBIK) and claiming its right to act as the sole executor of the founder's legacy in exercising the entrepreneurial ownership functions of Robert Bosch GmbH, there had, in purely formal terms, been no change in the distribution of authority, control, or power of direction among board of management, supervisory board, and RBIK. In his position as chairman of the RBIK shareholders' committee, Hans L. Merkle had kept hold of the reins of power, even after stepping down as chairman of the Bosch board of management [in 1984]. According to the RBIK partnership agreement, he was in fact meant to have relinquished this position in the summer of 1988 upon reaching the age limit of 75. However, the shareholders passed a special resolution enabling him to stay on until June 1993, just under six months past his 80th birthday in January.[119] Accepting the offer, Merkle announced that he still intended to give up his seat on the supervisory board punctually in June 1988. His justification was that at RBIK his function mainly concerned the internal affairs of the Bosch Group, whereas for a supervisory-board chairman there was a public-interest consideration.[120] That position was now assumed (until the "great reshuffle" of 1993) by Wolfgang Eychmüller, chairman of the board of management of Wieland-Werke in Ulm and an RBIK shareholder since 1984. So far as RBIK was concerned, Merkle proposed a further change: expanding the shareholders' committee from eight to nine. Under the Bosch constitution, Merkle argued, the advisory body could have seven or eight members, so RBIK could have nine members including Robert Bosch Jr.[121] As a result, instead of waiting for a vacancy as usual, the eight serving members of RBIK – namely Merkle, Adolff, Bierich, Bosch, Eychmüller, Guth (the then chairman of the supervisory board of Deutsche Bank had been elected as the "youngest" member as recently as mid-1986), Holzach, and Stein – were joined in June 1988 by a co-opted ninth member: Johan M. Goudswaard, vice-chairman of the board of directors at Unilever and already a member of the Bosch supervisory board.

In June 1993, Merkle finally did retire, to be replaced as RBIK chairman by Bierich, who at the same time took over chairmanship of the supervisory board. With this major reshuffle, certain changes also took place in the constellation of forces and in the internal make-up of corporate governance at Bosch. Unlike Merkle, Bierich did in many respects manifest the principles of the founder, though without quoting them all the time. "He gave these principles fresh impetus and new relevance by highlighting openness, fairness, future focus, and communication. These things now increasingly returned to the fore."[122] Moreover, Bierich was from the outset on good terms with the founder's son, who continued to represent the family regularly at RBIK meetings. This was in contrast to Merkle, who had hardly ever taken notice of him. The exceptional, non-voting status of Robert Bosch Jr. was stressed explicitly at the end of the minutes of each meeting, with regular mention of how under section five, sub-section two, of the RBIK guidelines he had attended in a purely advisory capacity. This was despite the fact that in April 1987 there had been a new agreement between RBIK and the members of the Bosch family regarding the establishment and function of the family council, with members of the family regularly being briefed by members of the Bosch board of management on all matters relating to corporate policy.[123] Bierich and Robert Bosch Jr. understood and trusted each other from the beginning, not least because of their shared love of philosophy.[124]

Even with Bierich in the chair, however, nothing changed in the meticulous preparation of the decision-making process at RBIK meetings. But when on June 23, 1994 (30 years after the founding of RBIK), the shareholders convened for their 100th meeting, they were joined, in the person of Hermann Scholl, by a forceful chairman of the Bosch board of management. Shortly afterward, Guth was replaced on the shareholders' committee by Hans Peter Stihl, himself a distinguished entrepreneur and at the same time president of the Federation of German Chambers of Industry and Commerce [*Deutscher Industrie- und Handelstag* or DIHT], and Stein made way for Friedrich Schiefer, the deputy chairman of the board of management. As the *Stuttgarter Zeitung* wrote on the occasion of Stihl's appointment, it was still "one of the finest positions to be had in the business world of Baden-Württemberg. [...] And it is to be seen not simply as a job, but more as an accolade to be asked to become a member of Robert Bosch Industrietreuhand KG."[125] As before, the principle was that the members had a dual role. On the one hand, they determined the strategic course that the Bosch Group would follow. On the other hand, they ensured that their supervisory functions accorded with the standards of the founder and that their joint actions reflected the imperatives of corporate governance as outlined in his guidelines. However, in the summer of 1996, shortly after Schiefer's death had propelled Tilman Todenhöfer prematurely into the ranks of the RBIK shareholders, there was intensive discussion about amending the partnership agreement of RBIK with regard to its cooptation procedure and to the relationship between continuity and flexibility when the shareholders' committee was faced with the task of adjusting to developments affecting the supervisory bodies of industrial enterprises as a whole. For one thing, the age limit for RBIK membership was lowered to 72 (though in justifiable exceptions a certain degree of flexibility was permitted) to bring it more into line with general rules applying to members of managing and supervisory boards.[126] For another, limited membership periods were introduced. As a general rule, future members were to be appointed for a ten-year term (although multiple extensions of five years at a time could be granted). Furthermore, any shareholder who had belonged to RBIK for more than ten years and who resigned on reaching the age of 65 could state a willingness to continue to make their experience available and, wherever possible, attend future meetings in an advisory capacity without the right to vote. In such cases, that shareholder would continue to receive all papers and minutes.[127]

Finally, in November 1999, a further personnel change in the RBIK shareholders' committee marked the end of an era in one respect, but continuity in another. After 30 years' membership, which made him the longest-serving shareholder of RBIK (albeit without full voting rights), Robert Bosch Jr. announced his retirement. Even though the family's right to send a representative to RBIK shareholders' meetings had long since lapsed, the committee decided that it still wished to include a member of the Bosch family among its ranks. With effect from November 26, 1999, it thus resolved to grant RBIK membership to Christof Bosch, one of the six children of Robert Bosch Jr. For him, too, an explicitly limited voting right applied, and he was appointed *ad personam* lest a legal precedent be set that would give the Bosch family the right to send a representative to RBIK meetings in the future.[128] Some years earlier, the members of the Bosch family had contributed their remaining shares in Robert Bosch GmbH to a family company especially set up for this

The Bosch family on a visit to the Abstatt engineering center (2008)

purpose, and in which the third generation also held a stake. As a result, the family's interests in dealings with Robert Bosch GmbH were represented by just one vote (or rather legal person). In March 2002, the RBIK committee members finally brought themselves to lift the voting-right restrictions on Christof Bosch and grant him full voting rights as an RBIK shareholder.[129] This also gave the family greater weight within RBIK.[130]

Outwardly, these changes were invisible. Even for the inner circle of members of the governing bodies of Bosch outside RBIK, their effect was barely noticeable at first. But after the spring of 2000, when Hermann Scholl had succeeded Bierich both as chairman of the board of management and of RBIK, the shareholders felt a growing need to discuss their own role, the way they saw themselves, and the practice of corporate governance at Bosch generally. This discussion was no doubt prompted in part by the debate then taking place in much of German business as well as among the general public about the principles and structures of "good corporate governance." After a long period in which Hans L. Merkle had dominated proceedings, debate became significantly more important in RBIK meetings, and the shareholders' committee began to evolve into an autonomously acting, direction-setting body. Although Scholl, like Merkle before him, now chaired the board of management and RBIK at the same time, there was talk of a "power vacuum up at the Schillerhöhe."[131] Whether such talk was accurate or not, there was no denying that relations between the RBIK shareholders and their chairman were very much on the agenda. And whatever the respective and diverse motives of Scholl and individual RBIK shareholders might have been, both sides now felt a need to know precisely, once and for all, what the responsibilities of RBIK shareholders really were. What were the rules, both in theory and in practice, governing relations between the shareholders and their chairman? Legally, each shareholder was an owner with equal rights. But when it actually came to exercising these entrepreneurial ownership rights, it was clear that the shareholders had not been so scrupulous in recent years. Above all, many of the RBIK shareholders from outside the company felt inadequately informed and called for greater influence in operational affairs. At the end of the year 2000, Peter Adolff (now the longest-serving RBIK shareholder) began a thorough study of the role of RBIK in Bosch corporate governance.[132] At the same time, the Bosch corporate legal department set about drafting a complementary paper that would provide a concise summary of the legal provisions relevant to everyday practice.[133] Adolff presented his study to Scholl and the other members of RBIK eighteen months later, at the end of May 2002. Here once again, for the first time in decades, was a detailed presentation of the "Bosch basic law." The study was also an expression of the sea-change that had happened at Bosch over the course of the 1990s. The basic principles of Robert Bosch, having increasingly faded into the background, had now begun to return to center stage within the company he had founded.[134] Indeed, explicit reference to Robert Bosch had become less and less frequent in the Merkle years and soon ceased altogether. Since the chairmanship of Hans Walz, no one had given any consideration to reinterpreting and adapting the "Bosch constitution" in light of altered circumstances. So a degree of reflection and renaissance seemed overdue at Bosch – not simply because there had been a significant shift in the parallelogram of forces underlying corporate governance at Bosch. Adolff's detailed paper derived the rights and duties of the RBIK shareholders in their ownership function from the founder's will. It stressed two things in particular. One was the goal of assuring the company's full independence by placing all the equity that carried voting rights into the hands of RBIK. The other was the principle of absolute equality of rights among its shareholders.[135]

Against this background, the RBIK meeting called on June 26, 2002, was a historic event in Bosch history. For the first time, shareholders discussed fundamental questions affecting RBIK. They looked at how they saw their own role, as well as their specific tasks and obligations. They considered RBIK's composition, internal structure, and *modus operandi*. And they talked about the way in which RBIK related to the board of management, the supervisory board, the Stiftung, and the Bosch family. There was fundamental agreement on the legal principles underpinning the organization. However, when it came to the way RBIK actually operated, there was heated debate – very likely for the first time in its history.[136] Eventually, the committee agreed to reduce the number of individual items submitted by the board of management for decision, and instead to focus much more on determining Bosch Group strategy. In the future, RBIK would come together for a strategy meeting once yearly. As for the now widely discussed topic of "corporate governance," the unanimous feeling was that, at Bosch, there was no urgent need for action. All the tools recommended by the Cromme Commission (the government body appointed to examine corporate governance in German industry) were available to the company and in actual use. "As to the [...] appointments made to the three positions of chairman of the board of management, chairman of the RBIK shareholders' committee, and chairman of the supervisory board, we found that no fundamental and particularly no unilateral decisions should be made. Rather RBIK, which in the end makes all direct or indirect decisions in this regard, should retain full flexibility and, depending on the company's situation and the personnel available, decide any case on its own merits."[137] Scholl's advent had ushered in a new discussion culture at RBIK. Coupled with a stronger right to demand information (including from the chairman) as well as to have a greater say in decision-making at an operational level, this led not least to a novel and perhaps timely rebalancing of corporate-governance structures in line with the substance and spirit of the "Bosch basic law."

Meanwhile, as the new millennium dawned, corporate management, (growth) strategy, and the development of its overall corporate culture were becoming key themes at Bosch. For instance, at the end of November 2000, RBIK had authorized Scholl to perform a capital increase of 547 million German marks, at the same time as converting its capital stock to the equivalent of 1.2 billion euros.[138] The company's equity base and its liquidity were both strengthened as a result. What was special about this was the so-called distribute/recapture method [*Schütt-aus-Hol-zurück-Verfahren*], which had already been used in November 1992, when a capital increase was carried out for the first time since 1985, raising capital stock in two stages to 1.2 billion German marks. First, Robert Bosch GmbH, using reserves and taking advantage of the lower rate of corporation tax that applied to distributions of profits, distributed an advance dividend of 1.5 billion German marks to its shareholders, who then contributed the net proceeds of the distribution back to the GmbH. The GmbH then used company funds to raise its capital in two stages (in December 1992 and June 1993) from a nominal 800 million German marks to 1.2 billion German marks.[139] In addition, the business share (2.9 percent of capital stock) held by Robert Bosch Industrieanlagen GmbH was transferred to Robert Bosch Stiftung, whose own share rose as a result from some 89 to 92 percent. Because it avoided the previously prohibitive levels of corporate income tax charged on reserves, the distribute/recapture method, carried out in close collaboration with the financial authorities, was the most tax-favorable way of achieving something that had become urgently necessary – namely, bringing capital stock into line with net assets and sales revenue. This distinctive method of raising funds for a capital increase was also employed at Bosch in October 1993 and again in 1998, progressively raising the company's capital stock to 1.8 billion German marks.[140] On each occasion, the family had likewise participated in these capital measures, commensurate with the 8 percent share they still held. But with the value of their interest in Bosch rocketing, they had long since been faced with the problem of growing fiscal obligations, notably in regard to wealth and inheritance tax – obligations that the dividends they received from the company no longer covered. Since the mid-1980s, therefore, thought had been given to finding a way of remedying this universally unsatisfactory situation and finding some other arrangement.[141] Merkle and Robert Bosch Jr. had corresponded on the subject for years. This made clear that "RB GmbH had a moral duty toward the family, a duty going beyond its legal commitment, in connection with the tax burden arising out of their respective shares in the business."[142] However, in March 1988 Merkle strongly recommended to family shareholders that some time in the next five years they should "think carefully about restructuring or transforming their holdings with the object of permanently reducing their wealth-tax burden or at least keeping the steady increase in that burden within bounds" – for instance, by obtaining profit-participating certificates.[143] However, the family had chosen to stay with direct share ownership.

In addition to the Bosch-specific path of acquiring capital by the company's own efforts and from its own funds, in the spring of 2001 Scholl again showed greater reliance on financing growth from external sources. For the first time in 17 years, the board of management engaged the services of ratings agencies and investment banks. For short-term financing from borrowed funds, it increased the existing commercial-paper program of Robert Bosch Finance Corporation from 0.3 billion to 2 billion U.S. dollars, and for longer-term financing from borrowed funds it issued bonds for up to four billion Ger-

The board of management of Robert Bosch GmbH.
Back row:
Peter Marks, Gerhard Kümmel, Wolfgang Drees, Tilman Todenhöfer, Kurt Liedtke.
Middle row:
Hermann Scholl, Wolfgang Chur, Bernd Bohr.
Front row:
Franz Fehrenbach, Siegfried Dais, Gotthard Romberg (2003).

man marks with a term of up to ten years.[144] "Bosch seeks fresh capital for acquisitions," was the headline in the *Financial Times Deutschland* in June 2001.[145] All these measures were part of a "value-driven management" program that had meanwhile been introduced at Bosch. This was the time when "shareholder-value" policies were at their height in listed companies the world over. Bosch itself, of course, was not in thrall to the capital market, but the board of management felt a need to "adapt its stance to an altered environment."[146] In mid-1999, with customers and competitors alike steering an increasingly value-driven course, Bosch had also resolved to introduce and develop appropriate mechanisms and tools to enhance the efficiency of its use of resources. Terms and concepts such as value contribution [*Wertbeitrag*], return on investment [*Kapitalrendite* or CFRoI] and minimum return [*Mindestrendite* or KKS], sustained cash flow [*nachhaltiger Cash Flow* or NCF] and capital turnover [*Kapitalumschlag*] became common usage in corporate accounting, and associates on all levels – division, business unit, plant, and department – wrestled with "value drivers." Value contribution indicated by how much result exceeded or fell below the expected return on capital employed. The expectation was that, compared to the former way of ascertaining operating result, this would provide a more sophisticated tool and a new and more efficient management variable. In a number of ways, Bosch reformed and revamped its financial and business management indicators. On the one hand, the way restructuring processes were handled was more complex; on the other, lasting incentives were provided for a permanent enhancement of the value of the company and its operating units.[147] Like the circumstances in which the "Bosch Production System" was implemented, the example of value-driven management shows how powerless the company was to escape the successive waves of management theory initiated or whipped up by the major management consultant firms. Not least, this was also true of the "change management" craze so widely propagated in the late 1990s or the debates about the rediscovery of corporate culture and the importance of company values and standards.

Before Scholl delivered his final address to the company's executives assembled at the GPI conference in June 2003, he brought in two further important changes. On the one hand, he extended the planning horizon at Bosch. The existing three-year business plan was to be supplemented by long-term planning with a ten-year timeframe. Implicitly, this was also an appeal for more willingness to take risks rather than cower behind bureaucratic firewalls. On the other, following long years of a largely defensive posture imposed by two major recessions, he proposed new and more aggressive profit and growth targets for the company. Under the cryptic slogans "RB Plus 10" and "Profit 05," and with greater definition of individual quantitative and qualitative regional and structural targets, the aim was to double total sales to 75 billion euros by 2010 and to consistently achieve a margin of 5 percent or more.[148] Ambitious it certainly was, calling for an average annual growth rate of 9 percent. The Bosch board of management knew full well that this was achievable only through considerably more external growth than in the past. More than half the sales growth was going to have to come from acquisitions.[149] And it involved substantial challenges as to how that growth was to be financed. Calculations showed that the company's thick liquidity cushion was going to become very much thinner, and there was a new readiness to accept a markedly higher level of debt.[150] Despite this clear preference for the external growth path, an in-house document of October 2002 warned that it was important not to lose sight of "strong internal growth," which had to be secured by a more project-specific, consistent management method, particularly since this growth path clearly involved less risk.[151] That much was evident from two key episodes in Bosch history. The first was the development of ABS, which had begun in 1969 but not reached break-even until 1985, after an accumulated upfront outlay equivalent to 112 million euros. However, even then the notional purchase price of ABS would have been 460 million euros, i. e., three times the upfront investment. From the perspective of 2001, the innovation was worth 1.4 billion euros to the company. The second success story was the lambda sensor. Its development had begun in 1970, with break-even being reached in 1981 following total upfront outlay of 9 million euros. The notional purchase price would have been 134 million euros, and its value to the company in 2001 was 226 million euros, plus accumulated and compounded cash flows of 434 million euros.[152] Clearly, if the right project was chosen, it was cheaper in the long run to develop business areas using the company's own resources (i. e., through internal growth) than to go down the acquisition route. Whatever the route chosen, the ambitious new growth target for the Bosch Group presupposed that *both* routes would offer a high "success rate."

In this address to the business policy briefing of June 2003, Scholl also attempted an initial, self-critical survey of his years as chairman of the Bosch board of management. He had been at the helm of the company during one of the more difficult periods in its history. The board had tried hard to improve its earning power structurally, yet its attempts had often been thwarted by external or internal developments. Serious earnings crashes and several daunting tasks (Blaupunkt, brakes, gasoline direct injection) had forced these endeavors onto the back burner, so to speak. All the same, intensive work on loss-making areas had been matched on the positive side by several milestones in the process of realignment and renewal at Bosch. There had been the quality drive, the improvement of project management, implementation of the company's own production system, further progress in globalization, the creation and expansion of a strong market position in China and Korea, divestment and structural readjustment in the loss-making communications technology business sector, fresh efforts toward diversification, and, not least, the beginnings of a change of generation at the top. The make-up of the Bosch Group had improved lastingly and moved forward over the past decade. But recessions, coupled with radical and rapid changes in market structure and competitive environment, had meant that staying on top of developments involved considerable effort. Navigation technology had proved more than Bosch could cope with, and the diesel boom had simply driven the company before it. "We simply rushed forward faster and faster, regardless of costs."[153] Looking back, Scholl conceded that he and his colleagues had not been able, on his watch, to achieve a good result. But many seeds had been sown, and the opportunities created and the conditions put in place would enable a rich harvest to be reaped. In a few years' time, he said, Bosch would be showing not simply a good operating result, but an excellent one.[154] Finally, Scholl sent his top managers away from the conference with 11 propositions and guiding principles, aimed mainly at encouraging them to take swift action at the first sign of trouble – be it at the first sign of a dip in earnings power, when areas of operation displayed doubtful prospects of success, or when there were glaring management weaknesses at or near the top. Moreover, he reminded them that it was above all through innovations of its own that Bosch had grown over the past decades. In the future as well, it would be absolutely essential to make these innovations happen, and this also called for perseverance and long-term product planning. As for acquisitions, care had to be taken to make greater use of the company's own store of skills and experience. If there were problems of integration, intervention had to be rigorous and prompt, using the company's own associates. Experience of working in other countries also had to be further extended. A critical shortage in the availability of skilled local managers needed to be overcome. And finally, when it came to regional expansion, the aim had to be for this to be pursued only through companies wholly owned by Bosch or in which Bosch had clear industrial leadership. "In the longer-term view, clear-cut management structures matter more than short-term market triumphs."[155]

4 Globalization, diversification, and focus on values (2003–2012)

"Driving change forward": new strategies and trends

In the autumn of 2002, it became apparent that the next change of leadership at Bosch was imminent. For some time, it had been clear that Hermann Scholl (then 68) would not be renewing his contract, which was due to expire in the summer of 2003. It was already a certainty that his successor would come from within the company. The candidates talked of by turns in the media were the four board members Bernd Bohr, Siegfried Dais, Franz Fehrenbach, and Tilman Todenhöfer.[1] In December, the white smoke duly appeared above the Schillerhöhe when Bosch announced that, effective July 1, 2003, the new chairman of the board of management would be Franz Fehrenbach, and Hermann Scholl would be chairing the supervisory board.[2] The switch was felt to be "typically Bosch-like," very much in the style of the company's management bodies: a handover without fuss to a successor who was appointed by the RBIK shareholders, came from within Bosch ranks, and had already worked alongside his predecessor for some time.

In Fehrenbach, the company was now headed by one of the "young braves" appointed to the board of management in 1998–99. Publicly, his elevation was seen not merely as an overdue injection of fresh blood (Fehrenbach was 14 years younger than Scholl), but also as a final farewell to the management style of Hans L. Merkle, who had died three years before. The newspaper *Süddeutsche Zeitung* introduced the new Bosch chief executive officer to its readers as "honest, straightforward, and not one to put on airs." Franz Fehrenbach, it assured them, was a "modern, approachable manager who had outgrown the generation of the legendary 'godfather.'"[3] Actually, the handover was in many ways characterized by continuity. Fehrenbach had been one of the principal influences behind the "culture of change" introduced under Scholl in the autumn of 1999. His promotion to the post of CEO was tantamount to a guarantee: namely, that this change would be driven forward energetically.

The new chairman was comparatively unknown outside the industry. Fehrenbach had come to Bosch as a 26-year-old trainee. He had then risen through the ranks in a determined but largely inconspicuous manner. However, there were several reasons why he was particularly well qualified for the top position. As an industrial engineer by training, he possessed both technical and business competence. Having held a leading management position in the U.S. regional company for some years, he also had international experience and was familiar with the U.S. market that had long been so difficult for Bosch. Before joining the board, he had headed Diesel Systems, the most successful division in Bosch's automotive technology business sector, and the one with the highest sales. But what most marked Fehrenbach out from the other, likewise highly qualified "young braves" was no doubt his preference for open communication and a cooperative style of management. In voting for him, the RBIK shareholders had also been voting for a different kind of image.

One of Fehrenbach's first acts as chairman of the board of management was to compose an e-mail and have it sent to all the associates in the company – a minor revolution in itself. The e-mail opened with the question: "What is the best thing about Bosch?" and closed with the answer: "the people who work here." In the body of his e-mail, Fehrenbach indicated the areas he would be focusing on. He confirmed his support for the "BeQIK" mission, for the Bosch values, and for the culture of change already visible in its outlines. He announced a deeper commitment to the company's non-automotive business as well as a shift in regional focus toward the Americas and Asia. All this his predecessor would also have subscribed to, but Fehrenbach actually pressed the "send" button. He addressed all associates directly, appealing to them to make it their personal responsibility to help rid the company of its structural rigidities.[4] His appeal aroused enormous expectations. The *Bosch-Zünder*, the in-house newspaper, published the first interview with the new Bosch CEO. Under the headline: "Urgent: driving change forward," Fehrenbach was pictured in a denim shirt, doing the gardening. His management style was said to be collaborative, and he was portrayed as willing to listen and open for suggestions.[5]

Fehrenbach did not disappoint these expectations. In fact he surprised many people who had underestimated this easygoing winegrower's son.[6] He was more aware of the importance of communication, both internal and external, than his predecessor had been. For him, communication was part of the culture of openness to which he felt committed. Yet this was not so much about the frequency of communication as its substance. At the 2003 LD-Forum, Fehrenbach demanded that corporate policy be presented clearly – from the reasons underlying it through to its implementation.[7] Three years later, at the same event, he went a step further, declaring that "our new corporate culture is about openness and transparency."[8] From 2005, the *Bosch-Zünder* appeared in nine languages. This was not merely because of the company's increasing globalization. Even before this, more than half its as-

Franz Fehrenbach (2009)

sociates were employed outside Germany. It was hoped that this new publication policy would also break down barriers to communication inside the company. Bosch associates in India had just as much right to be well informed about their company as their German colleagues "at home." And, of course, the internet was also becoming a more and more important medium. Since the introduction of the Bosch GlobalNet in 2009, associates with computerized workplaces have had a worldwide communication platform at their fingertips.[9]

A further signal was that names of divisions and abbreviations for the offices of board members were converted to English. As early as 2001, the designation codes for divisions, which outsiders could decipher only with difficulty, had been abolished in internal communications as well. For instance, the division formerly known as K3 had since been *Benzinsysteme*. It now became "Gasoline Systems," and the office (and person) of chairman of the board ceased to be referred to as F1 (*Führungsbereich* 1) and now became G1 (Group Executive Sector 1). But even Fehrenbach stuck in principle to the system of abbreviations for the offices of board members introduced in the Merkle era.

To help drive forward the process of change in corporate culture, Fehrenbach had already presented the final version of the catalogue of Bosch values at

"House of Orientation" workshop for associates (2005)

the GPI conference in June 2002. There were seven values: 1. Future and result focus [*Zukunfts- und Ertragsorientierung*], 2. Responsibility [*Verantwortlichkeit*], 3. Initiative and determination [*Initiative und Konsequenz*], 4. Openness and trust [*Offenheit und Vertrauen*], 5. Fairness [the English term was used], 6. Reliability, credibility, and legality [*Zuverlässigkeit, Glaubwürdigkeit und Legalität*], and 7. Cultural diversity [*Kulturelle Vielfalt*].[10] As a next step, the board members looked at questions of values-based management.[11] Fehrenbach was convinced that the only way of running a company as complex as Bosch was by giving its associates a frame of reference based on firm principles. The "BeQIK" mission and the Bosch values were to be embedded into such a framework, which board members and associates alike could then use as a guide for action. Worldwide, the process was accompanied by seminars about values. Under the [English-language] title "House of Orientation," the framework was ready for presentation in 2005. Its central image was formed by a three-tier pyramid comprising at its base the Bosch values and core competencies, superimposed onto which was the "BeQIK" mission and, at the top, the Bosch vision. The vision itself represented a "collective view of the future" whose purpose was to help the company's associates work together successfully in an increasingly globalized world.[12] Alongside this, in 2005 Bosch introduced the memorable slogan *Technik fürs Leben* ("Invented for life"). This was meant to serve the Bosch Group as a strategic imperative and to become part of the company's corporate identity. This is given graphic expression in the company's logo, in which the slogan is a kind of subtitle to the company's name. As had happened with "BeQIK," the "House of Orientation" permeated the Bosch Group from the top down – initially through seminars for executives but then through a brochure published in 13 languages under the title "What drives us, what we have in common, what we stand for." The title set out vividly what the "House of Orientation" wanted to achieve. It was to be a kind of bridge over which mission and values might pass and become cemented in everyday working practice. The brochure proved to be the most practicable way to achieve this end. It could be thrust into the hand of each associate, and no one, in the future, needed to sign up for a special seminar in order to become familiar with the company's principles. This is how the "House of Orientation" found an excellent reception, notably among the soaring numbers of associates in Asia.

But even this kind of guidance had its limits. In the end, no associate could be compelled to act in accordance with the maxims of the "House of Orientation" – nor should they, since these maxims ultimately pointed in the direction of individual initiative and responsibility. In practical terms, the frame of reference's main effect was to make it difficult to act against the Bosch values. Since Bosch associates identified strongly with their company, it seemed likely they would also have a strong desire to work with rather than against its values. Infringements were not punishable under labor law, but they could certainly lead to a degree of exclusion and act as barriers to promotion. Trainees were asked to declare adherence to the substance of the "House of Orientation." They were also advised to leave the company if they felt unable to identify with its mission and values.[13] Of course, how far anyone could in this way be persuaded to stay or to leave cannot be ascertained. Many will have accepted the "House of Orientation" simply because management expected them to and they were loathe to stick out. But the board itself now had to comply with the standards it had set, and came to realize that this was not always an easy task.

This preoccupation with "Bosch values" and the work on the "House of Orientation" may well have been partly why, with greater insistence than his predecessors, Fehrenbach invoked the person and principles of the founder. His address at the LD-Forum of December 2003 had taken as its theme: "Bosch kraftvoll weiterentwickeln" [Securing a strong development for Bosch]. This was an overt reference to the last will of Robert Bosch, which contained the injunction to secure for his company "a strong and meaningful development."[14] In the wake of the cultural transformation introduced in the autumn of 1999, Robert Bosch had been rediscovered. Fehrenbach referred to him more frequently and more directly than Scholl had done. He was also fond of citing the familiar words of the philosopher Odo Marquard: "Zukunft braucht Herkunft" [The future needs a past].[15] At the same time, the company's approach to its own history was undergoing a change. This approach had tended to be self-contained, even introverted, instead of being explicitly driven by a desire to communicate. For Fehrenbach, the Bosch heritage was more than just "a unique opportunity" to strengthen corporate identity. It could also be a "major competitive advantage."[16] The Bosch archives thus became the Historical Communications department and began promoting the company's history proactively and in an altogether more positive and open manner.

Operationally, Fehrenbach soon found himself embroiled in processes that flew in the face of the ambitious corporate mission he aspired to. In the autumn of 2003, a major disaster threatened Bosch in the shape of the SBC Sensotronic brake control, the electro-hydraulic brake system developed jointly with DaimlerChrysler and introduced two years earlier. The company had already let itself down badly in the course of 2001 over a major order from DaimlerChrysler, when Blaupunkt failed to supply navigation systems for the Mercedes E and S classes on time.[17] SBC reduced braking distance by adjusting hydraulic pressure in wheel brakes electronically. It was deemed a pioneering achievement, and engineers from both companies had won awards for it. But when DaimlerChrysler began fitting SBC in production models of its Mercedes E and SL classes, the system proved highly temperamental, with a marked tendency to break down if annual mileage was high. In May 2004, Mercedes-Benz felt compelled to recall 680,000 vehicles. A year later, an even bigger recall involved no fewer than 1.3 million vehicles.[18] DaimlerChrysler promptly ceased to fit SBC and asked Bosch's rival, Teves/Continental, to develop a conventional hydraulic brake. To the press, the reaction at Bosch was calm. Internally, however, the episode was a humiliation. It hit Bosch particularly hard, since it fell so far short of the quality commitment that formed part of its mission – the Q in "BeQIK." Fehrenbach felt obliged to severely admonish his executives, telling the GPI conference in June 2004: "This quality situation sits uncomfortably with the Bosch brand. Nor does it match our self-image, as enshrined in our 'BeQIK' mission."[19] Problems of quality had arisen before, in connection with common rail and other electronically controlled systems. But Bosch refused to tolerate them. It could not afford disgruntled major customers. And its intensive efforts to improve quality subsequently began to bear fruit. In the automotive technology business sector, total reported defects declined markedly. So far as zero-kilometer complaints were concerned, this started to happen in 2002. For components in vehicles already delivered, improvement began in 2004.[20]

In 2004, Bosch was able to record larger sales increases than in the years before. The largest increases were in two business sectors: the industrial technology sector on the one hand and the consumer goods and building technology sector on the other. These increases were largely due to the acquisition of Rexroth and Buderus, which in 2004 were consolidated in Bosch Group sales figures for the first time. However, the automotive technology business sector was also able to increase its sales by some 7 percent, compared to a modest plus of only 1 percent in the previous year. It looked as if the sector might be returning to the heady days of the pre-2001 diesel boom.[21] The medium-term planning target was for 8 percent sales growth, which was in line with a long-term empirical figure. A distinction was drawn in this connection between internal growth of 5 percent and a 3 percent sales increase as a result of acquisitions.[22] In its turn, this figure was the basis for the target margin, which in 2005 was set by the PP05 project. According to PP05, a pre-tax operating result of 7 to 8 percent was required so that planned growth could be financed through the company's own efforts (something Bosch continued to value very highly).[23]

In 2005, none of the business sectors disclosed increases as large as in the previous year. Sales growth still topped 5 percent in automotive technology and in the company as a whole, but targets were missed by a mile. Nonetheless, at the LD-Forum (which continued to provide the board of management with a platform for taking stock of the year just closed) in December of that year, Fehrenbach confirmed an annual growth target of 8 percent for the planning period up to 2008.[24] Both the upward trend in the automotive sector and the successful post-merger integration of Buderus and Rexroth bred hope. Bosch Rexroth AG especially was developing better than even optimists had expected. For this international market leader in mobile and industrial hydraulics, which produced gearboxes for wind turbines, electronic ship-steering systems, pumps, and valves, sales increased by over 60 percent in the period from 2003 to 2008, rising from some 3.7 billion euros to roughly 5.9 billion euros.[25] Another reason why these successes were so important to the board of management was that one of Fehrenbach's declared aims was to expand the non-automotive sectors at Bosch, reducing the company's dependence on the automobile, which as late as 2004 still accounted for over 60 percent of sales. The industrial technology sector had clearly gained in importance through Bosch Rexroth, becoming a third pillar alongside the automotive technology and the consumer goods and building technology sectors. Even so, with a 13 percent share of sales, it hardly constituted a proper counterweight to automotive technology. Everyone knew that after the Buderus and Rexroth takeovers the Schillerhöhe planned further investments outside the field of automotive engineering. The aim was to diversify the Bosch Group further after the loss of communications technology. At the 2005 LD-Forum, Fehrenbach hinted that, in 10 years' time, non-automotive sectors might account for more than 50 percent of sales.[26] For a future new business sector, the board had in mind sales of 5 billion euros.[27] It goes without saying that the project already had its own abbreviated designation: UBX [*Unternehmensbereich X*], or business sector X.

Table 19 Percentage shares of business sectors in Bosch Group sales (2000–10)[28]

Business sector	2000	2002	2004	2006	2008	2010
Automotive Technology	71	67	63	62	59	59
Consumer Goods and Building Technology	24	22	24	25	26	27
Industrial Technology	4	11	13	13	15	14
Communications Technology*	1					

* remainder

Clearly, a commitment to conglomerate, risk-spreading diversification has always been one of Bosch management's cast-iron principles. Like Merkle, Bierich, and Scholl before him, Fehrenbach considered an overdependence on automotive engineering too risky. But undoubtedly, Bosch's repeated attempts to tap into fields of business other than automotive engineering also had to do with the legal status and financial autonomy of the company. Had Bosch been a listed stock corporation, the capital market would have required greater concentration on its core business. Analysts usually assume that investors will go for a corporate profile that is as clear-cut as possible. They believe that diversity will tend to frighten money away. As the crisis in the U.S. automotive industry deepened in 2006 (particularly in the Chrysler Group, where huge losses led to massive job cuts at Daimler Chrysler, and eventually to the dissolution of the 1998 union between the two companies), Bosch once again felt the negative effects of its heavy reliance on the automotive industry.[29] In 2006, the automotive technology business sector (UBK) grew its sales by only 3.5 percent, while the industrial technology (UBI) and the consumer goods and building technology (UBG) sectors generated internal growth of 7 and 6 percent respectively. While such consumer goods divisions as Power Tools and BSH were going from strength to strength, the reverses in automotive technology meant that the Bosch Group as a whole was unable to increase sales by the 8 percent planned, but instead only by 5.4 percent.[30]

Fig. 16 Percentage year-on-year sales growth in the Bosch Group and individual business sectors, including acquisitions (2003–08)

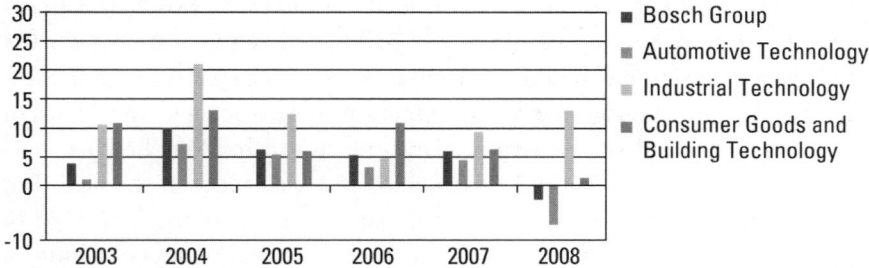

Source: Robert Bosch GmbH, annual reports for 2003–08

Against this background, the mood at the December 2006 LD-Forum was "depressed and burdened with self-doubt, notably in automotive technology."[31] Management personnel found themselves on the receiving end of a fiery address by G1, who also blamed the company's failure to achieve its targets on their having made too little effort. However, Fehrenbach's lecture also indicated a certain helplessness when faced with business developments that never kept pace with targets. "The consequence is that we find each year that we have fallen far short of our plans and once again put off any improvement to some future date."[32] Part of the reason, no doubt, is that Bosch had planned too optimistically. An average annual growth rate of 8 percent had been achieved in the period 1994–2003, but then the company had benefited from the exceptional economic circumstances resulting from the diesel boom. Now it did not.[33]

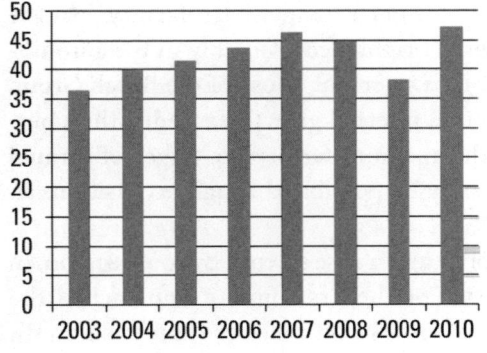

Fig. 17 Bosch Group sales (2003–10) in billions of euros

Source: Robert Bosch GmbH, annual reports for 2003–10

On top of the reverses in the U.S. business, Bosch had to swallow another bitter pill in 2006 in connection with automotive engineering, specifically for diesel injection. Volkswagen had decided to replace the Bosch unit-injector system with common rail. Since VW had been its only customer for the unit injector, Bosch now had to cut back its production, phasing it out completely at the end of 2009. The discontinuation was associated with losses of market share and a drop in margin.[34] Unit-injector technology had been developed especially for VW, and Bosch enjoyed a monopoly in the field. But when it came to common rail, VW could choose from among a number of suppliers. And indeed, the Wolfsburg company asked Siemens to build a common-rail plant in former East Germany. The shutdown of unit-injector production affected some 4,000 Bosch associates at the Feuerbach and Rommelsbach plants in Germany, as well as in Rodez (France) and Bursa (Turkey). Anxiety arose particularly in Feuerbach, when the works-council chairman Werner Neuffer announced that 2,670 jobs were under threat (2009 being also the year when production of distributor pumps was due to end). In 2006, the works council demanded that, as part of a "plan for Feuerbach's future," local management should waive any redundancies, continue to take on apprentices, and create replacements for any product lines about to be phased out.[35] A solution was found that would keep job losses at Feuerbach within limits and create fresh prospects for the site. In an agreement with the works council, Bosch promised to install five assembly lines for the new CP4 high-pressure diesel pump there. And in 2009, Feuerbach was also to become the lead plant for all common-rail pumps.[36] The Rommelsbach plant was eventually closed down in August 2009. However, there were no dismissals because Bosch had offered a guarantee of employment at its Reutlingen plants (of which Rommelsbach was one). And since Bosch had invested 600 million euros in the construction of a new semiconductor plant there, which was to produce eight-inch wafers, the Reutlingen location was able to cushion the closure. Opened in March 2010, this new plant absorbed many of the 620 associates from the former Rommelsbach facility.[37] In the 2007 financial year, the mood at Bosch brightened – notably in the automotive technology sector. Its sales rose by 4.5 percent, those of the Bosch Group as a whole by 6 percent.[38] Averaged out, internal growth exceeded the 5 percent target.[39] Even so, achieving the medium-term plan target of annual overall growth of 8 percent would only be possible through acquisitions in the years up to 2008.[40]

Total Bosch Group headcount once again rose steeply, by some 87,000, in the first decade of the new century. For the first time, it approached the 300,000 figure, having as recently as 2000 stood at fewer than 200,000. In

Germany alone, the number of Bosch Group associates increased by over 22,000 in the period 2000–10 (helped by the Buderus and Rexroth takeovers, admittedly), while in other European countries it went up by a total of some 26,000. But the largest increase in headcount came in Asia – notably in China. In Asia, Australia, and Africa, the number of Bosch associates shot up by almost 150 percent over the same 10-year period. As a result, the total share of Bosch associates employed in Germany (already less than half around the turn of the century) was down to 40 percent by 2010. The share in the Americas likewise declined over the same period, although Bosch had wanted to expand here in the new century. Originally, the Americas, together with Asia, had been among the chief points of emphasis in Fehrenbach's regional-diversification strategy. Following the decline of the automotive industry in the United States, such expansion plans had had to be abandoned in 2005.

Table 20 Regional employment structure of the Bosch Group (2000–10)[41]

	Germany	%	Rest of Europe	%	The Americas	%	Asia, Austr., Africa	%	Total
2000	91,000	46.2	47,068	23.9	33,118	16.8	25,694	13.1	196,880
2005	109,600	43.7	67,384	26.9	37,086	14.8	36,792	14.6	250,862
2010	113,557	40.0	73,045	25.8	33,689	11.9	63,216	22.3	283,507

Granted, Bosch still had a strongly European bias. In 2010, two-thirds of all associates still worked on the company's home continent. Nonetheless, because of the Bosch Group's strong growth in Asia, globalization was unquestionably an important feature of its development in these years. At Bosch, as with most major European companies, this globalization now picked up even more pace than in the 1990s. The Schillerhöhe saw this development (and continues to see it) as a form of diversification. The economies on the various continents were now developing so differently that a strong worldwide presence allowed risk to be spread in much the same way as being represented in a mixture of industrial sectors. For Fehrenbach, regional diversification was a key component of corporate strategy, and he wanted it to be pursued as deliberately as industrial diversification.

Another sign that globalization had acquired a new quality in the first decade of the new century was the regional distribution of sales. Up until 2005, there was little structural change here, but after that date the share accounted

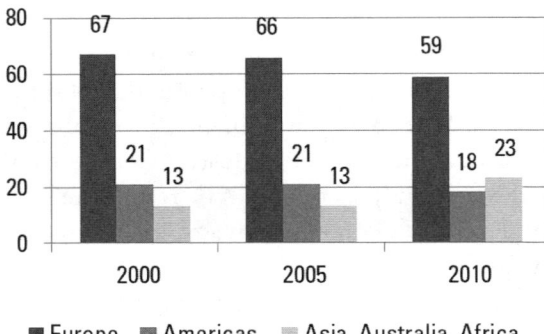

Fig. 18 Bosch Group sales structure by continent (2000–10)

for by Europe and the Americas declined markedly, while that of Asia, Australia, and Africa together rocketed from 13 to 23 percent. In 2010, the share of sales generated in Europe was lower than the share of associates employed there, since most Bosch Group plants were located in Europe. In the Americas, it was the other way around, and in Asia (taken together with Australia and Africa) both sales and headcount were more or less the same in percentage terms, at 22 and 23 percent respectively.

Under Fehrenbach, the members of the Bosch board of management redoubled their efforts to spot and to interpret emerging trends in order to identify future opportunities and to be able to react promptly to changes in the market. Their prime concern was to put their finger on the really big, long-term processes of change. Taking these megatrends as a starting point, the board of management and their in-house experts met several times a year to discuss what they meant for strategy. One megatrend that board members identified was how the focus of world economic growth was shifting increasingly toward Asia Pacific. In light of the rapid rise of China, whose economy had been growing at a steady 7 to 10 percent a year since the 1990s, this view enjoyed universal recognition. In 2005, the board of management launched its AP 25 program to profit from this Asia Pacific boom. Its aim was to raise the Asian contribution to Bosch Group sales to 25 percent within 10 years.[42] By 2010, that contribution already amounted to 23 percent if Australia and Africa are included.

Another megatrend identified by the board members and their strategists encompassed the issues of environment and energy. They were convinced that in the future, these issues would be more important than ever.[43] Under Fehrenbach, environmental protection and conservation of resources were vital elements of corporate strategy. Bosch manufacturing facilities the world over worked according to strict guidelines, which were considered so exemplary that Fehrenbach was named "Eco-Manager of the Year" in 2006. The BSH chief Robert Kugler had received the same award four years earlier. A field to which Fehrenbach attached particular importance was renewable energy, leading the press to dub him "Green Franz."[44] The Bosch Group was already represented in this area by Bosch Rexroth, which manufactured large gearboxes for wind turbines. This involvement increased when the company entered the solar energy field in 2008.[45] Some 45 percent of the company's research and development expenditure is now dedicated to sustainable and resource-conserving technologies.

Another area seen as offering great potential was electromobility. As early as 1967, there had been prototypes of vehicles fitted with Bosch electric power-trains, and six years later the company presented a trials vehicle featuring hybrid technology. These developments had not been pursued, however, because of the poor performance of batteries at that time and the extremely high price tag.[46] Some 40 years later, however, engineers were convinced that lithium-ion technology presented huge opportunities, and was the key to making electric vehicles viable. The company had already acquired a certain expertise in this area through its work on developing batteries for power tools.[47] In 2008, Bosch and the Samsung Group in Korea established SB LiMotive, a joint-venture company whose purpose was to develop and manufacture lithium-ion battery systems. Both parties stated the intention of investing some 500 million U.S. dollars in the new company.[48] However, four years later Bosch decided to terminate its collaboration with the Samsung SDI subsidary and continue development work in this field on its own for the time being.[49]

Lastly, planners already had their eye on a final megatrend. This was the long-term transition from an industrial to a service society. Their conclusion was that Bosch must stop seeing itself as a traditional industrial supplier and increasingly move into the service sector. The company now defined itself as a "leading technology and services company."[50] The services meant were not simply consulting and maintenance in the industrial sphere, services that are considered a standard part of all modern industrial supply. The Bosch Group now turned to the provision of services in a much broader sense – in the fields of communication and logistics, for instance.[51]

The company has enjoyed great success recently in areas where Bosch has long been represented. The power tools division has yet again proved a reliable earner. One extremely successful innovation (launched in the autumn of 2003) in this respect was the Ixo cordless drill/driver, the first cordless drill/driver to use lithium-ion technology. The Ixo soon became the world's widest-selling power tool, making a substantial contribution toward boosting power tools sales by nearly 60 percent between 2003 and 2011, from

2.4 billion to 3.8 billion euros.[52] In recent years, Bosch has expanded with similar success in security technology, an area that is oddly the last survivor of a business sector (communications technology) that was abandoned after heavy losses. Created in 2002, the Bosch Security Systems division has benefited from a soaring worldwide demand for monitoring and surveillance systems. CCTV for monitoring facilities and access-control systems are as much part of the product portfolio of Bosch Security Systems as fire alarms, burglar alarms, and evacuation-control systems.[53] In the business press, Bosch has been dubbed the "new star of the security world."[54] "E-call," the sophisticated emergency reporting system developed by Bosch, combines security technology and automotive electronics. As soon as sensors register an accident, the system automatically sends an emergency call to a Bosch control center, giving precise coordinates that allow the nearest emergency service to be alerted. Another part of the security systems division is public-address technology, which Bosch installs in airports, sports arenas, and football stadiums all over the world, often in conjunction with evacuation systems – as is the case at Changi Airport in Singapore.[55] Lastly, the division includes the Bosch Communications Center business unit, which acts as a control-center organization for monitoring and emergency-reporting systems and now has communication centers on three continents.[56]

"Getting the workforce through the crisis intact": Bosch in the financial and economic crisis of 2008–2009

The crisis that hit the U.S. real-estate market in the summer of 2007 soon put growing numbers of banks in the U.S. and Europe under pressure, after those banks had speculated in mortgage loans with low creditworthiness ratings – so-called "sub-prime" mortgages. In the first six months of 2008, the U.S. automobile market also collapsed. When the New York investment bank Lehman Brothers filed for bankruptcy on September 15, 2008, the world was plunged into its biggest financial crisis since the 1930s. The global financial system threatened to grind to a halt as banks stopped lending to each other.[57] Even though governments in the U.S. and Europe stepped in to rescue banks with bail-out programs on a scale never previously imagined, the crisis soon reached the "real economy." In Germany, too, the automobile sector suffered an unprecedented slump. "All assembly lines are at a standstill," the *Süddeutsche Zeitung* wrote on October 28, 2008. "At Mercedes in Sindelfingen. At BMW in Leipzig. At Opel in Bochum. Why? Customers are not buying cars. Not at the moment. Not in the middle of a crisis whose repercussions are very widely feared." The writer painted a gloomy outlook, shared by many at the time. The German automobile industry was "going into recession, as is the whole economy."[58]

At Bosch, too, certain parts of factories stood empty. In October 2008, sales in the automotive technology business sector were down 17 percent year on year. Associates at the Rommelsbach plant (which was to be closed the following year) were told to stay at home for a week.[59] Bosch followed other companies (Opel, Ford, ThyssenKrupp) in announcing shorter working weeks. From the beginning of November, 3,500 associates at the Bamberg plant were initially put on shorter hours for six months.[60] Bosch had already (in September) had to trim its 2008 sales forecast. Now, the company was expecting a disastrous operating result and a contraction of sales for the first time in 15 years. All medium-term growth targets had become so much waste paper. As December began, the board's reaction was to introduce further cuts. Associates at several plants (including the 6,500 employed in Feuerbach) were to be sent on leave from December 22 to January 7.[61] In January, application was made for statutory schemes for reduced working hours to be introduced at four plants: Bamberg, Eisenach, Reutlingen, and Salzgitter. The number of associates affected by such schemes rose to 9,000.[62]

What the press called "further bad tidings" was in fact part of a well-thought-out crisis strategy.[63] In Fehrenbach's view, business in Germany and throughout Europe did not face a lengthy depression. His assumption was that, having begun so abruptly, the crisis would not last long. Things would settle down toward the end of 2009. It was not a view unanimously shared by the RBIK shareholders.[64] Fehrenbach believed that Bosch would have to hold out for a year. He had in mind the lessons of the 1993 crisis. Back then, a confrontational crisis-management response had done a lot of damage to corporate culture. Cutting the workforce had been a mistake. Much know-how had been lost, and when the upturn came the company had found itself short of skilled workers.[65] Pondering on how that episode had affected management's reaction to the 2008–09 crisis, Fehrenbach said in retrospect: "For me that was a serious lesson. It [the experience of 1993] guided my actions during the recent crisis. It convinced me that taking the workforce through the crisis is always the right answer. Associates have to be convinced that we're doing the right thing. At Bosch, there's no alternative."[66]

The strategy with which Fehrenbach met the drastic setback of the autumn of 2008 was fixed that December. The RBIK shareholders gave it their approval on December 11.[67] Fehrenbach's plan included huge cuts, but projects with a promising future were to be spared. Research and development enjoyed particular immunity in this regard, but so did three specific projects: development of batteries for electric vehicles, acquisition of the ersol solar-energy company, and construction of the new semiconductor plant in Reutlingen. Research and development outlay for 2009 did in fact (at 3,603 million euros) come out some 7 percent down on the very high level reached in 2008 (3,889 million euros), although it still surpassed the 3,583 million euros spent in 2007. Capital expenditure, on the other hand, was curtailed drastically (2008: 3,276 million euros; 2009: 1,892 million euros).[68] When it came to cuts in personnel expenses, the board of management consulted closely with the works council. According to the account given by Alfred Löckle, chairman of the central works council, they had "first of all simply agreed, right from a very early stage, that we were going to get through this crisis and hang on to our core workforce."[69] "Getting everyone through the crisis" – that was the watchword.[70] To enable them to "hang on to the workforce," board and works council agreed to a package of measures concerning associates within Germany. To start with, worktime accounts were reduced. Then there was a reduction of the working week from 35 hours to 31.5 hours. When the crisis exceeded the worst expectations, the parties fell back on collective agreements to reduce working hours and statutory schemes for shorter working weeks. A portion of the costs incurred by the company as a result of such statutory schemes was spread over the whole workforce, in the form of a cut in income of between 1 and 1.5 percent. Löckle reports that this strategy was not without its opponents, both within management and on the employee side.[71] However, Fehrenbach and Löckle carried the day. According to the collective agreement for the safeguarding of jobs, if orders ran short the working week might be cut (with pay falling accordingly) to 30 hours. In that case, however, the associates concerned would have suffered a greater loss of income than under statutory schemes (where workers received compensation for hours lost from the Federal Employment Agency).

As the crisis wore on, Bosch associates at times waived a substantial portion of their income. The recession alone meant a roughly 10 percent drop in earnings. In return, management promised that there would be no dismissals. The works council had received assurances that burdens would be distributed in proportion to income, "the strong taking more strain, the weak less." The principle applied "from the bottom wage bracket up to Mr. Fehrenbach himself."[72] Management (board members included) received no salary increases for a total of more than two years, which lent the economy measures greater credibility. Moreover, performance-related bonuses shrank in line with operating result. In this crisis, Bosch was by no means alone in adopting the strategy of retaining its workforce by a range of means, including shorter hours. Most major companies in Germany did the same, having learned that the alternative (losing skilled workers) would cost them more.[73] What was exceptional was the way Fehrenbach managed the crisis. Having someone at the helm who placed great importance on open communication proved to be invaluable. Fehrenbach kept his managers informed in world-wide telephone conferences, and his workforce in letters to associates. Looking back, he said that "for the first time, [we] truly saw the value of communication."[74]

Meanwhile, Blaupunkt GmbH had become a chronic loss-maker. The subsidiary was in dire need of turnaround, and at the end of 2008 Bosch ceded parts of its business to the financial investor Aurelius. The parts affected were the Blaupunkt brand-name and the aftermarket business with car radios and navigation systems. The original-equipment side of the business stayed with Bosch. Before it was sold, Blaupunkt is said to have made losses totaling 20–30 million euros. With the advent of the financial and economic crisis it had become too much of a burden. Blaupunkt had been a traditional Bosch trademark, but Fehrenbach decided that enough was enough. It was agreed that the purchase price would not be disclosed. There was even talk of Bosch having paid Aurelius to take the patient on.[75]

It was in the first quarter of 2009 that the crisis hit Bosch with full force. While sales in the final quarter of 2008 had declined by 14.5 percent year on year, the January–March 2009 figure was 27 percent.[76] A collapse of such proportions had not been seen since the Second World War. Admittedly, from February various measures introduced by the German government kicked in. With the German parliament's *Konjunkturpaket II* ["Economic package II"], new arrangements governing shorter working weeks came into effect. State-funded allowances were extended from 6 months to 18 months (later, even to 24 months) and were now no longer conditional on one-third of a company's employees having first suffered a loss of earnings in excess of 10 percent. German companies made great use of this concession. Estimates suggest that some 300,000 jobs were saved during the 2008–09 crisis by means of this scheme.[77] Also introduced (alongside *Konjunkturpaket II*) was the "environmental premium" that the VDA had proposed back in October 2008. Popularly known as the *Abwrackprämie*, the "scrappage bonus scheme" gave any owner who junked an old automobile a state subsidy of 2,500 euros to buy a new one. The environmental premium soon proved an effective way of shoring up the automobile industry, automotive suppliers, and dealerships. At Bosch, it meant that sales in Germany fell less steeply than sales in the rest of the world. However, the premium was mainly used to purchase small cars, and in this segment of the market Bosch was less well represented with its injection and ESP systems.[78]

In mid-2009, Bosch management could still see no change for the better. Clearly they had underestimated the crisis, and they became edgy. In May, sales in the automotive technology business sector were down 36 percent year on year. In the industrial technology sector, the figure was 27 percent.[79] A 15 percent decline in sales had been predicted for 2009. Now Bernd Bohr, head of automotive technology, put it at 15–20 percent.[80] At the end of April, a total of 93,000 associates were working shorter hours, 58,000 of them in Germany. In countries with less flexible labor-market policies, even Bosch was laying people off. By the end of April, Bosch Group subsidiaries outside Germany had recorded 3,000 dismissals, as Wolfgang Malchow, the director of industrial relations, told a works-council conference in Bad Kissingen.[81] As the crisis wore on, that number increased sharply.

By this time, even Fehrenbach was expecting a "long difficult period."[82] For this reason, the board of management decided to approach the capital markets as a precautionary measure for securing the company's liquidity. On June 3, 2009, a bond for 1.1 billion euros was issued, divided into four- and eight-year tranches paying interest of 3.75 and 5.125 percent respectively.[83] Directed at institutional investors, the bond was well subscribed. But it was also a sign that Bosch was unsure how far the company was going to fall, and that, if push came to shove, management would always give top priority to the survival of Robert Bosch GmbH, even if that meant abandoning job guarantees. Back in the spring of 2009, Fehrenbach had stated at a workforce assembly: "We shall stick to this course just as long as we can."[84] From that it could be assumed that cooperation between management and works council was subject to certain reservations, and would not survive a prolonged crisis, since the works council left no one in doubt that it would not tolerate any deviation from the course steered up to that time.[85] Its watchword was: "Getting everyone through the crisis, however long it lasts!"[86]

The upturn took its time – but it came. On September 15, 2009, on the fringe of the Frankfurt International Motor Show, Fehrenbach was able to say: "The green shoots of recovery appear to be in sight."[87] In the fourth quarter of 2009, Bosch Group sales disclosed their first year-on-year growth – admittedly from a low recession-based level. The downward slide had been halted. Fehrenbach found his initial expectation confirmed – namely, that the crisis would take a V-shaped course, with a steep slump followed by an equally steep upswing. However, at the end of 2009 there were still 28,500 associates on statutory schemes for reduced working hours, 27,000 others were working reduced hours without compensation, and some 10,000 jobs had been shed outside Germany.[88] Summing up this worst year in Bosch's postwar history, the 2009 annual report disclosed a 15 percent drop in sales and an after-tax loss of

1.2 billion euros, which was equivalent to some 3 percent of total sales. For a longer or shorter period, nearly 112,000 associates had been affected by reduced working hours – around 65,000 of them in Germany. Worldwide, the total Bosch Group workforce had declined by some 3 percent from 282,758 (annual average for 2008) to 274,530 (annual average for 2009). Yet even the latter figure was well above the 2007 level.[89]

Compared with the sales decline right across the German automotive industry (down 20 percent) and across all German automotive suppliers (down 25 percent), Bosch got off quite lightly with its 15 percent fall.[90] Once again, the company had felt the downside of its heavy reliance on the automobile market. But at the same time, it saw that its relatively strong industrial technology business sector was unable to offset the collapse in its automotive technology business. At 24 percent, industrial technology had suffered an even greater sales decline over the previous year than had automotive technology (where sales were down 18 percent). And it was not automotive technology, but industrial technology that recorded the biggest loss in EBIT – at some 1.1 billion euros. The crisis had hit later there and the lowest point was reached only in the autumn of 2009. Particularly hard hit was Bosch Rexroth AG, which in past years had been among the Bosch Group's model companies. In October 2009, its management announced that 550 jobs (nearly 25 percent of the workforce) would be shed at the Schweinfurt and Volkach plants by means of severance agreements, partial retirement schemes, and early-retirement agreements.[91] In June 2010, by which time order books had begun filling up again, Bosch Rexroth was still insisting on these reductions. So there were protests. Job cuts were no longer mentioned when the 2010 financial year ended with a sales boost of 22 percent, but the 2010 sales figure remained below its 2008 level.[92] Within the Bosch Group, only the consumer goods and building technology business sector showed comparable stability (notably in heating systems and household appliances) with a 4.8 percent sales decline in 2009. Heating equipment and washing machines sold even during the recession. In the power tools division, sales were hit by the real-estate crisis in the U.S., but even here the decline in sales was only around 5 percent.[93]

So far as regional diversification was concerned, the company's Asia business offered a ray of hope during the crisis. "Business in Asia is a stabilizing factor," was a sub-heading in the Bosch 2009 annual report.[94] To be precise, this applied mainly to China, where 2009 sales were up 21 percent year on year in local currency terms and by as much as 26 percent in euro terms. In other words, Bosch had done the right thing by expanding its involvement in China in the years preceding the crisis. Strong growth in China and a stable business situation in India for the first time boosted Bosch Group sales to the point where Asia Pacific accounted for 20 percent of the group's earnings worldwide. In absolute terms, though, sales in the region declined, since Bosch did less business in Japan during the global financial crisis. However, the overall decline in sales here was under 2 percent, whereas in Europe it was 20 percent. In North America, where sales had already slumped in 2008 because of the sub-prime crisis, the decline was 11 percent, in South America 16 percent.[95]

Bosch was able to recover from the 2009 setback more quickly than most people in the company had thought possible. In 2010, sales throughout the Bosch Group rose by as much as 24 percent to 47.3 billion euros. That put them around 1 billion euros above the previous record level reached in 2007.[96] Economically, Bosch had withstood the ordeal well, as had German industry as a whole. But "Bosch culture," too, had come through the fire. It was partly this culture that had enabled the crisis to be overcome without social conflict of any note. The same was true of the "German model" generally, which had been much maligned as the process of globalization gathered pace. In fact, the German economic model had come through the harshest of crises (that of 2008–09) with flying colors. Boards of management, works councils, and unions had found constructive, mutually acceptable solutions. They had also received backing from the German government in the form of such timely measures as the extension of schemes to subsidize shorter working weeks. There is some doubt, however, as to whether the model would have continued to function had the crisis gone on much longer.

Even the causes of the crisis of 2008–09 provided confirmation that Bosch was committed to the right principles. "We deliberately reject short-term, short-sighted profit maximization," Fehrenbach told the LD-Forum in December 2010. "Instead, we stand by our sustained result focus and by the targets we have set for result."[97] On several occasions, the Bosch CEO publicly condemned the practices of investment banks. He actually broke off business relations with Goldman Sachs because of the excessive bonuses it was paying its bankers.[98] For the media, Fehrenbach was now something of a moral compass in the German business world. With the company's conservative financial policy, which even during the crisis gave the company an equity ratio of nearly 50 percent, Bosch did indeed provide a counter-model in the real economy to speculation in financial markets. This was acknowledged not only publicly and by the unions, but also by the ratings agencies. Even in June 2009, Standard and Poor's gave Bosch the best rating of all German industrial companies: an AA- with negative outlook.[99] A year later, the outlook was upgraded to "stable."

"Green Bosch": growth in renewables, losses in the solar business

Management at Bosch had long been aiming to reduce the company's dependence on automotive engineering. The approaches used to select fresh fields of operation were always changing. Under Fehrenbach, the procedure was systematized. First, the strategy department studied trends and distilled out proposals. The choice was then narrowed down at a retreat session with the board of management. If a proposal survived this selection process, a motion was submitted to the RBIK shareholders recommending that industrial operations commence in the chosen field. This is what happened in the summer of 2008, when Bosch acquired a majority holding in the Erfurt-based photovoltaics manufacturer ersol Solar Energy AG, a company with some 1,000 employees, and set up its Solar Energy division. Under every criterion the company applied, solar energy was a perfect match for Bosch's strategic direction and the way the company saw itself.

With its huge potential, solar energy had long been seen as the energy of the future. In Germany, thanks to the Renewable Energy Act (*Erneuerbare-Energien-Gesetz* or EEG) of 2000 and the EEG amendment of 2004, it had also become very good business. Massive government subsidies paid solar-power producers such high feed-in tariffs that demand climbed swiftly. Germany became the world's largest market for photovoltaics. Large numbers of solar companies started up, notably in the former East Germany – Thuringia, Saxony-Anhalt, and Saxony – where plenty of subsidies went into setting up these facilities and favorable tax incentives were available. Over the course of the decade, the number of new photovoltaic installations increased by leaps and bounds. The 900 MW generated in 2006 had become 7,400 MW by 2010.[100]

But it was not the high feed-in tariffs (already the subject of criticism in 2008) that persuaded Bosch to buy ersol Solar Energy AG. It was the fact that the solar cells, solar modules, and wafers manufactured there complemented the Bosch Group's product range well and looked like providing a further pillar in the area of non-automotive engineering. In 1997, the Bosch subsidiary BBT Thermotechnik GmbH had taken over the solar collector manufacturer Solar Diamant, which subsequently traded as Bosch Solarthermie GmbH.[101] In 2007, Junkers also began producing solar collectors, and in the same year Bosch agreed to collaborate with BASF on developing plastic solar cells to the point where they could be produced in series.[102] Furthermore, photovoltaics rounded out the Bosch Group's production portfolio in the renewable energy area. This included not only the wind- and marine-power systems manufactured by Bosch Rexroth but also the geothermal pumps made by BBT Thermotechnik. It was no secret that "eco-manager" Fehrenbach (as he was dubbed) had high hopes for "Green Bosch."

Of the share capital of ersol Solar Energy AG, 50.45 percent was held by the U.S. private-equity company Ventizz Capital. This was an opportunity for Bosch. Here was a financial investor for whom selling was simply a matter of the offer price. Ventizz Capital in fact sold Bosch its ersol holding for more than 60 percent above market value. Having paid 546 million euros for the Ventizz block, Bosch then offered the minority shareholders of ersol the same takeover price. The stock exchange judged the purchase price unreasonably excessive, and some analysts must have wondered why a company known for its conservative finance policy agreed to such a deal.[103] But Fehrenbach was determined to boost renewable energy-related sales, which in 2008 stood at 750 million euros, to 1.2 billion euros by 2010.[104] In relation to total Bosch Group sales, of course, this was only 3 percent – not enough for a separate business sector.

In 2009, ersol Solar Energy AG was renamed Bosch Solar Energy AG. Bosch, which now held more than 90 percent of the capital, decided to invest 530 million euros in building a new greenfield plant and giving the solar company a new center in Arnstadt (near Erfurt, the capital of Thuringia), to which the subsidiary's head office was later relocated.[105] The foundation stone of the new plant (where 1,100 new jobs were to be created) was laid in March 2009 in the presence of Chancellor Merkel, who hailed the project as a "real investment in the future."[106] Bosch Solar Energy AG subsequently expanded abroad, announcing the construction of subsidiaries in Vénissieux (France) and Batu Kawan (Malaysia). Also in 2009, Bosch acquired two other solar companies, Aleo Solar AG and Johanna Solar Technology GmbH. Aleo Solar AG brought in not only its home plant in Prenzlau, Germany, but also (which may have made it particularly interesting to Bosch) plants in Spain and China. The Solar Energy division (for which Siegfried Dais was the board member responsible) had about 3,500 associates by 2011 – not many so far as total workforce numbers in the Bosch Group were concerned, but a lot in comparison to other companies in the solar industry, which in Europe at least were mainly small and medium-sized enterprises.[107]

The takeover of Aleo Solar in October 2009 indicates that Bosch felt that the finance and economic crisis that had just passed vindicated its solar strategy. This was in spite of the crisis having hit both the solar business and wind power very hard.[108] In December 2009, a showpiece for Bosch Solar Energy was ready to go into operation. This was a 955 kWp photovoltaic array on the roof of the Bosch parking garage straddling the freeway next to Stuttgart Airport. For Bosch Solar Energy AG, the chief importance of this power station was as a reference. This was the subsidiary's debut as prime contractor for a major project. But for the Bosch Group as a whole, the installation was a declaration of faith in solar power. On both sides of the parking garage, power from the installation lit up huge Bosch signs, which with letters eight meters high were the largest in Europe. They could not fail to be seen by all associates and business partners flying into Stuttgart.[109]

Over the course of 2011, however, prospects for the German photovoltaics industry darkened. It experienced nothing short of disaster, in fact, as Chinese companies flooded the market with low-cost products. Despite high levels of subsidy through feed-in tariffs, German manufacturers stood no chance against such competition. Prices plummeted by no less than 40 percent within a year. Most companies lacked a generous financial cushion, so one by one the lights in the German solar-power industry went out. Big-name companies such as Solon and Solar Millennium were forced into bankruptcy – followed in the spring of 2012 by Q-Cells, the biggest of them all. "Technology of the future turns into industrial graveyard," ran one *Wirtschaftswoche* headline in October 2012.[110] But before this happened, Bosch Solar Energy reacted to the price collapse with the announcement that it was investing more than 500 million euros in building a plant in Malaysia. And it turned the crisis affecting the industry to advantage by taking over (in 2011–12) Voltwerk Electronics GmbH in Hamburg, a subsidiary of the ailing photovoltaics manufacturer Conergy.[111] However, the news that the Solar Energy division had lost around half a billion euros in 2011, with annual sales declining by some 9 percent, will doubtless have triggered a certain shock at senior-management level.[112] Bosch Solar Energy AG itself had not been an economic success in its early years. Bosch had been obliged to meet heavy losses in the solar division. For 2009 alone, those losses had topped 400 million euros. Yet up at the Schillerhöhe, people had still contrived to see all this as subsidizing a business with a promising future.[113] Following the disastrous 2011 result, however, things changed. In February 2012, the projected construction of the plant in Malaysia was put on hold. In June, Aleo Solar announced it was shutting its plant in Spain. And two months later, Bosch Solar Energy had to close its Erfurt plant, where some 100 associates had been employed.[114] Hope was fading for the solar-energy industry, with even the Chinese manufacturers recording losses by this time. There was worldwide overcapacity. Too many facilities had been built for too little demand. Associates at Aleo Solar and Bosch Solar Energy were placed on shorter working weeks. In the autumn of 2012, Bosch announced that it was re-examining the whole solar sector. Siemens had already decided to end its solar-power involvement.[115]

Senior management at Bosch found it hard to make up their minds. They would have liked to stay with solar technology, particularly since around 1.5 billion euros had been invested in it by this point. However, all efforts to compensate for the price collapse proved fruitless. In January 2013, the company was forced to admit that in the year just ended, the solar energy division had posted a record loss of some 1 billion euros. Only a few weeks later, on March 22, 2013, Bosch let it be known that the company was exiting solar technology. Production of ingots, wafers, cells, and modules would now cease in January 2014. Volkmar Denner, who had succeeded Franz Fehrenbach eight months previously, justified the decision on the grounds that it had proved impossible to find a "lastingly viable economic solution" for this area of operations.[116] The shareholders of Robert Bosch GmbH agreed unanimously. Nothing less was to be expected in connection with a decision of such magnitude. It was no secret that the Bosch family had agonized.[117] For Franz Fehrenbach, this was a particularly bitter step to take. As chairman of the supervisory board of Robert Bosch GmbH and managing partner of RBIK, he had to share responsibility for abandoning a field of operations that, on his watch, had been the subject of such momentous expectations. Interviewed alongside Denner in the Bosch in-house publication *Bosch-Zünder*, Fehrenbach told the magazine it was "possibly the most anguishing experience I have ever undergone in my professional career."[118] The Bosch Group's exit from photovoltaics directly affects a total of 3,000 associates of Bosch Solar Energy and Aleo Solar AG. The vast majority of them live in Thuringia and Brandenburg – *Länder* with above-average levels of unemployment. Bosch is anxious to offer former associates from the Solar Energy division other vacancies within the group, and it hopes to find buyers for all operations in this sphere. But the chairman of the board "deliberately [...] wishes to avoid creating high hopes."[119] Up until the decision to quit the field, Bosch's involvement in solar technology had cost the company around 2.4 billion euros altogether. Of that total, 750 million euros were operating losses. Capital expenditure of 1.56 billion euros had to be written down completely. Further losses were due to arise in the first quarter of 2013.[120]

How did this calamity come about? Presumably, the main reason why Bosch miscalculated so badly in connection with developing its solar-energy business was because the company believed that engineering expertise could win market share even in an area where low-cost mass production was what counted. But many other companies (not least Siemens) also failed to assess the situation properly. This suggests that the combination of heavy subsidies and a megatrend exerted enormous attraction. Here was a "technology of the future" in a rapidly growing market. No one wanted to miss the boat. What Bosch overlooked was that it could not, in the field of solar technology, bring its specific strengths to bear. It was having to enter an entirely new market with companies that were relatively small. In its earlier diversification attempts, the company had been successful whenever it had been able to take over established market and technology leaders that had access to a store of expertise. Junkers in 1932 and Rexroth in 2001 had been two such examples. Bosch Solar Energy and Aleo Solar, on the other hand, failed to develop such a technological lead. Bosch had similarly been unable to put its expertise to full use in communications technology. Here, then, was another occasion in Bosch history where an expensive diversification effort turned out to be a dead-end street. However, it seems likely that the company will continue to see renewable energy as an area with a promising future.

The China boom and growing markets in the other BRIC countries

In recent decades, Bosch's business in China has been an unprecedented success story. China has now overtaken Japan as the world's second-largest economy. Like many other German companies, Bosch could rely on China's continuing economic growth in the 2008–09 crisis. In the years after the crisis as well, German industry (notably its automotive sector) enjoyed a special boom thanks to the Chinese economy. As Germany's largest investor in China, the automotive industry now sells roughly one-fifth of its output there. For Bosch, China is now the third most important market after Germany and North America.[121]

Another reason for the company's success in China is that the name Bosch has long been a byword there. The first Bosch agency in China was established by the German trading company Walter Schärff und Co., based in Shanghai, in 1909. Due to the low level of motorization, the Chinese market was of minor importance to Bosch for a long time. Even so, many of the motorized vehicles on China's roads were heavy trucks, and as diesel engines are especially suitable for such trucks, Bosch diesel engineering was very much in demand. Back in the days of Mao Zedong, this was evident at the first German industrial exhibition, Technogerma, held in Beijing in 1975.[122] In 1984, following the start of Deng Xiaoping's policy of reform and opening-up, Bosch concluded licensing agreements with two Chinese companies concerning production of diesel injection pumps. For the first time since the Second World War, Bosch now expanded beyond purely aftermarket business in China into the original-equipment business. Two years later, Robert Bosch Hongkong Co. Ltd. was established, and in 1988 the first Bosch Car Service repair shop in the People's Republic of China opened in Beijing. A liaison office followed in 1989.[123] Initially, Bosch had the rather special problem that the name of the company did not translate easily into Chinese (i. e., Mandarin). Various translations were used on a provisional basis, relating to different product areas. For automotive-engineering purposes, the company was *poshu* (special wave). For refrigerators, it was *baixue* (white snow). After the opening of the new Beijing liaison office, a new name was looked for that would cover all the company's activities. On the advice of a linguist from Beijing University, the board settled for *boshi* – a compound of *bo* (broad, varied) and *shi* (world, lifetime).[124]

Following the opening of the liaison office, it was still to take a number of years before Bosch decided to set up a joint venture in China. This was despite the fact that Volkswagen, Bosch's largest customer, had reached joint venture agreements with the Chinese holding company SAIC as early as 1985 (Shanghai Volkswagen Automotive Company Ltd.) and with China's oldest automobile producer, FAW in Changchun, six years later (FAW-Volkswagen Automotive Company Ltd.). It seems likely that VW urged Bosch to expand into China. Yet although Bierich was himself determined to do so, there were clearly problems finding a suitable partner. The Chinese automotive-supply industry consisted of small players whose business was more of a local nature. However, in 1993 Bosch changed its approach. Its new plan for China looked beyond boosting selling activities and granting licenses, and aimed to set up joint ventures for diesel equipment, spark plugs, and aftermarket business with other Bosch products. The new approach held that, "as a result of its new liberalization," the People's Republic was becoming "a significant sales market for Bosch products."[125] A year later, it came a little closer to that goal. In April 1994, Bosch announced that it was concluding six joint-venture agreements in China and would be investing a total of 330 million U.S. dollars in the new companies. The *Bosch-Zünder* was already on the lookout for skilled workers and managers who were willing to go to China.[126] Meanwhile, the Chinese government, having seen that the country's automotive industry could develop no further without robust suppliers, was more than just metaphorically rolling the red carpet out for Bosch. On April 14, 1994, the then chairman of the board of management, Hermann Scholl, was received by Prime Minister Li Peng in the Great Hall of the People.[127] Li Peng, seen as a hardliner in the West since his proclamation of martial law in 1989, was at the same time among the most influential champions of the opening-up process. Bosch was able to agree an initial

Inauguration of the first Bosch Car Service repair shop in Guangzhou, China (2003)

joint venture with a company called CNEMS very quickly, in September 1994. And on the initiative of the board member Hansjörg Manger, a
joint-venture company named United Automotive Electronic Systems Co.
Ltd. (UAES) was established in Shanghai in 1995. Its business purpose was
to manufacture and sell systems and components for gasoline engines.[128] In
the early years, Bosch's China business was by no means a self-starter. In
fact, in 1997 the company had to admit that it had overestimated the capacity of the Chinese automobile market.[129] Two years later, Bosch brought all
its Chinese operations together under the roof of a single Shanghai-based
holding company, Bosch (China) Investment Ltd.

In China, the Stuttgart company had to adapt to a market that had developed under quite unique circumstances. The automotive industry there had
grown up only after the Second World War, and only with the economic reforms of the 1980s had it begun to grow rapidly. So when it came to serving a
growing market of individual car buyers, imports and joint ventures with
non-Chinese manufacturers were extremely important. Volkswagen was market leader with its Santana, produced in Shanghai from 1996 onward. But outside the urban centers of population, the market was dominated by vehicles of
a different sort – the simple, usually small models produced by Chinese manu-

facturers. It was to this situation that Bosch had to adapt, since it also wanted to become an original-equipment supplier to the indigenous automobile industry.

It was not until 2003 that China first graduated to the Bosch Group's top ten non-German markets. But even then, the world's most populous country came in only tenth, behind Austria and South Korea. In subsequent years, the situation changed. The establishment of Bosch Automotive Diesel Systems (RBCD) in 2004 marked the beginning of a third phase in Bosch's business operations in China. These operations now assumed a key role in corporate strategy, and became a new focal point of the Bosch Group's global activities. RBCD had been set up jointly with the Chinese Wuxi Weifu Group, but Bosch held 67 percent of the capital stock, giving it the majority shareholding in a Chinese company for the first time. The RBCD subsidiary built a large plant in Wuxi, near Shanghai. Wuxi was an extremely popular location with both Chinese and foreign investors, who liked to refer to it as "little Shanghai." Opened on November 18, 2005, the new plant initially employed a workforce of 1,800 to produce diesel injection systems. It was able to draw on the services of a diesel technical center which Bosch also built in Wuxi.[130] Almost in parallel, other plants were built in China by BSH, and by the power tools division to build industrial tools. In 2006, Bosch Rexroth built a plant in Beijing, and in Hangzhou, Bosch constructed a facility to manufacture packaging machinery.[131] A technical center in Suzhou and a winter test center in Inner Mongolia were added later. By 2010, Bosch had 22 subsidiaries in China.[132] Following a change in Chinese law, the vast majority of these new facilities were wholly owned by Bosch. This is also the preferred solution for foreign investors, since sole control makes it more difficult to "siphon off" technical know-how – something that Bosch had also experienced in China, much to its own cost.

From 2005 onward in China, the Bosch Group enjoyed growth on a scale that it had experienced only once before in its history – namely, in the pre-1914 United States. In the space of ten years, China leapt from twentieth to third in the sales ranking of Bosch markets. In 2009 alone, Bosch sales in China soared by more than 29 percent. In 2010, the increase was as much as 44 percent.[133] Associate numbers in China rose accordingly. In 2004, the Bosch Group employed some 10,700 people there. By 2011, this number was close to 30,000 – a figure that corresponds to some 10 percent of total Bosch headcount and makes China the country with the highest number of Bosch Group associates outside Germany.[134] With a traditional lion dance, the thousandth Bosch Car Service repair shop in China was inaugurated in Changzhou in July 2011. In the same year, Uwe Raschke (the Bosch board member with specific responsibility for Asia Pacific) announced that a further 40 regional sales offices would be opening in China.[135] The new Chinese headquarters in Shanghai inaugurated in April 2011 also gave architectural expression to the hopes Bosch now had of that market.

Such very rapid growth posed the problem of finding sufficient numbers of qualified workers. Bosch was also keen that most executive positions should be filled by Chinese personnel. A policy was adopted of forging links with large numbers of universities and presenting the company there through campus tours. In 2006 alone, some 20,000 students applied to Bosch for jobs.[136] The share of management posts held by Chinese natives has been successfully increased to 90 percent.[137] That may well be another reason why Bosch is so well thought of in China. Of the 500 foreign companies operating there, Bosch is among the 20 with the best image, according to a recent poll.[138] Many Bosch associates in the country believe that this is because the company is welcome there not only for its products but also for cultural reasons. Peter Pang, the former president of Bosch (China) Investment Ltd., sees no contradiction between Bosch values and Chinese culture: "Much of what Confucius teaches is also present in Bosch values."[139] However, there is no doubt that not all Bosch values are entirely respected in present-day China. Problems that may arise in this sphere are clear from the harsh criticism leveled in the German press at the sale to China of surveillance technology developed by Bosch Security Systems.[140]

In Asia, Bosch has strongly increased its presence in recent decades not only in China and Japan, but also in other eastern and southeast Asian countries. In South Korea, Bosch followed a similar pattern as in China, with a sales office being opened in 1982, joint ventures being concluded subsequently, and ultimately a regional company being established. As in other countries, however, there are certain differences. In Korea, for instance, Bosch is particularly well represented in the area of research and development, with its own technical center in Yongin, built in 1997. Joint ventures included, in 2011 Bosch had a total of 3,600 associates in Korea (although the company has since withdrawn from two major joint ventures, Kefico and SB LiMotive, so that figure is likely to go down). Singapore now plays an important role in Bosch's aftermarket business, in Taiwan the Unipoint Group was taken over in 2011, and in Vietnam a manufacturing facility has been set up.

Strong growth has also taken place over the past decade in Bosch's Indian business, although this has not been able to keep pace with developments in China. In terms of sales, India is not among Bosch's major non-German markets, but it is one of the countries with the largest number of Bosch Group as-

Training in the use of Bosch power tools in India (2011)

sociates. Bosch companies in India employ a total of 18,000 people. Starting in the 1950s, Bosch was represented in India by its MICO subsidiary, which for a long time manufactured only diesel products for the local market. Today the subsidiary trades as Bosch Ltd.,[141] with its principal location still in Bangalore. Inexpensive microcars are the vehicles in greatest demand in India, the market leaders being Maruti-Suzuki and Hyundai. Of the European automakers, the Volkswagen Group occupies pole position, with a comparatively modest sales figure of some 53,000 passenger cars per year. In 2008, Bosch in India fitted the Tata Nano, a microcar built by Tata Motors, with equipment including an electronic engine-management system. For this purpose, the sophisticated high-tech system had to be considerably simplified and adapted to regional requirements. Nonetheless, Bosch believed that, using a sort of "Intel inside" effect for inexpensive vehicles, such electronic engine-management systems would allow it to establish a foothold in the fast-growing Indian microcar market as well.[142] Today, a particularly large share of Bosch operations in India has to do with information technology. Robert Bosch Engineering and Business Solutions Ltd. develops software there for the Bosch Group, chiefly for engineering systems and products.

Bosch business in Russia developed along very different lines. At the beginning of 2013, the Bosch Group had only some 3,100 associates in the country, even though the share of non-Russian automobile makes has increased steeply once more following the market collapse during the 2008–09 recession, and despite a market in which roughly one-fifth of all new passenger-car registrations are now vehicles of German manufacture. The Bosch Group's main manufacturing location is the city of Engels, which lies opposite Saratov on the Volga River, about 900 kilometers from Moscow. The Bosch plant there produces spark plugs, lambda sensors, and parts for gasoline injection systems. Up to now, the company has lacked any strong local partners in the field of automotive engineering who might be in a position to assume responsibility for some of its manufacturing operations, and in this way allow it to avoid high import duties. The consumer goods business sector is represented in Russia by a power tools plant in Engels and a BSH household-appliance plant near St. Petersburg.

In Brazil, Bosch has long been one of the largest German companies after Volkswagen and Daimler-Benz. As far back as the 1980s, Brazil was one of Bosch's biggest markets outside Germany, and one of the countries with the highest number of Bosch associates. The Brazilian automotive industry is growing fast, with VW and Fiat currently leading the market. Bosch has had a plant in Campinas, a city some 100 kilometers north of São Paulo, since 1960. Campinas is also home to the headquarters of the regional company Robert Bosch Ltda. and to a plant belonging to Bosch Thermotechnik Lateinamerika. Since 1975, another important location has been Curitiba in the southern Brazilian federal state of Paraná. At the beginning of 2012, the diesel plant in Curitiba employed more than 3,000 associates. For a long time, sales in South America have failed to achieve the increases recorded in Asia. In fact, the Manaus plant had to be closed down. Now, however, Bosch is also pinning high hopes on Brazil's current economic boom. Thanks to around 1,000 Bosch Car Service repair shops, the company is among the country's best-known non-Brazilian businesses. Bosch Rexroth AG has also been represented in Brazil for some time, and some years ago commissioned a further plant in Pomerode (in the federal state of Santa Catarina) to manufacture hydraulics components and modules.

Looking beyond 125 years

Traditionally, anniversaries were never a Bosch strong point. When the company turned 50 in the autumn of 1936, the celebrations were overshadowed by clashes with the Stuttgart *Gauleitung*. For the 100th anniversary, the board of management determined that festivities would be "on a modest scale."[143] Instead of staging a costly ceremony, in 1986 the company preferred to set up the Robert Bosch Anniversary Foundation (a foundation for the promotion of science and young scientists, renamed "Hans L. Merkle Foundation" 11 years later). The 125th anniversary was to be different. This time, the aim was to get the company's key messages across, to highlight the brand name, and to make the company something people could experience for themselves. A total of 850 activities were meticulously planned. A special anniversary logo was used on placards, flags, and business correspondence. The climax was the anniversary gala, held at Stuttgart's new trade fair on May 19, 2011. The 2,000 guests included the then President of the German Federal Republic, Christian Wulff, the Governor of Baden-Württemberg, Winfried Kretschmann, and the former U.S. Secretary of State Henry A. Kissinger. Associates were involved far more than had been the case previously. At locations the world over, "Experience Days" were organized for them and their families. Celebrations were no longer to take place purely within the company, at the workplace, but also to be personal and emotive. Bosch projected a colorful, open image of itself as a company. The good mood among the workforce was of course helped by the fact that concerns about their job, which had been in everyone's thoughts only two years previously, had now been put completely aside. The company had emerged from the economic and financial crisis stronger than before, setting a new sales record.

With the anniversary year over, Bosch faced another change at the top – the sixth in the company's history. On June 30, 2012, Franz Fehrenbach stepped down from his post as chairman of the board of management to become chairman of the supervisory board and of RBIK. By this time, Fehrenbach was one of the few German entrepreneurs whose word carried weight beyond business circles. He was a business leader who said frankly that markets needed rules. His public castigation of bankers expressed what many people were thinking. It was also common knowledge that Chancellor Merkel thought highly of him and listened to his expert advice on the subject of the automotive industry.[144] The newspaper *Süddeutsche Zeitung* called Fehrenbach "one of Germany's most popular managers."[145] Yet he never courted popularity. He was listened to in the outside world mainly because he could not be fitted into a mold. He was a businessman who not only railed against the greed of many bankers but had also, as the CEO of the world's largest automotive supplier, been named "eco-manager of the year." However, those who admired Fehrenbach for this also had to acknowledge that he advocated a return to the 40-hour working week without any corresponding rise in pay, and rejected a law limiting excessive managerial pay as being an assault on the rights of supervisory boards and company shareholders.[146]

Inside the company, Fehrenbach did much to establish a culture of open communication. One method he used was to hold dialogue events that followed a uniform plan at Bosch locations all over the world. As facilitated

Franz Fehrenbach thanks all anniversary-project participants (2011)

discussions or as "town-hall meetings," these events might involve 1,000 associates or more. They were usually held whenever Fehrenbach visited the location concerned.[147] For the first time, large bodies of associates in a great many countries were able to rub shoulders with the chairman of the board of management. In China, for instance, 4,000 associates took part in two such meetings held in Wuxi and Suzhou in 2007. According to the *Bosch-Zünder*, the chance of meeting the Bosch CEO in the flesh was "a real crowd-puller."[148] It was the same in India when an event was held in Bangalore.[149] Fehrenbach was utterly convinced of the advantages of open communication. By reaching out to more associates than his predecessor had done, he not only met the expectations of a "communications society." He was also, as a result, able to convey to a large number of Bosch associates both the new mission and the old-established Bosch values, including the company's commitment to quality – and to do so in a way that was thought by many to be thoroughly credible.

Fehrenbach's successor as chairman of the board of management was Volkmar Denner. As in 2003, it was another handover between two associates who had "come up through the ranks." Once again, the new CEO came from the membership of the board of management. Once again, his predecessor moved up to chair the supervisory board and, from there, to oversee the board

Presentation of the Jewish Museum Berlin's Prize for Understanding and Tolerance to Robert Bosch GmbH. From left: Christof Bosch, Franz Fehrenbach, Henry A. Kissinger, W. Michael Blumenthal (November 14, 2009)

of management. Denner had likewise begun his professional career at Bosch and had shown himself consistently loyal to the company. In 1986, at the age of 29 and with a doctorate in physics from Stuttgart University, he had joined Bosch as a senior engineer in the division producing semiconductors and ECUs. Prior to his appointment to the board in January 2006, he had been president of the Automotive Electronics division. As a board member, he was given responsibility for research and development. Denner is considered the finest internet expert among the company's senior executives, is credited with a huge ability to motivate associates, and is felt to be capable of providing successful leadership in the "Web 3.0" era. "The man for Bosch 3.0" was how the *Frankfurter Allgemeine Zeitung* greeted his appointment as chairman of the board of management.[150] Two days before taking office on July 1, 2012, Denner wrote to associates. His letter emphasized that he wanted "to maintain continuity in the leadership of our company," as well as the importance of Bosch values. But it immediately placed a fresh accent: "We want Bosch to create exciting products, and by that I mean not only hardware and software, but also services – products that are created by people with passion." For ongoing formulation of the main points of corporate strategy (this too was new), he invited feedback from associates on two questions: "1. What has stood the test of time at Bosch, what should we keep on at all costs? 2. And if we want to make the most of our future opportunities, what do we need to change?"[151]

Denner will not be short of challenges. To begin with, there is the increasing size of the Bosch Group, whose workforce has now topped the 300,000 mark for the first time. Then there is the lack of balance in its production, management, and employment structure. Bosch is still heavily dependent on automotive engineering. In 2010, its automotive technology business sector accounted for 59 percent of sales.[152] In its corporate management, the gene pool is still very small. Very few board members have so far not been German nationals, and to this day there is not one woman among them. Granted, the number of women in managerial positions almost tripled between 1997 and 2012, reaching roughly 10 percent.[153] By contrast, the female contingent in the Bosch Group workforce in Germany sank to a new low of 21 percent in 2011 – having stood at around 30 percent in 1990 (a development that is of course due mainly to increasing automation and the fact that many "simple" tasks performed primarily by women have vanished).[154]

A few days before the change of leadership from Fehrenbach to Denner, Bosch announced an organizational change. Effective January 1, 2013, there would be a new business sector called "Energy and Building Technology" [*Energie- und Gebäudetechnik*].[155] The new business sector, which incorporates the Security Systems, Thermotechnology, and Solar Energy divisions, should (despite the exit from solar energy announced in March 2013) eventually be-

Table 21 Business sectors and divisions of the Bosch Group (January 1, 2013)

Automotive Technology	Industrial Technology	Consumer Goods	Energy and Building Technology
Gasoline Systems	Drive and Control Technology	Power Tools	Thermotechnology
Diesel Systems	Packaging Technology	Household Appliances	Security Systems
Chassis Systems Control			Solar Energy
Electrical Drives			
Starter Motors and Generators			
Car Multimedia			
Automotive Electronics			
Automotive Aftermarket			
Steering Systems			

Volkmar Denner (2012)

come a robust pillar of the company's non-automotive business. For some time now, the "internet of things and services" has been one of the company's most important projects for the future. Denner is encouraging the development of new business models in this area. Bosch believes that Web 3.0 offers huge potential, connecting vehicles with their surroundings and enabling products that have their own IP address to communicate with each other. The company expects that this connectivity will bring about a change in the global economy similar to that which followed the introduction of the internet itself. Bosch hopes that its software and systems unit Bosch Software Innovations will facilitate the smart connectivity of things and services (in the sphere of electromobility, for instance, where it will provide a platform for the networking of charge spots, vehicles, and energy suppliers).

Bosch also has plans to expand its research and development capabilities. In 2015, a new research and advance engineering center costing 310 million euros is to open in Renningen, a few kilometers to the west of the Schillerhöhe. This will be a new home for around 1,200 scientists, engineers, and technicians.[156] In automotive technology, this will reinforce an already existing trend for an ever greater share of R&D work to fall to suppliers. Another vision for the future, electromobility, is something that Bosch deems a long-term project, since the earliest point in time that significant numbers of electric vehicles can be expected on the roads is 2020.[157] Following the abandonment of the joint venture with Samsung SDI in September 2012, Bosch now intends to continue developing battery cells on its own in its newly established subsidiary Robert Bosch Battery Systems. The first all-electric vehicle to feature a Bosch battery pack, the Fiat 500e, went into series production in 2013.[158]

Services will feature more prominently within the Bosch Group in the future. The Bosch Communications Center with its roughly 5,000 associates already offers the company's business customers the opportunity of outsourcing their marketing, accounting, security, purchasing, IT, logistics, and human resources operations. In the services sector, there have been many start-ups in the Bosch Group since the late 1990s, many of which are now thriving. To name just a few examples: Bosch Engineering GmbH offers automotive engineering services, ETAS GmbH supplies engineering and calibration tools for electronic systems, SupplyOn AG provides an internet service for the automotive and manufacturing industries, and Bosch Energy and Building Solutions GmbH (BEBS) specializes in enhancing energy efficiency in commercial buildings.

Laying the foundation stone of the center for research and advance engineering in Renningen. Flanked by two journeymen, from left: Franz Fehrenbach, Winfried Kretschmann, Volkmar Denner, and Klaus Dieterich (September 27, 2012)

Final conclusions

Anybody coming to Bosch will sooner or later hear someone say that this company is "different." The reasons, they will be told, are "rooted in history." The fact is, Robert Bosch GmbH has always had a distinctive profile, one to which it has clung with remarkable consistency and to which it feels beholden to this day. This is true for its constitution as well as for its culture – for the "feel" of the company – and for a number of principles of its business policy. The quest for financial independence and an insistence on high quality standards have numbered among the company's doctrines for more than a hundred years now, as have a commitment to social responsibility and a certain culture of consensus. And while it is by no means in every respect that the company stands out from the mainstream of German and indeed European companies, Bosch is unmistakable through and through. Remarkably, the company's profile has lost none of its definition over the past 20 years of accelerated globalization. It therefore strikes us as fitting that Bosch is still based in Stuttgart, that its core business remains the same, and that the present chairman of the Bosch board of management is only its seventh in more than a century and a quarter. Yet this has not been somehow inevitable, a "given" which demands to be portrayed as such. It is the product of conscious decisions resulting from a number of factors. This is why the present study has set itself the task of finding out why specific courses of action were adopted, how challenges were responded to, and how setbacks were dealt with.

Of the many distinguishing features of the corporate history of Bosch, the main one is that the company cannot be understood without some examination of the person and influence of its founder. In many ways, Robert Bosch left an indelible mark on the company, both during his lifetime and beyond. He was not merely the founder and undisputed leading light of a business undertaking that, under his guidance, developed from a modest workshop in the west end of Stuttgart into a global brand. In a legal sense, Robert Bosch and the company were the same person, and this for more than 30 years. Only as the nineteenth century gave way to the twentieth did the rudiments of an institutionalized management emerge, and not until 1917, when what had been a sole proprietorship became a stock corporation, did that company become a legal person separate from its founder. But what remained was the substance.

Robert Bosch achieved his most lasting effect not through his business triumphs, impressive though these undoubtedly were, but by credibly championing principles and values that were then embedded in the culture of his company and that guided its entire business policy from the outset. These included social responsibility and international understanding, but also his claim to produce only "the finest products from the finest materials." Perhaps most pointedly, they gave rise to his famous maxim: "I would rather lose money than trust."[1] Robert Bosch saw his company as something more than just a commercial venture. He saw it as an ethical mission. Conversely, he believed that "good" conduct also paid off in business terms. His workers were able to benefit from this, as in the case of the early introduction of the eight-hour working day, yet they also defended themselves against the founder's will, as on the occasion of the strike in 1913. Nonetheless, the principles of Robert Bosch permeated the company like a set of unwritten works rules.

In his last will and a mass of supplementary guidelines, the founder sought to ensure that his company (which a few years before his death he arranged to have converted into a close corporation or GmbH) would continue to be run in a manner reflective of his spirit. To this end, he enlisted the support of a group of people whom he particularly trusted, making them his executors. Their job was not simply to administer his estate but also to carry the torch, as it were. Had there been a rebellious heir, as so often happens with family businesses, the history of Robert Bosch GmbH might have been different. As it was, the only potential heir Robert Bosch left the company on his death in 1942 was his underage son Robert Bosch Jr. The labyrinthine guidelines for the founder's executors left open the question of whether the son should at some point in time assume the leadership of the company as well as its majority shareholding, or whether the rights to Robert Bosch GmbH should pass to the trust administration company (VVB) which the founder had set up in 1921. In either case, the founder wanted his company's business activities to be carried out in accordance with his ideas and wishes.

Given this background, it comes as no surprise that the question of what the will meant turned into a power struggle within the company, especially after the war, while invoking the principles of Robert Bosch became a way of investing claims with authority. Together with his management board colleague Alfred Knoerzer, Hans Walz, the founder's successor as chairman, exerted pressure on Robert Bosch Jr., eventually forcing him out of the role of future head of the company. Under Hans L. Merkle, Bosch finally became a company in which the chairman of the board of management had sole say, even so far as the supervisory board was concerned. There was less talk now of Robert Bosch's values, although the company retained its special character. Its business policy, especially as regards the company's financial independence, continued to adhere to the maxims set out by the founder.

In 1964, the ownership and executive structures were created that still exist today. Once again, this was done with reference to the wishes of Robert Bosch. The executors persuaded the heirs of the founder (particularly his son, Robert Bosch Jr.) to agree to the company being taken into the ownership of VVB, which was subsequently renamed Robert Bosch Stiftung GmbH and restructured as a not-for-profit foundation. Robert Bosch Jr. had now given up his earlier ambitions of preserving the company as a family business and saw the setting up of such a foundation as a meaningful and constructive solution. None of those involved had any wish to turn the company into a publicly traded stock corporation. Today Robert Bosch GmbH provides a counter-model, through its corporate constitution, to the shareholder-value approach.

Set up in 1964, this special ownership structure, within the framework of which Robert Bosch Stiftung GmbH now holds 92 percent of the share capital in Robert Bosch GmbH while 93 percent of the voting rights lie with the industrial trust Robert Bosch Industrietreuhand KG (RBIK), led to a new form of consensus culture within the corporate governance of the company. While not directly derived from the legacy of Robert Bosch, neither does this constellation clash with it. Since there are always shareholders of RBIK who belong either to the supervisory board or to the board of management of Robert Bosch GmbH, and since the chairman of the board of management is always a shareholder of RBIK, any conflicts that occur can be carried out within these committees instead of between them. It therefore strikes us as consistent that for decades now, the retiring chairman of the board of management has moved smoothly into the chair of the supervisory board of Robert Bosch GmbH. The company has not fared badly with this model, though it defies all recent corporate-governance guidelines in being based more on consensus and securing continuity than on checks and balances. However, that is not to say that it will stay this way. If there comes a time when consensus cannot be reached, or if accelerating globalization no longer allows a company of this size to be managed by such a close-knit group of people, this way of managing things, though rooted in history, may prove a handicap.

The rise and rapid growth of the company in the decades preceding the First World War did not follow a master plan. At first, Robert Bosch did not even have a strategic concept for the company he had started up. His principles were reflected in his actions. At an early stage he was able (not least because he paid good wages) to build up a pool of skilled workers, to attract and retain talented associates, and to turn out products that were distinguished by high quality. But the main reason his business boomed was more coincidental than

intentional: with the magneto ignition device, he brought out the right product at the right time. Thanks to product innovation, notably the high-voltage
magneto ignition system produced from 1902, this technology was greatly improved – so much so that, as the motorization of road traffic gained momentum, the company's sales grew exponentially: indeed, by as much as 110 percent in 1906. The main focus of the company's production had thus shifted to
automotive technology, where it remains to this day.

As for historical continuity, it is also worthy of note that the company,
having established itself as one of the world's leading automotive suppliers, has
retained that place through thick and thin. This is especially remarkable when
we consider that the German automotive industry as a whole did not attain
that status in the international market until very much later. Bosch was able to
achieve this by repeatedly claiming technological leadership with outstanding
new products. The high-voltage magneto was followed by the diesel injection
pump. Then, in the 1960s, came electronically controlled gasoline injection,
later the electronic vehicle dynamics systems, and in the 1990s high-pressure
diesel injection. Of course, it was not only in automotive technology that
Bosch produced a steady stream of innovations. It did the same in the non-
automotive spheres – in communications technology, household appliances,
heating systems, power tools, and so on. The Bosch Group was involved in the
early days of television, just as it was in the development of navigation devices.
However, it was the state of the art in automotive technology that set the pace
for the company, not least because of the inherent dominance of this business
sector. Accordingly (and logically), this led to organizational and leadership
structures that were finely attuned to the automotive world and, ultimately,
responsive to that world only.

By no means was every Bosch innovation a business success, nor could the
company keep pace with every technological advance. In the 1920s, for instance, it was in danger of being left behind by the Americans, who were the
market leaders at that time. Yet Bosch always contrived to catch up, reaffirm-
ing market positions with fresh innovations. This was particularly the case
when the transition was made from electrical engineering to electronics and
microsystems technology – a paradigm shift in the automotive as well as in
other sectors. Often, Bosch was not the first mover in the race for new technologies, but first had to make up for the head start made by its competitors. In
other cases, however, only Bosch was able to make new designs ready for series
production, the common-rail diesel injection system being only one example.
The company's worldwide distribution network, the Bosch Car Service, and
Bosch power tools and household appliances certainly did their bit to establish
the brand. But it was technical innovations that were decisive, since they alone

could secure important business fields such as the automotive original-equipment business. For a leading automotive supplier, an innovation-driven approach is even more important than for an automaker, since design alone will not bring a supplier market share. As an automotive supplier, Bosch attained a strong position at a relatively early stage. Consequently, the company benefited from positive feedback effects from the market. It could produce in larger-scale series than most of its competitors, and so could keep its costs down. For the automakers that equipped large parts of their model range with Bosch products, switching supplier meant further expense.

All this gave Bosch an admirably strong position in the original-equipment market. But it also meant that, for a long time, too little attention was paid to the interests and requirements of its customers. Development times dragged on, and there were rigid hierarchies on every level. Bosch was seen as over-bureaucratic and too inflexible. The expansion of communications technology in the 1970s and 1980s did nothing to change this, especially as the largest contracts awarded here came from public authorities. But as competition became more global, structural rigidities of this kind increasingly proved to be a burden, which the board of management sought repeatedly to remove with new programs such as the continuous improvement process (CIP) launched in 1991 or the "BeQIK" mission (quality, innovation, customer orientation) brought in eight years later.

The internationalization of the company so evident at Bosch in its early days was closely bound up with the company's successful focus on the magneto in particular and automotive technology in general. Since the German automobile market hardly existed at all before the First World War, the only way for an automotive supplier to become a technology leader was to expand in the world market, notably in France and the United States, which were the key automotive markets of the age. This was what Bosch did with the aid of the magneto, establishing sales records in the U.S. market that exceeded all expectations. By 1913, the company was generating 88 percent of its sales outside Germany – though it was doing so in circumstances that bear no comparison with today's, for back then Bosch only really had one product. Yet the fact remains: only 20 years after Robert Bosch set up a workshop employing two people, his company name had become an international brand. This early international coup shaped the way the company saw itself. From now on, the world market, and especially the U.S. market, was the benchmark for business success. Following the loss of its most important international markets in the First World War, Bosch was determined to recover its former greatness, and launched a second internationalization drive. However, in the meantime its U.S. rivals had snatched the lead with their less expensive, mass-produced products, and after 1933 political events and German rearmament obstructed business outside Germany.

In the 1950s and 1960s, sales rose chiefly as a result of demand in the German market. In West Germany, those decades marked the transition to mass motorization. Business outside Germany was constantly being expanded, but two-thirds of sales and more were generated in Bosch's "home" market. It was not until the crisis year of 1974, after more than 40 years, that the share of business outside Germany once again exceeded 50 percent. There followed a third period of internationalization, during which Bosch once again built plants of its own in the United States. At the same time, through a combination of licensing agreements and joint ventures, Bosch entered the original-equipment business in Japan, where the automotive industry was going from strength to strength. Nonetheless, Europe still accounted for 83 percent of sales in 1990. Only with the accelerating pace of globalization in the 1990s and beyond did things begin to change. From 2005, this was due in the main to extremely rapid growth in China. Even in 2010, 59 percent of sales were still being posted in Europe (now including eastern Europe, of course), with Germany's share down to 23 percent. Apart from the two world wars, Bosch invariably suffered setbacks in the world market when price competition intensified, as it did in the 1920s and again in the 1980s. With its high standards of quality and its high development costs, the company found both periods heavy going, yet it was precisely these things that also accounted for its strength.

Bosch was already a multinational company a century ago – but one that developed its products exclusively in Germany and manufactured them without any explicit international division of labor. It was only after the mid-1990s, when the most recent wave of globalization started, that this began to change. Now, manufacturing processes within the Bosch Group were based on an international division of labor, local and regional associates were increasingly appointed to executive positions, also outside Europe, and communications became multilingual. Bosch is on the way to becoming a transnational company. However, in many respects, notably as regards the highest levels of leadership, it is still very much a German company. Granted, there is a board member with specific responsibility for Asia Pacific, but so far nobody from that region has ever become a board member.

If, taking account of the various strands of the company's development, we want to pick out the chief landmarks and turning points in Bosch history, the first one to mention is the company's dazzling rise before the First World War, when it grew from a small business to the world market leader for magnetos within just ten years. Later on, we see a major turning point in the second half of the 1920s. Following its recovery from the crisis of 1926, the company entered the diesel technology field in 1927, and made its first move into diversification with the start of power-tools production in 1928. This renewed and extended the foundations of the company. A further major turning point was the transfer of the Bosch family's shares to VVB (the precursor of Robert Bosch Stiftung GmbH) and the establishment of Robert Bosch Industriebeteiligung GmbH (the precursor of RBIK) in 1964, very soon after the start of the Merkle era. Finally, another new phase began around the turn of the millennium, when the company reacted to altered market structures brought about by accelerated globalization as well as to wider societal changes with a program of renewal. At the same time, Bosch's exit from communications technology marked the demise of the company's second largest business sector.

Viewed in this light, the Third Reich was not a period in which the course was set for the company's future. Nonetheless, it was an extremely important time for Bosch, which is why the present account also deals with it in such detail. The National Socialist dictatorship flew in the face of Bosch corporate culture. Yet the boom in the automotive industry following 1933 helped the company to increase its sales and profits substantially, while the armaments-related upturn was a further windfall. In consequence, the board of management under the chairmanship of Hans Walz attempted to perform a balancing act. To save the board of management from having to accept a dyed-in-the-wool National Socialist among its ranks, Walz and Karl Martell Wild joined the NSDAP. Walz also became a member of the SS and the *Freundeskreis Reichsführer SS* in order to gain useful political contacts. This did not prevent him (any more than it prevented Robert Bosch) from warning about Hitler's war plans. Yet at the same time, the new plants in Kleinmachnow and Hildesheim, built specifically to meet military requirements, carried out arms contracts of ever-increasing magnitude.

Unlike many other businessmen, the senior Bosch managers adhered to certain principles, though for the most part this remained hidden from the public gaze. The board of management and the human resources department spoke up for Jewish associates and associates of Jewish descent, and both Walz and Robert Bosch gave secret support to campaigns to aid persecuted Jews. Only to a comparatively limited extent was Bosch involved in the "Aryanization" of companies and real estate, and in most cases it was with the consent of the Jewish proprietors concerned. However, as the distance grew between Robert Bosch and his circle on the one hand and the National Socialist regime on the other, the amount of ordnance manufactured by Robert Bosch GmbH and its subsidiaries also continued to grow. The company had no alternative. Its products were indispensable for all motorized units in the German military – and above all for the *Luftwaffe* and the tank divisions. Nonetheless, in doing so it was following a path that was incompatible with the founder's principles.

In the First World War, too, military contracts had filled most of the Bosch order books. In the Third Reich, however, the situation was different. This time, Bosch was supplying the German armed forces with high technology for a war of aggression motivated by an ideology that was patently racist. It was serving a regime that cared nothing for "Bosch culture," and that cast many of its important principles to the winds. There were of course many who saw things in a different light, seeking to marry the ideas of Robert Bosch to the ideological aims of the National Socialists. They would point, for instance, to the company's focus on quality. They would praise its insistence on financial independence and the social benefits it granted. In the founder's final years, his principles were even hijacked by the National Socialists for propaganda purposes. There is ample reason to suppose that "Bosch culture" would sooner or later have been reinterpreted to suit the National Socialist ideal of industry or melded into a synthesis with the mounting influence of the military and weapons-procuring authorities on the company. The extremes to which Bosch felt forced to go as the war went on is plain from the fact that an approximate total of 20,000 forced laborers were deployed across the Bosch Group, including some 1,200 concentration-camp inmates. In defiance of every company principle, Russian workers and POWs were exposed to arbitrary acts of violence as well as to denunciation. In the Langenbielau plant, concentration-camp internees suffered savage maltreatment. At the same time, in Feuerbach the company saved so-called "half-Jews" from deportation, while Hans Walz and various other close friends of Robert Bosch supported the resistance movement as few other entrepreneurs did, actively plotting against Hitler within the "Bosch circle" headed by Carl Goerdeler, whom the company had employed as a consultant. In light of these sharp contrasts, any simplified assessment of Bosch in the Third Reich is bound to miss the mark. The company's special culture did not founder in the days of National Socialism, but glaring contradictions robbed it of its former power to integrate. For some, that culture provided a kind of protective cushion against the regime. Others saw it as a relic. And quite a few believed it was something the National Socialist system could exploit for its own purposes. Yet no permanent damage had been done. After the war, when the company's strong market position and the contribution it had made to the war effort brought it into the sights of Allied deconcentration policy, the company appealed more than ever to its traditional values.

It is understandable that such a position might come from the board of management. But the Bosch tradition also persisted among the workforce –

even though many workers had only been taken on during the armaments boom, and despite the considerable discontinuity caused by conscription during the war and redundancies at its end. Following the early postwar years, in which denazification and heated debate about the form the future economic order should take led to sharp disputes between works councils and management, a more balanced pattern of cooperation and conflict emerged as the "economic miracle" unfolded. Even the works councils came to see themselves as part of the Bosch corporate tradition: after all, Robert Bosch had been one of the few major industrialists to insist at an early stage that works councils be instated. By contrast, the company founder had found it hard to accept political agitation by trade-union representatives. Personally, Robert Bosch had long sympathized with the labor movement and voted Social Democrat. The left wing of the pre-1933 labor movement was strongly represented among the Bosch workforce, and in the years before and after the First World War, this had led to a number of politically motivated strikes. In postwar West Germany, the relatively well-paid Bosch workforce was willing to take industrial action when it came to disputes about shorter working weeks, higher wages, and better working conditions. There were strikes in 1963, 1967, 1971, 1973, 1978, and 1984, as *Boschler* fought first for the 40-hour working week and then for the 35-hour working week. Even so, relations between works councils and management were less confrontational than in many other large companies. A certain consensus existed. The two sides gave each other adequate notice of their intentions and then sought to reach agreement. During the 1974 recession, when for the first time in decades there were substantial job cuts, the revered works-council chairman Richard Rau sat down with Hans L. Merkle and negotiated extensive social compensation plans. Accordingly, when management decided to slash bonuses and make further huge job cuts as a response to the 1993 crisis, this was almost universally seen as a breach of the company's long-standing social tradition and a violation of "Bosch culture." Indeed, in retrospect the job cuts proved to have been a mistake on management's part, since there was a lack of skilled associates when the subsequent upswing came. The lesson was duly learned. In the economic downturns that followed, notably in the crisis of 2008–09, the company used shorter working weeks as a way of keeping headcount as stable as possible in its German plants. In effect, the board was re-affirming the founder's axiom that skilled associates were the company's most important asset.

For all the company's triumphs, the history of Bosch is also richly seamed with crises. Apart from the consequences of two world wars, these were crises of an economic nature. They hit the automotive industry particularly hard, and they usually caught the company inadequately prepared. The gravest of these, the crisis of 1926, is today largely forgotten. The reason for the steep drop in orders was not only a crisis in the automotive market. Bosch's manufacturing costs were also far too high. And as the preceding years of inflation had wiped out a substantial amount of equity, the company found itself on the brink of insolvency. Headcount shrank by over 40 percent within eight months, mainly as a result of dismissals. In the Great Depression of 1929–32, on the other hand, Bosch made more use of shorter working weeks than comparable large companies. In particular, it tried to hold on to its core of skilled workers for as long as possible. Admittedly, workforce numbers also dipped less sharply because the preceding crisis of 1926 had reduced them to a comparatively low level. But it may be that Robert Bosch and his management were keen to avoid the mass dismissals of 1926, since these had resulted in the company's losing too many skilled workers with valuable expertise. This suggests an analogy to the situation many years later, when the company had learned its lessons from the ruthless job cuts provoked by the 1993 crisis. The oil-price shocks of 1974 and 1979 were also experienced as a crisis at Bosch, since an excessively wide range of loss-making products made the company vulnerable. Merkle reacted by reducing the number of such products, which led to plant closures and redundancies. The 1979 crisis in particular made management aware that Bosch had to be better prepared for price competition – and that it was ill-equipped to do so. As it was, the adjustments that were made failed to keep pace with the growing price pressure that went hand in hand with the globalization of the automotive-supply sector. The 1993 recession affected the company all the more severely because its costs were still too high.

The crises examined here, including that of 2008–09, traced a similar curve at Bosch as in the automotive industry generally. As a supplier, Bosch was sometimes hit even harder. Yet over the past 80 years, the company has made huge efforts to reduce its dependence on automotive technology by diversifying its product portfolio. As early as 1928–32, disappointment at the slow growth of the automotive market prompted the first diversification drive, with the construction of power tools and refrigerators, the takeovers of Blaupunkt, Junkers, and Kino-Bauer, and the acquisition of a stake in Fernseh AG. A second diversification drive began in the Merkle era, with the establishment of Bosch Siemens Hausgeräte GmbH (BSHG) in 1967. It continued in the 1980s with the expansion of communications technology through the takeovers of ANT, Telenorma, and Teldix, and reached its high point in the Bierich era. After sustaining heavy losses, Bosch abandoned this sphere. The Rexroth and Buderus takeovers following the turn of the millennium marked the start of a fresh phase of diversification, a third drive. With some success, Bosch now expanded into capital goods, power engineering, and building technology.

However, its solar-power activities, begun in 2008, proved to be yet another loss-making venture, which it was then forced to abandon after just five years. In 2010, 59 percent of Bosch Group sales were still generated by automotive technology – well above the 1990 figure. In this search for additional business pillars, the company often failed to correctly assess the relevant markets and its own market position. Bosch has done best when it has bought up existing solid market leaders such as Junkers, Buderus, or Rexroth, which have held their own in the market on the basis of their own competence. The fact is, Bosch is still heavily dependent on the state of the automotive market. When that market collapses, Bosch is no less affected than the automakers themselves. But equally clearly, as was shown most recently in 2010, the company has so far always overcome such downturns, bouncing back as the market recovers.

Bosch has met the challenge of globalization while staying true to its exceptional, historically evolved identity. How successful the company has been is clear from the way the number of people it employs worldwide has increased by leaps and bounds. In 1970, Bosch Group associates numbered some 120,000. By 1990, the total had risen to some 180,000. And 20 years later, it had reached nearly 300,000. As an automotive supplier, the company today is looked upon as a model of success in the international market, mainly because of its independence of any single automaker, coupled with an outstanding international presence. By contrast, U.S. suppliers are stifled by the market strength of their major customers, while Japanese suppliers remain strongly oriented toward Japanese automakers. For the foreseeable future, automotive technology will continue to constitute Bosch's core business, particularly since electromobility seems to offer good long-term prospects that the company is well prepared to exploit. Other focal points in the near future will undoubtedly be power engineering and the expansion of the company's portfolio of services. But as the previous diversification efforts have shown, the crucial factor here will be Bosch's ability to establish itself in these areas with a distinctive image and competitive advantages.

In all likelihood, the company's worldwide success over the past 15 years is not merely due to its many innovations, but also to the fact that it has retained its identity. As a non-listed company, Bosch does not come under pressure from the capital market. It is not obliged to generate maximum profit in each quarter. It can set itself long-term goals and invest heavily in select projects that may be a commercial success only after many years. Granted, this brings the risk that failures will be clung to for longer than outside shareholders would allow. On the whole, though, the corporate constitution will likely continue to work to the Bosch Group's advantage, not that this rules out the possibility that it may yet change. The increasing globalization of recent decades has led the company to re-examine its roots. People at Bosch are now more aware of their own values and of their own corporate culture than was the case 20 years back. This is a point worth emphasizing, since it teaches a lesson of fundamental importance. With his basic principles and guidelines that have retained their validity to the present day, Robert Bosch is once again explicitly referred to as an authority. And while other companies are also rediscovering their historical heritage, at Bosch this process is bound up with a conscious declaration of faith in the principles of the man who founded the company. Financial sustainability, social responsibility, and a commitment to the public good – these are phrases one often hears at Bosch, not spouted as the usual fashionable slogans but honestly and credibly proclaimed, with a deep bow in the direction of the family of the founder and the activities of Robert Bosch Stiftung GmbH, as objectives to be achieved. Against this background, in a speech to mark the 125th anniversary of the company in May 2011, Christof Bosch, the founder's grandson, recalled how Robert Bosch had always seen his legacy: "Robert Bosch gave us the mission of ensuring that his work should be continued in the same spirit in which it had been created [...]. It would be wonderful if the company were to continue resolutely pursuing its objective of developing technology 'Invented for life' – and this worldwide. Technology that helps overcome the great challenges of the future, while at the same time – and just as my grandfather would have wanted – allowing the company's associates to live comfortably [...]. The task we have set ourselves is to write new chapters in this [astonishing] story [of our company] in the spirit of Robert Bosch. Our hope is that, if Robert Bosch were to encounter the Bosch name anywhere in the world in the future, he would still be proud."[2]

Appendix

Notes

Introduction

1 "Notiz vom 10.7.1996," in Robert Bosch GmbH, *Historische Kommunikation* [referred to in the following as RB] 1 016 175.
2 Cf. interview with Christof Bosch, September 22, 2010.
3 Kathrin Fastnacht, Dietrich Kuhlgatz, Dieter Schmitt, Christine Siegel, *Bosch 125 years. Invented for life*, Stuttgart, 2011.
4 Joachim Scholtyseck, *Robert Bosch und der liberale Widerstand gegen Hitler 1933–1945*, Munich, 1999.

I Early years and rise of the company (1886–1932)

1 Robert Bosch – portrait of a founder

1 Theodor Heuss, *Robert Bosch. Leben und Leistung*, new ed., Stuttgart, Leipzig, 2008 (1st ed. Tübingen, 1946), p. 24.
2 "Theodor Bäuerle, Robert Bosch," p. 21, RB 1 014 020. In Bäuerle's estimate, Servatius Bosch was worth some 200,000 marks.
3 Hans-Erhard Lessing, *Robert Bosch,* Reinbek, 2007, p. 14; Toni Pierenkemper, "Robert Bosch, der Industrielle. Zum Typus des deutschen Unternehmers in der Hochindustrialisierung," in *Kultur & Technik* 1987/1, p. 9.
4 Robert Bosch, "Lebenserinnerungen" (1921), p. 1, RB 1 014 006.
5 *Ibid.*
6 "Sei Mensch und ehre Menschenwürde." Quoted from Lessing, *Bosch*, p. 24.
7 *Ibid.*, p. 17.
8 "Theodor Bäuerle, Robert Bosch," p. 24, RB 1 014 020.
9 Margarete Fischer-Bosch, *Jugenderinnerungen an meinen Vater Robert Bosch*, Stuttgart, 1953, p. 10; Lessing, *Bosch*, p. 14.
10 Fischer-Bosch, *Jugenderinnerungen*, pp. 8 f.; Heuss, *Bosch*, p. 25.
11 "Robert Bosch an Margarete Bosch, 28.5.1940," RB 1 014 019.
12 Fischer-Bosch, *Jugenderinnerungen*, p. 9; "Bosch an Anna Kayser, 18.4.1885," RB 1 013 137.
13 Fastnacht, Kuhlgatz, Schmitt, Siegel, *125 years*, p. 11; Lessing, *Bosch*, 18 f.
14 "Robert Bosch, Lebenserinnerungen (1921)," p. 4, RB 1 014 006.
15 *Ibid.*, p. 5.
16 *Ibid.*, pp. 6 f.
17 *Ibid.*, p. 8.
18 "Aus den Jugendjahren unseres Herrn Robert Bosch," in *Bosch-Zünder* 1921/9, p. 233.

19 On April 18, 1885, Bosch wrote from New York City to his then fiancée Anna Kayser: "You see, I'm a socialist." RB 1 014 137.

20 Quoted in "Theodor Bäuerle, Robert Bosch," pp. 28 f., RB 1 014 020.

21 Fastnacht, Kuhlgatz, Schmitt, Siegel, *125 years*, p. 12.

22 Heuss, *Bosch*, pp. 101 f.; Lessing, *Bosch*, pp. 73 f.

23 Cf. Lessing, *Bosch*, p. 109.

24 Margarete Bosch (later Fischer-Bosch) completed her studies with a dissertation on agrarian history. Margarete Bosch, *Die wirtschaftlichen Bedingungen der Befreiung des Bauernstandes im Herzogtum Kleve und in der Grafschaft Mark im Rahmen der Agrargeschichte Westdeutschlands*, Berlin, 1920.

25 Lessing, *Bosch*, p. 132.

26 Cf. Joseph A. Schumpeter, *The theory of economic development*, Oxford, 1934; John Hagedoorn, "Innovation and entrepreneurship. Schumpeter revisited," in *Industrial and Corporate Change* 15, 1996/3, pp. 883–96.

27 *Sei Mensch und ehre Menschenwürde. Aufsätze, Reden und Gedanken von Robert Bosch* (Bosch-Schriftenreihe, vol. 1), Stuttgart, 1950, p. 56.

28 "Lieber Geld verlieren als Vertrauen," in *Bosch-Zünder* 1919/2, p. 21.

29 Pierenkemper, *Bosch*, p. 18.

30 Robert Bosch, "Von Vergangenheit, Gegenwart und Zukunft," in *Bosch-Zünder* 1926/10, p. 223.

31 "Social understanding," Bosch once wrote, "is something I inherited from my 'esteemed mother' – possibly, when all's said and done, from my father too." "Bosch an Closs, 23. 1. 1937," RB 1 014 415.

32 See p. 65.

33 Felix Pinner, *Deutsche Wirtschaftsführer*, Berlin, 1924, p. 206.

34 As emerges from a letter that Bosch wrote to a Heidenheim entrepreneur in January 1937, clearly this nickname did not first arise in connection with the introduction of the eight-hour working day: "The frequent attacks of hostility that I have had to bear just as much from colleagues in the trade unions and that resulted in my being dubbed 'Bosch the red' go back almost 50 years." "Bosch an Closs, 23. 1. 1937," RB 1 014 415.

35 "Robert Bosch, Lebenserinnerungen (1921)," p. 26, RB 1 014 006.

36 *Ibid.*

37 Robert Bosch, "Für Marx!," in *Frankfurter Zeitung*, April 21, 1925, RB 1 013 103; Robert Bosch, "Zur Kandidatur Hindenburg," in *Stuttgarter Neues Tagblatt*, April 21, 1925 [also in Bundesarchiv (BArch), DN 1/112736]; Robert Bosch, "Warum charakterlos?," in *Stuttgarter Neues Tagblatt*, March 11, 1932; "Bosch an Duisberg, 31. 3. 1932," Bayer-Archiv Leverkusen AS; Heuss, *Bosch*, pp. 468 ff.; Scholtyseck, *Bosch*, pp. 92 f.

38 Quoted from Joachim Scholtyseck, "Robert Bosch, die deutsch-französische Verständigung und das Ende der Weimarer Republik," in Rolf Becker, Joachim Scholtyseck, *Robert Bosch und die deutsch-französische Verständigung. Politisches Denken und Handeln im Spiegel der Briefwechsel*, Stuttgart [undated], p. 70.

39 Heuss, *Bosch*, pp. 181 f.

40 This donation to a foundation set up specifically for the purpose was to make it possible to develop the River Neckar between Mannheim and Esslingen. Until such time as the shipping lane was built, the interest was to be credited to the city of Stuttgart. Work on the project began after the First World War, but inflation soon devalued the capital of the foundation. Heuss, *Bosch*, pp. 268 ff.

41 Lessing, *Bosch*, p. 138. Cf. in this connection Claus-Michael Allmendinger, *Struktur,*

Aufgabe und Bedeutung der Stiftungen von Robert Bosch und seiner Firma. Ein Beitrag zur Geschichte des Stiftungswesens in Württemberg von 1900 bis 1964, Stuttgart, 1977.

42 On this subject, see pp. 245 f.

43 Christof Bosch, "Robert Bosch und die Boschhöfe." Article for *Königsdorfer Heimatbuch*, RB 1 014 299.

44 "Felix Olpp, Unser unvergesslicher Herr Bosch," p. 50, RB 1 014 003. On the "Jagdgemeinschaft Robert Bosch," see the papers in Landesarchiv Baden-Württemberg, Hauptstaatsarchiv Stuttgart P. 10.

45 Georg Escherich, "Jagderlebnisse," MS 1933–34, Bayerisches Hauptstaatsarchiv, Nachlass Georg Escherich, no. 35.

46 "Theodor Bäuerle, Robert Bosch. Persönliche Erinnerungen," p. 17 (sheet 18), RB 1 014 001.

47 *Ibid.*

48 Heuss, *Bosch*, pp. 45 f.

49 Robert Jütte, "The healing power of nature. Homeopath and 'lifestyle reformer'," in Robert Bosch GmbH (ed.), *Robert Bosch. His life and work* (*Journal of Bosch History*, supplement 1) [Stuttgart, 2009]. Cf., among other sources touching on this subject, Claus-Michael Allmendinger, "Robert Bosch und die homöopathische Bewegung in Württemberg," in Sigrid Heinze (ed.), *Homöopathie 1796–1996. Eine Heilkunde und ihre Geschichte*, Berlin, 1996, pp. 93–100.

50 Heuss, *Bosch*, pp. 538 ff.

51 *Ibid.*, pp. 488 ff.

52 "Theodor Bäuerle, Robert Bosch. Persönliche Erinnerungen," p. 8 (sheet 9), RB 1 014 001.

53 *Ibid.*, p. 34 (sheet 35).

54 Heuss, *Bosch*, p. 231.

55 "Festansprache von Hans Walz am 23. 9. 1941," RB 1 013 024.

56 "Lieber Geld verlieren als Vertrauen," in *Bosch-Zünder* 1919/2, p. 21.

57 *Ibid.*

2. The difficult early years

1 "Robert Bosch, Lebenserinnerungen (1921)," p. 10, RB 1 014 006.

2 The building at 75B Rothebühlstraße was destroyed in the Second World War. Today the Klett-Cotta publishing house occupies the site.

3 "Ergänzungen von Robert Bosch zu Theodor Bäuerle, 'Robert Bosch'," pp. 48 f., RB 1 014 009.

4 Otto Debatin, *Sie haben mitgeholfen. Lebensbilder verdienter Mitarbeiter des Hauses Bosch* (Bosch-Schriftenreihe, vol. 11), Stuttgart, 1963, pp. 70 f. Debatin bases his account on the reminiscences of a Bosch associate named Otto Fischer, who grew up at 75B Rotebühlstraße and subsequently worked for the company for over 40 years. Fischer should not be confused with the eponymous chief accountant and son-in-law of Robert Bosch. The reference to the Otto and Max Rosenfeld cigar business occurs in a communication from Robert Bosch's later associate Hugo Borst to Theodor Heuss. Borst considered it likely that the courtyard-entrance building belonged to the Rosenfelds. "Borst an Heuss, 20. 6. 1944 (note to p. 93)," RB 1 014 155.

5 "Robert Bosch, Lebenserinnerungen (1921)," p. 10, RB 1 014 006.

6 Heuss, *Bosch*, p. 91.

7 Lutz Pape, Hans-Jürgen Weinert, *Bottichwaschmaschine & Haustelegraph. Anfänge der Elektrotechnik im Haushalt*, Braunschweig, 1993, p. 62.

8 Marianne Erath, "Vom Fernschreiben zum Fernsprechen. Die Geschichte von Telegraph und Telefon im Südwesten," http://www.staatsanzeiger.de/kultur-und-geschichte/momente/archiv/momente-archiv/momente-ausgabe/175.

9 Wolfgang Leiner, "Paul Reisser. Ein württembergischer Pionier der Elektrotechnik," in Wolfgang Leiner (ed.), *Ausgewählte technikgeschichtliche Vorträge*, Stuttgart, 1984, pp. 174–84.

10 "Otto Fischer, Die Geschichte der Firma Robert Bosch 1886–1914 aus ihren Geschäftsbüchern (September 1942)," pp. 21, 31, 45, RB 1 003 062; Karl Erich Born, *Wirtschafts- und Sozialgeschichte des Deutschen Kaiserreichs (1867/71–1914)*, Stuttgart, 1985, p. 85.

11 "Robert Bosch, Lebenserinnerungen (1921)," p. 10, RB 1 014 006.

12 Ergänzungen von Robert Bosch zu Theodor Bäuerle, 'Robert Bosch'," p. 47, RB 1 014 009.

13 Wolfgang Leiner, *Geschichte der Elektrizitätswirtschaft in Württemberg*, vol. 1: *Grundlagen und Anfänge (bis 1895)*, Stuttgart, 1982, pp. 167 ff., 171 ff., 203.

14 Peter Strunk, *Die AEG. Aufstieg und Niedergang einer deutschen Industrielegende*, 2nd ed., Berlin, 2000, p. 24.

15 Lessing, *Bosch*, pp. 25, 60, 63. Schall and Robert Bosch had done their military service together in Ulm and remained friends. Lessing even sees Schall's offer as a crucial reason why Robert Bosch settled in Stuttgart.

16 "Otto Fischer, Die Geschichte der Firma Robert Bosch 1886–1914 aus ihren Geschäftsbüchern (September 1942)," pp. 9, 16, RB 1 003 062.

17 "Robert Bosch, Lebenserinnerungen (1921)," p. 10, RB 1 014 006.

18 Reinhart Seiffert, *Die Ära Gottlieb Daimlers. Neue Perspektiven zur Frühgeschichte des Automobils und seiner Technik*, Wiesbaden, 2009, pp. 66 f. The older patent held by Siegfried Marcus was easily circumvented. *Ibid.*, p. 18. On the biography of Nicolaus Otto, cf. Arnold Langen, *Nicolaus August Otto. Der Schöpfer des Verbrennungsmotors*, Stuttgart, 1949.

19 "Robert Bosch, Lebenserinnerungen (1921)," p. 10, RB 1 014 006; "Otto Fischer, Die Geschichte der Firma Robert Bosch 1886–1914 aus ihren Geschäftsbüchern (September 1942)," p. 16, RB 1 003 062.

20 "Otto Fischer, Die Geschichte der Firma Robert Bosch 1886–1914 aus ihren Geschäftsbüchern (September 1942)," pp. 15, 19, RB 1 003 062.

21 Robert Bosch, "Lebenserinnerungen" (1921), p. 10, RB 1 014 006.

22 "Otto Fischer, Die Geschichte der Firma Robert Bosch 1886–1914 aus ihren Geschäftsbüchern (September 1942)," pp. 17, 19, RB 1 003 062.

23 *Ibid.*, p. 28. Otto Fischer worked for Robert Bosch AG, initially as an office assistant, from 1918 onwards. In the period 1930–37, he was head of central accounts. He married Margarete Bosch, Robert Bosch's eldest daughter, in 1951, and from 1945 to 1960, he was a member of the Bosch board of management.

24 *Ibid.*, p. 45.

25 *Ibid.*, pp. 14, 22, 28.

26 Heuss, *Bosch*, p. 92.

27 Gottlob Honold, "Persönliche Erinnerungen," in *Bosch-Zünder* 1921/9, p. 235.

28 "Aus den Erinnerungen des Mechaniker-Mithelfers Schyle an das erste Jahrzehnt der Firma Bosch," in Debatin, *Sie haben mitgeholfen*, p. 172. Otto Fischer gives the same estimate as Honold for the year 1891: nine employees. "Otto Fischer, Die Geschichte der Firma Robert Bosch 1886–1914 aus ihren Geschäftsbüchern (September 1942)," p. 28, RB 1 003 062.

29 "Aus den Erinnerungen," p. 172.

30 "Otto Fischer, Die Geschichte der Firma Robert Bosch 1886–1914 aus ihren Geschäftsbüchern (September 1942)," p. 41, RB 1 003 062.

31 *Ibid.*, p. 28.

32 *Ibid.*, p. 33.

33 *Ibid.*, p. 45.

34 *Von der Glühbirne zum Mikroprozessor. 100 Jahre Elektrizität in Stuttgart*, ed. by Elektro-Innung Stuttgart, Stuttgart, 1984, p. 13.

35 Heuss, *Bosch*, p. 94; Gottlob Honold, "Persönliche Erinnerungen," in *Bosch-Zünder* 1921/9, p. 236.

36 Original words: "böse[s] Gewürge," cf. Fastnacht, Kuhlgatz, Schmitt, Siegel, *125 years*, p. 34.

37 "Otto Fischer, Die Geschichte der Firma Robert Bosch 1886–1914 aus ihren Geschäftsbüchern (September 1942)," p. 27, RB 1 003 062.

38 *Ibid.*, p. 42.

39 Leiner, *Geschichte*, pp. 204 ff., 209 ff.

40 *Ibid.*, pp. 215 ff. In 1902, the electricity works was taken over by the city of Stuttgart. Paul Sauer, *Das Werden einer Großstadt. Stuttgart zwischen Reichsgründung und Erstem Weltkrieg 1871 bis 1914*, Stuttgart, 1988, p. 129.

41 "Robert Bosch, Lebenserinnerungen (1921)," pp. 10 f., RB 1 014 006; Heuss, *Bosch*, p. 92; "Otto Fischer, Die Geschichte der Firma Robert Bosch 1886–1914 aus ihren Geschäftsbüchern (September 1942)," pp. 34, 45, RB 1 003 062.

42 Debatin, *Sie haben mitgeholfen*, p. 11.

43 *Ibid.*, pp. 13 ff.

44 *Ibid.*, p. 168; "Carl Beck, Aus alter Zeit" [undated], RB 1 044 001/3.

45 Debatin, *Sie haben mitgeholfen*, pp. 44 ff.

46 *Ibid.*, pp. 22 ff.

47 *Ibid.*, p. 171.

48 Original words: "altfränkische Idylle," Heuss, *Bosch*, p. 100.

49 *Ibid.*, p. 96.

50 "Theodor Bäuerle, Robert Bosch," p. 50, RB 1 014 020; Lessing, *Bosch*, pp. 69 f.

51 Cf. Fastnacht, Kuhlgatz, Schmitt, Siegel, *125 years*, p. 39.

52 Gottlob Honold, "Persönliche Erinnerungen," in *Bosch-Zünder* 1921/9, p. 235.

53 Debatin, *Sie haben mitgehofen*, p. 172; "Vor 50 Jahren führte Robert Bosch den Neunstundentag ein 1894–1944, 25. 4. 1944," RB 1 059 033.

3 The period of rapid growth

1 Quoted from Eugen Diesel, "Robert Bosch," in Eugen Diesel, Gustav Goldbeck, Friedrich Schildberger, *Vom Motor zum Auto. Fünf Männer und ihr Werk*, 3rd ed., Stuttgart, 1968, p. 269.

2 See the vivid account from the "automobile diary" kept by one of Austria's first drivers in Barbara Haubner, "Automobilismus im Kaiserreich. Auftakt zur Massenmobilisierung oder Freizeitvergnügen für Wohlhabende?," in Rudolf Boch (ed.), *Geschichte und Zukunft der deutschen Automobilindustrie. Tagung im Rahmen der "Chemnitzer Begegnungen" 2000*, Stuttgart, 2001, p. 25.

3 "50 Jahre Bosch-Zündung im Dienste der Kraftfahrt 1894–1944, 17. 2. 1944," RB 1 014 156.

4 Heuss, *Bosch*, p. 115.

5 "Produktionsstatistik ab 1887," RB 1 007 075.

6 Heuss, *Bosch*, p. 126; "Bilder aus der Vergangenheit," in *Bosch-Zünder* 1919/4, pp. 58 f.

7 Max J. B. Rauck, "Das Serienmotorrad wurde 90 Jahre alt," in *Kultur & Technik* 1986/2, pp. 92 f.

8 "Robert Bosch, Lebenserinnerungen (1921)," p. 12, RB 1 014 006; Heuss, *Bosch*, pp. 117 ff.; Lessing, *Bosch*, p. 78. The low-voltage magneto device developed by Zähringer was granted patent no. DRP 99399 of June 11, 1897 ("Elektrischer Funkengeber zur Zündung des Explosionsgemisches in Gasmotoren"). Heuss, *Bosch*, p. 118.

9 Rauck, "*Serienmotorrad*," p. 93. Rauck claims that Heuss's account is inaccurate in stating that the ignition device made for Rüb & Wegelin "failed to yield satisfactory results" and that Zähringer's invention came about in connection with a different job for Frederick R. Simms (De Dion-Bouton three-wheeler). Heuss, *Bosch*, pp. 115 ff. (quote on p. 115). However, Robert Bosch was correct in writing in his memoirs: "We succeeded in this and fitted the first such invention to a Heinle & Wegelin machine." But he gives the process the later date of 1899, which cannot be right. "Robert Bosch, Lebenserinnerungen (1921)," p. 12, RB 1 014 006.

10 Altogether Rüb & Wegelin bought 16 Bosch magnetos in the years 1896–97, and – as Heinle & Wegelin – remained an important Bosch customer in the years that followed. "Otto Fischer, Die Geschichte der Firma Robert Bosch 1886–1914 aus ihren Geschäftsbüchern (September 1942)," p. 53, RB 1 003 062.

11 "Bosch an Simms, 23. 10. 1897," RB 1 034 137.

12 "Frederick R. Simms, The History of the Magneto" (translation), pp. 2 ff., RB 1 034 155.

13 Wilfried Feldenkirchen, "*Vom Guten das Beste.*" *Von Daimler und Benz zur DaimlerChrysler AG*, vol. 1: *Die ersten 100 Jahre 1883–1983*, Munich, 2003, pp. 46 ff.

14 "Robert Bosch, Lebenserinnerungen (1921)," p. 12, RB 1 014 006. Lessing doubts Bosch's assertion and gives the estimate 500–600 rpm. Lessing, *Bosch*, p. 79.

15 "Robert Bosch, Lebenserinnerungen (1921)," p. 12, RB 1 014 006; Heuss, *Bosch*, pp. 117 ff.; "Beiträge von Simms zur Entwicklung der Magnetzündung 1897–98" (also evident from Robert Bosch's letters to Simms), RB 1 034 137.

16 Heuss, *Bosch*, p. 122.

17 Quoted from *ibid.*

18 "Bosch an Simms, 18. 2. 1898," RB 1 034 137 (with quote); "Robert Bosch, Lebenserinnerungen (1921)," pp. 12 f., RB 1 014 006.

19 "Robert Bosch, Lebenserinnerungen (1921)," p. 13, RB 1 014 006.

20 Christoph M. Merki, *Der holprige Siegeszug des Automobils 1895–1935. Die Motorisierung des Straßenverkehrs in Frankreich, Deutschland und der Schweiz*, Vienna, Cologne, 2002, pp. 52 ff., 268.

21 *Ibid.*, pp. 268 ff.; Feldenkirchen, *Daimler*, p. 59; "Robert Bosch, Lebenserinnerungen (1921)," pp. 13, 16, RB 1 014 006.

22 Merki, *Siegeszug*, p. 268; Feldenkirchen, *Daimler*, p. 59.

23 Merki, *Siegeszug*, p. 270.

24 "Gottlob Honold – Ein Pionier des Kraftverkehrs," p. 5, RB 1 013 245.

25 Heuss, *Bosch*, pp. 121 f.

26 "Geschichte des Hauses Bosch – Verkaufsorganisation" [undated], RB 1 029 003.

27 "Bosch an Simms, 26. 4. 1898," RB 1 034 137. In July, Bosch wrote to Simms that Wilhelm Maybach had paid him a visit and told him that "Mr. Daimler had been very indignant that I had gone back on my promise to let him sell my products." "Bosch an Simms, 25. 7. 1898," *ibid.*

28 *Ibid.*

29 "Geschichte des Hauses Bosch – Verkaufsorganisation" [undated], RB 1 029 003.

30 "Bosch an Simms, 17. 11. 1898," RB 1 034 137.

31 The words Robert Bosch used were "schmuckloser Kasten." Robert Bosch AG (ed.), *50 Jahre Bosch 1886–1936*, Stuttgart, 1936, p. 232; "Die Gebäude der Robert Bosch A.-G. in Stuttgart und Feuerbach," in *Bosch-Zünder* 1920/3, pp. 46 ff.

32 "Robert Bosch, Lebenserinnerungen (1921)," 1921, p. 14, RB 1 014 006; "Bilder aus der Vergangenheit," in *Bosch-Zünder* 1919/4, pp. 58 f.

33 "Produktionsstatistik ab 1887," RB 1 007 075.

34 "Robert Bosch, Lebenserinnerungen (1921)," p. 14, RB 1 014 006.

35 Lessing, *Bosch*, p. 87; Heuss, *Bosch*, p. 130.

36 "Bosch an Eugen Kayser, 25. 3. 1908," RB 1 014 552.

37 Debatin, *Sie haben mitgeholfen*, pp. 44 ff.

38 "Damit haben Sie den Vogel abgeschossen." Quoted from Heuss, *Bosch*, p. 139. On the subject of the development of the high-voltage magneto, cf. Gottlob Honold, "Wie entstand die Bosch-Lichtbogen-Zündung?," in *Bosch-Zünder* 1921/2, pp. 37 ff.; "Gottlob Honold – Ein Pionier des Kraftverkehrs," p. 10, RB 1 013 245; "Robert Bosch, Lebenserinnerungen (1921)," pp. 14 f., RB 1 014 006; Heuss, *Bosch*, pp. 139 ff.; Lessing, *Bosch*, pp. 89 f.

39 "Ergänzungen von Robert Bosch zu Theodor Bäuerle, Bosch," p. 79, RB 1 014 020.

40 "Robert Bosch, Lebenserinnerungen (1921)," pp. 14 f., RB 1 014 006; "Bosch an Eugen Kayser, 2. 11. 1908," RB 1 014 552.

41 Heuss, *Bosch*, pp. 138 f.

42 Gottlob Honold, "Wie entstand die Bosch-Lichtbogen-Zündung?," in *Bosch-Zünder* 1921/2, pp. 37 ff.; "Gottlob Honold – Ein Pionier des Kraftverkehrs," p. 11, RB 1 013 245.

43 "Gottlob Honold – Ein Pionier des Kraftverkehrs," pp. 10 f., RB 1 013 245.

44 *Ibid.*, p. 11.

45 "Produktionsstatistik ab 1887," RB 1 007 075.

46 Patent specification no. 156117, granted to "Robert Bosch in Stuttgart, Magnetelektrische Zündvorrichtung für Explosionskraftmaschinen," RB 1 013 245; Gottlob Honold, "Wie entstand die Bosch-Lichtbogen-Zündung?," in *Bosch-Zünder* 1921/2, p. 44.

47 Gottlob Honold, "Wie entstand die Bosch-Lichtbogen-Zündung?," in *Bosch-Zünder* 1921/2, p. 44.

48 "Otto Fischer, Die Geschichte der Firma Robert Bosch 1886–1914 aus ihren Geschäftsbüchern (September 1942)," p. 53, RB 1 003 062.

49 *Ibid.*, pp. 49, 53, 56.

50 "Bosch an die Direktion der Daimler-Motoren-Gesellschaft, 8. 1. 1910," RB 1 041 007 004.

51 When in 1906 Disconto-Gesellschaft, one of Germany's largest business banks, asked jointly with the AEG-owned Bank für elektrische Unternehmungen whether the Elektrotechnische Fabrik Robert Bosch might be interested in becoming a stock corporation [*Aktiengesellschaft* or AG], Robert Bosch reportedly replied that he did not have "the least intention of doing such a thing" [er "denke jedoch gar nicht daran, derartiges zu tun"]. Quoted in "Direction der Disconto-Gesellschaft an Bank für elektrische Unternehmungen, 15. 05. 1906," RB 1 014 249.

52 "Auskunft über die Firma Bosch 1908, Auskunftei W. Schimmelpfeng, Stuttgart, 19. 2. 1908," RB 1 010 024 061.

53 Merki, *Siegeszug*, pp. 52 ff., 60 ff.

54 Heidrun Edelmann, *Vom Luxusgut zum Gebrauchsgegenstand. Die Geschichte der Verbreitung von Personenkraftwagen in Deutschland*, Frankfurt am Main, 1989, p. 22.

55 Merki, *Siegeszug*, p. 40. The city of Stuttgart had around 263,000 inhabitants at the end of 1897.

56 *Ibid.*, pp. 60 ff.; Edelmann, *Luxusgut*, pp. 20 ff.

57 Reiner Flik, "Automobilindustrie und Motorisierung in Deutschland bis 1939," in Boch (ed.), *Geschichte*, p. 51.

58 "Robert Bosch, Lebenserinnerungen (1921)," p. 16, RB 1 014 006; "Robert Bosch, Warum ich mich von Frederick R. Simms trennen mußte. Zur Klarstellung" (copy), pp. 1 ff., RB 1 034 147.

59 "Frederick R. Simms, The History of the Magneto" (quoted from the German translation), pp. 5 f., 8 f., RB 1 034 155.

60 "Robert Bosch, Lebenserinnerungen (1921)," p. 17, RB 1 014 006.

61 *Ibid.*

62 "Robert Bosch, Warum ich mich von Frederick R. Simms trennen mußte. Zur Klarstellung" (copy), p. 4, RB 1 034 147; Heuss, *Bosch*, pp. 160 ff.

63 "Robert Bosch, Lebenserinnerungen (1921)," pp. 16 f., RB 1 014 006.

64 *Ibid.*, p. 17.

65 To this end, Borst worked at New York's Hardt von Bernuth bank from December 1904 to February 1906. See Wilfried Geissler, Sigrid Borst (eds.), *Hugo Borst 1881–1967. Familienvater, Kaufmännischer Direktor, Privater Kunstsammler und Förderer. Sammler von schöngeistiger und wissenschaftlicher Literatur*, Stuttgart, 2006, p. 10.

66 Rolf Becker, Frauke Engel, *"Unsere beste Reklame ist unsere Ware" Werbung bei Bosch von den Anfängen bis 1960* (Bosch-Archiv Schriftenreihe, vol. 2), Stuttgart, 1998, pp. 10, 20 (quote); "Borst an Heuss, 3. 6. 1943," RB 1 014 155.

67 Original words: "Eroberernatur", "Menschenfänger,"; Heuss, *Bosch*, p. 163. Original word: "Tausendsassa," Lessing, *Bosch*, p. 93.

68 "Robert Bosch, Lebenserinnerungen (1921)," p. 17, RB 1 014 006. On Klein's life history, see Heuss, *Bosch, pp. 163 ff.*

69 Russ Banham, *Bosch in the United States. The first 100 years*, Farmington Hills, 2006, p. 17.

70 Merki, *Siegeszug*, p. 19.

71 Banham, *Bosch*, pp. 17, 21.

72 Daniel Alef, *Charles and Frank Duryea. Brought us America's first gasoline-powered car*, Santa Barbara/CA, 2008.

73 Banham, *Bosch*, p. 22; Elke Sonnenberg, "'At last you can get them …' Bosch magnetos in the U.S.," in Robert Bosch Gmbh (ed.), *The emergence of a global player. The internationalization of the Bosch Group* (*Journal of Bosch History*, supplement [Stuttgart, 2008], pp. 12 f.; "Hermann Waker, Meine Jahre bei Bosch," p. 21, RB 1 832 018.

74 "Robert Bosch an Hermann Bosch, 27. 2. 1912," RB 1 014 278; Banham, *Bosch*, p. 26; Fastnacht, Kuhlgatz, Schmitt, Siegel, *125 years*, p. 202.

75 Banham, *Bosch*, pp. 23, 26.

76 "Official Bosch Distributors," in *The Bosch News*, vol. IV, no. 2, March 1913.

77 In the annotations he made to Bäuerle's Bosch biography, Robert Bosch ascribed this comment to his U.S. trip of April 1911. "Ergänzungen von Robert Bosch zu Theodor Bäuerle, 'Robert Bosch'," pp. 72 ff., RB 1 014 009. But in the memoir that he wrote himself in 1921 he said of the U.S. generally that "our foray into the market there was a veritable triumph [*Triumphzug*]." "Robert Bosch, Lebenserinnerungen (1921)," p. 17, RB 1 014 006.

78 Fastnacht, Kuhlgatz, Schmitt, Siegel, *125 years*, p. 202; Marlis Prinzing, *Der Streik bei Bosch im Jahre 1913. Ein Beitrag zur Geschichte von Rationalisierung und Arbeiterbewegung* (Zeitschrift für Unternehmensgeschichte, supplement 61) Stuttgart, 1989, p. 57.

79 Cornelius Torp, *Die Herausforderung der Globalisierung. Wirtschaft und Politik in Deutschland 1860–1914,* Göttingen, 2005, p. 105; Feldenkirchen, *Daimler,* p. 75; Wilfried Feldenkirchen, *Siemens 1918–1945,* Munich, 1995, p. 662.

80 Robert Bosch, "Von Vergangenheit, Gegenwart und Zukunft," in *Bosch-Zünder,* 1926/10, p. 222. On the crisis affecting the automotive industry in 1907, cf. Feldenkirchen, *Daimler,* p. 64.

81 Robert Bosch, "Von Vergangenheit, Gegenwart und Zukunft," in *Bosch-Zünder,* 1926/10, p. 222.

82 "Bosch an Eugen Kayser, 2. 2. 1908," RB 1 014 552.

83 Robert Bosch, "Von Vergangenheit, Gegenwart und Zukunft," in *Bosch-Zünder,* 1926/10, p. 222.

84 See appendix, p. 662, "Bosch Group headcount and sales revenue (1986–2012)."

85 The headcount at Daimler-Motoren-Gesellschaft was 3,510 at the end of 1904, rising to 5,050 by 1913. "Kennzahlen der Daimler-Motoren-Gesellschaft 1890–1925, Daimler AG," Mercedes-Benz Archives and Collection, cited in Feldenkirchen, *Daimler,* p. 71.

86 "Die Arbeiterbewegung bei Bosch," in *Der Beobachter,* June 10, 1913, RB 1 059 008; Prinzing, *Streik,* p. 2.

87 "Robert Bosch, Lebenserinnerungen (1921)," p. 31, RB 1 014 006.

88 Betriebsrat Bosch Feuerbach (ed.), … *auch beim Bosch gibt's nichts umsonst. 100 Jahre Arbeit und Leben in Feuerbach aus der Sicht der Beschäftigten. Ein Buch des Betriebsrats Bosch Feuerbach,* Stuttgart, 2009, pp. 16 ff.

89 Original word: "verpreußt." "Bosch an Kayser, 18. 11. 1908," RB 1 014 552.

90 "Robert Bosch, Lebenserinnerungen (1921)," p. 22, RB 1 014 006.

91 Prinzing, *Streik,* p. 20.

92 "Personalstatistik vom 01. 07. 1911 bis 11. 03. 1918," p. 1, RB 1 007 001.

93 Fastnacht, Kuhlgatz, Schmitt, Siegel, *125 years,* p. 165.

94 Prinzing, *Streik,* pp. 29 f.

95 Original words: "Ich zahle nicht gute Löhne, weil ich reich bin, sondern ich bin reich, weil ich gute Löhne zahle." Quoted from Heuss, *Bosch,* p. 403.

96 "Hermann Waker, Meine Jahre bei Bosch," p. 13, RB 1 832 018.

97 On the life story of Hugo Borst, see Geissler, Borst (eds.), *Borst*; Debatin, *Sie haben mitgeholfen,* pp. 36 ff.

98 On the life story of Ernst Ulmer, see Geissler, Borst (eds.), *Borst,* pp. 51 ff.

99 "Robert Bosch, Lebenserinnerungen (1921)," pp. 20 f., RB 1 014 006; Heuss, *Bosch,* pp. 168 f.

100 "Die Verkaufs-Organisation der Robert Bosch A.-G.," pp. 2 f., RB 1 029 003; for foundations and relocations of sales companies in the years 1909 to 1916, see *ibid.*

101 See p. 41.

102 Feldenkirchen, *Daimler,* p. 73.

103 "Arbeits-Ordnung der Firma Bosch, 16. 7. 1906," RB 1 006 005.

104 Heuss, *Bosch,* pp. 154 ff.

105 Robert Bosch on the eight-hour working day in "Sei Mensch," p. 43.

106 "Deutscher Metallarbeiter-Verband, Verwaltungsstelle Stuttgart-Kannstatt [sic] an Bosch, 26. 6. 1907," RB 1 059 033.

107 "Bosch an den Deutschen Metallarbeiter-Verband, Verwaltung Stuttgart, 26. 4. 1909," *ibid.*

108 Betriebsrat Bosch Feuerbach (ed.), … *auch beim Bosch*, pp. 20 f.; Heidrun Homburg, "Anfänge des Taylorsystems in Deutschland vor dem Ersten Weltkrieg. Eine Problemskizze unter besonderer Berücksichtigung der Arbeitskämpfe bei Bosch 1913," in *Geschichte und Gesellschaft* 4, 1978, pp. 180 ff.; Uta Stolle, *Arbeiterpolitik im Betrieb. Frauen und Männer, Reformisten und Radikale, Fach- und Massenarbeiter bei Bayer, Bosch und in Solingen (1900–1933)*, Frankfurt am Main, 1980, pp. 126 f.

109 Frederick Taylor, *The principles of scientific management*, London, 1911; Walter Hebeisen, *F. W. Taylor und der Taylorismus. Über das Wirken und die Lehre Taylors und die Kritik am Taylorismus*, Zurich, 1999.

110 Homburg, "Anfänge," pp. 182 ff.; Geissler, Borst (eds.), *Borst*, p. 12.

111 Betriebsrat Bosch Feuerbach (ed.), … *auch beim Bosch*, pp. 20 f.; Prinzing, *Streik*, pp. 8, 67 ff.

112 See p. 63.

113 Prinzing, *Streik*, p. 121.

114 *Ibid.*, pp. 85 f. In 1920, the local branch of the DMV concluded an agreement with the company to protect workers under the piecework system. Betriebsrat Bosch Feuerbach (ed.), … *auch beim Bosch*, p. 21.

115 Prinzing, *Streik*, pp. 7 f.

116 *Ibid.*, p. 9.

117 "Bosch an den DMV, Verwaltungsstelle Stuttgart, 6. 5. 1913," RB 1 002 073.

118 According to the company's weekly staff statistics, on May 26, 1913, 3,698 male and 238 female workers were employed at the factories, while on August 2, 1913, the respective figures were 3,466 and 233. So virtually no women workers took part in the rebellion. "Personalstatistik vom 01. 07. 1911 bis 11. 03. 1918," RB 1 007 001.

119 *Ibid.*

120 Prinzing, *Streik*, pp. 10 ff.

121 "Klein an Bosch Magneto Company, 10. 6. 1913," RB 1 059 048.

122 "Die Arbeiterbewegung bei Bosch," in *Der Beobachter*, June 10, 1913, RB 1 059 008.

123 "Klein an Bosch Magneto Company, 10. 6. 1913," RB 1 059 048; Prinzing, *Streik*, p. 12; Stolle, *Arbeiterpolitik*, p. 165.

124 "Klein an Heins, Bosch Magneto Company New York, 22. 7. 1913," RB 1 059 048. Looking back, Bosch gave slightly higher figures (800 strike breakers at the outset, 1,800 after a week). "Robert Bosch, Lebenserinnerungen (1921)," pp. 28 f., RB 1 014 006. In the company's own payroll statistics, weekly entries did not increase between July 14, 1913, and August 4, 1913. "Personalstatistik vom 01. 07. 1911 bis 11. 03. 1918," RB 1 007 001.

125 "Personalstatistik vom 01. 7. 1911 bis 11. 03. 1918," RB 1 007 001.

126 Prinzing, *Streik*, pp. 13 f.

127 Homburg, "Anfänge", p. 191, note 68.

128 *Ibid.*; Stolle, *Arbeiterpolitik*, pp. 166 ff.

129 Homburg, "Anfänge", pp. 192 ff.

130 Stolle, *Arbeiterpolitik*, pp. 161 ff.

131 Prinzing, *Streik*, pp. 128 ff.

132 *Ibid.*, p. 123.

133 *Ibid.*, pp. 121 ff., 126 f. On the life story of Westmeyer, cf. Theodor Bergmann, Wolfgang Haible, Galina Iwanowa, *Friedrich Westmeyer. Von der Sozialdemokratie zum Spartakusbund. Eine politische Biographie*, Hamburg, 1998.

134 "Keil an Walz, 12. 1. 1936," RB 1 059 008.

135 Prinzing, *Streik*, p. 131.

136 Lessing, *Bosch*, p. 112. The theory advanced there – namely, that Clara Zetkin used the Bosch strike to take revenge for her husband's unfaithfulness with Paula Bosch – is pure fantasy.

137 Betriebsrat Bosch Feuerbach (ed.), *... auch beim Bosch*, p. 29.

138 "Lieber Geld verlieren als Vertrauen," in *Bosch-Zünder* 1919/2, p. 21.

139 "Vorstand der Robert Bosch AG, Unsere Zukunft, Jan. 1919," p. 2, RB 1 832 067; "Hermann Waker, Meine Jahre bei Bosch," p. 18, RB 1 832 018.

140 "Chronologie der ersten Vertretungen und Fertigungen außerhalb Deutschlands," RB 1 010 024.

141 Cf. Mira Wilkins, "Multinational enterprise to 1930. Discontinuities and continuities," in Alfred D. Chandler, Bruce Mazlish (eds.), *Leviathans. Multinational corporations and the new global history*, Cambridge, 2005, pp. 52 f.

142 Bosch (China) Investment Ltd. (ed.), *100 years Bosch in China. Past, present, and future*, Shanghai, 2009, p. 63.

143 Johannes Bähr, Jörg Lesczenski, Katja Schmidtpott, *Winds of change. On the 150th anniversary of C. Illies & Co.*, Munich 2009, p. 119, p. 120.

144 "Anfänge der Bosch-Aktivitäten in Lateinamerika," RB 1 010 024 027.

145 Marcel Grauls, "One hundred years of success in Belgium," in Robert Bosch GmbH (ed.), *Bosch in Belgium 1907–2007*, Brussels, 2007, p. 40.

146 "Borst an Heuss, 20. 6. 1944," RB 1 014 155.

147 Becker, Engel, *Werbung*, pp. 11, 26, 32 ff.

148 "Borst an Heuss, 20. 6. 1944," RB 1 014 155.

149 Robert Bosch AG (ed.), *50 Jahre Bosch*, pp. 88 ff.

150 Robert Bosch GmbH (ed.), *Bosch Automotive. A product history* (Journal of Bosch History supplement 2) [Stuttgart, 2010], pp. 14 ff.

151 Robert Bosch AG (ed.), *50 Jahre Bosch*, pp. 88 ff.

152 Quoted from Heuss, *Bosch*, p. 201.

153 *Ibid.*, pp. 240, 275.

4 The First World War and its aftermath

1 "Personalstatistik vom 01. 07. 1911 bis 11. 03. 1918," RB 1 007 001; "Robert Bosch, Lebenserinnerungen (1921)," p. 31, RB 1 014 006.

2 "Robert Bosch an Anna Bosch, 31. 7. 1914," RB 1 014 140; Heuss, *Bosch*, p. 256.

3 "Bosch an Egnell, 28. 8. 1914," RB 1 014 057. A longer quotation from this letter can be found in Heuss, *Bosch,* p. 262.

4 Heuss, *Bosch*, p. 257.

5 *Ibid.*, p. 258.

6 "Robert Bosch, Lebenserinnerungen (1921)," p. 31, RB 1 014 006.

7 Heuss, *Bosch*, p. 260.

8 "Hermann Waker, Meine Jahre bei Bosch," p. 10, RB 1 832 018.

9 "Schreiben Ernst Eisemann & Co. GmbH, 6. 11. 1914," RB 1 014 562.

10 "Robert Bosch Personalabteilung an Wezel, 18. 8. 1914," RB 1 010 305.

11 "Bosch an Egnell, 28. 8. 1914," RB 1 014 057.

12 "Rüstungsproduktion WK 1. Tabellarische Übersicht zu Stückzahlen," RB 1 013 244; Fastnacht, Kuhlgatz, Schmitt, Siegel, *125 years*, p. 202.

13 See table 2, p. 81.

14 Quoted from Heuss, *Bosch*, p. 263.

15 "Rüstungsproduktion WK 1. Tabellarische Übersicht zu Stückzahlen," RB 1 013 244.

16 "Personalstatistik vom 01. 07. 1911 bis 11. 03. 1918," RB 1 007 001.

17 *Ibid.*

18 "Protokoll der Besprechung unter Vorsitz und Leitung Sr Exzellenz Herrn Graf von Zeppelin am 5. 9. 1914," RB 1 013 261.

19 Heuss, *Bosch*, p. 264.

20 "Robert Bosch, Hauptverwaltung, Hugo Borst, Rundschreiben Nr. 123, 28. 10. 1915," RB 1 013 261.

21 "Robert Bosch, Verwaltung, an Versuchsbau GmbH Gotha-Ost, 27. 10. 1915," *ibid.*

22 "Borst an Heuss, 9. 12. 1943," RB 1 014 155.

23 Heuss, *Bosch*, pp. 264 ff.

24 *Ibid.*, pp. 266 f.; "Robert Bosch, Lebenserinnerungen (1921)," p. 33, RB 1 014 006. Vollmoeller, the son of a Stuttgart industrialist and a former neighbor of the Bosch family, was an experienced and noted pilot. Before the war he had been a test pilot at the Rumpler aircraft works.

25 "Robert Bosch, Lebenserinnerungen (1921)," pp. 33 f. (quote on p. 34), RB 1 014 006.

26 Scholtyseck, *Bosch*, p. 41.

27 *Ibid.*, p. 39; Bernd Sösemann, "Politische Kommunikation im 'Reichsbelagerungszustand.' Programm, Struktur und Wirkungen des Clubs 'Deutsche Gesellschaft 1914'," in Manfred Bobrowsky, Wolfgang R. Langenbucher (eds.), *Wege zur Kommunikationsgeschichte*, Munich, 1987, pp. 630–49.

28 Scholtyseck, *Bosch*, p. 40.

29 *Ibid.*

30 *Ibid.*, p. 41.

31 "Robert Bosch, Lebenserinnerungen (1921)," p. 38, RB 1 014 006.

32 Heuss, *Bosch*, p. 268. On the donation to the Homeopathic Hospital Society, see Jütte, *Healing power*, p. 53.

33 "Robert Bosch AG, Unsere Zukunft, 23. 1. 1919," p. 1, RB 1 832 067.

34 Hans-Ulrich Wehler, *Deutsche Gesellschaftsgeschichte, vol. 4: Vom Beginn des Ersten Weltkrieges bis zur Gründung der beiden deutschen Staaten 1914–1949*, Munich, 2003, p. 65.

35 "Geschichte des Hauses Bosch – Verkaufsorganisation" [undated], p. 5, RB 1 029 003.

36 "Memorandum [an General Ludendorff] vom 11. 2. 1918," RB 1 014 053; "Jäckh an Bosch, 10. 2. 1918, RB 1 014 148. On this subject, see Eberhard Demm, *Ein Liberaler in Kaiserreich und Republik. Der politische Weg Alfred Webers bis 1920* (Schriften des Bundesarchivs, 38), Boppard am Rhein, 1990, p. 241.

37 "Bosch an Naumann, 29. 10. 1918," RB 1 014 055.

38 Robert Bosch AG (ed.), *50 Jahre Bosch*, p. 291.

39 "Hermann Waker, Meine Jahre bei Bosch," p. 21. RB 1 832 018.

40 "Bosch an Kayser, 13. 10. 1907," RB 1 014 552.

41 *Ibid.*

42 "Robert Bosch an Hermann Bosch, 27. 2. 1912," RB 1 014 278.

43 Paul Scheuing had been Robert Bosch's legal adviser since 1907. At that time, he had worked for *Justizrat* Ludwig Kielmayer, whom Bosch's colleague Hugo Borst had instructed to examine the Simms agreements. "Borst an Heuss, 20. 6. 1944," RB 1 014 155.

44 Heuss, *Bosch*, p. 274.

45 "Robert Bosch, Lebenserinnerungen (1921)," p. 35, RB 1 014 006.

46 "Niederschrift über die Aufsichtsratssitzung am 10. 12. 1937," p. 2, RB 1 002 005.

47 Robert Bosch AG (ed.), *50 Jahre Bosch*, p. 28.

48 "Vertrag zwischen Dr. ing. Robert Bosch und den Herren Gottlob Honold, Hugo Borst, Heinrich Kempter, Ernst Ulmer, Max Rall, 16. 7. 1917," RB 1 001 005.

49 Robert Bosch AG (ed.), *50 Jahre Bosch*, p. 28.

50 "Werner Schaubel, Untersuchungen über die Zweckbestimmung der VVB und RBTV, 5. 3. 1959," RB 1 001 289.

51 *Ibid.*, p. 2.

52 "Vertrag zwischen Herrn Dr. ing. Robert Bosch und der Vermögensverwaltung Bosch GmbH, 11. 3. 1921," RB 1 001 286.

53 "Werner Schaubel, Untersuchungen über die Zweckbestimmung der VVB und RBTV, 5. 3. 1959," p. 6, RB 1 001 289.

54 "Verkaufsangebot, 30. 4. 1924," RB 1 001 286.

55 "Walz an Schloßstein, 28. 11. 1947," quoted from *ibid.*, p. 49.

56 *Ibid.*

57 Banham, *Bosch*, pp. 27, 33. Subsequent investigations revealed that "Martin E. Kern" was in actual fact Edward Kern, an ex-prisoner with German nationality. Using this false identity, before the First World War he had risen to be vice-president of the truck manufacturer Mack Brothers and founded a bank. His real identity was exposed after he had begun an affair with an actress called Marion Davies, a lover of the press baron William Randolph Hearst. Kern's life story is said to have inspired the writer F. Scott Fitzgerald in penning his novel *The Great Gatsby*. Frank Whelan, *History's Headlines: Allentown Mansion Has a Scandalous Past*: URL: http://www. wfmz.com/features/History-s-Headlines/History-s-Headlines-Allentown-mansion-has-a-scandalous-past/-/11271212.

58 Peter E. Fäßler, *Globalisierung*, Cologne, Weimar, 2007, pp. 99 ff.

59 ABMC newspaper ad in the *New York Times* of January 6, 1919, reprinted in "Ich bin ein Amerikaner," in *Bosch-Zünder* 1919/1, p. 15; Becker, Engel, *Werbung*, p. 11.

60 Robert Bosch GmbH (ed.), *Emergence of a global player*, p. 18.

61 Heuss, *Bosch*, pp. 300 f.; Stoller, *Arbeiterpolitik*, p. 323.

62 "An die Angehörigen der Robert Bosch A.-G., Stuttgart und Feuerbach und der Bosch-Metallwerk A. G., Feuerbach, 15. 11. 1918," RB 1 010 305 001.

63 *Ibid.*

64 *Ibid.*

65 "Robert Bosch A. G., Unsere Zukunft, 23. 1. 1919," p. 3, RB 1 832 067; "An die Angehörigen der Robert Bosch A.-G., Stuttgart und Feuerbach und der Bosch-Metallwerk A. G., Feuerbach, 15. 11. 1918," RB 1 010 305 001.

66 "Robert Bosch A. G., Unsere Zukunft, 23. 1. 1919," p. 8, RB 1 832 067.

67 Fastnacht, Kuhlgatz, Schmitt, Siegel, *125 years*, p. 203. According to data published by Stolle, at the beginning of 1918, a total of 4,580 female blue-collar workers were employed at Bosch, in January 1919 only 1,820. In January 1914, the number of women employed on the shop floor at Bosch had stood at 308 only. Stolle, *Arbeiterpolitik*, p. 323.

68 Fastnacht, Kuhlgatz, Schmitt, Siegel, *125 years*, p. 203; "Kennzahlen der Daimler-Motoren-Gesellschaft 1890–1925," Daimler A. G., Mercedes-Benz Archives and Collection.

69 On Paul Hahn's life story and his work for Robert Bosch, see pp. 236, 242, and 245.

70 Heuss, *Bosch*, p. 316.

71 *Ibid.*, p. 316 (the quote); Scholtyseck, *Bosch*, p. 53.

72 "Aussperrung und Generalstreik (16. August bis 5. September 1920)," in *Bosch-Zünder* 1920/8, pp. 161 ff.; "Hermann Waker, Meine Jahre bei Bosch," p. 12, RB 1 832 018; Heuss, *Bosch*, p. 337. On the "tax war," cf. Stolle, *Arbeiterpolitik*, pp. 178 ff.

73 More extensive quotes from Robert Bosch's letter of April 29, 1919, are to be found in Heuss, *Bosch*, p. 324. An excerpt from this letter was printed in the associate newspaper *Bosch-Zünder*. On the question of works councils [*Betriebsräte*], see *Bosch-Zünder* 1919/5, p. 79.

74 Stolle, *Arbeiterpolitik*, p. 175.

75 *Ibid.*, pp. 168 f., 214 ff., 237 ff.

76 See appendix, p. 663, "Bosch Group headcount and sales revenue (1886–2012)."

77 "Robert Bosch A. G., Unsere Zukunft, 23. 1. 1919," p. 6, RB 1 832 067.

78 "VKS Referat 3, Die Organisation des Verkaufs der Bosch-Erzeugnisse", RB 1 029 003.

79 Dieter Schmitt, "Casa Bosch. First office opens in Argentina," in *Journal of Bosch History*, 2008, p. 12. It was during the 1921 crossing to Argentina on the *Brabantia* that Robert Bosch wrote the first part of his "Lebenserinnerungen." While he was in Argentina his son Robert passed away back in Stuttgart.

80 "Hermann Waker, Meine Jahre bei Bosch," RB 1 832 018; "Official Bosch Distributors," in *The Bosch News*, vol. IV, no. 2, March 1913.

81 "FEG an VH/ST/GL-T betr. Daten zur Geschichte der VH und BD, 27. 7. 1965," RB 1 029 003.

82 "40 Jahre Bosch-Dienst Hamburg 1921–1961," p. 6, RB 1 062 001. The proprietor of this first Bosch Service, Max Eisenmann, was Jewish, and in the Third Reich he was obliged to emigrate. The company was taken over by Alfred Kruse, a factory manager [*Werkleiter*] from Stuttgart.

83 "Geschichte des Hauses Bosch – Verkaufsorganisation" [undated], RB 1 029 003; "Daten zur Geschichte der VH und BD, 27. 7. 1965," *ibid.*

84 "Geschichte des Hauses Bosch – Verkaufsorganisation" [undated], p. 10, RB 1 029 003; "Aus unseren Verkaufshäusern und Vertretungen," in *Bosch-Zünder* 1923/10, p. 234.

85 "Daten zur Geschichte der VH und BD, 27. 7. 1965," RB 1 029 003.

86 Dietrich Worbs, "Funktionalität und Repräsentation. Das Bosch-Geschäftshaus in Berlin-Charlottenburg," in Zentralabteilung Anlagen und Bauten der Robert Bosch GmbH (ed.), *Art for innovation. Repräsentanz Berlin*, Stuttgart, 2003, pp. 8–17; "Geschichte des Hauses Bosch – Verkaufsorganisation" [undated], RB 1 029 003; "Bosch-Verkaufshäuser, 5. 3. 1931," *ibid.*; K. D. Heinrich, "75 Jahre Standort Berlin," in *Bosch-Zünder* 1984/10, p. 3.

87 "Geschichte des Hauses Bosch, – Verkaufsorganisation" [undated], RB 1 029 003

88 Robert Bosch AG (ed.), *50 Jahre Bosch*, pp. 165 ff., 240.

89 "Produktionsstatistik ab 1887," RB 1 007 075; *Bosch Automotive*, pp. 16 f.

90 Heuss, *Bosch*, p. 347; Robert Bosch AG (ed.), *50 Jahre Bosch*, pp. 132 ff.

91 Heuss, *Bosch*, p. 349.

92 "Aus unseren Verkaufshäusern und Vertretungen," in *Bosch-Zünder* 1923/10, p. 234. On the other hand, the "Bosch Bell" introduced in 1923 was not a success. This emitted a ringing sound to warn drivers when a tire was losing pressure and made sense only under the unusual conditions of the inflationary years, when rubber was scarce and tires exceptionally expensive. Cf. Robert Bosch AG (ed.), *50 Jahre Bosch*, p. 135.

93 See pp. 130 ff.

94 Robert Bosch AG (ed.), *50 Jahre Bosch*, p. 32.

95 Around that time Eisemann-Werke A. G. had been obliged to increase its capital, yet had no wish to become dependent on Dresdner Bank. According to Robert Bosch, he acquired his holding during the war. The investigative report into Bosch drawn up by the American military government after 1945 dates the episode to 1912. "Ergänzungen von Robert Bosch zu Theodor Bäuerle, 'Robert Bosch'," p. 160, RB 1 014 009; "Office of Military Government for Germany (U.S.) ['OMGUS'], Property Division, Decartelization Branch. In Sachen des Bosch-Konzerns, Feststellungen und Anordnungen," p. 19, RB 1 011 135.

96 Robert Bosch AG (ed.), *50 Jahre Bosch*, pp. 32, 242.

97 "Ausarbeitung betr. Mea, 26. 9. 1941," p. 2, RB 1 022 037.

98 *Ibid.*, pp. 1–8; "Bosch an Bücher, 18. 5. 1928," RB 1 014 401.

99 "Robert Bosch und die Presse" [undated, 1995], pp. 3 ff., 6 f., RB 1 014 787 001. As to the time of this involvement, opinions differ. *Ibid.*, p. 6.

100 Heuss, *Bosch*, p. 466. Hugenberg, having taken over Scherl-Verlag during the First World War, was building a media empire that under the Weimar Republic covered a large sector of Germany's media landscape.

101 On Reusch's dealings with the newspapers of the Gutehoffnungshütte Group, which owned not only the *Schwäbischer Merkur* but also the *Fränkischer Kurier* in Nuremberg and the *Münchner Neueste Nachrichten*, cf. Johannes Bähr, Ralf Banken, Thomas Flemming, *MAN. The history of a German industrial enterprise*, Munich, 2009, pp. 264 ff.

102 "Borst an Heuss, 5. 4. 1944," RB 1 014 155.

103 Heuss, *Bosch*, pp. 311 f.

104 *Ibid.*, p. 312.

105 Alexander Michel, *Von der Fabrikzeitung zum Führungsmittel. Werkzeitschriften industrieller Großunternehmen von 1890 bis 1945 (Beiträge zur Unternehmensgeschichte*, vol. 96), Stuttgart, 1997, p. 147.

106 Michel, *Fabrikzeitung*, p. 312. According to Michel, Debatin joined Robert Bosch A. G. on May 24, 1918. Heuss says it was September 1918. That was when Debatin switched to the secretariat of the board of management. Heuss, *Bosch*, p. 313; Michel, *Fabrikzeitung*, p. 152.

107 "Robert Bosch und die Presse" [undated, 1995], RB 1 014 787 001.

108 "Zum Geleit," in *Bosch-Zünder* 1919/1.

109 Dieter Schmitt, *Theodor Bäuerle (1882–1956). Engagement für Bildung in schwierigen Zeiten* ("Schriftenreihe zur Bosch-Geschichte," vol. 3), Stuttgart, 2005, pp. 56 ff.

110 "Debatin an Borst, Vorschläge für eine Zeitschrift der Arbeiterschaft der Robert Bosch A.-G.," RB 1 832 067.

111 Michel, *Fabrikzeitung*, p. 149.

112 *Ibid.*, pp. 156 ff.

113 *Ibid.*, pp. 149, 153, 163.

114 *Ibid.*, p. 128.

115 *Ibid.*, pp. 164 f.

116 *Ibid.*, p. 161.

117 "Lieber Geld verlieren als Vertrauen," in *Bosch-Zünder* 1919/2, p. 1.

118 Robert Bosch AG, "Bericht über das 5. Geschäftsjahr," in *Bosch-Zünder* 1922/4, p. 85; "Freiwillige Leistungen der Robert Bosch AG für ihre Gefolgschaft, Okt. 1937," p. 9, RB 1 043 002.

119 Pinner, *Wirtschaftsführer*, p. 210; "Otto Debatin, Robert Bosch GmbH und NSDAP," p. 3, RB 1 013 078.

120 "Freiwillige Leistungen der Robert Bosch AG für ihre Gefolgschaft, Okt. 1937," p. 9, RB 1 043 002.

121 Heuss, *Bosch*, pp. 404 f.

122 "Unser elftes Geschäftsjahr," in *Bosch-Zünder* 1928/5, p. 97; Heuss, *Bosch*, p. 405.

123 Heuss, *Bosch*, pp. 407 f.

124 *Ibid.*

125 *Ibid.*, p. 407.

126 *Ibid.*, p. 408.

127 *Ibid.*, pp. 408 ff.; "Unser zwölftes Geschäftsjahr," in *Bosch-Zünder* 1929/6, p. 122.

128 Heuss, *Bosch*, pp. 409 f.; "Unser elftes Geschäftsjahr," in *Bosch-Zünder* 1928/5, p. 97; "Unser zwölftes Geschäftsjahr," in *Bosch-Zünder* 1929/6, p. 122.

129 "Unser zwölftes Geschäftsjahr," in *Bosch-Zünder* 1929/6, p. 122.

130 For instance, the history chapter in the Festschrift published to mark the company's 50th anniversary was headed *Entwicklung des Hauses Bosch, 1886 bis 1936* ["Development of the House of Bosch, 1886 to 1936], Robert Bosch AG (ed.), *50 Jahre Bosch*, p. 19.

131 Heuss, *Bosch*, p. 409.

132 *Ibid.*, p. 406.

133 *Ibid.*, p. 407.

134 In this connection, cf. Martin L. Müller, *Bausparen in Deutschland zwischen Inflation und Währungsreform 1924–1948. Wohnungsbaufinanzierung im Spannungsfeld zwischen Staat und privaten und öffentlichen Bausparunternehmen* (Schriftenreihe der Zeitschrift für Unternehmensgeschichte, vol. 4), Munich, 1999, pp. 70 f.

135 "A. Utzinger," in *Elektrotechnische Zeitschrift*, December 28, 1922, p. 1539.

136 Ernst Durst, *Die Berufsausbildung des Mechanikers in der allgemeinen Feinmechanik*, 5th ed., Stuttgart, 1949.

137 Gottlob Honold, "Persönliche Erinnerungen," in *Bosch-Zünder* 1921/9, p. 236.

138 In the first 25 years, the apprentice department trained a total of 937 apprentices, only 288 of whom remained at Bosch. "Ansprache zum 25-jährigen Bestehen der Lehrlingsabteilung, 2. 7. 1938," RB 1 013 024.

139 "Die Lehrlings-Ausbildung bei der Robert Bosch A.-G." [Talk given by August Utzinger on November 26, 1921], in *Bosch-Zünder* 1922/1, p. 9.

140 "Lehrlingsausbildung bei den Bosch-Diensten," RB 1 043 008.

141 "Richtlinien für gewerbliche Lehrlinge der Robert Bosch A.-G." [undated], RB 1 043 008.

142 "Die Lehrlings-Ausbildung bei der Robert Bosch A.-G." [Talk given by August Utzinger on November 26, 1921], in *Bosch-Zünder* 1922/1, pp. 9 ff.

143 "Richtlinien für gewerbliche Lehrlinge der Robert Bosch A.-G." [undated], RB 1 043 008; Heuss, *Bosch*, p. 391.

144 Robert Bosch AG (ed.), *50 Jahre Bosch*, p. 274.

145 "Die Lehrlings-Ausbildung bei der Robert Bosch A.-G." [Talk given by August Utzinger on November 26, 1921], in *Bosch-Zünder* 1922/1, p. 9.

146 Robert Bosch AG (ed.), *50 Jahre Bosch*, p. 274.

147 Conrad Matschoß (ed.), *Robert Bosch und sein Werk*, Berlin, 1931, p. 85; Fastnacht, Kuhlgatz, Schmitt, Siegel, *125 years*, p. 203.

148 In this connection and on what follows, see Matschoß (ed.), *Bosch*, pp. 85 ff.; Robert Bosch AG (ed.), *50 Jahre Bosch*, pp. 232 ff.; "Die Gebäude der Robert Bosch A.-G. in Stuttgart und Feuerbach," in *Bosch-Zünder* 1920/3, pp. 46 ff.

149 "Die 'Bosch-Stadt'," in *Bosch-Zünder* 1930/1, p. 13.

5 The 1926 crisis, and diversification in the Great Depression

1 Heidrun Edelmann, "Der Umgang mit dem Rückstand. Deutschlands Automobil-industrie in der Zwischenkriegszeit," in Boch (ed.), *Geschichte*, pp. 42 f.; Flik, *Automobilindustrie*, pp. 71 f.
2 Merki, *Siegeszug*, p. 40.
3 Edelmann, *Luxusgut*, p. 111; Feldenkirchen, *Daimler*, p. 95; Flik, *Automobilindustrie*, p. 74.
4 Flik, *Automobilindustrie*, p. 74.
5 Carsten Thieme, "Krisenbewältigung durch Kooperation? Fusionsprozeß und Marktordnungsversuche bei Daimler-Benz 1924–1932," in Boch (ed.), *Geschichte*, pp. 95 f.; Gerald D. Feldman, "Die Deutsche Bank und die Automobilindustrie," in *Zeitschrift für Unternehmensgeschichte* 44, 1999/1, pp. 4 ff.; Feldenkirchen, *Daimler*, pp. 102 f.
6 Gerald D. Feldman, "The Deutsche Bank from World War to World Economic Crisis 1914–1933," in Lothar Gall, Gerald D. Feldman, Harold James, Carl-Ludwig Holtfrerich, Hans E. Büschgen, *The Deutsche Bank 1870–1995*, London, 1995, pp. 216 ff.
7 Günter Neliba, *Die Opel-Werke im Konzern von General Motors (1929–1948) in Rüsselsheim und Brandenburg. Produktion für Aufrüstung und Krieg ab 1935 unter nationalsozialistischer Herrschaft*, Frankfurt am Main, 2000, pp. 26 f., 32 ff.
8 In this connection, see pp. 130 ff.
9 Erich Klaiber, "Unsere neuen Magnetzünder," in *Bosch-Zünder* 1925/7, pp. 157 f.; Robert Bosch AG (ed.), *50 Jahre Bosch*, pp. 63 f.; Stolle, *Arbeiterpolitik*, p. 192.
10 Robert Bosch AG (ed.), *50 Jahre Bosch*, pp. 221 f.; Jürgen Bönig, *Die Einführung von Fließbandarbeit in Deutschland bis 1933. Zur Geschichte einer Sozialinnovation*, part 1, Münster, Hamburg, 1993, pp. 334, 340 ff.
11 "Friedrich Schildberger, Übersicht über den Bosch-Wettbewerb, 10. 9. 1948," pp. 1 f., RB 1 041 003. On battery-powered ignition systems, see also pp. 42 f., 77.
12 Quoted from Heuss, *Bosch*, p. 385.
13 In August 1925, 11,914 blue-collar and white-collar workers worked at Robert Bosch AG. With sales offices included, at the end of 1925 the Bosch payroll even stood at 12,862. "Jahresbericht für 1925," p. 1, RB 1 003 460; "Unser neuntes Geschäftsjahr," in *Bosch-Zünder* 1926/8, p. 175. Counting Robert Bosch Metallwerk AG as well, Bosch headcount totaled 14,188 at the end of 1925. Robert Bosch AG (ed.), *50 Jahre Bosch*, p. 292.
14 Robert Bosch, "Von Vergangenheit, Gegenwart und Zukunft," in *Bosch-Zünder* 1926/10, p. 223.
15 *Ibid.*
16 "Jahresbericht für 1926," p. 2, RB 1 003 461.
17 Cf. Ludwig Preller, *Sozialpolitik in der Weimarer Republik*, unamended reprint, Kronberg, Düsseldorf, 1978, pp. 364 ff.
18 Fastnacht, Kuhlgatz, Schmitt, Siegel, *125 years*, pp. 73 f.
19 Fritz Blaich, *Die Wirtschaftskrise von 1925/26 und die Reichsregierung. Von der Erwerbslosenfürsorge zur Konjunkturpolitik*, Kallmünz, 1977.
20 Thieme, "Krisenbewältigung," pp. 98 f.
21 "Lieber Geld verlieren als Vertrauen," in *Bosch-Zünder* 1919/2, p. 21.
22 "Jahresbericht für 1926," p. 2, RB 1 003 461.
23 Robert Bosch, "Von Vergangenheit, Gegenwart und Zukunft," in *Bosch-Zünder* 1926/10, p. 223.

24 "Unser neuntes Geschäftsjahr," in *Bosch-Zünder* 1926/8, p. 175.

25 Robert Bosch AG (ed.), *50 Jahre Bosch*, pp. 65 ff.; Robert Bosch GmbH (ed.), *Bosch Automotive*, p. 16.

26 "Friedrich Schildberger, Übersicht über den Bosch-Wettbewerb, 10. 9. 1948," p. 2, RB 1 041 003.

27 In this connection, see pp. 130 ff.

28 "Hans Walz, Grundsätzliche Betrachtungen, 1. 12. 1966," p. 4, RB 1 001 487.

29 *Ibid.*

30 "Price, Waterhouse & Co. an Robert Bosch AG, 13. 5. 1926," RB 1 003 015.

31 "Robert Bosch AG an Jakob Goldschmidt, 10. 4. 1926," BArch R 2/2006.

32 *Ibid.*

33 Robert Bosch AG (ed.), *50 Jahre Bosch*, p. 32; Heuss, *Bosch*, p. 385.

34 Heuss, *Bosch*, pp. 385 f.

35 "Ausarbeitung betr. Mea, 26. 9. 1941," p. 2, RB 1 022 037.

36 "Robert Bosch an Margarete Bosch, 14. 10. 1927," Zundel family private records, Nachlass Zundel [NL Zundel].

37 "Robert Bosch, Fortsetzung des Aufschriebs meiner Lebenserinnerungen, begonnen am 22. 5. 1930," p. 3, RB 1 014 007.

38 It is not clear whether the death of Hermann Borst, a brother of Hugo Borst who also worked for Bosch, had anything to do with these proceedings. Hermann Borst died in the spring of 1926. "Todesanzeige Hermann Borst," RB 1 044 001/4; Geissler, Borst (eds.), *Borst*, p. 16.

39 In this connection, see pp. 132 ff.

40 "Robert Bosch, Fortsetzung des Aufschriebs meiner Lebenserinnerungen, begonnen am 22. 5. 1930," p. 2, RB 1 014 007.

41 "Ergänzungen von Robert Bosch zu Theodor Bäuerle, 'Robert Bosch'," p. 76, RB 1 014 009.

42 "Borst an Heuss, 5. 5. 1944," RB 1 014 155.

43 Heuss, *Bosch*, p. 444.

44 "Robert Bosch, Fortsetzung des Aufschriebs meiner Lebenserinnerungen, begonnen am 22. 5. 1930," pp. 2 f., RB 1 014 007.

45 "Theodor Bäuerle, Robert Bosch. Persönliche Erinnerungen," p. 16 (sheet 17), RB 1 014 001.

46 Geissler, Borst (eds.), *Borst*, pp. 14 ff.

47 "Robert Bosch, Fortsetzung des Aufschriebs meiner Lebenserinnerungen, begonnen am 22. 5. 1930," p. 2, RB 1 014 007.

48 On Borst's death, his art collection passed to Stuttgart's *Staatsgalerie*, his library to the Württemberg *Landesbibliothek*.

49 The old board of management had consisted of Hugo Borst, Hermann Fellmeth, Otto Heins, Max Rall, Hans Walz, and Karl Martell Wild as full members and Hermann Bosch, Guido Gutmann, Richard Hochstetter, Emil Kirchdörfer, and Erich C. Rassbach as deputy members. In the new board of management appointed at the end of October 1926, Hans Walz, Karl Martell Wild, and Hermann Fellmeth were full members and Guido Gutmann, Max Rall, and Erich C. Rassbach deputies.

50 "Ungefähre Uebersicht über die Gliederung der Robert Bosch Aktiengesellschaft (1919)," RB 1 004 097.

51 "Umstrukturierung Anfang 1927" (organigram), *ibid.*

52 *Ibid.*, p. 83.

53 See above, p. 125.

54 See above, p. 109.

55 "Produktionsstatistik ab 1887," RB 1 007 075.

56 Stolle, *Arbeiterpolitik*, p. 200.

57 "Gliederung der Robert Bosch A.-G.," in *Bosch-Zünder* 1927/4, pp. 84 f.

58 Bönig, *Einführung*, p. 123.

59 "Denkschrift vom 28. 11. 1929," p. 3, RB 1 002 080.

60 *Ibid.*, pp. 3 f.

61 Bönig, *Einführung*, p. 335; Stolle, *Arbeiterpolitik*, pp. 191 f.

62 Stolle, *Arbeiterpolitik*, p. 202.

63 *Ibid.*, p. 195.

64 "FAL-Jahresberichte 1926–1929," RB 1 003 461–RB 1 003 464.

65 Stolle, *Arbeiterpolitik*, pp. 198 f., 324. Stolle takes a different view, concluding from a comparison with 1923 that "in the case of Bosch the theory of a rise in female labor remains unproven." *Ibid.*, p. 199.

66 Robert Bosch AG (ed.), *50 Jahre Bosch*, p. 143; Friedrich Schildberger, *Bosch und der Dieselmotor*, Stuttgart, 1950, pp. 22 f.

67 Bähr, Banken, Flemming, *MAN*, pp. 273 ff.

68 "Hermann Scholl, 40 Jahre elektronische Benzineinspritzung, Rede anlässlich des Symposiums in Frankfurt 11. 06. 2007," p. 5, RB 3 0005 764.

69 Robert Bosch AG (ed.), *50 Jahre Bosch*, p. 145; Robert Bosch GmbH (ed.), *Bosch Dieseleinspritzung. Höhepunkte eines Jahrhunderts. Ein Rundgang durch das Museum des Geschäftsbereichs Einspritzsysteme für Dieselmotoren*, Stuttgart [undated].

70 Robert Bosch AG (ed.), *50 Jahre Bosch*, p. 146.

71 Bähr, Banken, Flemming, *MAN*, p. 273.

72 Robert Bosch AG (ed.), *50 Jahre Bosch*, p. 146.

73 *Ibid.*, p. 147.

74 "Ergänzungen von Robert Bosch zu Theodor Bäuerle, 'Bosch'," p. 163, RB 1 014 009.

75 *Ibid.*

76 Lessing, *Bosch*, p. 127; "Wild an Rall 21./22. 1. 1925," RB 1 222 028 001.

77 "Ergänzungen von Robert Bosch zu Theodor Bäuerle, 'Robert Bosch'," p. 163, RB 1 014 009.

78 In November 1924, for instance, Kurt Wiesinger, professor of mechanical engineering at a major university, Zurich's ETH, attested to the Acro engine's "astonishingly favorable result," "Gutachten des Maschinen-Laboratoriums der Eidgenössischen Technischen Hochschule Zürich, Wiesinger, 17. 11. 1924," RB 1 222 028 001.

79 "Wild an Rall, 21./22. 1. 1925," *ibid.* (quotation); "Lippart an Debatin, 25. 2. 1952," RB 1 832 016. See also Lessing, *Bosch*, p. 128.

80 "Lippart an Debatin, 25. 2. 1952," RB 1 832 016; "Alfred Meyer, Erinnerungen," p. 10, *ibid.*; Lessing, *Bosch*, p. 128.

81 "Alfred Meyer, Erinnerungen," p. 10, RB 1 832 016.

82 "Bemerkung zu dem Entwurf eines Lizenzvertrages zwischen der Acro und Zoller (Mr/Kr.), 4. 2. 1925," RB 1 222 028 001.

83 Robert Bosch AG (ed.), *50 Jahre Bosch*, pp. 151 f.

84 *Ibid.*, p. 148.

85 *Ibid.*, p. 150.

86 "Alfred Meyer, Erinnerungen," p. 11, RB 1 832 016.

87 "Ergänzungen von Robert Bosch zu Theodor Bäuerle, 'Robert Bosch'," pp. 163 ff., RB 1 014 009.

88 In this connection, see pp. 121 ff.

89 Carl-Friedrich Baumann, *175 Jahre Henschel. Der ständige Weg in die Zukunft, 1810–1985*, Moers, 1985, p. 65.

90 Schildberger, *Bosch*, pp. 29 ff.; Eduard Klein, "50 Jahre M. A. N.-Fahrzeug-Dieselmotoren. Ein historischer Rückblick von der Geburtsstätte des Dieselmotors anlässlich des 50jährigen Jubiläums des kompressorlosen Fahrzeug-Dieselmotors," in *ATZ Automobiltechnische Zeitschrift*, 1973/4, pp. 115–17.

91 "Niederschrift über die Sitzung des Aufsichtsrats am 13. 9. 1932," RB 1 002 005.

92 "Mit diese Sache hast du deine Firma zum zweitenmal begründet." Fischer-Bosch, *Jugenderinnerungen*, p. 29. The quote also occurs in a similar form in "Ergänzungen von Robert Bosch zu Theodor Bäuerle, 'Robert Bosch',," pp. 163 ff., RB 1 014 009.

93 "Friedrich Schildberger, Übersicht über den Bosch-Wettbewerb, 10. 9. 1948," p. 2, RB 1 041 003.

94 "Denkschrift vom 28. 11. 1929," p. 3 (sheet 34), RB 1 002 080.

95 "Bosch an Bücher, 18. 5. 1928," RB 1 014 401.

96 "Denkschrift vom 28. 11. 1929," p. 3 (sheet 34), RB 1 002 080.

97 "Protokoll der 2. VAS am 12. 10. 1926," RB 1 002 077; Vera Dendler, "News from Barcelona. First office opens in Spain," in *Journal of Bosch History*, 2008, p. 7.

98 "Denkschrift vom 28. 11. 1929," p. 2 (sheet 33), RB 1 002 080.

99 "Protokoll der 26. VAS am 4. 12. 1929," *ibid.*

100 Vera Dendler, "The start of a lasting friendship. Franco-German manufacturing joint venture near Paris," in Robert Bosch GmbH (ed.), *Emergence of a global player*, pp. 27 f.

101 "Protokoll der 23. VAS am 1. 6. 1929," RB 1 002 080.

102 *Ibid.*

103 Heuss, *Bosch*, p. 430. Lucas had taken over its former rival C. A. Vandervell & Co. Ltd. (C.A.V.) in 1926.

104 "Niederschrift über die Aufsichtsratssitzung am 6. 6. 1930," RB 1 002 005.

105 "Umsätze RBMC ABMC, 7. 6. 1930," RB 1 011 016.

106 *Ibid.*; Banham, *Bosch*, pp. 32 f.

107 Banham, *Bosch*, pp. 32 f.

108 "Protokoll der 20. VAS am 7. 1. 1929," RB 1 002 080.

109 *Ibid.*

110 Banham, *Bosch*, p. 34.

111 *Ibid.*; Heuss, *Bosch*, pp. 379 f.

112 John Kenneth Galbraith, *The Great Crash 1929*, Boston, 1954.

113 "Denkschrift vom 28. 11. 1929," p. 16, RB 1 002 080.

114 "Protokoll der 26. VAS am 4. 12. 1929," *ibid.*; "American Bosch Corporation, 9. 6. 1941," p. 2d, RB 1 022 031 004.

115 "American Bosch Corporation, 9. 6. 1941," p. 1, RB 1 022 031 004.

116 Thieme, "Krisenbewältigung," p. 99. In 1926, 32,000 passenger cars were produced in Germany. In 1932, the number was 36,000. *Ibid.* In connection with the decline in sales in the automobile industry during the Great Depression, see also Edelmann, *Luxusgut*, pp. 129 ff.

117 "Unser vierzehntes Geschäftsjahr," in *Bosch-Zünder* 1931/6, p. 121.

118 *Ibid.*

119 Quoted in Thomas Schnabel, *Geschichte von Baden und Württemberg 1900–1952*, published by Haus der Geschichte Baden-Württemberg, Stuttgart, 2000, p. 135.

120 *Ibid.* In this connection, see also Thomas Schnabel, "'Warum geht es in Schwaben besser?' Württemberg in der Weltwirtschaftskrise 1928–1933," in Thomas Schnabel (ed.), *Die Machtergreifung in Südwestdeutschland. Das Ende der Weimarer Republik in Baden und Württemberg 1928–1933*, Stuttgart, 1982, pp. 184–209.

121 "Württemberg ist noch besser dran …," in *Bosch-Zünder* 1933/1, pp. 1 f.

122 "Jahresbericht der Fabrikleitung 1930," pp. 1, 4, RB 1 003 465.

123 "Jahresbericht der Fabrikleitung 1931," p. 1, RB 1 003 466.

124 Heinrich August Winkler, *Der Weg in die Katastrophe. Arbeiter und Arbeiterbewegung in der Weimarer Republik 1930 bis 1933*, Berlin, Bonn, 1987, p. 24.

125 "Jahresberichte der Fabrikleitung 1931–1933," RB 1 003 466–RB 1 003 468.

126 "Unser fünfzehntes Geschäftsjahr," in *Bosch-Zünder* 1932/9, p. 169.

127 *Ibid.*, pp. 169 f. For sales development, see the appendix, p. 663, "Bosch Group headcount and sales revenue (1886–2012)."

128 In 1930, the company's export sales came to roughly 20 million reichsmarks. In both 1931 und 1932 they stood at around 26 million reichsmarks. "Niederschrift über die Sitzung des Aufsichtsrats vom 7. 3. 1935," RB 1 002 005. For the percentage of exports in sales overall, see the appendix, p. 663, "Bosch Group headcount and sales revenue (1886–2012)."

129 "Produktionsstatistik ab 1887," RB 1 007 075.

130 "Jahresbericht der Fabrikleitung 1932," p. 1, RB 1 003 467; Feldenkirchen, *Siemens*, p. 663; "Kennzahlen der Daimler-Motoren-Gesellschaft, von Benz & Cie. und der Daimler-Benz AG," Daimler AG, Mercedes-Benz Archives and Collection; Christian Pierer, *Die Bayerischen Motorenwerke bis 1933. Eine Unternehmensgründung in Krieg, Inflation und Weltwirtschaftskrise*, Munich, 2011, p. 228; Manfred Grunert, Florian Triebel, *Das Unternehmen BMW seit 1916*, Munich, 2006, pp. 578 ff.; Bähr, Banken, Flemming, *MAN*, p. 268.

131 See table 9, p. 142.

132 *Ibid.*

133 "Unser sechzehntes Geschäftsjahr," in *Bosch-Zünder* 1933/3, p. 33.

134 At Daimler-Benz, differentiated working times of between 38 and 48 hours a week were introduced in 1932. Thilo Lang, *Das Investitionsverhalten Metall verarbeitender Unternehmen in Württemberg 1924–1936. Zwischen Rationalisierungsmaßnahmen und Kapazitätserweiterungen* (Stuttgarter historische Studien zur Landes- und Wirtschaftsgeschichte, vol. 5), Ostfildern, 2004, p. 114.

135 "Wir Arbeiter und die Wirtschaftskrise," in *Bosch-Zünder* 1931/11, p. 259.

136 *Ibid.*

137 "Jahresbericht der Fabrikleitung 1933," p. 1, RB 1 003 468.

138 Robert Bosch, *Die Verhütung künftiger Krisen in der Weltwirtschaft*, Stuttgart, 1932 (offprint from the periodical *Paneuropa*, May 1932). Quotes on pp. 19, 23.

139 "Bosch an Max Fischer, 5. 4. 1928," RB 1 014 566.

140 "Protokoll der 2. VAS vom 12. 10. 1926," RB 1 002 077.

141 "Ideal-Werke für drahtlose Telefonie A. G., 18. 9. 1941/9. 11. 1950," RB 1 011 140 001. On the conflict with AEG over AEG-Mea, see p. 100.

142 Robert Bosch AG (ed.), *50 Jahre Bosch*, p. 184.

143 "Produktionsstatistik ab 1887," RB 1 007 075.

144 Robert Bosch AG (ed.), *50 Jahre Bosch*, pp. 184 ff.

145 *Ibid.*, pp. 191 ff.; Bettina Höcherl, "A helping hand in every kitchen. The Bosch refrigerator," in *Journal of Bosch History*, 2008, pp. 18 f.

146 "Niederschrift der Aufsichtsratssitzung vom 9. 3. 1933," RB 1 002 005.

147 Robert Bosch AG (ed.), *50 Jahre Bosch*, p. 191.

148 "10-Jahresbericht des BTH3 (1. 4. 1930–31. 3. 1940)," pp. 1 f., RB 1 010 443.

149 *Ibid.*, pp. 1 ff.; "Daten zur Geschichte der Bosch-Erzeugnisse 1887–1939, 7. 3. 1960," RB 1 010 024 006.

150 Blaupunkt GmbH (ed.), *Blaupunkt. Die Werbegeschichte einer Marke*, Hildesheim, 2007, p. 11; Manfred Overesch, *Bosch in Hildesheim 1937–1945. Freies Unternehmertum und nationalsozialistische Rüstungspolitik*, Göttingen, 2008, p. 278.

151 See p. 150.

152 "Ideal-Werke für drahtlose Telefonie A. G., 18. 9. 1941/9. 11. 1950," RB 1 011 140 001.

153 "Bericht des Vorstandes über das vierzehnte Geschäftsjahr," in *Bosch-Zünder* 1931/6, p. 122.

154 "Bericht des Vorstandes über das siebzehnte Geschäftsjahr," in *Bosch-Zünder* 1934/3, p. 41.

155 Kilian J. L. Steiner, *Ortsempfänger, Volksempfänger und Optaphon. Die Entwicklung der deutschen Radio- und Fernsehindustrie und das Unternehmen Loewe, 1923–1962*, Essen, 2005, pp. 125 ff.

156 *Ibid.*, pp. 123 ff.; Otto R. Oeschner, "50 Jahre Fernsehtechnik bei Bosch," in "Bosch Fernseh 1929–1979," MS, 1979, RB 1 610 021.

157 Steiner, *Ortsempfänger*, p. 124.

158 Rainer Haus, Hans Sarkowicz, *Using energy more efficiently. 75 years of thermotechnology from Bosch*, Munich, 2007, pp. 99 ff. On the foundation of Junkers & Co. GmbH and how Hugo Junkers saw himself as an entrepreneur, see also Lutz Budraß, *Flugzeugindustrie und Luftrüstung in Deutschland 1918–1945* (Schriften des Bundesarchivs, 50), Düsseldorf, 1998, pp. 42 ff.

159 "OMGUS, Property Division, Decartelization Branch. In Sachen des Bosch-Konzerns, Feststellungen und Anordnungen," pp. 19 f., RB 1 011 135; Heuss, *Bosch*, p. 452.

160 "OMGUS, Property Division, Decartelization Branch. In Sachen des Bosch-Konzerns, Feststellungen und Anordnungen," pp. 19 f., RB 1 011 135. According to a different version, the trustee installed at Junkers by Deutsche Bank approached Bosch in connection with the search for a buyer. "Aktennotiz über den Verkauf von Junkers & Co. GmbH, 29. 8. 1941," Landeshauptarchiv Sachsen-Anhalt, Abt. Dessau [subsequently LHASA, DE] "Junkers Wärmetechnik Dessau," no. 35, sheet 1; "Bosch an Junkers, 15. 11. 1932," *ibid.*, sheet 43. On the history of Junkers and the 1932 sale, see also "Kurzer Abriss aus der Geschichte der Firma Junkers & Co. G.m.b.H., Dessau (Ico)," LHASA, DE "Junkers, Wärmetechnik Dessau," sheet 51.

161 "Aktennotiz über den Verkauf von Junkers & Co. GmbH, 29. 8. 1941," LHASA, DE, "Junkers Wärmetechnik Dessau," no. 35, sheet 1; "Bosch an Junkers, 15. 11. 1932," *ibid.*, sheet. 43.

162 Budraß, *Flugzeugindustrie*, pp. 320 ff.; Haus, Sarkowicz, *Using energy*, pp. 112 f.

163 Heuss, *Bosch*, pp. 458 f.; "OMGUS, Property Division, Decartelization Branch. In Sachen des Bosch-Konzerns, Feststellungen und Anordnungen," p. 21, RB 1 011 135.

164 "OMGUS, Property Division, Decartelization Branch. In Sachen des Bosch-Konzerns, Feststellungen und Anordnungen," pp. 21 f., RB 1 011 135. On Scintilla AG, see p. 161.

165 "Die 'Noris' Zünd-Licht A. G. vom 1. 1. 1926 bis 31. 12. 1926," pp. 1 ff., 7, RB 1 022 036 007. From 1957, Noris Zündlicht AG was run as the Nuremberg plant of Robert Bosch GmbH. On Südinteressen GmbH, see "OMGUS, Property Division, Decartelization Branch. In Sachen des Bosch-Konzerns, Feststellungen und Anordnungen," p. 21 f., RB 1 011 135.

166 "OMGUS, Property Division, Decartelization Branch. In Sachen des Bosch-Konzerns, Feststellungen und Anordnungen," p. 21, RB 1 011 135.

167 Eisemann-Werke, Noris Zünd-Licht AG, and Eugen Bauer GmbH subsequently became part of Robert Bosch GmbH, while Junkers & Co. was absorbed into Bosch Thermotechnik GmbH and Blaupunkt GmbH into the Car Multimedia division. Bosch parted company with the Blaupunkt brand and the car-radio and navigation-system aftermarket business in 2008.

II. Bosch in the Third Reich (1933–1945)

1 The Bosch Group in the economic upswing of National Socialism (1933–1939)

1 Christoph Buchheim, "Die Erholung von der Weltwirtschaftskrise 1932/33 in Deutschland," in *Jahrbuch für Wirtschaftsgeschichte*, 2003, 1, pp. 13 ff.

2 "Unser sechzehntes Geschäftsjahr," in *Bosch-Zünder* 1933/3, p. 33.

3 Buchheim, "Erholung," pp. 18 ff.

4 "Gesetz über Änderung des Kraftfahrzeugsteuergesetzes.? Vom 10. April 1932," in *RGBl.* I 1933, p. 192. A few weeks later owners of older vehicles were allowed to defray all future automobile license taxation with a single lump-sum payment.

5 Feldenkirchen, *Daimler*, p. 123; Edelmann, *Luxusgut*, pp. 157 ff.

6 Edelmann, *Luxusgut*, p. 167.

7 Dorothee Hochstetter, *Motorisierung und "Volksgemeinschaft." Das Nationalsozialistische Kraftfahr-Korps (NSKK) 1931–1945*, Munich, 2005, p. 185. See also Edelmann, *Luxusgut*, p. 167.

8 As late as 1938 the army accounted for barely 5 percent of sales in the German automotive industry. Edelmann, *Luxusgut*, pp. 196 f.

9 "Bericht des Vorstandes über das siebzehnte Geschäftsjahr," in *Bosch-Zünder* 1934/3, p. 41.

10 Robert Bosch, "Das Auto für das ganze Volk," in *Bosch-Zünder* 1933/3, p. 36.

11 Robert Bosch AG, 1934 annual report, Stuttgart, 1935, p. 3.

12 Unlike in the tax balance sheet, hidden reserves did not have to be shown in the commercial balance sheet. The tax balance sheets of Robert Bosch AG/GmbH from this period could not be found. On the problem of the various assessment provisions in commercial and tax balance sheets at this time, see also Mark Spoerer, *Von Scheingewinnen zum Rüstungsboom. Die Eigenkapitalrentabilität der deutschen Industrieaktiengesellschaften 1925–1941 (VSWG, supplement 123)*, Stuttgart, 1996, pp. 62 ff.

13 According to these, in the 1940 financial year Bosch made a net profit of approximately 29.9 million reichsmarks, whereas the profit shown in the annual report was 3.4 million reichsmarks. The hidden reserves formed by the end of 1940 came to 106 million reichsmarks. "Bericht der Deutschen Revisions- und Treuhand-Aktiengesellschaft Berlin über die bei der Robert Bosch GmbH, Stuttgart, vorgenommene Prüfung des Jahresabschlusses zum 31. 12. 1940," p. 17, RB 1 003 093; Robert Bosch GmbH, 1940 annual report, p. 14.

14 "Unser achtes Geschäftsjahr," in *Bosch-Zünder* 1925/7, p. 155; Robert Bosch GmbH, 1941 annual report, p. 18.

15 "Bericht der Deutschen Revisions- und Treuhand-Aktiengesellschaft Berlin über die bei der Robert Bosch GmbH vorgenommene Prüfung des Jahresabschlusses zum 31. 12. 1940," p. 62, RB 1 003 093.

16 So said Erich Carl Rassbach in the board of management meeting of June 8, 1938. See "Protokoll der Vorstandssitzung am 8. 6. 1938," RB 1 002 088.

17 "Bipartite Control Office, Bipartite Decartelization Commission, Bosch Report, vol. I, Final Determination and Order," p. 3, U.S. National Archives and Records Administration [subsequently, NARA] RG 260, 17/252/1–1; "OMGUS, Property Division, Decartelization Branch. In Sachen des Bosch-Konzerns, Feststellungen und Anordnungen," p. 3, RB 1 011 135.

18 See the appendix, p. 663 ff., "Bosch group headcount and sales revenue (1886–2012)."

19 Robert Bosch AG, 1936 annual report, p. 3.

20 On the conversion to a GmbH, see, p. 166 ff. The main difference between the board of management of the GmbH and the AG was that henceforth Robert Bosch belonged to the former as chairman, having chaired the supervisory board hitherto. Otherwise, there were only two changes. In 1933, Erich Carl Rassbach, a former deputy member of the board of management, became a full *Geschäftsführer,* and at the same time Ernst Durst, who had not been a member of the board of management of the AG, rose to become a deputy *Geschäftsführer.*

21 Robert Bosch AG, 1936 annual report, p. 7.

22 Robert Bosch AG, 1935 annual report, p. 8; Robert Bosch GmbH, 1938 annual report, p. 11; "WOL Jahresbericht 1941," p. 1, RB 1 003 476.

23 "Jahresbericht der Fabrikleitung 1933," RB 1 003 468; "WOL Jahresbericht 1941," p. 1, RB 1 003 476.

24 Robert Bosch AG (ed.), *50 Jahre Bosch*, pp. 264 f.

25 Otto Debatin, "Freiwillige Leistungen der Robert Bosch A.-G. für ihre Gefolgschaft," in *Bosch-Zünder* 1927/10, p. 181. In this connection, see also Robert Bosch AG (ed.), *50 Jahre Bosch*, p. 269. On the development of wages in the Württemberg metal-working industry at the time, see also Lang, *Investitionsverhalten*, pp. 182 ff.

26 Robert Bosch AG (ed.), *50 Jahre Bosch*, pp. 262, 267. For more about this publication, see p. 175.

27 "10-Jahresbericht des BTH3 (1. 4. 1930–31. 3. 1940), 19. 4. 1940," p. 14, RB 1 010 443.

28 Robert Bosch AG, 1935 annual report, p. 5; Robert Bosch AG, 1936 annual report, p. 5; Hans-Christoph Graf von Seherr-Thoss, *Die deutsche Automobilindustrie. Eine Dokumentation von 1886 bis heute,* Stuttgart, 1974, p. 315.

29 "Protokoll der Vorstandssitzung am 8. 6. 1938," RB 1 002 088.

30 On the emergence of the Volkswagen factory, see Hans Mommsen, Manfred Grieger, *Das Volkswagenwerk und seine Arbeiter im Dritten Reich*, Düsseldorf, 1996.

31 Robert Bosch GmbH, 1938 annual report, p. 5; Heuss, *Bosch*, pp. 576 f.

32 "Protokoll der Vorstandssitzung am 8. 6. 1938," RB 1 002 088.

33 *Ibid.*

34 *Ibid.*

35 *Ibid.*

36 Karl Martell Wild provided this information. *Ibid.*

37 "Protokoll der Vorstandssitzung am 8. 6. 1938," RB 1 002 088.

38 Edelmann, *Luxusgut*, pp. 193 ff.

39 In this connection, see pp. 202 ff.

40 "OMGUS, Property Division, Decartelization Branch. In Sachen des Bosch-Konzerns, Feststellungen und Anordnungen," p. 22, RB 1 011 135.

41 Bosch purchased 50.9 percent of the capital stock of Scintilla in 1935. Initially, this holding was in the possession of two of the Bosch Group's Swiss asset-management companies, Industria Kontor AG and Robertina AG, headed by a Zurich attorney, Gustav Hürlimann. The development of the Bosch holding in Scintilla AG is documented in RB 1 022 054. See also "Gouvernement Provisoire de la République Française, Ministère des Finances, Affaire Scintilla" [undated], Archives du Ministère des affaires étrangères et européennes, La Courneuve, 2 AEF 3168. On the history of Scintilla AG, see "Geschichte der Scintilla AG," MS, RB 1 608 001; "25 Jahre deutsch-schweizerische Verwaltungsbank AG 1933–1958," MS, pp. 30 ff., RB 1 608 002.

42 "10-Jahresbericht des BTH3 (1. 4. 1930–31. 3. 1940)," p. 2, RB 1 010 443.

43 "Bericht des Wirtschaftsprüfers Dr. Gustav Trauth über die Prüfung der wirtschaftlichen Entwicklung von Kriegsende bis zum 20. 6. 1948 bei der Metallerzbergbau Westmark GmbH, Traben-Trarbach," Landeshauptarchiv Koblenz [subsequently LHA Koblenz] 540, 001, no. 486; "Rechtsanwälte Dr. Pfander, Dr. Drescher, Peter Rößler, Dr. Franck an die Restitutionskammer beim Landgericht Koblenz, 11. 5. 1949," LHA Koblenz 583.1, no. 4020.

44 "OMGUS, Property Division, Decartelization Branch. In Sachen des Bosch-Konzerns, Feststellungen und Anordnungen," p. 20, RB 1 011 135.

45 Robert Bosch GmbH, 1937 annual report, p. 8.

46 "Aktenvermerk über eine Rücksprache mit Herrn Dr. Banneitz am 21. 1. 1935 und mit Herrn Staatssekretär Ohnesorge und Herrn Dr. Banneitz im Reichspostministerium am 31. 1. 1935," RB 1 610 021.

47 On the "aryanization" of Loewe's holding in FESE, see pp. 191 f. See also Steiner, *Ortsempfänger*, pp. 222 ff., 229 ff.

48 Otto R. Oeschner, "50 Jahre Fernsehtechnik bei Bosch," in "Bosch Fernseh 1929–1979," MS, 1979, p. 2, RB 1 610 021.

49 "Prospekt der Fernseh Aktiengesellschaft, Berlin (1938)," RB 1 610 002; "Der Einheits-Fernsehempfänger E 1," *ibid.*

50 Robert Bosch AG, 1936–1937 annual reports; Haus, Sarkowicz, *Using energy*, p. 114.

51 Robert Bosch AG, 1938 annual report, p. 8; Haus, Sarkowicz, *Using energy*, p. 114; "OMGUS, Property Division, Decartelization Branch. In Sachen des Bosch-Konzerns, Feststellungen und Anordnungen," p. 20, RB 1 011 135.

52 Robert Bosch GmbH, 1938 annual report, p. 9; Robert Bosch AG, 1935 annual report, p. 6.

53 Robert Bosch GmbH, 1936–1938 annual reports.

54 Wolfgang König, "Der Volksempfänger und die Radioindustrie. Ein Beitrag zum Verhältnis von Wirtschaft und Politik im Nationalsozialismus," in *Vierteljahrschrift für Sozial- und Wirtschaftsgeschichte* 90, 2003, p. 269–89; Wolfgang König, *Volkswagen, Volksempfänger, Volksgemeinschaft. "Volksprodukte" im Dritten Reich. Vom Scheitern einer nationalsozialistischen Konsumgesellschaft*, Paderborn, 2004.

55 Robert Bosch GmbH, 1938 annual report, p. 9.

56 "Blaupunkt-Werke GmbH an Robert Bosch GmbH, Patent- und Lizenzabteilung, 27. 9. 1948," RB 1 011 137 001; Robert Bosch GmbH, 1938 annual report, p. 9.

57 "Bericht Körber über einen Besuch bei Magneti-Marelli am 29. 4. 1935," RB 1 034 046; "Bericht Körber über eine Unterredung mit Herrn Bruno Quintavalle, Marelli-MABO, am 30. 10. 1936," *ibid.*; Robert Bosch GmbH (ed.), *Bosch dal 1904 in Italia*, Milan, 2004, pp. 43 ff.

58 On the establishment of C.A.V.-Bosch Ltd., see p. 137.

59 "Lucas said that it was the approach of the 1939 war which enabled it to do that." Competition Commission, *Report on the Supply of Electrical Equipment for Mechanically Propelled Land Vehicles, 18. 12. 1963*, part II, p. 32, http://webarchive.

nationalarchives.gov.uk/20140402141250////www.competition-commission.org. uk/rep_pub/reports/1960_1969/ fulltext/025c03.pdf.

60 The sale was clearly thought of as a temporary solution only, as the Bosch legal adviser Karl Eugen Thomä reported in a discussion held in November 1940: "On the basis of certain agreements made with Lucas at the time and because of our engineering capabilities, there is reason to hope that, regardless of the military outcome of hostilities with Britain, in years to come we shall be able to re-occupy what for us – technically and financially speaking – is a favorable position vis-à-vis C A.V." "Karl Thomä, Aufzeichnung vom 5. 11. 1940," RB 1 011 107.

61 Heuss, *Bosch*, p. 601; Dendler, "Start," pp. 26 ff.

62 "Karl Thomä, Aufzeichnung vom 5. 11. 1940," p. 7, RB 1 011 107; Scholtyseck, *Bosch*, p. 420. On the cession of the foreign holdings to the Mendelssohn Group in Amsterdam and their repurchase during the war, see pp. 203 f., 206 f.

63 UABC sales stood at 3.4 million USD in 1933 and rose to 9.2 million USD by 1937 before falling, after the sale of the radio business, to 3.5 million USD in 1938. "American Bosch Corporation, 21. 12. 1939 (Abschrift des Berichts Dr. Fischer)," RB 1 011 081.

64 *Ibid.* On the sale of UABC shares to the Mendelssohn Group in Amsterdam and their repurchase during the war, see pp. 203 ff.

65 Distribution of proprietary rights was disguised with the aid of two Czech attorneys. Following the occupation of Prague, Ideal Radio AG was able to reveal its true identity, which was welcomed at Bosch. "Karl Thomä, Aufzeichnung vom 5. 11. 1940," p. 8, RB 1 011 107.

66 "Bericht über die Robert Bosch GmbH, Prag" [undated], RB 1 022 029.

67 "Karl Thomä, Aufzeichnung vom 5. 11. 1940," p. 8, RB 1 011 107.

68 Among the consequences of the second Sino-Japanese war were the establishment of a new Bosch Service garage in Peking and new Bosch departments in the Manchuria region. Walter Genthner, "Ein Bosch-Mann reist nach China," in *Bosch-Zünder* 1939/5, pp. 98 ff.; Bähr, Lesczenski, Schmidtpott, *Handel*, pp. 144 f.

69 Fastnacht, Kuhlgatz, Schmitt, Siegel, *125 years*, pp. 202 f.

70 In this connection, see pp. 193 ff.

71 According to Deutsche Revisions- und Treuhand AG (DRT), between 1939 and 1940 sales at Robert Bosch GmbH increased from 223.6 million reichsmarks to 229.1 million reichsmarks. However, subtracting DMLG sales over the same period leaves a decline from 199.7 million reichsmarks (1939) to 185.2 million reichsmarks (1940). "Bericht der Deutschen Revisions- und Treuhand-Aktiengesellschaft Berlin über die bei der Robert Bosch GmbH vorgenommene Prüfung des Jahresabschlusses zum 31. 12. 1940," pp. 21 f., RB 1 003 093.

72 *Ibid.*

73 Heuss also took the view that it was of purely "formal significance," because the company had never been an anonymous stock corporation, but had always retained "the character of a private family enterprise." Heuss, *Bosch*, p. 602.

74 Heuss even assumed that, taken together, heirs whom Robert Bosch did not know occupied "in power terms, a stronger position" than the founder's own heirs. *Ibid.*, p. 277.

75 In this connection, see pp. 122 ff.

76 "Nur die Tatsache ist mir bekannt: die Stunde der Gründung war eine der schwersten meines Lebens." Quoted from Heuss, *Bosch*, p. 275.

77 Johannes Bähr, Axel Drecoll, Bernhard Gotto, *Flick im Dritten Reich*, Munich, 2008, pp. 111 f.

78 Prompted by lessons learnt during the Great Depression, an emergency decree of September 1931 had already introduced important reforms. In this connection, see Sylvia Engelke, Reni Maltschew, "Weltwirtschaftskrise, Aktienskandale und Reaktionen des Gesetzgebers durch Notverordnungen im Jahre 1931," in Walter Bayer, Mathias Habersack (eds.), *Aktienrecht im Wandel, vol. I: Entwicklung des Aktienrechts*, Tübingen, 2007, pp. 570–618.

79 "Gesetz über Aktiengesellschaften und Kommanditgesellschaften auf Aktien vom 30. 1. 1937," in *RGBl.* I 1937, pp. 107–65. In this connection, see also Johannes Bähr, "Unternehmens- und Kapitalmarktrecht im 'Dritten Reich'. Die Aktienrechtsreform und das Anleihestockgesetz," in Johannes Bähr, Ralf Banken (eds.), *Wirtschaftssteuerung durch Recht im Nationalsozialismus. Studien zur Entwicklung des Wirtschaftsrechts im Interventionsstaat des "Dritten Reichs"* (Studien zur europäischen Rechtsgeschichte, vol. 199), Frankfurt am Main, 2006, pp. 50 ff.

80 "Gesetz über Aktiengesellschaften und Kommanditgesellschaften auf Aktien vom 30. 1. 1937," in *RGBl.* I 1937, pp. 159 f. (§ 257).

81 "Niederschrift über die Aufsichtsratssitzung am 10. 12. 1937," p. 3, RB 1 002 005.

82 This view can still be found in the chronicle published to mark the company's centenary. See Hans Konradin Herdt, *Bosch 1886–1986. Porträt eines Unternehmens*, Stuttgart, 1986, p. 85.

83 E.g. "Robert Bosch AG wird GmbH," in *Berliner Tageblatt*, 11. 12. 1937. Between 1935 and 1938, the number of AGs in Germany fell from 7,840 to 5,353. Bähr, "Unternehmens- und Kapitalmarktrecht," p. 55.

84 "Niederschrift über die Aufsichtsratssitzung am 10. 12. 1937," RB 1 002 005.

2 "Corporate community" versus "people's community": Bosch, the NSDAP, and the National Socialist regime

1 Bosch and Walz, together with Theodor Bäuerle, had jointly founded the local Stuttgart branch of the League of Defense against Anti-Semitism [*Verein zur Abwehr des Antisemitismus*] in 1926. Created in Berlin in 1890, the League had since the 1920s worked hand-in-hand with the German Democratic Party [DDP], to which Bosch was sympathetic.

2 Otto Schwarz, "Vom Werden und Wirken der Betriebszelle Bosch der NSBO," in *Bosch-Zünder* 1934/4, pp. 74 f.

3 "Hans Walz, Beilage zum Fragebogen: Kurze Darstellung der Beziehungen zur NSDAP und SS, 27. 8. 1945," p. 1, RB 1 013 033.

4 See also Scholtyseck, *Verständigung*; "Willy Schloßstein, Betrifft: Einstellung des Herrn Robert Bosch und seiner Mitarbeiter zum Nazi-Regime, 20. 1. 1947," p. 3, Staatsarchiv Ludwigsburg [subsequently StA Ludwigsburg] EL 902/20, Bü 87568.

5 "Bosch an Keppler, 23. 2. 1933," reprinted in Becker, Scholtyseck, *Bosch*, p. 178. In March 1933, following a conversation with Robert Bosch in Berlin, Georg Escherich noted that "[Bosch] is clever enough to come to terms with the present situation" and that he had "established contact with the new government." "Tagebuch Georg Escherich 1933, Eintrag 17. 3.," Bayerisches Hauptstaatsarchiv, Nachlass Escherich 20; Scholtyseck, *Bosch*, p. 119.

6 Paul Sauer, *Württemberg in der Zeit des Nationalsozialismus*, Ulm, 1975, pp. 26 ff.; Thomas Schnabel, *Württemberg zwischen Weimar und Bonn 1928 bis 1945/46* (Schriften zur politischen Landeskunde Baden-Württembergs, vol. 143), Stuttgart, 1986, pp. 181 ff. For biographical details of Murr, see Paul Sauer, *Wilhelm Murr. Hit-*

lers Statthalter in Württemberg, Tübingen, 1998; Joachim Scholtyseck, "'Der Mann aus dem Volk.' Wilhelm Murr, Gauleiter und Reichsstatthalter in Württemberg-Hohenzollern," in Michael Kißener, Joachim Scholtyseck (eds.), *Die Führer der Provinz. NS-Biographien aus Baden und Württemberg* (Karlsruher Beiträge zur Geschichte, 2), Konstanz, 1997, pp. 477–502; Walter Nachtmann, "Wilhelm Murr und Karl Strölin. Die 'Führer' der Nazis in Stuttgart," in Hermann G. Abmayr (ed.), *Stuttgarter NS-Täter. Vom Mitläufer bis zum Massenmörder*, Stuttgart, 2009, pp. 187–97.

7 Schnabel, *Württemberg*, p. 183. Under the Reichstag Fire Decree of February 27, 1933, anyone suspected of "views hostile to the state" could be arrested without charge and without evidence and taken into "preventive custody."

8 Quoted from Scholtyseck, *Verständigung*, p. 82.

9 "Hans Walz, Beilage zum Fragebogen: Kurze Darstellung der Beziehungen zur NSDAP und SS, 27. 8. 1945," p. 1, RB 1 013 033; Scholtyseck, *Bosch*, pp. 119 f.

10 "Bosch an Escherich, 15. 3. 1933," reprinted in Becker, Scholtyseck, *Bosch*, pp. 180 ff.

11 "Bosch an Rümelin, 12. 4. 1933," quoted from Scholtyseck, *Bosch*, p. 120.

12 "Bosch an Escherich, 15. 5. 1933," reprinted in Becker, Scholtyseck, *Bosch*, p. 180.

13 "Schloßstein an die Spruchkammer Stuttgart, 20. 7. 1947," p. 12, RB 1 013 109.

14 "Bosch an Mauk, 22. 9. 1933," RB 1 014 081; Scholtyseck, *Bosch*, pp. 127 f.

15 "Bosch an Mauk, 3. 10. 1933," RB 1 014 081; "Bosch an Keppler, 9. 1. 1934," RB 1 014 582 (quote); "Bosch an Keppler, 13. 1. 1934," *ibid.*; Scholtyseck, *Bosch*, p. 128.

16 Heuss, *Bosch*, p. 597; Sabine Brantl, *Haus der Kunst, München. Ein Ort und seine Geschichte im Nationalsozialismus*, published by Haus der Kunst, München, Munich, 2007, pp. 56–63.

17 "Hans Walz, Beilage zum Fragebogen: Kurze Darstellung der Beziehungen zur NSDAP und SS, 27. 8. 1945," RB 1 013 033. For a similar view, see "Otto Debatin, Robert Bosch GmbH und NSDAP," p. 3, RB 1 013 078.

18 "NSDAP-Mitgliedskarte Hans Walz," BArch 31XX Reichskartei der NSDAP; Scholtyseck, *Bosch*, p. 153. Schloßstein's NSDAP membership was in fact subsequently declared invalid on the grounds that he was married to a "half-Jewess." "Schloßstein an die Spruchkammer Stuttgart, 20. 7. 1947," RB 1 013 109, sheets 2 ff.

19 Scholtyseck writes that Fellmeth applied for admittance to the NSDAP together with Walz and Wild, which is incorrect. Fellmeth became a supporting member of the SS (often chosen as an "alternative" to NSDAP membership) in 1934. Scholtyseck, *Bosch*, p. 153; "Spruchkammer Stuttgart, Spruch gegen Hermann Fellmeth vom 6. 3. 1947," p. 7, StA Ludwigsburg EL 902/20, Bü 93826; "Erklärung Fellmeth vom 23. 1. 1947," RB 1 013 060, sheet 11.

20 The fact that Rassbach became a supporting member of the SS is particularly noteworthy since he was American and took German citizenship (in response to political pressure) only in the autumn of 1940. "Meldebogen Erich Carl Rassbach, 25. 4. 1946," StA Ludwigsburg EL 902/20, Bü 104068; "Erich C. Rassbach, Eidesstattliche Erklärung, 13. 10. 1947," *ibid.*

21 According to Heuss, the state's top hunting official [*Landesjägermeister*] made a vain attempt to convince Robert Bosch to join the NSDAP. Heuss, *Bosch*, p. 597. A second, likewise unsuccessful attempt was made by the SS officer Gottlob Berger, who knew Bosch well. Scholtyseck, *Bosch*, pp. 152, 602, note 199. On the Berger connection, see pp. 177 f.

22 On the subject of Daimler-Benz, see also Feldenkirchen, *Daimler*, pp. 137 f.; Hans Pohl, Stephanie Habeth, Beate Brüninghaus, *Die Daimler-Benz AG in den Jahren*

1933 bis 1945. Eine Dokumentation (Zeitschrift für Unternehmensgeschichte, Supplement 47), Stuttgart, 1986, pp. 19 f.

23 Scholtyseck, *Bosch*, p. 159; "Gottlob Berger, Zur Geschichte der Robert Bosch GmbH 1933–1948," p. 3, RB 1 013 084.

24 "Anlage I/ zu Frage 8 (Anhang zu: Hans Walz, Beilage zum Fragebogen: Kurze Darstellung der Beziehungen zur NSDAP und SS, 27. 8. 1945)," RB 1 013 033, sheet 16. The available personal files of the SS do not give the date of joining. Walz's SS officer file begins only with his appointment as *Untersturmführer* in September 1938. "SS-Personalbogen Hans Walz," BArch SSO/220B. Initially Walz meant to join the SA, but Murr blocked this.

25 As Walz described it, the connection with the SS was through payments that this organization literally extorted from Bosch and other companies. In return, the SS offered the prospect of protection from intervention by the party machine and "investing our people, the better to protect their companies, with a rank in the SS." Robert Bosch and his colleagues on the board of management had asked him (he said) "to make this personal sacrifice in the interests of the company." "Hans Walz, Beilage zum Fragebogen: Kurze Darstellung der Beziehungen zur NSDAP und SS, 27. 8. 1945," pp. 2 ff., RB 1 013 033.

26 Otto Debatin, "Zum 1. Mai," in *Bosch-Zünder* 1933/4, p. 51. In this connection, see also Scholtyseck, *Bosch*, p. 152.

27 In this connection, see p. 103.

28 Scholtyseck, *Bosch*, p. 152.

29 "Spruchkammer 11 Stuttgart, Spruch gegen Otto Debatin, 28./29. 5. 1948," p. 8, StA Ludwigsburg EL 902/20, Bü 103816; "Otto Debatin, Bescheinigung für Erwin Kussing, 8. 3. 1948," RB 1 832 058.

30 "NSDAP-Mitgliedskarte Ernst Durst," BArch 31XX Reichskartei der NSDAP.

31 "Otto Henne, Vertraulicher Bericht an die Direktion z. Hd. Dr. Otto Fischer, 15. 4. 1947," RB 1 832 058.

32 *Ibid.*

33 Menzel demanded severance pay of 1 million reichsmarks. At the insistence of the state government, Bosch had to consent to a settlement, paying compensation of 100,000 reichsmarks. "AGL an PSH betr. Dr. Menzel, 7. 1. 1957," RB 1 094 006/7.

34 According to the Bosch annual report for 1946, toward the end of the war some 3,300 blue-collar and 1,450 white-collar associates belonged to the NSDAP or its affiliate organizations, the SA and the SS. On the shop floor this was approximately 15 percent, among white-collar associates 28 percent. Projected onto total workforce numbers, this corresponds to 17.5 percent. As part of a "Campaign to Purge National Socialists" that the works council carried out immediately after the war's end, questionnaires went out to a total workforce (blue-collar and white-collar associates) of some 6,900. According to information supplied by Eugen Eberle, who chaired the works council, approximately one-fifth had been members of the NSDAP and its subdivisions, comprising 11.8 percent of shop-floor staff, 36 percent of office staff, and 73 percent of senior white-collar associates. Robert Bosch GmbH, annual report January 1, 1945 to June 30, 1946, p. 11. Eugen Eberle, Peter Grohmann, *Die schlaflosen Nächte des Eugen E., Erinnerungen eines neuen schwäbischen Jacobiners*, Stuttgart, 1982, p. 163.

35 On the percentage of NSDAP members at Trillke-Werke, see p. 603, note 58.

36 "Berufsausschuß Hildesheim (Review Board), Entnazifizierung, an die Militärregierung 117, Special Branch, Hildesheim, 1. 12. 1947," Niedersächsisches Landesarchiv, Hauptstaatsarchiv Hannover, Nds 171 Hildesheim no. 70820; "Betriebsrat Blaupunktwerke Berlin-Wilmersdorf an Betriebsrat Blaupunkt Apparatebau GmbH, 22. 10. 1946," RB 1 707 001; "Betriebsrat Blaupunkt Apparatebau GmbH an Hans Teich, 1. 11. 1946," *ibid.*

37 In this connection, see pp. 184 f.

38 "Waren wir ein nationalsozialistischer Betrieb?," in *Bosch-Zünder* 1947/1–3, p. 1.

39 "Spruchkammer 11 Stuttgart, Spruch gegen Otto Debatin, 28./29. 5. 1948," p. 7, StA Ludwigsburg EL 902/20, Bü 103816.

40 "Waren wir ein nationalsozialistischer Betrieb?," in *Bosch-Zünder* 1947/1–3, p. 1.

41 Eberle, Grohmann, *Nächte*, p. 74. Eberle, a toolmaker, had been a member of the Communist Party since 1928. Following the National Socialist assumption of power he had been taken into "protective custody" and had lost his job at Kodak. Bosch had taken him on in refrigerator production in January 1934. From 1945 to 1952, Eberle chaired the works council of Robert Bosch GmbH. In February 1952, he and two other works-council members were dismissed without notice for tabling a resolution against re-armament at a company meeting. From 1948 to 1984, Eberle was a Stuttgart city councillor.

42 "Otto Debatin, Robert Bosch GmbH und NSDAP," p. 4, RB 1 013 078. Walz considered the amount recorded by Debatin for "donations to churches and Jews" to be excessively low. He reckoned it had been in the region of 1.1 million reichsmarks. "Hans Walz, Erklärung, 28. 7. 1948," p. 21, RB 1 013 036.

43 "Die Feier des 21. März bei der Robert Bosch A.-G.," in *Bosch-Zünder* 1934/3, p. 52.

44 "Bericht über die Besprechung zwecks Beilegung der Differenzen zwischen der Firma Robert Bosch AG Stuttgart und der Deutschen Arbeitsfront am 1. 12. 1937," p. 3, StA Ludwigsburg PL 502/29, Bü 96.

45 "Man dürfe aber 'Boschgemeinschaft' nicht mit 'Volksgemeinschaft' vergleichen." *Ibid.*, p. 6.

46 Heuss, *Bosch*, p. 466.

47 "Scheißdemokratenblättle" is the word quoted in Scholtyseck, *Bosch*, p. 154. On the *Gleichschaltung* or forced coordination of the press in Württemberg after 1933, see also Schnabel, *Württemberg*, pp. 352 ff.

48 Scholtyseck, *Bosch*, pp. 154 f.

49 *Ibid.*, pp. 155 f.

50 *Ibid.*, pp. 40, 184.

51 For biographical details of Schacht, see Christopher Kopper, *Hjalmar Schacht. Aufstieg und Fall von Hitlers mächtigstem Bankier*, Munich, Vienna, 2006.

52 Scholtyseck, *Bosch*, pp. 184 f.

53 Robert Bosch AG (ed.), *50 Jahre Bosch*, p. 242. On this Festschrift, see also pp. 159 f.

54 "Otto Debatin, Robert Bosch GmbH und NSDAP," p. 10, RB 1 013 078.

55 *Ibid.*, pp. 2 f.

56 Hartmut Berghoff, Cornelia Rauh-Kühne, *Fritz K. Ein deutsches Leben im 20. Jahrhundert*, Stuttgart, Munich, 2000, pp. 105 ff.

57 Reinhard Vogelsang, *Der Freundeskreis Himmler*, Göttingen, 1972, pp. 22 ff.

58 Initially, members were invited to the party rallies in Nuremberg. From 1938, there were also monthly lecture evenings in Berlin's "House of the Aviators" [*Haus der Flieger*]. Kranefuß also organized several group excursions, including to the Dachau and Sachsenhausen concentration camps. *Ibid.* Whether Walz went on these outings cannot be established. No lists of excursionists have come down to us. The likelihood is that none were compiled.

59 "SS-Personalbogen Hans Walz," BArch SSO/220B. According to Gottlob Berger, Walz was admitted to the SS as an *Unterscharführer*, which corresponded to the rank of NCO. "Gottlob Berger, Zur Geschichte der Robert Bosch GmbH 1933–1948," p. 3, RB 1 013 084.

60 Scholtyseck, *Bosch*, p. 159.

61 Scholtyseck, on the other hand, suspects that Walz did already belong to the group founded by Keppler and would have stayed on in order to retain "'party backing' against Gauleiter Murr." *Ibid.* When Walz did in fact join the *Freundeskreis Reichsführer SS* cannot be shown conclusively, no contemporary document having survived that gives the date. The SS officer file for Hans Walz that has survived starts with an entry dated September 11, 1938. "SS-Personalbogen Hans Walz," BArch SSO/220B. The Bremen businessman Karl Lindemann, who likewise belonged to "Himmler's Friendship Circle," supposed after the war that Walz had joined only in 1935. "Karl Lindemann, Erklärung unter Eid 28. 2. 1947 (NI-5514)," cited from Vogelsang, *Freundeskreis*, p. 153. According to his attorney, Rudolf Scheuing, it was only from 1937 onward that Walz was invited to "Friendship Circle" meetings. "Rudolf Scheuing an die Spruchkammer 6, Stuttgart-Bad Cannstatt, 22. 4. 1948," p. 8, StA Ludwigsburg EL 902/20, Bü 87568. On Walz's entry into the SS, see p. 172.

62 Unlike the *Gauleiter's* office, the SS did not boycott the Bosch anniversary celebrations. When Walz was officially investigated after the anniversary, he could say, "the SS is concerned to stress that it [the SS] takes no exception to the Festschrift." Quoted from "Bericht über die Besprechung zwecks Beilegung der Differenzen zwischen der Firma Robert Bosch AG Stuttgart und der Deutschen Arbeitsfront am 1. 12. 1937," p. 5, StA Ludwigsburg PL 502/29, Bü 96. The SS was represented at the anniversary celebrations by *Obersturmbannführer* Ludolf-Hermann von Alvensleben, head of the organization's Stuttgart section.

63 Scholtyseck, *Bosch*, pp. 162 f.

64 *Ibid.*, pp. 161 ff. For biographical information about Berger, see Joachim Scholtyseck, "Der 'Schwabenherzog.' Gottlob Berger, SS-Obergruppenführer," in Kissener, Scholtyseck (eds.), *Führer*, pp. 77–110.

65 "Der Weg zum Frieden," in *Bosch-Zünder* 1935/7, pp. 135–40.

66 For an overview of this, see Adam Tooze, *The wages of destruction. The making and breaking of the Nazi economy*, London, 2006, pp. 229–43.

67 Cited from "Willy Schloßstein, Einstellung des Herrn B. und seiner Firma zum Nazi-Regime, Juli 1945," p. 5, RB 1 013 076. In this connection, see also Scholtyseck, *Bosch*, p. 206.

68 "Otto Debatin, Robert Bosch GmbH und NSDAP," p. 10, RB 1 013 078.

69 "Rundschreiben Walz betr. Politischer Schulungskurs, 20. 2. 1939," RB 1 043 024/6. "Der Schulungskurs der Betriebsgemeinschaft der Robert Bosch GmbH vom 13. März bis 30. Juni 1939 (DAF-Schulungslehrgang Nr. 96)," RB 1 043 024/6; "Otto Debatin, Robert Bosch GmbH und NSDAP," p. 13, RB 1 013 078.

70 For biographical details of Bühler, see Gerhard Taddey, "Zwischen Widerstand und Gestapo. Dr. Hugo Bühler, Abwehrbeauftragter der Firma Bosch in Stuttgart," in *Zeitschrift für Württembergische Landesgeschichte* 70, 2011, pp. 455–88. Taddey relies exclusively on the defense testimony in Bühler's denazification tribunal [*Spruchkammer*] files. At Bosch, the first man given responsibility for defense was Otto Debatin, head of personnel and deputy "factory leader" [*Betriebsführer*]. On Bühler's conduct as counter-intelligence officer at Robert Bosch GmbH, see pp. 184, 186, 233 f.

71 "Debatin an Wild, 29. 3. 1947," RB 1 832 058. The deputy board member Ernst Durst wrote to colleagues instructing them that only with his assent were communications to be passed to Bühler. "Auszug aus den Aussagen des Herrn Hermann Müller, früher ZW/BWL Assistent bei Dr. Sw. Vom 29. 3. [o. J.]," StA Ludwigsburg EL 902/20, Bü 97890.

72 "Felix Olpp, Unser unvergesslicher Herr Bosch," p. 12, RB 1 014 003. In connection with the "Sudeten crisis" of 1938, see Heinrich August Winkler, *Geschichte des Westens. Die Zeit der Weltkriege 1914–1945*, Munich, 2011, pp. 852 ff.

73 "Meine Herrâ, der Kerle isch a Verbrecher." Quoted from "Felix Olpp, Unser unvergesslicher Herr Bosch," p. 12, RB 1 014 003.

74 "Kundgebung für Freundschaft und Frieden," in *Bosch-Zünder* 1938/10, p. 186.

75 *Ibid.*

76 "Willy Schloßstein, Einstellung des Herrn B. und seiner Firma zum Nazi-Regime, Juli 1945," p. 7, RB 1 013 076. On the links with Schairer and Mannheimer, see Scholtyseck, *Bosch*, pp. 228, 230 ff.

77 "So, nun wissen wir wenigstens, woran wir sind." Quoted from Scholtyseck, *Bosch*, p. 286.

78 "Otto Debatin, Robert Bosch GmbH und NSDAP," pp. 12 f., RB 1 013 078. According to this source, Bosch was the 416th company in Germany to be granted the title "National Socialist Model Enterprise."

79 *Ibid.*, p. 13.

80 In this connection, see p. 246.

81 See pp. 247 f.

82 "Hans Walz, Beilage zum Fragebogen: Kurze Darstellung der Beziehungen zur NSDAP und SS, 27. 8. 1945," pp. 1 f., RB 1 013 033; Scholtyseck, *Bosch*, p. 162.

83 Scholtyseck, *Bosch*, p. 162. Apart from an ominous reference by Berger, there is nothing to suggest that there was documentary proof of what he alleged. The rumor must be put down to Berger's fertile imagination. On Berger's credibility, see Scholtyseck, "'Schwabenherzog'," p. 99. An equally dodgy witness was Friedrich Menzel, the sacked head of development who is said to have backed up Berger's contention. "Vermerk betr. Gottlob Berger, 27. 9. 1973," RB 1 013 084.

84 See "Hans Walz, Beilage zum Fragebogen: Kurze Darstellung der Beziehungen zur NSDAP und SS, 27. 8. 1945," pp. 1 f., RB 1 013 033.

85 Heuss, *Bosch*, p. 621. In this connection, see also Scholtyseck, *Bosch*, p. 415. The quote (er werde die Nebenregierung Bosch nicht länger dulden) is also found in "Theodor Heuss, Reinhold Maier, Theodor Bäuerle, Hermann Binder, Erklärung für Hans Walz, 18. 2. 1946," RB 1 013 034; "Hans Walz, Beilage zum Fragebogen: Kurze Darstellung der Beziehungen zur NSDAP und SS, 27. 8. 1945," p. 7, RB 1 013 033.

86 Extract from the published "Tagebuch des hingerichteten früheren deutschen Botschafters von Hassell, 11. 8. 1939, Anlage 49 zum Ermittlerbericht im Spruchkammerverfahren gegen Hermann Fellmeth, 3. 12. 1946." The same quote is found in Scholtyseck, *Bosch*, p. 302.

87 "Der Chef der Sicherheitspolizei und des SD an den Reichsführer SS, Feldkommandostelle, 5. 10. 1943," BArch SSO/220B (SS-Offiziersakte Hans Walz).

88 "Der SS-Richter beim Reichsführer SS und Chef der Deutschen Polizei an das Hauptamt SS-Gericht, München, 21. 5. 1943," *ibid.*; "Der SS-Richter beim Reichsführer SS und Chef der Deutschen Polizei an den Chef der Sicherheitspolizei und des SD, 5. 12. 1943," *ibid.*

89 "Vermerk über Telefongespräch mit SS-Oberführer Kranefuß, 30. 4. 1943," *ibid.*; "Vermerk über Telefongespräch mit SS-Gruppenführer Berger, 30. 4. 1943," *ibid.*

90 "Kranefuß an Himmler, 21. 4. 1943," reprinted in Vogelsang, *Freundeskreis*, pp. 145 ff. (quote on p. 147).

91 Johannes Bähr, "'Bankenrationalisierung' und Großbankenfrage. Der Konflikt um die Ordnung des deutschen Kreditgewerbes während des Zweiten Weltkrieges," in Harald Wixforth (ed.), *Finanzinstitutionen in Mitteleuropa während des National-sozialismus* (Geld und Kapital, vol. 4), Stuttgart, 2001, pp. 71–94.

92 "Erwin Bohner, Zeugnis, 11. 2. 1946," RB 1 013 038; Scholtyseck, *Bosch*, p. 367; Bähr, "'Bankenrationalisierung'," pp. 88 ff.

93 Despite becoming known subsequently as the "Feuerbach address," the speech was in fact delivered in the administration building of Robert Bosch GmbH on Stuttgart's Militärstraße (the present Breitscheidstraße). "Rede Walz vom 12. 7. 1943," RB 1 013 024 (also in RB 1 013 241 and in StA Ludwigsburg EL 902/20, Bü 87568, Anlage 42a, where it is given the date 17. 7. 1943).

94 *Ibid.*, p. 1. See also Scholtyseck, *Bosch*, pp. 364, 366.

95 Scholtyseck, *Bosch*, p. 366; "Hans Walz, Beilage zum Fragebogen: Kurze Darstellung der Beziehungen zur NSDAP und SS, 27. 8. 1945," p. 6, RB 1 013 033.

96 Original words: "auf's Schafott." Quoted from Scholtyseck, *Bosch*, p. 366.

97 Scholtyseck, *Bosch*, p. 384 (quote); Tilman Fichter, Eugen Eberle, *Kampf um Bosch*, Berlin, 1974, p. 158; "Luckau an Bühler, 17. 1. 1947," StA Ludwigsburg EL 902/20, Bü 97890.

98 Wolfgang Kress, "Anton Hummler und Max Wagner – zwei Arbeiter leisten Widerstand." URL: http://www.stolpersteine-stuttgart.de; Hans Teich, *Hildesheim und seine Antifaschisten. Widerstandskampf gegen den Hitlerfaschismus und demokratischer Neubeginn 1945 in Hildesheim*, Hildesheim, 1979, pp. 125 ff.

99 "Spruchkammer Stuttgart, Aussage Ernst Rogowski, 13. 2. 1947," StA Ludwigsburg EL 902/20, Bü 70680; "Greiner an Gönnenwein, 30. 4. 1947," *ibid.* According to Rogowski's *Aussage* or witness statement, the German "counter-intelligence officer" at Lavalette was killed by a resistance group.

3 Bosch and the Jews

1 The Stuttgart group of the *Verein zur Abwehr des Antisemitismus* with its 200 or so members failed to gain much influence among the city's bourgeoisie. Martin Ulmer, *Antisemitismus in Stuttgart. Studien zum öffentlichen Diskurs und Alltag*, Berlin, 2011, pp. 365 f.

2 Scholtyseck, *Bosch*, pp. 267 f.

3 See p. 189.

4 On the Landauer case, see p. 185.

5 *Ibid.*

6 In this connection, see also Scholtyseck, *Bosch*, p. 281.

7 "Aufstellung von Juden und Halbjuden, die in den letzten 12 Jahren in der Robert Bosch GmbH in Beschäftigung standen bzw. noch stehen, 20. 9. 1945," RB 1 013 068.

8 Jörg Kurz, *Chronik der Stadt Stuttgart 1933–1945* (Veröffentlichungen des Archivs der Stadt Stuttgart, vol. 30), Stuttgart, 1982, p. 39; a similar source is Ulmer, *Antisemitismus*, p. 23.

9 Scholtyseck, *Bosch*, p. 268.

10 "Aufstellung von Juden und Halbjuden, die in den letzten 12 Jahren in der Robert Bosch GmbH in Beschäftigung standen bzw. noch stehen, 20. 9. 1945," RB 1 013 068.

11 Because of the attacks on Landauer, his department had been balloted. Most colleagues voted in his favor. There seem to have been only a few agitators. But Landauer had decided to leave the country. "Otto Debatin, Robert Bosch GmbH und NSDAP," p. 9, RB 1 013 078.

12 How Landauer survived until the war's end is not known. However, Bosch helped him by giving his non-Jewish wife a clerking job at the company. "Aufstellung von Juden und Halbjuden, die in den letzten 12 Jahren in der Robert Bosch GmbH in Beschäftigung standen bzw. noch stehen, 20. 9. 1945," RB 1 013 068.

13 "Auszug aus einem Bericht des Dr. Friedrich Menzel an Gauleiter Murr (Februar 1942), Anlage 41 zum Ermittlerbericht im Spruchkammerverfahren gegen Hermann Fellmeth, 3. 12. 1946," StA Ludwigsburg EL 902/20, Bü 93826 EA (denacitication court files, Hermann Fellmeth).

14 "Otto Debatin an die Spruchkammer 11, Stuttgart-N, Klageschrift-Erwiderung, 7. 1. 1948," p. 11, StA Ludwigsburg EL 902/20, Bü 103816. Debatin is here quoting from Menzel's February 24, 1942, report to Murr. Fritz Landauer later lived as Fred Salomon in Long Island near New York. StA Ludwigsburg EL 350I, Bü 28247.

15 "Otto Debatin, Robert Bosch GmbH und NSDAP," pp. 8 f., RB 1 013 078. After the war, the counter-intelligence officer Hugo Bühler described his rival Debatin's behavior in the Johanan case differently. "Hugo Bühler, Tätigkeit bei der Firma Bosch GmbH" [undated], p. 9, RB 1 010 195.

16 "Aufstellung von Juden und Halbjuden, die in den letzten 12 Jahren in der Robert Bosch GmbH in Beschäftigung standen bzw. noch stehen, 20. 9. 1945," RB 1 013 068.

17 "Nichtarische Vertreter der Robert Bosch GmbH, 2. 10. 1945," *ibid.*

18 "Junkers & Co. GmbH an Firma Curt Reinhardt, Leipzig, (Vertraulich), 25. 2. 1938," LHASA, DE Junkers Wärmetechnik Dessau no. 96.

19 "Aufstellung von Juden und Halbjuden, die in den letzten 12 Jahren in der Robert Bosch GmbH in Beschäftigung standen bzw. noch stehen, 20. 9. 1945," RB 1 013 068.

20 Beate Meyer, *"Jüdische Mischlinge." Rassenpolitik und Verfolgungswahn 1933–1945*, Hamburg, 2001, pp. 237 ff.

21 Scholtyseck, *Bosch*, p. 281; "Interview mit Fritz Nast-Kolb" [undated], RB 1 842; "Fritz Nast-Kolb, 'Ich überlebte, weil Bosch half'," *ibid.*; Fritz Nast-Kolb, "Jahrgang 1916," in Johannes Steinhoff, Peter Pechel, Dennis Showalter (eds.), *Deutsche im Zweiten Weltkrieg. Zeitzeugen sprechen*, Munich, 1989, pp. 408–10; Losten interview of September 23, 2010; "Hugo Bühler, Tätigkeit bei der Firma Bosch GmbH" [undated], p. 12, RB 1 010 195.

22 Eberhard Röhm, Jörg Thierfelder, "Schützende Hände über 'Juden' und 'Mischlingen'. Die Stuttgarter Firmen Paul Lechler und Robert Bosch," in Eberhard Röhm, Jörg Thierfelder, *Juden, Christen, Deutsche 1933–1945*, vol. 4: 1941–1945, part 2, Stuttgart, 2007, pp. 460 f., 465; "Hugo Bühler, Tätigkeit bei der Firma Bosch GmbH" [undated], p. 12, RB 1 010 195.

23 Röhm, Thierfelder, "Hände," pp. 469 ff. Friedrich Haarburger was a son of the Reutlingen industrialist Karl Haarburger. The painter Alice Haarburger, murdered in a concentration camp in 1942, was an aunt of Friedrich Haarburger. He was not directly related to the chemist Martha Haarburger.

24 "Hugo Bühler, Tätigkeit bei der Firma Bosch GmbH" [undated], p. 12, RB 1 010 195.

25 *Ibid.*, p. 10; "Interview mit Fritz Nast-Kolb" [undated], RB 1 842.

26 "Hugo Bühler, Tätigkeit bei der Firma Bosch GmbH" [undated], p. 10, RB 1 010 195. Probably at the same time Bühler was able to have his student friend Konrad Wittwer assigned to Bosch by the Labor Office and given a job in the new facility.

His contacts had already made it possible not only for Wittwer's sister, Marianne Seligmann-Heilner, to escape deportation to Auschwitz, together with her husband and their son, but also for the whole (Jewish) family to travel to Switzerland. "Hugo Bühler, Tätigkeit bei der Firma Bosch GmbH" [undated], p. 11, RB 1 010 195.

27 In this connection, see p. 222.

28 See pp. 225 f.

29 Scholtyseck, *Bosch*, p. 274.

30 For biographical details of Adler, see Fritz Richert, *Karl Adler. Musiker, Verfolgter, Helfer. Ein Lebensbild*, Stuttgart, 1990.

31 Cited from Richert, *Adler*, pp. 64 f.

32 Scholtyseck, *Bosch*, p. 273.

33 Richert, *Adler*, p. 70.

34 Kurz, *Chronik*, pp. 778, 794.

35 "Stellungnahme zur Frage der Zwangsarbeiter-Entschädigung, Stand 20. 8. 1998," RB 1 012 037. According to Scholtyseck, the payments that passed through the account in Amsterdam were alone worth the equivalent of some 500,000 reichsmarks. Scholtyseck, *Bosch*, p. 273.

36 In this connection and in connection with what follows, see Scholtyseck, *Bosch*, pp. 280 f.; Röhm, Thierfelder, "Hände," pp. 474 ff.; Maria Zelzer, *Weg und Schicksal der Stuttgarter Juden. Ein Gedenkbuch*, published by the city of Stuttgart (Veröffentlichungen des Archivs der Stadt Stuttgart, special issue), Stuttgart, 1964, pp. 230–40, and http://www.zeichen-der-erinnerung.org/n5_1_haarburger_martha.htm.

37 Paul Sauer, "Ganze Familien wurden in den Tod geschickt. Die Deportation von württembergischen und hohenzollerischen Juden am 1. Dezember 1941 von Stuttgart nach Riga," in Konrad Pflug, Ulrike Raab-Nicolai, Reinhold Weber (eds.), *Orte des Gedenkens und Erinnerns in Baden-Württemberg*, Stuttgart, 2007, pp. 304–10.

38 Contact may well have come about through a female friend of Haarburger. However, the chemist was also a cousin of Bona Schloßstein, whose husband headed Robert Bosch's private secretariat. "Bona Schloßstein, Erklärung, 2. 2. 1946," RB 1 013 034.

39 Taddey, "Widerstand," p. 473; "Martha Haarburger, Bescheinigung für Hugo Bühler, 14. 1. 1946," StA Ludwigsburg EL 902/20, Bü 97890.

40 Zelzer, *Weg*, pp. 228, 238 ff.; Scholtyseck, *Bosch*, pp. 280 f.; Röhm, Thierfelder, "Hände," pp. 474 ff.; Susanne Rueß, *Stuttgarter jüdische Ärzte während des Nationalsozialismus*, Würzburg, 2009, pp. 322 ff.; Klaus Steinke, "'In den Abgrund – und jenseits wieder hinauf.' Umgangsweisen mit dem Bösen: Dr. med. Marga Wolf und ihre Helferinnen und Helfer." URL: http://www.stolpersteine-stuttgart.de.

41 Walz received his "Righteous among the Nations" award on January 2, 1969. The citation was handed to him by the Israeli ambassador in Stuttgart on March 13, 1970. Richert, *Adler*, pp. 80 ff.; "Walz, Hans," in Daniel Fraenkel, Jakob Borut (eds.), *Lexikon der Gerechten unter den Völkern. Deutsche und Österreicher*, Göttingen, 2005, pp. 278 f.

42 "Walz an Adler, 4. 4. 1970." Quoted from Scholtyseck, *Bosch*, p. 282.

43 "Felix Olpp, Unser unvergesslicher Herr Bosch," p. 14a, RB 1 014 003; Scholtyseck, *Bosch*, p. 270.

44 After the war, the sellers of the building at 8 Affalterstraße confirmed to Bosch that the price of 260,000 reichsmarks named in the purchase agreement of September 21, 1938, had been a fair one. So they waived any right to restitution. In return, they received from Bosch buildings in Bad Boll and Stuttgart-Feuerbach. "Vergleich zwischen den Erben und Erbeserben des am 1.9.1930 verstorbenen Herrn Leo Meyer und der Firma Robert Bosch GmbH, 6. 3. 1950," RB 1 024 114; "Beschreibung der Ersatzgrundstücke," *ibid.* The building at 102a Büchsenstraße belonged to the Levy family until October 1938, and they rented part of it out to Robert Bosch GmbH. A realty firm invited Bosch to make an offer for the entire site, probably because the owners had to emigrate. According to later accounts, at 68,000 reichsmarks the purchase price was reasonable. However, after the war the transaction was found to have been incorrectly entered in the land register and was therefore legally invalid. Since the site still belonged legally to the Levys, in 1950 the heirs ceded their rights to the purchase price to Bosch. "Amtsgericht Stuttgart, Schlichter für Wiedergutmachung, Vergleich in der Rückerstattungssache Max Lane und andere gegen die Firma Robert Bosch GmbH, 9. 8. 1950," RB 1 024 115.

45 Otto Rosenfeld was also the president of the Stuttgart Chess Club. Peter Schweickhardt's *Ehrenvorsitzender Rosenblum. Eine Erzählung*, Stuttgart, 2007 retells in literary form his life and fate during the Third Reich.

46 "Jewish Restitution Successor Organization [JRSO], Stuttgart Regional Office, an Pulkowski, 15. 6. 1951," RB 1 024 602 001; "Martini an Schoenfeldt (JRSO), 12. 7. 1951," *ibid.*; "Aktennotiz betr. Erwerb des Grundstücks Herdweg 63, 21. 10. 1949," *ibid.* The house at Herdweg 63 was destroyed in the war. In 1953, Bosch sold the site as a ruin to a publishing company, Thieme-Verlag.

47 "Amtsgericht Stuttgart, Schlichter für Wiedergutmachung, Vergleich vom 25. 11. 1949," RB 1 024 116 001.

48 "Rechtsanwälte Dr. Ostertag und Dr. Ulmer an den Schlichter, Wiedergutmachungsbehörde Stuttgart, Rückerstattungsantrag Namens Dr. h. c. Richard Heilner gegen Firma Robert Bosch GmbH und andere, 23. 11. 1948," pp. 3 f., 6 f., RB 1 024 304. Heilner had once persuaded Bosch to join the Paneuropean Union. Both men had also been members of the Franco-German Society. Anita Ziegenhofer, *Botschafter Europas. Richard Nikolaus Coudenhove-Kalergi und die Paneuropa-Bewegung in den zwanziger und dreißiger Jahren*, Vienna, Cologne, 2004, pp. 111 f.; Scholtyseck, *Bosch*, pp. 103, 193. Some biographical details of Heilner may be found at http://www.dillmann-gymnasium.de/gymnasium/organisation/geschichte-schulstatistik/ehemalige/; "Die Heilner-Brüder aus Urspringen," at http://www.hdbg.de/auswanderung/docs/heilner_bio.pdf.

49 "Rechtsanwälte Dr. Ostertag und Dr. Ulmer an den Schlichter, Wiedergutmachungsbehörde Stuttgart, Rückerstattungsantrag Namens Dr. h. c. Richard Heilner gegen Firma Robert Bosch GmbH und andere, 23. 11. 1948," pp. 6 f., RB 1 024 304; "Dr. Ing. Friedrich Bihl, Wertschätzung des Grundstücks Herdweg 94 und 94/1, 19. 1. 1939," *ibid.*; "REA an FIH, EEA/Th, BW/WEL u. a., 3. 5. 1949," *ibid.*

50 "Knoerzer an REA betr. Rückerstattungsantrag Heilner, 5. 5. 1949," *ibid.* Knoerzer and Heilner had first become acquainted at the Weißenhof tennis club. *Ibid.*

51 "Amtsgericht Stuttgart, Schlichter für Wiedergutmachungssachen, Vergleich in der Rückerstattungssache des Dr. Richard Heilner, Aktenzeichen S 1262, 10. 9. 1949," RB 1 024 305.

52 This is true of a building at 56 Bismarckallee in Frankfurt-Bockenheim that had belonged to Adler & Oppenheimer AG and passed to Robert Bosch GmbH on March 18, 1937, for 46,000 reichsmarks. Regarding two plots in Budapest that Bosch bought in 1936 and 1939 respectively, it is not clear that the woman selling them was of Jewish origin. "Aufstellung über jüdische Fabriken und Geschäftshäuser gekauft seit 1933, 23. 8. 1945," RB 1 024 502; "Aufstellung über jüdische Wohnhäuser und

Grundstücke, gekauft seit 1933, 23. 8. 1945," *ibid.*; "Ungeklärt, ob jüd. Besitz, 23. 8. 1945," *ibid.*

53 "Protokoll der öffentlichen Sitzung der Spruchkammer Stuttgart-Schönleinstr. 11 am 6. 3. 1947," p. 2, StA Ludwigsburg EL 902/20, Bü 93826.

54 "Rechtsanwalt Rupp an die Herren Testamentsvollstrecker, 31. 8. 1951," RB 1 001 258; "Abschrift der Verhandlung vor dem Preußischen Notar im Bezirke des Oberlandesgerichts Frankfurt a. M., 7. 3. 1934," RB 1 013 267; "Vertragsantrag vom 9. 11. 1934," *ibid.*

55 "Vermerk betr. Privatsekretariat Dr. Robert Bosch, 5. 3. 1937," BArch R 8136/3397. According to this source, Schloßstein was originally interested in the Bavarian blanket manufacturer Bruckmühl AG, which was not Jewish-owned. Since there was no connection with Bosch Group products in either case, the transaction may well have been an investment on Bosch's part.

56 "Felix Olpp, Unser unvergesslicher Herr Bosch," p. 14i, RB 1 014 003; (some of Olpp's portrayal of this matter is incorrect. He also gives the wrong name to the Reichskreditgesellschaft negotiating partner Otto Gerlitz); "Verlagerungsbetriebe, Stand 1. 1. 1945," RB 1 013 156; "Aktenvermerk über die Besprechung mit Herrn Schloßstein, 26. 10. 1939," BArch R 8136/3734; "Niederschrift über die Sitzung der RBTV am 17. 11. 1950," p. 6, RB 1 001 258.

57 "Felix Olpp, Unser unvergesslicher Herr Bosch," p. 14i, RB 1 014 003.

58 "Schloßstein an Testamentsvollstrecker, 12. 3. 1951," p. 8, RB 1 001 258; "Felix Olpp, Unser unvergesslicher Herr Bosch," pp. 17 f., RB 1 014 003.

59 "Felix Olpp, Unser unvergesslicher Herr Bosch," pp. 17 f., RB 1 014 003.

60 *Ibid.*, pp. 14g f.; "Schloßstein an Testamentsvollstrecker, 8. 11. 1950," p. 8, RB 1 001 258; "Schloßstein an Testamentsvollstrecker, 12. 3. 1951," p. 7, *ibid.* Once the Victoria shares in the Robert Bosch inheritance were unfrozen, Olpp persuaded Bosch's grandson Georg Zundel to let them count towards his portion of the inheritance. The block of shares later rose steeply in value and Zundel sold some of them to Kurt Hamann to pay for a forest estate that he (Zundel) was buying in Carinthia. The proceeds further enabled him to build a student hall of residence in Tübingen-Lustnau. "Felix Olpp, Unser unvergesslicher Herr Bosch," pp. 14d f., RB 1 014 003. According to Olpp's account, Zundel did in fact subsequently sell the rest of his Victoria shares on the stock exchange. *Ibid.*

61 "Niederschrift über eine Sitzung des Aufsichtsrats der Robert Bosch GmbH am 18. 10. 1949," RB 1 002 008. On the "aryanization" of Metallerzbergbau Westmark, see p. 162.

62 Steiner, *Ortsempfänger*, pp. 225 f. Siegmund Loewe, having quit the Jewish community in 1934, was deemed to be a "person of mixed blood" on account of his Jewish father. *Ibid.*, pp. 35, 231.

63 Goerz aimed to have the national Ministry of Economic Affairs appoint Robert Bosch as fiduciary at Loewe as early as 1934. Steiner, *Ortsempfänger*, pp. 29 f.

64 "Niederschrift über eine Sitzung des Aufsichtsrats der Robert Bosch GmbH am 18. 10. 1949," RB 1 002 008. On the ancestry of Paul Goerz's wife, see "Goerz an die Militär-Regierung Det. 122, Hildesheim, 21. 8. 1945," Niedersächsisches Landesarchiv, Hauptstaatsarchiv Hannover, Nds 171 Hildesheim no. 70820. On Rassbach, see below, p. 590, note 20.

65 "Aktennotiz über eine Besprechung am 30. 11. 1937," Landesarchiv Berlin B Rep. 025–08, no. 4331/55 (WGA, Akten der Wiedergutmachungsämter [files of the Berlin restitution offices]).

66 *Ibid.*; Steiner, *Ortsempfänger*, p. 230.

67 The Loewe company was indeed taken over by the Reich Air Ministry soon after its withdrawal from FESE. Steiner, *Ortsempfänger*, pp. 235 ff.

68 "Vermerk REA betr. Rückerstattungsfälle, 13. 11. 1950," RB 1 013 156.

69 Steiner, *Ortsempfänger*, pp. 307 ff.; "Vergleich in der Rückerstattungssache 81 WGA 386.51, 14. 1. 1965," RB 1 610 026. In this connection, see also pp. 379 f.

4 Involvement in rearmament and arms production in the Second World War

1 On the expropriation of Junkers-Flugzeugwerk AG and Junkers-Motorenbau GmbH in 1933, see Budraß, *Flugzeugindustrie*, pp. 320 ff.

2 "10-Jahresbericht des BTH3 (1. 4. 1930 – 31. 3. 1940), 19. 4. 1940," pp. 12 f., RB 1 010 443.

3 Certainly, there can be no question of a "policy of obstructionism" (Scholtyseck) or "delaying tactics" (Lessing) on the part of the company in its dealings with the Air Ministry and the Army Procurement Office. Scholtyseck, *Bosch*, p. 134; Lessing, *Bosch*, p. 137. Scholtyseck here relies solely on a note that Robert Bosch wrote on April 24, 1936, turning down an appeal for donations to the party with reference to the construction of back-up plants [*Ausweichwerke*] and other financial commitments. *Ibid.*, p. 596, note 102; Heuss, *Bosch*, p. 597. The suggestion that Bosch deliberately disobeyed military instructions here is based on apologias written after the war. See for instance "Willy Schloßstein, Einstellung des Herrn B. und seiner Firma zum Nazi-Regime, Juli 1945," RB 1 013 076.

4 Scholtyseck and Lessing date the establishment of the Dreilinden plant to 1937. Scholtyseck, *Bosch*, p. 134; Lessing, *Bosch*, p. 137. On the building of Dreilindenwerk, see pp. 195 ff.

5 On Knoblauch's role, see also p. 195.

6 "Aussage George Hansen vom 24. 2. 1948," quoted from "Hans Walz, Erklärung, 28. 7. 1948," p. 2, RB 1 013 036.

7 Becker, Scholtyseck, *Bosch*, p. 204.

8 *Ibid.*

9 "Bericht der Deutschen Revisions- und Treuhand-Aktiengesellschaft Berlin über die bei der Robert Bosch GmbH vorgenommene Prüfung des Jahresabschlusses zum 31. 12. 1940," p. 53, RB 1 003 093 (figures exclude transitory DLMG sales).

10 In 1940, 51 percent of the sales of Robert Bosch GmbH (excluding transitory DLMG sales) went to 30 major customers. Daimler-Benz alone took deliveries worth some 23 million reichsmarks, which represented around a 10 percent share. Direct supplies to military authorities (the Air Ministry in particular) totaled 12.5 million reichsmarks. *Ibid.*, p. 22.

11 "Rede Walz vom 12. 7. 1934," RB 1 013 024, see p. 181.

12 Pierer, *Bayerische Motorenwerke*, p. 44.

13 Budraß, *Flugzeugindustrie*, p. 210. Even back then the main suppliers to the aviation industry, including Bosch as a manufacturer of ignition devices, were to be moved to central Germany for security reasons. For reasons of cost, however, this relocation could not be carried out. *Ibid.*

14 "Bosch an Mauk, 22. 12. 1933," in Becker, Scholtyseck, *Bosch*, p. 204.

15 Budraß, *Flugzeugindustrie*, p. 352.

16 "Besprechungen am 16. 6. 1934," BArchM [Abt. Militärarchiv] RL 3/287. Knoblauch had been a head of department at the Army Procurement Office [*Heereswaffenamt*] from 1927 to 1931. Presumably Bosch took him on especially for the negotiations with the military authorities. How Knoblauch's connection with Robert Bosch AG came about can no longer be established. Knoblauch worked at Bosch until 1939 as "Representative of Robert Bosch A.-G. Stuttgart, Berlin-Charlottenburg Sales Office." For further biographical details of Knoblauch, see Dermot Bradley, Karl-Friedrich Hildebrand, Markus Rövekamp, *Die Generale des Heeres 1921–1945*, vol. 7: *Knabe–Luz*, Osnabrück, 2004, pp. 22 f.

17 "Vertrag zwischen dem Reichsluftfahrtministerium und der Firma Robert Bosch Aktiengesellschaft, Stuttgart, 16. 8. 1934/3. 9. 1934," RB 1 606 003. Bosch placed great importance on funding the project itself rather than through government loans, because it was a company principle never to make itself dependent on borrowed capital. "Kreditprotokoll Nr. 257/39, 14. 10. 1940," BArch R 8121/286.

18 "Besprechungen am 25. 5. 1934," BArchM RL 3/287. On the creation of the Drei-linden plant and the history of Dreilinden Maschinenbau GmbH, see also Angela Martin, *Ich sah den Namen Bosch. Polnische Frauen als KZ-Häftlinge in der Drei-linden Maschinenbau GmbH*, published by Berliner Geschichtswerkstatt, Berlin, 2002, pp. 215–99.

19 "Vertrag zwischen dem Reichsluftfahrtministerium und der Firma Robert Bosch Aktiengesellschaft, Stuttgart, 16. 8. 1934/3. 9. 1934," RB 1 606 003.

20 Johannes Bähr, *Industrie im geteilten Berlin (1945–1990): Die elektrotechnische Industrie und der Maschinenbau im Ost-West-Vergleich: Branchenentwicklung, Technologien und Handlungsstrukturen* (Einzelveröffentlichungen der Historischen Kommission zu Berlin, vol. 83), Munich, 2001, pp. 23 ff.; Sigfrid von Weiher, *Berlins Weg zur Elektropolis. Ein Beitrag zur Technik- und Industriegeschichte an der Spree*, Göttingen, Zürich, 1987, pp. 137 ff.

21 "Bericht über die Sitzung am 1. 10. 1934 im Reichswirtschaftsministerium, Abteilung VIII, betr. Bauvorhaben der Firma Bosch in Dreilinden," BArch R 3901/20712.

22 "Hermann Bauer, Bosch und seine Beteiligung an der Rüstung," p. 1, RB 1 013 062.

23 For instance, a note on a meeting held on July 27, 1934, reads as follows: "In most cases, the differences between the proposals of L. D. [*Luftwaffenverwaltungsamt*] and the company are resolved by Bosch giving in." "Besprechungen am 27. 7. 1934," BArchM RL 3/287. Bosch was concerned that the Dreilinden project might attract undesirable competition, as a note about a discussion held on September 11, 1935, reveals: "The company [i. e., Bosch] is worried about some development work starting up at Siemens. It receives express confirmation that the Dreilinden agreement has full validity." "Besprechungen am 11. 9. 1935," BArchM RL 3/299.

24 "Reichsminister der Luftfahrt an Robert Bosch AG, Direktion, 3. 9. 1934," RB 1 606 003; "Besprechungen am 19. 8. 1935," BArchM RL 3/287.

25 Paul Vogelgsang had joined Robert Bosch Metallwerk AG in Feuerbach in 1920. Since 1924 he had been commercial manager there. Heinrich Walchenbach had worked for Bosch since 1928. On Vogelgsang, see "Paul Vogelgsang tritt in den Ruhestand," in *Bosch-Zünder* 1957/12, p. 254; "Otto Debatin, Paul Vogelgsang," RB 1 044 005/3. A handwritten manuscript of the memoirs of Vogelgsang may be found at RB 1 606 004.

26 Budraß, *Flugzeugindustrie*, p. 353; Budraß, "Zwischen Unternehmen und Luftwaffe. Die Luftfahrtforschung im 'Dritten Reich'," in Helmut Maier (ed.), *Rüstungsforschung im Nationalsozialismus. Organisation, Mobilisierung und Entgrenzung der Technikwissenschaften* (Geschichte der Kaiser-Wilhelm-Gesellschaft im Nationalsozialismus, vol. 3), Göttingen, 2001, pp. 161 f.; Constanze Werner, *Kriegswirtschaft und Zwangsarbeit bei* BMW, Munich, 2005, pp. 32 ff.

27 Richard van Basshuysen (ed.), *Ottomotoren mit Direkteinspritzung. Verfahren, Systeme, Entwicklung, Potenzial*, Wiesbaden, 2007, p. 11; Kyrill von Gersdorff, Kurt Grasmann, *Flugmotoren und Strahltriebwerke*, Munich, 1981, pp. 169 f.; Pohl, Habeth, Brüninghaus, *Daimler-Benz*, pp. 98 ff.; "Bosch-Benzindirekteinspritzung für Flugmotoren, 12. 1. 2012," RB Luftfahrt 016/005.

28 "Daimler-Benz AG an das Reichsministerium der Luftfahrt, Abt. LC 3, Herrn Flieger-Hauptstabsingenieur Eisenlohr, 23. 8. 1939," BArchM RL 3/587.

29 "G.F.C.C., Étude sur le groupe Robert Bosch en Allemagne et à l'étranger, Sept. 1947," Archives du Ministère des affaires étrangères et européennes, La Courneuve, GMFB 2/312/2.

30 The targets called for production of 100 injection pumps a month by the end of 1938. At Bosch these were seen as "exceptional, quite unforeseen demands calling for new hires, retraining, etc." "Robert Bosch GmbH (Durst/Lippart) an das Reichsluftfahrtministerium, z. H. Dipl. Ing. Mahnke, 22. 7. 1938," RB 1 606 003.

31 *Ibid.*; "Kreditprotokoll Nr. 257/39, 14. 10. 1940," BArch R 8121/286; "Bericht der Deutschen Revisions- und Treuhand-Aktiengesellschaft Berlin über die bei der Robert Bosch GmbH vorgenommene Prüfung des Jahresabschlusses zum 31. 12. 1940," p. 22, RB 1 003 093. According to this report, profits at DLMG in the 1939 financial year amounted to 900,000 reichsmarks.

32 "Das grenzt ja geradezu an Sabotage. Wenn das Werk in einem halben Jahr nicht flott liefert, dann geschieht etwas." Quoted from "Hermann Bauer, Bosch und seine Beteiligung an der Rüstung," RB 1 013 062.

33 *Ibid.*

34 Total capital expenditure came to 24 million reichsmarks, of which Bosch contributed 10.8 million reichsmarks from its own resources. A further loan of 13.2 million reichsmarks was put up by the nationally owned Luftkontor GmbH (renamed Bank der deutschen Luftfahrt or German Aviation Bank in 1940). "Reichsminister der Luftfahrt und Oberbefehlshaber der Luftwaffe, LF 3, von Hellingrath, an Luftkontor GmbH Berlin-Schöneberg, 21. 11. 1939," BArch R 8121/286.

35 "Produktionsstatistik seit 1887," RB 1 007 075.

36 "Bosch-Benzindirekteinspritzung für Flugmotoren, 12. 1. 2012," RB Luftfahrt 016/005.

37 "Besprechungen am 19. 8. 1935," BArchM RL 3/299.

38 "Besprechungen am 11. 9. 1935," *ibid.*

39 "Dietrich Steiner, Firmenchronik der Blaupunkt-Werke," p. 7, RB 1 010 024 073.

40 In 1944, 45 percent of the production of Blaupunkt GmbH was accounted for by orders from Bosch and DLMG, 55 percent by orders coming directly from army and air force. The company now possessed one of the best equipped high-frequency laboratories in Germany. "Vermerk über eine Besprechung am 20. 1. 1944 betr. Blaupunktwerke GmbH, Wilmersdorf," BArch R 8121/148; "Auszug aus dem Aktenvermerk vom 26. 8. 1943 wegen Dreilinden Maschinenbau GmbH, Kleinmachnow," *ibid.*

41 Overesch, *Bosch*, pp. 24 f., 28 f., 40 ff.

42 *Ibid.*, p. 45.

43 Overesch, *Bosch*, p. 40.

44 *Ibid.*, pp. 40 ff., 43 ff., 52 f.; "Niederschrift über Besprechungen in Berlin, betr. Standortwahl für AW II am 8./9. 9. 1937, 13. 9. 1937," Werksarchiv Bosch Hildesheim I/2; "Bericht über die Entwicklung des Werkes bis zum Herbst 1953, 25. 10. 1953," *ibid.*

45 "Otto Debatin, Robert Bosch GmbH und NSDAP," p. 21, RB 1 013 078.

46 Bosch had not meant the search for a site to go on for so long. The fault lay with the vagueness of the specifications and lobbying by the various authorities involved. Overesch sees a further reason as having been "a persistent reluctance on the part of Robert Bosch GmbH to contribute to the armaments economy." Overesch, *Bosch*, p. 54. He refers here to the attitude of Hans Walz toward National Socialism and Walz's connection with Goerdeler. However, both things were quite unrelated to the decision regarding the back-up plant in northern Germany.

47 Original words: "nur Grobschmiede," quoted from Overesch, *Bosch*, p. 41.

48 Barbara Hopmann, *Von der Montan zur Industrieverwaltungsgesellschaft* (IVG), 1916–1951, Stuttgart, 1996, pp. 71 ff.; Bähr, Drecoll, Gotto, *Flick-Konzern*, p. 143.

49 "Kurze Zusammenfassung der wichtigsten Punkte aus der Besprechung vom 28. 6. 1937 im Heereswaffenamt, betreffend Ausweichwerk II (AW II)," Werksarchiv Bosch Hildesheim I/2.

50 "Mantelvertrag zwischen dem Deutschen Reich, vertreten durch das Oberkommando des Heeres, und der Firma Robert Bosch GmbH, 2. 11./20. 12. 1938," *ibid.*

51 "Bericht über die Entwicklung des Werkes bis zum Herbst 1953, 25. 10. 1953," Werksarchiv Bosch Hildesheim I/2; Overesch, *Bosch*, p. 31. The ELFI shares were held 98 percent by Robert Bosch GmbH and 2 percent by Eugen Bauer GmbH.

52 Carl Martin Dolezalek, who came from a well-known engineering family, was considered one of the most promising figures in German mechanical engineering. However, he had received no university chair because he was not a member of the NSDAP, joining the party only in 1940. After the war, Dolezalek was given a chair at the Technische Hochschule Stuttgart. In Stuttgart, he founded the Institut für Industrielle Fertigung und Fabrikbetrieb, now known as the Fraunhofer-Institut für Produktionstechnik und Automatisierung. Otto Kienzler, "Carl Martin Dolezalek 70 Jahre," in *VDI-Nachrichten*, October 15, 1969, p. 25; Overesch, *Bosch*, esp. pp. 261 f.; Helmut Trischler, Rüdiger vom Bruch, *Forschung für den Markt. Geschichte der Fraunhofer-Gesellschaft*, Munich, 1999, pp. 371 ff.; "Öffentliche Sitzung des Entnazifizierungs-Hauptausschusses Hildesheim, 30. 5. 1949," Niedersächsisches Landesarchiv, Hauptstaatsarchiv Hannover, Nds 171 Hildesheim, C. M. Dolezalek. The former regular officer Max Clostermeyer had worked for Bosch since 1923. He belonged to the NSDAP as well as to the SS. Overesch, *Bosch*, p. 78; "Spruchgericht 18, Spruchkammer, Urteil in dem Spruchgerichtsverfahren gegen Max Clostermeyer, 22. 11. 1948," Niedersächsisches Landesarchiv, Hauptstaatsarchiv Hannover, Nds 171 Hannover, no. 17494. In 1951, Clostermeyer returned to Bosch, becoming technical director of its ignition plant. "Lebenslauf Max Clostermeyer," RB 1 094 001/17.

53 "Bericht über die Entwicklung des Werkes bis zum Herbst 1953, 25. 10. 1953," Werksarchiv Bosch Hildesheim I/2; Overesch, *Bosch*, pp. 32 f.

54 Original words: "eine der schönsten Werksanlagen [...] die je gebaut wurden." Quoted from Overesch, *Bosch*, p. 63.

55 *Ibid.*, p. 165; "Elektro- und Feinmechanische Industrie GmbH, Denkschrift der Geschäftsleitung, 9. 6. 1941," p. 7, Werksarchiv Bosch Hildesheim I/2.

56 Overesch, *Bosch*, p. 217.

57 "Elektro- und Feinmechanische Industrie GmbH, Denkschrift der Geschäftsleitung, 9. 6. 1941," p. 7, Werksarchiv Bosch Hildesheim I/2.

58 According to Trillke-Werke figures, 300 out of 2,208 German associates (13.6 percent) belonged to the NSDAP on March 1, 1945. For the male German workforce, however, the figure was 27 percent. "Stand der Belegschaft und Rückgang des NS-Einflusses in den Trillke-Werken," Werksarchiv Bosch Hildesheim. See also Overesch, *Bosch*, p. 252. At Robert Bosch GmbH, the ratio of NSDAP members to total numbers of German associates was just under 19 percent. See p. 173.

59 "Bericht über die Entwicklung der Firma Trillke-Werke GmbH Hildesheim (Stand März 1944)," Werksarchiv Bosch Hildesheim I/8; Overesch, *Bosch*, p. 33.

60 Original words: "[sich] auf die für Sonderfahrzeuge des Heeres (Panzerwagen-, Zugmaschinen-, Funkwagen-Aggregate und dergleichen) benötigten Ausrüstungsteile beschränken." Quoted from Overesch, *Bosch*, p. 151.

61 Original words: "[für die] schnellen Truppen." *Ibid.*

62 Overesch, *Bosch*, pp. 152 f.

63 *Ibid.*, p. 31; Fricke interview of May 6/7, 2010.

64 "Bericht über die Entwicklung des Werkes bis zum Herbst 1953, 25. 10. 1953," Werksarchiv Bosch Hildesheim I/2; Overesch, *Bosch*, p. 31.

65 Overesch, *Bosch*, pp. 38, 163, 237; Fricke interview of May 6/7, 2010.

66 "Oeffentliche Urkunde über die Gründung der 'Industria Aktiengesellschaft,' mit Sitz in Chur, 22. 5. 1930," RB 1 011 039; "Aufstellung, 14. 1. 1931," *ibid.*; "Hans Walz, Darstellung zur Industria Kontor AG und zur Robertina AG (März 1931)," RB 1 011 138 001; "Vermerk ZR vom 26. 8. 1985," RB 1 011 149 002.

67 "Hans Walz, Darstellung zur Industria Kontor AG und zur Robertina AG (März 1931)," RB 1 011 138 001.

68 "Vermerk ZR vom 26. 8. 1985," RB 1 011 149 002; "Abschrift REA/Gr 26. 3. 1952 betr. American Bosch Corporation," pp. 2 f., RB 1 022 031 004. Nakib was founded in 1929 by Danatbank and Stockholms Enskilda Bank. At the start of 1934, Bosch controlled approximately 82 percent of ABC shares issued. Of the Bosch shareholding in UABC, 39.4 percent was owned by Nakib, 16.9 percent belonged formally to Mendelssohn Amsterdam, 39.2 percent belonged to Industria Kontor AG and Robertina AG, and 4.5 percent belonged to Eisemann. *Ibid.*

69 "Aktennotiz Willy Schloßstein, 21. 11. 1947," RB 1 013 039. A contributory factor may have been that the Swiss government had decided to stop allowing revenue from German stocks and shares kept in Switzerland to be transferred. "S. Kuhn an O. Fischer, 13. 7. 1936," RB 1 011 086 007.

70 Quoted from "Aktennotiz Willy Schloßstein, 21. 11. 1947," RB 1 013 039. Scholtyseck feels that Bosch was trying to protect the non-German subsidiaries from confiscation by the regime, but this is not the case. See Scholtyseck, *Bosch*, p. 232. In fact the German authorities expressly agreed to the transaction. It brought in precisely what Göring had asked companies to provide in October 1936 – namely, large amounts of foreign exchange for the government. In any case, the shares concerned were already in Switzerland and the Netherlands – but in the possession of companies belonging to the Bosch Group.

71 "Vertrag zwischen der Robert Bosch GmbH und Mendelssohn & Co., Amsterdam, 6./7. 4. 1937," RB 1 022 071; "Gegenüberstellung der Verkaufs- und Rückkaufspreise, 26. 9. 1940," RB 1 022 071; "Karl Thomä, Aufzeichnung vom 5. 11. 1940," p. 6, RB 1 011 107; "Abschrift REA/Gr 26. 3. 1952 betr. American Bosch Corporation," pp. 2 f., RB 1 022 031 004; Scholtyseck, *Bosch*, p. 233. Mendelssohn Amsterdam later took over Scintilla AG/Guma and Ascot Water Heaters Ltd. In total, Mendelssohn Amsterdam paid Bosch the equivalent of some 7.37 million reichsmarks. "Gegenüberstellung der Verkaufs- und Rückkaufspreise, 26. 9. 1940," RB 1 022 071.

72 "Robert Bosch AG an die Wirtschaftsgruppe der Elektro-Industrie, Berlin, 26. 6. 1935," RB 1 011 086 007.

73 On Mannheimer's origins and business practices, see Julius H. Schoeps, *Das Erbe der Mendelssohns. Biographie einer Familie*, 2nd ed., Frankfurt am Main, 2011, pp. 316 ff.; André Kostolany, *Mehr als Geld und Gier*, 2nd ed., Munich, 2006, pp. 15 f.; Scholtyseck, *Bosch*, pp. 230 ff.

74 See p. 139.

75 *Ibid.*, pp. 320 f.; Christoph Kreutzmüller, *Händler und Handlungsgehilfen. Der Finanzplatz Amsterdam und die deutschen Großbanken (1918–1945)*, Stuttgart, 2005, p. 45. The former parent company in Berlin, Mendelssohn & Co., had already gone into liquidation at the end of 1938, following "aryanization" by Deutsche Bank.

76 "Karl Thomä, Aufzeichnung vom 5. 11. 1940," p. 2, RB 1 011 107.

77 *Ibid.*, p. 3.

78 Scholtyseck, *Bosch*, p. 293; Ulf Olsson, *Stockholms Enskilda Bank and the Bosch Group 1939–1950*, Stockholm, 1998, pp. 14 f.; "Aktennote betr. Besprechung mit Baron Waldemar von Oppenheim, 3. 11. 1939," RB 1 011 107.

79 "Vertrag zwischen der SEB, der AB Planeten und der Robert Bosch GmbH, 5. 12. 1939," RB 1 011 120 001; Olsson, *Stockholms Enskilda Bank*, pp. 14 f. See also Gerald Aalders, Cees Wiebes, "Stockholms Enskilda Bank, German Bosch and I. G. Farben. A short history of cloaking," in *Scandinavian Economic History Review*, 33, 1985/1, pp. 25–50; "Gegenüberstellung der Verkaufs- und Rückkaufspreise, 26. 9. 1940," RB 1 022 071.

80 Olsson, *Stockholms Enskilda Bank*, pp. 14 ff.

81 "Abschrift REA/Gr 26. 3. 1952 betr. American Bosch Corporation," p. 2k, RB 1 022 031 004; Olsson, *Stockholms Enskilda Bank*, pp. 16 ff.; "Aktennote vom 14. 6. 1945," RB 1 194 019; "Gegenüberstellung der Verkaufs- und Rückkaufspreise, 26. 9. 1940," RB 1 022 071.

82 "Karl Thomä, Aufzeichnung vom 5. 11. 1940," pp. 5 ff., RB 1 011 107; "Gegenüberstellung der Verkaufs- und Rückkaufspreise, 26. 9. 1940," RB 1 022 071. The holding in the British company, Ascot, was bought from Nakib by a Dutch company.

83 These were as follows: American Bosch Corp. (New York/Springfield), Robo AB (Stockholm), A/S Magneto (Copenhagen), A/S Automagnet (Oslo), SA Allumage Lumière (Brussels), Robert Bosch AG (Geneva), Equipo Bosch SA (Barcelona), Robert Bosch SA (Buenos Aires), Scintilla AG/Guma (Solothurn), Industria Kontor AG (Chur), Robertina AG (Glarus), Amsterdamsche Maatschappij voor Nijverheidsbelangen (Amsterdam), and N. V. Internationale Trust & Administratie Maatschappij "Fundus" (Maastricht). "Gegenüberstellung der Verkaufs- und Rückkaufspreise, 26. 9. 1940," RB 1 022 071.

84 *Ibid.*

85 *Ibid.*, pp. 21 f.; Scholtyseck, *Bosch*, p. 425.

86 "Department of Justice, War Division, Economic Warfare Section, Report on the Activities of Robert Bosch G.m.b.H. in the Fuel Injection Industry, 16. 6. 1943," pp. 24 ff., NARA RG 122, Box 2.

87 Fritz Mannheimer had deposited the shares there as collateral for a loan. "Abschrift REA/Gr 26. 3. 1952 betr. American Bosch Corporation," p. 2n, RB 1 022 031 004; *Office of Alien Property Custodian. Annual report for the period March 11, 1942 to June 30, 1943*, reprint, New York, 1977, p. 63.

88 Olsson, *Stockholms Enskilda Bank*, pp. 22 ff.

89 *Ibid.*, p. 25.

90 *Ibid.* Robert Bosch GmbH, Geneva, and shares in Scintilla AG/Guma had been sold in Switzerland as early as 1941.

91 "Excerpt from Documents pertaining to the Gold Transaction," pp. 9 ff., 18, RB 1 104 019 001.

92 Ralf Banken, *Edelmetallmangel und Großraubwirtschaft. Die Entwicklung des deutschen Edelmetallsektors im "Dritten Reich" 1933–1945* (Jahrbuch für Wirtschaftsgeschichte, supplement 13), Berlin, 2009; Unabhängige Expertenkommission Schweiz – Zweiter Weltkrieg, *Die Schweiz und die Goldtransaktionen im Zweiten Weltkrieg* (Veröffentlichungen der UEK, vol. 16), Zurich, 2002, pp. 43 f., 55 ff.

93 In the London Declaration of January 5, 1943, the Allies had already warned neutral countries not to perform transactions involving stolen property from the German sphere of domination. Unabhängige Expertenkommission Schweiz – Zweiter Weltkrieg, *Schweiz*, p. 149.

94 "Excerpt from Documents pertaining to the Gold Transaction," p. 21, RB 1 104 019 001.

95 The securities remained on deposit at Bankhaus Leu until the end of the war. The account was in the name of Célestine Frei-Meyer, the wife of Bosch's Swiss agent, Max Frei. *Ibid.*, pp. 23 ff., 29.

96 Mira Wilkins, *The history of foreign investments in the United States, 1914–1945* (Harvard Studies in Business History, 43), Cambridge/Mass., p. 541.

97 Olsson, *Stockholms Enskilda Bank*, pp. 28 ff.

98 "G. F.C. C., Étude sur le groupe Robert Bosch en Allemagne et à l'étranger, Sept. 1947," Archives du Ministère des affaires étrangères et européennes, La Courneuve, GMFB 2/312/2; "Dreilinden Maschinenbau GmbH, Kleinmachnow, Bericht der Geschäftsführer über das 5. Geschäftsjahr (Kalenderjahr 1940)," BArch R 8121/286; Martin, *Bosch*, p. 249.

99 But see p. 161.

100 Willi Glasbrenner, *Arbeit und Rüstung. Die Geschichte des Arbeitsdienstes und der Firma "Bosch" in Crailsheim 1933–1945*, Crailsheim, 2009, pp. 95 ff., 106 ff.

101 *Ibid.*, p. 141. The company gave a different reason after the war. Despite what the authorities had promised, Bosch said, not enough suitable workers had been found in Crailsheim. "Hermann Bauer, Bosch und seine Beteiligung an der Rüstung," p. 2, RB 1 013 062; "Betriebsgeschichte des Außenwerkes Bamberg, 17. 7. 1954," p. 1, RB 1 070 005.

102 Glasbrenner, *Arbeit*, pp. 141, 160; "Schreiben Az.2 f.-X-Dr. L./Sto., 16. 3. 1942," BArchM RW 21–65/12.

103 "Zweigstelle Nürnberg des Landesarbeitsamts Bayern an den Planungsreferenten beim Reichsstatthalter in Bayern, Flierl, 10. 8. 1939," RB 1 070 144 001; "Betriebsgeschichte des Außenwerks Bamberg, 17. 7. 1954," RB 1 070 005; "Das Außenwerk 1 – Bamberg," RB 1 070 144 001.

104 "Das Außenwerk 1 – Bamberg," RB 1 070 144 001.

105 "Betriebsgeschichte des Außenwerkes Bamberg, 17. 7. 1954," pp. 2 ff., RB 1 070 005.

106 Manurhin made meat-processing machinery, ammunition-producing machinery, and pistols. In the spring of 1940, the entire board of management had fled. The company's head office had been relocated to Cusset, near Vichy. "Deutsche Revisions- und Treuhand AG, Niederlassung Straßburg, Bericht des kommissarischen Verwalters betreffend Maschinenbauwerke AG, Mülhausen/Elsass, 20. 5. 1941," Archives Départementales du Haut-Rhin, Colmar, Purg 54075; "Rüstungskommando Straßburg, Aktennotiz vom 17. 10. 1940," *ibid.*

107 "Aktenvermerk, 9. 9. 1940," *ibid.* Bosch already had the status of "chief interested party" [*Hauptinteressent*] in the Bourtzwiller Manurhin plant. *Ibid.*

108 "Rundschreiben WOL Rosenberg betr. Foa 2 – Bosch Gliederung/Neues Außenwerk, 29. 10. 1940," RB 1 004 088; "Mietvertrag, 8. 10. 1940," Archives Départementales du Haut-Rhin, Colmar, Purg 54075; "Kaufvertrag, 10. 10. 1940," *ibid.*; "Vereinbarung über Einräumung eines Vorkaufsrechts, 8. 10. 1940," *ibid.*

109 Joachim Scholtyseck, *Der Aufstieg der Quandts. Eine deutsche Unternehmerdynastie*, Munich, 2011, p. 570.

110 "Hermann Bauer, Bosch und seine Beteiligung an der Rüstung," RB 1 013 062.

111 In September 1943, Sundgau Maschinenbau GmbH employed 3,213 persons. These included not only 2,872 Alsatians, 160 Germans, 30 French, and forced labor from several countries, but also a number of Swiss nationals. "Sundgau Maschinenbau GmbH, Zusammenstellung der in den geschützten Betrieben des A. O. III Rü Straßburg i. E. beschäftigten Arbeitskräfte nach dem Stand vom 21. 9. 1943," BArchM RW 20–5/41.

112 In this connection, see pp. 203 ff.

113 "Economic Warfare Section, Department of Justice, Confidential Report June 16, 1943," in "Department of Justice, War Division, Economic Warfare Section, Report on the Activities of Robert Bosch G.m.b.H. in the Fuel Injection Industry, 16. 6. 1943," p. 38, NARA RG 122, Box 2 (also in RB 1 010 249). Headcount at Lavalette rose to 437 by June 1943. "Zahl der mit Geräten oder Teilen nach Bosch-Konstruktion Beschäftigten bei den Nachbauern, Zulieferern und Außenwerkstätten, sowie zusätzlicher Leutebedarf," RB 1 051 062.

114 "Hans Walz, Erklärung, 28. 7. 1948," p. 23, RB 1 013 036.

115 "Robert Bosch GmbH, Verkaufshaus Berlin, Bericht über die Ostreise von Ernst Gmelin (Leiter des Verkaufshauses Berlin) in der Zeit vom 1. 5.–13. 5. 1944, 2. 6. 1944," RB 1 013 148. The BDK plants were army-owned but operated by Bosch on a fiduciary basis.

116 Fastnacht, Kuhlgatz, Schmitt, Siegel, *125 years*, p. 203.

117 On the number of drafts, see Robert Bosch GmbH, 1946 annual report, p. 10. On forced labor, see pp. 218–35.

118 See table 14, p. 210.

119 See the appendix, p. 663, Bosch Group headcount and sales revenue (1886–2012)."

120 "G.F.C.C., Étude sur le groupe Robert Bosch en Allemagne et à l'étranger, Sept. 1947," Archives du Ministère des affaires étrangères et européennes, La Courneuve, GMFB 2/312/2; "Personalstand vom 31. 12. 1944," RB 1 007 086.

121 "G.F.C.C., Étude sur le groupe Robert Bosch en Allemagne et à l'étranger, Sept. 1947," Archives du Ministère des affaires étrangères et européennes, La Courneuve, GMFB 2/312/2. Sales at Blaupunkt were 30 million reichsmarks in 1939, 17.5 million reichsmarks in 1940, and 28.5 million reichsmarks in 1941. *Ibid.*

122 *B.I.O.S. Final report No. 551, German Wireless Communication, mainly with reference to Cm, Dm and Pulse Technique*, London, 1946; Wolfgang Scharschmidt, *Röhrenhistorie. Die Technikgeschichte der Elektronenröhre*, vol. 4: *Deutsche Wehrmachtsröhren*, Dessau, 2010.

123 Overesch, *Bosch*, p. 218; "Zahl der mit Geräten oder Teilen nach Bosch-Konstruktion Beschäftigten bei den Nachbauern, Zulieferern und Außenwerkstätten, sowie zusätzlicher Leutebedarf," RB 1 051 062; Robert Bosch GmbH, 1944 annual report, p. 4.

124 Joseph Hoppe, "Fernsehen als Waffe. Militär und Fernsehen in Deutschland 1935–1950," in Museum für Verkehr und Technik (ed.), *Ich diente nur der Technik. Sieben Karrieren zwischen 1940 und 1950* (Schriftenreihe des Museums für Verkehr und Technik, vol. 13), Berlin, 1995, p. 76.

125 *Ibid.*, pp. 67 ff.

126 *Ibid.*, p. 78.

127 Speer believed "that the Reich ought not to become involved with private corporations unless some utterly compelling necessity presented itself." *Ibid.*, pp. 74 ff., 78 f.

128 That was how Paul Goerz described the situation in a letter to Eric C. Rassbach.
"Goerz an Rassbach, 14. 1. 1944," RB 1 610 021. See also Hoppe, *Fernsehen*, pp. 80 f.

129 The group overseeing electrical equipment for the armed forces was headed by
Erich Carl Rassbach, a member of the Bosch board of management, the special T–15
committee by his colleague Ernst Durst.

130 "Der Reichsminister für Bewaffnung und Munition an die Geschäftsführung der
Robert Bosch GmbH, 3. 3. 1943," RB 1 013 064.

131 "Walter Schiedt, Erklärung, 11. 12. 1946," RB 1 013 064; "Leistungsbericht der Siling-
Werke GmbH, erstattet zur Erlangung der ersten Anerkennungsurkunde im Leis-
tungswettkampf deutscher Betriebe (Mai 1944)," RB 1 611 001/2. On the history of
Christian Dierig AG, see Christian Dierig AG Augsburg (ed.), *Das Werk von fünf
Generationen – 150 Jahre Dierig*, Augsburg, 1955.

132 "Hermann Bauer, Bosch und seine Beteiligung an der Rüstung," RB 1 013 062.

133 Alfred Konieczny, "Das KZ Groß-Rosen in Niederschlesien," in Ulrich Herbert,
Karin Orth, Christoph Dieckmann (eds.), *Die nationalsozialistischen Konzentrationslager. Entwicklung und Struktur*, vol. 1, Göttingen, 1998, p. 317.

134 "Siling-Apparatebau GmbH an die Kriminalpolizei Stuttgart, 26. 2. 1952," ITS Digitales Archiv Doc. No. 82111434#1.

135 Theodor Baumann had worked for Bosch as an engineer since 1921, and since 1929
he had been technical manager of the oiler plant. "Personalstammkarte Theodor
Baumann," RB 1 094 011; "Leitende Bosch-Männer, Baumann," in *Bosch-Zünder*
1959/5, p. 103. Alfred Brack had joined Robert Bosch GmbH in 1936. Among other
posts in the company he had filled that of commercial-organization adviser to contract factories. "Lebenslauf Alfred Brack," RB 1 611 003.

136 "Leistungsbericht der Siling-Werke GmbH, erstattet zur Erlangung der ersten
Anerkennungsurkunde im Leistungswettkampf deutscher Betriebe (Mai 1944),"
pp. 5 f., RB 1 611 001/2. According to a later statement, up to 1,200 personnel were
transferred from Stuttgart to Langenbielau. "Spruchkammer Stuttgart, Kammer 7,
Feuerbach, Aufgliederung der Spruchbegründung zum Verfahren Langenbielau,
durchgeführt in der Zeit vom 22. 9.–24. 10. 1947," p. 8, RB 1 611 002.

137 "Leistungsbericht der Siling-Werke GmbH, erstattet zur Erlangung der ersten
Anerkennungsurkunde im Leistungswettkampf deutscher Betriebe (Mai 1944),"
RB 1 611 001/2.

138 "Hermann Bauer, Eidesstattliche Erklärung, 20. 3. 1946," StA Ludwigsburg EL 902/20,
Bü 90857 (denazification court files, Hermann Bauer).

139 "Spruchkammer Stuttgart, Kammer 7, Feuerbach, Aufgliederung der Spruchbegründung zum Verfahren Langenbielau, durchgeführt in der Zeit vom 22. 9.–
24. 10. 1947," pp. 59 f., RB 1 611 002. External camps belonging to the Groß-Rosen
concentration camp had been built in Langenbielau and Reichenbach. Alfred
Konieczny, "Langenbielau I (Bielawa)," in Wolfgang Benz, Barbara Distel (eds.), *Der
Ort des Terrors. Geschichte der nationalsozialistischen Konzentrationslager*, vol. 6:
Natzweiler, Groß-Rosen, Stutthof, Munich, 2007, pp. 377–80.

140 On this relocation, see p. 202. See also Overesch, *Bosch*, p. 237.

141 "Hermann Bauer, Eidesstattliche Erklärung, 20. 3. 1946," StA Ludwigsburg
EL 902/20, Bü 90857 (denazification court files, Hermann Bauer). Bauer was standing in at this meeting for Ernst Durst, who headed special group T–15.

142 *Ibid.* In regard to Bosch, Milch is said to have told Bauer: "Such obstinacy as you and your company display I have never encountered before." *Ibid.*

143 "Bericht des BW Mai 1945 – Dezember 1949, Flieger-Angriffe auf die Feuerbacher- und Stuttgarter-Werke," RB 1 024 454.

144 "Hermann Bauer, Bosch und seine Beteiligung an der Rüstung," p. 3, RB 1 013 062.

145 In the towns and villages around Bruttig, it was soon being rumored that Bosch was going to assemble Hitler's "miracle weapon," the V2. In fact, the tunnel accommodated only a small and relatively simple production operation involving spark plugs. Ernst Heimes, *Ich habe immer nur den Zaun gesehen. Suche nach dem KZ-Außenlager Cochem*, 4th ed., Koblenz, 1999, p. 170.

146 "Hermann Bauer, Bosch und seine Beteiligung an der Rüstung," p. 3, RB 1 013 062; "Robert Bosch GmbH, Abteilung Widu/WEL an Bauleitung A7, 6. 4. 1944," RB 1 636 001.

147 "Bericht über die Besichtigung der Grube 'Rothe Erde' in Deutschoth am 3./4. 6. 1944," RB 1 024 350; "ROWA GmbH an die Bauleitung 'Rothe Erde'," 21. 8. 1944," *ibid.*

148 "Verlagerung der Einspritzpumpenfertigung von der Dreilinden Maschinenbau GmbH, Kleinmachnow, in die Flugmotorenwerke Ostmark/Brünn," RB 1 606 004; "Abschlussbericht über die Tätigkeit des Bosch Stoßtrupps in FO-Brünn in der Zeit vom 5. 8. 1943 bis 4. 4. 1944," RB 1 606 003. In Boletice, Bosch found a temporary home at Konkordia-Spinnerei Stöhr & Co.

149 In the so-called "Blaupunkt-Bunker" (measuring approximately 2,000 m²) beneath the stadium stands, the company produced condensers. "Fertigungsverlagerungen Stand 1. 1. 1945," RB 1 013 156; "Blaupunkt-Werke GmbH an Studio Bochum, 19. 2. 1990," RB 1 707 027. It is not true that Blaupunkt had been manufacturing fuses for anti-aircraft guns there since 1938 – an account found in Thomas Schmidt, *Das Berliner Olympia-Stadion und seine Geschichte*, Berlin, 1983, p. 19.

150 "Der Gauleiter und Reichsstatthalter im Sudetengau, Verlagerungsausschuss, an Firma Junkers & Co, GmbH, 11. 8. 1944," LHASA, DE Junkers Wärmetechnik Dessau no. 122.

151 "Das Außenwerk 1 – Bamberg," RB 1 070 144 001.

152 "Aktennotiz, 5. 10. 1944," RB 1 024 475.

153 "Liste derjenigen Gegenstände, die von der Robert Bosch GmbH Stuttgart zum Schutz gegen Luftangriffe in der Grube der Salzwerk AG Heilbronn untergebracht wurden, 27. 6. 1945," RB 1 024 488; "Liste der Kunstwerke, die von der Robert Bosch GmbH, Stuttgart, im Salzbergwerk Heilbronn verlagert sind [sic], 9. 10. 1945," *ibid.*

154 "Zusammenstellung der Verlagerungsorte und Verlagerungsbetriebe der Robert Bosch GmbH (einschl. SGMG)," RB 1 024 453.

155 Holger Lange, "Bosch im Krieg," in *Reutlinger Nachrichten,* April 23, 2011.

156 "Zusammenstellung der Verlagerungsorte und Verlagerungsbetriebe der Robert Bosch GmbH (einschl. SGMG)," RB 1 024 453; Robert Bosch GmbH, 1945 annual report.

157 The Giengen engineering-works site was later bought by Bosch. The company built a household-appliances plant there, which now belongs to BSH Bosch und Siemens Hausgeräte GmbH. In Reutlingen after the war, Bosch continued to run a branch manufacturing operation until 1953. In 1964, the Ulrich Gminder AG plant was taken over by Bosch.

158 See "Jahresbericht 1947, Belegschafts-Verhältnis einschl. Außenwerke und Außenstellen (ohne TOGE)," RB 1 003 478.

159 See "Personalstand am 31. 12. 1944," RB 1 007 086.

160 "Stand am 23. 12. 1942," RB 1 007 086; "Personalstand vom 31. 12. 1944," *ibid.*; "Das Außenwerk 1 – Bamberg," RB 1 070 144 001.

161 See also Tooze, *Wages*, pp. 358 ff.

162 "Unsere Betriebsgemeinschaft. Ein Leistungsbericht der Robert Bosch GmbH Kriegsjahr 1940/41," MS, Stuttgart, 1941, pp. 191 ff., RB 700 004.

163 "Helmut Leinss, Vor zwanzig Jahren," RB 1 044 003/4.

164 *Ibid.*; "Niederschrift der Sitzung des Aufsichtsrats der Robert Bosch GmbH am 21. 10. 1948," RB 1 002 007.

165 In the retreat, only 25–30 freight-car loads of machinery could be recovered. About 20 of those made it back to Stuttgart. That corresponded to less than 10 percent of the plant equipment that Bosch had transported to Langenbielau in 300 freight cars in 1943. "Hermann Bauer, Bosch und seine Beteiligung an der Rüstung," p. 5, RB 1 013 062.

166 On the war's end in Hildesheim, see Overesch, *Bosch*, p. 248.

167 "Vermerk betr. Bericht von Kretschmer über Reise nach Berlin, Dessau und Apolda vom 2.–24. 7. 1945, 26. 7. 1945," RB 1 606 003.

168 "Paul Vogelgsang tritt in den Ruhestand," in *Bosch-Zünder* 1957/12, p. 254; "Auszug aus dem Journal des NKWD/MWD-Speziallagers Buchenwald über Heinrich Walschtenbach [*sic*], 21. 12. 1998," RB 1 606 025.

169 Kurz, *Chronik*, pp. 1020 ff.; Sauer, *Murr*, pp. 150 ff.; Roland Müller, *Stuttgart zur Zeit des Nationalsozialismus*, Stuttgart, 1988, pp. 529 ff.; Nachtmann, "Murr," p. 197; Scholtyseck, *Bosch*, p. 536.

170 Robert Bosch GmbH, 1946 annual report, p. 10.

171 Overesch, *Bosch*, pp. 282 ff.

172 "G.F.C.C., Étude sur le groupe Robert Bosch en Allemagne et à l'étranger, Sept. 1947," Archives du Ministère des affaires étrangères et européennes, La Courneuve, GMFB 2/312/2.

173 In connection with the 1940 hidden reserves, see p. 585, note 13; on the development of sales, see the table in the appendix, "Bosch Group headcount and sales revenue (1886–2012)," p. 663.

5 Beyond the bounds of the "Bosch community": forced labor

1 Mark Spoerer, *Zwangsarbeit unter dem Hakenkreuz*, Stuttgart, 2001, pp. 15, 223. See also Ulrich Herbert, *Fremdarbeiter. Politik und Praxis des "Ausländer-Einsatzes" in der Kriegswirtschaft des Dritten Reiches*, 3rd ed., Bonn, 1999.

2 *Ibid.*, pp. 221 ff., 226.

3 Provisions contained in sections 6 and 52 of the Convention respecting the Laws and Customs of War on Land of October 18, 1907.

4 Spoerer, *Zwangsarbeit*, pp. 151 f.

5 *Ibid.*, p. 158.

6 Soviet POWs received around 8 reichsmarks a week, other POWs around 16 reichsmarks a week, whereas the average German industrial worker earned 51 reichsmarks a week. Furthermore, POWs were paid only in camp money. *Ibid.*, pp. 165 f.

7 Ulrich Herbert, "Zwangsarbeit im 'Dritten Reich.' Kenntnisstand, offene Fragen, Forschungsprobleme," in Gabrielle Hauch (ed.), *Industrie und Zwangsarbeit im Nationalsozialismus. Mercedes-Benz – VW – Reichswerke Hermann Göring in Linz und Salzgitter*, Innsbruck, 2003, p. 16; Tooze, *Wages*, p. 537.

8 Mark Spoerer, "Profitierten Unternehmen von KZ-Arbeit? Eine kritische Analyse der Literatur," in *Historische Zeitschrift*, 268, 1999/1, pp. 61–91.

9 "Luckau an Wild, 16. 6. 1947," RB 1 012 003.

10 "Hans Walz, Erklärung vom 22. 7. 1947," p. 22, RB 1 013 036.

11 "Hans Walz, Erklärung, 22. 7. 1947," RB 1 013 034, sheet 68.

12 "Otto Debatin, Robert Bosch GmbH und NSDAP," p. 18, RB 1 013 078.

13 "Hans Walz, Erklärung, 28. 7. 1948," p. 22, RB 1 013 036.

14 RB 1 012 046 (Feuerbach incl. Crailsheim); RB 1 012 042–1 012 044 (Langenbielau).

15 *Zwangsarbeit in Stuttgart, 1939–1945. Ein Gedenkblatt*, ed. by Stiftung Geißstraße Sieben, Stuttgart 2000, p. 5.

16 "Rundschreiben BOL 1 betr. Arbeitseinsatz von Kriegsgefangenen bei Bosch, 31. 12. 1940," RB 1 012 004. On deployment of forced labor in Stuttgart, see also Müller, *Stuttgart*, pp. 411–25.

17 "Rundschreiben PEL betr. Unterkunft für ausländische Arbeitskräfte, 28. 3. 1941," RB 1 012 005.

18 Spoerer, *Zwangsarbeit*, pp. 81 f.

19 "PEL (Debatin) an alle Leitungen und an die Abteilungsvorstände der Verwaltung, 6. 11. 1942," RB 1 012 005.

20 "Personalstatistik Stand 23. 12. 1942," RB 1 007 086.

21 "Aktenvermerk über eine Besprechung am 18. 11. 1942," BArch R 8121/197.

22 "Robert Bosch GmbH, Abt. BPL 2, Beschäftigtenmeldung 30. 11. 1944," RB 1 012 003, sheet 12.

23 "Namenslisten Werke Feuerbach," RB 1 012 025 and RB 1 025 027.

24 Prison labor did not begin in the Third Reich, of course. However, since at that time penitentiaries contained a great many victims of political persecution, these too presumably suffered their share of National Socialist injustice. The reports of Alfred Hausser give some impression of this. As the head of an illegal Communist youth league, Hausser had been sentenced to 15 years' imprisonment. From 1939 he had to work for Bosch. Manfred Dautel, *Ehemalige Zwangsarbeiterinnen und Zwangsarbeiter in Stuttgart. Ein Beitrag zur noch nicht erforschten Geschichte der Stadt Stuttgart*, published by IG Metall Stuttgart, VVN-BdA Stuttgart, and Interessengemeinschaft der ehemaligen Zwangsarbeiterinnen und Zwangsarbeiter unter dem Naziregime, Stuttgart, 1997, pp. 12 ff.

25 The number of Ludwigsburg penitentiary inmates working for Bosch grew during the war, reaching almost 300. At the end of 1944, 232 inmates of Celle penitentiary and 41 inmates of the one in Brandenburg were on the books of Bosch, or rather Trillke-Werke and DLMG. Siling-Werke had 70 female inmates of Jauer/Eulengebirge penitentiary working for them in November 1944. Records of numbers employed on production operations in the penitentiary in Schwäbisch Hall are unknown. Documents on this subject can be found at RB 1 012 003, RB 1 012 006, and RB 1 013 165.

26 "Hans Walz, Erklärung, 28. 7. 1948," p. 22, RB 1 013 036.

27 "Luckau an Wild, 16. 6. 1947," RB 1 012 003. Luckau's 1947 letter still uses National Socialist terminology, mentioning "Angehörige der jüdischen Rasse oder jüdisch versippte ("members of the Jewish race or mixed-race Jews").

28 "Liste Zwangsarbeiter Trillke-Werke GmbH, Hildesheim," RB 1 012 007. According to this, a total of 2,711 non-German civilian workers and prisoners of war were employed at ELFI/Trillke-Werke during the war, including 14 from Bulgaria, Spain, and Switzerland, and 9 stateless persons.

29 Martin, *Bosch*, pp. 33, 265, 269.

30 *Ibid.*, pp. 275 ff.

31 *Ibid.*, p. 270.

32 Haus, Sarkowicz, *Using energy*, pp. 114 f. Wilhelm Stoll, who headed the company during the war, said something different. By his account, at the end of the war 1,800 non-German workers were employed in the Dessau and Asch plants. "Öffentliche Sitzung der Spruchkammer 3 Vaihingen, Protokoll der öffentlichen Sitzung am 14. 6. 1948 im Verfahren gegen Wilhelm Stoll," StA Ludwigsburg EL 920/20, Bü 74674.

33 On this and what follows, see table 15 on p. 224.

34 "Personalstand vom 31. 12. 1944," RB 1 007 086.

35 "Beschäftigtenmeldung vom 30. 11. 1944," RB 1 012 003.

36 6,451 forced laborers assigned to Langenbielau less 261 in Siling-Werke. Lists of names in RB 1 012 025 and RB 1 012 027.

37 As at March 5, 1945 (number of non-German workers [male and female] in group accommodation). Martin, *Bosch*, p. 270.

38 As at September 30, 1944. Overesch, *Bosch*, p. 251.

39 "Liste Zwangsarbeiter Trillke-Werke GmbH, Hildesheim," RB 1 012 007. In this connection, see note 28 above.

40 As at May 1, 1944, "Leistungsbericht der Siling-Werke GmbH (Mai 1944)," p. 6, RB 1 611 001/2.

41 Lists of names in RB 1 012 025 and RB 1 012 027.

42 RB 1 012 014.

43 Haus, Sarkowicz, *Using energy*, pp. 114 f.

44 "Verlagerungsbetriebe Blaupunkt, 1. 1. 1945," RB 1 012 003.

45 According to a newspaper report. See Heimes, *Zaun*, p. 179.

46 "Hans Walz, Erklärung, 22. 7. 1947," RB 1 013 034, sheet 68.

47 On the Crailsheim operation, see Glasbrenner, *Arbeit*, p. 160; on the Bamberg back-up plant, see "Ausländereinsatz während des Krieges in AW1," RB 1 070 144 001.

48 Scholtyseck, *Bosch*, p. 382.

49 Martin, *Bosch*; Angela Martin, Ewa Czerwiakowski (eds.), *Muster des Erinnerns. Polnische Frauen als KZ-Häftlinge in einer Tarnfabrik von Bosch*, Berlin, 2005, pp. 51 f.; Overesch, *Bosch*, pp. 213 ff.; Stefan A. Oyen, Manfred Overesch, "'Starter für den Krieg.' Bosch Hildesheim im Dritten Reich," in Andreas Heusler, Mark Spoerer, Helmuth Trischler (eds.), *Rüstung, Kriegswirtschaft und Zwangsarbeit im "Dritten Reich*," Munich, 2010, pp. 107–37.

50 Spoerer, *Zwangsarbeit*, p. 226.

51 Martin, *Bosch*, pp. 275 ff.; "Verlagerungsbetriebe Blaupunkt, 1. 1. 1945," RB 1 012 003; "Jan Pankiewicz, Erinnerungsbericht (quote on p. 4 and p. 9)," Archiwum Muzeum Gross-Rosen, 4293/DP; "Leistungsbericht der Siling-Werke GmbH (Mai 1944)," RB 1 611 001/2.

52 http://www.fhxb-museum.de/zwangsarbeit/index.htm. According to this source, 19 female Jewish forced laborers worked at Blaupunkt-Werk II in Berlin's Köpenicker Str. until 1942–43. We know from what happened to the Samuel family (as documented by Götz Aly) that Jews liable for compulsory service (and who were later deported) were also forced to work at other Blaupunkt locations in Berlin. Götz Aly, *Im Tunnel. Das kurze Leben der Marion Samuel 1931–1943*, Frankfurt am Main, 2004. Other references to Jewish labor deployment at Blaupunkt can be found in Wolf Gruner, *Der geschlossene Arbeitseinsatz deutscher Juden*, Berlin, 1997, pp. 164, 226.

53 "Verlagerungsbetriebe Blaupunkt, 1.1.1945," RB 1 012 003; "Jan Pankiewicz, Erinnerungsbericht (quote on p. 4 and p. 9)," Archiwum Muzeum Groß-Rosen, 4293/DP. The reports and papers examined from the Groß-Rosen Memorial contain no reference to any connection with another "commando," a center for high-frequency research called the "Weather Station Commando" (likewise relocated to Groß-Rosen from Dachau concentration camp in 1943). On this research center, see Alfred Konieczny, *Das "Kommando Wetterstelle" im KL Groß-Rosen*, Wałbrzych, 1994; on the Groß-Rosen concentration camp, see Isabell Sprenger, *Groß-Rosen. Ein Konzentrationslager in Schlesien*, Cologne, 1996; Isabell Sprenger, Walter Kumpmann, "Groß-Rosen – Stammlager," in Benz, Distel (eds.), *Ort*, vol. 6, pp. 195–221; Konieczny, "Groß-Rosen."

54 On the Langenbielau subcamp, see Konieczny, "Langenbielau," pp. 377 ff.

55 "DLMG/KGL betr. Besuch in Deutschoth, 9. 8. 1944," RB 1 024 350; "Bericht über Besprechung betr. Küchenerrichtung für ROWA am 18. 8. 1944, 18. 8. 1944," *ibid.*; "ROWA GmbH an die Bauleitung 'Rothe Erde,' 21. 8. 1944," *ibid.* At the time an annex of Natzweiler concentration camp already existed in Audun-le-Tiche, where an underground factory was also fitted out for Volkswagen.

56 Evacuated on September 1, 1944, the inmates of the subcamp were subsequently put to work in the Kochendorf salt mine near Heilbronn. Klaus Riexinger, "Deutsch-Oth (Audun-le-Tiche)," in Benz, Distel (eds.), *Ort*, vol. 6, pp. 75 f.

57 "Robert Bosch GmbH, Abteilung Widu/WEL an Bauleitung A7, 6.4.1944," RB 1 636 001.

58 See Heimes, *Zaun*, p. 180.

59 "Hans Walz, Erklärung 22. 7. 1947," RB 1 013 034.

60 "Spruchkammer 11 Stuttgart, Spruch gegen Otto Debatin, 28./29. 5. 1948," p. 8, RB 1 832 001. A former Stalag administrator was among those giving assurances that POWs received "decent, humane treatment from Robert Bosch GmbH representatives." "Wilhelm Dick, Erklärung, 7. 12. 1946," StA Ludwigsburg EL 902/20, Bü 103816.

61 "Auslandsbriefprüfstelle Wien, Stimmungsbericht, 4. 9. 1942 (NI-1208)," NARA T-301, Roll 12/1201. In this connection, see also Scholtyseck, *Bosch*, p. 380.

62 "Zeugenaussage Eberle im Spruchkammerverfahren Hans Walz," EL 902/20, Bü 87568.

63 Dautel, *Zwangsarbeiterinnen*, p. 4.

64 "Rundschreiben 1. 2. 1945 betr. Boschstollen am Siegelberg," RB 1 013 268.

65 Letter from Emil Schmid to the Mühlhausen works council, August 29, 1947," cited in Dautel, *Zwangsarbeiterinnen*, p. 6.

66 "Protokoll über die Verpflegung russischer Kriegsgefangener im Arbeitskommando 3096 bei der Robert Bosch GmbH, Stuttgart, Betriebsteil Mühlhausen a. N., 18. 10. 1945," RB 1 012 003.

67 "De Gületen an Abt, 11. 10. 1946," StA Ludwigsburg EL 902/20, Bü 103816.

68 "Oskar Kiess, Wesentliche Gesichtspunkte über die Behandlung und den Einsatz ausländischer Arbeitskräfte im Lichtwerk, 18. 2. 1948," RB 1 012 003.

69 "PEL (Debatin) an alle Leitungen und an die Abteilungsvorstände der Verwaltung, 6. 11. 1942," RB 1 012 005.

70 *Ibid.*

71 Ruud de Koning, *Brieven van mijn vader Henk de Koning uit Duitsland en Tsjechië 1942–1945*, Assen, 2008.

72 Martin, Czerwiakowski (eds.), *Muster*, pp. 51 f.

73 Martin, *Bosch*, pp. 161, 195; Martin, Czerwiakowski (eds.), *Muster*, p. 51.

74 Martin, *Bosch*, p. 151.

75 "[Das Unternehmen] habe hier die soziale Tradition seines Hauses aktivieren können." Overesch, *Bosch*, pp. 231, 233 (quote); Fricke interview of May 6/7, 2010.

76 Overesch, *Bosch*, p. 239; "De Gületen an Abt, 11. 10. 1946," StA Ludwigsburg EL 902/20, Bü 103816. Hans Teich, who after the war chaired the works council at Trillke-Werke, reported that in the tool-building shed convicts had to work in a locked wire cage. Teich, *Hildesheim*, p. 66.

77 Oyen, Overesch, "'Starter für den Krieg'," p. 131.

78 Overesch, *Bosch*, p. 239.

79 Quoted from *ibid.*, p. 227.

80 Fricke interview of May 6/7, 2010.

81 "Spruchkammer Stuttgart, Kammer 7, Feuerbach, Aufgliederung der Spruchbegründung zum Verfahren Langenbielau, durchgeführt in der Zeit vom 22. 9.–24. 10. 1947," p. 9, StA Ludwigsburg EL 902/20, Bü 78868 (see also RB 1 611 002).

82 *Ibid.*, pp. 17 ff. Veronika Dietz, the fellow-worker to whom Adler had given the food and money, was denounced to the Gestapo and sent to a concentration camp.

83 *Ibid.*, pp. 22, 55. Adler's widow later unsuccessfully filed charges against Robert Bosch GmbH. The court took the view that willful murder could not be proven. By then, the crime had lapsed. StA Ludwigsburg EL 317 III, Bü 114.

84 "Spruchkammerverfahren gegen Hans Walz," StA Ludwigsburg EL 902/20, Bü 87568; "Debatin an Wild, 29. 3. 1947," RB 1 832 058.

85 "Zeugenaussage Eberle im Spruchkammerverfahren gegen Hans Walz, Protokoll der öffentlichen Sitzung der Spruchkammer Bad Cannstatt am 9. 6. 1948," StA Ludwigsburg EL 902/20, Bü 87568.

86 "Debatin an Wild, 29. 3. 1947," RB 1 832 058.

87 "Spruchkammer Stuttgart, Kammer 7, Verfahren Langenbielau, 24. 10. 1947," StA Ludwigsburg EL 902/20, Bü 78868; "Zentral-Spruchkammer Nord-Württemberg, Spruch gegen Theodor Baumann, 31. 8. 1950," *ibid.*, sheets 183, 187; "Personalstammkarte Theodor Baumann," RB 1 094 011; "Leitende Bosch-Männer, Baumann," in *Bosch-Zünder* 1959/5, p. 103.

88 "Spruchkammer Stuttgart, Kammer 7, Feuerbach, Aufgliederung der Spruchbegründung zum Verfahren Langenbielau, durchgeführt in der Zeit vom 22. 9.–24. 10. 1947," StA Ludwigsburg EL 902/20, Bü 78868.

89 "Jan Pankiewicz, Erinnerungsbericht (quoted on p. 4 and p. 9)," Archiwum Muzeum Groß-Rosen, 4293/DP. When Groß-Rosen was evacuated in January 1944, the Blaupunkt Commando detainees were moved to Mittelbau-Dora concentration camp. From there, shortly before the end of the war they were taken to Bergen-Belsen, where they too were obliged to undertake one of the notorious death marches.

90 "Ob es deutsche Frauen und Mädchen im politischen Russland wohl ebenso gut hätten? Und wie in Russland unsere deutschen Kriegsgefangenen behandelt werden, weiss niemand. Wir appellieren an die Denkenden unserer Gefolgschaft und bitten sie, auch ihrerseits dafür zu sorgen, dass deutsche Gutmütigkeit nicht in Würdelosigkeit ausartet." Quoted from "Spruchkammer 11, Stuttgart, Spruch gegen Otto Debatin, 28./29. 5. 1948," p. 8, RB 1 832 001 (StA Ludwigsburg EL 902/20, Bü 103816). A fuller version of the quote from Debatin's notice may be found in Scholtyseck, *Bosch*, p. 380.

91 Cited in "Spruchkammer 11 Stuttgart, Spruch gegen Otto Debatin, 28./29. 5. 1948," p. 8, RB 1 832 001.

92 Bühler may even have played an active part in the case, although police investigations after the war could no longer prove this. "Polizeipräsidium Stuttgart, Informationsdienst, an die Spruchkammer Stuttgart, 12. 12. 1946," RB 1 010 195.

93 "Debatin an Wild, 29. 3. 1947," RB 1 832 058. In this connection, see also Scholtyseck, *Bosch*, p. 381.

94 "Leistungsgrad der ausländischen Zivilarbeiter und Kriegsgefangenen, alle Werke, 23. 6. 1943," RB 1 012 005.

95 In this connection, see also the details of an investigation by the national chamber of commerce [*Reichswirtschaftskammer*], a study covering the Rhineland and Westphalia, and the well-known Krupp study in Spoerer, *Zwangsarbeit*, pp. 186 ff.; Tooze, *Wages*, p. 537. These investigations ranked the output of French civilian workers at some 80–90 percent of the German norm, that of male civilian workers from the Soviet Union between 60 and 100 percent, while female civilian workers from eastern Europe performed to the same level as their German counterparts. Only concentration-camp inmates and Soviet POWs deployed in the construction industry had a markedly lower output at 50 percent of the German norm or less. On the productivity of forced labor at Trillke-Werke, see p. 230.

96 On forced-labor counts among German companies prior to 2000, see Spoerer, *Zwangsarbeit*, p. 248. Regarding Bosch, see also the article "Bosch muss Zwangsarbeiter nicht entschädigen," in *Stuttgarter Nachrichten*, January 26, 2000.

97 "Karl Gutbrod, Gedankenskizze zum Thema Zwangsarbeit, 21. 2. 1999," RB 1 012 037. A similar source is "Stellungnahme zur Frage der Zwangsarbeiter-Entschädigung, 20. 8. 1998," RB 1 012 037.

98 "Ise Bosch an Bierich, 10. 12. 1998," RB 1 016 730. See also Bierich's reply, dated December 12, 1998, and a note of February 2, 1999, *ibid.*

99 Susanne-Sophia Spiliotis, *Verantwortung und Rechtsfrieden. Die Stiftungsinitiative der deutschen Wirtschaft*, Frankfurt am Main, 2003, p. 49.

100 Original words: "keine moralische Schuld, wenn auch eine materielle Verpflichtung der deutschen Wirtschaft." "Hans L. Merkle, Stellungnahme zu dem Grundsatzpapier für das Bundeskanzleramt, 12. 2. 1999," RB 1 012 037.

101 Original words: "moralische Verantwortung der deutschen Wirtschaft." Quotes in this and the previous note from Spiliotis, *Verantwortung*, p. 286.

6 The Bosch circle and resistance to Hitler

1 The *Württembergischer Metallindustriellenverband* and the *Vereinigung württembergischer Arbeitgeberverbände* respectively. Scholtyseck, *Bosch*, pp. 200 f.

2 Der "Rote Hahn". Künstler, Polizeidirektor, Widerständler 1883–1952. Ein Gedenkblatt, ed. by Stiftung Geißstraße Sieben, Stuttgart 2003; "Willy Schloßstein, Einstellung des Herrn B. und seiner Firma zum Nazi-Regime, Juli 1945," p. 6, RB 1 013 076.

3 Heuss, *Bosch*, p. 544.

4 Schmitt, *Bäuerle*.

5 Original word: "Lobhudelei." *Ibid.*, p. 97.

6 Christoph Markschies, "Carl und Friedrich Goerdeler," in Joachim Mehlhausen (ed.), *Zeugen des Widerstands*. Ehemalige Studenten der Universität Tübingen, die im Kampf gegen den Nationalsozialismus starben, 2nd ed., Tübingen, 1999, pp. 151 ff., 161 ff.; Sabine Gillmann, Hans Mommsen (eds.), *Politische Schriften und Briefe Carl Goerdelers*, Munich, 2003; Daniela Rüther, *Der Widerstand des 20. Juli* *auf dem Weg in die Soziale Marktwirtschaft. Die wirtschaftspolitischen Vorstellungen der bürgerlichen Opposition gegen Hitler*, Paderborn, 2002, pp. 315 ff.; Hans Mommsen, *Alternatives to Hitler. German resistance under the Third Reich*, London, 2003. On the controversy over where Goerdeler stood on antisemitism, see also Peter Hoffmann, *Carl Goerdeler and the Jewish question, 1933–1942*, Cambridge, 2011; Christof Dipper, "Der deutsche Widerstand und die Juden," in *Geschichte und Gesellschaft* 9, 1983, pp. 349–80. A paean of hero worship from one of Goerdeler's friends is Gerhard Ritter, *Carl Friedrich Goerdeler und die deutsche Widerstandsbewegung*, Stuttgart, 1954.

7 Werner Abelshauser, "Rüstungsschmiede der Nation? Der Kruppkonzern im Dritten Reich und in der Nachkriegszeit 1933 bis 1951," in Lothar Gall (ed.), *Krupp im 20. Jahrhundert. Die Geschichte des Unternehmens vom Ersten Weltkrieg bis zur Gründung der Stiftung*, Berlin, 2002, pp. 303 ff.

8 "Hans Walz, Meine Mitarbeit an der Aktion Goerdeler," p. 1, StA Ludwigsburg EL 902/20, Bü 87568. Scholtyseck accepts Walz's account without question. Scholtyseck, *Bosch*, pp. 208 f.

9 Markschies, *Goerdeler*, p. 166.

10 "Karl E. Thomä, Erinnerungen an die Zusammenarbeit mit Dr. Karl Goerdeler" [undated, 1974], p. 1, RB 1 013 178.

11 In this connection, see p. 204.

12 "Willy Schloßstein, Einstellung des Herrn B. und seiner Firma zum Nazi-Regime, Juli 1945," p. 7, RB 1 013 076.

13 Markschies, *Goerdeler*, p. 164.

14 "Hans Walz, Meine Mitarbeit an der Aktion Goerdeler," p. 4, StA Ludwigsburg EL 902/20, Bü 87568.

15 Scholtyseck, *Bosch*, p. 226.

16 See also Klaus-Jürgen Müller, *Generaloberst Ludwig Beck. Eine Biographie*, 2nd ed., Paderborn, 2009.

17 Scholtyseck, *Bosch*, p. 300.

18 Quoted from Susanne Preuß: "Warum bringt denn den Kerle niemand um?," in *FAZ.NET [Frankfurter Allgemeine Zeitung]*, August 16, 2011.

19 Scholtyseck, *Bosch*, pp. 332 ff.

20 Quoted from *ibid.*, p. 336.

21 According to a reconstruction made in August 1945, Goerdeler received the following payments from Robert Bosch GmbH: 20,000 reichsmarks in 1937, 60,000 reichsmarks in 1938, 60,000 reichsmarks in 1939, 70,000 reichsmarks in 1940, 80,000 reichsmarks in 1941, 100,000 reichsmarks in 1942, 100,000 reichsmarks in 1943, and 50,000 reichsmarks in 1944. The only payments for which there is voucher evidence totaled 181,000 reichsmarks. There was also a loan to Goerdeler of 60,000 reichsmarks. "Zahlungen an Herrn Dr. Goerdeler, 24. 8. 1945," RB 1 013 082. With Bosch backing, in 1943 Goerdeler was able to purchase the Katharinenplaisir estate near Heilbronn. Scholtyseck assumes that Goerdeler received around 250,000 reichsmarks in salary and 450,000 reichsmarks for "conspiratorial purposes." Joachim Scholtyseck, "Robert Bosch und der Boschkreis als finanzielle, geistige und politische Unterstützer des Widerstands vom 20. Juli 1944," in Detlev J. Blesgen (ed.), *Financiers, Finanzen und Finanzierungsformen des Widerstands* (Schriftenreihe der Forschungsgemeinschaft 20. Juli 1944 e. V., vol. 5), Berlin, 2006, p. 40.

22 "Hans Walz, Meine Mitarbeit an der Aktion Goerdeler," p. 9, StA Ludwigsburg EL 902/20, Bü 87568.

23 *Ibid.*

24 Scholtyseck, *Bosch*, p. 482.

25 Schmitt, *Bäuerle*, pp. 102 ff.; Scholtyseck, *Bosch*, pp. 161 f. On Berger's connection with the Bosch circle, see pp. 177 f.

26 Scholtyseck, *Bosch*, pp. 393 ff.

27 *Ibid.*, p. 390.

28 See above, p. 181.

29 Scholtyseck, *Bosch*, pp. 481 f.

30 Gert Nylander, *German resistance movement and England. Carl Goerdeler and the Wallenberg brothers*, Stockholm, 1999, pp. 31 ff., 46 ff. (Carl Goerdeler, undated memorandum, which was written in Stockholm on May 20, 1943).

31 Scholtyseck, *Bosch*, pp. 432 f.

32 "Karl E. Thomä, Erinnerungen an die Zusammenarbeit mit Dr. Karl Goerdeler" [undated, 1974], p. 7, RB 1 013 178.

33 Heinz Bardua, *Stuttgart im Luftkrieg*, Stuttgart, 1967; "Bericht des BW Mai 1945 – Dezember 1949, Flieger-Angriffe auf die Feuerbacher- und Stuttgarter-Werke," RB 1 024 454; Scholtyseck, *Bosch*, p. 532.

34 Original words: "[dass] die Aktion gegen Hitler unmittelbar bevorstehe." Quoted from Scholtyseck, *Bosch*, p. 498.

35 *Ibid.*, pp. 498 f.

36 *Ibid.*, pp. 503 ff.

37 *Ibid.*, pp. 502 f. On Fischer's appointment by Goerdeler, see *ibid.*, p. 482.

38 *Ibid.*, pp. 504 f.

39 *Ibid.*, pp. 505 ff., 512 ff.

40 *Ibid.*, pp. 522 ff.; Frank had been the conspirators' political commissioner for Baden, Fischer for Württemberg.

41 *Ibid.*, pp. 525 f.

42 *Ibid.*, pp. 526 f. The same account can be found in "Walz an Kiesinger, 29. 4. 1960," RB 1 013 084.

43 Scholtyseck, *Bosch*, pp. 528 f.

44 On the instructions of Berger, who had been put in charge of POW matters, Albrecht Fischer was released from Sachsenhausen concentration camp before the war's end. Hahn was freed from Brandenburg penitentiary by the Red Army. *Ibid.*, pp. 528, 531.

45 *Ibid.*, p. 525.

46 Berger was released as early as 1951. Bosch helped him to assemble supporting statements for denazification proceedings and gave him a job as premises and machinery administrator at Stuttgarter Zeitungsverlag, in which the Bosch family held shares through DVA. Here Berger was very soon dismissed for right-wing agitation. He subsequently found employment at the curtain-rail manufacturer MHZ in Musberg, near Böblingen. Robert Bosch GmbH paid for an attorney to secure a pension for Berger arising out of his former job as a teacher. Walz lent his weight to a clemency plea when in 1960 Berger received a prison sentence for treasonable relations. By providing financial assistance and offering various commissions (including his memoirs of the NS years), the company supported Berger until his death. Scholtyseck, "'Schwabenherzog'," pp. 107 ff.; "Walz an Kiesinger, 29. 4. 1960," RB 1 013 084; "Vermerk Schreiber betr. Gottlob Berger, 27. 9. 1973," *ibid.*

47 On the definition and delimitation of these categories of historical resistance, see Gerhard Botz, "Methoden- und Theorieprobleme der historischen Widerstandsforschung," in Helmut Konrad, Wolfgang Neugebauer (eds.), *Arbeiterbewegung –*

Faschismus – Nationalbewußtsein. Festschrift zum 20jährigen Bestand des Doku-mentationsarchivs des österreichischen Widerstandes und zum 60. Geburtstag von Herbert Steiner, Vienna, Munich, 1983, pp. 137–51.

48 Scholtyseck, *Bosch.*

7 Death and legacy of Robert Bosch

1 See also, in this connection, pp. 28 and 30.

2 "Ansprache des Herrn Bosch," in *Bosch-Zünder* 1940/5–6," p. 49. See also Heuss, *Bosch,* pp. 637 f. On the donation for Stiftung Homöopathisches Krankenhaus Stuttgart: "Oberfinanzpräsident Württemberg an Reichsminister der Finanzen, 7. 1. 1944," BArch R 2/20902.

3 *Bosch-Zünder* 1941/10–12, pp. 81, 83. According to Scholtyseck, Bosch had Gottlob Berger to thank for this award. Berger had extorted it from Ley, the DAF head, with the threat that otherwise he would arrange for Hitler to decorate Bosch himself. It seems likely that this was one of the fairy tales with which Berger was constantly trying to impress. Scholtyseck bases his account on a remark by Bäuerle (another man who was very ready to believe Berger's stories in other instances). Scholtyseck, *Bosch,* p. 358. See also, in this connection, p. 242 and p. 594, note 83.

4 "Reusch an Margarete Bosch, 13. 8. 1941," Rheinisch-Westfälisches Wirtschafts-archiv [subsequently RWWA] 130–400101290, sheet 16; "Informationsdienst der Stadt der Auslandsdeutschen Stuttgart, 22. 9. 1941," Stadtarchiv Stuttgart 13/93.

5 "Reusch an Margarete Bosch, 3. 10. 1941," RWWA 130–400101290, sheet 10; "Felix Olpp, Unser unvergesslicher Herr Bosch," pp. 20 ff. (sheets 39 ff.), RB 1 014 003.

6 Heuss, *Bosch,* p. 617.

7 "Bosch an Heuss, 4. 3. 1942," RB 1 014 154. Initially, the historian Johannes Haller had been considered for the task. Another possibility was the historian of technology Conrad Matschoß, who like Heuss had brought out a book about Robert Bosch back in 1931. "Debatin an Heuss, 17. 7. 1946," RB 1 832 058; "Bosch an Haller, 20. 3. 1942," RB 1 014 014.

8 "Heuss an Bosch, 6. 3. 1942," RB 1 014 154.

9 Theodor Heuss (ed.), *Robert Bosch,* Stuttgart 1931.

10 "Heuss an Margarete Bosch, 20. 11. 1945," RB 1 014 738.

11 Ernst Wolfgang Becker, *Theodor Heuss. Bürger im Zeitalter der Extreme,* Stuttgart, 2011; Elke Seefried (ed.), *Theodor Heuss. In der Defensive. Briefe 1933–1945,* Munich, 2009, pp. 44 f.

12 "Hans Walz, Anmerkung zu Werner Schaubel, Untersuchungen über die Zweck-bestimmung der VVB und RBT, S. 44 unten, 7. 4. 1959," RB 1 001 289, p. 54; "Felix Olpp, Unser unvergesslicher Herr Bosch," p. 29 (sheet 51), RB 1 014 003.

13 *Bosch-Zünder,* special issue of March 12, 1942, pp. 5 ff.

14 *Ibid.,* pp. 12 f.; footage in *Die Deutsche Wochenschau,* no. 603, March 1942.

15 *Bosch-Zünder,* special issue of March 12, 1942, pp. 15 ff.; Heuss, *Bosch,* p. 18.

16 Bosch's eldest daughter later told her step-sister: "How ashamed we all felt!," Eva Madelung interview of March 16, 2011.

17 *Ibid.*

18 Elly Heuss-Knapp, *Bürgerin zweier Welten. Ein Leben in Briefen und Aufzeichnun-gen,* ed. by Margarethe Vater, 3rd ed., Tübingen, 1963, p. 287; Seefried (ed.), *Heuss,* pp. 465 ff.

19 "Robert Bosch GmbH an das Arbeitsamt Heidelberg, 16. 8. 1944," RB 1 832 058.

20 See pp. 90 f.

21 "Karl Schreiber, Diskussionsbeitrag über die Robert Bosch Stiftung, 31. 5. 1978," p. 18, RB 1 044 005/2.

22 In his deliberations about succession arrangements, Bosch had been thinking about an "heir director" [*Erbendirektor*] since 1924. He later termed this figure *Familiendirektor*. "Werner Schaubel, Untersuchungen über die Zweckbestimmung der VVB und RBTV, 5. 3. 1959," pp. 14 ff., RB 1 001 289.

23 "Robert Bosch, Verfügung von Todes wegen, 31. 5. 1938," RB 1 001 081. Leinss, Scheuing, and Stribeck had been VVB shareholders since as far back as 1921, Walz and Fellmeth since 1924, and Wild since 1927. Bohner joined them in 1939. Suitable executors were named in the May 31, 1938, will as: Carl Bosch, Otto Debatin, Alfred Knoerzer, Max Rall, Erich C. Rassbach, Ernst Rupp, and Willy Schloßstein. Carl Bosch having died in 1940, Carl Goerdeler was entered in his place as "substitute executor" [*Ersatz-Testamentsvollstrecker*].

24 *Ibid.*, p. 7.

25 *Ibid.*, pp. 7 f.

26 According to those guidelines, the latest version of which dates from December 23, 1937, a family director was to receive the majority shareholding on one condition. He must perform "the task assigned to him, namely that of providing leadership for the companies belonging to Robert Bosch GmbH, in the proper fashion – that is to say, in the manner and to the extent to which I did so myself." "Richtlinien für die Vermögensverwaltung Bosch GmbH vom 19. 7. 1935 mit Nachtrag vom 23. 12. 1937," RB 1 001 198.

27 "Robert Bosch der Ältere. an Robert Bosch der Jüngere (Januar 1939), Abschrift vom 18. 7. 1953," RB 1 001 260. See also the quote from this letter on p. 278.

28 The capital contributions totaled 280,000 reichsmarks. Of this sum, 200,000 reichsmarks belonged to the community of heirs. Partners Hermann Fellmeth, Arthur Leinss, Richard Stribeck, Paul Scheuing, Hans Walz, and Karl Martell Wild held 10,000 reichsmarks each, while Erwin Bohner held 20,000 reichsmarks. "Liste der Gesellschafter der Vermögensverwaltung Bosch GmbH nach dem Stand am 31. 12. 1942," RB 1 058 098.

29 "Vermögensverwaltung Bosch GmbH an den Reichsminister der Finanzen, 30. 7. 1943," BArch R 2/20902, sheets 104 ff.; "Oberfinanzpräsident Württemberg an Reichsminister der Finanzen, 7. 1. 1944," *ibid.*, sheets 101 f.; "Finanzamt für Körperschaften in Stuttgart an den Oberfinanzpräsidenten Württemberg, 20. 10. 1942," *ibid.*, sheets 111 ff.

30 "Vermögensverwaltung Bosch GmbH an den Reichsminister der Finanzen, 30. 7. 1943," *ibid.*, sheet 107.

31 "Telegramm Goerdelers an Ministerialrat Meuschel, Reichsfinanzministerium, 6. 6. 1944," *ibid.*, sheet 123; "Vermerk Reichsfinanzministerium betr. Auflösung der Vermögensverwaltung Bosch GmbH, 8. 7. 1944," *ibid.*, sheet 128; "Reichsfinanzminister an den Oberfinanzpräsidenten Württemberg, 8. 9. 1944," *ibid.*, sheet 129.

32 "Rechtsanwalt Ludwig Meyer an Ministerialrat Meuschel, 10. 10. 1944," *ibid.*, sheet 131.

III Adaptation and change between economic boom and economic crises (1945–1983)

1 Reconstruction in the shadow of Allied decartelization policy and disagreements within the company

1 See "Schreiben vom 8. 9. 1945," RB 1 001 487.
2 In this connection, see "Notiz vom 18. 10. 1945" in (retrospective) conjunction with "Notiz vom 1. 11. 1948," RB 1 002 193.
3 In this connection, see "Erklärung vom 7. 3. 1947," RB 1 010 163, and (though written more than a year earlier) Knoerzer's letter to the supervisory board of April 8, 1946, RB 1 001 487. On the protagonists' biographical backgrounds and careers at Bosch, see the brief portraits in *Bosch-Zünder* 1952/4, p. 61 (Otto Fischer), *Bosch-Zünder* 1952/5–6, p. 88 (Alfred Knoerzer), *ibid.*, p. 89 (Walter Lippart). See also "Niederschrift der Aufsichtsratssitzung vom 22. 5. 1946," RB 1 002 007.
4 See "Niederschrift der Sitzung vom 30. 10. 1945," RB 1 001 256.
5 In this connection, see the 53-page "Gutachten von Schaubel zu 'Untersuchungen über die Zweckbestimmung der VVB und der RBVT'," dated March 5, 1959, RB 1 001 289.
6 A final agreement by the heirs regarding distribution of the estate was reached in late 1951. In this connection, see the "Auseinandersetzungsplan" appended to the "Niederschrift der TV-Sitzung (TVS) vom 22. 10. 1951," RB 1 001 259, and the "'Abschließender Bericht' der TV über die Durchführung der Nachlassauseinandersetzung vom 13. 1. 1954," RB 1 001 261.
7 See *ibid.*, p. 45.
8 See "Notiz über 'die Entwicklung der Anweisungen der Gesellschafter an die Geschäftsführer vom Jahre 1947 bis heute' vom 12. 11. 1958," RB 1 001 270.
9 "Notiz der Beratungen des TV-Gremiums vom 2. 12. 1947," RB 1 001 257.
10 "Besprechungsnotiz vom 10. 4. 1947," RB 1 001 257.
11 In this connection, see, among other sources, Albrecht Fischer's thorough account "Betr. Inhaftierung von Herrn Walz 1945–1947," RB 1 013 034.
12 In this connection, see the example of managers in other companies given in Paul Erker, Toni Pierenkemper (eds.), *Deutsche Unternehmer zwischen Kriegswirtschaft und Wiederaufbau. Studien zur Erfahrungsbildung von Industrieeliten*, Munich, 1999.
13 "Placing my own life in danger, I was among the most active opponents of the Nazi regime ever," Walz wrote in one of his petitions for release. See the memoranda in RB 1 012 050 and the copies of petitions for release in RB 1 013 034.
14 Walz's "Notiz vom 22. 7. 1947" and "Brief vom 16. 7. 1947," RB 1 013 034 (original documents in StA Ludwigsburg, EL 902/20, Bü 87568).
15 See the papers relating to the trial-court proceedings in RB 1 012 050.
16 On this and what follows, see "Niederschrift der TVS vom 5. 11. 1948," RB 1 001 257.
17 *Ibid.*
18 *Ibid.*
19 *Ibid.*, p. 3. Incidentally a later, differently constituted working committee of the supervisory board was explicitly refused such a wide range of powers.
20 *Ibid.*, p. 5.
21 *Ibid.* See also the detailed "Notiz zur RBTV Robert Bosch GmbH vom 1. 11. 1948," in

the same minutes. On the wider debate, see also "Niederschrift über die TV-Sitzung vom 3. 12. 1948," in *ibid.*

22 See "'Vorschläge zur Änderung des Gesellschaftsvertrags der Robert Bosch GmbH, die zweckmäßigerweise vor Inkrafttreten des Betriebsverfassungsgesetzes getroffen werden sollten,' Schreiben Schloßstein an die TV vom 28. 10. 1952," RB 1 001 259.

23 See "Niederschrift über die TV-Sitzung vom 5. 11. 1952," in *ibid.* Fellmeth had been dead since mid-December 1948.

24 "Niederschrift der TVS vom 3. 12. 1952," RB 1 001 259. Walz laid claim from that moment to the position of "Chairman of the Board of Management" [*Vorsitzender der Geschäftsführung*], and had notepaper printed accordingly, regardless of the fact that no such term existed in the relevant law. Only in a shareholder resolution adopted on February 25, 1953, did Walz (for internal purposes, at least) receive that title.

25 "Niederschrift der TVS vom 3. 12. 1952," RB 1 001 259, p. 6.

26 *Ibid.*, p. 3.

27 *Ibid.*, p. 4.

28 In this connection, see Betriebsrat Bosch Feuerbach (ed.), *... auch beim Bosch*, pp. 63 f., and Richard Rau's interview of November 9, 2005, in RB 1 229 067. For a thorough treatment of this period from Eberle's standpoint, see Fichter, Eberle, *Kampf*.

29 For a general account, see also in this connection Paul Erker, *Ernährungskrise und Nachkriegsgesellschaft. Bauern und Arbeiterschaft in Bayern 1943 bis 1953*, Stuttgart, 1990.

30 In this connection, see also the brief note in *Bosch-Zünder* 1947/1–3, p. 2.

31 However, within Bosch itself there was persistent discussion about the existing wage groups of skilled workers paid by the hour (A) and semi-skilled or unskilled B and C piece-workers and relations between them. Among other sources on this subject, see *Bosch-Zünder* 1952/9, p. 210.

32 In this connection, see the statement in *Bosch-Zünder* 1951/4–5, pp. 61 f.

33 "Bericht der GF an den Aufsichtsrat für die Zeit vom 1. 4.–30. 6. 1953," p. 5, RB 1 002 901.

34 For an overview of Allied antitrust policy, see Volker Berghahn, *Unternehmer und Politik in der Bundesrepublik*, Frankfurt am Main, 1985, pp. 84 ff.

35 In this connection, cf. "BIOS Final Report No. 60, Robert Bosch GmbH vom 6. 7. 1945," for example, RB 1 011 142 008. See also "BIOS Report No. C29 342 vom 5.–12. 10. 1945," and "CIOS Target Report No. 545 vom 25.–29. 6. 1945," and "FIAT Final Report No. 573 vom 4. 12. 1945," in *ibid.*

36 In this connection, see also "Bewertung des von den Alliierten entnommenen geistigen Eigentums," June 1948, RB 1 011 137 004 and 005.

37 For the Bosch standpoint on this, see "Bericht vom 22. 9. 1948," RB 1 011 143 001, and the 30-page "Gutachten vom 20. 12. 1948," a Bosch-commissioned opinion as to the legality of the whole operation, RB 1 011 137 002. For the point of view of the French sequestrator, see the report of January 1, 1946, in Archives du Ministère des affaires étrangères et européennes, La Courneuve, 2 AEF 183 and AB 232 3. Finally, see the report "G.F.C.C., Étude sur le groupe Robert Bosch en Allemagne et à l'étranger, Sept. 1947," GMFB 2/312/2.

38 Not until 1960 was Bosch able to reacquire its evacuated facility and integrate it in the parent company once more. In this connection, see also the (somewhat cursory) talk by Merkle, *Ein deutsches Unternehmen in Frankreich. Die Bosch-Gruppe und der Neubeginn in den deutsch-französischen Beziehungen ab 1945*, reprinted Bonn, 1995.

39 On this and what follows, see the detailed account by Alfred Knoerzer, "Die Bosch-Entflechtung – ein Rückblick," in *Bosch-Zünder* 1952/2, pp. 26–31, as well as the extensive account (likewise worked up from the files) by Wilhelm Lampert, then head of the Bosch patent and license department, "Geschichte des Entflechtungs- und Entkartellierungsverfahrens der Robert Bosch GmbH 1947–1952," 61 manuscript pages, March 1987, RB 1 011 149 001.

40 "Niederschrift der TVS vom 17. 3. 1947," RB 1 001 257.

41 See "Protokoll der TVS vom 2. 12. 1947," in *ibid.*

42 "Notiz FAL vom 11. 8. 1947," RB 1 011 138 002.

43 *Ibid.*

44 See "Schreiben an das Wirtschaftsministerium vom 19. 8. 1947," in RB 1 011 144 006.

45 See in detail in this connection Lampert, "Entflechtungs- und Entkartellierungsverfahren," p. 21; also the report in *Bosch-Zünder* 1948/4–5, pp. 1 ff. See also, in connection with the directive, RB 1 011 130 002.

46 In this connection, see the 14-page "Notiz von Knoerzer und Fischer über 'Die wirtschaftlichen Wirkungen der geplanten Entflechtung des Bosch-Firmenverbandes' vom 31. 8. 1948," RB 1 011 143 001. Essentially, what was predicted was a substantial technological setback for the German automotive industry with all the economic consequences that were bound to follow.

47 See the line of argument traced in detail in "Robert Bosch GmbH, Einwandserklärung vom Mai 1948," in RB 1 011 132 002. On the debate about negotiating strategy, see also "Niederschrift der TVS vom 15. 4. 1948," RB 1 001 257.

48 In this connection, Bosch's first task had been meticulously to acquire the relevant legal literature from America. A further very costly exercise was the "dismissal campaign" [*Einstellungsaktion*] in which Bosch was obliged, in respect of all its business partners, to terminate or suspend contract negotiations that were either questionable or forbidden under Law no. 56 and Law no. 78, which at the time meant 65 licensing and business agreements, 117 Bosch Service agreements, 1,868 supply agreements, and countless other certificates of formal obligation toward retailers of Bosch products. For a detailed account of this, see Lampert, "Entflechtungs- und Entkartellierungsverfahren," pp. 39–44.

49 Once again detailed, in part verbatim minutes of the oral hearing may be found in Lampert, "Entflechtungs- und Entkartellierungsverfahren." Regarding the course the hearing took, see also the impressive account *ibid.*, pp. 34 ff. On the sometimes detailed memoranda of the works councils (e.g. that of the Hildesheim plant), see RB 1 011 138 003. See also the article "Betriebsräte gegen Bosch-Entflechtung," in the *Hannoversche Presse* of October 19, 1948.

50 For instance, the "implementation timetable" submitted by Bosch was structured over four years. In this connection, see Knoerzer, "Bosch-Entflechtung," p. 28. See also a 53-page report that the bi-zonal Administration for Trade and Industry (forerunner of the Federal Ministry of Trade and Industry) issued in February 1949 under the title "Das Dezentralisierungsverfahren Nr. 1 gegen die Firma Robert Bosch GmbH, Stuttgart," RB 1 011 145 002.

51 See the order itself, RB 1 011 155 007.

52 Lampert states in his account that this writ could not be found in the Bosch archives and may well have been lost. In fact, it is contained in the document "In the Court of Deconcentration Appeals, in the Matter of Bosch, Bipartite Deconcentration Action No. 1, on Appeal from the Bipartite Decartellization Commission – Brief of Robert Bosch GmbH and the Executors under the will of Robert Bosch by

Rudolf Mueller" (the other attorneys named are George Nebolsine, John Foster, Pierre Lepaulle, Karl Eugen Thomä, Wilhelm Lampert, and Hans W. Kamberg), RB 1 011 129 002.

53 In this connection, see also the documents in RB 1 011 137 001.

54 The same argument is advanced in a memorandum dated July 21, 1951, p. 20, RB 1 011 145 001.

55 See the letter and a detailed "Darstellung des Dekartellierungsverfahrens durch Knoerzer an Erhard vom 24. 2. 1949," RB 1 011 145 003.

56 See "Memorandum," RB 1 011 145 001. See also Lampert, "Entflechtungs- und Entkartellierungsverfahren," pp. 49 f.

57 "Bericht der GF auf der TVS am 15. 6. 1951," RB 1 002 007.

58 *Ibid.*, p. 2.

59 "Memorandum," RB 1 011 146 002.

60 "Schreiben McCloys an Ministerpräsident Maier vom 3. 1. 1952," RB 1 011 146 003.

61 For details in this connection, see "Verhandlungsnotizen," "Protokolle," and "Erlass," RB 1 011 146 001 to RB 1 011 146 003. Internally the Bosch management had decided that, should settlement talks fail, they would make no further concessions but simply "accept the ruling." See "Protokoll der TVS vom 11. 1. 1952," p. 8, RB 1 001 260.

62 See in this connection Merkle's note, dated July 13, 1972, of a conversation he had with one of the attorneys involved at the time, RB 1 015 052.

63 On the lengthy prehistory of the Act against Restraints on Competition [*Gesetz gegen Wettbewerbsbeschränkungen* or GWB], see Berghahn, *Unternehmer und Politik*, pp. 152 ff. See also Lisa Murach-Brand, *Antitrust auf deutsch. Der Einfluß der amerikanischen Alliierten auf das Gesetz gegen Wettbewerbsbeschränkungen nach 1945*, Tübingen 2004.

64 Knoerzer, "Bosch-Entflechtung," p. 30. See also "Bericht Knoerzers in der TVS am 20. 2. 1952," RB 1 001 260.

65 Which is also how Knoerzer saw the situation in "Bosch-Entflechtung," p. 31.

66 See the detailed account in the company report for the period January 1, 1945, to June 30, 1946, as well as the separate company report addressed to the supervisory board for the period July 1 to December 31, 1945, in RB 1 001 119.

67 See also the detailed company report for the period July 1, 1946 to December 31, 1947, in *ibid.*

68 See Knoerzer's 20-page report concerning his U.S. trip from November 4 to December 8, 1952, RB 1 002 101.

69 *Ibid.*

70 *Ibid.*, p. 16.

71 "Notiz von Walz an die TVS vom 18. 5. 1953," RB 1 001 260.

72 Quoted from "Gerhard Greiner, Bericht über eine Konzernuntersuchung bei der Firma Robert Bosch GmbH vom Juli 1963," p. 153, RB 1 035.

73 In January 1955, for example, the transfer of the new Feuerbach dynamo plant to new production premises was completed. This work had begun in May 1953 – almost two years previously. See *Bosch-Zünder* 1955/1, pp. 27–9.

74 See also, in this connection, information provided by Greiner (see note 72 above), notably in part 2 of the section "Marktstellung des Konzerns," p. 2/126, RB 1 035.

75 "Protokoll der TVS vom 11. 6. 1956," RB 1 001 263.

76 See also "Protokoll der Aufsichtsratssitzung vom 8. 12. 1954," RB 1 011 135 002. In 1952, the company's equity ratio was still 51.2 percent. By 1955 it was already down to 41.6 percent, and in ensuing years it dipped below the 30-percent mark.

77 "Niederschrift der TV-Sitzung vom 11. 10. 1955," RB 1 001 262.

78 In this connection, see also "Zusammenstellung VKM vom 25. 8. 1953," RB 1 002 102.

2 From family-run business to foundation-owned company: the long march to a new Bosch constitution

1 "Protokoll der TVS vom 11. 1. 1952," RB 1 001 260.

2 Walz's letter of May 12, 1952, reproduced in Zundel's autobiography. See Georg Zundel, *"Es muss viel geschehen!" Erinnerungen eines friedenspolitisch engagierten Naturwissenschaftlers*, Berlin, 2006, p. 108.

3 A copy of the January 1939 letter was made on July 18, 1953. See RB 1 001 260.

4 On January 29, 1953, when Robert Bosch Jr. turned 25, the administrative responsibility of the executors regarding his assets not encumbered by pre- or post-bequest orders came to an end. However, he agreed to have the group of executors continue to exercise this responsibility.

5 In this connection, see the various exchanges of letters and the notes concerning the very full debate about the nature and extent of that training program (a debate that went on until the autumn of 1953), in RB 1 002 102.

6 "Protokoll der TVS vom 17. 8. 1953," in *ibid.*

7 See the *Denkschrift*, submitted by the assembled representatives of the committee of executors, the supervisory board, and the board of management, drafted by Eugen Diesel, and reprinted in *Bosch-Zünder* 1953/3, pp. 26–9.

8 "Rede von Walz auf dem Herrenabend vom 21. 12. 1953," pp. 9 f., RB 1 013 025.

9 "Protokoll der TVS vom 12. 10. 1953," RB 1 001 260. This also prompted extensive debate about the future composition of the group of executors and the replacement of retiring members. See also the very thorough "Protokoll der TVS vom 13. 6. 1953," RB 1 001 260. At the October meeting Walz no longer stood in the way of Knoerzer's possible accession to the committee. Ultimately, this was about drawing up new standing orders to sort out the question of voluntary or compulsory resignation on grounds of age or ill-health.

10 "Niederschrift der TVS vom 5. 2. 1953," RB 1 001 260.

11 "Niederschrift der TVS vom 25. 11. 1954," p. 4, RB 1 001 261.

12 "Niederschrift der TVS vom 15. 12. 1954," in *ibid.*

13 "Rede von Walz auf dem Herrenabend am 20. 12. 1954," RB 1 013 025.

14 *Ibid.*, pp. 2 f.

15 "Protokoll der TVS am 14. 11. 1956," p. 25, RB 1 001 263.

16 In this connection, see "Bericht Robert Boschs d. J. auf der TVS am 25. 11. 1959," pp. 3–6., RB 1 001 266.

17 In this connection, see "Protokoll der TVS vom 5. 2. 1959," RB 1 001 266.

18 See "Denkschrift von Walz über die Nachfolgefrage vom November 1956," RB 1 013 026.

19 On the retirement of Max Dehn, who signed a letter of resignation only under pressure, see "TVS vom 24. 4. 1959," RB 1 001 266.

20 *Ibid.*, p. 6.

21 *Ibid.*, p. 14. On the brief, consensual discussion of the memorandum, see "TVS vom 4. 12. 1956," pp. 7 ff., RB 1 001 263. However, the question arises as to how far Walz adhered to his own principles subsequently, given that in December 1958, when the appointment of replacement members of the group of executors again stood on the agenda, Walz proposed Frei (then a member of the board of management) "as perfect Bosch material." Alfred Knoerzer proposed Lippart, also a current member of the Bosch board of management. In December 1958, Walz made a note of several changes of mind on his part, relative to his November 1956 memorandum. See his "Notiz vom 8.12.1958 als vorbereitende Ausführungen zur TVS am 12.12.1958," RB 1 001 265.

22 In this connection, see the thorough "Debatte in der TVS am 24.1.1957," pp. 5 ff., RB 1 001 264.

23 On this and what follows, see "Niederschrift der TVS vom 12.3.1958," RB 1 001 265.

24 *Ibid.*, p. 5.

25 Most of the alterations and additions concerned two points. The first was how the right to vote was to be exercised and underage shareholders represented, as laid down in section 13. In this connection, see Walz's detailed preparatory work in "Gedanken und Motive zur Änderung des § 13 des Gesellschaftsvertrags der RB GmbH vom 4.12.1956," RB 1 001 263, and "Protokoll der TVS vom 14.11.1956," pp. 6 ff., in *ibid.* The second concerned calculation of the so-called "notional share price," which was the price paid to shareholders who wished or were compelled to sell their shares. In this connection, see Walz's detailed "Denkschrift vom November 1956 über den Kaufpreis von Geschäftsanteilen der Robert Bosch GmbH mit umfangreichen Anlagen und weiteren Kommentaren der Rechts- und Bilanzabteilung," RB 1 013 026.

26 See also "Niederschrift der Sitzung des TV-Arbeitsausschusses vom 27.1.1959," RB 1 001 266.

27 "Schaubel-Gutachten vom 5.3.1959," p. 52, RB 1 001 289.

28 "Notiz von Walz vom 7.4.1959," RB 1 001 289.

29 This is evident from "Protokoll der TVS vom 5.12.1960," pp. 11 f., RB 1 001 267, and "Protokoll der TVS vom 23.3.1961," in *ibid.*

30 See the report of January 1959, RB 1 001 490, which significantly was found in NL Knoerzer.

31 *Ibid.*, p. 2.

32 The resignation of Otto Fischer was evidently preceded by differences of opinion and a row between him and Knoerzer. At least, that is how Fischer describes the situation in a letter to Walz dated June 3, 1956, RB 1 001 263. See also the discussion of the matter at the executors' meeting of June 22, 1956, in *ibid.* Not long afterwards (in October 1962), Walter Lippart's seat became vacant as a result of his unexpected death.

33 "Protokoll der TVS vom 29.3.1960," p. 2, RB 1 001 267.

34 "Brief vom 25.11.1960," RB 1 001 487.

35 See "TVS vom 12.12.1958," p. 10, RB 1 001 265.

36 Knoerzer's account of the matter in his "Gesprächsnotiz vom 13.2.1961," in *ibid.*

37 Hans Walz, "Robert Bosch. Der Mann und das Werk," in *Bosch-Zünder* 1961/9, pp. 197–206. The other ceremonial speeches are reprinted in the same issue.

38 "Niederschrift der Sitzung des TV-Arbeitsausschusses vom 27.1.1959," RB 1 001 266.

39 *Ibid.*, p. 5.

40 *Ibid.*, p. 4.

41 *Ibid.*, p. 5.

42 *Ibid.*

43 See also "Protokoll der TVS vom 8.12.1961," p. 23, RB 1 001 268.

44 "Protokoll der Versammlung der Familienmitglieder am 7.5.1962," RB 1 001 269. See also the extensive "Bericht über den gegenwärtigen Stand der Untersuchungen zur Frage VVB-Weg vom 15.6.1962," RB 1 001 269.

45 "Niederschrift der TVS vom 28. 6. 1962," p. 4, RB 1 001 269. See also "Stellungnahme zu dem von Frau FiBo gestellten Wunsch nach einem Mitbestimmungsrecht in der VVB vom 22. 6. 1962," in *ibid.*

46 "Protokoll der Versammlung der Familienmitglieder am 7. 5. 1962," pp. 6 ff., RB 1 001 269.

47 Original words: "tollste Verdrehungen." See also the letter "Fischer-Bosch an Zundel, 21. 12. 1962," in NL Zundel. The later account of these problems in Zundel's biography is also somewhat cryptic as well as being corrupted by hindsight. Zundel, *"Es muss viel geschehen!"*, p. 164.

48 "Notiz über eine Besprechung Zundels mit Margarete Fischer-Bosch sowie Olpp und Schaubel vom Sekretariat Bosch am 20. 12. 1962," in *ibid.*

49 "Protokoll der TVS vom 28. 6. 1962," p. 7, RB 1 001 269, and "Besprechungsnotiz von Rupp mit Fischer-Bosch vom 10. 7. 1962," in *ibid.* See also "Bericht von Walz vom 21. 2. 1963 über die Unterredung mit Zundel am 18. 1. 1963," in NL Zundel.

50 "Gutachten vom 21. 2. 1963," in NL Zundel.

51 *Ibid.*, p. 37.

52 *Ibid.*, p. 64.

53 See also "Brief der TV 'an die Erben des Herrn Robert Bosch' vom 18. 4. 1963," in NL Zundel. The subcommittee comprised attorney Ernst Rupp as family representative in the group of executors, Knoerzer, Heinz Küppenbender (a member of the board of management of Carl Zeiss who had been co-opted to the group of executors), and lastly Hans L. Merkle.

54 In this connection, see the notes and letter from Felix Olpp to Zundel of May 5 and May 25, 1963, respectively, relating to Zundel's meeting with Knoerzer on May 28, 1963, in NL Zundel. Here Olpp clearly takes the side of the family and advises Zundel against making hasty promises.

55 See also "Niederschrift der TVS vom 31. 5. 1963," pp. 8 ff., RB 1 001 270.

56 *Ibid.*, p. 9.

57 *Ibid.*

58 *Ibid.*

59 In this connection, see "TV-Beschluss vom 15. 10. 1963," in RB 1 001 270, and "Brief Knoerzers an Paula Zundel vom 27. 9. 1963," in NL Zundel.

60 "Niederschrift der TVS vom 20. 3. 1963," RB 1 001 270.

61 The text of the letter had in fact been composed by Walz himself, as Knoerzer noted on a later occasion. "Transkript Notizen Knoerzers vom 6. 10. 2005," RB 1 001 492.

62 "Niederschrift der TVS vom 28. 11. 1963," RB 1 001 270.

63 *Ibid.*, p. 3.

64 *Ibid.*, p. 5.

65 *Ibid.*

66 *Ibid.*

67 "Robert Bosch Jr. an Knoerzer 21. 4. 64, Abschnitt Anlage 1 zu vertraulicher TV-Sitzung am 23. 4. 64," RB 1 017 253.

68 "Niederschrift der TVS vom 23. 3. 1964," p. 2, RB 1 001 271.

69 "Aktenvermerk vom 31. 3. 1964," in NL Zundel.

70 "Protokoll der TV-Verhandlungsausschuss-Sitzung vom 2. 4. 1964," in *ibid.* See also in this connection "Entwurf des Schreibens an Zundel," RB 1 001 272.

71 See "Protokoll der TVS-Besprechung vom 2. 6. 1964," RB 1 001 271.

72 *Ibid.*

73 *Ibid.*, p. 4.

74 In this connection, see "Rahmenprotokoll über die Inkraftsetzung des Vertrag-swerks VVB RBIG am 26. 6. 1964," in NL Zundel. Initial pre-agreements regarding VVB had been reached as early as March 26, 1964. These are documented in RB 1 017 435.

75 "Fischer-Bosch an Knoerzer, 26. 6. 1964," RB 1 001 271. The compromise eventually settled on was that the following addendum, composed by Georg Zundel, should be tacked on to the statement of discharge: "I, however, believe that it would be my grandfather's wish today to let me take a hand in what becomes of the company." In this connection, see "Besprechungsnotiz vom 27. 6. 1964," *ibid.*

76 How far that renunciation of voting rights was legally correct and did not infringe GmbH law was not really examined at the time. Only later did it become a problem.

77 In this connection, see also "Graf zu Dohna, 'Die Rolle der Robert Bosch Industrie-treuhand KG aus rechtlicher Sicht,' 3. 6. 2002" and "Peter Adolff, 'Die Rolle der Robert Bosch Industrietreuhand KG im Rahmen der Bosch-Unternehmensverfas-sung,' 30. 5. 2002," in RB 1 848 061 and RB 1 848 063 respectively.

78 *Ibid.*

79 In this connection, see the 12-page "Vereinbarung vom 26. 6. 1964" signed by all members of the family, in RB 1 001 490.

80 *Ibid.* See the whole bundle of papers relating to the "Vertragswerk des Hauses Bosch vom 26. Juni 1964", in RB 1 017 434.

81 "Hans Walz, Grundsätzliche Betrachtungen vom 1. 12. 1966," RB 1 001 487.

82 *Ibid.*

83 "Particularly the decisions that those holding shares in our company had to make in relation to their shares concern me deeply," Felix Olpp wrote later (in December 1964) to Paula Zundel. "After all, I know from experience what our unforgettable Mr. Bosch wished to see set down and established in his last will and testament. All the prettification attempted subsequently cannot alter that fact. However, it is done now, and all we can do is hope things will turn out right." Letter of December 25, 1964, in NL Zundel.

84 This was also how Christof Bosch, Robert Bosch's grandson, saw the matter in the interview of February 19, 2008 (transcript, p. 9), in RB 1 229 055 as well as in the interview of September 9, 2010.

85 See the Christof Bosch interview of February 19, 2008, transcript p. 35, in RB 1 229 055.

86 "Niederschrift über die Gesellschafterversammlung der VVB vom 30. 9. 1964," in *ibid.*

87 Subsequently, Robert Bosch Jr. launched the *Gute Arbeit* ("good work") campaign that underpinned further quality management at Bosch. In this connection, see (among other sources) the article in *Bosch-Zünder* 1971/1, p. 5.

88 "Memorandum vom 9. 11. 1966," RB 1 001 312.

89 *Ibid.*, p. 1.

90 *Ibid.*, p. 5. In this connection, see also a complementary document that argues in the same direction: "Hans Walz, Grundsätzliche Betrachtungen vom 1. 12. 1966," RB 1 001 493.

91 "Niederschrift der RBIG-Sitzung vom 26. 11. 1970," RB 1 001 329.

92 "Richtlinien für die RBIG vom 22. 6. 1965," RB 1 001 306.

93 *Ibid.*, p. 9.

94 "Niederschrift der RBIG-Sitzung vom 25. 3. 1971," RB 1 001 331.

95 Robert Bosch and Eva Madelung set up Stiftung für Bildung und Behindertenförde-rung GmbH in mid–1971 (it was renamed Heidehof Stiftung GmbH in 2005). In

November 1971, Georg Zundel was also planning a new foundation, which materialized at the end of that same year as Berghof-Stiftung für Konfliktforschung.

96 In this connection, see "Niederschrift der RBIG-Sitzung vom 27./28. 5. 1971,"
RB 1 001 332.

97 In this connection, see "Ansprache von Merkle bei der Trauerfeier am 30. 4. 1974,"
RB 1 013 015.

98 "Notiz vom 18. 2. 1974," RB 1 022 236.

99 For the details, see "Protokoll der RBIG-Sitzung vom 25. 3. 1976," RB 1 001 359.

100 "Niederschrift der RBIK-Sitzung vom 31. 3. 1977," pp. 10 ff., RB 1 001 361.

101 On the complex details of carrying out the capital increase and negotiating with the
family beforehand, see the extensive documentation in NL Stein (RB 1 017 670) – for
instance, Stein's "Notiz vom 16. 5. 1977."

102 In this connection, see "Notiz Stein vom 28. 1. 1976," RB 1 017 669.

103 "Niederschrift der RBIK-Versammlung vom 30. 6. 1977," RB 1 001 362.

104 *Ibid.*, p. 8.

105 In this connection, see the letter "Bosch an Stein, 7. 7. 1978," RB 1 017 671. On the
various models of and problems surrounding worker participation, see "Niederschrift der RBIK vom 6. 4. 1978," RB 1 001 368. As late as February 1980 the subject is
alluded to in a note written by Stein: "We are still in touch with Georg Zundel and
have to keep him informed occasionally."

106 "Niederschrift der RBIG vom 23. 6. 1976," RB 1 001 360. See also "Notiz Schaubel,
17. 7. 1978," RB 1 001 369.

107 "Niederschrift der RBIK-Sitzung vom 5. 4. 1979," RB 1 001 374.

108 See also "Notiz vom 13. 2. 1978," RB 1 001 368.

109 For details in this connection, see "Niederschrift der RBIK vom 12. 6. 1982,"
RB 1 001 388, and "Rundschreiben IK 90 von Merkle/Stein am 21. 6. 1982," in *ibid.*

110 In this connection, see also "Unterlagen zur RBIK vom 24. 11. 1982," RB 1 001 391,
and "Unterlagen zur RBIK vom 23. 6. 1983," RB 1 001 392.

111 See also Christof Bosch interview of September 22, 2010. Another example of this is
the wish expressed by Robert Bosch Jr. to RBIG in April to retain the family-repre-
sentative arrangement even after all obligations arising out of the 1964 agreement
had been discharged. This was more than Merkle as chairman of the RBIG shareholders could bring himself to accept. He had in mind (he said) issuing a "declaration of goodwill" rather than making any actual concessions to Robert Bosch Jr.
The latter should simply receive a promise that the advisory group [meaning the
body of shareholders] would at some time look at whether and to what extent
Bosch's ideas could be realized. See "Niederschrift der RBIG vom 10. 4. 1975," RB
1 001 354.

112 "Peter Adolff, 'Die Rolle der Robert Bosch Industrietreuhand KG im Rahmen der
Bosch-Unternehmensverfassung,' 30. 5. 2002," p. 3, RB 1 848 063.

113 Back at the end of April 1978, the then chairman of the board of trustees of the
Bosch Stiftung, Karl Schreiber, had written to Merkle, reacting almost with fury to
the company's decision to cut the dividend announced for 1977 and hence the funds
passing to the Stiftung from 40 million to 36 million German marks. See "Schreiber
an Merkle, 27. 4. 1978" and "Merkle an Schreiber, 18. 5. 1978," in NL Stein (RB 1 017 408).
There was a similar exchange between Stiftung and company in May 1982 concerning the dividend policy for 1981. In this connection, see "Merkle an Schreiber,
17. 5. 1982," in *ibid.* In February 1981, Robert Bosch Jr. had also written to RBIG, or
rather Merkle, on behalf of the family shareholders, pointing out that the preferen-

tial dividend approved by the company was no longer sufficient to balance out the rising tax burden on the family shareholders resulting from the increase in value of the shares in Robert Bosch GmbH held by family members. Particularly in view of future wealth-tax and income-tax legislation, that tax burden far exceeded the family's financial possibilities. See "Bosch an Merkle, 4. 2. 1981," RB 1 017 408.

114 In this connection, see Adolff interview of March 15, 2010.

115 In this connection, see also Christof Bosch, in Robert Bosch GmbH (ed.), *Robert Bosch 1928–2004. Zum Gedenken an Robert Bosch 29. Januar 1928 – 2. August 2004. Ansprachen der Trauerfeier am 28. September 2004 Gerlingen-Schillerhöhe*, Stuttgart, 2004, p. 35.

116 Christof Bosch interview of February 19, 2008, tanscript p. 10, RB 1 229 055. Robert Bosch Jr. subsequently embarked on a second professional career as a psychologist and psychotherapist. See the detailed appreciation in the speeches at his funeral on September 28, 2004, in Robert Bosch GmbH (ed.), *Robert Bosch 1928–2004.*

117 Addressing the group of executors on June 28, 1962, Walz had said: «RB is entitled to have his executors show some understanding of his aims. They must not adopt divergent views or pursue obscure legal paths of interpretation but execute the will of RB himself." "TVS vom 28. 6. 1962," RB 1 001 269.

118 See, for instance, Nina Grunenberg, *Die Wundertäter. Netzwerke der deutschen Wirtschaft 1942 bis 1966*, Frankfurt am Main, 2008, p. 199.

119 In this connection, see also the Christof Bosch interview of September 22, 2010.

3 Corporate organization and corporate strategy between economic miracle and oil-price shock

1 "Schreiben der WOL vom 16. 3. 1953," RB 1 002 093.

2 "Niederschrift der TVS vom 17. 5. 1960," p. 6, RB 1 001 267.

3 "Abschlussbericht vom 13. 3. 1962" and "Sitzungsprotokolle vom 2. 2. 1961 bis zum 12. 2. 1962," RB 1 047 116.

4 "Präsentation des Berichts auf der TVS am 28. 6. 1962," pp. 9 ff., RB 1 001 269.

5 There were also such general organizational categories as corporate departments, divisions, manufacturing units, and sales organizations. See "Anlage zur GFS vom 20. 7. 1965," RB 1 002 105.

6 See also, in this connection, "Schreiben Merkles über die Änderungen in der Zuständigkeit der Führungsbereiche vom 24. 2. 1967," RB 1 017 086.

7 "Grundsätze in der Fassung vom 20. 2. 1967," RB 1 017 242.

8 The eight members of the board of management were Hans L. Merkle, Klaus G. Alberts, Hans Bacher, Willi Hofmann, Kurt Losten, Karl Schreiber, Paul A. Stein, and Gustav Wagner. Robert Bosch Jr. had quit the board of management on May 27, 1971. The three deputies were Konrad Eckert, Alfred Hetzel, and Rudolf Scharpff, while the two new members were Ulrich Mertz and Kurt Schips. See the detailed list of 111 directors and board of management members comprising the senior management team at Bosch in the 1971 annual report, pp. 5–7.

9 See also, in this connection, the detailed "Notiz Merkles vom 9. 9. 1971" appended to "Niederschrift der RBIG vom 21. 9. 1971," RB 1 001 335, and the highly confidential "Sonderprotokoll über die GFS am 30. 8. 1971," RB 1 230 002 015.

10 See Merkle's newspaper article "Aufruf an die Unternehmer," in *Frankfurter Allgemeine Zeitung*, July 12, 1971.

11 See also, in this connection, Hans L. Merkle, "Führung im multinationalen Unternehmen," in Hans L. Merkle, *Dienen und Führen. Erkenntnisse eines Unternehmers*, Stuttgart, 2001, pp. 183 ff.

12 The occasion was the resignation of Rudolf Scharpff, who as board member responsible for consumer goods business at Bosch was forced out by Merkle in the aftermath of the Blaupunkt crisis. In this connection, see "Niederschrift der GFS vom 27. 3. 1979," RB 1 001 374, and "Merkle an die RBIK, 22. 1. 1979," in *ibid.* See also the article "F1 soll sich von F5 getrennt haben. Hans Merkle irritiert die Führungskräfte der Bosch-Gruppe mit seiner neuen Personalpolitik," in *TOPICS*, no. 4, year 3, March 12, 1979, pp. 3–4.

13 "Niederschrift der RBIK vom 24. 11. 1982," RB 1 001 389.

14 In this connection, see *Manager Magazin* 1978/1, and the major Merkle interview in *Manager Magazin* 1983/3, pp. 76–88. In the "Manager of the Year" poll Merkle made only third place behind the Siemens CEO, Berhard Plettner, and Walter Deuss, chairman of the board of management at the retail giant Karstadt. See *Industriemagazin* 12, 1977, pp. 14–16.

15 In this connection, see also "Merkle an die RBIK-Gesellschafter, 3. 5. 1974," RB 1 001 347.

16 A further addition in the spring of 1983 was an International Advisory Board for Research and Development, on which the president of Exxon sat, among others. Precisely how the web functioned is tricky to reconstruct. Its chief function may well have been to host rapid exchange of information and ideas – a kind of diplomatic network in the sphere of industrial business. One spectacular development in this connection was a further political step taken by Merkle in June 1979: only days after the CDU and CSU had nominated Franz Josef Strauß as their candidate for the chancellorship, Merkle resigned his CDU membership.

17 Among the few exceptions was Merkle's speech at the centenary celebrations in September 1986. Entitled "Robert Bosch and his achievement," it is reproduced in Merkle, *Dienen und Führen*, pp. 239–66.

18 "Das Sensorium für das Kommende." *Ibid.*, p. 250.

19 Initial plans for this had been laid nearly 14 years earlier, following a special study trip to the U.S. to view dozens of administration buildings. See the 43-page report (!) presented in November 1964 under the title "Studium der Lösungen von Verwaltungsgebäuden im Hinblick auf das neue Verwaltungszentrum in Gerlingen," RB 1 028 050 002.

20 An example: "Einer der grundlegenden ökonomischen Irrtümer unserer Zeit ist, man könne sich leisten, was man sich leistet, auch wenn man sich mehr leistet, als man selbst leistet."

21 See the anthology published as Hans L. Merkle, *Dienen und Führen. Erkenntnisse eines Unternehmers*, Stuttgart, 2001.

22 "GFS vom 17. 3. 1965," RB 1 002 105.

23 In this connection, see also the Gutbrod interview of October 27, 2005, transcript p. 4 and manuscript appendix, in RB 1 229 072.

24 "Protokoll der GFS vom 5. 10. 1965," and "Protokoll der GFS vom 19. 10. 1965," RB 1 002 105.

25 "Maßnahmeplan zur Straffung der Führung, zur Produktionsanpassung und zur Kostensenkung," in "Niederschrift der RBIG vom 25. 11. 1965," RB 1 001 309.

26 Although there had actually, in a series of other branches such as textiles and chemicals, been signs of crisis for a long time before the 1967 crash.

27 See the relevant pieces from *Frankfurter Allgemeine Zeitung, Industriekurier, Süd-*

deutsche Zeitung, and *Handelsblatt* of October 28, 1965, reproduced as "Pressespiegel-Anhang zum Protokoll der RBIG-Sitzung vom 25. 11. 1965," RB 1 001 309.

28 "Pressespiegel zur Bilanzpressekonferenz am 6. 7. 1966, als Anhang zum Protokoll der RBIG vom 30. 7. 1966," RB 1 001 315.

29 On the state of budgetary accounting at Bosch, see "Memorandum vom 23. 3. 1966," RB 1 018 007 1.

30 "Protokoll der RBIG vom 15. 3. 1967," RB 1 001 306.

31 "Pressespiegel zur Bilanzpressekonferenz am 12. 7. 1967, als Anhang zum Protokoll der RBIG vom 29. 7. 1967," RB 1 001 325.

32 *Bosch-Zünder* 1971/3, pp. 50–3.

33 "Organigramm Stand 3. 6. 1977," RB 1 001 364. See also Robert Bosch GmbH, annual reports for 1974 ff.

34 "Bericht vom 14. 6. 1974," RB 1 016 888.

35 "Niederschrift der Sonder-GFS vom 26. 7. 1974," RB 1 230 005 022.

36 *Ibid.*

37 *Ibid.*, p. 3.

38 "Pressedokumentation zur Bilanzpressekonferenz vom 13. 7. 1976," in *ibid.*

39 In this connection, see "Ausführungen mit angehängter Grafik auf der GPI-Tagung am 1. 12. 1977 zur Lagebeschreibung der Bosch-Gruppe," RB 1 002 885.

40 "Schreiben vom 29. 1. 1979," RB 1 001 374.

41 *Ibid.*, p. 7.

42 "Niederschrift der GFS vom 25. 8. 1980," in *ibid.*

43 "Niederschrift der GFS vom 6. 4. 1981," RB 1 001 384.

44 "Niederschrift der GFS vom 18. 5. 1981," in *ibid.*

45 The literature dealing with supply systems in the automotive industry is now extensive. For some examples, see Stephanie Tilly, "Das Zulieferproblem aus institutionenökonomischer Sicht. Die westdeutsche Automobil-Zulieferindustrie zwischen Produktions- und Marktorientierung (1960–1980)," in *Jahrbuch für Wirtschaftsgeschichte*, 2010, 1, pp. 137–60; Manfred Deiß, Volker Döhl (eds.), *Vernetzte Produktion. Automobilzulieferer zwischen Kontrolle und Autonomie*, Frankfurt am Main, 1992; Heinz-Rudolf Meißner, *Die Teile und die Herrschaft. Die Reorganisation der Automobilproduktion und der Zulieferbeziehungen*, Berlin, 1994.

46 Schnabel interview of December 18, 2006, transcript p. 5.

47 For a detailed treatment of these engineering developments, see Walter Kaiser, *Bosch und das Kraftfahrzeug. Rückblick 1950–2003*, Stuttgart, 2004 (published in English as *Bosch and the automobile, 1950–2003: a review*, Stuttgart, 2008).

48 See note dated April 28, 1955, in RB 1 002 103.

49 In connection with this and what follows, see "Gerhard Greiner, Bericht über eine Konzernuntersuchung bei der Firma Robert Bosch GmbH vom Juli 1963," especially part 2: "Marktstellung des Konzerns," RB 1 035.

50 In this connection, see the tables in *ibid.*, pp. 230, 235.

51 *Ibid.*, p. 19.

52 "Protokoll der TVS vom 23. 3. 1964," p. 17, RB 1 001 271.

53 For details of the development of the original-equipment business between 1952 and 1982, see the automotive technology business sector sales figures set out in the monthly reports of the board of management to the supervisory board, as well as the reports to RBIK, RB 1 001 306 ff., 1 002 902, 1 002 931, 1 002 933, 1 002 936, 1 002 939.

54 In this connection, see (for example) "Protokoll der GFS vom 23. 9. 1975," p. 6, RB 1 230 006 025.

55 In this connection, for the 1975–81 period, together with forecasts and plans for 1982–85, see table of sales and capital expenditure in these two fields, July 2, 1982, RB 1 230 013 017.

56 "Merkle an die Gesellschafter der RBIK, vom 26. 3. 1979," RB 1 001 374. In this connection, see also Richard Gaul's article "Computer am Steuer," ["Computers at the wheel"] in *Die Zeit*, March 23, 1979, p. 19.

57 In this connection, see also the address by Bacher at the official opening of the center on April 30, 1970, RB 1 018 007 2, as well as Bacher's talks on the growing role of electronics in vehicles, April 18, 1977, RB 1 018 007 4, and "Kraftfahrzeugausrüstung – Möglichkeiten und Aufgaben für Bosch," autumn 1976, RB 1 018 007 3.

58 "Protokoll der GFS vom 14. 8. 1978," RB 1 230 009 020.

59 See the list drawn up in June 1973, RB 1 015 267.

60 "Notiz Stein, 17. 1. 1975," RB 1 017 503 1.

61 "Bericht Merkles auf der RBIK vom 10. 4. 1975," RB 1 001 352. In this connection, see also Merkle's detailed account of developments in "GPI-Tagung vom 27. 8. 1975," RB 1 015 021.

62 In this connection, see also the article "Aufsichtsrats-Diplomatie," in *Frankfurter Allgemeine Zeitung*, June 4, 1975.

63 "Vermerk Merkles über Telefonat mit Ulrich von der Deutschen Bank am 12. 9. 1975 und am 1. 12. 1975," RB 1 015 021.

64 Scholl was responsible for divisions K1 to K4, Eckert for K5 and K6.

65 "Economically, the present situation is felt to be the most precarious one we have faced since the currency reform," we read in "Protokoll der Sitzung des Beirats der Herstellergruppe Teile und Zubehör vom 30. 5. 1975," pp. 4 ff., RB 1 015 267. In this connection, see also "Protokoll der Herstellergruppenversammlung vom 26. 9. 1974," in *ibid.*

66 The "spare parts dispute" first emerged in the early 1950s. Stretching over many years, it reached its climax toward the end of the 1970s. For a detailed treatment, see Tilly, *Zulieferproblem*, pp. 150 ff.

67 "Protokoll der Herstellergruppenversammlung vom 10. 11. 1977," p. 4, RB 1 015 267. In connection with the concentration process then affecting automotive suppliers, see the article by Peter Odrich, "Zulieferer in der Klemme," in *Frankfurter Allgemeine Zeitung*, June 2, 1979.

68 "Merkle an die Gesellschafter der RBIG, 22. 11. 1973," RB 1 001 345.

69 "Protokoll der GFS vom 12. 12. 1977," RB 1 230 008 030. In connection with the rapidly changing demands, which also repeatedly occurred later (in the diesel division, for instance), see also the Riesenberg interview of April 4, 2007, transcript p. 15, RB 1 229 040.

70 "Protokoll der GFS vom 17. 5. 1976," RB 1 230 007 012.

71 In this connection, see the article "VW gegen Bosch," in *Der Spiegel*, January 30, 1978, p. 97.

72 "Protokoll der GFS vom 19. 2. 1979," RB 1 230 010 001 and "Protokoll der GFS vom 2. 4. 1979," RB 1 230 010 008.

73 "Niederschrift der Sitzung der RBIK vom 27. 11. 1980," p. 8, RB 1 001 381.

74 In this connection, see the discussions at Bosch's original-equipment conference on May 30, 1983, in *Bosch-Zünder* 1983/6 p. 1.

75 The story of MICO and Bosch in India virtually serves to exemplify the problems and political intricacies of the foreign investments made by Germany in India and the Asian region in the 1970s. It is time it was examined in detail. In this connection, see the thorough documentation in RB 1 017 527 1–2.

76 For the deliberations about investing in Brazil, see *ibid.*

77 In this connection, see the details of Bosch's foreign holdings in "Gerhard Greiner, Bericht über eine Konzenuntersuchung bei der Firma Robert Bosch GmbH vom Juli 1963," pp. 165 ff. RB 1 035, See also Karl Eugen Thomä's account, "Der Wiederaufbau unserer Auslandsbeziehungen," in *Bosch-Zünder* 1954/6–7, pp. 86–7.

78 "Niederschrift der TVS vom 20. 3. 1963," p. 12, RB 1 001 270.

79 Robert Bosch GmbH, 1960 annual report; *Handelsblatt*, September 22, 1961; "Gerhard Greiner, Bericht über eine Konzenuntersuchung bei der Firma Robert Bosch GmbH vom Juli 1963," pp. 177 ff. RB 1 035.

80 For details, see "Aufstellung vom 31. 12. 1967," RB 1 696 096.

81 See "Presseberichterstattung zur Ankündigung Merkles am 20. 3. 1969 als Anlage zum Protokoll der RBIG vom 27. 3. 1969," RB 1 002 111.

82 A forerunner was Netola Verwaltungs AG, based in Glarus, Switzerland, founded in 1956. In this connection, see RB 1 022 054.

83 See Merkle's comments of July 11, 1968, January 19, 1971, and February 2, 1971, RB 1 696 096.

84 See "Übersicht über die Ertragslage in den Regionalgesellschaften vom 2. 4. 1974," RB 1 696 004.

85 "Protokoll der GFS vom 23. 5. 1967," p. 2, RB 1 002 107. See also "Besuchsnotiz Knoerzer in Birmingham bei Lucas am 13./14. 4. 1961," RB 1 002 101; Harold Nockolds, *Lucas – The first 100 years*, London, 1979, pp. 127 ff., 231 ff. As an instance of the Bosch view, see "Protokoll der GFS vom 6. 3. 1978," p. 11, RB 1 230 009 006.

86 In connection with the relevant talks and negotiations, including those held in October 1952 and November 1955, see RB 1 002 102.

87 "Protokoll der GFS vom 12. 2. 1968," p. 5, RB 1 230 001.

88 "Protokoll der GFS vom 15. 6. 1970," *ibid.* Soon afterwards, however, the plans for a takeover, including Bosch's participation, came to nothing.

89 "Antrag zur GFS vom 5. 7. 1976," RB 1 230 006 001.

90 "Protokoll der GFS vom 21. 2. 1977," RB 1 230 008 001.

91 "Protokoll der GFS vom 6. 2. 1978," p. 6, RB 1 230 009 003.

92 In this connection, see also Scholl and Todenhöfer interviews.

93 "Protokoll der GFS vom 24. 11. 1983," p. 15, RB 1 230 014 030.

94 "Notiz zu den 'Aktivitäten der Bosch-Gruppe in Südostasien' vom 7. 6. 1972," RB 1 230 003 021.

95 "Protokoll der GFS vom 26. 4. 1966," RB 1 002 106.

96 For the context, see Christopher Neumaier, *Dieselautos in Deutschland und den USA. Zum Verhältnis von Technologie, Konsum und Politik 1949 bis 2005*, Stuttgart, 2010.

97 "Protokoll der GFS vom 26. 6. 1972," RB 1 230 003 021.

98 "Brief von Borg-Warner vom 11. 6. 1975," RB 1 017 501–1.

99 "Antrag zur GFS vom 16. 12. 1976" and "Schreiben an die RBIK-Gesellschafter vom 21. 12. 1976," RB 1 001 365.

100 In June 1977, Bosch had had an opportunity of increasing its U.S. involvement in the electronics sphere. American Microsystems Inc. (AMI), which had only been in existence for 12 years, offered Bosch a 25-percent partnership for the equivalent of 30 million German marks. With a workforce of 3,600 and sales of 67 million dollars, the company chiefly possessed R&D expertise in integrated circuits and in the MOS technology so important to Bosch. In connection with the development of semiconductor technology and associated know-how at Bosch, which soon brought the Stutt-

gart company into direct competition with such major electronics producers as Motorola and Siemens, see Kaiser, *Bosch*, pp. 129–45. Other sources include a talk given by Callsen, then head of development for automotive electrics, under the title "The place of semiconductors in Bosch automotive production", see "Vortrag von Callsen [...] vor dem Testamentsvollstrecker-Gremium am 23. 3. 1961," RB 1 001 268. On semiconductor strategy at Bosch, see also "Bericht zum 'Stand der gegenwärtigen Halbleiteraktivitäten bei RB' auf der GFS vom 7. 2. 1977," RB 1 230 008 001; "Papier vom 30. 11. 1979," RB 1 847 116, and a presentation by Baur, "'Halbleiter-Studie Baur' vom November 1982," RB 1 230 013 028.

101 "Protokoll der GFS vom 9. 4. 1979," RB 1 230 010 012.

102 List dated November 14, 1979, RB 1 230 010 033.

103 "Protokoll der GFS vom 10. 11. 1980," p. 6, RB 1 230 011 029.

104 See the documents "Benutzung des Namens BOSCH in USA," dated March 25, 1969, RB 1 230 002 001–030, and "Geschichte der Rechte am Namen und an der Marke BOSCH in USA" [undated], RB 1 241 040.

105 *Ibid.*, p. 2.

106 "Notiz zur RBIK vom 23. 3. 1983," RB 1 001 391.

107 "GF-Mitteilung vom 6. 11. 1981," RB 1 230 012 030.

108 *Ibid.*

109 "Notiz vom 9. 6. 1981," RB 1 017 039, and "Reisebericht Indien vom 16. 9. 1980," RB 1 017 040.

110 Robert Bosch GmbH, 1970 annual report, pp. 13 f.

111 For a general view, see Frank Uekötter, *Umweltgeschichte im 19. und 20. Jahrhundert*, Munich, 2007.

112 Merkle's talk, entitled *Der Regelkreis unternehmerischer Planung*, is reprinted in *Deutsche Zeitung*, November 10, 1972, pp. 31–4.

113 *Ibid.*

114 "Protokoll der GFS vom 19. 11. 1973," RB 1 230 004 026.

115 For an example, see the informative and critical booklet by Klaus Möbius of the Kiel Institute for World Economy: *Das Umweltproblem aus wirtschaftlicher Sicht* (Kieler Diskussionsbeiträge zu aktuellen wirtschaftspolitischen Fragen, 14) Kiel, 1971.

116 "Aufstellung vom 8. 1. 1974," RB 1 046 057, and "Zusammenstellung für eine Erhebung der IHK Stuttgart vom 7. 3. 1972," RB 1 046 049 001.

117 "Notiz," RB 1 046 057.

118 "Aufstellung der zwischen Dezember 1971 und April 1973 erschienenen *Bosch-Zünder*-Artikel vom 25. 10. 1973," RB 1 046 057.

119 "'Entwicklungstendenzen auf dem Gebiet des Umweltschutzes,' Referat vom 6. 7. 1972," RB 1 046 086.

120 "GF-Richtlinie vom 15. 1. 1973," RB 1 005 016.

121 Robert Bosch GmbH, 1976 annual report, p. 10, and "Anhang zum Protokoll des GFS vom 20. 7. 1976," RB 1 230 007 018.

122 "Protokoll der Ratio-Tagung vom 4./5. 6. 1975," RB 1 027 001 1. In mid-January 1979, a study was made of the health risks resulting from asbestos and lead. See "Gesundheitsgefahren durch Asbest und Blei. Bericht über Stand der Sicherheitsmaßnahmen bei Robert Bosch," RB 1 030 087. And two years later, Bosch presented its first separate "Energy Report". The report combined a brief description of the international energy situation and energy developments at Bosch with a detailed catalogue of action including the principal energy-saving measures currently in place at Bosch or planned for the future. See "Energiereport Robert Bosch GmbH 1980," RB 1 030 072.

Clearly, though, this was a "one-off." No more reports were published in the years that followed.

123 "Unterlagen zur GFS vom 19. 11. 1979," RB 1 030 010 009.

124 "Notiz der ZT vom 8. 2. 1980," RB 1 030 061.

125 In this connection, see among other sources the "Fuel Cell" report in *Bosch-Zünder* 1964/8–10, pp. 66–8.

126 Particularly on the early phase (1880s to 1930s) see Gijs Mom, *The electric vehicle. Technology and expectations in the automobile age*, Illinois, 2004.

127 See the fuel-cell report of October 10, 1961, as well as a further report on lead batteries, RB 1 047 017.

128 In this connection, see (among other sources) "Vortrag 'Bosch im Elektromobil' vom 8. 5. 1967," RB 1 069 001, and "Notiz vom 22. 12. 1967," in *ibid*.

129 See the various newspaper and periodical articles gathered together in RB 1 069 002 1.

130 "Reisebericht vom 16. 3. 1967," RB 1 047 016.

131 "Protokoll der GFS vom 13. 4. 1970," p. 5, RB 1 230 001 001. See also the various 1973 development reports in RB 1 010 302.

132 For instance, Bosch experimented with fuel cells powered by methanol and acid electrolytes. In this connection, see also the report of the Schwieberdingen engineering center for automotive electrics: Robert Bosch GmbH (ed.), *Bosch HEUTE, Informationen Schwieberdingen. Der neue Standort)*, Stuttgart, 1970, p. 15, RB 1 001 350.

133 At first, this applied primarily to CO_2 emissions. Emissions of unburned hydrocarbons remained a problem. In this connection, see also Hermann Scholl, "Elektronisch gesteuerte Benzineinspritzung – Weiterentwicklung der Jetronic," in *Bosch Technische Berichte* 1, November 1969, pp. 1–12.

134 In this connection, see (among other sources) Robert Bosch GmbH, 1972 annual report, p. 13, and 1973 annual report, p. 10.

135 "Protokoll der GFS vom 29. 11. 1973," p. 15, RB 1 001 345.

136 "Entwicklungsziel Umweltschutz," reprinted in *Bosch-Zünder* 1971/10, pp. 240–1. In this connection, see also Robert Bosch GmbH (ed.), *Bosch HEUTE,* pp. 4 f., RB 1 001 350.

137 "Protokoll der GFS vom 19. 11. 1973," RB 1 230 004 026.

138 For the press release with the list of projects, see RB 1974 1104.

139 "Pressemitteilung vom Mai 1975," RB 1975 0506.

140 "Protokoll der GFS vom 10. 2. 1975," p. 2, RB 1 230 006 003.

141 "Rede Bachers am 7. 1. 1981," RB 1 018 007 4.

142 See "Notiz vom 12. 10. 1973" and "Notiz vom 30. 10. 1979," both in RB 1 022 301.

143 "Rede Bachers am 28. 10. 1981," RB 1 018 007 4.

144 "[…] beim Kampf um umweltfreundliche Kraftfahrzeuge," was how it was put in an article in the March 1974 issue of *Bosch-Zünder*.

145 "Rede Bachers am 28. 10. 1981," RB 1 018 007 4.

146 "Protokoll der GFS vom 24. 11. 1983," pp. 6 ff. RB 1 230 014 030.

4 Between Americanization and Japanization: manufacturing organization and work environment

1 For a comprehensive treatment of this subject, see Harm G. Schröter, *Americanization of the European economy. A compact survey of American economic influence in Europe since the 1880s*, Dordrecht, 2005. For details of German companies, see also Christian Kleinschmidt, *Der produktive Blick. Wahrnehmung amerikanischer und japanischer Management- und Produktionsmethoden durch deutsche Unternehmer*

1950–1985, Berlin, 2002, and Susanne Hilger, *"Amerikanisierung" deutscher Unternehmen. Wettbewerbsstrategien und Unternehmenspolitik bei Henkel, Siemens und Daimler-Benz (1945/49–1975)*, Wiesbaden, 2004. Volker Berghahn's study of the Americanization of the German economy is still of fundamental significance: *Unternehmer und Politik in der Bundesrepublik*, Frankfurt am Main, 1985.

2 "Berichte und Fragenkataloge," RB 1 128 002 005–7.

3 *Ibid.*, p. 33.

4 "Amerika-Reise 1955, BSP 1 Wagner," RB 1 028 030 001.

5 See (to take two examples of the earlier meetings) "Protokoll der 30. FWS vom 25. 3. 1954" (with many individual references to problems of detail), RB 1 027 012 8, or "Protokoll der 40. FWS vom 21. 7. 1955," RB 1 027 013 2. See also "Protokoll der 1. Rationalisierungs-Tagung vom 27. 4. 1956," RB 1 027 013 4.

6 "Bericht auf der GFS vom 24. 6. 1959," RB 1 002 093.

7 "Bericht über die 86. Werksleiter-Tagung vom 29. 4. 1960," RB 1 047 122.

8 "Betriebsanalyse Gesamt-Bosch von 1959," RB 1 068 001 1. See also the nearly 180-page WOL annual reports for 1951 and 1961, RB 1 003 481.

9 "Amerika-Bericht 1960 von Hofmann, Kilgus, Bacher, Hohnacker," p. 11, RB 1 028 056 001.

10 "TVS-Protokoll vom 1. 7. 1958," RB 1 001 265.

11 "Denkschrift vom 2. 4. 1959," RB 1 002 095.

12 In this connection, see also "Zusammenstellung der Freiwilligen Sozialleistungen der Robert Bosch GmbH für 1960," RB 1 001 267.

13 "Protokoll der 6. Ratio-Tagung vom 30. 10. 1958," RB 1 027 006 3. The conference had as its general heading "Stepping up our rationalization efforts with a view to making ourselves more competitive in export markets and given the imminence of the European Common Market."

14 This method, using predetermined times, had been developed in America back in 1940 by the consultant engineers Maynard, Stegemerten, and Schwab. In 1948, the three had published their findings in a book entitled *Methods-time measurement*, which caused an immediate stir far beyond American shores. In 1951, Maynard founded the MTM Association for Standards and Research, firmly establishing the quality of a method that went on to conquer the globe.

15 In this connection, see also the detailed introductory texts and data-sheets in RB 1 046 112.

16 "Einführung in das MTM-Verfahren, 5. 10. 1960," *ibid.*

17 U.S. consultancy companies brought MTM to Europe in the early 1950s – initially to Sweden, where the first European MTM association was set up in 1955, then to Switzerland, the Netherlands, and France. In connection with the historical evolution of the process, see the *Festschrift* published by Deutsche MTM-Vereinigung e. V. to mark its fortieth anniversary, *MTM – Von Anfang an richtig*, Hamburg, 2002, pp. 9–28.

18 "'Survey of Manufacturing of Bosch' von B. Payne vom 16. 12. 1959," p. 1, RB 1 002 103.

19 *Ibid.*, pp. 2 ff.

20 "Protokoll TVS vom 29. 6. 1960," pp. 4 f., RB 1 001 267.

21 In this connection, see the individual discussion reports from July 1960 to the summer of 1961 in RB 1 068 001 2.

22 In this connection, see "B. Payne, 'Summary of Management Control Area' 5. 1. 1961," RB 1 068 001 1. See also "Besprechungsnotiz vom 15. 12. 1960," RB 1 068 001 2, and "Besprechungsbericht vom 11. 4. 1961," *ibid.*

23 "Bericht über eine FEH-Besprechung vom 17. 4. 1961," RB 1 068 001 1. On the introduction of MTM in the *Lichtwerk*, see also the relevant piece in *Bosch-Zünder* 1964/2, pp. 28–31.

24 In this connection, for a provisional review of six years of "successful implementation of the MTM system" see (among other sources) the article about MTM published on the occasion of the fourth international MTM conference held in Stuttgart, *Bosch-Zünder* 1966/9, pp. 172–5. Bruce Payne was again engaged by Bosch in an advisory capacity between April 1971 and November 1972, this time in the sphere of sales and administration. However, unlike in 1962, the work of the consulting engineers was in this instance deemed less successful. See the documents in RB 1 068 002 2.

25 In this connection, see also Betriebsrat Bosch Feuerbach (ed.), … *auch beim Bosch*, pp. 94 f.

26 Franziska Böhles, "'Der Capo hat uns die Werkstatt gezeigt,' Arbeitsmigration bei Bosch, Die ersten 'Gastarbeiter' am Standort Feuerbach," in Reinhard Johler, Felicia Sparacio (eds.), *Abfahren. Ankommen. Boschler sein. Lebensgeschichten aus der Arbeitswelt*, 2nd ed., Tübingen, 2011, p. 240; Wolfgang Malchow, "Die Rolle der Italiener für die Wirtschaft in Baden-Württemberg," address given at the Italian Consulate-General in Stuttgart on July 15, 2005, marking the 50th anniversary of the German-Italian agreement on recruiting Italian labor and bringing it to Germany, RB 1 044 017.

27 Ulrich Herbert, *Geschichte der Ausländerpolitik in Deutschland. Saisonarbeiter, Zwangsarbeiter, Gastarbeiter, Flüchtlinge*, Munich, 2001, p. 205.

28 *Ibid.*, pp. 223 ff.; Werner Abelshauser, *Deutsche Wirtschaftsgeschichte seit 1945*, Munich, 2004, pp. 319 f.; Miriam Hessler, "'Ich habe viele Erinnerungen an hier'. Wie aus 'Gastarbeitern' Mitbürger geworden sind," in Johler, Sparacio (eds.), *Abfahren*, p. 305.

29 "Personalstatistik, Beschäftigtenstand 31. 12. 1960," RB 1 007 087; "Ausländische Arbeiter 1969–75," RB 1 007 088 f.; "Beschäftigung ausländischer Mitarbeiter bei RB und TOGE, Vergleich 1967 zu 1970," 30. 10. 1970, RB 1 158 008.

30 "Ausländische Arbeiter 1969–1975," RB 1 007 088 f.; "Personalstatistik, Beschäftigtenstand 1. 12. 1973," RB 1 007 089; and "Beschäftigtenstand 1. 1. 1976," RB 1 007 090.

31 Malchow, "Die Rolle der Italiener," RB 1 044 017.

32 See table 16, p. 360.

33 Monika Mattes, *"Gastarbeiterinnen" in der Bundesrepublik. Anwerbepolitik, Migration und Geschlecht in den 50er bis 70er Jahren*, Frankfurt am Main, 2005, pp. 129, 186; see also "Gastarbeiter. Entwicklungshilfe für Reiche?," in *Der Spiegel*, November 22, 1971, pp. 138 ff.

34 "Beschäftigung ausländischer Mitarbeiter bei RB und TOGE, Vergleich 1967 zu 1970, 30. 10. 1970," RB 1 158 008.

35 *Ibid.*

36 *Ibid.*

37 Sautter, interview of October 19, 2010.

38 "Personalstatistik, Beschäftigtenstand 31. 12. 1960," RB 1 007 087, and "Beschäftigtenstand 1. 1. 1976," RB 1 007 090; "Beschäftigung ausländischer Mitarbeiter bei RB und TOGE, Vergleich 1967 zu 1970, 30. 10. 1970," RB 1 158 008; "Ausländische Mitarbeiter Bosch-Gruppe Inland, 4. 2. 1976," *ibid.*

39 Sautter interview, October 19, 2010.

40 *Ibid.*

41 *Ibid.*
42 "Per Moneta," in *Der Spiegel*, October 7, 1964, pp. 44 ff.
43 Sautter interview, October 19, 2010.
44 "Bericht der 86. Werksleiter-Tagung vom 16. 5. 1960," RB 1 047 122.
45 The words "Sklavenaufpasser im Mittelalter" come from a letter written by a Turkish worker named Aram M. They are reproduced in Karin Hunn, *"Nächstes Jahr kehren wir zurück." Die Geschichte der türkischen "Gastarbeiter" in der Bundesrepublik*, Göttingen, 2005, p. 214, n. 35. See also Betül Özyakan, "Es gibt keine Probleme, es gibt nur Herausforderungen," in Johler, Sparacio (eds.), *Abfahren*, pp. 143 f.
46 "Schreiber an Springer, 10. 3. 1965," RB 1 059 001.
47 "Bosch nimmt ausländische Arbeiter in Schutz," press release dated March 11, 1965, RB 1965 0305.
48 "Beschlüsse der GFS am 24. 9. 1973," RB 1 230 004 021.
49 "Beschäftigung ausländischer Mitarbeiter bei RB und TOGE, Vergleich 1967 zu 1970, 30. 10. 1970," RB 1 158 008.
50 Mattes, *"Gastarbeiterinnen,"* p. 319.
51 "Beschäftigung ausländischer Mitarbeiter bei RB und TOGE, Vergleich 1967 zu 1970, 30. 10. 1970," RB 1 158 008.
52 *Ibid.*
53 "[...] diese Entwicklung nicht machen können," quoted from Böhles, "'Der Capo ...'," p. 250.
54 See "Bericht vom 1. 7. 1963," RB 1 059 002. The committee's report comprised 15 pages.
55 In this connection, see "Anweisung Nr. 2, Lohnauseinandersetzungen 1966," RB 1 093 003.
56 See also, in this connection, Robert Bosch GmbH, 1965 annual report, p. 12.
57 In this connection, see also (among other sources) "Reisebericht USA 1964 von Kilgus, Haas," RB 1 027 012 13.
58 See also, in this connection, the presentation "'Wertanalyse – eine Methode zur Kostensenkung,' auf der 16. Ratio-Tagung vom 1. 10. 1964," RB 1 027 001 9.
59 "Rede Bachers," RB 1 018 007 2.
60 This was why, among other changes made in the late 1950s, the lubrication-pump business had been sold and production of headlights and dynamos for bicycles shut down.
61 "Protokoll der GPI vom 20. 12. 1973," pp. 3 f., RB 1 002 882.
62 "Vortrag Raible auf der 23. Ratio-Tagung vom 4./5. 6. 1975," RB 1 027 001 1.
63 "Protokoll der GPI vom 20. 12. 1973," p. 4, RB 1 002 882.
64 "Vortrag Bachers vom 21. 10. 1976," RB 1 018 007 4.
65 See "Besuchsbericht Kilgus, Wunderlich vom Oktober 1962," RB 1 028 018 011, and "Notiz vom 10. 11. 1965," RB 1 028 026 006.
66 In this connection, see "Besuchsberichte von der Werkzeugmaschinen-Ausstellung 1970 in Chicago," RB 1 028 026 007, and "Besuchsberichte von der Europäischen Werkzeugmaschinenausstellung 1977 in Hannover," RB 1 028 055 002.
67 In this connection, see "GFS-Protokoll vom 8. 9. 1980 zu den Beratungen über Dialogsysteme für Materialwirtschaft und Fertigung in den Feuerbacher Werken," RB 1 230 011 024. This fundamental process (dialogue systems for materials management and production) for German companies has yet to be examined in any detail. For an overview, see James W. Cortada, *The digital hand. How computers changed the work of American manufacturing, transportation, and retail industries*, Oxford, 2003.

68 "Protokoll der GFS vom 29. 9. 1981," p. 4, RB 1 230 012 026.
69 "Notiz der Personalstelle vom 28. 9. 1970," RB 1 093 008.
70 "Gedächtnisniederschrift der Gespräche vom 10. 9. 1970," RB 1 093 008.
71 In this connection, see also Betriebsrat Bosch Feuerbach (ed.), … *auch beim Bosch*, pp. 93 f.
72 *Ibid.* See also the transcript of the Rau interview, RB 1 229 067.
73 "Protokoll der GFS vom 15. 10. 1973," p. 1, RB 1 230 004 032.
74 "GFS-Beschluss vom 12. 11. 1973," RB 1 230 004 025.
75 For instance, a "Feuerbach General Plan" drawn up in the summer of 1970 provided for comprehensive renovation and extension or redevelopment of the plant at a cost of 100 million German marks spread over the next ten years. It was a huge project, and in fact only about a third of it had been completed by 1976. Space on the site was so tight that no new buildings could be put up until the old ones had been demolished. See the discussions at the board of management meetings of June 28 and November 25, 1976, RB 1 001 360.
76 "Zusammenstellung für die Jahre 1973 bis 1982," RB 1 007 096. From 1977 to 1981, there was again a significant decrease, before the crisis year of 1982 once again saw a steep rise in shorter working weeks (152,000 man-days).
77 "Bericht Merkle auf der RBIK vom 29. 9. 1977," RB 1 001 363.
78 "Bericht auf der GFS vom 20. 3. 1978," RB 1 230 009 019. In this connection, see also Betriebsrat Bosch Feuerbach (ed.), … *auch beim Bosch*, p. 106.
79 See the various calls for strikes and strike progress reports, RB 1 059 002.
80 "Protokoll der GFS vom 15. 11. 1982," p. 2, RB 1 002 236; in this connection, see also "GFS vom 24. 7. 1981," RB 1 002 221, "GFS vom 19. 10. 1981," RB 1 002 219, and "Anlage zur GFS vom 7. 5. 1982 zur künftigen Modifizierung der Entlohnung," RB 1 059 002.
81 In this connection, see the report in the June 23, 1983, issue of *Handelsblatt*, which was also discussed at RBIK on June 23, 1983, RB 1 001 392.
82 Report in the June 23, 1983, issue of *Handelsblatt*.
83 In this connection, see Karl Lauschke, *Mehr Demokratie in der Wirtschaft. Die Entstehungsgeschichte des Mitbestimmungsgesetzes von 1976*, Düsseldorf, 2006; Ralph Greifenstein, Leo Kißler, *Mitbestimmung im Spiegel der Forschung. Eine Bilanz der empirischen Untersuchungen 1952–2010*, Berlin, 2010.
84 "Protokoll der GFS vom 14. 6. 1971," RB 1 230 001 001.
85 In this connection, see the newspaper article "Mitbestimmung bei Bosch erst 1978," in *Stuttgarter Zeitung*, July 16, 1976; see also "Merkle an die Gesellschafter der RBIK, 28. 7. 1976," RB 1 001 388.
86 "Protokoll der GFS vom 2. 5. 1977," pp. 7 f., RB 1 230 008 020.
87 "Erklärung des Konzern- und Gesamtbetriebsrats der Robert Bosch GmbH," RB 1 230 008 021.
88 "Brief vom 11. 7. 1977," *ibid.*
89 In this connection, see the mass of documents and internal working papers on the constitutional complaint in the papers of Paul Stein, the board of management member responsible for legal affairs, RB 1 022 236.
90 *Ibid.*
91 In this connection, see the article in the November 11, 1978, issue of *Stuttgarter Nachrichten*, RB 1 022 236. See also Knud Andresen, Ursula Bitzegeio, Jürgen Mittag (eds.), *Nach dem Strukturbruch? Kontinuität und Wandel von Arbeitsbeziehungen und Arbeitswelt(en) seit den 1970er-Jahren*, Bonn, 2011.
92 Interview with Rau, November 9, 2005, transcript p. 8, RB 1 229 067.

93 *Ibid.*

94 *Ibid.*, p. 14.

95 "Reisebericht vom 23.2. bis 14. 3. 1964" (28 pages), RB 1 028 051 001.

96 "Japan-Reise vom September 1968" and particularly the bulky (160-page) "Japan-Studie vom März 1969," RB 1 028 052.

97 See also, in this connection, "Rede Bachers vom 29. 11. 1971 über 'Eindrücke von einer Japanreise'," RB 1 018 007 3.

98 "Bericht vom November 1974," RB 1 114 00 1, and "Bericht vom Februar 1976," RB 1 047 115.

99 In connection with Merkle's visit to Japan, see the documents in RB 1 690 005 and "Notiz vom 20. 6. 1980," RB 1 028 057.

100 Kleinschmidt, *Blick*, pp. 366 ff.

101 "Ausführlicher Bericht vom 29. 1. 1981," RB 1 127 219.

102 *Ibid.*, pp. 5 f.

103 "Bericht der Studiengruppe auf der Geschäftspolitischen Informationstagung am 27. 2. 1981," RB 1 002 889, and "Protokoll der GFS vom 9. 2. 1981," RB 1 230 012 002.

104 "Protokoll der 1. Sitzung vom 10. 4. 1981" and minutes of subsequent meetings, RB 1 127 219.

105 "Diskussionsgrundlage für die GFS am 19. 2. 1982," RB 1 230 013 002.

106 "Rede Bachers vom 25. 5. 1982," RB 1 018 007 4. Another reason why this manufacturing conference was so important was that this was the first time in four years that the Bosch Group executives responsible for manufacturing (all 255 of them) had got together. See also the article "Kosten senken, Kosten senken ...," in *Bosch-Zünder* 1982/5, p. 1.

107 "Besprechungsbericht vom 2. 9. 1981," RB 1 018 007 4. See also the very thorough "'Gedanken zur Fertigung in den 80er Jahren – Gesetzliche und tarifpolitische Entwicklung,' vorgetragen auf der GPI am 2. 12. 1981," RB 1 002 889.

108 In this connection, see some of the papers in RB 1 127 126.

109 "Vortrag Kochs über 'Die zukünftige Fertigung bei RB' am 8. 5. 1984," p. 16, RB 1 127 126.

5 The phase of "indiscriminate diversification": strategic alliances and the move into new areas of business

1 Bosch made other diversification attempts, too, though these were soon abandoned as failures. In the early 1970s, for instance, acting in collaboration with the Wüstenrot savings and loan association, the group moved into prefabricated-building construction. For a sample source in this connection, see "Merkle an die RBIK, 20. 11. 1973," RB 1 001 345.

2 A good general source in this connection is Morten Reitmayer, Ruth Rosenberger (eds.), *Unternehmen am Ende des "goldenen Zeitalters." Die 1970er Jahre als Gegenstand der Unternehmens- und Wirtschaftsgeschichte*, Essen, 2008.

3 On Gerling, see (among other sources) "Merkle an Schieren, 6. 10. 1975," RB 1 015 309 045, and on the Allianz holding "Merkle an Schieren, 30. 7. 1981," *ibid.*

4 "Notiz vom 21. 9. 1961," RB 1 047 059.

5 "Protokoll der TVS vom 28. 11. 1963," RB 1 001 280.

6 *Ibid.*

7 "Aktennotiz über eine Besprechung vom 25. 3. 1964," RB 1 064 001–1, and "Bericht Merkles auf der RBIG vom 26. 11. 1964," RB 1 001 306.

8 "Besprechungsnotiz vom 21. 7. 1965," RB 1 064 001–1.

9 "Brief an das Bundeskartellamt vom 13. 1. 1966" and "Zusammenstellung namhafter Zusammenschlüsse der Industrie elektrischer Konsumgüter seit 1958," *ibid.*

10 Article in the *Süddeutsche Zeitung* of March 12, 1966; see *ibid.*

11 "Bericht Merkles auf der RBIG-Sitzung vom 24. 3. 1966," RB 1 001 310.

12 "Notiz vom 19. 4. 1966" and a detailed account of developments, both *ibid.*

13 That, for instance, was the title of a talk given by Günther, president of the Federal Cartel Authority, to the Baden-Baden Entrepreneurs' Colloquy on March 8, 1966. In this connection, see "Notiz Merkles vom 11. 3. 1966," *ibid.* Incidentally, Merkle was himself involved in the consultations over amendment of the Act against Restraints on Competition held at the Federal Chancellery in February 1965, consultations in which representatives of the business world evidently voiced certain misgivings; see "Merkle an Bundeswirtschaftsminister Schmücker, 12. 2. 1965," RB 1 015 033.

14 See the detailed "Memorandum zum 'zweiten Weg' der Hausgeräte-Zusammenarbeit Bosch Siemens vom 2. 5. 1966," RB 1 064 008.

15 Detailed reports and minutes of meetings between June and September 1966, RB 1 064 001–2.

16 "Bericht Merkles auf der GFS vom 5. 12. 1966," RB 1 002 106. See also "Fernschreiben des Bundeskartellamts an Bosch vom 22. 11. 1966," RB 1 064 001.

17 In this connection, see also the "survey of the European market for household appliances" by F. W. Hohage (one of the distribution managers of BSHG) presented on July 2, 1967, in "Pressemitteilung vom Juli 1967," RB 1967 0705.

18 More precisely, in 1981 total profit of 55 million German marks was recorded. By 1983 the figure was 94.4 million, which represented a margin of just 2 to 3 percent. See RB 1 015 016–003. For a detailed record of sales according to product area, broken down into the three main brands Bosch, Siemens, and Constructa for the period 1975 to 1977, see RB 1 064 001–1.

19 See "Protokoll der GFS vom 22. 4. 1968," RB 1 002 108, and the annual reports for 1967 (pp. 15 f.), 1968 (pp. 12 f.), 1969 (pp. 23 f.), and 1970 (pp. 24 ff.). However, that did not mark the end of the troubled history of the precarious (in terms of cartel law) organization of Bosch's household-appliances business. Late November 1972 brought an initial reorganization of its joint household-appliances operations. This chiefly involved switching from a group based on contracts to a group based on shareholder relationships. Then on January 1, 1978, the Bosch-Siemens partnership in the field of household appliances underwent another reorganization. This comprised more tightening-up of management organization and a merger of its personnel to create a single BSHG workforce. The final act (for the time being) followed in October 1982, when a crisis-hit AEG shed its household-appliance interests and Bosch-Siemens promptly bought up Neff GmbH, for which after a formal investigation the Federal Cartel Authority once again gave the green light.

20 In this connection, see also Robert Bosch GmbH (ed.), *Bosch Fernseh 1929–1979 (Festvorträge zum Firmenjubiläum am 31. 5. 1979)*, Darmstadt, 1979.

21 "Zusammenstellung der Verkaufsumsätze der Tochtergesellschaften 1948 bis 1977," RB 1 003 072.

22 In connection with this and what follows, see the papers in RB 1 610 026, specifically "Memorandum vom 11. 7. 1963."

23 "Notiz vom 6. 11. 1963," *ibid.* On the history of Loewe and the industry, see Steiner, *Ortsempfänger.*

24 See (among other sources) "Besprechungsnotizen Bosch-Siemens vom 22. 6. 1967," RB 1 017 520.

25 "Auszug aus dem Protokoll der RBIG vom 29. 6. 1967," RB 1 017 520.

26 Robert Bosch GmbH, 1973 annual report, p. 16.

27 Horst Sandvoß interview, transcript pp. 6 f., RB 1 229 087. Sandvoß had been the spokesman of the Blaupunkt board in 1968.

28 "Protokoll der GFS vom 20. 3. 1978," p. 11, RB 1 030 009.

29 "Protokoll der GFS vom 13. 3. 1978," p. 13, *ibid.*

30 As one former Blaupunkt manager observed retrospectively in an interview. See RB 1 229 087.

31 Among other sources for this, see "Niederschrift der RBIK vom 28. 9. 1978," pp. 6 f., RB 1 001 374.

32 As Merkle himself said at a board meeting, see "Protokoll der GFS vom 2. 7. 1979," p. 7, RB 1 030 010.

33 See "Protokoll der GFS vom 19. 3. 1979," RB 1 230 001, and "Niederschrift der RBIK vom 5. 4. 1979," pp. 14 ff., RB 1 001 374.

34 Nearly 40 million German marks of which, however, could be offset against tax under a profit and loss transfer agreement between Blaupunkt and Robert Bosch GmbH. The net loss was roughly 16 million German marks.

35 "Niederschrift der RBIK vom 28. 6. 1979," RB 1 001 376.

36 "Interne Prognoserechnung und Markteinschätzung vom 13. 2. 1981," RB 1 017 217.

37 "Merkle an Plettner, 12. 10. 1978," RB 1 017 511.

38 In the summer of 1983, in fact, talks reopened regarding potential alliances between Philips Grundig, Siemens, and Bosch Blaupunkt. See "Gesprächsvermerk Schips vom 14. 6. 1983," RB 1 017 519.

39 See "Bericht auf der GFS vom 26. 5. 1975" and "Aktennotiz vom 21. 4. 1975," RB 1 230 006 001.

40 "Bericht auf der GFS vom 26. 5. 1975," p. 5. There had been repeated contacts and negotiations between Bosch and Messerschmitt before. The first time had been in 1964, when use of manufacturing facilities had been the issue. On that occasion, Messerschmitt had evidently tabled a direct 26 percent partnership with Bosch, which the latter had turned down as "unacceptable in view of the risks of the aviation and aerospace industry." See "Protokoll GFS vom 18. 2. 1964," RB 1 002 098.

41 "Ausführliche Notiz zu MBB vom 17. 12. 1976," pp. 2 f., RB 1 022 397.

42 Listed in *ibid.* On the history of MBB in the context of the development of the German aviation and aerospace industry, see (among other sources) Christopher Magnus Andres, *Die bundesdeutsche Luft- und Raumfahrtindustrie 1945–1970. Ein Industriebereich im Spannungsfeld von Politik, Wirtschaft und Militär*, Frankfurt am Main, 1996, and Hartmut Schneider, *Neue politische Ökonomie und Technologiepolitik. Fallstudie am Beispiel der Luftfahrtindustrie*, Berlin, 1980.

43 "Protokoll der GFS vom 20. 12. 1976," p. 5, RB 1 230 008.

44 "Notiz zur Verhandlungslinie vom 21. 7. 1977," RB 1 022 397.

45 See *Deutsche Zeitung*, July 7, 1978, p. 14, among other press reports in RB 1 022 397.

46 "Protokoll der GFS vom 9. 10. 1978," in *ibid.*

47 "Merkle an Plettner vom 28. 12. 1978," in RB 1 022 379–1.

48 *Ibid.*

49 "Studie vom 13. 2. 1979," RB 1 030 072.

50 In this connection, see for instance the lecture given by Hans Gissel, member of the board of AEG-Telefunken, under the title "Kommunikationstechnik – Auf dem Weg zur Integration der Dienste" at a technical colloquium on October 8, 1981, a printed version of which may be found in RB 1 017 486. For a general view of technical change in the field, see Oskar Blumtritt, *Nachrichtentechnik. Sender, Empfänger, Übertragung, Vermittlung*, Munich, 2005. Two English-language sources are Gerald Brock, *The second information revolution*, Cambridge, 2003, and Alfred D. Chandler, *Inventing the electronic century. The epic story of the consumer electronics and the computer industries*, New York, 2001.

51 For a general account, see Peter Strunk, *Die AEG. Aufstieg und Niedergang einer Industrielegende*, Berlin, 2000, pp. 104 ff.

52 "Protokoll der GFS vom 29. 11. 1979," p. 18, RB 1 001 376.

53 The planned term was ten years with an effective yield of 6.43 percent, albeit without any kind of security.

54 "Dürr an Merkle vom 20. 3. 1981," RB 1 017 509 –1.

55 See, for example, the minutes of the RBIK shareholders' meeting of March 26, 1981.

56 "*Stuttgarter Zeitung* vom 7. 8. 1981," RB 1 017 483 (where there are other press cuttings as well).

57 In this connection, see the detailed "Bericht über den Stand der Verhandlungen auf der RBIK-Sitzung vom 25. 6. 1981," RB 1 001 384.

58 "Protokoll der RBIK-Sitzung am 25. 6. 1981," pp. 11 ff., RB 1 001 384.

59 "AEG-Poker: SEL oder Bosch," in *Stuttgarter Nachrichten*, August 14, 1981.

60 See "Protokoll der GFS zum Verhandlungsstand 'TC' vom 14. 9. 1981," RB 1 017 483.

61 Echoed in "Bericht Merkles auf der RBIK-Sitzung vom 2. 12. 1981," RB 1 001 386.

62 "Protokoll der RBIK vom 28. 9. 1981," *ibid.*

63 "'Dossier TC' vom 24. 9. 1981," *ibid.* On the intricate details of corporate law, see also the very full "Bericht Steins an den Aufsichtsrat vom 19. 10. 1981," *ibid.*

64 In this connection, see also the very extensive (it runs to nearly 200 pages) study commissioned from Rolf-Dieter Leister of the Advisory Institute for Information and Telecommunications Technology, "Bericht über den Telematik-Verbund und seine strategische Ausrichtung und Marktchancen vom 2. 12. 1981," RB 1 017 490 –1.

65 *Ibid.* Handwritten notes by the person taking down the minutes.

66 "Vermerk Merkles vom 6. 11. 1981 über ein Gespräch mit Christians von der Deutschen Bank im Bundeskanzleramt," RB 1 017 485.

67 "Notiz 'Absicherung des AEG-Risikos' vom 29. 9. 1981," RB 1 017 490 –2. See also "Vermerk Merkles über Gespräche mit Bundeswirtschaftsminister Graf Lambsdorff vom 5. 11. 1981," RB 1 017 485.

68 "Vertragswerk Telekommunikation vom 20. 11. und 1. 12. 1981," RB 1 017 482.

69 See, for instance, the article in *Börsen-Zeitung*, December 3, 1981. In addition to Allianz AG (with its 9 percent holding), in January 1982 Bosch saw another partner climb aboard. This was J. M. Voith GmbH, which as a pure capital investor joined Telenorma with a sub-holding of 24.9 percent that carried no voting rights.

70 For details, see Strunk, *AEG*, pp. 130 ff., and Dürr's account in his autobiography: Heinz Dürr, *In der ersten Reihe. Aufzeichnungen eines Unerschrockenen*, Berlin, 2008, pp. 201 ff.

71 "Aktennotiz der Bosch-Rechtsabteilung vom 14. 9. 1982," RB 1 017 484.

72 "Briefwechsel zwischen Bosch und AEG von Januar / Februar 1983," RB 1 017 486.

73 "Merkle an Dürr, 24. 6. 1983," *ibid.*

74 See "Fall AEG – Kein Lehrstück für eine erfolgreiche Sanierung," in *Frankfurter Rundschau*, September 17, 1984, *ibid.*

75 "Protokoll der GFS vom 22. 12. 1981," RB 1 001 387.

76 "Protokoll der GFS vom 18. 1. 1982," *ibid.*

77 "Niederschrift der Sonder-GFS vom 9. 2. 1982," *ibid.*

6 Initial conclusions

1 "Protokoll der GFS vom 26. 5. 1964," RB 1 002 098.

2 For the individual earnings figures of the various product categories, see "Anhang zur Niederschrift der GFS vom 1. 10. 1982," RB 1 230 013 001–037.

3 In this connection, see also Peter Adolff's interview of March 15 and April 17, 2010.

4 "Wir sind ein moderner Großkonzern mit alten mittelständischen Strukturen. Man kann darüber lächeln, aber das ist die Realität." Quoted from the still-pertinent character study of Bosch in Rainer Frenkel's article "Das Erbe des 'roten Bosch'," in *Die Zeit*, July 9, 1976, p. 19.

IV. Bosch and the challenges of globalization (1984–2012)

1 Radical change and continuity in the shadow of economic turbulence (1984–1993)

1 In this connection, see among other sources Franz Fehrenbach, "Er war ein durch und durch glaubwürdiger Mann" ["He was a thoroughly trustworthy man"], in *Marcus Bierich. Im Spiegel seiner Familie, Freunde und Weggefährten*, Frankfurt am Main, 2010, pp. 352 ff.

2 "Ein einziger Motivationsschub": Quoted from the character sketch in *Industriemagazin*, October 1985, p. 22.

3 "Vortrag Bierichs auf dem ersten LD-Forum am 6. 9. 1985," RB 1 017 147.

4 *Ibid.*, p. 8.

5 *Ibid.*, p. 12.

6 *Ibid.*, pp. 36 f.

7 *Ibid.*, p. 25.

8 *Ibid.*, p. 30.

9 "Bosch ist nicht zu bremsen," in *Industriemagazin*, October, 1985, pp. 29–32.

10 Robert Bosch GmbH, 1984 annual report and 1987 annual report.

11 "Marcus Bierich macht bei Bosch mobil," in *Die Welt*, July 8, 1988, p. 10.

12 In this connection, see (among other sources) press reports in the *Hannoversche Allgemeine Zeitung*, July 7, 1988, and the *Heilbronner Stimme*, July 8, 1988.

13 "Protokoll der RBIK vom 27. 6. 1984," RB 1 848 006.

14 In this connection, see the piece "Duell der Giganten," in *Manager Magazin* 1985/12, pp. 8–10, and newspaper articles in *Stuttgarter Zeitung*, November 22, 1985, p. 7, and *Welt am Sonntag*, July 31, 1988, p. 23.

15 "Rede Bierichs auf der GPI vom 21. 12. 1987," pp. 12 f., RB 1 002 898.

16 "Anlage 4 zum Protokoll der Aufsichtsratssitzung vom 29. 4. 1987," p. 4, RB 1 848 025.

17 "Anlage 2 zum Protokoll der Aufsichtsratssitzung vom 30. 6. 1989," pp. 3 f., RB 1 848 027.

18 In this connection, see the presentation of the Automotive Technology ("K") business sector in "Protokoll der Aufsichtsratssitzung am 25. 6. 1990," pp. 8 f., RB 1 848 028.

19 "Anlage 4 zum Protokoll der Aufsichtsratssitzung vom 29. 4. 1987," p. 5, RB 1 848 025.

20 "Bosch stärkt sein Engagement in Frankreich," in *Bosch-Zünder* 1989/10, p. 1; Adolf Ahnefeld, "Große Wachstumschancen vorhanden," *ibid.*, p. 4.

21 Hermann Scholl interview of October 21, 2010.

22 "Antrag zur GFS 19. 3. 1990, DDR: Standort für K-Fertigung," RB 3 0005 047 001. VW had already concluded a joint-venture agreement with the VEB IFA Kombinat Pkw to build a production plant for passenger cars in Zwickau, while Daimler-Benz had agreed with the IFA combine to establish joint commercial-vehicle production facilities in Ludwigsfelde, now a southern suburb of Berlin.

23 *Ibid.*

24 *Ibid.*

25 Hermann Scholl interview of October 21, 2010.

26 "Protokoll vom 21. 12. 1984" (10 pages), RB 1 016 832 002.

27 "Aktennotiz zum McKinsey-Projekt vom 29. 1. 1985," RB 1 016 832 001.

28 *Ibid.*

29 See the various reports of discussions in *ibid.*

30 In this connection, see (among other sources) "Bericht Bierich auf der RBIK vom 28. 11. 1985," p. 9, RB 1 848 005.

31 "Notiz vom 3. 5. 1985," RB 1 016 832 001.

32 "Protokoll der RBIK-Sitzung vom 26. 11. 1987," p. 7, RB 1 848 007.

33 In this connection, see (among other sources) "Bericht Schips F6 auf der Aufsichtsratssitzung vom 1. 7. 1986," RB 1 848 024.

34 "Protokoll der RBIK-Sitzung vom 27. 3. 1987," p. 8, RB 1 848 008.

35 "Rede Bierichs auf der GPI vom 21. 12. 1987," p. 26, RB 1 002 898.

36 See also "Bericht auf der RBIK-Sitzung vom 10. 6. 1989," pp. 8 f., RB 1 848 008.

37 *Ibid.*

38 See, for instance, "Anlage 3 zum Aufsichtsratssitzungsprotokoll vom 30. 6. 1989," RB 1 848 027. and "Unterlage zur GFS am 22. 5. 1989," RB 1 016 832 002.

39 See Ahnefeld's interview of August 6, 2012.

40 "Protokoll der RBIK-Sitzung vom 25. 3. 1993," p. 4, RB 1 848 010.

41 "Schreiben Gutbrod an Adolff vom 31. 1. 1989," RB 1 848 008.

42 "Vortrag Weber vom 14. 3. 1991," RB 1 848 029.

43 "Notiz vom 9. 7. 1991," RB 1 016 832 002. See also the then three-year-old article "Suche nach Alliierten," in *Wirtschaftswoche*, June 3, 1988, pp. 48–64.

44 "Tischvorlage zur RBIK-Sitzung vom 20. 3. 1990," RB 1 848 009.

45 "Niederschrift der RBIK-Versammlung vom 24. 11. 1994," pp. 6 ff., RB 1 848 011.

46 Schiefer in his report to the Bosch supervisory board. See "Anlage 3 zur Niederschrift der Aufsichtsratssitzung vom 27. 4. 1995," RB 1 002 751.

47 See the article in the *Stuttgarter Zeitung* of July 1, 1994, "Jetzt kocht der Bosch-Vize selbst."

48 "Debatte im Aufsichtsrat vom 27. 4. 1995," RB 1 002 751.

49 In this connection, see "Gesprächsleitfaden für Besprechung F1 mit Aufsichtsratsmitgliedern von Blaupunkt am 26. 4. 1993," RB 1 016 218.

50 "Bericht zur Geschäftslage auf der RBIK-Sitzung vom 27. 6. 1996," RB 1 848 012.

51 See also "Lagebericht auf der RBIK-Sitzung vom 20. 3. 1997," RB 1 848 013.

52 *Ibid.*, p. 5.

53 "Niederschrift der RBIK-Sitzung vom 20. 3. 1997," p. 8, RB 1 848 013.

54 "Brief vom 24. 9. 1998," RB 1 848 014.

55 "Bericht auf der RBIK-Sitzung vom 18. 3. 1999" and "Bericht auf der RBIK-Sitzung und vom 22. 6. 1999," RB 1 848 014.

56 "Protokoll der RBIK-Sitzung vom 16. 3. 2000," RB 1 848 060.

57 Robert Bosch GmbH, 1970 annual report, p. 45; Robert Bosch GmbH, 1980 annual report, p. 27.

58 Robert Bosch GmbH, 1980 annual report, pp. 22 ff.; Robert Bosch GmbH (ed.), *Emergence of a global player.*

59 Robert Bosch GmbH (ed.), *Emergence of a global player*, p. 35.

60 Banham, *Bosch*, p. 64.

61 *Ibid.*

62 *Ibid.*

63 Robert Forrant, *Metal fatigue. American Bosch and the demise of metalworking in the Connecticut River Valley*, Amityville, 2009.

64 Banham, *Bosch*, p. 65.

65 "Hans L. Merkle, The economic situation and the business in the Bosch Group in 1985, 22. 10. 1985," RB 1 015 1334.

66 Robert Bosch GmbH, 1990 annual report, p. 15.

67 See article "US-Markt wird zum 'Schlachtfeld'," in *Stuttgarter Zeitung*, September 16, 1987.

68 Robert Bosch GmbH, annual reports for the relevant years.

69 In North, Central, and South America, the Bosch Group generated sales of some 3.5 billion German marks in 1985, and slightly under 3.4 billion German marks in 1990; see Robert Bosch GmbH, 1995 annual report, p. 5. Figures for 1990 calculated from data given in Robert Bosch GmbH, 1990 annual report, pp. 4, 26.

70 Robert Bosch GmbH, 1995 annual report, p. 23.

71 See table 17, p. 424.

72 Hans K. Herdt, "Bosch bleibt Bosch," in *Börsen-Zeitung*, July 10, 1993.

73 Robert Bosch GmbH, 1990 annual report, p. 26.

74 "GFS Fernost vom 12. 11. 1992," RB 1 021 082.

75 "GPI-Vortrag am 28. 5. 1990, Dr. F. Scholl/F7," RB 3 0005 047 002.

76 Scholl's interview of October 21, 2010; Robert Bosch GmbH, 1972 annual report, pp. 23 f.; Robert Bosch GmbH, 1973 annual report, p. 25.

77 Robert Bosch GmbH, 1999 annual report, p. 12.

78 Article "Japan-Autos – Europa kommt unter die Räder," in *Der Spiegel*, July 21, 1980; Konrad Seitz, *Die japanisch-amerikanische Herausforderung. Deutschlands Hochtechnologie-Industrien kämpfen ums Überleben*, 2nd ed., Munich, Bonn, 1991, p. 192.

79 Seitz, *Herausforderung*, p. 210.

80 From the article about Bosch in *Industriemagazin*, October 1985, p. 18.

81 In this connection, see the detailed analysis of weaknesses in the automotive business sector and how to eliminate them ("Schwächen des UBK – und wie sie überwunden werden können") presented at an internal retreat session on April 11, 1991, pp. 15 ff., RB 1 016 838.

82 *Ibid.*, p. 21.

83 "Aktennotiz zur Lage im Unternehmensbereich K vom 4. 9. 1990," RB 1 016 838.

84 Robert Bosch GmbH, 1989 annual report, p. 2.

85 "Referatmanuskript zur GPI vom 18. 12. 1989," RB 1 016 822 001.

86 In this connection, see the detailed report, "Bericht von Zimmerer (K5/L) auf der GPI-Tagung am 16. 12. 1991," RB 1 101 020 1.

87 *Ibid.*, p. 2.

88 *Ibid.*, p. 4.

89 *Ibid.*, pp. 8 ff.

90 "Bericht Zimmerer als Anlage 3 zur Niederschrift der Aufsichtsratssitzung vom 27. 6. 1996," RB 1 002 751.

91 *Ibid.*, p. 6.

92 *Ibid.*, p. 8.

93 *Ibid.*, p. 9.

94 "Vortrag auf der GPI vom 19. 12. 1997," pp. 8 f., RB 3 0005 764.

95 In this connection, see the unsparing analysis carried out by the consultants of the Thomas Group, particularly the presentation given by Philip J. Lovell to the top-level LD-Forum on September 9, 1999, "Interne Prozesse bei Bosch: Anmerkungen eines Außenstehenden," p. 3, RB 1 217 032.

96 *Ibid.*

97 *Ibid.*

98 "Vortrag Rojahn (F4A) auf der F-Klausur am 2.5.2001," RB 1 214 055 003.

99 *Ibid.*, p. 5.

100 In this connection, see also "Vortrag von Peter J. Marks über das Bosch Production System vor dem Aufsichtsrat am 21.3.2003," RB 1 848 066.

101 The term comes from the Japanese and translates literally as "load load."

102 In this connection, see also the description in Betriebsrat Bosch Feuerbach (ed.), … *auch beim Bosch*, p. 131.

103 "Im Würgegriff der Konzerne," in *Der Spiegel*, April 26, 1993, pp. 118 ff.

104 "Siemens AG. Mehrheit an Bendix Electronics erworben," in *Handelsblatt*, July 18, 1988.

105 "Die Branche will einen zweiten Bosch" (Walter Kunerth). Kunerth headed the automotive-engineering business sector of Siemens AG. His words are quoted from "Machtkämpfe unter der Motorhaube," in *Industriemagazin*, July 1989, p. 97.

106 "Vermerk betr. BMW, Besprechung am 23.1.1991," RB 1 195 027 (quotation); "Vermerk betr. BMW, LZV für SG," 30.11.1990, *ibid.*

107 "Vermerk betr. BMW, LZV für SG, 30.11.1990," *ibid.*

108 "Protokoll der RBIK-Sitzung vom 23.11.1990" and "Protokoll der RBIK-Sitzung vom 9.4.1991," RB 1 848 009.

109 In this connection, see also the detailed "Antrag zu den Kostenanpassungsmaß-nahmen auf der GFS vom 5.3.1991," RB 1 002 428.

110 "Protokoll der RBIK-Sitzung vom 9.4.1991," p. 11, RB 1 848 009.

111 "Bosch bereitet sich auf wachstumsschwache Jahre vor," *Börsen-Zeitung*, July 5, 1991. See also the commentary entitled "Ein hoher Preis," in *ibid.*, July 6, 1991.

112 Original words: "Die Tarifpolitik der Gewerkschaft vernichtet Arbeitsplätze in Deutschland." In this connection, see also *The Wall Street Journal*, July 5, 1991.

113 *Manager Magazin*, 1991/8, pp. 15–24, including an interview with Bierich.

114 *Ibid.*, p. 15.

115 *Ibid.*

116 *Ibid.*

117 "Vortrag auf der GPI vom 3.6.1991," pp. 46 ff., RB 1 016 823 002.

118 *Ibid.*, p. 65.

119 In this connection, see also the very thorough "Bericht über die Entwicklung des Unternehmensbereichs K durch Scholl am 26.11.1991 vor dem Aufsichtsrat," RB 1 848 030.

120 In this connection, see also the very thorough "Bericht über 'Entwicklungen in der Zulieferindustrie' auf der Aufsichtsratssitzung vom 28.4.1992," RB 1 848 030.

121 "Protokoll der RBIK-Sitzung vom 24.11.1992," RB 1 848 009.

122 "Anlage zum Protokoll der Aufsichtsratssitzung vom 17.6.1993," RB 1 002 751.

123 *Ibid.*, p. 3.

124 *Ibid.*, p. 6.

125 "ARS 23.11.1993 – Personal- und Strukturmaßnahmen 1991–1993," RB 1 230 024 027.

126 "Informationskonzept zur Personalkostensenkung, Bl. 2, Anlage 2 zur Unterlage zur GFS 25.1.1993," RB 1 230 024 003.

127 *Auto 92/93*, the VDA's annual report for 1992/93, p. 21.

128 "Notiz zum Gespräch mit dem GBR am 27. 1. 1993," RB 1 016 838.

129 "Protokoll der RBIK-Sitzung vom 25. 3. 1993," p. 16, RB 1 848 010.

130 "Erklärung des Konzernbetriebsrats der Bosch-Gruppe Inland zum Personal- und Sozialabbau sowie zur Tarifsituation," RB 1 016 254 001.

131 *Ibid.*

132 "Protest vor der Zentrale," in *Bosch-Zünder* 1993/4, p. 2; "GFS 26. 4. 1993," RB 1 230 024 011; Löckle interview of November 4, 2011. According to Löckle, the number taking part was around 15,000.

133 Fehrenbach, in *Marcus Bierich*, p. 360. See also *ibid.*, p. 355, for an assessment of the 1993 clash.

134 Löckle interview of November 4, 2011.

135 Ahnefeld interview of August 6, 2012. In this connection, see also the Todenhöfer interview of July 5, 2010, pp. 25 f.

136 Todenhöfer interview of July 5, 2010.

137 "Vortrag Bierich auf der GPI vom 24. 5. 1993," RB 1 016 655 001.

138 *Ibid.*, p. 9.

139 "Protokoll der RBIK vom 25. 3. 1993," RB 1 848 010.

140 *Ibid.*, p. 3.

141 Franz Fehrenbach thought the same. See *Marcus Bierich*, p. 356.

142 In this connection, see also the copy of a private letter written by Bierich in May 1993 and reproduced in *ibid.*, pp. 256 ff.

143 Robert Bosch GmbH, 1993 annual report.

144 *Ibid.*, p. 59; "Referat F1 zur Geschäftslage, GFS 20. 6. 1994," RB 3 0005 764.

145 In the middle of 1993, the board was given a negative operating result of 313 million German marks for the fourth quarter of the year. This included "outgoings for workforce adjustments" of 370 million German marks. "Finanzprogramm 1993/Ausgabe Juni der Robert Bosch GmbH und Bosch-Gruppe Welt, 1. 6. 1993," RB 1 230 024 015.

146 Robert Bosch GmbH, 1993 annual report, pp. 7 (quotation), 44.

147 As Tilman Todenhöfer commented in his reminiscence in *Marcus Bierich*, pp. 421 ff.

148 Robert Bosch GmbH, annual reports.

149 Robert Bosch GmbH, 1938–1992 annual reports; see also "Tabelle Mitarbeiterstruktur: Frauen-Männer, Bosch-Gruppe Inland 1989–2012," RB 1 007 198.

150 In this connection, see also Betriebsrat Bosch Feuerbach (ed.), … *auch beim Bosch*, pp. 110 f.

151 "Bericht auf der GFS vom 18. 5. 1992," RB 1 002 428.

152 *Ibid.*

153 "Notiz bzw. Unterlage zur GFS vom 4. 5. 1992," *ibid.*

154 "Schreiben vom 10. 11. 1992," RB 1 016 254 001. See also other protest letters and the documents "Resolution des Gesamtbetriebsrats vom 29. 10. 1992" and "Antwortschreiben der Geschäftsleitung vom 6. 11. 1992," in which cutting the non-union supplements is defended with reference to the hard times that lay ahead for the company; *ibid.*

155 "Bericht Bierich auf der RBIK vom 30. 6. 1988," p. 13, RB 1 848 008.

156 "Strukturveränderungen am Standort Feuerbach," press release dated March 12, 1993, RB 1 230 024 027.

157 In this connection, see "Lageanalyse zu Bosch aus dem Jahr 1992 von gewerkschaftlicher Seite," p. 38, RB 1 016 254 001.

158 Quoted from Betriebsrat Bosch Feuerbach (ed.), … *auch beim Bosch*, p. 123.

159 "Notiz vom 29. 3. 1993," RB 1 016 838; "ARS 23. 11. 1993 – Personal- und Strukturmaßnahmen 1991–1993, 18. 11. 1993," RB 1 230 024 027.

160 "Niederschrift der GFS-Klausur vom 21./22. 12. 1993," RB 1 192 307.

161 *Ibid.*

162 The report was entitled *Bündnis für Arbeit – Standortbestimmung Bosch* [Alliance for
Employment – Where does Bosch stand?]. Attachment 3, "Niederschrift der Aufsichtsratssitzung vom 16. 4. 1996," RB 1 002 751.

163 *Ibid.*, p. 2.

164 *Ibid.*, p. 4.

165 In this connection, see (among other sources) the report in *Stuttgarter Nachrichten*,
May 10, 1996.

166 In this connection, see "Scholl und Todenhöfer an die Fraktionsvorsitzenden der
rot-grünen Regierungskoalition, 13. 6. 2001," RB 1 848 059.

167 "Interne Notiz vom 26. 4. 1999," RB 1 245 007.

168 "Protokoll der Aufsichtsratssitzung vom 29. 11. 2001," RB 1 848 066.

169 "Protokoll der Aufsichtsratssitzung vom 10. 12. 2003," *ibid.*

170 Betriebsrat Bosch Feuerbach (ed.), … *auch beim Bosch*, pp. 126 f.; in this connection,
see also *ibid.*, p. 520.

2 Into the digital age

1 Hermann Scholl interview of October 21, 2010.

2 Johannes Bähr, "Die 'amerikanische Herausforderung.' Anfänge der Technologiepolitik in der Bundesrepublik Deutschland," in *Archiv für Sozialgeschichte* 35, 1995,
p. 118.

3 Kaiser, *Bosch*, pp. 222 ff.

4 "ZBR, Kommentar zur Analyse der FuE-Aktivitäten, 18. 12. 1989," RB 3 0005 047 001.

5 Kaiser, *Bosch*, p. 220.

6 See, for instance, the retrospective survey that Hermann Scholl presented to the
GPI meeting before he became chairman of the supervisory board: "Entwicklung
der Bosch-Gruppe: Rückblick und Ausblick, GPI vom 23. 6. 2003," p. 7, RB 3 0005 764.

7 Kaiser, *Bosch*, pp. 234 f.

8 "FuE-Aufwendungen der Bosch-Gruppe 1984–1989," RB 3 0005 047 002.

9 See pp. 460 ff.; see also p. 483 ff.

10 "Beschluss über die Errichtung eines Beirats für Forschung und Entwicklung bei
der Robert Bosch GmbH (Entwurf), 13. 3. 1979," RB 1 030 066.

11 Kaiser, *Bosch*, p. 236.

12 "LD-Forum vom 13./14. 6. 1996," p. 1, RB 3 0005 764.

13 Robert Bosch GmbH, 1999 annual report, p. 10; Robert Bosch GmbH, 1989 annual
report, p. 9.

14 Robert Bosch GmbH, 2010 annual report, pp. 23, 25.

15 Average R&D spending among German automotive suppliers in 2001 was 5.2 percent
of sales. In 2010, Siemens AG spent 5.1 percent of sales on R&D, the BMW Group 4.6
percent. Steffen Kinkel, Gunter Lay, "Automobilzulieferer in der Klemme. Vom Spagat zwischen strategischer Ausrichtung und Auslandsorientierung," in Hans Böckler
Stiftung and Fraunhofer Institut für Systemtechnik und Innovationsforschung (eds.),
Mitteilungen aus der Produktionsinnovationserhebung, no. 32, March 2004; Siemens
AG, *2010 Annual report*, Munich, 2011, p. 2; BMW Group, *2010 Annual report*, Munich, 2011, p. 36. On R&D spending at Bosch, see Fig. 11 (p. 455).

16 Kaiser, *Bosch*, p. 109.

17 "Hermann Scholl, 40 Jahre elektronische Benzineinspritzung. Rede anlässlich Symposium in Frankfurt 11. 9. 2007," RB 3 0005 764; Kaiser, *Bosch*, pp. 110 f.; Holger Bingmann, "Antiblockiersystem und Benzineinspritzung (Anti-Blocking System and Fuel Injection)," in Horst Albach, *Culture and technical innovation. A cross-cultural analysis and policy recommendations* (Akademie der Wissenschaften zu Berlin, research report 9), Berlin, New York, 1994, pp. 760 ff.

18 Kaiser, *Bosch*, pp. 111 f.; Holger Bingmann, "Mensch – Politik – Kultur. Einflüsse auf die technische Entwicklung bei Daimler-Benz," Diss. rer. pol. Freie Universität Berlin, Berlin, 1990, pp. 281 ff.

19 Kaiser, *Bosch*, p. 114.

20 *Ibid.*, p. 121.

21 *Ibid.*, p. 122.

22 *Ibid.*, p. 121; see also Scholl interview of July 5, 2010.

23 Robert Bosch GmbH (ed.). *Bosch Automotive*, p. 43.

24 Scholl interview of October 21, 2010.

25 Kaiser, *Bosch*, pp. 126 ff.

26 "Hermann Scholl, 40 Jahre elektronische Benzineinspritzung, Rede anlässlich Symposium in Frankfurt 11. 9. 2007," p. 15, RB 3 0005 764.

27 Kaiser, *Bosch*, p. 148; Bingmann, "Antiblockiersystem," p. 771.

28 Bingmann, "Antiblockiersystem," p. 772.

29 Kaiser, *Bosch*, p. 151.

30 In this connection, see also Kaiser, *Bosch*, p. 156; Bingmann, "Mensch," pp. 301 ff.

31 Kaiser, *Bosch*, p. 147; Bingmann, "Antiblockiersystem," p. 775.

32 "Vermerk F42 betr. ABS Entwicklung des Geschäftszweiges bei RB, 24. 7. 1986," RB 1 010 072.

33 Bingmann, "Mensch," pp. 309 ff.; Kaiser, *Bosch*, p. 161 (quotation).

34 Kaiser, *Bosch*, p. 166.

35 Bingmann, "Antiblockiersystem," pp. 789 f.; Kaiser, *Bosch*, p. 165.

36 Bingmann, "Antiblockiersystem," p. 805.

37 Kaiser, *Bosch*, pp. 166, 168.

38 *Ibid.*, p. 166.

39 *Ibid.*, pp. 166 ff.

40 *Ibid.*, pp. 170, 183 (on the 2003 market share); "Wachsen oder weichen," in *Wirtschaftswoche*, July 5, 1990, p. 117 (on the 1990 market share).

41 Kaiser, *Bosch*, pp. 171 ff.

42 *Ibid.*, pp. 174 ff.

43 *Ibid.*, p. 180.

44 "Tanz um die Gummihütchen," in *Der Spiegel*, November 3, 1997, pp. 248–57; Hermann Winner, "Mercedes und der Elch: die perfekte Blamage," in *Die Welt*, October 21, 2007.

45 "Tanz um die Gummihütchen," in *Der Spiegel*, November 3, 1997, p. 256.

46 Kaiser, *Bosch*, pp. 181 f.

47 "Wir bringen Boxberg ins Haus," *Bosch-Zünder* 1999/8–9, p. 9.

48 *Ibid.*

49 Kaiser, *Bosch*, pp. 183, 185 f.

50 *Ibid.*, pp. 183 ff.; Robert Bosch GmbH, 2005 annual report, p. 39.

51 "Hermann Scholl, 'Rückblick und Ausblick,' GPI vom 23. 6. 2003," RB 3 0005 764.

52 *Ibid.*

53 In this connection, see also pp. 409–420.

54 Kaiser, *Bosch*, pp. 192 f.

55 *Ibid.*, p. 195.

56 "Von der Karte zum Pfadfinder," in *Auto Bild*, February 23, 2006.

3   From restructuring to change: the process of renewal in the 1990s (1993–2003)

1 In this connection, see also the article "Bosch bleibt Bosch," *Börsen-Zeitung*, July 10, 1993; see also *Stuttgarter Zeitung*, June 6, 1993, and the interview with Scholl in *Stuttgarter Zeitung*, October 28, 1993.

2 "Einleitungsrede Scholls auf dem ersten LD-Forum am 13./14. 6. 1996," RB 1 142 036.

3 "Vortrag Scholl auf der GPI vom 19. 12. 1997," p. 10, RB 3 0005 764.

4 *Ibid.*

5 *Ibid.*, p. 12.

6 Fehrenbach, in *Marcus Bierich*, p. 357.

7 Over these years, however, margin remained stagnant at just above 2 percent.

8 "Unterlagen zum Gespräch GF und LD-Kreis vom 29.9./1. 10. 1993," RB 1 192 307.

9 "Referat-Manuskript Scholls zur geschäftspolitischen Lage, u. a. auch auf der GPI am 16. 12. 1993 vorgetragen," p. 13, RB 3 0005 764.

10 *Ibid.*

11 *Ibid.*, pp. 38 f.

12 *Ibid.*, p. 45.

13 In this connection, see also "Protokoll der LD-Gespräche vom 9. 2. 1994," RB 1 192 310, and above all "Protokoll der F-Klausur vom 9./10. 5. 1994," RB 1 192 308.

14 Interview, *Stuttgarter Zeitung*, October 28, 1993.

15 *Ibid.*

16 In this connection, see (among other sources) a report in *Börsen-Zeitung*, July 1, 1994.

17 In this connection, see also the reports in *Börsen-Zeitung*, May 10, 1996, in *Handelsblatt*, May 9, 1996, and in *Frankfurter Allgemeine Zeitung*, May 16, 1997. On the subject of economic planning for 1997, see also the detailed "Unterlagen zur RBIK vom 26. 11. 1996," RB 1 848 012.

18 "Vortrag Scholls auf der GPI vom 18. 12. 1995," p. 7, RB 3 0005 764.

19 "Vortrag Scholls auf dem LD-Forum am 13./14. 6. 1996," *ibid.*

20 "Erzeugnisklassenrechnung 1987 als Unterlage zur GFS vom 26. 9. 1988," RB 1 230 019 013.

21 "EZKL-Erfolgsrechnung 1995, Unterlage zur GFS vom 3. 6. 1996," RB 1 230 027 011; see also "Vortrag Scholls auf der GPI am 16. 12. 1996," pp. 9 f., RB 3 0005 764.

22 *Ibid.*, p. 10.

23 "Vortrag Scholls auf der GPI vom 19. 12. 1997," p. 15, RB 3 0005 764.

24 *Ibid.*

25 "Protokoll der RBIK vom 23. 6. 1994," p. 9, RB 1 848 011.

26 "Protokoll der RBIK vom 23. 3. 1995," p. 3, *ibid.*

27 "Scholl auf der Aufsichtsratssitzung vom 27. 4. 1995," *ibid.* In this, however, Bosch was unsuccessful. "Protokoll der Aufsichtsratssitzung vom 12. 12. 2002," p. 4, RB 1 848 066.

28 "Bericht von F4D über 'Kraftfahrzeugausrüstung – Herausforderungen und Chancen des Marktes für Erstausrüstung' auf der Aufsichtsratssitzung vom 22. 4. 1997," RB 1 848 013; see also the earlier, identically titled "Vortrag auf der GPI vom 16. 12. 1996," RB 1 002 697.

29 "Pressemeldung vom 12. 4. 1996," RB 1 016 496 001.

30 "Notiz vom 10. 6. 1985," *ibid.*

31 "Bündnis gegen Bosch," in *Manager Magazin* 1988/2, pp. 8–11.

32 In this connection, see also the detailed "Notiz vom 21. 2. 1996," as presented to the RBIK, RB 1 848 012.

33 As reported in *Stuttgarter Zeitung*, February 20, 1996.

34 "Schreiben K1/LV an F40, 17. 4. 1989," RB 1 016 496 002.

35 "Notiz vom 17. 4. 1989," RB 1 016 496 001, as well as the various Bosch-AlliedSignal negotiation minutes of January and February 1990 and (following interruptions) June–October 1992, *ibid.*

36 In this connection, see (among other sources) "Bericht Scholls auf der Aufsichtsratssitzung vom 20. 3. 1996," RB 1 002 751.

37 Another joint-venture company involving Knorr-Bremse and AlliedSignal had been founded in October 1998 to produce brake systems for commercial vehicles. See "Bericht auf der RBIK vom 26. 11. 1998," RB 1 848 014.

38 "Rede Scholls auf dem LD-Forum am 29./30. 6. 1998," RB 3 0005 764; see also Scholl's remarks in "Protokoll der RBIK-Sitzung vom 26. 11. 1998," RB 1 848 014.

39 *Ibid.*, p. 4.

40 In this connection, see also (among other sources) "Vortrag von Wolfgang Chur über 'Verbesserung der Kundenbeziehungen' auf der Aufsichtsratssitzung vom 25. 11. 1999," RB 1 848 066.

41 "Aufstellung über die Umsätze mit den zehn größten Abnehmern 1993 und 1994," RB 1 848 010.

42 "Vortrag Lovell auf dem LD-Forum vom 9./10. 9. 1999," p. 1, RB 1 217 032.

43 "Ansprache Scholls auf der GPI-Versammlung am 17. 12. 1998," p. 22, RB 3 0005 764.

44 "Sonder-Niederschrift der GFS vom 9. 7. 1999," RB 1 214 056 001.

45 "Vortrag Scholls auf dem GPI-Treffen vom 18. 6. 2001," RB 3 0005 764; see also the detailed "Erzeugnisklassen-Erfolgsrechnung für 2000 als Anlage zur GFS vom 11. 6. 2001," RB 1 230 032 011.

46 See also the further "Status-Bericht zu den Verlustgebieten auf der F-Klausur vom 21./22. 1. 2003," RB 1 242 187.

47 In this connection, see (among other sources) "Rede Scholls auf dem LD-Forum am 15. 12. 2000," RB 3 0005 764.

48 "Rede Scholls auf dem LD-Forum vom 17. 12. 2001," *ibid.*

49 "Bericht Scholls zur Geschäftslage auf der RBIK-Sitzung vom 28. 11. 2002," RB 1 848 061.

50 *Auto 94/95*, VDA annual report, p. 25; Robert Bosch GmbH, 2004 annual report, p. 31.

51 Original words: "eine Technik, mit der es sich zu beschäftigen lohnt." Max Straubel, "Elektronische Dieseleinspritzregelung (EDC)," in *Bosch-Zünder* 1987/1, p. 5.

52 Kaiser, *Bosch*, p. 89.

53 "Protokoll der GPI vom 23. 6. 2003," RB 3 0005 764.

54 Kaiser, *Bosch*, pp. 92 f.

55 *Ibid.*, pp. 89 f.

56 *Ibid.*, p. 94.

57 "Referat F 1, GPI 17. 12. 1998," RB 3 0005 764.

58 Ludger Meyer, "Dieselboom bringt Arbeit," in *Bosch-Zünder* 1–2, 1999, p. 1.

59 *Ibid.*; see also "Referat F 1, GPI 17. 12. 1998," RB 3 0005 764.

60 In this connection, see also the detailed "'Statusbericht Diesel' auf der Aufsichtsratssitzung vom 25. 11. 1999," RB 1 848 066.

61 Guido Reinking, Thomas Fröhlich, "Quasi-Monopolist Bosch kommt beim Diesel unter Druck," *Financial Times Deutschland*, August 31, 2000.

62 "Ansprache Scholl auf der GPI-Versammlung am 17. 12. 1998," pp. 5 f., RB 3 0005 764.

63 Guido Reinking, Thomas Fröhlich, "Quasi-Monopolist Bosch kommt beim Diesel unter Druck," *Financial Times Deutschland*, August 31, 2000. The report led Bosch to intervene directly with the VW board. See the letter to Martin Winterkorn, then R&D chief at VW, dated September 6, 2000, RB 1 848 060.

64 See p. 520.

65 VDA [German Automobile Association], Auto 1995 annual report, pp. 17 f.; Auto 2001 annual report, p. 36; Auto 2006 annual report, p. 35. See also Robert Bosch GmbH, 2010 annual report, p. 41.

66 "Diesel-Marktanteil bald 41 Prozent. Vom Stinker zum Hightech-Motor. Selbstzünder sind in Deutschland beliebter denn je," article in *Auto Bild*, June 5, 2002.

67 VDA annual reports.

68 Thomas Fromm, "Deutschlands Diesel-Missionare," *Süddeutsche Zeitung*, January 7, 2012.

69 In this connection and for what follows, see the detailed "Bericht über den Unternehmensbereich Produktionsgüter auf der Aufsichtsratssitzung vom 23. 11. 1990," RB 1 848 028.

70 See "Bericht auf der Aufsichtsratssitzung vom 26. 6. 1997," RB 1 002 750.

71 "Protokoll der Aufsichtsratssitzung vom 27. 7. 1996," pp. 3 f., RB 1 002 751.

72 In this connection, see also (among other sources) reports in *Frankfurter Allgemeine Zeitung*, April 19, 2000, and *Süddeutsche Zeitung*, April 6, 2000, p. 29.

73 In this connection, see also (among other sources) "Bericht auf der RBIK-Sitzung vom 30. 11. 2000," RB 1 848 060.

74 "Bericht zum Stand der Integration auf der RBIK-Sitzung vom 15. 3. 2001," *ibid*.

75 In this connection and on what follows, see the detailed "Vortrag von Wörner über 'Struktur, Steuerung und Situation der BSHG' auf der GPI vom 16. 12. 1991," RB 1 101 020 1.

76 *Ibid.*, p. 9.

77 *Ibid.*, p. 11.

78 "Bericht und strategischer Rückblick BSHG vom 2. 2. 2004," RB 1 244 001 003 1/2.

79 "Bericht auf der RBIK-Sitzung vom 4. 5. 2001," RB 1 848 060.

80 *Ibid.*, p. 3.

81 *Ibid.*, p. 5.

82 "Bericht zum Stand des Buderus-Erwerbs auf der Sitzung der RBIK am 29. 10. 2001," RB 1 848 061.

83 *Ibid.*

84 *Ibid.*

85 "Bericht auf der Aufsichtsratssitzung vom 10. 12. 2003," RB 1 848 066.

86 *Ibid.*, p. 2.

87 "Rede Scholl zur geschäftspolitischen Ausrichtung der Bosch-Gruppe auf dem GPI vom 18. 6. 2001," RB 3 0005 764.

88 Robert Bosch GmbH, 1999 annual report, p. 5.

89 Fehrenbach interview of July 23, 2010.

90 Quoted from Ludger Meyer's article, "Haben Sie mehr Mut," *Bosch-Zünder* 1999/6–7, p. 1.

91 Scholl made explicit reference to these issues in "Vortrag vor der GPI am 17. 12. 1998" and "Vortrag vor der GPI vom 16. 12. 1999," RB 3 0005 764.

92 See p. 465.

93 "Schlußwort F1, LD-Forum 9./10. 9. 1999," pp. 3 f., RB 3 0005 764.

94 *Ibid.*, pp. 6 f.

95 *Ibid.*, pp. 18 f.

96 "Stärker um unsere Kunden kämpfen," in *Bosch-Zünder* 1999/10–11, p. 1.

97 *Ibid.*

98 "Was tun Sie für Ihre Kunden?," *ibid.*, p. 3; Ludger Meyer, "BMW erlebt einen neuen Bosch," *ibid.*

99 "Status Projekt 'BeQIK' – Laufende Aktivitäten (Anlage 6 zum Schreiben F4E vom 9. 11. 1999)," RB 1 232 043 62.

100 "Status Projekt 'BeQIK' – Programmname/Logo (Anlage 4 zum Schreiben F4E vom 9. 11. 1999)," *ibid.*

101 "Status Projekt 'BeQIK', 24. 9. 1999 (Unterlage zur GFS am 4. 10. 1999)," *ibid.*

102 Robert Bosch GmbH, 1999 annual report, p. 11.

103 "Und für BeQIK gingen sie sogar ins Kloster," in *Bosch-Zünder* 2000/12, p. 4.

104 "Rückmeldungen der Teilnehmer in den sechs LD-Seminaren 'BeQIK: Mut zur Veränderung,' Februar bis Juli 2000, 30. 8. 2000," RB 1 232 419.

105 "Hüter des Grals," in *Manager Magazin*, March 22, 2001.

106 Franz Fehrenbach, "Auf der Grundlage von CIP," in *Bosch-Zünder* 2000/1–2, p. 3.

107 Fehrenbach interview of July 23, 2010.

108 "Bericht F4B zu Tagesordnungspunkt 5 der ARS der RB GmbH am 25. 11. 1999," RB 1 002 769.

109 Gunter Epple, "Wir unternehmen den Wandel," in *Bosch-Zünder* 2001/5–6, p. 1.

110 Original word: "Reformstau." See the article "Hüter des Grals," as well as Dietmar H. Lamparter, "Kulturrevolution auf schwäbische Art," in *Die Zeit*, August 30, 2001, and Karsten Langer, "Ritter der Tafelrunde," in *Manager Magazin*, December 18, 2003.

111 "Antworten auf BeQIK-Fragen," in *Bosch-Zünder* 2000/12, p. 4.

112 Bundesministerium für Arbeit und Sozialordnung, *Unternehmenskultur, Arbeitsqualität und Mitarbeiterengagement in den Unternehmen in Deutschland*, Berlin, 2008.

113 "Franz Fehrenbach, Bosch kraftvoll weiterentwickeln, LD-Forum 18./19. 12. 2003," RB 1 204 513.

114 "Be Bosch – Unsere Werte. Stand und weiteres Vorgehen, Notiz vom 25. 4. 2001," RB 1 214 055 003.

115 "Hermann Scholl, 'Be Bosch – Unsere Werte,' LD-Forum 17./18. 12. 2001," RB 3 0005 764.

116 *Ibid.*

117 "Statusberichte 'Bosch-Werte' – Befragung durch Unicorn (Unterlage zur F-Klausur am 16. 10. 2001), 11. 10. 2001," RB 1 232 0351.

118 *Ibid.*; "Unicorn Consultants GmbH, 'Werteorientierung und Kulturwandel bei Bosch'," RB 1 242 291.

119 "Protokoll der RBIK-Sitzung vom 25. 3. 1988," RB 1 848 008.

120 *Ibid.*

121 *Ibid.*, p. 4.

122 This was Ahnefeld's assessment in *Marcus Bierich*, p. 412.

123 "Abkommen in der Neufassung vom 29. 4. 1987" and "Liste der GF Referate in den Familienratssitzungen zwischen 1968 und 1985," RB 1 016 730.

124 According to the memoirs of Irmgard Bosch, in *Marcus Bierich*, p. 346.

125 *Stuttgarter Zeitung*, July 20, 1995, p. 8.

126 In this connection, see also "Protokoll der RBIK-Sitzung vom 26. 11. 1996," RB 1 848 012, and "Adolff an Bierich, 1. 8. 1996," RB 1 016 178 001.

127 "Protokoll der RBIK-Sitzung vom 26. 11. 1996," RB 1 848 012.

128 "Protokoll der RBIK vom 25. 11. 1999," RB 1 848 014.

129 "Rundschreiben der RBIK vom 6. 3. 2002," RB 1 848 061.

130 Robert Bosch Jr. died in August 2004. In this connection, see also the speeches and eulogy in the commemorative volume *Robert Bosch 1928–2004*, published by Robert Bosch GmbH. Bierich had already retired from RBIK in mid-March 2000. He died (two months after Merkle) on November 25, 2000.

131 "Ein Machtvakuum auf der Schillerhöhe." That was how the *Stuttgarter Nachrichten* put it on September 29, 2000, but there were other voices saying the same thing.

132 Adolff was an RBIK partner for 31 years – longer than anyone. He had also, under various chairmen (Merkle, Bierich, Scholl), served for 23 years as a member of the human-resources committee, which made appointments to the board of management.

133 "Graf zu Dohna, 'Die Rolle der Robert Bosch Industrietreuhand KG aus rechtlicher Sicht,' 3. 6. 2002," MS, 19 pages, RB 1 848 061. Regardless of its partly different style of presentation and argumentation, this was not a "rebuttal" of Adolff but was written in close consultation with him. That is why it repeatedly makes direct reference to Adolff's paper.

134 "Peter Adolff, 'Die Rolle der Robert Bosch Industrietreuhand KG im Rahmen der Bosch-Unternehmensverfassung,' 30. 5. 2002," 37-page MS, RB 1 848 063. As to how the document came about, see also the Adolff interview of March 15 and April 17, 2010.

135 Scholl paid tribute to the study later (on the occasion of Adolff's retirement at the end of June 2007) as a "legally grounded analysis of the office of partner" and as an "important basis for consensus." See the MS of Scholl's address of June 25, 2007.

136 "Notiz der Besprechung vom 26. 6. 2002," RB 1 848 061.

137 *Ibid.* At the time of writing, the RBIK shareholders comprise ten persons: Christof Bosch, Siegfried Dais, Volkmar Denner, Franz Fehrenbach, Jürgen Hambrecht (ex-chairman of the board at BASF), Olaf Kübler (ex-president of ETH Zürich), Lars G. Josefsson (ex-president and CEO of Vattenfall AB), Michael Otto (chairman of the supervisory board, Otto Group), Urs Rinderknecht (former director-general of UBS), and Tilman Todenhöfer. Two long-serving former partners have attended meetings: Peter Adolff (former board member of Allianz) and Bo Berggren (ex-president and CEO of the Swedish copper-mining company Stora Kopparberget – which incidentally is the world's oldest business organization.)

138 "Protokoll der RBIK-Sitzung vom 30. 11. 2000," pp. 10 ff., RB 1 848 060.

139 "Pressemitteilung Bosch vom 27. 11. 1992" and the detailed "Bericht zur Kapitalerhöhung auf der Aufsichtsratssitzung vom 24. 11. 1992," RB 1 848 030.

140 "Protokoll der RBIK-Sitzung vom 25. 11. 1997," RB 1 848 013.

141 On the subject of family dividends, see (among other sources) "Notiz vom 8. 3. 1985" and "Notiz vom 26. 3. 1987," RB 1 016 730.

142 *Ibid.*

143 "Notiz vom 14. 11. 1991," *ibid.*

144 "Protokoll der RBIK-Sitzung vom 28. 2. 2001," p. 6, RB 1 848 060.

145 *Ibid.*

146 "Vortrag F3 zur Aufsichtsratssitzung vom 29. 11. 2001," RB 1 848 066.

147 In this connection, see also "Diskussionsgrundlage zur F-Klausur vom 2. 5. 2001," RB 1 214 055 003.

148 "Notiz zur F-Klausur vom 16. 10. 2001," RB 1 214 056 001.

149 In this connection, see also "Bericht zur Langfristplanung der Bosch-Gruppe auf der RBIK Sitzung vom 13. 6. 2002," RB 1 848 065.

150 *Ibid.*

151 "Unterlage zur 'Behandlung interner Wachstumsprojekte' für die F-Klausur vom 4. 11. 2002," RB 1 232 0581.

152 *Ibid.*, pp. 2 f.

153 "Rede Scholl auf dem LD-Forum am 20. 12. 2002," RB 3 0005 764 3.

154 *Ibid.*

155 "Rede Scholl auf dem GPI-Treffen vom 23. 6. 2003," p. 12, RB 3 0005 764.

4 Globalization, diversification, and focus on values (2003–2012)

1 "Navigation ins Aus," in *Manager Magazin*, November 23, 2001; "Spätzünder," in *Manager Magazin*, October 25, 2002.

2 "Neuer Bosch-Chef kommt aus dem Hause," in *Frankfurter Allgemeine Zeitung*, December 13, 2002.

3 "Gottvater" was Merkle's nickname within the company. Dagmar Deckstein, "Ein 'Junger Wilder' hält die Zündkerze," in *Süddeutsche Zeitung*, December 14, 2002.

4 "Franz Fehrenbach (F1) an die Mitarbeiter der Bosch-Gruppe/To the Associates of the Bosch Group, 1. 7. 2003," RB 1 204 997.

5 "Wichtig: Den Wandel vorantreiben," in *Bosch-Zünder* 2003/7–8, p. 3.

6 In this connection, see also "Der Unterschätzte," in *Frankfurter Allgemeine Zeitung*, November 18, 2004, and "Der Kulturrevolutionär," in *Financial Times Deutschland*, January 9, 2004.

7 "Vortrag F1/Fehrenbach LD-Forum 18./19. 12. 2003," RB 1 204 513.

8 "Vortrag G1/Fehrenbach LD-Forum 20./21. 12. 2006," RB 1 204 516.

9 "Bosch-Welt rückt enger zusammen," in *Bosch-Zünder* 2009/1, p. 1.

10 "Vortrag Fehrenbach, GPI, 21. 06. 2002," RB 1 204 521.

11 "Protokoll der Geschäftsführer-Klausur-Sitzung am 10. 10. 2003," RB 1 242 322.

12 "Vortrag G1/Fehrenbach LD-Forum 17. 12. 2004," RB 1 204 514.

13 "'Wissen über die Herkunft stärkt die Corporate Identity von Organisationen'"; Bosch-Chef Franz Fehrenbach über die Bedeutung von Geschichtsbewusstsein," in Heike Bühler, Uta-Micaela Dürig (eds.), *Tradition kommunizieren. Das Handbuch der Heritage Communication. Wie Unternehmen ihre Wurzeln professionell vermitteln*, Frankfurt am Main, 2008, p. 149.

14 "Vortrag G1/Fehrenbach LD-Forum 18./19. 12. 2003," RB 1 204 513. For the wording in Robert Bosch's will see the quote on pp. 249 f. and "Robert Bosch, Verfügung von Todes wegen, 31. 5. 1938," RB 1 001 081.

15 Fehrenbach, "Wissen über die Herkunft," p. 143.

16 "Vortrag G1/Fehrenbach LD-Forum 17. 12. 2004," p. 51, RB 1 204 514; (quotations) Fehrenbach interview of July 23, 2010.

17 "Navigation ins Aus," in *Manager Magazin*, November 23, 2001.

18 "Probleme mit der Wunderbremse," in *Auto Bild*, May 11, 2004.

19 "Vortrag G1/Fehrenbach, 'Geschäftslage und Weiterentwicklung der Bosch Gruppe,' GPI 30. 06. 2004," p. 35, RB 1 204 523.

20 "Grafiken BA20&21 (0-mileage) und BA40&42 (field) Bosch responsibility," RB 1 204 559.

21 Robert Bosch GmbH, 2004 annual report.

22 Fehrenbach interview of May 26, 2011. From the beginning of the 1980s to 2010, sales grew by an annual average of 7.5 percent in total and 5 percent internally. "Vortrag G1/Fehrenbach, LD-Forum 22. 12. 2010," p. 5, RB 1 204 519.

23 Fehrenbach interview of July 23, 2010.

24 "Vortrag G1/Fehrenbach, LD-Forum 21. 12. 2005," RB 1 204 515.

25 Workforce numbers at Bosch Rexroth also went up from 15,049 to 18,701 over the same period. "Umsätze und Mitarbeiter Bosch Rexroth AG 2001–2011," RB 1 706 032.

26 "Vortrag G1/Fehrenbach, LD-Forum 21. 12. 2005," RB 1 204 515.

27 *Ibid.*

28 Robert Bosch GmbH, annual reports for 2000–2010.

29 "Bosch leidet mit der US-Autoindustrie," in *Handelsblatt*, February 1, 2007.

30 Robert Bosch GmbH, 2006 annual report.

31 "Vortrag G1/Fehrenbach LD-Forum 19./20. 12. 2007," RB 1 204 517.

32 "Vortrag G1/Fehrenbach LD-Forum 20./21. 12. 2006," RB 1 204 516.

33 Robert Bosch GmbH, 2003 annual report, p. 19.

34 "Vortrag G1/Fehrenbach LD-Forum 20./21. 12. 2006," RB 1 204 516.

35 "Dialog. Informationen der IGM-Betriebsräte und Vertrauensleute für die Beschäftigten bei Bosch Feuerbach," no. 5, July 2006.

36 Betriebsrat Bosch Feuerbach (ed.), … *auch beim Bosch*, p. 127.

37 "550 Mio. Euro für Reutlingen," in *Manager Magazin online*, June 14, 2006; "Bosch-Werk in Rommelsbach: Am 24. August schließen die Tore," in *Reutlinger General-Anzeiger*, July 19, 2009; "Köhler und Mappus bei Bosch," in *Reutlinger General-Anzeiger*, October 18, 2010.

38 Robert Bosch GmbH, 2007 annual report.

39 "Franz Fehrenbach, 'From strategic direction to action [talk titled in English],' LD-Forum 19./20. 12. 2007," RB 1 204 517.

40 Robert Bosch GmbH, 2007 annual report.

41 Robert Bosch GmbH, annual reports for 2000–2010.

42 "Vortrag G1/Fehrenbach, LD-Forum 21. 12. 2005," RB 1 204 515.

43 Fehrenbach interview of July 23, 2010.

44 Martin-W. Buchenau, "Der grüne Franz," in *Handelsblatt*, June 4, 2008.

45 In this connection, see also pp. 531.

46 Robert Bosch GmbH (ed.), *Bosch Automotive*, pp. 46 ff. See also Robert Bosch GmbH, 1967 annual report; "Entwicklungsbericht Fahrzeug mit Hybridantrieb 1973," RB 1 010 032; "Presseinfo 1973, 'Ein neuer Hybridantrieb für Kraftfahrzeuge'," RB 1973 0810.

47 "Rendite muss steigen," in *Automobilwoche*, May 19, 2008 (Bernd Bohr interview with *Automotive News Europe*).

48 "Bosch-Chef schmiedet Batteriepakt. Autozulieferer gründet mit Samsung Gemeinschaftsunternehmen für alternative Energietechnik," in *Handelsblatt*, June 17, 2008; "Joint Venture von Bosch und Samsung SDI auf dem Erfolgskurs. SB LiMotive startet Fertigung von Lithium-Ionen-Batterien," press release, November 2010.

49 "Bosch und Samsung gehen getrennte Wege bei den Batterien," in *Financial Times Deutschland*, September 5, 2012.

50 Robert Bosch GmbH, 2008 annual report ("Bosch Vision").

51 In this connection, see also p. 547.

52 "Entwicklung Bosch-Geschäftsbereich Power Tools 2001–2011," RB 1 010 024 074; Christoph Herrmann, Günter Moeller, *Innovation – Marke – Design. Grundlagen einer neuen Corporate Governance*, Düsseldorf, 2006, pp. 107 f.

53 Bosch Sicherheitssysteme GmbH (ed.), *Sicherheitslösungen mit System. Individueller Schutz für Menschen, Objekte und Werte*, Munich, 2010.

54 Martin-W. Buchenau, "Der neue Star der Sicherheitsbranche," in *Wirtschaftswoche*, June 22, 2012.

55 "Gert van Iperen, Bosch ist mit Sicherheitssystemen weltweit auf Wachstumskurs, 25.12.2012," press release, RB 2012 09520.

56 Bosch Sicherheitssysteme GmbH (ed.), *Sicherheitslösungen*.

57 Bernd Rudolph, "Hintergründe und Verlauf der globalen Finanzkrise 2008," in Johannes Bähr, Bernd Rudolph, *Finanzkrisen 1931–2008*, Munich, 2011, pp. 143–241.

58 Ulrich Schäfer, "Alle Bänder stehen still," in *Süddeutsche Zeitung*, October 28, 2008.

59 "Absatzflaute: BMW stoppt Produktion, Bosch schickt Mitarbeiter in den Urlaub," in *Spiegel Online Wirtschaft*, October 27, 2008.

60 "Die Kurzarbeit kommt wieder," in *Stuttgarter Nachrichten*, October 28, 2008; "Kurzarbeit bei Bosch," in *Süddeutsche Zeitung*, November 6, 2008.

61 "Bosch schickt Zehntausende in verlängerte Ferien," in *Spiegel Online Wirtschaft*, December 12, 2008.

62 "Bosch meldet Kurzarbeit an," in *Stuttgarter Zeitung*, January 12, 2009.

63 "Bosch reagiert mit Kurzarbeit auf die Absatzflaute," in *Spiegel Online Wirtschaft*, January 12, 2009.

64 "Niederschrift über die Gesellschafterversammlung der RBIK am 11.12.2008," RB 1 001 499.

65 In this connection, see pp. 440 ff.

66 Fehrenbach interview of July 23, 2010.

67 "Niederschrift über die Gesellschafterversammlung der RBIK am 11.12.2008," RB 1 001 499.

68 Robert Bosch GmbH, annual reports for 2008 and 2009.

69 Löckle interview, November 4, 2011.

70 *Ibid.*

71 *Ibid.*

72 *Ibid.*

73 In this connection, see also (among other sources) VDA, 2010 annual report, p. 10.

74 Fehrenbach interview, July 23, 2010.

75 "Bosch verkauft Blaupunkt," in *Handelsblatt*, December 18, 2008; "Bosch verschenkt Traditionsmarke," in *Süddeutsche Zeitung*, May 17, 2010.

76 "Niederschrift über die Gesellschafterversammlung der RBIK am 15.12.2009," RB 1 001 499; Fehrenbach interview, July 23, 2010.

77 "Kurzarbeit rettet 300 000 Jobs," in *Süddeutsche Zeitung*, January 2, 2010.

78 Martin-W. Buchenau, "Bosch sieht noch kein Ende der Krise," in *Handelsblatt*, June 17, 2009.

79 "Niederschrift über die Gesellschafterversammlung der RBIK am 30.06.2009," RB 1 001 499.

80 Buchenau, "Bosch sieht noch kein Ende der Krise," in *Handelsblatt*, June 17, 2009.

81 "Personalkosten rasch anpassen," in *Bosch-Zünder* 2009/3, p. 5.

82 "Den Dialog weiter stärken," in *Bosch-Zünder* 2009/3, p. 5.

83 "Bosch begibt Anleihe in Höhe von 1,1 Milliarden Euro," press release dated June 4, 2009, RB 2009 0602.

84 Original words: Wir wollen an diesem Kurs weiter festhalten, solange es irgendwie nur geht. Quoted from Löckle interview, November 4, 2011.

85 *Ibid.*

86 "Den Dialog weiter stärken," in *Bosch-Zünder* 2009/3, p. 5.
87 "Durststrecke bis 2009," in *Manager Magazin*, September 15, 2009.
88 "Kurzarbeit rettet 300 000 Jobs," in *Süddeutsche Zeitung* 2, 2010.
89 Robert Bosch GmbH, 2009 annual report, pp. 18, 70; see also appendix, p. 665, "Bosch Group headcount and sales revenue (1886–2012)."
90 VDA, 2010 annual report, pp. 22 f.
91 Robert Bosch GmbH, 2009 annual report; "Personalabbau bei Bosch-Rexroth: Von Teilzeit bis Abfindung mit Turboprämie," in *Mainpost*, February 24, 2010.
92 "Auftragsbücher von Bosch Rexroth füllen sich rasant," in *Frankfurter Allgemeine Zeitung*, May 2, 2011; "Umsätze und Mitarbeiter Bosch Rexroth AG 2001–2011," RB 1 706 032.
93 Robert Bosch GmbH, 2009 annual report: "Entwicklung Geschäftsbereich Power Tools 2001–2011," RB 1 010 024 074.
94 Robert Bosch GmbH, 2009 annual report, p. 17.
95 *Ibid.*
96 Robert Bosch GmbH, 2010 annual report, p. 16.
97 "Vortrag G1/Fehrenbach, LD-Forum 22. 12. 2010," RB 1 204 519.
98 Susanne Preuß, "Boschs Bankenschelte," in *Frankfurter Allgemeine Zeitung*, January 28, 2010; "Bosch kündigt erster Bank die Zusammenarbeit [Bosch ends relationship with first bank]," in *Financial Times Deutschland*, January 28, 2010; "Bosch-Chef bejubelt Goldman-Ermittlungen," in *Financial Times Deutschland*, April 21, 2010; "Unternehmer knöpfen sich die Banken vor," in *Handelsblatt*, September 7, 2011.
99 Martin-W. Buchenau, "Fehrenbach und sein AA–," in *Handelsblatt*, June 30, 2009.
100 "Bosch verschiebt Baubeginn für Solarfabrik," in *Frankfurter Allgemeine Zeitung*, February 6, 2012.
101 Haus, Sarkowicz, *Using energy*, p. 91.
102 *Ibid.*, p. 121; "Das Fenster wird zum Kraftwerk," *Bosch-Zünder* 2007/4, p. 4.
103 "Bosch kauft Solarfirma Ersol," in *Frankfurter Allgemeine Zeitung*, June 2, 2008.
104 *Ibid.*
105 "Über ersol strahlt die Sonne," *Bosch-Zünder*, 2009/1, p. 1.
106 Address by Chancellor Merkel at the laying of the foundation stone of the new solar-cell facility at ersol Solar Energy AG (Bosch Group), March 24, 2009. URL: http://www.bundesregierung.de/content/DE/Bulletin/2009/03/27-3-bk-solar.html (quotation); "Grundstein für Ausbau der Solarproduktion gelegt. Bei ersol entstehen 1100 neue Arbeitsplätze," press release dated March 24, 2009.
107 "Bosch greift nach Aleo Solar," in *Frankfurter Allgemeine Zeitung*, August 3, 2009; "Bosch fürchtet fünf harte Jahre im Solargeschäft," in *Financial Times Deutschland*, June 22, 2011; "Bosch verschiebt Baubeginn für Solarfabrik," in *Frankfurter Allgemeine Zeitung*, February 6, 2012.
108 "Bosch verschiebt Baubeginn für Solarfabrik," in *Frankfurter Allgemeine Zeitung*, February 6, 2012.
109 "Bosch Solar Energy erstmals als Generalübernehmer. Solarstromanlage auf den Dächern des Bosch-Parkhauses versorgt 250 Haushalte, Januar 2010," press release, RB 2010 0110.
110 "Zukunftstechnik wird zur Pleitebranche," in *Wirtschaftswoche*, October 23, 2012.
111 "Bosch plant neue Solarfabrik in Malaysia. Statement von Franz Fehrenbach," press release dated June 22, 2012; "Bosch schlägt bei Conergy zu," in *Financial Times Deutschland*, December 21, 2011.

112 "Bosch verschiebt Baubeginn für Solarfabrik," in *Frankfurter Allgemeine Zeitung*, February 6, 2012.

113 *Ibid.*

114 *Ibid.*; "Bosch-Tochter macht Werk in Spanien dicht," in *Handelsblatt*, June 11, 2012; "Bosch zieht den Stecker," in *Handelsblatt*, August 29, 2012.

115 "Bosch stellt die Fotovoltaik auf den Prüfstand," in *Stuttgarter Zeitung*, November 1, 2012; "Bei Siemens geht die Sonne unter," in *Süddeutsche Zeitung*, October 22, 2012.

116 "Entscheidung getroffen. Bosch beendet Aktivität im Bereich Photovoltaik, 22. 3. 2013," press release, RB 2013 03015.

117 "Robert Bosch stößt sein Solargeschäft ab," in *Frankfurter Allgemeine Zeitung*, March 23, 2013.

118 "Fakten muss man akzeptieren," in *Bosch-Zünder online*, March 22, 2013.

119 "Bosch steigt aus der Fotovoltaik aus," http: // www.stuttgarter-zeitung.de, March 22, 2013.

120 "Robert Bosch stößt sein Solargeschäft ab," in *Frankfurter Allgemeine Zeitung*, March 23, 2012.

121 "China jetzt die Nummer drei in der Bosch-Welt," in *Bosch-Zünder* 2011/2, p. 7.

122 Bosch (China) Investment Ltd. (ed.), *100 years Bosch in China*, pp. 85 ff.

123 *Ibid.*, p. 95.

124 *Ibid.*, p. 97.

125 "GFS 8. 2. 1993," RB 1 230 024 004.

126 Bosch (China) Investment Ltd. (ed.), *100 years Bosch in China*, p. 101; "Mitarbeiter gesucht," in *Bosch-Zünder* 1993/1, p. 3.

127 "Bosch-Chef Scholl verhandelt mit Li Peng in Peking," in *Stuttgarter Zeitung*, April 15, 1994; "'Wir wollen rasch produzieren.' Hermann Scholl in China," in *Bosch-Zünder* 1994/4, p. 1.

128 "Neues Unternehmen in China," in *Bosch-Zünder* 1994/8, p. 1; Bosch (China) Investment Ltd. (ed.), *100 years Bosch in China*, p. 103.

129 "Bericht F4D über den Markt für Erstausrüstung Kfz-Technik, Aufsichtsratssitzung vom 22. 4. 1997," RB 1 002 767.

130 "China nimmt Fahrt auf und Bosch ist dabei," in *Bosch-Zünder* 2007/1, p. 8.

131 *Ibid.*

132 Robert Bosch GmbH, 2010 annual report, pp. 126 f.

133 Robert Bosch GmbH, 2009 annual report, p. 17; Robert Bosch GmbH, 2010 annual report, p. 17. "China wird der größte Markt sein," in *Bosch-Zünder* 2011/1, p. 7; "China jetzt die Nummer drei in der Bosch-Welt," in *Bosch-Zünder* 2011/2, p. 7.

134 Robert Bosch GmbH, 2004 annual report, p. 54; Michael Freitag, "Ohne China fehlte einiges," in *Manager Magazin*, October 20, 2010.

135 "Bosch Opens Its 1000th Bosch Car Service Center in China, July 2011," RB 2011 00711; "China wird der größte Markt sein," in *Bosch-Zünder* 2011/1, p. 7.

136 Robert Bosch GmbH, 2006 annual report, p. 66.

137 Bosch (China) Investment Ltd. (ed.), *100 years Bosch in China*, p. 113.

138 *Ibid.*

139 Quoted in "Zur rechten Zeit am richtigen Ort," in *Bosch-Zünder* 2007/1, p. 9.

140 Christoph Giesen, Max Hägler, "Bosch will Überwachungstechnik nach China verkaufen," in *Süddeutsche Zeitung*, December 8, 2012.

141 Dietrich Kuhlgatz, "Water for the fields, power for cars. Bosch in India," in Robert Bosch GmbH (ed.), *Emergence of a global player*, pp. 40 ff.

142 Dietmar H. Lamparter, "Bosch macht die Inder stark," in *Die Zeit*, May 15, 2008.

IV   4   Globalization, diversification, and focus on values   **661**

143 "GFS 13. 2. 1984," RB 1 230 015 005.
144 "Merkels erster Mann für gewisse Fragen," in *Handelsblatt*, April 22, 2010.
145 "Bosch bekommt einen neuen Chef," in *Süddeutsche Zeitung*, March 30, 2012.
146 "Vortrag G1/Fehrenbach, LD-Forum 18./19. 12. 2003," RB 1 204 513; "Die Büchse der Pandora ist geöffnet. Interview mit Bosch-Chef Franz Fehrenbach," in *Handelsblatt*, December 12, 2007.
147 "Corporate Dialogveranstaltungen, 6. 4. 2006," RB 1 252 039.
148 "An zwei Orten mit 4000 Mitarbeitern im Gespräch," in *Bosch-Zünder* 2008/6 (German national edition), p. 7.
149 "Indien: Treff mit dem Chef," in *Bosch-Zünder* 2006/6, p. 7.
150 "Der Mann für Bosch 3.0," in *Frankfurter Allgemeine Zeitung*, March 30, 2012.
151 "Information von Volkmar Denner, Mitglied der Geschäftsführung, 29. 6. 2012," RB 1 253 001.
152 Robert Bosch GmbH, 2010 annual report.
153 "Diversity bei Bosch. Entwicklung Frauenanteil in Führungspositionen SL1–LD 1997–2012," RB 1 235 049.
154 "Mitarbeiterstruktur: Frauen-Männer, Bosch-Gruppe Inland 1989–2012," *ibid*.
155 "Änderungen in der Geschäftsführung der Robert Bosch GmbH," press release dated June 29, 2012.
156 "Bosch legt Grundstein zu neuem Zentrum für Forschung und Vorausentwicklung," press release dated September 27, 2012.
157 "Bosch besinnt sich auf die alte Stärke," in *Handelsblatt*, March 19, 2012; "Elektroautos: Durchbruch erst ab 2020," in *Bosch-Zünder* 2013/1, p. 20.
158 "Robert Bosch Battery Systems gegründet. Bosch baut Entwicklung und Produktion effizienter Speichertechnologie aus, 13. 12. 2012," press release, RB 2012 1208.

Final conclusions

1 "Lieber Geld verlieren als Vertrauen," in *Bosch-Zünder* 1919/2, p. 21.
2 "Rede Christof Boschs bei der Jubiläumsgala am 19. 5. 2011," pp. 2 ff., RB 2011 05506.

Bosch Group headcount and sales revenue (1886–2012)

Year	Headcount[1]	Sales revenue in marks/RM/DM/euros	Share of sales revenue outside Germany (%)
		mark	
1886/1887	3		
1887		5,700	
1888		9,300	1
1889		15,000	1.7
1890		19,000	1.5
1891	10	25,500	2.2
1892	25	35,100	12.9
1893	2	27,600	22.4
1894	4	30,000	7.4
1895		38,900	8.5
1896	14	80,600	3.3
1897		101,700	9.4
1898	9	163,300	14.7
1899	28	236,000	15.8
1900	37	295,900	
1901	54	369,500	
1902	77	untraceable	
1903	145	untraceable	
1904	283	842,500	
1905	472	1,726,000	
1906	611	3,624,000	78.9
1907	944	untraceable	86.7
1908	1,103	7,938,000	87.7
1909	2,066	12,836,000	89.6
1910	3,002	19,628,000	87.2
1911	3,552	22,286,000	86.5
1912	4,959	33,147,000	83.8
1913	4,542	26,862,000	88.7
1914	3,611	23,560,000	77.1
1915	3,895	33,126,000	12.7
1916	5,639	47,513,000	9.8
1917	8,253	77,652,000	8.5

Year	Headcount[1]	Sales revenue in marks/RM/DM/euros	Share of sales revenue outside Germany (%)
1918	9,249	73,462,000	8.5
1919	6,208	62,539,000	14.8
1920	7,794	inflation	57.4
1921	6,444	inflation	40.2
1922	8,491	inflation	49.2
1923	10,621	inflation	inflation
		reichsmark (RM)	
1924	9,769	49,445,000	34.6
1925	13,808	72,825,000	31.6
1926	6,752	47,521,000	41.1
1927	10,267	71,370,000	34.1
1928	11,333	83,029,000	40.6
1929	10,292	85,227,000	43.5
1930	8,367	67,465,000	46.5
1931	8,658	55,940,000	48.6
1932	8,548	48,443,000	55.7
1933	11,455	60,314,000	34.8
1934	15,216	96,605,000	22.0
1935	16,396	111,129,000	16.5
1936	18,599	134,705,000	15.9
1937	19,817	158,319,000	17.4
1938	23,103	182,900,000	11.6
1939	21,580	217,927,000	9.3
1940	23,161	225,446,000	10.3
1941	24,650	248,080,000	9.9
1942	25,288	328,782,000	11.1
1943	22,879	368,845,000	12.7
1944	22,124	364,652,000	7.4
1945	4,975	50,351,000	0
1946	9,432	49,209,000	0
1947	10,541	57,137,000	4.1
		German marks (DM)	
1948	10,812	85m	5.4
1949	12,533	188m	10.3
1950	20,836	258m	10.5
1951	19,432	385m	13.3
1952	20,493	419m	13.6
1953	26,441	469m	16.7
1954	31,357	599m	18.0

Year	Headcount[1]	Sales revenue in marks/RM/DM/euros	Share of sales revenue outside Germany (%)
1955	37,997	757m	17.0
1956	38,488	860m	18.8
1957	44,459	967m	18.4
1958	51,001	1,153m	19.8
1959	60,000[2]	1,495m	19.2
1960	71,000	1,741m	19.1
1961	70,000	1,883m	20.5
1962	69,500	2,031m	19.6
1963	75,048	2,232m	35 (21)[3]
1964	87,112	2,650m	35
1965	89,723	2,970m	34
1966	85,720	3,168m	36
1967[4]	84,714	3,051m	39
1968	93,367	3,751m	40
1969	109,897	4,719m	40
1970	119,502	5,508m	39
1971	114,800	5,606m	40
1972	107,483	5,765m	46
1973	113,023	6,461m	48
1974	115,171	7,076m	52
1975	105,553	7,281m	52
1976	105,827	8,319m	51
1977	110,459	9,160m	49
1978	117,754	9,618m	49
1979	120,487	10,804m	51
1980	121,584	11,809m	54
1981	115,869	12,950m	56
1982	112,154	13,812m	56
1983[5]	109,660	14,352m	55
1984	131,882	18,373m	53
1985	140,374	21,223m	54
1986[6]	147,378	21,719m	51
1987	161,343	25,365m	50
1988	165,732	27,675m	51
1989	174,742	30,588m	52
1990	179,636	31,824m	51
1991	181,498	33,600m	48
1992	177,183	34,432m	47
1993	164,506	32,469m	49
1994	156,464	34,478m	54

Year	Headcount[1]	Sales revenue in marks/RM/DM/euros	Share of sales revenue outside Germany (%)
1995	158,372	35,844m	56
1996	172,359	41,146m	61
1997	179,719	46,851m	65
1998	188,017	50,333m	65
1999	194,335	54,579m	66
2000	196,880	61,717m	72
		euros (EUR)	
2001	218,377	34,029m	72
2002	225,897	34,977m	72
2003	229,439	36,357m	71
2004[7]	238,847	40,007m	72
2005[8]	248,853	41,461m	73
2006	257,754	43,684m	74
2007	267,562	46,320m	75
2008	282,758	45,127m	74
2009	274,530	38,174m	76
2010	276,418	47,259m	77
2011	295,256	51,494m	77
2012	306,272	52,464m	77

1 Through 1966, headcount is recorded at year's end. From 1967, the annual average is given. Up to 1958, regional organizations and subsidiary companies are not included.

2 From 1959 through 1962, only round numbers are available for associates.

3 Up to 1962, exports as percentage of total sales; from 1963, exports plus external sales by companies outside Germany.

4 Effective January 1, 1968, all sales were treated as net amounts (without VAT). Sales figures before 1968 were calculated as gross amounts, inclusive of VAT in its old form. By way of comparison, 1967 sales using the old method of calculation came to 3,210 million German marks.

5 Effective January 1, 1984, the sales of the Telefonbau und Normalzeit Lehner & Co (Telenorma) group of consolidated companies were included for the first time. By way of comparison, 1983 sales including Telenorma came to 16,126 million German marks.

6 In 1987, the German operations of Bosch-Siemens Hausgeräte, as well as ANT Nachrichtentechnik GmbH, were included in the financial statements on a pro rata basis. By way of comparison, 1986 sales including these two affiliated companies on a pro rata basis came to 23,807 million German marks.

7 Restrospective calculation for 2004 according to International Financial Reporting Standards (IFRS) results in the following figures: sales 38,954 million euros; global headcount (average for the year) 234,000 (rounded); of which in Germany 107,000 (rounded).

8 The consolidated financial statements for 2005 were prepared for the first time using IFRS. Before this, the accounting standards of the German Commercial Code were used.

List of abbreviations

Bosch-internal abbreviations

ABC	American Bosch Corporation
ABM Beteiligungs GmbH	Allianz Bosch MTU Beteiligungsgesellschaft
ABMC	American Bosch Magneto Corporation
AGL	Leitung für Angestelltenfragen (corporate human resources)
ALI	Autofahrer-Leit- und Informationssystem (driver guidance and information system)
AMBAC	American Bosch Arma Corporation
ARS	Aufsichtsratssitzung (supervisory board meeting)
ASR	Antriebsschlupfregelung (traction control system)
AW	Außenwerk (branch operation)
BBT	BBT Thermotechnik GmbH
BD	Bosch-Dienst (Bosch Car Service)
BDK-Werke	Bosch-Dienst K-Werke (Bosch Car Service automotive plants)
BEGE	Beteiligungsgesellschaft (affiliated company)
BEBS	Bosch Energy and Building Solutions GmbH
BeQIK	[Name of a company mission, from the German words *Betriebsergebnis* (operating result), *Qualität* (quality), *Innovation* (innovation), and *Kundenorientierung* (customer orientation)]
BOL	Büro der Leitung für Wirtschaftskontrolle und Organisation (corporate business management and organization)
BP	Blaupunkt
BPL	Büro der Personalleitung (corporate human resources)
BPS	Bosch Production System
BPWG	Blaupunkt-Werke GmbH
BSH	BSH Bosch und Siemens Hausgeräte GmbH
BSHG	Bosch-Siemens Hausgeräte GmbH
BTH	Büro der Technischen Hauptleitung (investigative office reporting to corporate engineering department)
BüW	Bühl/Bühlertal plant
BW	Bautenwerk (real estate and buildings)
C	Unternehmensbereich Kommunikationstechnik (communications technology business sector)
DLMG	Dreilinden Maschinenbau GmbH
EDC	Electronic diesel control
EKL	Einkaufsleitung (corporate purchasing)
ELFI	Elektro- und Feinmechanische Industrie GmbH
EZKL	Erzeugnisklasse (product class)

F 1 to 8	Führungsbereiche (group executive sectors) 1 to 8
FAL	Fabrikleitung (factory management)
FDR	Fahrdynamikregelung (vehicle dynamics control)
FESE	Fernseh AG/GmbH
FIS	Führungsinformationssitzung (business policy briefing)
FSV	Zentralbereich Forschung, Stoffe und Verfahren (corporate sector for research, materials, and process engineering)
G1	Group executive sector 1
GBR	Gesamtbetriebsrat (central works council)
GF	Geschäftsführung (board of management)
GFS	Geschäftsführersitzung (board of management meeting)
GPI	Geschäftspolitische Information (business policy briefing)
IW	Isolitwerk
K 1 to 9	Divisions of the automotive technology business sector
KFL	Kaufmännische Fabrikleitung (factory management commercial)
KGL	Kaufmännische Geschäftsleitung (executive vice president commercial)
LD	Leitungen und Direktoren (senior executives)
LW	Lichtwerk (light works)
MC	Mobile communications division
MIPS	Materials-flow-based information, production, and control system
MW	Metallwerk (metal works)
Nakib	N.V. Administratiekontoor voor Internationale Belegging
NK-Bereich	Non-automotive division
NT	Northern Telecom
PEL	Personalleitung (corporate human resources)
PSH	Personal- und Sozialhauptleitung (corporate department for human resources and social services)
RB	Robert Bosch GmbH
RBCD	Bosch Automotive Diesel Systems Co., Ltd.
RBES	Robert Bosch Española SA
RBIG	Robert Bosch Industriebeteiligung GmbH
RBIK	Robert Bosch Industrietreuhand KG
RBMC	Robert Bosch Magneto Company
RBTV	Robert Bosch Testamentsvollstrecker (group of executors of Robert Bosch's will)
RBUS	Robert Bosch Corporation (USA)
REA	Rechtsabteilung (legal department)
ROWA	Subsidiary company, name taken from the first letters of Rogowski and Walz
SAVEM	[Bosch sales company in France]
SBC	Sensotronic brake control
SG	Starter Motors and Generators division
SGMG	Sundgau Maschinenbau GmbH
TCS	Traction control system
TEH	Technische Hauptleitung (corporate engineering department)
TFL	Technische Fabrikleitung (factory management – technical)

TN	Telefonbau und Normalzeit Lehner & Co.
TOGE	Tochtergesellschaften (subsidiary or subsidiaries)
TOL	Technische Oberleitung (technical general management)
TT	Thermotechnology division
TV	Testamentsvollstrecker (executor(s))
TVS	Sitzung der Testamentsvollstrecker (meeting of the group of executors)
UABC	United American Bosch Corporation
UAES	United Automotive Electronic Systems Co., Ltd.
UBG	Unternehmensbereich Gebrauchsgüter und Gebäudetechnik (consumer goods and building technology business sector)
UBI	Unternehmensbereich Industrietechnik (industrial technology business sector)
UBK	Unternehmensbereich Kraftfahrzeugtechnik (automotive technology business sector)
UC	Unternehmensbereich Kommunikationstechnik (communications technology business sector)
VDC	Vehicle dynamics control
VGO	Versuchsbau GmbH Gotha-Ost
VH	Verkaufshaus (sales office)
VKH	Verkaufs-Hauptleitung (corporate sales)
VVB	Vermögensverwaltung Bosch GmbH (Bosch trust administration)
VWH	Verwaltungs-Hauptleitung (corporate administration)
WEL	Werksleitung (plant management)
WIDU GmbH	Subsidiary company, name comes from the first letters of Wild and Durst
ZT	Zentralbereich Technik (corporate sector for engineering)
ZW	Zünderwerk (spark-plug plant)

Other abbreviations

AB	Aktiebolag (Swedish: stock corporation)
ABS	Antiblockiersystem (antilock braking system)
Acro	American Crude Oil Corporation
AEG	Allgemeine Elektricitäts-Gesellschaft
AG	Aktiengesellschaft (stock corporation)
Agfa	Aktiengesellschaft für Anilinfabrikation
AKZO	Algemene Koninklijke Zout Organon
AMI	American Microsystems, Inc.
ANT	ANT Nachrichtentechnik GmbH
AT&T	American Telephone & Telegraph Company
ATN	AEG-Telefunken Nachrichtentechnik GmbH
ATZ	Automobiltechnische Zeitschrift
BArch	Bundesarchiv
BArchM	Bundesarchiv, Abteilung Militärarchiv
BASF	Badische Anilin- & Soda-Fabrik
BDC	Berlin Document Center
BDI	Bundesverband der deutschen Industrie (Federation of German Industries)

BIOS	British Intelligence Objectives Sub-Committee
BMW	Bayerische Motoren Werke
BRIC	Brazil, Russia, India, China
BTX	Bildschirmtext (videotext)
CAV or C.A.V.	C. A. Vandervell & Co. Ltd.
CIP	continuous improvement process
CDU	Christlich Demokratische Union Deutschlands (Christian Democratic Union of Germany)
CeBIT	Centrum für Büroautomation, Informationstechnologie und Telekommunikation (Center for Office Automation, Information Technology, and Telecommunications; IT trade fair)
CFRoI	cash flow return on investment
CIOS	Combined Intelligence Objectives Sub-Committee
CNC	computerized numerical control
CNEMS	Chinese Engine Management Systems Corp. Ltd.
Corp.	corporation
D-Jetronic	[electronic gasoline injection system, controlled by pressure; D stands for *Druck* or pressure]
DAF	Deutsche Arbeitsfront (German Labor Front)
DB	Daimler-Benz
DDP	Deutsche Demokratische Partei (German Democratic Party)
DDR	Deutsche Demokratische Republik (German Democratic Republic; East Germany)
DEC	Digital Equipment Corporation
Delco	Dayton Engineering Laboratories Company
DIHT	Deutscher Industrie- und Handelstag (Association of German Chambers of Commerce and Industry)
DM	Deutsche Mark (German mark)
DMV	Deutscher Metallarbeiter-Verband (Association of German Metal Workers)
DRT	Deutsche Revisions- und Treuhand AG
DV	Datenverarbeitung (data processing)
DVA	Deutsche Verlags-Anstalt
DVP	Demokratische Volkspartei (Democratic People's Party)
EBIT	earnings before interest and taxes
ECU	electronic control unit
e. V.	eingetragener Verein (registered association)
EEG	Erneuerbare-Energien-Gesetz (German Renewable Energy Act)
EETPU	Electrical, Electronic, Telecommunications, and Plumbing Union
EFTA	European Free Trade Association
EG	Europäische Gemeinschaft (European Community)
EPA	Environmental Protection Agency
ESP	Elektronisches Stabilitätsprogramm (electronic stability program)
ETAS	Engineering Tools, Applications and Services GmbH
ETH	Eidgenössische Technische Hochschule
EVA	Elektronischer Verkehrslotse für Autofahrer (electronic traffic pilot for drivers)

EWG	Europäische Wirtschaftsgemeinschaft (European Economic Community)
FAW	First Automotive Works
FEA	Société Financière d'Equipment Automobile
FEMSA	Fabrica Española Magneto S.A.
FIAT	Field Investigation Agency, Technical
Fiat	Fabbrica Italiana Automobili Torino
FuE	Forschung und Entwicklung (research and development)
G.F.C.C.	Groupe Français du Conseil de Contrôle
GEC	General Electric Company
Gestapo	Geheime Staatspolizei
GM	General Motors
GmbH	Gesellschaft mit beschränkter Haftung (close corporation)
GSM	Global System for Mobile Communications
GWB	Gesetz gegen Wettbewerbsbeschränkungen (Act against Restraints on Competition)
h. c.	honoris causa
I. G. Farben/ IG Farben	Interessengemeinschaft Farbenindustrie
IBM	International Business Machines Corporation
IE	Industrial engineering
IFRS	International Financial Reporting Standards
IG Metall	Industriegewerkschaft Metall (metalworkers union)
IHK	Industrie- und Handelskammer (chamber of commerce)
Inc.	Incorporated company
ISDN	Integrated services digital network
IT	Informationstechnik (information technology)
ITS	International tracing service
ITT	International Telephone & Telegraph Corp.
IVG	Industrieverwaltungsgesellschaft (state-owned real estate management company)
JCO	Junkers & Co GmbH
Jr.	Junior
JRSO	Jewish Restitution Successor Organization
K-Jetronic	[Mechanically controlled gasoline injection system; K stands for *kontinuierliche* or continuous]
KdF	Kraft durch Freude (strength through joy)
KG	Kommanditgesellschaft (limited partnership)
KHD	Klöckner-Humboldt-Deutz
KKR	Kohlberg Kravis Roberts & Co.
KKS	Kapitalkostensatz (cost of capital)
KL	Konzentrationslager (concentration camp)
KPD	Kommunistische Partei Deutschlands (German Communist Party)
KZ	Konzentrationslager (concentration camp)
L-Jetronic	[Electronic gasoline-injection system, controlled by air flow; L stands for *Luft* or air]
LHA	Landeshauptarchiv
LHASA	Landeshauptarchiv Sachsen-Anhalt
Lkw	Lastkraftwagen (truck)

Ltd.	limited
M	mark
MABO S.A.	Bosch joint venture in Italy, from the first letters of Marelli and Bosch
MAN	Maschinenfabrik Augsburg-Nürnberg
Manurhin	Manufacture de Machines du Haut-Rhin
MBB	Messerschmitt-Bölkow-Blohm
MHZ	Mechanischer Hachtel-Zug
MICO	Motor Industries Co. Ltd.
MIT	Massachusetts Institute of Technology
Montan GmbH	Verwertungsgesellschaft für Montaninteressen GmbH
MOS	metal-oxide semiconductor
MS/Ms.	Manuskript (manuscript)
MTM	methods-time measurement
MTU	Motoren- und Turbinen-Union Friedrichshafen GmbH
MW	megawatt
MWD	Soviet Ministry of Internal Affairs (English: MVD)
NABCO	Nippon Air Brake Co. Ltd.
NARA	National Archives and Records Administration
NC	numerical control
NCF	Nachhaltiger Cash Flow (sustainable cash flow)
NKWD	Narodny kommissariat vnutrennich del (People's Commissariat for Internal Affairs, NKVD in English)
NL	Nachlass ([literary] estate)
NS	Nationalsozialismus (National Socialism)
NSBO	Nationalsozialistische Betriebszellenorganisation (National Socialist Factory Cell Organization)
NSDAP	Nationalsozialistische Deutsche Arbeiterpartei (National Socialist German Workers' Party)
NSKK	Nationalsozialistisches Kraftfahr-Korps (National Socialist Motor Corps)
NT	Nachrichtentechnik (telecommunications)
o. J.	ohne Jahr (undated)
OMGUS	Office of Military Government for Germany (U.S.)
Opec	Organization of the Petroleum Exporting Countries
Pkw	Personenkraftwagen (passenger car)
PS	Pferdestärke (horsepower)
plc	public limited company
pty	proprietary limited company
RCA	Radio Corporation of America
RGBl.	Reichsgesetzblatt
RM	Reichsmark
RWE	Rheinisch-Westfälisches Elektrizitätswerk AG
RWTH	Rheinisch-Westfälische Technische Hochschule
RWWA	Rheinisch-Westfälisches Wirtschaftsarchiv
S&H	Siemens & Halske
SA	Sturmabteilung
S. A.	Sociedad Anónima/Société Anonyme
SAIC	Shanghai Automotive Industry Corporation

SD	Sicherheitsdienst des Reichsführers SS
SEB	Stockholms Enskilda Bank
SEL	Standard Elektrik Lorenz
SEV Marchal	Société Anonyme pour l'Equipement Electrique des Vehicules
SNIAS	Société Nationale Industrielle Aérospatiale
SPC	statistical process control
SPD	Sozialdemokratische Partei Deutschlands (German Social Democratic Party)
SS	Schutzstaffel
StA	Staatsarchiv
Stalag	Stammlager (prisoner-of-war camp)
T&N	Telefonbau und Normalzeit Lehner & Co.
TDI	turbocharged direct injection
TQM	total quality management
TTM	time to market
UBS	Union Bank of Switzerland/Union de Banques Suisses
UEK	Unabhängige Expertenkommission Schweiz – Zweiter Weltkrieg
URL	uniform resource locator
UTC	United Technologies Corporation
V2	Vergeltungswaffe 2
VAT	value-added tax
VDA	Verband der Automobilindustrie e. V. (German Association of the Automotive Industry)
VDI	Verein Deutscher Ingenieure (Association of German Engineers)
VDO	Vereinigte Deuta-Ota
VEB	Volkseigener Betrieb (state-owned enterprise) in the German Democratic Republic
VHS	video home system
VSWG	Vierteljahrschrift für Sozial- und Wirtschaftsgeschichte
VW	Volkswagen AG

Photo credits

Sources and bibliography

A Unpublished sources

Bosch archives

Robert Bosch GmbH, Historical Communications, Stuttgart-Feuerbach (RB)

1 001   *Gesellschafter* [shareholders] (1895–2004)
1 002   *Aufsichtsrat und Geschäftsführung* [supervisory board and board of management] (1909–2004)
1 003   *Rechnungswesen* [accounts] (1887–2006)
1 004   *Gliederungspläne und Organisation* [organizational charts and organization] (1914–2007)
1 006   *Arbeitsordnungen, Betriebsvereinbarungen, Tarife* [work rules, works agreements, pay scales] (1901–2007)
1 007   *Personalstatistiken, Löhne, Gehälter, Statistiken* [HR statistics, wages, salaries, other statistics] (1886–2008)
1 010   *Kleine Ablieferungen* [minor packages of materials] (1889–2010)
1 011   *Entflechtungsverfahren Bosch* [Bosch deconcentration proceedings] (1926–1997)
1 012   *Ausländer- und Gefangeneneinsatz WK II* [use of foreign labor and prisoners of war in the Second World War] (1939–2007)
1 013   Hans Walz (1912–2007)
1 014   Robert Bosch (1883–2007)
1 015   Hans L. Merkle (1935–2003)
1 016   Marcus Bierich (1983–1993)
1 017   Paul Adolf Stein (1942–2007)
1 018   Hans Bacher (1968–1982)
1 020   Hermann Scholl (1962–1994)
1 022   *Zentralabteilung Recht (ZR); Verträge und Vereinbarungen* [corporate legal affairs; contracts and agreements] (1892–2003)
1 024   *Liegenschaften* [real estate] (1900–2006)
1 025   *Marktforschung* [market research] (1954–1970)
1 027   *Rationalisierungstagungen* [rationalization conferences] (1946–1986)
1 028   *Reiseberichte* [travelogues] (1928–1986)
1 029   *Verkaufshäuser* [sales offices] (1918–2003)
1 030   *Zentralbereich Technik (ZT)* [corporate engineering] (1977–1983)
1 034   *Auslandsvertretungen, Auslandsgesellschaften* [agencies and companies outside Germany] (1898–2005)
1 035   *Konzentrationsakten* [concentration] (1962/63)
1 038   Continuous improvement process (CIP) (1994–2008)
1 039   *Bosch-Archiv (ZÖF)* [Bosch archives]; *Historische Kommunikation* [Historical Communications] (1918–2010)

1 041   *Verkauf, Marketing* [sales, marketing] (1887–1981)

1 043   *Sozialwesen, Ausbildung, Weiterbildung* [social benefits, occupational and further training] (1904–2008)

1 044   *Mitarbeiter* [personnel] (1886–2007)

1 046   *Büro der Fertigungshauptleitung (BFE)* [corporate manufacturing planning] (1933–1981)

1 047   *Fertigungsentwicklungs-Leitung (FWL)* [corporate operations planning] (1935–1976)

1 051   *Markenrecht* [trademark rights] (1909–1968)

1 058   Robert Bosch Stiftung, Robert-Bosch-Krankenhaus (1939–2009)

1 059   *Arbeitskämpfe, Betriebsrat* [industrial disputes, works council] (1906–2004)

1 062   *Bosch-Dienste* [Bosch Car Service operations] (1921–2006)

1 064   Bosch-Siemens-Hausgeräte GmbH (1944–2004)

1 065   *Fertigung WKII, Kriegsschäden* [manufacturing in the Second World War, war damage] (1910–1994)

1 068   *Zusammenarbeit mit Unternehmensberatern* [work with management consultants] (1960–1981)

1 070   *Werk Bamberg* [Bamberg plant] (1933–2005)

1 093   Günter Bensinger (1954–1992)

1 094   *Personalakten* [personnel records] (1880–1991)

1 099   *Geschäftsbereich K6/Hydraulik/Pneumatik* [K6 division/hydraulics/pneumatics] (1962–1988)

1 101   Marcus Bierich (1976–1994)

1 102   *Geschäftsbereich K5/Diesel-Einspritzsysteme* [K5 division/diesel injection systems] (1946–2001)

1 104   *K-Verkaufsorganisation* [automotive sales organization] (1982–1988)

1 116   *Zentralabteilung Recht (ZR)* [corporate legal affairs] (1974–1992)

1 118   *Zentralabteilung Recht (ZR)* [corporate legal affairs] (1955–1995)

1 122   Tilman Todenhöfer (1950–1994)

1 127   Hubert Zimmerer (1964–1995)

1 131   *Zentralabteilung Recht (ZR)* [corporate legal affairs] (1965–1995)

1 132   Robert Bosch d. J. [Robert Bosch Jr.] (1963–1996)

1 158   *Personal- und Sozialwesen (PSW)* [human resources and workforce welfare] (1919–2007)

1 192   Tilman Todenhöfer (1970–2005)

1 194   *Verkauf der Bosch REGEs vor dem Zweiten Weltkrieg* [sale of Bosch regional subsidiaries before the Second World War] (1937–1999)

1 195   Hermann Eisele und Hubert Zimmerer (1986–1999)

1 204   Franz Fehrenbach (1961–2004)

1 214   Robert Oswald und Kurt Liedtke (1984–2007)

1 217   Peter Marks (1997–2005)

1 219   *Zentralabteilung Controlling, Planung, M&A* [corporate department for controlling, planning, and M&A] (1969–1994)

1 222   *Acro-Motor* [Acro engine] (1894–1955)

1 229   *Interviews mit ausgeschiedenen und noch aktiven leitenden Mitarbeitern/Zeitzeugen (Transkripte)* [transcripts of interviews with senior executives and other persons, either retired or still in service]

    040   Klaus Riesenberg, April 11, 2007

    055   Christof Bosch, February 19, 2008

067	Richard Rau, November 9, 2005
072	Karl Gutbrod, October 27, 2005
087	Horst Sandvoß
088	Dieter Schnabel, December 18, 2006

1 230   *Geschäftsführersitzungen* (GFS) [board of management meetings] (1969–1999)

1 232   Wolfgang Chur (1999–2008)

1 235   *Familie und Beruf – Frauen – Mitarbeiternetzwerke*
[family and career – women – associate networks] (2009)

1 241   *Zentralabteilung C/IP* [corporate department for intellectual property]
(1907–1974)

1 242   Wolfgang Drees (1997–2005)

1 244   Gotthard Romberg (1995–2009)

1 245   Wolfgang Malchow (1972–2002)

1 252   *Zentralabteilung C/HD* [human resources development and organizational
development with CIP coordination] (up to 2008)

1 253   Volkmar Denner (2012)

1 606   Dreilinden Maschinenbau (DLMG) (1934–2008)

1 608   Scintilla (1920–2004)

1 610   Fernseh GmbH/AG (FESE) (1929–2003)

1 611   Siling-Werke GmbH (1919–1949)

1 636   WIDU GmbH (1944–1947)

1 676   Borg Warner Corp. (1973–1988)

1 696   Robert Bosch Internationale Beteiligungen AG (1954–2004)

1 706   Bosch-Rexroth AG (2001–2005)

1 707   Blaupunkt (BP) (1943–2007)

1 832   *Nachlass Otto Debatin* [literary remains of Otto Debatin] (1918–1994)

1 842   *Nachlass Fritz Nast-Kolb* [literary remains of Fritz Nast-Kolb] (1916–2000)

1 848   *Ablage Peter Adolff* [files of Peter Adolff] (1976–2009)

3 000   *Pressedokumentation* [press documentation]

3 0005   *C/CC-Ablieferungen (Unternehmenskommunikation)* [materials submitted
by corporate communications]

6 001   *Fotosammlung* [photographic collection]

RB   Technische Dokumentation, Luftfahrt 016 [technical documentation, aircraft]

Other archives

Archives Départementales du Haut-Rhin, Colmar
Purg 54075

Archives du Ministère des affairs étrangères et européennes, La Courneuve
2 AEF 3168
GMFB 2/312/2

Archiwum Muzeum Gross-Rosen, Wałbrzych
4293/DP

Bayer-Archiv Leverkusen
Autographensammlung (AS)

Bayerisches Hauptstaatsarchiv, Munich
Nachlass Georg Escherich (literary remains of Georg Escherich)

Bundesarchiv, Berlin (BArch)
Abt. R – Deutsches Reich

R 2	Reichsfinanzministerium
R 3901	Reichsarbeitsministerium
R 8121	Bank der deutschen Luftfahrt AG
R 8136	Reichskreditgesellschaft AG
SSO	SS-Offiziersakten [formerly BDC]
31XX	Reichskartei der NSDAP [formerly BDC]

Abt. DDR

DN 1	Ministerium der Finanzen

Abt. Militärarchiv, Freiburg i. Br. (BArchM)

RL 3	Generalluftzeugmeister
RW 20	Rüstungsinspektionen
RW 21	Rüstungskommandos

Daimler AG, Mercedes-Benz Archives & Collection
Kennzahlen der Daimler-Motoren-Gesellschaft, Benz & Cie. und Daimler-Benz AG

Internationaler Suchdienst, Bad Arolsen (ITS), Digitales Archiv
Doc. No. 82111434#1

Landesarchiv Baden-Württemberg – Hauptstaatsarchiv Stuttgart

P 10	Jagdgemeinschaft Robert Bosch

Landeshauptarchiv Koblenz (LHA Koblenz)

540	Bezirksämter für Wiedergutmachung und verwaltete Vermögen
583,1	Landgericht Koblenz

Landeshauptarchiv Sachsen-Anhalt, Abteilung Dessau (LHASA, DE)
Junkers Wärmetechnik Dessau

Landesarchiv Berlin

B Rep. 025–08	Wiedergutmachungsämter (WGA) von Berlin

Niedersächsisches Landesarchiv, Hauptstaatsarchiv Hannover

Nds 171 Hannover	Entnazifizierungsbehörden im Regierungsbezirk Hannover
Nds 171 Hildesheim	Entnazifizierungsbehörden im Regierungsbezirk Hildesheim

Privatarchiv Familie Zundel, Salzburg
NL Zundel

Rheinisch-Westfälisches Wirtschaftsarchiv, Cologne (RWWA)

130–400101	Gutehoffnungshütte Oberhausen AG, Nachlass Paul Reusch (literary remains of Paul Reusch)

Staatsarchiv Ludwigsburg (StA Ludwigsburg)

EL 317 III	Staatsanwaltschaft Stuttgart, Nationalsozialistische Gewaltverbrechen
EL 350 I	Landesamt für die Wiedergutmachung Baden-Württemberg: Einzelfallakten
EL 902/20	Spruchkammer 37 – Stuttgart: Verfahrensakten
PL 502	Sammlungsgut der US-Militärregierung zur Dokumentation der NS-Belastung

Stadtarchiv Stuttgart

13/93	Informationsdienst der Stadt der Auslandsdeutschen Stuttgart

U.S. National Archives and Records Administration, College Park, Maryland
RG 122   Federal Trade Commission
RG 260   Records of the U.S. Occupation Headquarters, World War II
T-301   Records of the U.S. Chief of Counsel for War Crimes, Nuremberg
                      Military Tribunals

Werksarchiv Bosch Hildesheim
I/2   Gründung, Verträge
I/8   Elfi, Trillke, Bosch

B Interviews

Dr. Peter Adolff, March 15, 2010, and April 17, 2010
Dr. Adolf Ahnefeld, August 6, 2012
Dr. Christof Bosch, September 22, 2010
Franz Fehrenbach, July 23, 2010, and May 26, 2011
Karl Josef Fricke, May 6 and 7, 2010
Alfred Löckle, November 4, 2011
Kurt Losten, September 23, 2010
Dr. Eva Madelung, March 16, 2011
Hermann Meyer, March 29, 2011
Gerhard Sautter, October 19, 2010
Prof. Dr.-Ing. Hermann Scholl, July 7, 2010, and October 21, 2010
Tilman Todenhöfer, July 5, 2010, and October 21, 2010
Renate Zundel, March 8, 2011

C Published sources

Annual reports

Robert Bosch AG, annual reports 1917–1936
Robert Bosch GmbH, annual reports 1937–2012
VDA, annual reports 1992–2010

Official gazettes

Reichsgesetzblatt (RGBl.) [Reich legal gazette]

Other Bosch publications

Betriebsrat Bosch Feuerbach (ed.), *... auch beim Bosch gibt's nichts umsonst. 100 Jahre Arbeit und Leben in Feuerbach aus Sicht der Beschäftigten. Ein Buch des Betriebsrats Bosch Feuerbach*, Stuttgart, 2009.
Bosch (China) Investment Ltd. (ed.), *100 years Bosch in China. Past, present, and future*, Shanghai, 2009.
Bosch Sicherheitssysteme GmbH (ed.), *Sicherheitslösungen mit System. Individueller Schutz für Menschen, Objekte und Werte*, Munich, 2010.
Fastnacht, Kathrin/Kuhlgatz, Dietrich/Schmitt, Dieter/Siegel, Christine: *Bosch 125 years. Invented for life*, Stuttgart, 2011.

Robert Bosch AG (ed.), *50 Jahre Bosch 1886–1936*, Stuttgart, 1936.

Robert Bosch GmbH (ed.), *Bosch Automotive. A product history* (Journal of Bosch History, supplement 2) [Stuttgart, 2010].

Robert Bosch GmbH (ed.), *Bosch dal 1904 in Italia*, Milan, 2004.

Robert Bosch GmbH (ed.), *Bosch Dieseleinspritzung. Höhepunkte eines Jahrhunderts. Ein Rundgang durch das Museum des Geschäftsbereichs Einspritzsysteme für Dieselmotoren*, Stuttgart [undated].

Robert Bosch GmbH (ed.), *Bosch Fernseh 1929–1979 (Festvorträge zum Firmenjubiläum am 31. 5. 1979)*, Darmstadt, 1979.

Robert Bosch GmbH (ed.), *Bosch HEUTE. Informationen Schwieberdingen. Der neue Standort.* Stuttgart, 1970.

Robert Bosch GmbH (ed.), *Bosch in Belgium 1907–2007*, Brussels, 2007.

Robert Bosch GmbH (ed.), *Robert Bosch. His life and work* (Journal of Bosch History, supplement 1) [Stuttgart, 2009].

Robert Bosch GmbH (ed.), *Robert Bosch 1928–2004. Ansprachen der Trauerfeier am 28. September 2004* Gerlingen-Schillerhöhe, Stuttgart, 2004.

Robert Bosch GmbH (ed.), *The emergence of a global player. The internationalization of the Bosch Group* (Journal of Bosch History, supplement 3) [Stuttgart, 2008].

Zentralabteilung Anlagen und Bauten der Robert Bosch GmbH (ed.), *Art for innovation. Repräsentanz Berlin*, Stuttgart, 2003.

The Bosch News 1913
Journal of Bosch History 2008
Bosch Technische Berichte 1969
Bosch-Zünder, years 1919–2013 (English edition May 2005 ff.)
Bosch-Zünder online 2013

Writings and speeches by Robert Bosch, reminiscences of Robert Bosch

Bäuerle, Theodor	"Robert Bosch," RB 1 014 020
Bosch, Robert	"Lebenserinnerungen [Memoirs] (1921)," RB 1 014 006
Bosch, Robert	"Die Verhütung künftiger Krisen in der Weltwirtschaft [Preventing future crises in the world economy]," (offprint from journal *Paneuropa*, May 1932), Stuttgart, 1932
Bosch, Robert	*Sei Mensch und ehre Menschenwürde. Aufsätze, Reden und Gedanken von Robert Bosch* [Never forget your humanity, and respect human dignity in your dealings with others. Essays, speeches, and thoughts of Robert Bosch] (Bosch-Schriftenreihe, vol. 1), Stuttgart, 1950
Fischer-Bosch, Margarete	*Jugenderinnerungen an meinen Vater Robert Bosch* [Youthful reminiscences of my father, Robert Bosch], Stuttgart, 1953
Olpp, Felix	"Unser unvergesslicher Herr Bosch [Our unforgettable Mr. Bosch]," RB 1 014 003
Walz, Hans	"Robert Bosch. Der Mann und das Werk [Robert Bosch. The man and the achievement]," *Bosch-Zünder* 9, 1961, pp. 197–206

Writings of Hans L. Merkle

Merkle, Hans L.   *Dienen und Führen. Erkenntnisse eines Unternehmers* [Serving and leading. Insights of an entrepreneur], Stuttgart, 2001

Merkle, Hans L.   *Ein deutsches Unternehmen in Frankreich. Die Bosch-Gruppe und der Neubeginn in den deutsch-französischen Beziehungen ab 1945* [A German company in France. The Bosch Group and the new beginnings of Franco-German relations from 1945], Bonn, 1995

D Newspapers and periodicals

Auto Bild
ATZ Automobiltechnische Zeitschrift
Automobilwoche
Der Beobachter
Berliner Tageblatt
Bild-Zeitung
Börsen-Zeitung
Deutsche Zeitung
Elektrotechnische Zeitschrift
Financial Times Deutschland
Frankfurter Rundschau
Frankfurter Zeitung/Frankfurter Allgemeine Zeitung/FAZ.NET
Handelsblatt
Hannoversche Allgemeine Zeitung
Hannoversche Presse
Harvard Business Review
Heilbronner Stimme
Industrial and Corporate Change
Industriekurier
Industriemagazin
Kultur & Technik
Mainpost
Manager Magazin
Manager Magazin online
The New York Times
Reutlinger General-Anzeiger
Reutlinger Nachrichten
Scandinavian Economic History Review
Der Spiegel
Spiegel online Wirtschaft
Süddeutsche Zeitung
Stuttgarter Nachrichten
Stuttgarter Neues Tagblatt
Stuttgarter Zeitung
Teknikens Värld
Topics
VDI-Nachrichten
The Wall Street Journal

Die Welt
Welt am Sonntag
WirtschaftsWoche
Die Zeit

E Internet and film sources

http://de.wikipedia.org/wiki/Wirtschaftszahlen_zum_Automobil#cite_note-OICA-1
http://vda.de/de/publikationen/jahresberichte/index.html
http://webarchive.nationalarchives.gov.uk/20140402141250/http://www.competition-
        commission.org.uk//rep_pub//reports/1960_1969/fulltext/025c03.pdf
http://www.bundesregierung.de/Content/DE/Bulletin/2009/03/37-3-bk-solar.html
http://www.dillmann-gymnasium.de/gymnasium/organisation/geschichte-schul-
        statistik/ehemalige/
http://www.fhxb-museum.de/zwangsarbeit/index.htm
http://www.staatsanzeiger.de/kultur-und-geschichte/momente/archiv/momente-
        archiv/momente-ausgabe/175/
http://www.stuttgarter-zeitung.de
http://www.wfmz.com/features/History-s-Headlines/History-s-Headlines-Allentown-
        mansion-has-a-scandalous-past/11271212

F Bibliography

Aalders, Gerald/Wiebes, Cees: "Stockholms Enskilda Bank, German Bosch and I. G. Farben. A short history of cloaking," in *Scandinavian Economic History Review* 33, 1985/1, pp. 25–50.

Abelshauser, Werner: "Rüstungsschmiede der Nation? Der Kruppkonzern im Dritten Reich und in der Nachkriegszeit 1933 bis 1951," in Lothar Gall (ed.): *Krupp im 20. Jahrhundert. Die Geschichte des Unternehmens vom Ersten Weltkrieg bis zur Gründung der Stiftung*, Berlin, 2002, pp. 267–472.

Abelshauser, Werner: *Deutsche Wirtschaftsgeschichte seit 1945*, Munich, 2004.

Ahnefeld, Adolf: "Für viele waren es Sternstunden," Bierich, *Spiegel*, pp. 409–14.

Alef, Daniel: *Charles and Frank Duryea. Brought us America's first gasoline-powered car*, Santa Barbara/Ca., 2008.

Allmendinger, Claus-Michael: "Robert Bosch und die homöopathische Bewegung in Württemberg," in Sigrid Heinze (ed.): *Homöopathie 1796–1996. Eine Heilkunde und ihre Geschichte*, Berlin, 1996, pp. 93–100.

Allmendinger, Claus-Michael: *Struktur, Aufgabe und Bedeutung der Stiftungen von Robert Bosch und seiner Firma. Ein Beitrag zur Geschichte des Stiftungswesens in Württemberg von 1900 bis 1964*, Stuttgart,1977.

Aly, Götz: *Im Tunnel. Das kurze Leben der Marion Samuel 1931–1943*, Frankfurt am Main 2004.

Andres, Christopher Magnus: *Die bundesdeutsche Luft- und Raumfahrtindustrie 1945– 1970. Ein Industriebereich im Spanungsfeld von Politik, Wirtschaft und Militär*, Frankfurt am Main, 1996.

Andresen, Knud/Bitzegeio, Ursula/Mittag, Jürgen (eds.): *Nach dem Strukturbruch? Kontinuität und Wandel von Arbeitsbeziehungen und Arbeitswelt(en) seit den 1970er-Jahren*, Bonn, 2011.

Bähr, Johannes: "'Die amerikanische Herausforderung.' Anfänge der Technologiepolitik in der Bundesrepublik Deutschland," in *Archiv für Sozialgeschichte* 35, 1995, pp. 115–30.

Bähr, Johannes: "'Bankenrationalisierung' und Großbankenfrage. Der Konflikt um die Ordnung des deutschen Kreditgewerbes während des Zweiten Weltkrieges," in Harald Wixforth (ed.): *Finanzinstitutionen in Mitteleuropa während des Nationalsozialismus* (Geld und Kapital, vol. 4), Stuttgart, 2001, pp. 71–94.

Bähr, Johannes: *Industrie im geteilten Berlin (1945–1990). Die elektrotechnische Industrie und der Maschinenbau im Ost-West-Vergleich: Branchenentwicklung, Technologien und Handlungsstrukturen* (Einzelveröffentlichungen der Historischen Kommission zu Berlin, vol. 83), Munich, 2001.

Bähr, Johannes: "Unternehmens- und Kapitalmarktrecht im 'Dritten Reich.' Die Aktienrechtsreform und das Anleihestockgesetz," in Johannes Bähr and Ralf Banken (eds.): *Wirtschaftssteuerung durch Recht im Nationalsozialismus. Studien zur Entwicklung des Wirtschaftsrechts im Interventionsstaat des "Dritten Reichs"* (Studien zur europäischen Rechtsgeschichte, vol. 199), Frankfurt am Main, 2006, pp. 35–69.

Bähr, Johannes/Drecoll, Axel/Gotto, Bernhard: *Flick im Dritten Reich*, Munich 2008.

Bähr, Johannes/Banken, Ralf/Flemming, Thomas: *MAN. The history of a German industrial enterprise*, Munich, 2009.

Bähr, Johannes/Lesczenski, Jörg/Schmidtpott, Katja: *Winds of change. On the 150th anniversary of C. Illies & Co.*, Munich, 2009.

Banham, Russ: *Bosch in the United States. The first 100 years*, Farmington Hills 2006.

Banken, Ralf: *Edelmetallmangel und Großraubwirtschaft. Die Entwicklung des deutschen Edelmetallsektors im "Dritten Reich" 1933–1945* (*Jahrbuch für Wirtschaftsgeschichte*, supplement 13), Berlin, 2009.

Bardua, Heinz, *Stuttgart im Luftkrieg 1939–1945*, (Veröffentlichungen des Archivs der Stadt Stuttgart, vol. 23), Stuttgart, 1967.

Basshuysen, Richard van (ed.): *Ottomotoren mit Direkteinspritzung. Verfahren, Systeme, Entwicklung, Potenzial*, Wiesbaden, 2007.

Baumann, Carl-Friedrich: *175 Jahre Henschel. Der ständige Weg in die Zukunft, 1810–1985*, Moers, 1985.

Becker, Ernst Wolfgang: *Theodor Heuss. Bürger im Zeitalter der Extreme*, Stuttgart, 2011.

Becker, Rolf/Engel, Frauke: *"Unsere beste Reklame ist unsere Ware." Werbung bei Bosch von den Anfängen bis 1960* (Bosch-Archiv Schriftenreihe, vol. 2), Stuttgart 1998.

Becker, Rolf/Scholtyseck, Joachim: *Robert Bosch und die deutsch-französische Verständigung. Politisches Denken und Handeln im Spiegel der Briefwechsel*, Stuttgart [undated].

Benz, Wolfgang/Distel, Barbara (eds.): *Der Ort des Terrors. Geschichte der nationalsozialistischen Konzentrationslager*, vol. 6: *Natzweiler, Groß-Rosen, Stutthof*, Munich, 2007.

Berghahn, Volker: *Unternehmer und Politik in der Bundesrepublik*, Frankfurt am Main, 1985.

Berghoff, Hartmut/Rauh-Kühne, Cornelia: *Fritz K. Ein deutsches Leben im 20. Jahrhundert*, Stuttgart, Munich, 2000.

Bergmann, Theodor/Haible, Wolfgang/Iwanowa, Galina: *Friedrich Westmeyer. Von der Sozialdemokratie zum Spartakusbund. Eine politische Biographie*, Hamburg, 1998.

Bingmann, Holger: "Antiblockiersystem und Benzineinspritzung (Anti-Blocking System and Fuel Injection)," in Horst Albach: *Culture and technical innovation. A cross-cultural analysis and policy Recommendations* (Akademie der Wissenschaften zu Berlin, research report 9), Berlin, New York, 1994, pp. 736–821.

Bingmann, Holger: *Mensch – Politik – Kultur. Einflüsse auf die technische Entwicklung bei Daimler-Benz*, doctoral thesis. Freie Universität Berlin, Berlin, 1990.

Blaich, Fritz: *Die Wirtschaftskrise von 1925/26 und die Reichsregierung. Von der Erwerbslosenfürsorge zur Konjunkturpolitik*, Kallmünz, 1977.

Blaupunkt GmbH (ed.): *Blaupunkt. Die Werbegeschichte einer Marke*, Hildesheim, 2007.

Blumtritt, Oskar: *Nachrichtentechnik. Sender, Empfänger, Übertragung, Vermittlung*, Munich, 2005.

Boch, Rudolf (ed.): *Geschichte und Zukunft der deutschen Automobilindustrie. Tagung im Rahmen der "Chemnitzer Begegnungen" 2000*, Stuttgart, 2001.

Böhles, Franziska: "'Der Capo hat uns die Werkstatt gezeigt,' Arbeitsmigration bei Bosch, Die ersten 'Gastarbeiter' am Standort Feuerbach," in Johler/Sparacio (eds.): *Abfahren*, pp. 237–51.

Böhles, Franziska: "Es gibt keine Probleme, es gibt nur Herausforderungen – Betül Özyakan," in: Johler/Sparacio (eds.), *Abfahren*, pp. 141–47.

Bönig, Jürgen: *Die Einführung von Fließbandarbeit in Deutschland bis 1933. Zur Geschichte einer Sozialinnovation*, part 1, Münster, Hamburg, 1993.

Born, Karl Erich: *Wirtschafts- und Sozialgeschichte des Deutschen Kaiserreichs (1867/71–1914)*, Stuttgart, 1985.

Bosch, Margarete: *Die wirtschaftlichen Bedingungen der Befreiung des Bauernstandes im Herzogtum Kleve und in der Grafschaft Mark im Rahmen der Agrargeschichte Westdeutschlands*, Berlin, 1920.

Botz, Gerhard: "Methoden- und Theorieprobleme der historischen Widerstandsforschung," in Helmut Konrad/Wolfgang Neugebauer (eds.): *Arbeiterbewegung – Faschismus – Nationalbewußtsein. Festschrift zum 20jährigen Bestand des Dokumentationsarchivs des österreichischen Widerstandes und zum 60. Geburtstag von Herbert Steiner*, Vienna, Munich, 1983, pp. 137–51.

Bradley, Dermot/Hildebrand, Karl-Friedrich/Rövekamp, Markus: *Die Generale des Heeres 1921–1945*, vol. 7: *Knabe–Luz*, Osnabrück, 2004.

Brantl, Sabine: *Haus der Kunst, München. Ein Ort und seine Geschichte im Nationalsozialismus*, published by Haus der Kunst, München, Munich, 2007.

Brock, Gerald: *The second information revolution*, Cambridge, 2003.

Buchheim, Christoph: "Die Erholung von der Weltwirtschaftskrise 1932/33 in Deutschland," in *Jahrbuch für Wirtschaftsgeschichte* 2003/1, pp. 13–26.

Budraß, Lutz: *Flugzeugindustrie und Luftrüstung in Deutschland 1918–1945* (Schriften des Bundesarchivs, 50), Düsseldorf, 1998.

Budraß, Lutz: "Zwischen Unternehmen und Luftwaffe. Die Luftfahrtforschung im 'Dritten Reich'," in Helmut Maier (ed.): *Rüstungsforschung im Nationalsozialismus. Organisation, Mobilisierung und Entgrenzung der Technikwissenschaften (Geschichte der Kaiser-Wilhelm-Gesellschaft im Nationalsozialismus*, vol. 3), Göttingen, 2002, pp. 142–82.

Bühler, Heike/Dürig, Uta-Micaela (eds.), *Tradition kommunizieren. Das Handbuch der Heritage-Communication. Wie Unternehmen ihre Wurzeln professionell vermitteln*, Frankfurt am Main, 2008.

Bundesministerium für Arbeit und Sozialordnung, *Unternehmenskultur, Arbeitsqualität und Mitarbeiterengagement in den Unternehmen in Deutschland*, Berlin, 2008.

Chandler, Alfred D.: *Inventing the electronic century. The epic story of the consumer electronics and the computer industries*, New York, 2001.

Christian Dierig AG Augsburg (ed.), *Das Werk von fünf Generationen – 150 Jahre Dierig*, Augsburg, 1955.

Cortada, James W.: *The digital hand: How computers changed the work of American manufacturing, transportation, and retail industries*, Oxford, 2003.

Dautel, Manfred (ed.): *Ehemalige Zwangsarbeiterinnen und Zwangsarbeiter in Stuttgart. Ein Beitrag zur noch nicht erforschten Geschichte der Stadt Stuttgart*, published by IG Metall Stuttgart, VVN-BdA Stuttgart, and Interessengemeinschaft der ehemaligen Zwangsarbeiterinnen und Zwangsarbeiter unter dem Naziregime, Stuttgart, 1997.

Debatin, Otto: *Sie haben mitgeholfen. Lebensbilder verdienter Mitarbeiter des Hauses Bosch* (Bosch-Schriftenreihe, vol. 11), Stuttgart, 1963.

Deiß, Manfred/Döhl, Volker (eds.): *Vernetzte Produktion. Automobilzulieferer zwischen Kontrolle und Autonomie*, Frankfurt am Main, 1992.

Demm, Eberhard: *Ein Liberaler in Kaiserreich und Republik. Der politische Weg Alfred Webers bis 1920* (Schriften des Bundesarchivs, 38), Boppard am Rhein, 1990.

Dendler, Vera: "The start of a lasting friendship. Franco-German manufacturing joint venture near Paris," in Robert Bosch GmbH (ed.): *The emergence of a global player. The internationalization of the Bosch Group* (*Journal of Bosch History*, supplement 3) [Stuttgart 2008], pp. 26–9.

Dendler, Vera: "News from Barcelona. First office opens in Spain," in *Journal of Bosch History*, 2008, pp. 6–9.

Deutsche MTM-Vereinigung (ed.): *MTM – Von Anfang an richtig*, Hamburg, 2002.

Diesel, Eugen: "Robert Bosch," in Eugen Diesel/Gustav Goldbeck/Friedrich Schildberger: *Vom Motor zum Auto. Fünf Männer und ihr Werk*, 3rd ed., Stuttgart, 1968, pp. 257–308.

Dipper, Christof: "Der deutsche Widerstand und die Juden," in *Geschichte und Gesellschaft* 9, 1983, pp. 349–80.

Dürr, Heinz: *In der ersten Reihe. Aufzeichnungen eines Unerschrockenen*, Berlin, 2008.

Durst, Ernst: *Die Berufsausbildung des Mechanikers in der allgemeinen Feinmechanik*, 5th ed., Stuttgart 1949.

Eberle, Eugen/Grohmann, Peter: *Die schlaflosen Nächte des Eugen E., Erinnerungen eines neuen schwäbischen Jacobiners*, Stuttgart, 1982.

Edelmann, Heidrun: "Der Umgang mit dem Rückstand. Deutschlands Automobilindustrie in der Zwischenkriegszeit," in Boch (ed.): *Geschichte*, pp. 41–8.

Edelmann, Heidrun: *Vom Luxusgut zum Gebrauchsgegenstand. Die Geschichte der Verbreitung von Personenkraftwagen in Deutschland*, Frankfurt am Main, 1989.

Engelke, Sylvia/Maltschew, Reni: "Weltwirtschaftskrise, Aktienskandale und Reaktionen des Gesetzgebers durch Notverordnungen im Jahre 1931," in Walter Bayer/Mathias Habersack (eds.): *Aktienrecht im Wandel*, vol. I: *Entwicklung des Aktienrechts*, Tübingen, 2007, pp. 570–618.

Erker, Paul: *Ernährungskrise und Nachkriegsgesellschaft. Bauern und Arbeiterschaft in Bayern 1943 bis 1953*, Stuttgart, 1990.

Erker, Paul/Pierenkemper, Toni (eds.): *Deutsche Unternehmer zwischen Kriegswirtschaft und Wiederaufbau. Studien zur Erfahrungsbildung von Industrieeliten*, Munich, 1999.

Fäßler, Peter E.: *Globalisierung*, Cologne, Weimar, 2007.

Fehrenbach, Franz: "Er war ein durch und durch glaubwürdiger Mann," in *Marcus Bierich*, pp. 352–62.

Feldenkirchen, Wilfried: *Siemens 1918–1945*, Munich, 1995.

Feldenkirchen, Wilfried: *"Vom Guten das Beste." Von Daimler und Benz zur Daimler-Chrysler AG*, vol. 1: *Die ersten 100 Jahre 1883–1983*, Munich, 2003.

Feldman, Gerald D.: "Die Deutsche Bank und die Automobilindustrie," in *Zeitschrift für Unternehmensgeschichte* 44, 1999/1, pp. 3–14.

Feldman, Gerald D.: "Die Deutsche Bank vom Ersten Weltkrieg bis zur Weltwirtschaftskrise 1914–1933," in Lothar Gall/Gerald D. Feldman/Harold James/Carl-Ludwig Holtfrerich/Hans E. Büschgen: *Die Deutsche Bank 1870–1995*, Munich, 1995, pp. 137–314.

Fichter, Tilman/Eberle, Eugen: *Kampf um Bosch*, Berlin, 1974.

Flik, Reiner: "Automobilindustrie und Motorisierung in Deutschland bis 1939," in Boch (ed.): *Geschichte*, pp. 49–84.

Forrant, Robert: *Metal fatigue. American Bosch and the demise of metalworking in the Connecticut River Valley*, Amityville, 2009.

Fraenkel, Daniel/Borut, Jakob (eds.): *Lexikon der Gerechten unter den Völkern. Deutsche und Österreicher*, Göttingen, 2005.

Galbraith, John Kenneth: *The Great Crash 1929*, Boston, 1954.

Geissler, Wilfried/Borst, Sigrid (eds.): *Hugo Borst 1881–1967. Familienvater, Kaufmännischer Direktor, Privater Kunstsammler und Förderer. Sammler von schöngeistiger und wissenschaftlicher Literatur*, Stuttgart, 2006.

Gersdorff, Kyrill von/Grasmann, Kurt: *Flugmotoren und Strahltriebwerke*, Munich, 1981.

Gillmann, Sabine/Mommsen, Hans (eds.): *Politische Schriften und Briefe Carl Goerdelers*, Munich, 2003.

Glasbrenner, Willi: *Arbeit und Rüstung. Die Geschichte des Arbeitsdienstes und der Firma "Bosch" in Crailsheim 1933–1945*, Crailsheim, 2009.

Grauls, Marcel: "One hundred years of success in Belgium," in Robert Bosch GmbH (ed.), *Bosch in Belgium 1907–2007*, Brussels, 2007.

Greifenstein, Ralph/Kißler, Leo: *Mitbestimmung im Spiegel der Forschung. Eine Bilanz der empirischen Untersuchungen 1952–2010*, Berlin, 2010.

Grunenberg, Nina: *Die Wundertäter. Netzwerke der deutschen Wirtschaft 1942 bis 1966*, Frankfurt am Main, 2008.

Gruner, Wolf: *Der geschlossene Arbeitseinsatz deutscher Juden*, Berlin, 1997.

Grunert, Manfred/Triebel, Florian: *Das Unternehmen BMW seit 1916*, Munich, 2006.

Hagedoorn, John: "Innovation and entrepreneurship. Schumpeter revisited," in *Industrial and Corporate Change* 5, 1996/3, pp. 883–96.

Haubner, Barbara: "Automobilismus im Kaiserreich. Auftakt zur Massenmobilisierung oder Freizeitvergnügen für Wohlhabende?," in Boch (ed.): *Geschichte*, pp. 23–40.

Haus, Rainer/Sarkowicz, Hans: *Using energy more efficiently. 75 years of thermotechnology from Bosch*, Munich, 2007.

Hebeisen, Walter: *F. W. Taylor und der Taylorismus. Über das Wirken und die Lehre Taylors und die Kritik am Taylorismus*, Zurich, 1999.

Heimes, Ernst: *Ich habe immer nur den Zaun gesehen. Suche nach dem KZ-Außenlager Cochem*, 4th ed., Koblenz, 1999.

Herbert, Ulrich: *Fremdarbeiter. Politik und Praxis des "Ausländer-Einsatzes" in der Kriegswirtschaft des Dritten Reiches*, 3rd ed., Bonn, 1999.

Herbert, Ulrich: *Geschichte der Ausländerpolitik in Deutschland. Saisonarbeiter, Zwangsarbeiter, Gastarbeiter, Flüchtlinge*, Munich, 2001.

Herbert, Ulrich: "Zwangsarbeit im 'Dritten Reich.' Kenntnisstand, offene Fragen, Forschungsprobleme," in Gabrielle Hauch (ed.), *Industrie und Zwangsarbeit im Nationalsozialismus. Mercedes-Benz – VW – Reichswerke Hermann Göring in Linz und Salzgitter*, Innsbruck, 2003.

Herdt, Hans Konradin: *Bosch 1886–1986. Porträt eines Unternehmens*, Stuttgart, 1986.

Herrmann, Christoph/Moeller, Günter: *Innovation – Marke – Design. Grundlagen einer neuen Corporate Governance*, Düsseldorf, 2006.

Hessler, Miriam: "'Ich habe viele Erinnerungen an hier.' Wie aus 'Gastarbeitern' Mitbürger geworden sind," in Johler/Sparacio (eds.): *Abfahren*, pp. 305–20.

Heuss, Theodor: *Robert Bosch. Leben und Leistung*, new ed., Stuttgart, Leipzig, 2008 (first printed Tübingen, 1946).

Heuss, Theodor (ed.): *Robert Bosch*, Stuttgart, 1931.

Heuss-Knapp, Elly: *Bürgerin zweier Welten. Ein Leben in Briefen und Aufzeichnungen*, published by Margarethe Vater, 3rd ed., Tübingen, 1963.

Hilger, Susanne: *"Amerikanisierung" deutscher Unternehmen. Wettbewerbsstrategien und Unternehmenspolitik bei Henkel, Siemens und Daimler-Benz (1945/49–1975)*, Wiesbaden, 2004.

Hochstetter, Dorothee: *"Motorisierung und Volksgemeinschaft." Das Nationalsozialistische Kraftfahr-Korps (NSKK) 1931–1945*, Munich, 2005.

Höcherl, Bettina: "A helping hand in every kitchen. The Bosch refrigerator," in *Journal of Bosch History*, 2008, pp. 16–9.

Hoffmann, Peter: *Carl Goerdeler and the Jewish question, 1933–1942*, Cambridge, 2011.

Homburg, Heidrun: "Anfänge des Taylorsystems in Deutschland vor dem Ersten Weltkrieg. Eine Problemskizze unter besonderer Berücksichtigung der Arbeitskämpfe bei Bosch 1913," in *Geschichte und Gesellschaft* 4, 1978, pp. 170–194.

Hopmann, Barbara: *Von der MONTAN zur Industrieverwaltungsgesellschaft (IVG), 1916–1951*, Stuttgart, 1996.

Hoppe, Joseph: "Fernsehen als Waffe. Militär und Fernsehen in Deutschland 1935–1950," in *Ich diente nur der Technik. Sieben Karrieren zwischen 1940 und 1950* (Schriftenreihe des Museums für Verkehr und Technik Berlin, vol. 13), Berlin, 1995, pp. 53–88.

Hunn, Karin: *"Nächstes Jahr kehren wir zurück." Die Geschichte der türkischen "Gastarbeiter" in der Bundesrepublik*, Göttingen, 2005.

Johler, Reinhard/Sparacio, Felicia (eds.): *Abfahren. Ankommen. Boschler sein. Lebensgeschichten aus der Arbeitswelt*, 2nd ed., Tübingen, 2011.

Jütte, Robert: "The healing power of nature. Homeopath and 'lifestyle reformer',," in Robert Bosch GmbH (ed.), *Robert Bosch. His life and work* (Journal of Bosch History, Supplement 1) [Stuttgart, 2009], pp. 52–5.

Kaiser, Walter: *Bosch and the automobile, 1950–2003: a review*, Stuttgart, 2008.

Kinkel, Steffen/Lay, Gunter: "Automobilzulieferer in der Klemme. Vom Spagat zwischen strategischer Ausrichtung und Auslandsorientierung," in *Mitteilungen aus der Produktionsinnovationserhebung*, published by Hans Böckler Stiftung and Fraunhofer Institut für Systemtechnik und Innovationsforschung, No. 32, March 2004.

Kißener, Michael/Scholtyseck, Joachim (eds.): *Die Führer der Provinz. NS-Biographien aus Baden und Württemberg* (Karlsruher Beiträge zur Geschichte, 2), Konstanz, 1997.

Klein, Eduard: "50 Jahre M.A.N.-Fahrzeug-Dieselmotoren. Ein historischer Rückblick von der Geburtsstätte des Dieselmotors anlässlich des 50jährigen Jubiläums des kompressorlosen Fahrzeug-Dieselmotors," in *ATZ Automobiltechnische Zeitschrift* 75, 1973/4, pp. 115–7.

Kleinschmidt, Christian: *Der produktive Blick. Wahrnehmung amerikanischer und japanischer Management- und Produktionsmethoden durch deutsche Unternehmer 1950–1985*, Berlin, 2002.

König, Wolfgang: "Der Volksempfänger und die Radioindustrie. Ein Beitrag zum Verhältnis von Wirtschaft und Politik im Nationalsozialismus," in *Vierteljahrschrift für Sozial- und Wirtschaftsgeschichte* 90, 2003, pp. 269–89.

König, Wolfgang: *Volkswagen, Volksempfänger, Volksgemeinschaft. "Volksprodukte" im Dritten Reich. Vom Scheitern einer nationalsozialistischen Konsumgesellschaft*, Paderborn, 2004.

Konieczny, Alfred: *Das "Kommando Wetterstelle" im KL Groß-Rosen*, Wałbrzych, 1994.

Konieczny, Alfred: "Das KZ Groß-Rosen in Niederschlesien," in Ulrich Herbert/Karin Orth/Christoph Dieckmann (eds.): *Die nationalsozialistischen Konzentrationslager. Entwicklung und Struktur*, vol. 1, Göttingen, 1998, pp. 309–26.

Konieczny, Alfred: "Langenbielau I (Bielawa)," in Benz/Distel (eds.): *Ort des Terrors*, vol. 6, pp. 377–9.

Koning, Ruud de: *Brieven van mijn vader Henk de Koning uit Duitsland en Tsjechië 1942–1945*, Assen, 2008.

Kopper, Christopher: *Hjalmar Schacht. Aufstieg und Fall von Hitlers mächtigstem Bankier*, Munich, Vienna 2006.

Kostolany, André: *Mehr als Geld und Gier*, 2nd ed., Munich, 2006.

Kreutzmüller, Christoph: *Händler und Handlungsgehilfen. Der Finanzplatz Amsterdam und die deutschen Großbanken (1918–1945)*, Stuttgart, 2005.

Kuhlgatz, Dietrich: "Water for the fields, power for cars. Bosch in India," in Robert Bosch GmbH (ed.), *The emergence of a global player. The internationalization of the Bosch Group* (Jounal of Bosch History, supplement 3) [Stuttart, 2008].

Kurz, Jörg: *Chronik der Stadt Stuttgart 1933–1945* (Veröffentlichungen des Archivs der Stadt Stuttgart, vol. 30), Stuttgart, 1982.

Lang, Thilo: *Das Investitionsverhalten Metall verarbeitender Unternehmen in Württemberg 1924–1936. Zwischen Rationalisierungsmaßnahmen und Kapazitätserweiterungen* (Stuttgarter historische Studien zur Landes- und Wirtschaftsgeschichte, vol. 5), Ostfildern, 2004.

Langen, Arnold: *Nicolaus August Otto. Der Schöpfer des Verbrennungsmotors*, Stuttgart, 1949.

Lauschke, Karl: *Mehr Demokratie in der Wirtschaft. Die Entstehungsgeschichte des Mitbestimmungsgesetzes von 1976*, Düsseldorf, 2006.

Leiner, Wolfgang: *Geschichte der Elektrizitätswirtschaft in Württemberg*, vol. 1: *Grundlagen und Anfänge (bis 1895)*, Stuttgart, 1982.

Leiner, Wolfgang: "Paul Reisser. Ein württembergischer Pionier der Elektrotechnik," in Wolfgang Leiner (ed.), *Ausgewählte technikgeschichtliche Vorträge*, Stuttgart, 1984, pp. 174–84.

Lessing, Hans-Erhard: *Robert Bosch*, Reinbek, 2007.

Marcus Bierich. Im Spiegel seiner Familie, Freunde und Weggefährten, Frankfurt am Main, 2010.

Markschies, Christoph: "Carl und Friedrich Goerdeler," in Joachim Mehlhausen (ed.): *Zeugen des Widerstands. Ehemalige Studenten der Universität Tübingen, die im Kampf gegen den Nationalsozialismus starben*, 2nd ed., Tübingen, 1998, pp. 142–72.

Martin, Angela: *Ich sah den Namen Bosch. Polnische Frauen als KZ-Häftlinge in der Dreilinden Maschinenbau GmbH*, published by Berliner Geschichtswerkstatt, Berlin, 2002.

Martin, Angela/Czerwiakowski, Ewa (eds.): *Muster des Erinnerns. Polnische Frauen als KZ-Häftlinge in einer Tarnfabrik von Bosch*, Berlin, 2005.

Matschoß, Conrad (ed.): *Robert Bosch und sein Werk*, Berlin, 1931.

Mattes, Monika: *"Gastarbeiterinnen" in der Bundesrepublik. Anwerbepolitik, Migration und Geschlecht in den 5oer bis 7oer Jahren*, Frankfurt am Main, 2005.

Meißner, Heinz-Rudolf: *Die Teile und die Herrschaft. Die Reorganisation der Automobil-produktion und der Zulieferbeziehungen*, Berlin, 1994.

Merki, Christoph M.: *Der holprige Siegeszug des Automobils 1895–1935. Zur Motorisierung des Straßenverkehrs in Frankreich, Deutschland und der Schweiz*, Vienna, Cologne, 2002.

Meyer, Beate: *"Jüdische Mischlinge." Rassenpolitik und Verfolgungswahn 1933–1945*, Hamburg, 2001.

Michel, Alexander: *Von der Fabrikzeitung zum Führungsmittel. Werkschriften industrieller Großunternehmen von 1890 bis 1945* (Beiträge zur Unternehmensgeschichte, vol. 96), Stuttgart, 1997.

Möbius, Klaus: *Das Umweltproblem aus wirtschaftlicher Sicht* (Kieler Diskussionsbeiträge zu aktuellen wirtschaftspolitischen Fragen, 14), Kiel, 1971.

Mom, Gijs: *The electric vehicle. Technology and expectations in the automobile age*, Illinois, 2004.

Mommsen, Hans: *Alternatives to Hitler. German resistance under the Third Reich*, London, 2003.

Mommsen, Hans/Grieger, Manfred: *Das Volkswagenwerk und seine Arbeiter im Dritten Reich*, Düsseldorf, 1996.

Müller, Klaus-Jürgen: *Generaloberst Ludwig Beck. Eine Biographie*, 2nd ed., Paderborn, 2009.

Müller, Martin L.: *Bausparen in Deutschland zwischen Inflation und Währungsreform 1924–1948. Wohnungsbaufinanzierung im Spannungsfeld zwischen Staat und privaten und öffentlichen Bausparunternehmen* (Schriftenreihe der Zeitschrift für Unternehmensgeschichte, vol. 4), Munich, 1999.

Müller, Roland: *Stuttgart zur Zeit des Nationalsozialismus*, Stuttgart, 1998.

Murach-Brand, Lisa: *Antitrust auf Deutsch. Der Einfluß der amerikanischen Alliierten auf das Gesetz gegen Wettbewerbsbeschränkungen nach 1945*, Tübingen. 2004.

Nachtmann, Walter: "Wilhelm Murr und Karl Strölin. Die 'Führer' der Nazis in Stuttgart," in Hermann G. Abmayr (ed.): *Stuttgarter NS-Täter. Vom Mitläufer bis zum Massenmörder*, Stuttgart. 2009, pp. 186–97.

Nast-Kolb, Fritz: "Jahrgang 1916," in Johannes Steinhoff/Peter Pechel/Dennis Showalter (eds.): *Deutsche im Zweiten Weltkrieg. Zeitzeugen sprechen*, Munich, 1989, pp. 408–10.

Neliba, Günter: *Die Opel-Werke im Konzern von General Motors (1929–1948) in Rüsselsheim und Brandenburg. Produktion für Aufrüstung und Krieg ab 1935 unter nationalsozialistischer Herrschaft*, Frankfurt am Main. 2000.

Neumaier, Christopher: *Dieselautos in Deutschland und den USA. Zum Verhältnis von Technologie, Konsum und Politik 1949 bis 2005*, Stuttgart, 2010.

Nockolds, Harold: *Lucas – The first 100 years*, London, 1979.

Nylander, Gert: *German resistance movement and England. Carl Goerdeler and the Wallenberg brothers*, Stockholm, 1999.

Olsson, Ulf: *Stockholms Enskilda Bank and the Bosch Group 1939–1950*, Stockholm, 1998.

Overesch, Manfred: *Bosch in Hildesheim 1937–1945. Freies Unternehmertum und nationalsozialistische Rüstungspolitik*, Göttingen, 2008.

Oyen, Stefan A./Overesch, Manfred: "'Starter für den Krieg.' Bosch Hildesheim im Dritten Reich," in Andreas Heusler/Mark Spoerer/Helmuth Trischler (eds.): *Rüstung, Kriegswirtschaft und Zwangsarbeit im "Dritten Reich"*, Munich, 2010, pp. 107–37.

Pape, Lutz/Weinert, Hans-Jürgen: *Bottichwaschmaschine & Haustelegraph. Anfänge der Elektrotechnik im Haushalt*, Braunschweig, 1993.

Pierenkemper, Toni: "Robert Bosch, der Industrielle. Zum Typus des deutschen Unternehmers in der Hochindustrialisierung," in *Kultur & Technik* 1987/1, pp. 4–18.

Pierer, Christian: *Die Bayerischen Motorenwerke bis 1933. Eine Unternehmensgründung in Krieg, Inflation und Weltwirtschaftskrise*, Munich, 2011.

Pinner, Felix: *Deutsche Wirtschaftsführer*, Berlin, 1924.

Pohl, Hans/Habeth, Stephanie/Brüninghaus, Beate: *Die Daimler-Benz AG in den Jahren 1933 bis 1945. Eine Dokumentation* (Zeitschrift für Unternehmensgeschichte, supplement 47), Stuttgart, 1986.

Preller, Ludwig: *Sozialpolitik in der Weimarer Republik*, unamended reprint, Kronberg, Düsseldorf, 1978.

Prinzing, Marlis: *Der Streik bei Bosch im Jahre 1913. Ein Beitrag zur Geschichte von Rationalisierung und Arbeiterbewegung* (Zeitschrift für Unternehmensgeschichte, supplement 61), Stuttgart, 1989.

Rauck, Max J. B.: "Das Serienmotorrad wurde 90 Jahre alt," in *Kultur & Technik* 1986/2, pp. 82–94.

Reitmayer, Morten/Rosenberger, Ruth (eds.): *Unternehmen am Ende des "goldenen Zeitalters". Die 1970er Jahre als Gegenstand der Unternehmens- und Wirtschaftsgeschichte*, Essen, 2008.

Richert, Fritz: *Karl Adler. Musiker, Verfolgter, Helfer. Ein Lebensbild*, Stuttgart, 1990.

Riexinger, Klaus: "Deutsch-Oth (Audun-le-Tiche)," in Benz/Distel (eds.), *Ort des Terrors*, vol. 6, pp. 75–6.

Ritter, Gerhard: *Carl Friedrich Goerdeler und die deutsche Widerstandsbewegung*, Stuttgart, 1954.

Röhm, Eberhard/Thierfelder, Jörg: "Schützende Hände über 'Juden' und 'Mischlingen': Die Stuttgarter Firmen Paul Lechler und Robert Bosch," in Eberhard Röhm/Jörg Thierfelder: *Juden, Christen, Deutsche 1933–1945*, vol. 4: *1941–1945*, part 2, Stuttgart, 2007, pp. 451–77.

Rudolph, Bernd: "Hintergründe und Verlauf der globalen Finanzkrise 2008," in Johannes Bähr/Bernd Rudolph, *Finanzkrisen 1931 und 2008*, Munich, 2011, pp. 143–241.

Rueß, Susanne: *Stuttgarter jüdische Ärzte während des Nationalsozialismus*, Würzburg, 2009.

Rüther, Daniela: *Der Widerstand des 20. Juli auf dem Weg in die Soziale Marktwirtschaft. Die wirtschaftspolitischen Vorstellungen der bürgerlichen Opposition gegen Hitler*, Paderborn, 2002.

Sauer, Paul: "Ganze Familien wurden in den Tod geschickt. Die Deportation der württembergischen und hohenzollerischen Juden am 1. Dezember 1941 von Stuttgart nach Riga," in Konrad Pflug/Ulrike Raab-Nicolai/Reinhold Weber (eds.): *Orte des Gedenkens und Erinnerns in Baden-Württemberg*, Stuttgart, 2007, pp. 304–10.

Sauer, Paul: *Das Werden einer Großstadt. Stuttgart zwischen Reichsgründung und Erstem Weltkrieg. 1871 bis 1914*, Stuttgart, 1988.

Sauer, Paul: *Wilhelm Murr. Hitlers Statthalter in Württemberg*, Tübingen, 1998.

Sauer, Paul: *Württemberg in der Zeit des Nationalsozialismus*, Ulm, 1975.

Scharschmidt, Wolfgang: *Röhrenhistorie. Die Geschichte der Elektronenröhre*, vol. 4: *Deutsche Wehrmachtsröhren*, Dessau, 2010.

Schildberger, Friedrich: *Bosch und der Dieselmotor*, Stuttgart, 1950.

Schmitt, Dieter: "Casa Bosch. First office opens in Argentina," in *Journal of Bosch History*, 2008, pp. 10–3.

Schmitt, Dieter: *Theodor Bäuerle (1882–1956). Engagement für Bildung in schwierigen Zeiten* (Schriftenreihe zur Bosch-Geschichte, vol. 3), Stuttgart, 2005.

Schnabel, Thomas: *Geschichte von Baden und Württemberg 1900–1952*, published by Haus der Geschichte Baden-Württemberg, Stuttgart, 2000.

Schnabel, Thomas: "'Warum geht es in Schwaben besser?' Württemberg in der Weltwirtschaftskrise 1928–1933," in: Thomas Schnabel (ed.): *Die Machtergreifung in Südwestdeutschland. Das Ende der Weimarer Republik in Baden und Württemberg 1928–1933*, Stuttgart, 1982, pp. 184–209.

Schnabel, Thomas: *Württemberg zwischen Weimar und Bonn 1928 bis 1945/46* (Schriften zur politischen Landeskunde Baden-Württembergs, vol. 143), Stuttgart, 1986.

Schneider, Hartmut: *Neue politische Ökonomie und Technologiepolitik. Fallstudie am Beispiel der Luftfahrtindustrie*, Berlin, 1980.

Schoeps, Julius H.: *Das Erbe der Mendelssohns. Biographie einer Familie*, 2nd ed., Frankfurt am Main, 2011.

Scholtyseck, Joachim: *Der Aufstieg der Quandts. Eine deutsche Unternehmerdynastie*, Munich, 2011.

Scholtyseck, Joachim: "'Der Mann aus dem Volk.' Wilhelm Murr, Gauleiter und Reichsstatthalter in Württemberg-Hohenzollern," in Kißener/Scholtyseck (eds.): *Die Führer der Provinz*, pp. 477–502.

Scholtyseck, Joachim: *Robert Bosch und der liberale Widerstand gegen Hitler 1933–1945*, Munich, 1999.

Scholtyseck, Joachim: "Robert Bosch und der Boschkreis als finanzielle, geistige und politische Unterstützer des Widerstands vom 20. Juli 1944," in Detlev J. Blesgen (ed.): *Financiers, Finanzen und Finanzierungsformen des Widerstands* (Schriftenreihe der Forschungsgemeinschaft 20. Juli 1944 e. V., vol. 5), Berlin, 2006, pp. 33–51.

Scholtyseck, Joachim: "Robert Bosch, die deutsch-französische Verständigung und das Ende der Weimarer Republik," in Becker/Scholtyseck, *Bosch*, pp. 44–116.

Scholtyseck, Joachim: "Der 'Schwabenherzog.' Gottlob Berger, SS-Obergruppenführer," in Kißener/Scholtyseck (eds.): *Die Führer der Provinz*, pp. 77–110.

Schröter, Harm G.: *Americanization of the European economy. A compact survey of American economic influence in Europe since the 1880s*, Dordrecht, 2005.

Schumpeter, Joseph A.: *The theory of economic development*, Oxford, 1934.

Schweickhardt, Peter: *Ehrenvorsitzender Rosenblum. Eine Erzählung*, Stuttgart, 2007.

Seefried, Elke (ed.): *Theodor Heuss. In der Defensive. Briefe 1933–1945*, Munich, 2009.

Seherr-Thoss, Hans-Christoph Graf von: *Die deutsche Automobilindustrie*, Eine Dokumentation von 1886 bis heute, Stuttgart, 1974.

Seitz, Konrad: *Die japanisch-amerikanische Herausforderung. Deutschlands Hochtechnologie-Industrien kämpfen ums Überleben*, 2nd ed., Munich, Bonn, 1991.

Seiffert, Reinhard: *Die Ära Gottlieb Daimlers. Neue Perspektiven zur Frühgeschichte des Automobils und seiner Technik*, Wiesbaden, 2009.

Sösemann, Bernd: "Politische Kommunikation im 'Reichsbelagerungszustand', Programm, Struktur und Wirkungen des Klubs 'Deutsche Gesellschaft 1914'," in Manfred Bobrowsky/Wolfgang R. Langenbucher (eds.): *Wege zur Kommunikationsgeschichte*, Munich, 1987, pp. 630–49.

Sonnenberg, Elke: "'At last you can get them …' Bosch magnetos in the U.S.," in Robert Bosch GmbH (ed.), *The emergence of a global player. The internationalization of the Bosch Group* (Journal of Bosch History, supplement 3) [Stuttgart, 2008], pp. 12–5.

Spiliotis, Susanne-Sophia: *Verantwortung und Rechtsfrieden. Die Stiftungsinitiative der deutschen Wirtschaft*, Frankfurt am Main, 2003.

Spoerer, Mark: "Profitierten Unternehmen von KZ-Arbeit? Eine kritische Analyse der Literatur," in *Historische Zeitschrift* 268, 1999/1, pp. 61–91.

Spoerer, Mark: *Von Scheingewinnen zum Rüstungsboom. Die Eigenkapitalrentabilität der deutschen Industrieaktiengesellschaften 1925–1941* (VSWG, supplement 123), Stuttgart, 1996.

Spoerer, Mark: *Zwangsarbeit unter dem Hakenkreuz*, Stuttgart, 2001.

Sprenger, Isabell: *Groß-Rosen. Ein Konzentrationslager in Schlesien*, Cologne, 1996.

Sprenger, Isabell/Kumpmann, Walter: "Groß-Rosen – Stammlager," in: Benz/Distel (eds.): *Ort des Terrors*, vol. 6, pp. 195–221.

Steiner, Kilian J. L.: *Ortsempfänger, Volksempfänger und Optaphon. Die Entwicklung der deutschen Radio- und Fernsehindustrie und das Unternehmen Loewe, 1923–1962*, Essen, 2005.

Stiftung Geißstraße Sieben (ed.): *Der "Rote Hahn." Künstler, Polizeidirektor, Widerständler 1883–1952. Ein Gedenkblatt*, Stuttgart 2003.

Stiftung Geißstraße Sieben (ed.), *Zwangsarbeit in Stuttgart, 1939–1945*, Stuttgart 2000.

Stolle, Uta: *Arbeiterpolitik im Betrieb. Frauen und Männer, Reformisten und Radikale, Fach- und Massenarbeiter bei Bayer, BASF, Bosch und in Solingen (1900–1933)*, Frankfurt am Main, 1980.

Strunk, Peter: *Die AEG. Aufstieg und Niedergang einer deutschen Industrielegende*, 2nd ed., Berlin, 2000.

Taddey, Gerhard: "Zwischen Widerstand und Gestapo. Dr. Hugo Bühler, Abwehrbeauftragter der Firma Bosch in Stuttgart," in *Zeitschrift für Württembergische Landesgeschichte* 70, 2011, pp. 455–88.

Taylor, Frederick W.: *The principles of scientific management*, London, 1911.

Teich, Hans: *Hildesheim und seine Antifaschisten. Widerstandskampf gegen den Hitlerfaschismus und demokratischer Neubeginn 1945 in Hildesheim*, Hildesheim, 1979.

Thieme, Carsten: "Krisenbewältigung durch Kooperation? Fusionsprozeß und Marktordnungsversuche bei Daimler-Benz 1924–1932," in Boch (ed.): *Geschichte*, pp. 85–108.

Tilly, Stephanie: "Das Zulieferproblem aus institutionenökonomischer Sicht. Die westdeutsche Automobil-Zulieferindustrie zwischen Produktions- und Marktorientierung (1960–1980)," in *Jahrbuch für Wirtschaftsgeschichte* 2010/1, pp. 137–60.

Tooze, Adam: *The wages of destruction. The making and breaking of the Nazi economy*, London, 2006.

Torp, Cornelius: *Die Herausforderung der Globalisierung. Wirtschaft und Politik in Deutschland 1860–1914*, Göttingen, 2005.

Trischler, Helmut/Bruch, Rüdiger vom: *Forschung für den Markt. Geschichte der Fraunhofer-Gesellschaft*, Munich, 1999.

Uekötter, Frank: *Umweltgeschichte im 19. und 20. Jahrhundert*, Munich, 2007.

Ulmer, Martin: *Antisemitismus in Stuttgart. Studien zum öffentlichen Diskurs und Alltag*, Berlin, 2011.

Unabhängige Expertenkommission Schweiz – Zweiter Weltkrieg: *Die Schweiz und die Goldtransaktionen im Zweiten Weltkrieg* (Veröffentlichungen der UEK, vol. 16), Zurich, 2002.

Vogelsang, Reinhard: *Der Freundeskreis Himmler*, Göttingen, 1972.

Von der Glühbirne zum Mikroprozessor. 100 Jahre Elektrizität in Stuttgart, ed. by Elektro-Innung Stuttgart, Stuttgart, 1984.

Wehler, Hans-Ulrich: *Deutsche Gesellschaftsgeschichte*, vol. 4: *Vom Beginn des Ersten Weltkrieges bis zur Gründung der beiden deutschen Staaten 1914–1949*, Munich, 2003.

Weiher, Sigfrid von: *Berlins Weg zur Elektropolis. Technik- und Industriegeschichte an der Spree*, Göttingen, Zurich, 1987.

Werner, Constanze: *Kriegswirtschaft und Zwangsarbeit bei BMW*, Munich, 2005.

Wilkins, Mira: *The history of foreign investments in the United States, 1914–1945* (*Harvard Studies in Business History*, 43), Cambridge/Mass., 2004.

Wilkins, Mira: "Multinational enterprise to 1930. Discontinuities and continuities," in Alfred D. Chandler/Bruce Mazlish (eds.): *Leviathans. Multinational corporations and the new global history*, Cambridge 2005, pp. 45–80.

Winkler, Heinrich August: *Geschichte des Westens. Die Zeit der Weltkriege 1914–1945*, Munich, 2011.

Winkler, Heinrich August: *Der Weg in die Katastrophe. Arbeiter und Arbeiterbewegung in der Weimarer Republik 1930 bis 1933*, Berlin, Bonn, 1987.

Zelzer, Maria: *Weg und Schicksal der Stuttgarter Juden. Ein Gedenkbuch*, published by Stadt Stuttgart (Veröffentlichungen des Archivs der Stadt Stuttgart, special issue), Stuttgart, 1964.

Ziegenhofer, Anita: *Botschafter Europas. Richard Nikolaus Coudenhove-Kalergi und die Paneuropa-Bewegung in den zwanziger und dreißiger Jahren*, Vienna, Cologne, 2004.

Zundel, Georg: *"Es muss viel geschehen!" Erinnerungen eines friedenspolitisch engagierten Naturwissenschaftlers*, Berlin, 2006.

Index of persons

Page numbers in italics refer to picture captions

Index of companies

Excluding Robert Bosch GmbH and its legal predecessors